C000294991

The
Yorkshire County
Cricket Club Limited

Registered Number 28929R

YEARBOOK
2014

116th EDITION

Sponsors of

THE YORKSHIRE COUNTY CRICKET CLUB

Editor:

DAVID WARNER

Records and Statistics

Yorkshire First Eleven:

JOHN T POTTER

Yorkshire Second Eleven:

HOWARD CLAYTON

Production Editor:

JAMES M. GREENFIELD

Published by
THE YORKSHIRE COUNTY CRICKET CLUB
HEADINGLEY CRICKET GROUND
KIRKSTALL LANE
LEEDS LS6 3DP
Tel: 0843 504 3113   Fax: 01132 784099
Internet: http://www.yorkshireccc.com
e-mail: cricket@yorkshireccc.com

Solicitors: *Auditors:*

DLA PIPER UK LLP   KPMG Audit plc

Medical Officer: Dr NIGEL MAYERS, MBChB, MRCGP

Burley Park Medical Centre, 273 Burley Road, Leeds LS4 2EL

The opinions expressed by contributors are not necessarily those of the Board.

1

TELEPHONE AND FAX NUMBERS

HEADINGLEY CRICKET GROUND	**Tel: 0843 504 3113** Fax: 01132 784099
NORTH MARINE ROAD, SCARBOROUGH	**Tel: 01723 365625** Fax: 01723 364287
BURNLEY ROAD, TODMORDEN	**Tel: 01706 813140**
SHIPTON ROAD, YORK	**Tel: 01904 623602**
BRADFORD & BINGLEY	**Tel: 01274 775441**
STAMFORD BRIDGE	**Tel: 01759 371545**

© The Yorkshire County Cricket Club 2014

Produced by:

Great Northern Books
PO Box 213, Ilkley LS29 9WS
www.greatnorthernbooks.co.uk

ISBN: 978-0-9928193-1-6

CONTENTS

Officers for 2014

THE BOARD

Mr C J GRAVES (Executive Chairman)
Mr R A SMITH TD, DL (Director)
Mr S DENISON (Director)
Mr M FARRINGTON (Leeds City Council)
MR M P VAUGHAN OBE (Director)
MR S WILLIS (Leeds Metropolitan University)

MEMBERS' COMMITTEE

Chairman: Mr S J MANN

ELECTED MEMBERS

Ms C EVERS	Mr R LEVIN
Mr S J MANN	Mr E STEPHENS

APPOINTED MEMBERS

Mr A KILBURN   Mr R W STOTT
Mr R A SMITH (On behalf of the board)

MUSEUM DIRECTOR

Mr D S HALL CBE, TD

ARCHIVES COMMITTEE

Chairman: Mr J C D ALLAN

Mr J C D ALLAN	Mr H CLAYTON
Mr P E DYSON	Mr J M GREENFIELD
Mr M POPE	Mr B SANDERSON
Mr D O SMITH	Mr D WARNER

Mr R D WILKINSON

Changes announced after February 25 will be recorded in the 2015 edition of the Yorkshire County Cricket Club Yearbook

NEXT PRESIDENT CONTINUES THE LINK WITH BARNSLEY

By David Warner

One former Barnsley batsman bowed out as President of Yorkshire County Cricket Club at the annual meeting in March...and another was due to be elected in his place. Geoffrey Boycott OBE completed his momentous two-year period in office, and the Yorkshire Board had nominated Harold "Dickie" Bird OBE to replace him.

The two men are as different as chalk from cheese, both in character and in what made them into international personalities on the sporting scene, but they are as one in their love of Yorkshire cricket and their loyalty and dedication to the county club.

No one needs reminding that Yorkshire celebrated their sesquicentenary last year, and that it proved to be such a big success is due in no small measure to Geoffrey's involvement throughout — from the big night at the Crucible Theatre in Sheffield on January 8, which marked exactly 150 years since the Club was formed, right through to the spectacular gala dinner at Elland Road, Leeds, on October 3.

In between Geoffrey was on hand at numerous functions as well as inviting many of the Club's most committed members to take afternoon tea with him on match days at Headingley, an experience enjoyed by all who were fortunate enough to be asked.

Mention must also be made of the considerable contribution made towards the success of the big events by Geoffrey's wife, Rachael, who was responsible for much of the meticulous planning along with other members of a special subcommittee formed to carry out this essential behind-the-scenes work.

YORKSHIRE PRIDE President Boycott addresses members at the Gala Dinner

When Geoffrey was elected President in 2012, he said in these pages that he considered his appointment to be the icing on the cake of his long involvement with Yorkshire — and Dickie was expressing

6

181 not out v. Glamorgan at Bradford in 1959, left, was "Dickie" Bird's finest hour as a Yorkshire player...but it was as a world-class umpire that he was to achieve immortality with the unveiling of a bronze statue in his native Barnsley 50 years later

similar sentiments even before his nomination was confirmed. In the final pages of his book, *Dickie Bird 80 Not Out*, published last year, he wrote: "Now I sit back in my favourite chair and look back on all those years with a sense of pride and satisfaction. I'm content. I've done it all. Well, almost. If there is one other thing that would really be the icing on a fabulous cake for me, it would be to become President of Yorkshire County Cricket Club. How wonderful would that be. The son of a coalminer, a county cricketer turned umpire, following in the footsteps of such famous past presidents..."

And now his wish has come true!

Just as Geoffrey scaled the heights as a Yorkshire and England batsman, so Dickie has an equal claim to fame as one of the greatest and best-loved umpires the game has known. His record of officiating in three World Cup finals, four World Cup tournaments, 66 Test matches and 92 one-day internationals is testimony to that, not to mention standing in The Queen's Silver Jubilee Test match between England and Australia at Lord's in 1977 and the England v. Australia Centenary Test, also at headquarters, in 1980.

Let us not forget that it was for his native county that Dickie began his first-class career in 1956, and he was a member of Yorkshire's 1959 Championship-winning squad before moving to Leicestershire in 1960 and later becoming a first-class umpire. His passion for the White Rose has never left him, and it goes without saying that he will be seen far more often than not at Yorkshire matches during his term of presidency.

Officials of the Yorkshire County Cricket Club

President	Treasurer	Captain	Captain (Contd)
T R Barker 1863	M J Ellison 1863-1893	R Iddison 1863-1872	D L Bairstow 1984-1986
M J Ellison 1864-97	M Ellison, jun 1894-1898	J Rowbotham 1873	P Carrick 1987-1989
Lord Hawke 1898-1938	Chas Stokes 1899-1912	L Greenwood 1874	M D Moxon 1990-1995
Rt Hon Sir F S Jackson 1939-1947	R T Heselton 1913-1931	J Rowbotham 1875	D Byas 1996-2001
T L Taylor 1948-1960	A Wyndham Heselton 1932-1962	E Lockwood 1876-1877	D S Lehmann 2002
Sir W A Worsley Bart 1961-1973	M G Crawford 1963-1979	T Emmett 1878-1882	A McGrath 2003
Sir K Parkinson 1974-1981	J D Welch 1980-1984	Hon M B (Lord) Hawke 1883-1910	C White 2004-6
N W D Yardley 1981-1983	P W Townend 1984-2002	E J R H Radcliffe 1911	D Gough 2007-8
		Sir A W White 1912-1918	A McGrath 2009
The Viscount Mountgarret 1984-1989	*Chairman*	D C F Burton 1919-1921	A W Gale 2010-
Sir Leonard Hutton 1989-1990	A H Connell, DL 1971-1979	Geoff Wilson 1922-1924	*Secretary*
Sir Lawrence Byford QPM, LLD, DL 1991-1999	M G Crawford 1980-1984	A W Lupton 1925-1927	Geo Padley 1863
	H R Kirk 1984-1985	W A Worsley 1928-1929	J B Wostinholm 1864-1902
R A Smith TD, LLB, DL 1999-2004	B Walsh, QC 1986-1991	A T Barber 1930	F C (Sir Fredk.) Toone 1903-1930
David Jones CBE 2004-6	Sir Lawrence Byford CBE, QPM, LLD, DL 1991-1998	F E Greenwood 1931-1932	J H Nash 1931-1971
Robert Appleyard 2006-8	K H Moss MBE 1998-2002	A B Sellers 1933-1947	J Lister 1972-1991
Brian Close CBE 2008-10	G A Cope 2002	N W D Yardley 1948-1955	D M Ryder 1991-2002
	R A Smith TD, LLB, DL 2002-5	W H H Sutcliffe 1956-1957	*Company Secretary*
Raymond Illingworth CBE 2010-12	Colin J Graves 2005-	J R Burnet 1958-1959	B Bouttell 2002-5
		J V Wilson 1960-1962	Charles Hartwell 2011-
Geoffrey Boycott OBE 2012-13		D B Close 1963-1970	*Chief Executive*
		G Boycott 1971-1978	C D Hassell 1991-2002
		J H Hampshire 1979-1980	Colin J Graves 2002-5
		C M Old 1981-1982	Stewart Regan 2006-10
		R Illingworth 1982-1983	Colin J Graves 2012-2013
			Mark Arthur 2013-

DONT MISS ENGLAND AT HEADINGLEY

ENGLAND v SRI LANKA
2ND INVESTEC TEST MATCH | 20th – 24th JUNE 2014

ENGLAND v INDIA
ROYAL LONDON ONE-DAY SERIES | 5th SEPTEMBER 2014

COUNTY FIXTURES — 2014

LV COUNTY CHAMPIONSHIP — Division 1
(All four-day matches)

Date			Opponents	Venue
Sun	13-16	April	Somerset	Taunton
SUN	**20-23**	**APRIL**	**NORTHAMPTONSHIRE**	**HEADINGLEY**
Sun	27-30	April	Middlesex	Lord's
Sun	4-7	May 14	Durham	Riverside
SUN	**11-14**	**MAY**	**WARWICKSHIRE**	**HEADINGLEY**
SUN	**25-28**	**MAY**	**LANCASHIRE**	**HEADINGLEY**
Sat	31-3	May-June	Northamptonshire	Northampton
SUN	**8-11**	**JUNE**	**NOTTINGHAMSHIRE**	**HEADINGLEY**
Mon	16-19	June	Sussex	Arundel
Sun	22-25	June	Warwickshire	Edgbaston
MON	**7-10**	**JULY**	**DURHAM**	**HEADINGLEY**
SAT	**19-22**	**JULY**	**MIDDLESEX**	**SCARBOROUGH**
FRI	**15-18**	**AUGUST**	**SUSSEX**	**SCARBOROUGH**
Sun	31-3	Aug/Sept	Lancashire	Old Trafford
Tue	9-12	September	Nottinghamshire	Trent Bridge
TUE	**23-26**	**SEPTEMBER**	**SOMERSET**	**HEADINGLEY**

ROYAL LONDON 50-OVER CUP

Sat	26	July	Lancashire	Old Trafford
TUE	**29**	**JULY**	**GLOUCESTERSHIRE**	**HEADINGLEY**
Tue	5	August	Northamptonshire	Northampton
THU	**7**	**AUGUST**	**WORCESTERSHIRE**	**HEADINGLEY**
Fri	8	August	Leicestershire	Leicester
MON	**11**	**AUGUST**	**ESSEX**	**SCARBOROUGH**
WED	**13**	**AUGUST**	**DERBYSHIRE**	**SCARBOROUGH**
Thu	21	August	Hampshire	Southampton
Tue/Thu/Fri	26,28,29	August	Quarter-Finals	TBC
Thu/Sat	4-6	September	Semi-Finals	TBC
Sat	20	September	Final	Lord's

NATWEST T20 BLAST CUP

FRI	**16**	**MAY**	**NORTHAMPTONSHIRE**	**HEADINGLEY**
Fri	23	May	Warwickshire	Edgbaston
FRI	**30**	**MAY**	**DERBYSHIRE**	**HEADINGLEY**
Fri	6	June	Lancashire	Old Trafford
Fri	13	June	Northamptonshire	Northampton
FRI	**27**	**JUNE**	**LANCASHIRE**	**HEADINGLEY**
Sat	28	June	Nottinghamshire	Trent Bridge
TUE	**1**	**JULY**	**LEICESTERSHIRE**	**HEADINGLEY**
WED	**2**	**JULY**	**DURHAM**	**HEADINGLEY**
Fri	4	July	Worcestershire	Worcester
Fri	11	July	Durham	Riverside
Sun	13	July	Derbyshire	Chesterfield
FRI	**18**	**JULY**	**WARWICKSHIRE**	**HEADINGLEY**
FRI	**25**	**JULY**	**NOTTINGHAMSHIRE**	**HEADINGLEY**
Fri/Sat/Sun	1,2,3	August	Quarter-Finals	TBC
Sat	23	August	Semi-Finals and Final	Edgbaston

OTHER MATCHES

TUE	**1-3**	**APRIL**	**LEEDS/BRADFORD MCCU**	**HEADINGLEY**
Tue	8-11	April	Northamptonshire	Northampton

10

INVESTEC TEST MATCHES
(All five-day matches)
ENGLAND V. SRI LANKA

Thu June 12 . . . . .Lord's   **FRI JUNE 20** . . . . . .**HEADINGLEY**

ENGLAND v. INDIA

Wed July 9 . . . . .Trent Bridge   Thu July 17 . . . . .Lord's
Sun July 27 . . . . .Southampton   Thu August 7 . . . . .Old Trafford
Fri August 15 . . . . .The Oval

ROYAL LONDON ONE-DAY INTERNATIONALS

Thu	22	May	England v. Sri Lanka . . . . .The Oval (Day/Night)
Sun	25	May	England v. Sri Lanka . . . . .Emirates Durham ICG
Wed	28	May	England v. Sri Lanka . . . . .Old Trafford (Day/Night)
Sat	31	May	England v. Sri Lanka . . . . .Lord's
Tue	3	June	England v. Sri Lanka . . . . .Edgbaston (Day/Night)
Mon	25	August	England v. India . . . . .Bristol
Wed	27	August	England v. India . . . . .SWALEC Stadium, Cardiff
Sat	30	August	England v. India . . . . .Trent Bridge
Tue	2	September	England v. India . . . . .Edgbaston
FRI	**5**	**SEPTEMBER**	**ENGLAND v. INDIA** . . . .**HEADINGLEY**

NATWEST INTERNATIONAL T20

Tue	20	May	England v. Sri Lanka . . . . .The Oval (Floodlit)
Sun	7	September	England v. India . . . . .Edgbaston

SECOND ELEVEN CHAMPIONSHIP

Wed	9-11	April	Glamorgan . . . . .Cardiff
Tue	15-17	April	Nottinghamshire . . . . .Nottinghamshire Sports Club
MON	**2-4**	**JUNE**	**WARWICKSHIRE** . . . .**STAMFORD BRIDGE**
Tue	10-12	June	Lancashire . . . . .Northern CC, Crosby
TUE	**15-17**	**JULY**	**WORCESTERSHIRE** . . . .**YORK**
WED	**23-25**	**JULY**	**DURHAM** . . . .**HARROGATE**
TUE	**5-7**	**AUGUST**	**LEICESTERSHIRE** . . . .**YORK**
Tue	12-14	August	MCC Young Cricketers . . . . .Shenley
Wed	27-29	August	Derbyshire . . . . .Away (TBC)
Wed	11	September	Final . . . . .TBC

SECOND ELEVEN TROPHY

Tue	8	April	Glamorgan . . . . .Cardiff
Mon	14	April	Nottinghamshire . . . . .Nottinghamshire Sports Club
Mon	9	June	Lancashire . . . . .Todmorden
MON	**16**	**JUNE**	**WARWICKSHIRE** . . . .**PUDSEY CONGS**
Thu	3	July	Derbyshire . . . . .Away (TBC)
MON	**14**	**JULY**	**WORCESTERSHIRE** . . . .**STAMFORD BRIDGE**
TUE	**22**	**JULY**	**DURHAM** . . . .**MARSKE**
MON	**4**	**AUGUST**	**LEICESTERSHIRE** . . . .**BARNSLEY**
Mon	11	August	MCC Young Cricketers . . . . .Shenley
Tue	27	August	Semi-Final

SECOND ELEVEN TWENTY20 (TWO MATCHES IN THE SAME DAY)

TUE	**6**	**MAY**	**DURHAM** . . . .**YORK**
FRI	**9**	**MAY**	**LANCASHIRE** . . .**ABBEYDALE PARK, SHEFFIELD**
Wed	14	May	Nottinghamshire . . . . .Trent College
Thu	15	May	Derbyshire . . . . .Away (TBC)
Fri	12	July	Semi-Finals and Final . . . . .TBC

SECOND ELEVEN FRIENDLIES

Tue	22-24	April	Lancashire	Northop Hall
MON	**28-30**	**APRIL**	**LANCASHIRE**	**HEADINGLEY**
FRI	**2**	**MAY**	**LANCASHIRE**	**HEADINGLEY (T20X2))**
TUE	**27-29**	**MAY**	**KENT**	**SCARBOROUGH**
TUE	**24-26**	**JUNE**	**SCOTLAND A**	**SCARBOROUGH**
Mon	7-10	July	Gloucestershire	Bristol
WED	**10-12**	**SEPTEMBER**	**LANCASHIRE**	**HEADINGLEY**
Tue	16-18	September	Somerset	Taunton Vale CC

YORKSHIRE ACADEMY IN THE YORKSHIRE LEAGUE

Sat	19	April	York	Away
SAT	**26**	**APRIL**	**DRIFFIELD**	**WEETWOOD**
Sat	3	May	Sheffield Collegiate	Away
Mon	5	May	Sheffield United	Away
SAT	**10**	**MAY**	**BARNSLEY**	**WEETWOOD**
Sat	17	May	Appleby Frodingham	Away
SAT	**24**	**MAY**	**CASTLEFORD**	**WEETWOOD**
MON	**26**	**MAY**	**DONCASTER**	**WEETWOOD**
SAT	**7**	**JUNE**	**ROTHERHAM**	**WEETWOOD**
Sat	14	June	Scarborough	Away
SAT	**21**	**JUNE**	**CLEETHORPES**	**WEETWOOD**
Sat	28	June	Harrogate	Away
SAT	**5**	**JULY**	**YORK**	**WEETWOOD**
Sat	12	July	Driffield	Away
SAT	**19**	**JULY**	**SHEFFIELD COLLEGIATE**	**WEETWOOD**
Sat	26	July	Barnsley	Away
FRI	**1**	**AUGUST**	**APPLEBY FRODINGHAM**	**WEETWOOD**
SAT	**2**	**AUGUST**	**SHEFFIELD UNITED**	**WEETWOOD**
Sat	9	August	Castleford	Away
Sat	23	August	Rotherham	Away
Mon	25	August	Doncaster	Away
SAT	**30**	**AUGUST**	**SCARBOROUGH**	**HOME (TBC)**
Sat	6	September	Cleethorpes	Away
SAT	**13**	**SEPTEMBER**	**HARROGATE**	**HOME (TBC)**

YORKSHIRE ACADEMY IN THE YORKSHIRE LEAGUE CUP

Sun	18	May	Rotherham Town	Away

YORKSHIRE ACADEMY IN THE YORKSHIRE LEAGUE T20

Sun	8	June	Castleford	Castleford

YORKSHIRE ACADEMY FRIENDLIES

Sun	13	April	Sheriff Hutton Bridge	Away
Wed	30	April	Sedbergh School	Away
Mon	19	May	Derbyshire Academy	Away (TBC)
MON	**30-2**	**JUNE/JULY**	**SCOTLAND DEVELOPMENT SQUAD**	**WEETWOOD**

YORKSHIRE UNDER-17s in ONE-DAY AND TWO-DAY
NATIONAL CHAMPIONSHIPs

Tue	8-9	July	Durham	Away (TBC)
Thu	10	July	Durham	Away (TBC)
TUE	**22-23**	**JULY**	**DERBYSHIRE**	**WEETWOOD**
THU	**24**	**JULY**	**DERBYSHIRE**	**WEETWOOD**
Tue	5-6	August	Cheshire	Away (TBC)
Thu	7	August	Cheshire	Away (TBC)
TUE	**12-13**	**AUGUST**	**LANCASHIRE**	**WEETWOOD**
THU	**14**	**AUGUST**	**LANCASHIRE**	**WEETWOOD**
TUE	**20-21**	**AUGUST**	**SEMI-FINALS**	**WEETWOOD**
Thu	29-30	August	Two-Day Final	TBC
Sun	1	September	One-Day Final	TBC

*In an exclusive interview for the Yorkshire Yearbook,
Chief Executive MARK ARTHUR maps out the route
he has planned for the White Rose club*

WE ARE ON A JOURNEY, JOIN
US ON THE ROAD AHEAD

By David Warner

Mark Arthur is a man on two missions. He is well on the road to achieving one of them, while the other is strewn with obstacles which, if they can be successfully removed, will lead to Headingley being pre-eminent among the Test match grounds.

When the former Nottinghamshire CCC and Nottingham Forest chief executive took on a similar role with Yorkshire last May he could not stand accused of coming with his head buried in the sand.

He was fully aware of the Club's multi-million pound debt, and knew that the perilous financial situation had to be addressed, but it was a challenge he was prepared to accept because he also knew that Yorkshire was the best known cricket club in the world, and he wanted to head the team that would try to put it back on the highest of pedestals.

Within the boundaries of the Broad Acres, 117,000 people over the age of 14 play cricket every weekend and there are 747 league clubs, all competing with an intensity that is unique to the county itself.

Mark appreciated that no other county club could tap into such a rich source, and he arrived with the long-term aim of strengthening links with local schools and clubs. He and his executive team rolled up their sleeves, and got cracking to such an extent that they visited over 40 clubs and leagues this winter to spread the word, and they intend to be just as pro-active when the nights draw in again.

The response to these visits has been remarkable with the clubs and their players feeling that they have become part of the Yorkshire family. If Mark can similarly succeed in his other ambition of further developing Headingley and filling the stadium for international matches, he will indeed be a happy man.

When the post of Yorkshire Chief Executive was advertised early last year what was it that made Mark want to apply for it? "During all the years I have been involved in professional sport and cricket, Yorkshire CCC was set apart from the other counties because it was a sporting institution with an almost indefinable uniqueness of history and tradition, a great Club which, nevertheless, had never owned its own land

MARK ARTHUR: Cricket first

until Headingley became its home in recent years," he said. "It was also a club which provided players for the England team but had a history of infighting and, at times, of tearing itself apart. On top of all that, there was the largess of the county itself with so many cricket clubs to draw its talent from.

"So, when the post was advertised I spoke to a number of confidants about it, and while very excited about the prospect of the job itself, the big worry sign was the debt the Club was carrying.

"During the interview process, I had to convince myself it was something I was prepared to address, along with the members of the Board and the executive team already in place. Now, having been in the job for some nine months, whilst enormously challenging I can see a route ahead.

"On that route I will always put cricket first and I want us to challenge for trophies to fill what has recently been a fairly empty cupboard — but we have to do it with caution and live within our means.

"With a guarantee of international cricket at Headingley until 2019 we have to make the most of that opportunity, and if we don't then our international future could be very bleak."

This, indeed, is a stark warning, but action to prevent it coming about is already being taken, and one of the priorities is to make sure that Headingley posts big attendances at all of the Test matches up to the time their agreement with the ECB runs out.

Mark and his team failed to fill all the seats for the May Test match against New Zealand last year, but the signs are far more encouraging for Sri Lanka's first Test appearance at the ground in their game against England starting on June 20.

"At the time of writing we are five months ahead of last year with sales of Test match tickets, and I am anticipating an enjoyable and successful event," said Mark. "The difference this year is that we have a new ticketing system which enables us to service our members and supporters in a far more customer-friendly and efficient manner. We have also reduced prices in many areas of the ground and we gave all purchasers an early bird discount if they bought tickets before the end of January. In addition, we have reconfigured what was the West Stand into four distinct enclosures under the new name of the White Rose Stand, and this was to define certain types of behaviour that may or may not be tolerated in that vicinity.

"We are keen to make sure that a day at the Test match is a very enjoyable event for ordinary spectators, and Headingley will be adorned with blue, yellow and white flowers at both the St Michael's Lane and Sir Leonard Hutton Gates entrances. This will improve the initial appearance of the ground and will make Headingley welcoming to everyone.

"Our regular stewards will be dressed in Yorkshire CCC blazers, which will be Cambridge Blue with a Yorkshire rose on the breast pocket. We are an international cricket ground of repute and we want to make sure the initial experience is a good one and that spectators will have a fantastic time and want to return the following year."

For Headingley's future to be secure, however, much more needs to be done than just to pack 'em into the ground — as Mark is only too well aware. "There is a move to reduce the number of international Test venues in order that the Test match grounds which are chosen can stage regular Test match cricket, thereby being able to develop sustainable business plans," said Mark. "We and Durham are the only Test match venues not to have floodlights, and the area of the ground at the rugby stand end is at the moment below acceptable international standards.

"We have to improve income streams and find the mechanism to reduce the Club's debt and then improve the fabric of the ground. We have put in a planning application to Leeds City Council, and if this is granted in the Spring the next task will be to fund the floodlights which will cost £1.8m, of which there will be an ECB grant of £700,000 and the remaining £1.1m will have to be found by ourselves. But we will not be able to undertake this work until the finance is in place. We cannot add to the debt so we have to find the right source of income.

"Although we are guaranteed international cricket until 2019, the ICC (International Cricket Council) may well make a requirement that all Test match staging grounds have floodlights. There is no timescale as yet, but we know that the clock is ticking.

"One of the strengths of Yorkshire's case to the ECB for continuing to stage Test matches at Headingley in the long term is that we represent a county that has more cricket clubs and more players than any other county in England but, that said, we need to prove there is an appetite among those people to watch international cricket, and we must make sure Headingley is a ground fit for purpose.

"The present capacity is around 17,000 and we need to increase it to over 20,000. Members will be as aware as the Board that the facilities in

**VISION OF THE FUTURE: Headingley under floodlights.
Natwest Pro40 — Yorkshire v. Middlesex, August 8, 2007**

some areas of the ground are below those enjoyed by other Test grounds, but on the plus side Headingley has a fantastic history of staging thrilling and memorable Test matches going right back to 1899. No-one must under-estimate the value of history and tradition."

No-one should take too lightly, either, the financial restraints which are currently reining in Yorkshire in their obvious desire to have out-standing facilities on all four sides of the Headingley ground. Make no mistake about it, the will is there, and if circumstances arise which allow for the major re-development of the rugby stand area they will be taken with all possible speed.

At the moment, Mark wants everyone to keep faith in the future. "I thank all sponsors, partners, members and supporters of Yorkshire County Cricket Club," he said. "We are on a journey and hopefully you will all stick with us and we will gain a few more on the road ahead. This is a magnificent club, a magnificent brand and we want to make the most of it."

FINE BALLANCE REWARDED
WITH ASHES CALL-UP

By Graham Hardcastle

So many Yorkshire players were picked by England at various levels last summer that you could be forgiven for forgetting the odd one or two. One of the 14 you will not forget is Gary Ballance!

The left-hander topped 1,000 County Championship runs for the first time in 2013 — a tally boosted by two centuries in the final week of the season against Surrey The Oval.

There may not have been much on the game, with Yorkshire already assured of second place and Surrey relegated, but Ballance, who had been called to England's winter *Ashes* squad the day before the match, had everything to play for. He had skipper Alastair Cook and coach Andy Flower to impress further so that his name would be to the fore in the coming months "down under". In doing so, he became the 13th Yorkshire player to score centuries in both innings of a match and the first since Pakistani Younus Khan in 2007.

Ballance's game has come on leaps and bounds during the last two summers. He has played innings of note for the *White Rose* in every format, including the two 40-over centuries against the Unicorns in 2012 and 2013, the match-clinching 64 not out off 37 balls against Trinidad and Tobago at Centurion in the Champions League t20 qualifiers in October 2012, and his maiden Championship century for Yorkshire — the 111 against Warwickshire at Edgbaston in August 2011.

Why single out that one from all of the eight first-class centuries he has scored for his county? It came after passing 50 for Yorkshire 10 times that summer, and while a number of those innings were not out and did not present him with the opportunity to reach three figures this would have been in the back of his mind.

Born in Harare, Zimbabwe, he moved to England as a 16-year-old. Initially, he lived with former Zimbabwe international Dave Houghton, whose wife is the cousin of Gary's dad. He was signed to the Derbyshire Academy at the age of 16 in 2006, and finished his education at Harrow School. He played four one-day games for Derbyshire, scoring 48 against a West Indies 'A' attack led by Tino Best while he was still 16, and hit 73 on his competitive debut for Derbyshire, a Pro40 match against Hampshire at the Rose Bowl.

Ballance was offered a place in the Yorkshire Academy in 2007, but he had to wait until the following year to see first-team action with the county he now calls his own.

He said in the *All Out Cricket* magazine last October: "I like to think of myself as a true Yorkshireman. The people here say Yorkshire is its own country, and I've enjoyed every minute.

"Leeds is my favourite city in the country. I've had some great times, and made some very good mates up in Yorkshire. It's a really good place, and the people have been very welcoming."

Ballance, prolific in Yorkshire Second Eleven and Yorkshire League cricket for Barnsley, debuted for the White Rose in a Championship match against Kent at Canterbury in July 2008, scoring one and five.

GARY BALLANCE: Topped 1,000 runs for the first time

He would play only one Championship match in just less than the next three years, but quickly stamped his authority on his return in the pressure-cooker environment of a *Roses* match at Liverpool in May 2011 with a second-innings 57. It was the first of those 10 half-centuries before reaching three figures, including a run of five 50s in five games.

Two winters of domestic cricket in Zimbabwe for MidWest Rhinos under the guidance of Jason Gillespie, ironically, in 2010-11 and 2011-12 helped the former Zimbabwe Under-19s player's development. His career-best 210 came for them in their four-day Logan Cup competition.

Ballance has proved himself to be one of Yorkshire's most potent weapons in one-day and *Twenty20* cricket, demonstrating significant power on numerous occasions, none more so than against T&T in South Africa as he fired the county through to the group stages, where they would come up against powerhouses Sachin Tendulkar and MS Dhoni.

"Gaz has a very mature approach to his cricket," Gillespie said. "He

Catch in the cold: Gary Ballance clings on to Steve Magoffin on the second day of Yorkshire's Champion ship match v. Sussex at Headingley on April 11

understands the game. He's made runs in all three forms, in all different situations, under pressure. That's a very important trait to have as a batsman. He's been there at the end when we've won games of cricket in all forms, and that is the mark of a mature player."

The second half of the 2013 summer was a purple patch for the affable 24-year-old (then 23), with three successive hundreds for Yorkshire and the England Lions in August. It was a run of form that earned Ballance a one-day international debut for England against Ireland at Malahide in early September, in which he unfortunately made a two-ball duck, but ultimately a place on England's winter *Ashes* tour — when he started with a one-ball duck!

His *Ashes* call came at the beginning of the final week of the season — in which he scored those two hundreds against Surrey. It was no surprise to hear him say: "I think the past week is up there with the best of my career. To get the call about my England selection at the beginning of it was a great feeling, and to finish off the season with two hundreds was fantastic. I'm really happy with the way the season's gone.

"I got the phone call from Geoff Miller. The first thing he said was, 'Are you sitting down for this?' Then he said, 'We'd like you to come to Australia on the tour.' I was very shocked when I heard it, very surprised. But, at the same time, very excited. The Yorkshire lads were excited and happy for me as well.

"Personally, I had the target of getting 1,000 runs in the Championship at the start of the season, and this is the first time I've done it, so that was very satisfying, also."

He had to wait patiently for his Ashes chance, making his debut in the Fifth Test at Sydney when the series was gone, but in a first-innings 18 he showed enough to leave the vast majority of fans and pundits calling for him to retain his place ahead of the home series with Sri Lanka. He then made an immediate impact in the one-day series with Australia.

The future is definitely bright for Gary Ballance.

NOW ONE-DAY FORM NEEDS TO MATCH CHAMPIONSHIP

By Graham Hardcastle

Yorkshire endured a mixed campaign in 2013. Limited-overs cricket was not so great, but they made significant strides in the Championship, finishing second after putting up a serious title challenge for large parts of the season. Heading into 2014, the squad are confident that they can clinch their first four-day title since 2001.

Let us start on white-ball cricket — and get the bad bit out of the way:

The Vikings won only three of their 12 Yorkshire Bank 40 matches, a record which only the Unicorns failed to better in Group C...and the Unicorns, a team of players hopeful of either breaking into or back into county cricket, are no longer in operation.

Yorkshire brought in a host of young players for the YB40, including record-breaking 15-year-old fast bowler Matthew Fisher, who will be better for the experience in the long-term. Fisher became the youngest post-Second World War county cricketer at 15 years and 212 days when he was selected for his first-team debut against Leicestershire at Scarborough on June 9. But the team's overall record in the competition was not good enough for a county of Yorkshire's standing, whether they be concentrating on LV= County Championship cricket or not.

Now they have been handed a favourable draw in the 50-over competition, which replaces the 40 League, and they need to put in a serious challenge for the four quarter-final places up for grabs from each of the two nine-team groups. You can rest assured, because coach Jason Gillespie says he wants to give the competition "a real hot crack".

The former Australian Test star said of the return of 50-over cricket to the county schedule for the first time since 2009: "We are really excited about it. We'll be giving it our very best. We had to rest and manage a few of our players, especially our bowlers, throughout the 40-over season last summer. With the 50-over programme being blocked off a little bit more, we can really go and work hard to win that tournament."

The White Rose *Twenty20* performances were no better — Yorkshire finishing bottom of the North Division with two wins from 10 matches. Yet, coming on the heels of a Finals Day appearance the season before their slide was more understandable, given the number of key absentees. Overseas duo Mitchell Starc and David Miller were unavailable, as was

England new boy Joe Root.

An embarrassing eight-wicket *Twenty20* defeat with nine overs to spare away to Lancashire, when the Vikings failed to defend 125, was the lowlight of a dreadful limited-overs campaign, in which the county lost 16 out of 22 matches in both competitions.

Concentrating on the red-ball premier competition in the domestic schedule, Gillespie's troops enjoyed a hugely

Youngest since the war: Matthew Fisher plays for Yorkshire's first team at 15 years and 212 days

encouraging Championship campaign in their 150th anniversary year. It may have ended in the disappointment of letting slip a 25-and-a-half-point lead over eventual champions Durham with four matches left, but the signs are good for success. Recruits Jack Brooks and Liam Plunkett settled in well, and Plunkett's re-emergence as an all-round force was particularly pleasing with 36 wickets and 394 runs from 12 matches.

Captain Andrew Gale recovered from a difficult start to score 1,000 runs for the first time, as did Gary Ballance — who went to Australia as part of England's 2013-14 *Ashes* squad. Ballance scooped the Players' Player of the Year award in early October.

The emergence of 20-year-old opener Alex Lees was a major plus. He enjoyed one of the innings of the summer — 275 not out in the win against Derbyshire at Chesterfield — and became the county's youngest double centurion at 20 years and 95 days to join Ballance in the awards as Young Player of the Year. Gale and Root also scored Championship double-centuries, Gale against Nottinghamshire at Scarborough and Root against Derbyshire at Headingley.

Adil Rashid's early form with the bat, including three successive centuries, is worthy of note, especially given the controversy surrounding the leg-spinner on the eve of the season, following published comments which cast doubt on his future with the county.

Overseas signing Kane Williamson, who has agreed to return to the

Club on a more permanent basis for the forthcoming summer, enjoyed the end of the season, the Kiwi scoring four half-centuries in five Championship innings at one stage.

In the bowling department pacemen Ryan Sidebottom, the Members' Player of the Year, and Steven Patterson had impressive campaigns yet again, leading the way with 49 and 46 wickets, Plunkett coming third with 36 and Brooks bagging 34 from 11 matches.

There was even a maiden first-class wicket for former Australian Test batsman Phil Jaques against Sussex at Hove in his 187th outing, albeit in contrived circumstances. Jaques left the county at the end of the season to pursue a career in coaching, initially with Sydney grade club Sutherland, where Yorkshire Colt Jack Leaning spent his winter.

Leaning made his Championship debut in the draw against Surrey at Headingley after some excellent form in Second Eleven and club cricket. Unfortunately, he posted a two-ball duck, but he also played a handful of limited-overs matches, scoring 60 in the YB40 defeat against Somerset at Taunton in mid- August two days after capturing 5-22 with his off-spinners against the Unicorns at Headingley.

Yorkshire won Championship matches against Durham, Derbyshire twice, Warwickshire, Middlesex twice and Nottinghamshire. There were 10-wicket wins over Middlesex at Lord's and Nottinghamshire at Trent Bridge. The away win against Durham in April came when Root scored a brilliant 182 to anchor a successful pursuit of 336, and the home win against Derbyshire the following week was achieved despite conceding 475 in the first innings. Root responded with 236 and Jonny Bairstow with 186 to help Yorkshire to 677-7 declared, and then Brooks took 5-40 to bowl Derbyshire out for 163 during an exciting last day.

It was the clinical 139-run win over defending champions Warwickshire at Edgbaston in mid-May which was the highlight of 2013. Yorkshire bowled Warwickshire out for 128, replied with 407 and bowled the hosts out again for 140. Patterson and Plunkett led the way with six wickets each and Rashid a century in a match which saw Yorkshire serve notice to all that they were genuine title contenders in their first season back in Division 1. Yorkshire also deserve praise for their production line: 14 of their players from Under-17 level upwards gained England recognition at some point during the summer.

Director of Professional Cricket Martyn Moxon is confident of another title challenge this summer — so long as the players do not become complacent: "This division is very tough. You only have to look at Surrey being relegated after being favourites to win the Championship at the start of the season. So we can't take anything for granted.

"I think we're a good team, and I don't think there are too many weaknesses. But there are percentages here and there that we can

OVERSEAS FIND: Kane Williamson, who hit 84 and 97 as the Championship slipped away at Scarborough

improve upon. The key is not to get complacent, and to try and work hard and improve. We played some really good cricket last year, yet we only finished second. So it's a lesson for us going forward. We have to maintain our standards."

While Gillespie described a second-place finish as "a fantastic achievement" a year after earning promotion from Division 2, he pointed to the defeat against Durham at Scarborough in late August as the defining moment in the title race: "Durham completely outplayed us in that game at Scarborough, and they deserved to win," he said. "If we'd managed to win that or at least save the game we may have found ourselves with an opportunity. But all we can do is congratulate Durham.

"It was hard to fault our lads' attitude or effort. As a support staff we managed our players as best we could, especially our fast bowling. It would have been a fairytale had we got promoted and then gone on to win the title, but we always knew we were a strong team."

ALL-ROUND PERFORMANCES
MATCH THE SUNNY WEATHER

By Howard Clayton

There was a definite and sustained improvement in the weather with the result that Yorkshire Seconds lost only three full days in the Championship and one in the Trophy compared with 18 the year before across all three formats.

The team played well on occasions, ending up fourth in the Northern section with three wins and two draws, and the only disappointment in the major format was that the season ended with consecutive defeats by Lancashire and Nottinghamshire. Yorkshire entered those last two games hoping to qualify for the Championship playoff if they had enough points, but it was not to be as Lancashire won in two days and Nottinghamshire successfully chased almost 250 on the last afternoon.

Batting had been the weak link in 2012, but this time the players gained welcome pre-season practice in the many "friendlies" before competitive action began on May 28. Yorkshire ran up 480 against Leicestershire in the Championship, and passed 300 three more times. Leading run-scorers were Jack Leaning, 391, Dan Hodgson, 385, and newcomer Ollie Robinson, 329. There were four centuries — two by Alex Lees and maiden centuries for Eliot Callis and Will Rhodes.

Robinson completed an impressive first year by also becoming the leading wicket-taker with 15 scalps. Moin Ashraf had 12, bowling quickly at times, and Iain Wardlaw, Karl Carver and Steven Patterson each took 11. Hodgson led the way behind the stumps with 11 catches.

There was a batting disaster at Barnt Green, where Yorkshire were put out for 68 and 67, their lowest totals ever against Worcestershire. They lost by an innings and 121 runs, one of their heaviest defeats.

The Trophy saw a similar move up the table to fourth place. Two games were lost — the opener against Derbyshire and the final game against Lancashire. There were four wins, one tie and two rain-affected matches. The winners of the last one-dayer against Lancashire at Todmorden would qualify for the semi-finals...but it was not to be for Yorkshire as the *Red Rose* inflicted a five-wicket defeat. The tied game against MCC Young Cricketers was Yorkshire's first in Second Eleven one-day cricket, and it prevented a first defeat at the hands of the Young Cricketers by the skin of their teeth. Yorkshire batted well for 279-9 in the 40 overs, Adam Lyth leading the way with 102, and at tea it looked

Wings of a dove: Leading run-scorer Jack Leaning more than proved his worth as an acrobatic fielder

in the bag. Confidence ebbed away as MCC replied with 182-3 until a burst of wickets made it 206-8. From 237-9 with 43 needed in six overs Yorkshire should have finished it, but it went all the way to the wire: Wardlaw was bowling the third ball of the last over when Zain Shahzad, who had batted so well for his 39, decided to go for glory...he mis-hit to long-on, where Joe Sayers took a good catch, and a subdued Yorkshire realised they had pocketed a point they hardly deserved.

Another good score of 248-5 against Leicestershire included five penalty runs, as Leicestershire had not completed their overs in the allotted time. There was a quite magnificent spell from Matthew Fisher of 7-1-25-6, the second-best figures for Yorkshire in Second Eleven one-day cricket, beaten only by Paul Booth's 6-21 v. Nottinghamshire in 1986.

Phil Jaques made 105 to prove his fitness after injury in the 252-6 against Nottinghamshire, a game which almost fell away as from 89-7 Brett Hutton, 64, and George Bacon, 58, added 127 in 74 balls. This was the highest eighth-wicket stand against Yorkshire by any opponents in the one-day competition. The leading run-scorer was Hodgson, 237, with Azeem Rafiq and Leaning totalling 138 runs each. The leading wicket-takers were Ashraf with nine and Rafiq, eight. Wicket-keeper

Hodgson snapped up 13 victims, 10 caught and three stumped. Yorkshire in the *T20* competition showed a welcome improvement, moving from bottom to third place in the group with nine points from four victories and one abandonment. The other three games were lost.

There were two high-scoring friendly matches before competitive play began at Headingley against Nottinghamshire and a 150 run chase ended successfully. The second game got as far as 19 overs with Nottinghamshire batting when rain set in.

Both games against Lancashire at Marske were lost, Karl Brown seeking form with the *Red Rose* Seconds and finding it with 101 not out in the first game. Liam Livingstone hit 100 in the second as Lancashire ran up 224-4, at that time the highest total since the inception of the Second Eleven *T20* competition. Yorkshire played the EDP Under-19s at Loughborough next day and won both games by batting first.

The programme was completed three days later at Denby against Derbyshire. Bundled out for 81 in the first game, the players arrived for lunch with some advice from the coaches ringing in their ears and duly turned the tables in match two. The best sustained performance in 2013 came from Rafiq, who took 10 wickets over the eight matches, and his 4-11 against Derbyshire was the best analysis for Yorkshire in the *T20*.

Yorkshire Seconds had a lot of friendly cricket, beginning a six-week programme in mid-April at Hartlepool. A good game, in which Sayers made an unbeaten 100, brought a creditable draw and a useful introduction for Jonathan Tattersall into multi-day cricket with an unbeaten 20. Sayers, 91, and Lees, 121 not out, helped to hold Lancashire to a draw at Scarborough, where rain wiped out the final afternoon. Alex Davies, 119, and Jordan Clark, 102, helped Lancashire to a substantial lead — Clark smiting six sixes in one over from Gurman Randhawa, all pulled over mid-wicket towards the main entrance.

It was Lancashire again as the circus moved to North Wales and Northop Hall. This brought a magnificent five-wicket win as Yorkshire scored the required 354 in 81.2 overs. Solid batting all the way down, led by Hodgson, 87, and Andrew Hodd, 74 — finished off by 40 in 27 deliveries by Leaning — ensured a splendid victory. It was not the only contribution Hodd made to the Seconds' cause: he scored well in other friendly games and in those Championship fixtures where Jonathan Bairstow's presence in the first team forced a wicket-keeping rejig.

Next came Canterbury and a four-dayer against the combined might of Kent and Surrey. This was a high-scoring draw in which Hodgson, 115, registered his second century of the season as he led Yorkshire to their highest 2013 total of 485. Kent used 10 bowlers in the 148.5 overs they needed to get Yorkshire out. Finally, it was Lancashire again, this time at Aigburth in what became a three-dayer and a one-dayer. The one-day game was lost by seven wickets, but Ben Coad, 3-31, took all three and did his reputation no harm at all.

The three-dayer was severely hampered by the weather, and forfeitures were needed from each side to contrive a target. Yorkshire failed by 144 to reach the 321 needed, but not before Eliot Callis had compiled his maiden 50.

The season ended with two more three-day friendlies. First, it was down to Merchant Taylor's School in Northwood to meet Middlesex. The first day was lost to rain, but the second and third and two forfeitures saw Yorkshire win.

Hodd led the way with a sumptuous 165, the highest individual score of the season for Yorkshire Seconds, ably supported by another 50 from Hodgson. Middlesex were going well at 148-1, but

ANDREW HODD: Sumptuous

Carver produced the season's second-best bowling figures for 2013 in any Yorkshire second-team game, 6-43, his personal best. A win by 93 runs over the team who finished as joint county champions with Lancashire, beaten finalists in the *T20* and one-day beaten semi-finalists, was no mean feat. So to Weetwood, and a final outing against Durham, where the last day was washed out with an interesting finish in prospect.

Five regular players, Karl Carver, Matt Fisher, Will Rhodes — who made a splendid century against Pakistan — Josh Shaw and Jonathan Tattersall, who captained the side, all represented England Under-19s in the Tri-Series against Bangladesh and Pakistan. When Fisher played in the first one-dayer on August 6 he became the youngest ever to represent the England Under-19s at 15 years and 270 days. The five retained their places in December for the Under-19 Tri-Series in the United Arab Emirates against the home side and Pakistan, and there were three Yorkshire representatives in the England Under-17 squad — Ryan Gibson, Mosun Hussain and Jared Warner. All except Warner have already made Yorkshire second-team debuts.

Warner and Hussain have retained their places in the EDP Under-17 squad, and will undergo rigorous training at the National Performance Centre at Loughborough before a trip to Sri Lanka this April. With Bairstow, Ballance, Bresnan and Root in the England set-up and Lees in the back-up squad, the coaching staff must be doing something right.

*Howard Clayton is the Yorkshire CCC Second Eleven Scorer

CURTAIN BROUGHT DOWN
WITH FIVE WINS ON TROT

By Harold D Galley

Season 2013 began brightly with a 27-run victory over Castleford, in which younger squad members Mosun Hussain scored 50 and Karl Carver took five wickets. Alex Lees scored a superb 91 not out in the 10-wicket victory over Sheffield United, and he followed this with an unbeaten 163 as Rotherham lost by nine wickets at Clifton Lane.

There was a League defeat against Driffield, who went on to win the Yorkshire League Cup and the *Twenty20* competition, but continued good form kept the Colts in second place to eventual champions York most of the season. They faltered against teams who had experienced ex-county players: this was the case in the first round of the Cup against Doncaster Town, where a poor batting display saw the Academy all out for 109 and the vastly experienced Doncaster opener Simon Widdup's fine 65 not out took the home side to victory.

Unlike the previous season, few matches were cancelled or abandoned because of the weather.

The first match in August was an opportunity to defeat York and go top of the table. This looked highly unlikely when the Academy were 40-5 and all out for 65, only one batsman reaching double figures, but the pace bowlers reduced York to 30-5. Hopes rose, but Tom Pringle at No. 8 hit five fours in an aggressive 22 and Ryan McKendry was unbeaten at the close, steering York home by three wickets. An outright win would have put the Academy on the top of the table.

The boys finished the season in fine style with successive victories over Appleby Frodingham, Hull, Barnsley, Sheffield Collegiate and Cleethorpes. Some outstanding batting performances will linger long in spectators' memories, namely Callis's 168 v. Hull, Yaaser Imtiaz's 81 on his debut in the same match, and Ryan Gibson's excellent 139 off 116 balls v. Harrogate.

Carver's 5-29 in the opening League match was an indication of his fine season to come. Two quicker bowlers had five wicket hauls — Ben Coad taking 5-27 v. Sheffield Collegiate and Lewis Stabler 5-20 in the last League match against Cleethorpes.

*Harold Galley is the Yorkshire Academy Scorer

FESTIVALS ARE FEAST DAYS
FOR SEVERAL AGE GROUPS

By Chris Hassell

Another eventful and enjoyable year with some exciting performances at the lower-age group levels, the Under-11s excelling themselves. Most fixtures were completed with minimal interference from the weather. The Under-10s, 11s and 13s all won their festivals, as did the 14B team at both Scarborough and Wolverhampton: the 90th-anniversary match was staged at Scarborough's magnificent facility on North Marine Road against Lancashire Under-15s, followed by a most enjoyable celebration dinner attended by parents and officials from both sides. A total of 190 matches were played at county level. For next season an Under-10 B team will be introduced to accommodate the increasing number of aspiring young players.

15 A: P13, W9, L2, D1, Ab1. A satisfying season, but without the success we might have achieved, albeit with a number of highlights. For the first time an Under-15 player, Matthew Fisher from Easingwold School, was unavailable because of commitments at a higher level — indeed the highest, with selection for Yorkshire's First Eleven in the Yorkshire Bank 40 against Leicestershire at Scarborough to become the youngest post-war county cricketer at 15 years and 212 days. He spent the season with Yorkshire's Second Eleven and Academy teams.

The season started well, the team winning the northern section of the ECB County Cup with seven victories and one no-result to earn a home tie in the quarter-final against Staffordshire. Even allowing for the boys not being at full strength there was a woeful batting performance in chasing a modest 169 and losing by 39 runs with nine overs remaining. A great opportunity was missed to meet Surrey again — they won the trophy with overs to spare. Other than that one regrettable lapse of concentration there were some very good performances, with seven boys selected for the north team at the Bunbury Festival — Ed Morrison, St Wilfred's Catholic HS; Mustafa Rafique, Roundhay HS, and Jonathan Read, Lady Lumley's School, put in some very good performances, whilst Ed Barnes, King James's, Knaresborough; James Brown, Winterhill Comprehensive; Yassar Imtiaz, Royd's Hall School, and James Logan, Freeston Academy, went on to make significant contributions for the Academy. Yassar captained the county as well as the north team, and secured the "most refreshing approach" award at the Bunbury with Ed Barnes taking the best-bowler award and a scholarship to attend the National Performance Centre at Loughborough. Our 90th-anniversary clash with Lancashire was played as a time game, and after frequent interruptions for rain was narrowly lost.

Team Manager: Andy Rowsell. Coaches: Andrew Chadwick and Richard Damms.

15 B: P14, W11, D1, L2. An excellent season with good performances from a many of the boys. Daniel McLean, Worksop College, flourished as captain, and performed magnificently to gain his county cap for his all-round contribution. Sam Wigglesworth, Outwood School, took the batting honours with more than 500 runs. Matthew Taylor, St Thomas A'Beckett School, won the Fox Trophy most-improved-player award, and Ryan Gaughan, Malton School, gained the bowling award for his persistency and accuracy. On the southern tour there was a good win over London in a two-dayer and a close encounter with a strong Middlesex team, also over two days. On the way home there was an excellent win over a strong Northamptonshire. A total of 24 boys played in the squad, which showed how many were knocking on the door.

Team Manager: Bob Wincer, Woodhouse Grove. Coach: Peter Hepworth.

14 A: P23, W15, L7, Ab1. A somewhat disappointing season with a lack of success in the ECB County Cup and at the Taunton Festival. James Pick, Driffield School, was a very capable captain, and scored 788 runs. Sam Woodcock, Brinsworth Comprehensive, won the Brian Willey Player of the Year Trophy with a number of good returns. Harry Brook, Ilkley GS, with 818 runs took the batting award and is now with the Yorkshire Academy and performing well. Matthew Rees, Kettlethorpe HS, with 28 wickets won the bowling award. Most-improved player was Adam Ahmed, Belle Vue Boys. The team won four out of five matches at the Scarborough Festival, but finished as runners-up. There was a good win over Lancashire and against the Yorkshire B team who actually won the Festival.

Team Manager/Coach: Tony Pickersgill. Assistant: Jack Bethel.

14 B: P26, W19, L5, Ab2. A very satisfying season. The boys were undefeated at the Midlands Festival, winning the trophy against some very good A teams. They also won the Scarborough Festival, where the final match was on the main ground at North Marine Road. This was a fantastic day for Yorkshire, the A team playing the B team and the B team winning the trophy. Archie Scott, Pudsey Crawshaw, captained the side very well, scoring 501 runs and taking 29 wickets. The batting award went to Will Huffer, St Peter's School, and the bowling award to Ted Patmore, St Peter's School.

Team Manager/Coach: Tony Pickersgill. Coaches: Bren Terry, Adrian Grayson and John Terry.

*The Service of Thanksgiving for the 150th Anniversary
of Yorkshire County Cricket Club in York Minster
on June 14, 2013, was one of the highlights of the year.
The sermon was preached by the Bishop of Hull,
The Right Reverend Richard Frith, and the address was
given by the President of MCC, Mike Griffiths.
Here we give their addresses in full*

THE BISHOP'S SERMON

To say how pleased I am to have been invited to preach today is an understatement. As a lifelong cricket addict I was thrilled and delighted to be asked, especially as a Southerner who still, I'm afraid, admits to being a Somerset supporter.

But as today has drawn nearer that pleasure has given way to apprehension, as I've pondered what on earth I can say from the pulpit beyond a heartfelt: "Thank God for cricket in general and Yorkshire CCC in particular."

150 Years – it's quite a story. As David Warner has reminded us in his book, *The Sweetest Rose*, there are records of cricket in Yorkshire going back as far as 1750, but this year we celebrate the formation of Yorkshire CCC itself in 1863. Today is not the first link between Yorkshire Cricket and this Minster. There was the Yorkshire player who introduced Lord Hawke to the county. He was the Rev. Edmund Sardinson Carter, a distinguished musician here at York Minster. I am told he retained his sense of humour, even when serving on the Committee of Yorkshire CCC!

And many clergy have had a love of Yorkshire cricket. The Vicar of Riddlesden, the Rev. Hugh Hunter, wrote to *The Times* on August 26, 1938: "Sir, I called out to a very small boy in the village here this evening as he was slogging a ball up the street, 'Hello Bradman'. He replied, "I'm not Bradman, I'm Utton'. I apologised immediately. Don Bradman had held the Test record of 334 until the previous day, when Len Hutton scored 364 against Australia at The Oval. 'I'm not Bradman, I'm Utton', of course."

Preparing for today, one of the questions I asked myself was whether I should reflect on a history of rows, personality clashes, controversy, times when performances have been blown off course by jealousy, intrigue and personal rivalry. But I decided that, no, this is not the time for me to go on about the Church of England!

Of all that the CofE and Yorkshire CCC have in common, it's the reminder — in the words of the old strapline of the *News of the World* — "All human life is here".

Yes, cricket and the Church have much in common: arguments — women bishops or overseas players, finance, buildings, leadership, patterns of play — 20/20 or Test matches on the one hand, happy-clappy or matins on the other.

Even a quick glance at the history of the Club gives plenty of reminders of the remarkable mixture which makes up human nature. On the one hand, made in the image of God, what the Bible calls (Psalm 8) "little less than God and crowned with glory and honour."

BISHOP RICHARD FRITH
Thank god for cricket
and the faith

It's not blasphemous to talk of God-like cricketers, divine attributes, glimpses of heaven; we're talking God-given gifts here.

On the other hand, there are indications with every match of the fallibility of human beings, in the mistakes we make in relationships with each other as much as in the use of our gifts.

Cricket lends itself to all sorts of analogies about life, some of them pretty feeble, but dropped catches, faulty calling and wrong shot selection are evident not just in the sports pages of the newspaper.

For much of Yorkshire's history there has been the backdrop of the relationship between amateurs and professionals, gentlemen and players. I love the story of Major Arthur Lupton, whose playing record was, shall we say, modest — 700 runs in 104 matches — but was appointed captain in 1927 at the age of 44, and is credited with restoring discipline to the side.

It was harmless enough that the amateur had initials before and professionals after their surnames written on the scorecard so that the announcer at Lord's could issue a correction to the scorecard, that "for F J Titmus, please read Titmus F J". Or even that Lord Hawke said: "Pray God that no professional will ever captain England."

But I don't want to over-romanticise gentlemen and players. Episodes like the way in which Harold Larwood was treated by the establishment after the bodyline series in Australia, as opposed to how his captain, the amateur Douglas Jardine was, are far from glorious.

And in Yorkshire there has at times been much tension focused on issues of class. But nonetheless, at its best, the interaction between the

BALLANCING ACT: Gary Ballance became Yorkshire's latest Test player when he made his debut for England against Australia on last winter's *Ashes* tour before also taking part in the one-day series.

YORKSHIRE — 2013

APRIL LINE-UP: Back row, left to right: Richard Damms, Development Manager; Daniel Hodgson, James Wainman, Joe Sayers, Vice-Captain; Azeem Rafiq, Jack Leaning, Andrew Hodd, Gurman Randhawa and Tony Pickersgill, Development Coach. Middle row: Tom Summers, Strength and Conditioning Coach; Ian Dews, Director of Cricket Development; Gary Ballance, Richard Pyrah, Steven Patterson, Liam Plunkett, Iain Wardlaw, Alex Lees, Jack Brooks, Moin Ashraf, Scot McAllister, Physiotherapist, and Paul Farbrace, Second Team Coach. Front row: Martyn Moxon, Director of Cricket; Ryan Sidebottom, Adil Rashid, Jonathan Bairstow, Andrew Gale, Captain; Tim Bresnan, Adam Lyth, Phil Jaques and Jason Gillespie, First Team Coach. Absent: Joe Root. *(Photo: VAUGHN RIDLEY)*

BENEFIT BOY: Yorkshire and England fast-bowling all-rounder Tim Bresnan, who has been awarded a benefit this year by his county club. Tim is eager to express his thanks by collecting a large crop of wickets and a sackful of runs.

FOCUS ON YOUTH — MATTHEW FISHER

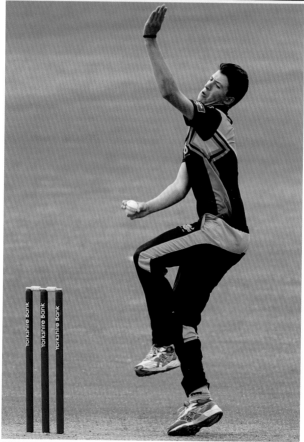

THE YOUNGEST ONE: Matthew Fisher became the youngest English player to be selected for a competitive county match when he made his Yorkshire debut at 15 years and 212 days in the 2013 YB40 League fixture against Leicestershire at Scarborough on June 9.

TOP MAN: Alex Lees acknowledges the applause upon leaving the field at Chesterfield after hitting an unbeaten 270 against Derbyshire to become Yorkshire's youngest double-century maker. *(photo: David Griffin).*

OVER THE TOP: Jonny Bairstow brought gasps of delight from the Headingley crowd when he scored 64 and put on 124 for the fifth wicket with Joe Root in the Second Test against New Zealand, a stand which helped England to win by 247 runs and clinch the series.

FIRST TEST HUNDRED: Joe Root raised the roof in the victorious Headingley Test against New Zealand upon completing his maiden Test century off 156 balls with nine fours. He was out for 104.

YORKSHIRE'S 2013 TEST HEROES

180 AT LORD'S: Joe Root at the crease during his second-innings epic for England against Australia in the Second Investec Test. **BELOW:** Who should be on hand as 12th man, drinks waiter, glove-carrier and chief sledger but brother Billy. *(Photos: MATT ROOT)*

amateur and the professional, gentlemen and players, brought to cricket something quite special.

Michael Marshall in his book, *Gentlemen and Players*, wrote of "the chemistry involving the carefree amateur and the dedicated professional."

The formal distinction between gentlemen and players may have gone — thankfully, I'd say — but the attitudes, characteristics and strengths indicated by each of them remain – in both cricket and, I would claim, for life, lived as God would have us live.

150 not out...Yorkshire's next President, Harold 'Dickie' Bird, arrives at the Minster

In the cultures of both cricket and the Church a caricature of both the professional and the amateur can give us the worst of both worlds. *Amateur* can mean incompetent, as in a bunch of amateurs. And similarly *professional* can have negative overtones, about money or professional fouls. But what if we see both *amateur* and *professional* positively? After all, *amateur* actually means, for the love of it. And *professional* taking seriously, developing skills, maximising ability.

Watching Joe Root and Jonny Bairstow batting together at Headingley last month, there was evident from both of them a sense of the skill and dedication of the professional and the enjoyment, smiles, and delight in each other's success of an amateur.

Both the amateur and the professional emphasis were there in our Bible reading earlier. After being told to clothe ourselves with compassion, kindness, humility, gentleness and patience, St Paul says: "Over all these virtues put on love." In other words, be an amateur. And then he goes on to say "...whatever you do, whether in word or deed, do it all in the name of the Lord Jesus." In other words, according to your profession, be it of faith or of cricket.

I unashamedly want to pass on a love of cricket and of faith from generation to generation. Thank God for those who introduced us to both cricket and faith. We give thanks today, as we take a fresh guard, setting our sights on not simply a double century but on whatever kind of innings is demanded by the circumstances, in the interests of the team.

Thank God for Yorkshire County Cricket Club.

THE MCC PRESIDENT'S ADDRESS

I feel very privileged that my term of office as MCC President coincides with the Yorkshire County Cricket Club's 150th anniversary celebrations and the opportunity to visit and speak in this wonderful building.

Like most county cricketers in the 1960s, my career bore an imprint from Yorkshire.

Either you played for Yorkshire and were phenomenally successful — and possibly prone to having the odd disagreement — or you played against them, and you cursed your luck that you were of the same era as so many outstanding players.

Playing against Yorkshire was the closest many of us came to replicating the experience and demands of Test cricket because of the tough,

MIKE GRIFFITHS
Yorkshire has provided
an inestimable legacy

uncompromising and, of course, intensely skilful nature of our opposition. Runs or wickets against Yorkshire were special. Caught Sharpe bowled Trueman was a dismissal to remember.

Of course, Yorkshire and MCC have been very closely linked over the years. Both MCC and cricket have benefited so much from Yorkshire. Indeed, if it were not for a certain Yorkshireman MCC might not exist.

In 1787 Thomas Lord, who was born in Thirsk, barely 20 miles from here, was commissioned by the request of the White Conduit Club to find and manage a venue for their fixtures. He bought his first ground in what is now Dorset Square, and it was here that MCC was formed. Subsequently, Lord moved the Club to another ground before settling in 1814 at the present site of Lord's Cricket Ground in St John's Wood. The rest, as they say, is history...except it could easily have been so different.

Lord was an entrepreneur first and cricketer second. His new ground struggled financially, and his head turned to property development; bricks and mortar, he thought, would be more profitable than leather and willow. Thankfully, he was persuaded to sell the ground to a prominent Member and Bank of England director, William Ward, and everyone was happy. Lord got his money and his place in cricket history, and MCC safeguarded its cricket ground.

This all happened in 1825 — the same year MCC played its first match in Yorkshire, on Sheffield Wednesday's ground at Darnall.

Another 38 years passed before the Yorkshire County Cricket Club was founded in1863, but it was well worth the wait.

I was intrigued to discover that, unlike any other county cricket club, its Sheffield founders, when creating the club, officially designated it *THE Yorkshire County Cricket Club* with the intention of warding off competition from other towns and cities in the county that had their own ideas about forming a county club and selecting teams to play under the name of Yorkshire. How dare they?

This Club was to be the definitive article, the real deal.

Since then Yorkshire cricket has bestrode the cricketing world — it has even provided four MCC Presidents, and many people think it should have been more. The first was Lord Hawke, who exceptionally held the post for five years while the Great War was raging. He was followed by Sir Stanley Jackson in 1921 and Sir William Worsley in 1963.

After a gap of 50 years, the untitled Phillip Hodson assumed the throne, and while he may not have achieved similar feats at first-class level to his illustrious predecessors he holds the distinction of having played in more than 300 out matches for MCC, and could still be found bowling his inimitable medium-pacers during his Presidency last year.

Yorkshire also set itself apart from other counties with its policy of playing only cricketers born within the county boundary, although this unwritten regulation was often breached in the early years — probably from a lack of information about where people were born — and in the case of amateurs was often disregarded. In any event the county had so many available players that there was little need to get them from anywhere else!

It took the county 30 years to win its first County Championship, but in the subsequent 75 years 29 more were won. It would have been more but for Surrey's dominance in the 1950s, in which Yorkshire had to make do with being runners-up for half of that time. Nevertheless, Yorkshire had its own halcyon periods, notably the early 1900s, the 1920s and '30s and the 1960s.

These achievements would not have been possible without a system that has produced some of the game's greatest cricketers. Time is too short to mention them all, but I would mention two who typified the ethos of the Hawke era — Wilfred Rhodes and George Hirst — whose respective feats of over 4,000 first-class wickets and the double of 2,000 runs and 200 wickets in a season will never be surpassed.

But Yorkshire cricket extends beyond affairs of the county club. The number of people playing at recreational level continues to grow, which makes one wonder what it is that gives Yorkshire people such an affinity with the aptitude for the game. Yorkshire people are not slow to express their individuality but at the same time have an innate desire to contribute to a team effort and be accepted by one's fellow men.

One explanation I have seen for the historical aptitude for cricket ascribes it to the occupation of handloom-weaving of a large part of the population prior to the Industrial Revolution. Apparently, the practice of catching and throwing a shuttle back and across the loom developed an extraordinary hand-to-eye co-ordination that befitted the catching and hitting of a cricket ball.

The county's contribution to the game of cricket has been inestimable. At national level over 80 Yorkshire players have represented the country. It was often said that when Yorkshire were strong England were strong. Yorkshire has produced many successful England captains.

The county's extensive league and club system has also played its part, and the Bradford League became the virtual centre of the game during the two world wars, attracting players from all over the country.

The England team that inflicted the heaviest defeat ever on an opponent — Australia at The Oval in 1938 — contained five Yorkshire players, one of whom, of course, Sir Leonard Hutton, scored 364, and I'm sure I was not alone watching the exploits of two young Yorkshire batsmen at Headingley last month and being touched by the pride and affection in which they were held by their home crowd.

So much work has gone into securing the future of Headingley for Yorkshire County Cricket Club, led tirelessly by your current Chairman, Colin Graves, who was also recently appointed Deputy Chairman of ECB and able, therefore, to more influence the wider first-class game.

MCC will continue to forge close associations with Yorkshire cricket at all levels. For example, this year we have a Root in our MCC Young Cricketers group, and father Matt Root currently plays in our recreational out match programme. Even Granddad was at Lord's to watch the action when England beat New Zealand.

For many years the county opened and closed its season with first-class matches against MCC, the first at Lord's in early May and the second as a feature of the Scarborough Cricket Festival in early September. More Yorkshire players than I can possibly mention wore the MCC colours with distinction while representing England overseas. But, most of all, if it wasn't for one Yorkshireman who had the foresight to buy land for the men of the White Conduit Club to play their cricket in privacy cricket would be all the poorer.

So, MCC salutes Yorkshire. Yorkshire has already provided an inestimable legacy to all cricket in its first 150 years. The links between our two clubs are as strong as ever. Above all, countless cricketers have derived hours of enjoyment from Yorkshire County Cricket Club's unfailing support for all levels of the game.

*Music was provided by the Bradford Cathedral Consort directed by Jonathan Eyre, Assistant Director of Music at Bradford Cathedral, and the organ was played by Robert Sharpe, Director of Music at York Minster. The Bidding Prayer and the Final Prayer and Blessing were given by the Yorkshire Chaplain, Canon Max Wigley. Prayers were said by Canon Peer Moger, Precentor of York Minster, and the Blessing was given by the Dean of York, the Very Rev. Vivienne Faull. Readings were given by David Kelly, chairman of Yorkshire Gentlemen's Cricket Club, and Bob Stott, of Yorkshire CCC's 150th Anniversary Committee.

This award for outstanding service to Yorkshire County Cricket Club was inaugurated in 2008. It was shared last year between RON DEATON, a former member of the Yorkshire Archives Committee who is an expert on the County's history and has helped in numerous ways to identify its past, and JOAN PICKERING, membership secretary of the Yorkshire CC Supporters' Association who runs their Kabin at Headingley Cricket Stadium, along with Veronica Denby, a previous recipient of the Medal. Here, Ron and Joan tell their own stories.

THE LOVE AFFAIR THAT STILL BURNS BRIGHTLY

By Ron Deaton

My earliest cricketing memory is of being taken by my brother, Ken, to watch a match at Bilton (Harrogate) some time during the summer of 1951.

To this day I don't know why he opted to view from a lofty perch in an ash tree just beyond the boundary while I was instructed to sit quietly on the ground below. Maybe it was because he was a teenager and could do as he liked, and I was only six.

Today the tree still stands, albeit in the garden of a house on the Hill Top estate, the club having removed to their present ground at the end of the 1951 season.

Thereafter, my interest in cricket steadily grew, and I well remember volunteering to fetch my neighbour's evening paper from the corner shop if only because the STOP PRESS revealed how Yorkshire had been doing that day.

My love affair with the Yorkshire Club was consummated not long after my 10th birthday. To be precise on July 6, 1955. By that time I knew enough about Yorkshire cricket to not only know the names of those who played but, thanks to images on cigarette cards and the like and fuzzy photos in newspapers and magazines, I knew what most of them looked like. But I hadn't actually seen any of them in the flesh.

The chance to put that right came in the summer of 1955 when a plot was hatched, along with several school friends, to hotfoot it after school to St George's Road to see the last session on the first day of the match

37

between Yorkshire and Glamorgan. The expectations were enormous. Would we see Len Hutton score another hundred? Would we see Fred Trueman in full flow? And would Bob Appleyard — recently returned from the 1954-55 *Ashes* triumph in Australia — be playing? We also had high expectations of a Yorkshire victory.

The big day arrived, and when the bell rang at four o'clock there was no hanging around. We were off on the two-and-a-half mile trek from Bilton Grange Primary School to the County Ground in St George's Road. I know for sure we arrived before play resumed after tea. In those days tea was taken from 4.15 until 4.35pm. I can also remember that we didn't need to pay to get in. That was important, because it meant that I had an unexpected shilling to spend.

Threepence was immediately invested in a scorecard, and that was the very first item of cricket memorabilia I purchased.

So, we'd arrived safe and sound. The ground seemed to be packed, but we managed to find seats together on the Mound facing the pavilion. Deep joy. Yorkshire were batting and, as expected, going very well. But when we perused the scorecard, shock horror! For starters there was no Len Hutton. Although we didn't know it at the time Leonard had played his last match for Yorkshire the previous week at Bournemouth. I missed seeing him play by just one week! The end of a glorious career.

Equally disappointing was the absence of Fred Trueman and Bob Appleyard. Both out injured. But there was still plenty to get excited about with Billy Sutcliffe flaying the bowling on his way to a career-best 161 not out. There was a new face in the team. A teenager from Hull — James Graham Binks — who, although he had made his first-team debut a couple of weeks earlier, was making his first Championship appearance in Yorkshire. Perhaps the biggest shock of all came on the third day when Glamorgan secured victory by four wickets and, in so doing, recorded their very first win in Yorkshire.

For me the result really didn't matter all that much. What did matter was that I'd seen my heroes in action. Not only that — and to my absolute delight —I'd managed to get a few autographs after the match, signed with my blotchy school fountain pen on the threepenny scorecard I'd bought at teatime. That was not only the start of a lifelong love affair with Yorkshire County Cricket Club, but also the start of my passion for collecting Yorkshire cricketers' autographs.

Half-a-century later, during the 2005 Scarborough Cricket Festival, I was invited to join the Yorkshire County Cricket Club Archives Committee and, although I'd have preferred to have opened the batting with Ken Taylor or Bryan Stott in the 1960s, I regarded it as an honour to have been asked and a privilege to have served the Club in this way.

Probably the most significant achievement during my time on the committee was working with colleagues to organise the Club's "legitimate" Archive in such a way that all items produced by the Club —

including minute books, scorebooks, financial ledgers and a whole host of other publications and paperwork — were categorised, described, referenced and listed. Similarly, the Club's library of Yorkshire-related cricket books, together with a wide range of three-dimensional items — including bats, balls, clothing, ceramics and metalware — were referenced and listed.

Apart from the methodical archive work I also enjoyed the start-to-finish involvement with the production of the 12 *Yorkshire Cricketing Legends* DVDs but, without doubt, the labour of love that gave me the greatest personal satisfaction was being entrusted with organising the wonderful collection of memorabilia assembled by Wilfred Rhodes and given to the Club by his granddaughter, Mrs Margaret Garton, in 2010.

Thankfully the flame that was sparked by my brother and kindled at St George's Road almost 60 years ago still burns brightly today. In conclusion it would be remiss of me not to say how surprised, grateful and embarrassed I was to be awarded the President's Medal in 2013.

Many thanks; for everything.

THURSDAY'S CHILD HAS GONE FAR WITH YORKSHIRE

One of my earliest memories — it just so happens to be of cricket — was being taken by my mother as a four-year-old to our village ground to watch the team and my grandfather umpire the game.

My mother was taking her turn at preparing the teas, and on reflection I was much more interested in the tea than the cricket!

Over the years there have been many memorable cricket moments for me with both Yorkshire and England. At the forefront must be the games where I witnessed Yorkshire win-

By Joan Pickering

ning the Championship — firstly at my (now) home town ground, St George's Road, Harrogate, in 1967, and secondly at North Marine Road, Scarborough, in 2001.

Test-match cricket also figures strongly, watching England take on Australia at Headingley back in 1964, again in 1972 and, more recently, in 2009. In August 1977 I found myself sitting in the "Coconut Shies" with a gang of cricket nuts from my office and witnessing Geoffrey Boycott achieve his 100th century — that was indeed special.

Everyone has lovely memories of cricket at Scarborough, I'm sure. Back in the 1980s I recall watching games that Michael Parkinson had organised, with many international stars playing on both sides. In 1987 I was at a packed North Marine Road when Yorkshire paraded the Benson & Hedges Cup they had won the day before at Lord's, and in 2013 I saw several records broken for Yorkshire, including a match featuring Matthew Fisher, at 15 years and 212 days the youngest cricketer post–war to play in a competitive county fixture.

Headingley highlights include Darren Lehmann scoring 339 against Durham in 2006 and Mark Ramprakash scoring his 100th first-class century in 2008 — days to remember. In the late 80s and early 90s I enjoyed the Harrogate Cricket Festival (sadly no more) and also the Scarborough Festival. I made many friends at both venues — happy days.

I joined the Yorkshire County Cricket Supporters' Association in the autumn of 1995. Being at most of the YCCSA winter meetings I assisted in various tasks, and in the course of time I was asked to consider joining the committee. I agreed, and am now the membership secretary and serve in the Kabin on match days. In the distant past, when the YCCSA ran coaches to away matches, I recall travelling down from Leeds to Lord's in 2002 for the final of the Cheltenham & Gloucester Trophy — Yorkshire v. Somerset — what a happy day that was, and Yorkshire triumphed !

I've always enjoyed travelling — must be something to do with being born on a Thursday according to the rhyme: "Thursday's Child has far to go". In 2000 I embarked on my first overseas pre-season tour with Yorkshire to Australia. I enjoyed it so much that I went on the next two, to South Africa, and then Grenada. In the last few years I have travelled to Australia twice and South Africa three times — each holiday included an international cricket match, of course! All-in-all, I'm having a wonderful time, seeing so many new places and different cultures.

Over the years I have been watching cricket I've made some wonderful enduring friendships, both here and abroad. I would like to say a huge "thank-you" to all the people I have met through my involvement with the YCCSA and all manner of folk who come to the Kabin to buy and to chat. Most importantly, may I say what an honour and a pleasure it is to have been awarded the President's Medal in this the Club's 150th Anniversary Year.

The Queen's reign

That cricket was never more popular than it is at this time is certain. The public interest was never keener...the history of athletics cannot, indeed, show anything more gratifying from the standpoint of public interest or of public morality than the record of cricket during the Queen's reign.

Illustrated News (Diamond Jubilee Number) 1897

DETERMINED LEFT-HANDER WHO SET A CLUB RECORD

By David Warner

JOE SAYERS: Patience of Job

After failing to command a regular first team place last season — largely through a combination of injury, loss of form and the rising fortunes of young opening batsman Alex Lees, Joe Sayers announced his retirement from first-class cricket in the New Year.

A likable and strongly determined left-hander with the patience of Job, Sayers perhaps never quite achieved the heights to which he seemed destined to climb during his days at Oxford University where he gained a cricket Blue in 2002-2004 and captained the Oxford UCCE side.

He also led England at Under-17 and Under-19 level and many believed he was an England Test captain in the making.

Sayers made his first one-day appearance for Yorkshire in 2003 and his first-class debut for his native county the following year. Joe enjoyed a couple of seasons of outstanding form, and set a county record of which he can be justly proud — becoming the only left-hander in the Club's history twice to carry his bat. The first occasion was against Middlesex at Scarborough in 2006 when he spent just under seven hours (420 minutes) compiling an unbeaten 122 out of 376. The following summer he showed even greater stubbornness against Durham at Headingley, holding out for 553-minutes while accumulating an unbeaten 149 out of 414, Yorkshire

41

going on to win by nine wickets. In both games he was unbeaten in the second innings, and he was on the field the whole of each match. The only other left-hander to carry his bat for the *White Rose* was Bryan Stott with 144 out of 262 against Worcestershire at Worcester in 1959, but he performed the feat only once.

Appointed Yorkshire's vice-captain ahead of the 2012 season, Sayers played in 97 first-class matches, scoring 4,855 runs at an average of 32.58. He made nine centuries, with a top score of 187 against Kent at Tunbridge Wells in 2007. Sayers was in splendid early-season form that year, hitting three centuries in the first six Championship matches, but he was even more successful overall in 2009 when he topped 1,000 runs for the first time and ended up with 1,150 first-class runs at 42.59.

In early July the following year Sayers was floored by what was diagnosed as post-viral fatigue, and it was 10 months before he was fit to resume his first-class career, the illness hitting him just when he should have been at his best in terms of age and fitness. On his return he showed on pre-season tours that he could score just as quickly as anyone in the one-day game, and he demonstrated this on occasions last season.

Also last year, Sayers wrote *Rose-Tinted Summer: The Dressing Room Diary*, which gave a detailed account of the Club's highs and lows during its sesquicentennial year.

Phil Jaques

A second farewell was paid to Australia's former left-hander Phil Jaques, when he left Headingley at the end of a two-year spell following his previous summers in a Yorkshire cap in 2004 and 2005.

A thorough professional who was much admired and respected by his teammates, Jaques never gave anything less than his best, and he left Yorkshire with the highest first-class average for the county of any of the crop of current players — a much envied 51.12 from 53 matches, which brought him 4,039 runs with 11 centuries and a top score of 243 against Hampshire at the Rose Bowl in 2004. Even by then Yorkshire were well aware of his ability to score double-hundreds, for he had made 222 against them for Northamptonshire at Wantage Road the year before.

Jaques was brought back to Yorkshire immediately after their shock relegation to Division Two of the Championship in 2011, and he played a substantial part in making sure they went straight back up again by becoming their leading scorer in the competition in 2012 with 792 runs from 15 matches including two centuries.

He was similarly consistent last season, when he missed two games because of injuries, but still compiled 770 Championship runs with two centuries — the first being 139 against Derbyshire at Chesterfield, when he and Alex Lees piled up 311 together, Yorkshire's highest partnership for the second wicket in matches between the two sides.

Oliver Hannon-Dalby

The 6ft 7in fast bowler never quite fulfilled his promise before moving to Warwickshire for the start of last season, but he did enjoy one summer of outstanding success which contributed greatly to Yorkshire almost winning the Championship against all the odds.

They narrowly avoiding relegation in 2009, and prospects looked even bleaker in 2010 with the departure of pacemen Matthew Hoggard and Deon Kruis. Hannon-Dalby, 21, aided by Steven Patterson and Ajmal Shahzad, made sure that the experienced duo were hardly missed.

Halifax-born Hannon-Dalby made his debut in the Championship clash

Outstanding season: Paceman Oliver Hannon-Dalby took Yorkshire close to 2010 title

against Surrey at The Oval in May 2008, claiming Mark Ramprakash as his maiden victim, but he did not appear in the competition again until 2010 under new captain Andrew Gale. In the first match against Warwickshire at Edgbaston he grabbed 5-68, and in the next game against Somerset at Headingley he emerged with identical figures as Yorkshire opened up with two consecutive victories.

While never scaling such heights again, he bowled consistently all season, and never missed a match, ending up with 34 wickets at 38.20 runs apiece. Yorkshire wisely preserved his energy and fitness by playing him in Championship fixtures only. Hannon-Dalby played in 24 first-class matches for Yorkshire, claiming 43 wickets at 45.06, and he also took part in five 40-over matches, collecting five wickets.

Iain Wardlaw

The right-arm fast bowler was almost 26 when he was unexpectedly plucked from league cricket in 2011 by Yorkshire, who were keen to see if he could make it at county level. He played in the Bradford League for Cleckheaton, skipper Andrew Gale's club, and it was soon evident that he was not short of pace, although he occasionally lacked control. His first-team debut was in the *Twenty20* match against Nottinghamshire at Headingley in July, when he was Yorkshire's most successful bowler with 2-17 from 3.1 overs in a hefty defeat. That month he made his Championship debut in the *Roses* thriller at Headingley, capturing Tom Smith, but he did not see out the match because Tim Bresnan returned from the England Test squad to take his place.

With several young fast bowlers breaking through last season, Yorkshire probably felt that there was little chance of a permanent place for Wardlaw, although he did make his mark in the *YB40* competition. He turned out in eight matches, and after a quiet start he three times claimed three wickets in the innings to total 14 victims — one fewer than leading wicket-taker Richard Pyrah.

Wardlaw lacked nothing in keenness, which was just as intense when he became a regular in Scotland's international team last year. He took four wickets in four first-class appearances for Yorkshire, and in 16 40-over games he notched 22 scalps. He had two in eight *Twenty20* fixtures.

Paul Farbrace

Yorkshire reluctantly said farewell to second-team coach Paul Farbrace, when he took up the post of head coach of the Sri Lanka senior side and joined them on their tour against Pakistan in the United Arab Emirates. Paul was Sri Lanka's assistant coach from 2007 to 2009.

The former Kent wicket-keeper/batsman and head coach joined Yorkshire in their new structure ahead of the 2012 season, and the benefits of the fielding plan he brought with him could soon be seen at first-team level, particularly in the *Twenty20*, where they reached Finals Day.

Yorkshire Chairman Colin Graves said: "Paul's departure is a loss, and I would like to thank him for his effort over the past two years."

Paul was expected at Headingley this June for the Sri Lanka Test.

Scot McAllister

Eleven years of dedicated service as first-team physiotherapist ended when Scot McAllister left to take up an appointment as clinical manager and lead physiotherapist with Scotland Rugby Union Sevens. Highly regarded by Yorkshire's playing staff, Scot also enjoyed spells as physiotherapist for England Lions and the England Performance Programme.

Scot was replaced as Yorkshire CCC physiotherapist by Kunwar Bansil, who previously worked for Super League Club Hull FC and who came highly recommended both by Scot and medical consultant, Wayne Morton, the former Yorkshire and England physiotherapist.

*Yorkshire also said farewell to strength-and-conditioning coach Tom Summers, who left after six years to take up a post in Hong Kong. Yorkshire appointed their former left-arm spinner, Ian Fisher, as senior strength-and-conditioning coach, with Blaine Clancy as a strength-and-conditioning coach. Ian also had playing spells with Gloucestershire and Worcestershire before joining Essex as senior strength-and-conditioning coach. Blaine spent last season as an intern with Yorkshire.

JOSEPH JOHN SAYERS

FIRST-CLASS CRICKET FOR YORKSHIRE 2004 TO 2013

Left-hand Batsman	Right-arm bowler

Born: Leeds   November 5, 1983

Debut: For Oxford University   v Worcestershire at Oxford   April 13, 2002

Debut for Yorkshire   v. Leicestershire at Leicester   August 19, 2004

Last played: Yorkshire v. Surrey at Leeds   June 21, 2013

Capped: June 16, 2007

BATTING AND FIELDING

Season	M	I	NO	Runs	HS	Avge	100s	50s	Ct
2004	5	9	0	311	62	34.55	0	3	0
2005	10	17	1	592	115	37.00	2	2	11
2006	13	21	3	590	122*	32.77	1	3	7
2007	14	22	3	644	187	33.89	3	1	5
2008	6	9	0	76	22	8.44	0	0	6
2009	17	29	2	1150	173	42.59	2	5	16
2010	9	14	0	395	63	28.21	0	5	3
2011	11	22	2	773	139	38.65	1	6	5
2012	6	9	1	241	45	30.12	0	0	3
2013	6	9	1	83	25*	10.37	0	0	4
	97	161	13	4855	187	32.80	9	25	60

BOWLING

Season	Matches	Overs	Mdns	Runs	Wkts	Avge	Best	5wI
2005	10	7	0	35	0	—	—	—
2006	13	2	0	7	0	—	—	—
2009	17	10.5	0	32	3	10.66	3-20	—
2010	9	24	3	61	0	—	—	—
2011	11	13.2	3	31	3	10.33	3-15	—
	97	57.1	6	166	6	27.66	3-15	—

Centuries (9)

104	v. Leicestershire	at Scarborough	2005
115	v. Bangladesh A	at Leeds	2005
122*	v. Middlesex	at Scarborough	2006
149*	v. Durham	at Leeds	2007
123	v. Worcestershire	at Leeds	2007
187	v. Kent	at Tunbridge Wells	2007
173	v. Warwickshire	at Birmingham	2009
152	v. Somerset	at Taunton	2009
139	v. Durham MCCU	at Durham	2011

ALL FIRST-CLASS MATCHES

BATTING AND FIELDING

M	I	NO	Runs	HS	Avge	100s	50s	Ct
108	179	14	5457	187	33.07	11	28	63

BOWLING

Matches	Overs	Mdns	Runs	Wkts	Avge	Best	5wI
108	60.1	7	178	6	29.66	3-15	—

DOMESTIC LIST A CRICKET FOR YORKSHIRE 2003-2013

Debut: National League 45   v. Gloucestershire   at Leeds   September 21, 2003
Last played: Yorkshire Bank 40   v. Middlesex   at Leeds   June 20, 2013

BATTING AND FIELDING

Season	M	I	NO	Runs	HS	Avge	100s	50s	Ct
2003	1	1	0	62	62	62.00	0	1	0
2004	1	1	0	7	7	7.00	0	0	0
2005	7	7	2	130	54*	26.00	0	1	0
2006	3	3	0	33	13	11.00	0	0	0
2009	7	7	0	166	55	23.71	0	2	1
2010	1	1	0	29	29	29.00	0	0	1
2011	6	6	0	71	25	11.83	0	0	0
2012	1	1	0	1	1	1.00	0	0	0
2013	3	2	0	78	58	39.00	0	1	0
	30	29	2	577	148	21.37	0	5	2

BOWLING

Season	Matches	Overs	Mdns	Runs	Wkts	Avge	Best	4wI
2005	7	9	0	71	1	71.00	1-31	—
2011	6	1	0	8	0	—	—	—
	30	10	0	79	1	71.00	1-31	—

ALL LIST A MATCHES FOR YORKSHIRE

BATTING AND FIELDING

Matches	Innings	Not Out	Runs	Highest Score	Avge	100s	50s	Ct
31	30	2	594	62	21.21	0	5	2

BOWLING

Overs	Maidens	Runs	Wickets	Average	Best	4wI
10	0	79	1	79.00	1-31	—

DOMESTIC TWENTY20 CRICKET FOR YORKSHIRE 2005-2013

Debut: v. Nottinghamshire   at Leeds   July 3, 2005
Last played: v. Lancashire   at Manchester   July 24, 2013

BATTING AND FIELDING

Season	M	I	NO	Runs	HS	Avge	100s	50s	Ct
2005	3	1	0	12	12	12.00	0	0	2
2009	2	2	0	6	5	3.00	0	0	0
2011	7	6	0	154	44	25.66	0	0	0
2013	5	5	0	81	38	16.20	0	0	3
	17	14	0	253	44	18.07	0	0	5

FIFTY YEARS SERVICE FROM HEAD OF GRAYSON FAMILY

Last year Adrian Grayson was Chairman of the English Schools' Cricket Association. The honour was in recognition of 50 years of service to schools cricket, beginning at the school in Bedale where he taught, and then many years with North Riding and later North Yorkshire teams.

He was also involved with the full Yorkshire Schools' sides and with ESCA North. He has been player, coach, team manager, administrator and organiser of matches, and is still very much involved.

We met at Bedale Cricket Club on home ground. Adrian played at Bedale from 1975 to 1995, and has been secretary and chairman there. He captained the York and District League representative side, and is proud of their victory over the Bradford League. He also captained the Yorkshire Over-50s team when they beat Wales in the final of the national competition in 1998.

It is as a coach that Adrian has found most satisfaction, and he has gained a high reputation for his work with young cricketers. Carol and Adrian have two sons — Simon, who played football professionally for several clubs and after managing Leeds United and Huddersfield Town is manager at Preston North End, and Paul, who played first-class cricket for Yorkshire and Essex, where he is now chief coach.

In 2007 Adrian received an OSCA — Outstanding Service to Cricket Award...no Hollywood catwalks here — from the Yorkshire Cricket Board, and in June 2012 he was awarded the British Empire Medal for services to sport in Bedale.

Bedale has an attractive, wide main street and market square with a 14th Century market cross. You go uphill to St Gregory's Church and Rectory. You pass Bedale Hall and the golf club to come to the tree-lined cricket ground on Leyburn Road, where Adrian has spent so much time.

It was way back in 1828 that Bedale Cricket Club was founded, and the town was an important centre of Yorkshire cricket in its very early days. It has produced three Yorkshire and England cricketers: George Anderson played for Yorkshire from 1850 to 1869, represented the All England Eleven before Test cricket was formally organised, and toured

Chain of office: Adrian at his installation as Chairman of the English Schools' Cricket Association, flanked by cricket and footballing sons Simon, left, and Paul

Australia in 1863-1864. When Old Ebor interviewed George "in a snug room in a comfortable house in Aiskew" in 1898 he was told: "I was born in Bedale, have lived here all my life and hope to die here", which he did. Roger Iddison captained Yorkshire in their first official county match at The Oval in 1863, held that office for 10 seasons, and also toured Australia. The third international cricketer from Bedale, of course, is Adrian's son, Paul who played two one-day internationals in Kenya and Zimbabwe.

I asked Adrian about his early life, and how he became a teacher at Bedale: "I was born in Pickering, where my father was a corn merchant, and went to Lady Lumley's Grammar School. When I was 18 I was offered a job at Bedale School by Bill Pearson, the North Riding PE Adviser, and I stayed two years as an unqualified teacher helping in the PE Department. Then I went off to London to Borough Road College at Isleworth, taking PE and Geography. When I qualified I got a job back at Bedale, where I have stayed.

"Roy Mitchinson, the headmaster, had been a good cricketer, and he made sure we had good facilities at the school. I played for Yorkshire Under-15s at both cricket and football, and I remember a match against Lancashire at Preston with Graham Boothroyd and Billy Roberts in 1956. I played cricket at Pickering from age 15 to 26, then had six years at Northallerton. I came to Bedale in 1974 to take the club by the scruff of the neck!"

Bedale were then in Division 3 of the York and District League. Adrian was involved in their revival, and also in the building of the new clubhouse in Leyburn Road as a founder member of the Sports Association. Adrian's interest and ability at football were inherited by both sons, and his life would have been different if he had accepted York City's offer of professional terms when he was 19. He played many times for the Reserves at Bootham Crescent.

We discovered that we were both in the crowd on a snowy February Saturday at Bootham Crescent in 1955 when York City beat a Tottenham Hotspur side including Alf Ramsey, Danny Blanchflower and Eddie Bailey as well as George Robb, an amateur who played one full international for England against Hungary. Adrian did his teaching practice at George Robb's school in Finchley.

He was a founder member of Bedale Athletic and Sports Association in 1972, and has served many years as secretary. He has been secretary, chairman and president of the football club.

Adrian is a first-rate cricket coach, and has been fully involved in the organisation and management of school cricket. We talked first about coaching: "I first qualified at Borough Road when I got the MCC coaching certificate. Jim Sims, the old Middlesex player, used to come to Borough Road. So I began coaching in 1964 when I returned to Bedale.

"I did my advanced certificate at Scarborough, along with Doug Padgett. We used Bedale Sports Hall for evening classes, and it became a centre for weekend courses for younger boys. There were special elite courses, and I remember Arnie and Ryan Sidebottom staying at the pub on the village green at Thornton Watless. Paul helped with these courses, and batted with coins on the stumps.

"In 2014 I shall have had 50 years of schools cricket, including 20 years as manager of North Yorkshire Schools. I pick up the *Yorkshire Post* and see so many names I know: Adam Lyth, Victor Craven, John Inglis and York players like the McKendrys, Pringle and Snell. Our job is to produce good club cricketers, to set standards and to show how the game should be played. You build up relationships with parents and grandparents and follow the careers of those who do well, but it is just as satisfying when a boy rings up to say: 'I got 25 for Crakehall today'. I do get recognised everywhere, and when I sold my car to an ex-pupil he told me that 'whenever I go near a cricket ground the car automatically turns in'.

"I also got involved in helping the coaches with England Schools at Lilleshall and Bisham Abbey. I was an assistant to Keith Andrew, Les Lenham and Graham Saville in the 1970s and 1980s. I remember Alec Stewart and Mark Ramprakash. We also coached at Gateshead, where I first met Michael Atherton and had Ronnie Irani in my group."

The appointment as Chairman of the English Schools' Cricket

Association is a well deserved recognition of many years of commitment to helping young cricketers.

We met at the Bunbury Festival in Durham, where Adrian was wearing his badge of office. This is a competition in which the best under-15 boys play over a week representing the North, Midlands, London and the East and the South and West. It was held at Durham University on the ground where Sachin Tendulkar made his Yorkshire century and at Maiden Castle. Next year it will be at Oakham School in Rutland. As chairman Adrian was at Arundel for the finals of the under-15 competition for individual schools, but the big day was at Lord's for a match between ESCA and MCC Schools, when Jared Warner and Jordan Thompson represented Yorkshire.

The Bedale sporting story continues with the achievements of Simon and Paul. Carol, Adrian's wife, who has had multiple sclerosis for many years, has been involved in everything he has done and has been a great support, especially when the boys were young. "Simon, the eldest, is a good cricketer, but his career has been in football," Adrian says. "He was in the last 25 for England Schools Under-15s, and signed as an apprentice with Leeds United, playing alongside David Batty and Gary Speed. He moved to Leicester City, then Aston Villa, and he now manages Preston North End. Paul is only 18 months younger, and the boys have always been very competitive.

"Paul started at Ralph Middlebrook's cricket school, and was in the first intake of boys just before the Academy was set up. Darren Gough was his closest friend, and each has been best man at the other's wedding. He played with Ralph at Pudsey Congs, and was picked for the England Under-19s tour to Australia. He played for Yorkshire for five years, made a century at Worcester which I was lucky enough to see, and he left reluctantly as all our contacts were in Yorkshire.

"But he has had a successful time at Essex, and is now the county coach. Paul and Alison have two children, Beth and Oliver, who now goes to Felsted School, where his mother is a nurse and matron. Simon's boy, Joseph, shows promise as a footballer at Blackburn Academy."

I enjoyed my visit to Bedale and my conversations with Adrian. I was impressed by talking with someone who has devoted so much time and effort encouraging youngsters to play cricket, and he has been rewarded not only by those who have gone on to play at a high level, but also by so many who enjoy the game.

In paying tribute to Adrian Grayson's achievements we also recognise the efforts of so many in Yorkshire who work hard in various voluntary capacities and particularly parents, grandparents and other relatives who must clock up a good mileage in the cause of schools cricket. Many Yorkshire cars are going to turn automatically into cricket grounds.

NOT FOR THE FIRST TIME THE DAYS THEY ARE A-CHANGIN'

By Andrew Bosi

If the game has been transformed out of all recognition since our centenary year, so has the experience of those watching it.

Soon after the Second World War, when the posters went up at London Bridge station to warn that the gates had been closed at The Oval, there would have been few visiting supporters among the full house that this notice portrayed when Yorkshire were the visitors.

It was only in the late 1960s, following the growth of the universities, that the population became more mobile and the London economy increasingly dependent on Yorkshire folk for its success. The Yorkshire Southern Group was formed in 1980 in recognition of this.

Country members were allocated to the Leeds section unless requesting otherwise, but for all that the Sheffield members occupied 28 pages of the *Yorkshire Yearbook* to Leeds's 27 and Bradford's 19, with 17 pages covering Doncaster and Barnsley. Sheffield, Leeds and Bradford had three or four three-day matches each season, and large numbers of those members would have attended their local games each summer.

For the more adventurous there was usually a week-long tour with Sunday off: in 1963 Taunton was followed by Bristol, and Lord's by Clacton. This persisted into the era of a reduced programme of County Championship matches, and I can recall Canterbury and Hove in 1979 and Weston and Cheltenham in 1982. By 2011 we find Yorkshire on the road from May 18 to June 1, but the distances travelled between venues rather more challenging.

Our experience as spectators changes with the phases of life. In the early years cricket-watching was confined to school holidays, and I was fortunate that the first day of Worcestershire v. Yorkshire in 1966 coincided with such a holiday and that the following year the same fixture fell in the half-term break. Last year the Taunton game was in half-term, and there have been just three games in the summer holidays — not much opportunity for introducing the next generation to proper cricket.

In the days of full-time employment, with not as much annual leave as now, it became attractive to watch a single day of as many games as possible. In the 1980s, even with the reduced programme of Championship matches, there might have been a dozen Saturdays with first-class cricket, perhaps a bank-holiday Monday or two, and with 17 days leave it was possible to sample a little of most games. In those days the bread and butter one-day competition was the Sunday League, which involved breaking off in the middle of a Championship match.

Between 1983 and 1988 the Championship fixtures were on a three-year cycle and the Sunday League a two-year cycle. This made it impossible to dovetail the two, and a calamity arose in 1987 when it appeared to some that Yorkshire's anxiety to get from the Championship game at Hastings to Bristol and back resulted in the abandonment of play on the Saturday — which might have been the only chance of getting on to the drying outfield at the historic Sussex ground.

The advent of four-day cricket and the end of the blank day in the middle of the fixture made watching a full match a much better proposition. With so few games left the annual leave entitlement stretched further, and a switch to part-time work made mid-week games more attractive, as they do not generally clash with league cricket. Three nights in a town or city is usually an enjoyable experience, although I know that one or two found the 2012 weather in Colwyn Bay made for hard going!

This coming season sees the trial of Sunday starts for the vast majority of Championship matches, an ECB response to an ill-defined request for more first-class cricket at weekends. Of course, if you ask someone with a Monday to Friday job what would encourage them to watch more cricket they will say games at weekends. What I think they really want are games that start on a Saturday when there is usually public transport more readily available. Unfortunately, that is simply not possible given the financial imperative of playing *Twenty20* games on Friday nights.

In glorious weather for last year's Cheltenham Festival it was noticeable how good the crowds were on the first three days and how poor on the Saturday, even though in the first game the last day had been set up with a run chase which was always likely to go to the wire, and which duly lasted for almost eight hours.

Yorkshire have commendably talked of delaying the start to 12 noon in order to mitigate the public-transport problems, although reaching Scarborough at this hour would still present a challenge. Scarborough, in my opinion, would be better served by a Sunday afternoon *Twenty20* game and a mid-week Championship match.

I doubt if the Sunday starts will last long. Nothing has lasted long over the last 50 years. Somerset, and to a lesser extent Worcestershire and Gloucestershire, will be adversely affected by the transport issue, and if the era of austerity persists outside London other venues could be without buses just at the time county treasurers would hope to see them.

* Andrew Bosi is a member of Yorkshire County Cricket Club Southern Group and a regular attender of all Yorkshire Championship matches

BOOTH AND DRAKE DAZZLE — AND ARE GONE FOR EVER

By Derek Hodgson

While in 1939 Hitler was obliging enough to wait until the first-class season was virtually over before invading Poland, the Kaiser was less forthcoming in 1914, attacking Belgium on August 3.

In those days of heady, sunny excitement, with crowds in Paris and Berlin applauding each successive declaration of war, there was every expectation that it would be "over by Christmas" and cricket, like most civilised segments of society, expected a possibly nasty but short interruption to the progress of an ever-improving world.

In fact, the world had changed for ever, and not for the better.

Yorkshire began the season in fine fettle with successive innings victories against Northamptonshire, MCC and Essex, and celebrated Hawke's presidency of MCC in the centenary year of the Lord's ground.

Hampshire, on a flat Southampton pitch, stopped the gallop with a double-century from Mead, although Denton and Hirst raised 312 for

Test-class all-rounder and gallant warrior: One of the *Wisden* Cricketers of the Year in 1914, Booth received a commission in the West Yorkshire Regiment, became a second lieutenant, and died just under a year later when he went over the top on July 1, 1916, the first day of the Battle of the Somme *(Photo: Ron Deaton Archive)*

53

Yorkshire's fourth wicket. Surrey then won at Bradford, reinforcing the impression that Yorkshire were less incisive on dry pitches.

Hirst took an injury, and Kilner, after a winter illness, was not fully fit. Two defeats by Kent were a serious setback, Blythe taking 8-55 at Bramall Lane.

From mid-July, Yorkshire were rampant, winning 11 of their 12 remaining fixtures, including by an innings at Old Trafford, but winning half their 28 matches was not good enough in 1914, their final

CAPTAIN SIR ARCHIBALD WHITE
Yorkshire's skipper was called back to the Royal Horse Artillery shortly after the completion of the 1914 Roses match at Old Trafford
(Photo: Ron Deaton Archive)

position being fourth. Not surprisingly, the summer finished in some confusion. On the outbreak of war Surrey, the leaders, cancelled their two remaining fixtures, and after some argument MCC, then the governing body, declared them champions in November. Kent, with 16 wins from 28 games against Surrey's 15 from 26, were again hard done by.

Benny Wilson scored 208 against Sussex at Bradford before Yorkshire cancelled their last two home games, both friendlies, and set off on their last tour for five years, winning at Bristol and Weston and drawing at Brighton. Booth, 155 wickets, and Drake 158 — both scoring more than 800 runs — were to die before county cricket was seen again, Booth on the first day of the Battle of the Somme.

He and Kilner immediately volunteered for the Army — "it's our duty," they told Old Ebor — while Drake, unfit for military service, died of an illness in February 1919. On that last tour of the golden age Booth and Drake bowled unchanged against Gloucestershire before Drake took all 10 in Somerset's second innings — the first time this feat had been achieved by a Yorkshire player. Equally impressive was Drake's remarkable achievement against Derbyshire at Chesterfield of taking four wickets in four balls, the only time this has been done by a Yorkshire bowler.

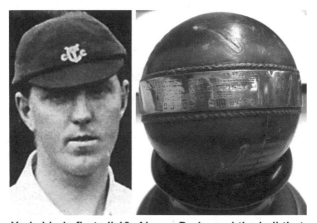

Yorkshire's first all 10: Alonzo Drake and the ball that was mounted for him after his historic spell against Gloucestershire. A look at the scorebook, below, says it all *(Photos: www.adelphiarchive.co.uk)*

BOWLERS	1	2	3	ANALYSIS OF BOWLING					
				4	5	6	7	8	9
Booth									
Drake									

Yorkshire's office, then in Leeds city centre, became the headquarters of the West Riding Volunteers, a regiment that grew to 20 battalions, such was the enthusiasm in the early months. Major Lord Hawke, a militia man in the previous century, became county adjutant and, on promotion to Colonel, was succeeded in that office by Captain Frederick Toone, Yorkshire's Secretary. Almost 500 parcels of cricket gear were dispatched to various military camps at home and abroad, and £20,000 — add two noughts today — was raised for wartime charities by the playing of exhibition marches.

With Hawke banging the drum, Yorkshire made it quite clear that ongoing remuneration and re-engagement of players after the war would depend on all concerned either enlisting or taking up munitions work. Nearly all did the necessary, but Drake was unable to conform for medical reasons, and was twice rejected for service. On the other hand,

Dewsbury 1914: Warwickshire are batting, and the bowler is Major Booth. He scored 91 for once out
(Photo: www.adelphiarchive.co.uk)

Wilson neither enlisted nor involved himself with appropriate war work — and he did not play for Yorkshire again.

The Scarborough Cricket Festival, scheduled to be played in early September, was cancelled in its entirety, and within weeks the town was being bombarded by German battlecruisers.

Away from cricket, in January in Milan priests thundered against the tango. A suffragette ruined a Velasquez painting in the National Gallery; Pancho Villa marched on Mexico City; the heir to the Austrian throne was assassinated in Sarajevo on June 29; Rasputin was murdered in Moscow in July — and the following month Europe was at war, ending an era of enormous hope and promise of improving health and prosperity. Five years later the world was greyer, grimmer and more frantic. The Germans, starving and racked by reparations, smouldered.

Partners of the future: Lance Corporal Herbert Sutcliffe, above, had yet to play for Yorkshire when war was declared, but Percy Holmes, right, was in his second year

BENNY WILSON
Never played again

YORKSHIRE'S FIRST-CLASS HIGHLIGHTS OF 1914

Wins by an innings (11)

Gloucestershire (94 and 84) lost to Yorkshire (405) by an innings and 227 runs at Bristol

Yorkshire (443) beat Sussex (111 and 149) by an innings and 183 runs at Bradford

Yorkshire (378) beat Northamptonshire (117 and 105) by an innings and 156 runs at Northampton

Yorkshire (372) beat Somerset (90 and 127) by an innings and 155 runs at Sheffield

Yorkshire (292) beat MCC (39 and 134) by an innings and 119 runs at Lord's

Gloucestershire (185 and 146) lost to Yorkshire (449) by an innings and 118 runs at Harrogate

Derbyshire (181 and 68) lost to Yorkshire (297) by an innings and 48 runs at Chesterfield

Essex (259 and 141) lost to Yorkshire (441) by an innings and 41 runs at Leyton

Yorkshire (346) beat Northamptonshire (146 and 192) by an innings and 8 runs at Huddersfield

Cambridge University (131 and 159) lost to Yorkshire (296) by an innings and 6 runs at Cambridge

Derbyshire (157 and 90) lost to Yorkshire (252-9 dec) by an innings and 5 runs at Leeds

Wins by 10 wickets (1)

:Lancashire (162 and 83) lost to Yorkshire (190 and 56-0) by 10 wickets at Manchester

Totals of 400 and over (6)

461	v. Sussex at Brighton
449	v. Gloucestershire at Harrogate
443	v. Sussex at Bradford
441	v. Essex at Leyton
426 for 3 wkts dec	v. Hampshire at Southampton
405	v. Gloucestershire at Bristol

Opponents dismissed for under 100 (10)

96	Warwickshire at Birmingham	84	Gloucestershire at Bristol (2nd innings)
94	Gloucestershire at Bristol (1st innings)	83	Lancashire at Manchester
90	Derbyshire at Leeds	68	Derbyshire at Chesterfield
90	Somerset at Sheffield	44	Somerset at Weston-super-Mare (1st innings)
90	Somerset at Weston-super-Mare (2nd innings)	39	MCC at Lord's

Century Partnerships (19)

For the 1st wicket (1)

115	B B Wilson and T J D Birtles	v. Lancashire at Sheffield

For the 2nd wicket (2)

124	B B Wilson and A Dolphin	v. Essex at Leyton
103	T J D Birtles and D Denton	v. Lancashire at Sheffield

57

Century Partnerships *(Continued)*

For the 3rd wicket (6)

177	D Denton and R Kilner	v. Sussex at Brighton
119	B B Wilson and R Kilner	v. Gloucestershire at Harrogate
114	W Rhodes and R Kilner	v. Surrey at Bradford
110	B B Wilson and R Kilner	v. Sussex at Bradford
102	W Rhodes and R Kilner	v. Northamptonshire at Huddersfield
102	D Denton and R Kilner	v. Derbyshire at Chesterfield

For the 4th wicket (5)

312	D Denton and G H Hirst	v. Hampshire at Southampton
271	B B Wilson and W Rhodes	v. Sussex at Bradford
111	B B Wilson and G H Hirst	v. Hampshire at Hull
107	R Kilner and G H Hirst	v. Northamptonshire at Northampton
104	W Rhodes and G H Hirst	v. Nottinghamshire at Nottingham

For the 5th wicket (3)

128	R Kilner and M W Booth	v. Cambridge University at Cambridge
103	W Rhodes and G H Hirst	v. Lancashire at Hull (Non Championship)
102	D Denton and G H Hirst	v. Somerset at Sheffield

For the 6th wicket (1)

101	G H Hirst and D C F Burton	v. Essex at Leyton

For the 7th wicket (1)

107	D Denton and A Drake	v. Middlesex at Sheffield

Centuries (14)

B B Wilson (4)

208	v. Sussex at Bradford
106	v. Essex at Leyton
102	v. Gloucestershire at Harrogate
101	v. Derbyshire at Leeds

D Denton (3)

168*	v. Hampshire at Southampton
129	v. Middlesex at Sheffield
124	v. Sussex at Brighton

G H Hirst (3)

146	v. Hampshire at Southampton
107	v. Somerset at Sheffield
105 *	v. Northamptonshire at Huddersfield

W Rhodes (2)

118	v. Sussex at Bradford
105 *	v. Lancashire at Hull (Non Championship)

T J D Birtles (1)

104	v. Lancashire at Sheffield

R Kilner (1)

169	v. Gloucestershire at Bristol

5 wickets in an innings (34)

M W Booth (13)

8 for 64   v. Essex at Leyton (2nd innings)
7 for 21   v. MCC at Lord's
7 for 69   v. Northamptonshire at Huddersfield
6 for 41   v. Gloucestershire at Bristol (2nd innings)
6 for 48   v. Gloucestershire at Bristol (1st innings)
6 for 96   v. Essex at Leyton (1st innings)
6 for 98   v. Lancashire at Sheffield
5 for 27   v. Somerset at Weston-super-Mare
5 for 36   v. Kent at Sheffield (2nd innings)
5 for 39   v.Warwickshire at Birmingham
5 for 43   v.Kent at Sheffield (1st innings)
5 for 56   v.Sussex at Bradford
5 for 60   v.Somerset at Sheffield

A Drake (11)

10 for 35   v.Somerset at Weston-super-Mare (2nd innings)
6 for 39   v.Cambridge University at Cambridge
6 for 40   v.Northamptonshire at Northampton
6 for 54   v.Middlesex at Lord's
5 for 6   v. Derbyshire at Chesterfield
5 for 16   v.Somerset at Weston-super-Mare (1st innings)
5 for 33   v.Lancashire at Manchester
5 for 37   v.Hampshire at Hull
5 for 45   v.MCC at Lord's
5 for 48   v.Warwickshire at Birmingham
5 for 53   v.Lancashire at Hull (Non Championship)

W Rhodes (5)

7 for 19   v.Derbyshire at Leeds
6 for 68   v.Middlesex at Sheffield
6 for109   v.Surrey at Bradford (1st innings)
5 for 56   v.Surrey at Bradford (2nd innings)
5 for 93   v.Kent at Tonbridge

G H Hirst (3)

6 for 34   v.Northamptonshire at Northampton
5 for 24   v.Hampshire at Hull
5 for 94   v.Leicestershire at Leicester

E Smith (1)

6 for 40   v.Leicestershire at Bradford

C P Whiting (1)

5 for 46   v.Essex at Leeds

10 wickets in a match (6)

M W Booth (4)

14 for 160 (6 for 96 and 8 for 64)   v. Essex at Leyton
10 for 79 (5 for 43 and 5 for 36)   v. Kent at Sheffield
12 for 89 (6 for 48 and 6 for 41)   v. Gloucestershire at Bristol
11 for 42 (7 for 21 and 4 for 21)   v. MCC at Lord's

A Drake (1)

15 for 62 (5 for 27 and 10 for 35)   v. Somerset at Weston-super-Mare

W Rhodes (1)

11 for 165 (6 for109 and 5 for 56)   v. Surrey at Bradford

The Double (all First-Class matches) (1)

W Rhodes

    1,325 runs @ 29.44   117 wickets @ 18.11

3 catches in an innings (10)

A Dolphin (6)

4	v. Gloucestershire at Bristol
3	v. Essex at Leyton
3	v. Surrey at Bradford
3	v. Gloucestershire at Harrogate
3	v. Sussex at Bradford (1st innings)
3	v. Sussex at Bradford (2nd innings)

W Rhodes (2)

4	v. Northamptonshire at Huddersfield
3	v. Lancashire at Sheffield

D C F Burton (1)

3	v. Northamptonshire at Northampton

E R Wilson (1)

3	v. Warwickshire at Birmingham

3 dismissals in an innings (4)

A Dolphin (4)

5 (4ct, 1st)	v.	Gloucestershire at Bristol
4 (3ct, 1st)	v.	Essex at Leyton
3 (2ct, 1st)	v.	Derbyshire at Chesterfield
3 (1ct, 2st)	v.	Somerset at Weston-super-Mare

5 dismissals in a match (5)

A Dolphin (4)

5 (4ct, 1st)	v.	Essex at Leyton
5 (5ct)	v.	Gloucestershire at Harrogate
6 (6ct)	v.	Sussex at Bradford
6 (5ct, 1st)	v.	Gloucestershire at Bristol

W Rhodes (1)

5 (5ct)	v.	Northamptonshire at Northampton

Debuts (4)

In first-class cricket: H M Claughton, G H Crawford, E Smith and C P Whiting

---

Sunny days

Given to George Hirst as a reward for 12 years of splendid service, the Bank Holiday match at Leeds was favoured by fine weather, and during the three days 78,681 spectators visited the Headingley ground, the proceeds of the benefit (£3,702) exceeding all records.

Wisden 1905

100 YEARS AGO

YORKSHIRE AVERAGES 1914

ALL FIRST-CLASS MATCHES

Played 31   Won 16   Lost 4   Drawn 11

(Yorkshire matches scheduled v. An England XI at Harrogate on August 20, 21 and 22
and v. MCC at Scarborough on September 3 ,4 and 5
were abandoned on the outbreak of the First World War)

County Championship: Played 28   Won 14   Lost 4   Drawn 10

BATTING AND FIELDING *(Qualification 10 completed innings)*

Player	M.	I.	N.O.	Runs	H.S.	Avge	100s	50s	ct/st
G H Hirst	29	45	6	1655	146	42.43	3	8	22
D Denton	31	49	1	1728	168*	36.00	3	11	17
B B Wilson	31	50	1	1605	208	32.75	4	9	6
R Kilner	29	44	1	1329	169	30.90	1	11	18
W Rhodes	30	47	2	1325	113	29.44	2	8	36
M W Booth	30	46	6	871	60	21.77	0	5	22
A Drake	31	44	2	828	80	19.71	0	4	17
T J D Birtles	18	28	6	427	104	19.40	1	1	7
P Holmes	12	17	3	222	61	15.85	0	1	7
E Oldroyd	14	24	3	327	51	15.57	0	1	9
D C F Burton	16	21	3	272	36	15.11	0	0	10
A W White	24	33	9	321	51	13.37	0	1	17
A Dolphin	30	38	10	371	66	13.25	0	3	54/18
Also batted									
R C Burton	2	2	0	47	47	23.50	0	0	3
H Watson	1	2	0	41	41	20.50	0	0	1/1
C P White	4	7	2	72	26	14.40	0	0	1
E Smith	3	5	1	45	34	11.25	0	0	1
E R Wilson	2	3	1	14	13*	7.00	0	0	3
H M Claughton	1	2	0	7	4	3.50	0	0	0
G H Crawford	2	2	0	5	5	2.50	0	0	2
A C Williams	1	1	1	5	5*	—	0	0	1

BOWLING *(Qualification 10 wickets)*

Player	Overs	Mdns	Runs	Wkts	Avge	Best	5wI	10wM
E Smith	48	10	126	10	12.60	6-40	1	0
A Drake	1017.2	283	2418	158	15.30	10-35	11	1
M W Booth	946.5	170	2697	155	17.40	8-64	13	4
W Rhodes	824.4	209	2120	117	18.11	7-19	5	1
G H Hirst	479.4	117	1244	42	29.61	6-34	3	0
Also bowled								
R C Burton	17	2	73	6	12.16	3-11	0	0
A C Williams	28	4	103	5	20.60	3-81	0	0
C P Whiting	82	19	242	9	26.88	5-46	1	0
E Oldroyd	49	6	158	5	31.60	2-53	0	0
H M Claughton	12	3	32	1	32.00	1-32	0	0
G H Crawford	43	12	109	3	36.33	3-90	0	0
R Kilner	84	15	305	1	305.00	1-59	0	0
E R Wilson	13	4	36	0	—	0-36	0	0
T J D Birtles	6	1	20	0	—	0-20	0	0
B B Wilson	5	0	18	0	—	0-9	0	0
D Denton	3	1	7	0	—	0-7	0	0

TITLE HAT-TRICK BID FAILS BUT ILLINGWORTH DOES DOUBLE

By Anthony Bradbury

The Yorkshire side of 1964 will have looked forward to their coming season in a comfortable frame of mind.

In four of the previous five seasons they had been County Champions, and now they were seeking a hat-trick of titles, having won under Vic Wilson in 1962 and Brian Close in 1963.

They were the clear favourites to win again, but a nasty surprise was forthcoming, for their destiny in 1964 was to finish in fifth place.

Worcestershire, who had 18 wins in 28 games, won the Championship for the first time, and did so emphatically — 41 points clear of Midland rivals Warwickshire.

RAYMOND ILLINGWORTH: Did the last double for Yorkshire
(Photo: Ron Deaton Archive)

Then came Northamptonshire and Surrey, both above Yorkshire who managed 11 victories. Yorkshire still had a remarkably good side and Brian Close, again a strong captain, Raymond Illingworth, Jimmy Binks, Doug Padgett and Don Wilson played in every match. Philip Sharpe and John Hampshire were each in 25 of the matches, and Fred Trueman, Geoff Boycott, Ken Taylor, Mel Ryan and Tony Nicholson all played in more than half of the Championship games. Perhaps the key

62

Embarrassed in pumps: Scorer Ted Lester is persuaded to turn out in the Gillette Cup against Middlesex at Lord's in borrowed kit because John Hampshire had been taken ill, and Yorkshire had travelled without a substitute. Lester, then 44, had not played in the first team for nine years

(Photo: Ron Deaton Archive)

to this brief decline in Yorkshire status was the inability of Trueman to fulfil the high standard of past years — 67 wickets at 20.05 would seem today to be a good return, but the previous year he had taken 76 wickets at 12.84.

Even so, the old campaigner was still good enough to play in four Tests against Australia and to take his 300th Test wicket.

The best individual player was Illingworth. Fred Titmus was preferred to him in the Tests, so Illingworth played for Yorkshire throughout the season and did the "double" in Championship games with 104 wickets and 1,055 runs. A "double" by a Yorkshire player has never been achieved since, and with the restriction of first-class matches today no one is ever likely to do so again.

Boycott, who had so impressed in 1963, now started his England career with games against Australia, but he was still able to play many matches for Yorkshire — quite unlike the modern fraternity — and in all games for his county he scored 1,639 runs, including 122 against the Australians at Bradford. In the other match against the Australians, at Sheffield, Ken Taylor made a wonderful 160 in a losing cause.

Yorkshire took these matches against the tourists very seriously, and the Sheffield match included 10 who had or would play for England. The only man who did not achieve that accolade was the steadfast Nicholson, who was chosen for the MCC side to tour South Africa in 1964-5, and might have played in Tests, but who had to withdraw with

History at The Oval: Skipper Ted Dexter congratulates Freddie Trueman as England leave the field in the Fifth Test after Trueman had become the first man to take 300 Test wickets. His final tally of 307 was to remain a record until 1975-6 *(Photo: www.adelphiarchive.co.uk)*

back trouble before the tour started. He had been top of the Yorkshire averages in 1964 with 76 wickets at 15.69, and third in the national bowling averages behind the Worcestershire pair of James Standen and Len Coldwell, which may explain in part why that side won the Championship — though in Tom Graveney and Basil d'Oliveira, Worcestershire had two batsmen in the top four of the national averages.

One of the most exceptional results in the Championship occurred at Bristol on September 2 and 3, when the Yorkshire challenge for the title was already over. It was their last Championship match — another contrast with dates for 2014 — and they defeated Gloucestershire by a remarkable innings and 294 runs. Boycott scored 177, and Gloucestershire "on turf enlivened by morning rain", said *Wisden*, were bowled out for 47 and 84 in less than four hours. Gloucestershire lost their first 14 wickets for 59 runs, and Trueman had match figures of 7-36. Two months earlier the boot had been on the other foot when Yorkshire at Edgbaston had been put out for 54, the Warwickshire and Barbadian bowler Rudi Webster having the extraordinary analysis of 12.4-7-6-7 and match figures of 12-58.

Another match with an exceptional player performance was against Kent at the lovely Crabble ground, Dover, where first-class cricket has long stopped being played. Yorkshire batted first, and on a rain-affected surface totalled 256. Illingworth, coming in when Yorkshire were 41-4, totally dominated a partnership of 110 with his captain, Close, and went on to a wonderful 135. Next day Illingworth twice assumed complete control on the bowling front to take 14 wickets (7-49 and 7-52). It was as comprehensive a one-man show as any one might ever imagine.

There was another player who has cause to recall that game: Yorkshire gave a debut to George Bloom, a diminutive batsman from Scarborough. Coming in at No. 8, he scored two, then held two magnificent catches at long-on. He never played for the Yorkshire first team again, but he will always remember being a part of that extraordinary match of Raymond Illingworth.

The 1964 season was the second of the one-day competition, now for the first time named the Gillette Cup. Yorkshire played only one match, and were knocked out by Middlesex at Lord's. An unwelcome curiosity was that they had chosen to travel without a 12th man.

John Hampshire was taken ill with serum fever, and Yorkshire Scorer Ted Lester, who had not held a bat for three years, nor played for the first team for nine years, gallantly accepted a request to play. To use a familiar phrase, he did not trouble his replacement scorer. Yorkshire were bowled out for 90, a sad exit in May from a competition which was to thrive and thrive. In echoes of past years Johnny Wardle appeared for Cambridgeshire against Essex in a contest where Sir Leonard Hutton was man-of-the-match adjudicator.

Another man from a past era to return to the first-class stage was Don Brennan, who captained MCC against Yorkshire at Scarborough. He was 44 — and might have taken special delight in the stumping of Illingworth. In this last Yorkshire game of the season Richard Hutton, as an opening batsman in his county of birth for the first time, scored 39 and 89, and the same match allowed both Trueman and Wilson to complete their 100 wickets for the season. This game provided interest, excitement, festival cricket at its best and a satisfying Yorkshire win.

Wicket-keepers born in Yorkshire had little chance of being in the side when Binks had control of the gloves, but the rarest of opportunities came to Geoffrey Hodgson when Binks was called up to play for MCC v. Surrey. Yorkshire were playing Oxford University on the same dates, so Hodgson, who had been playing for Yorkshire Second Eleven since 1957, played his only Yorkshire first-class game — and with two stumpings and no catches he may be the only Yorkshire wicket-keeper to have more stumpings than catches. He later played one game for Lancashire, unusual but not unknown for past Yorkshire players.

The Annual Report recorded at the end of the season that "the First Eleven made an unofficial tour of North America and Bermuda, and the tour created great interest in the various centres visited and should do much to encourage cricket in those parts". The team actually visited

YORKSHIRE 1964. Back row, left to right: Geoffrey Boycott, Doug Padgett, Mel Ryan, Don Wilson, John Hampshire, Tony Nicholson and Philip Sharpe. Front row: Jimmy Binks, Freddie Trueman, Brian Close (captain) Raymond Illingworth and Ken Taylor
(Photo: Ron Deaton Archive)

such diverse places as Mount Vernon, Washington, Toronto, Calgary, Vancouver, Hollywood, and Hamilton in Bermuda. G S Sobers...yes the great Sir Garfield Sobers...made seven guest appearances for the Yorkshire side, and on one occasion batted for a time with Boycott, each scoring a century. As none of the matches in which Sobers appeared was first class his name does not appear within Yorkshire Records sections of the *Yearbook*. Sadly, it cannot really be said that cricket has flourished in North America since the heady days for the players on that tour.

Away from the playing arena the *Yearbook* for 1964 named a total of 44 people as officers or on the main Committee of the Club, and 21 were then were on the Grounds and Membership Sub-Committee. The membership list occupied 216 closely typed pages in that *Yearbook*. Many may regret that data-protection issues prevent the publication of such a list today.

Those who paid at the gate for first and second-team games totalled 132,077. That figure did not include the thousands of members who attended home fixtures. The way in which Yorkshire CCC is structured and managed in 2014, and indeed supported, in comparison with 1964 is just as wholly different as the forms of cricket that the Yorkshire team have to play half a century later.

YORKSHIRE'S FIRST-CLASS
HIGHLIGHTS OF 1964

Win by an innings (5)

Yorkshire (425-7 dec) defeated Gloucestershire (47 and 84) by an innings and 294 runs at Bristol

$ Lancashire (101 and 120) lost to Yorkshire (352) by an innings and 131 runs at Leeds

Yorkshire (288) defeated Glamorgan (55 and 194) by an innings and 39 runs at Leeds

$ Nottinghamshire (112 and 193) lost to Yorkshire (339-6 dec) by an innings and 34 runs at Nottingham

Yorkshire (256) defeated Kent (97 and 146) by an innings and 13 runs at Dover

$ Consecutive matches

Wins by 10 wickets (1)

Middlesex (309-6 dec and 132) lost to Yorkshire (413 and 29-0) by 10 wickets at Leeds

Totals of 400 and over (2)

413	v. Middlesex at Leeds
423-7 dec	v. Gloucestershire at Bristol

Opponents dismissed for under 100 (4)

55	Glamorgan at Leeds	84	Gloucestershire at Bristol
47	Gloucestershire at Bristol		(2nd innings)
	(1st innings)	97	Kent at Dover

Century Partnerships (20)

For the 1st wicket (7)

236	G Boycott and K Taylor	v. Lancashire at Manchester
129	G Boycott and K Taylor	v. Surrey at Bradford
128	G Boycott and P J Sharpe	v. Glamorgan at Swansea
123	G Boycott and K Taylor	v. Middlesex at Leeds
116	K Taylor and J H Hampshire	v. Oxford University at Oxford (1st innings)
114*	J H Hampshire and K Taylor	v. Oxford University at Oxford (2nd innings)

(partnership ended when J H Hampshire retired ill on 67)*

108	G Boycott and P J Sharpe	v. Gloucestershire at Bristol

For the 2nd wicket (2)

197	G Boycott and D E V Padgett	v. Australia at Sheffield
129	G Boycott and D E V Padgett	v. Essex at Hull

For the 3rd wicket (3)

171	D E V Padgett and D B Close	v. Nottinghamshire at Nottingham
114*	J H Hampshire and P J Sharpe	v. Derbyshire at Sheffield
107	D E V Padgett and D B Close	v. Warwickshire at Birmingham

For the 4th wicket (3)

205*	G Boycott and P J Sharpe	v. Leicestershire at Leicester
151	G Boycott and D B Close	v. Gloucestershire at Bristol
107	J H Hampshire and R Illingworth	v. Leicester at Bradford

For the 5th wicket (3)

131	R Illingworth and D B Close	v. MCC at Scarborough
110	D B Close and R Illingworth	v. Kent at Dover
105	J H Hampshire and R Illingworth	v. Hampshire at Portsmouth

Century Partnerships *(Continued)*

For the 7th wicket (2)

126	J C Balderstone and J G Binks	v. Middlesex at Lord's
118	R A Hutton and J G Binks	v. Lancashire at Leeds

Centuries (14)

G Boycott (5)

177	v. Gloucestershire at Bristol
151*	v. Leicestershire at Leicester
151	v. Middlesex at Leeds
131	v. Lancashire at Manchester
122	v. Australia at Bradford

J H Hampshire (2)

150	v. Leicestershire at Bradford
110	v. Hampshire at Portsmouth

R Illingworth (2)

135	v. Kent at Dover
103	v. MCC at Scarborough

D E V Padgett (2)

112	v. Derbyshire at Chesterfield
110	v. Nottinghamshire at Nottingham

K Taylor (2)

160	v. Australia at Sheffield
153	v. Lancashire at Manchester

D B Close (1)

100*	v. Surrey at Bradford

5 wickets in an innings (22)

R Illingworth (7)

$	7 for 49	v. Kent at Dover (1st innings)
$	7 for 52	v. Kent at Dover (2nd innings)
$	7 for 62	v. Surrey at The Oval
	7 for 89	v. Nottinghamshire at Scarborough
	6 for 30	v. Oxford University at Oxford
	6 for 50	v. Middlesex at Leeds
	5 for 40	v. Glamorgan at Swansea

$ consecutive innings

A G Nicholson (6)

7 for 32	v. Lancashire at Leeds
6 for 29	v. Glamorgan at Leeds (1st innings)
6 for 44	v. Glamorgan at Leeds (2nd innings)
6 for 82	v. Worcestershire at Scarborough
5 for 27	v. Nottinghamshire at Nottingham
5 for 28	v. Nottinghamshire at Scarborough

D Wilson (3)

6 for 51	v. Surrey at The Oval
6 for 62	v. MCC at Scarborough (1st innings)
5 for 65	v. MCC at Scarborough (2nd innings)

M Ryan (2)

5 for 38	v. Hampshire at Portsmouth
5 for 72	v. Leicestershire at Bradford

F S Trueman (2)

5 for 49	v. Gloucestershire at Sheffield
5 for 53	v. Leicestershire at Leicester

5 wickets in an innings *(Continued)*

    D B Close (1)

        6 for 29 v. Kent at Bradford

    R A Hutton (1)

        5 for 34 v. Hampshire at Portsmouth

10 wickets in a match (3)

    R Illingworth (1)

        14 for 101 (7 for 49 and 7 for 52)   v. Kent at Dover

    A G Nicholson (1)

        12 for 73 (6 for 29 and 6 for 44)   v. Glamorgan at Leeds

    D Wilson (1)

        11 for 127 (6 for 62 and 5 for 65)   v. MCC at Scarborough

3 catches in an innings (12)

    J G Binks (4)

        4   v. MCC at Scarborough

        3   v. Kent at Bradford

        3   v. Leicestershire at Leicester

        3   v. Lancashire at Leeds

    D B Close (2)

        3   v. Nottinghamshire at Scarborough

        3   v. Gloucestershire at Bristol

    P J Sharpe (2)

        3   v. Warwickshire at Birmingham

        3   v. Glamorgan at Swansea

    J H Hampshire (1)

        3   v. MCC at Lord's

    R Illingworth (1)

        3   v. Sussex at Hove

    K Taylor (1)

        3   v. Surrey at Bradford

    D Wilson (1)

        3   v. Glamorgan at Leeds

3 dismissals in an innings (4)

    J G Binks (4)

        4 (3ct, 1st) v. Kent at Bradford

        3 (2ct, 1st) v. Northamptonshire at Sheffield

        3 (2ct, 1st) v. Worcestershire at Scarborough

        3 (2ct, 1st) v. MCC at Scarborough

5 catches in a match (1)

    J G Binks (1)

        6 (2 + 4) v. MCC at Scarborough

5 dismissals in a match (1)

    J G Binks (1)

        7 (6ct, 1st) v. MCC at Scarborough

Debuts (3)
In first-class cricket: G R Bloom, G Hodgson and B Wood

Capped (1)

R A Hutton   August 3, 1964

YORKSHIRE AVERAGES 1964

ALL FIRST-CLASS MATCHES

Played 33	Won 12	Lost 4	Drawn 17
County Championship: Played 28	Won 11	Lost 3	Drawn 14

BATTING AND FIELDING *(Qualification 10 completed innings)*

Player	M.	I.	N.O.	Runs	H.S.	Avge	100s	50s	ct/st
G Boycott	19	31	4	1639	177	60.70	5	7	6
K Taylor	20	31	2	1149	160	39.62	2	6	11
R Illingworth	33	44	9	1301	135	37.17	2	7	17
P J Sharpe	30	49	8	1273	79*	31.04	0	9	29
D B Close	33	50	7	1281	100*	29.79	1	7	45
J G Binks	32	38	10	826	95	29.50	0	4	55/11
J H Hampshire	30	49	5	1280	150	29.09	2	8	20
D E V Padgett	33	51	2	1380	112	28.16	2	6	19
R A Hutton	10	14	1	346	89	26.61	0	2	11
F S Trueman	24	29	3	480	77	18.46	0	4	15
J C Balderstone	11	14	1	234	58	18.00	0	2	3
D Wilson	33	41	7	526	46	15.47	0	0	16
M Ryan	23	23	11	112	21	9.33	0	0	7
A G Nicholson	22	17	6	76	25	6.90	0	0	9

Also batted

Player	M.	I.	N.O.	Runs	H.S.	Avge	100s	50s	ct/st
B Wood	5	7	2	63	35	12.60	0	0	4
M C Fearnley	1	2	0	8	8	4.00	0	0	0
G Hodgson	1	1	0	4	4	4.00	0	0	0/2
J S Waring	2	2	0	4	3	2.00	0	0	0
G R Bloom	1	1	0	2	2	2.00	0	0	2

BOWLING *(Qualification 10 wickets)*

Player	Overs	Mdns	Runs	Wkts	Avge	Best	5wI	10wM
A G Nicholson	581.4	159	1193	76	15.69	7-32	6	1
J C Balderstone	81.1	37	187	11	17.00	3-28	0	0
R Illingworth	1012.2	374	2131	122	17.46	7-49	7	1
F S Trueman	633.2	137	1562	75	20.82	5-49	2	0
D Wilson	928.2	348	1978	93	21.26	6-51	3	1
R A Hutton	128.2	35	355	16	22.18	5-34	1	0
M Ryan	418.3	102	1006	44	22.86	5-38	2	0
D B Close	539.5	195	1243	52	23.90	6-29	1	0

Also bowled

Player	Overs	Mdns	Runs	Wkts	Avge	Best	5wI	10wM
M C Fearnley	12.5	2	25	2	12.50	2-19	0	0
D E V Padgett	11	5	27	1	27.00	1-2	0	0
J H Hampshire	29	5	81	1	81.00	1-15	0	0
K Taylor	77	14	204	1	204.00	1-34	0	0
J S Waring	16	4	36	0	—	0-11	0	0
G Boycott	16	4	52	0	—	0-1	0	0
P J Sharpe	3	0	17	0	—	0-8	0	0
J G Binks	1	0	12	0	—	0-12	0	0

50 YEARS AGO

YORKSHIRE AVERAGES 1964

LIST A KNOCKOUT COMPETITION — GILLETTE CUP

Played 1   Lost 1

BATTING AND FIELDING

Player	M.	I.	N.O.	Runs	H.S.	Avge	100s	50s	ct/st
R Illingworth	1	1	0	23	23	23.00	0	0	0
G Boycott	1	1	0	16	16	16.00	0	0	0
D E V Padgett	1	1	0	13	13	13.00	0	0	1
D Wilson	1	1	0	7	7	7.00	0	0	0
K Taylor	1	1	0	2	2	2.00	0	0	0
F S Trueman	1	1	0	2	2	2.00	0	0	0
D B Close	1	1	0	1	1	1.00	0	0	1
M Ryan	1	1	0	1	0	1.00	0	0	0
E I Lester	1	1	0	0	0	0.00	0	0	0
P J Sharpe	1	1	0	0	0	0.00	0	0	3
J G Binks	1	1	1	21	21*	—	0	0	1/1

BOWLING

Player	Overs	Mdns	Runs	Wkts	Avge	Best	4wI	RPO
R Illingworth	4.2	1	6	1	6.00	1-6	0	1.38
K Taylor	11	4	19	3	6.33	3-19	0	1.72
M Ryan	13	2	32	2	16.00	2-32	0	2.46
D B Close	11	1	35	2	17.50	2-35	0	3.18
F S Trueman	13	1	47	1	47.00	1-47	0	3.61

Wheer's t'brass

I like the Tykes because they are never false to their nature. When Trueman's team came into the dressing room, I afterwards learned, they did not indulge themselves in any paeans of self-praise. Far from it. They got stuck into a first-class row as to whether individual money prizes — the brass — should go into a communal fund.

Jack Fingleton, Wisden 1968

YORKSHIRE AVERAGES 1964

TOUR TO NORTH AMERICA AND CANADA

Played 13   Won 9   Drawn 3   Abandoned 1

BATTING AND FIELDING

Player	M.	I.	N.O.	Runs	H.S.	Avge	100s	50s	ct/st
G S Sobers	4	4	0	198	117	49.50	1	1	2
R Illingworth	11	11	1	466	144	46.60	2	1	3
G Boycott	11	11	0	370	108	33.63	1	1	4
R A Hutton	12	12	1	291	46	26.45	0	0	4
F S Trueman	11	10	2	190	41	23.75	0	0	1
D B Close	11	11	1	228	76	22.80	0	1	2/1
P J Sharpe	12	11	0	249	114	22.63	1	0	3
J H Hampshire	11	11	0	239	76	21.72	0	2	1
M Ryan	11	9	7	41	14*	20.50	0	0	1
D E V Padgett	12	11	0	214	77	19.45	0	2	1
J G Binks	11	10	0	192	69	19.20	0	1	7/8
R A Roberts	4	2	1	14	14	14.00	0	0	0
D Wilson	11	9	0	78	62	8.66	0	1	5

BOWLING

Player	Overs	Mdns	Runs	Wkts	Avge	Best	4wI	RPO
G S Sobers	43	19	98	16	6.12	4-11	4	2.27
F S Trueman	80	22	168	27	6.22	6-21	3	2.10
R Illingworth	46	18	115	14	8.21	4-17	1	2.50
R A Hutton	35.1	9	94	9	10.44	3-12	0	2.67
D Wilson	63.5	15	183	17	10.76	6-11	2	2.86
D B Close	32	11	98	5	19.60	2-7	0	3.06
G Boycott	4	0	20	1	20.00	1-20	0	5.00
M Ryan	54	15	131	6	21.83	1-8	0	2.42
J H Hampshire	2	0	11	0	—	0-11	0	5.50

Wardle dropped

In that dusty (1949) summer Wardle bowled more than 1,000 overs for his 100 wickets despite being dropped for the Committee to assess another left-arm spinner, Alan Mason, of Addingham, who took 37 wickets at an average of 28. Close also bowled 920 overs for his 101 wickets at 25, an extraordinary performance for a bowler of 18, for he also batted 42 times for his 958 runs for the county at 28.

The Carnegie History

UNITED VENTURE BRINGS BOBBY PEEL HEADSTONE

By J C David Allan

One of the highlights of an industrious and rewarding year for the Archives Committee was the provision and dedication of a headstone in Bruntcliffe Cemetery, Morley, at the grave of Bobby Peel, one of the greatest left-arm slow bowlers Yorkshire and England have ever seen.

A moving ceremony conducted by Yorkshire County Cricket Club's chaplain, Canon Max Wigley, took place on Saturday, October 19, attended by proud descendants of Peel and representatives of Yorkshire CCC, including available members of the Archives Committee.

Money for the tasteful black marble headstone was raised by Peel's relatives with a contribution from the Archives Committee. The White Rose adorns the top left-hand corner of the headstone, upon which is written:

> **IN MEMORY OF**
> **R. (BOBBY) PEEL**
> **1857-1941**
> **YORKSHIRE AND ENGLAND**
> **CRICKETER**
> **Also His Wife**
> **ANNIE LOUISA**
> **1858-1933**

The placing of a headstone upon Peel's previously unmarked grave came to fruition as a direct result of a remarkable coincidence in the later part of 2011, when two descendants of Peel quite independently and at markedly different times of the year made enquiries to Archives Committee member Paul Dyson about their illustrious ancestor's cricketing career.

The older of the two, Robin Barron, from Wakefield, having been given the telephone number of the other, made the necessary contact call, but before doing so he recognised that the number had a Lancashire dialling code. This led him to wonder if he was about to re-engage with an arm of the family that had been lost to him. He only had one name to work with — "Verna".

The call was made, an Andrew Clarke responded, and he was soon confirming that he was a great-great grandson of Bobby Peel and that his mother was Verna. They all arranged to meet at Brighouse, and spent an enjoyable lunch and afternoon catching up on family history as well as agreeing what do next.

They were unanimous that the great man should be suitably honoured. Andrew had already confirmed that Bobby was buried in Bruntcliffe Cemetery, Morley, and been given a plot number.

Robin made two unsuccessful trawls of the cemetery before contacting the Crematorium Department in Leeds, where he received great help in terms of the grave's location, but it was unmarked. Mission accomplished, he reported back to the others.

A further enquiry of the Department was needed to find out what was required in order to erect a headstone. A mass of paperwork followed for the ownership of the grave to be transferred, and then permission given to erect a tone.

While all this was going on Robin was maintaining contact with Paul Dyson and, through him, the Archives Committee.

A meeting of that Committee

BOBBY PEEL: Yorkshire and England all-rounder
(Photo: Ron Deaton Archive)

agreed that it wished to be involved in the next phase, and Yorkshire Board member Robin Smith gave permission for the Yorkshire Rose to be used on the stone. Work on the final stage could begin, and it ended with the installation and dedication of the stone.

Those able to attend the ceremony, meticulously organised by Robin Barron, included direct descendants of three of Bobby's children — the fourth was killed in Great War — from one grandchild through multiple great-grandchildren and a nice spread of great-great-grandchildren. Other relatives included a good representation from the line descending from Bobby's brother, Solomon; a descendant of Thomas Foster, one of about 30 players who were born out of Yorkshire yet played for them before the boundaries were opened; Clive McManus, Chair of Morley Historical Society; Coun. Judith Elliott, one of the Local Authority members for Morley Ward; Richard Taylor, representing the MCC, and both the Chair and Secretary of Wombwell Cricket Lovers' Society.

The County Club were represented by Board member Robin Smith, Members' Committee representatives Stephen Mann, chairman, and Eric Stephens; Players' Association members Geoff Cope, secretary, and Bryan Stott, former chairman, and Howard Clayton, Ron Deaton, James Greenfield, Mick Pope, Brian Sanderson and David Warner from the Archives Committee. Unfortunately, David Allan and Paul Dyson were unable to attend because of previous engagements.

The party adjourned to the Commercial Inn, Churwell, where Bobby was once the popular landlord. An excellent meal provided a suitable base for further cricketing discussion and family catch-up. Robin Barron told the party how the provision of the headstone had come about, and Robin Smith expressed his thanks to the family on behalf of Yorkshire County Cricket Club, emphasising what a great cricketer Peel had been and that he was held in high regard by the Club.

Following Ted Peate in the line of great Yorkshire left-arm bowlers, Peel played in 318 matches for Yorkshire between 1882 and 1897 when he was dismissed by Lord Hawke. By then, he had captured for his native county 1,311 wickets at a miserly average of 15.74, and scored 9,322 runs with nine centuries and one double-century.

In 20 Test matches he took 101 wickets at 16.8 runs apiece, and hit 427 runs with a top score of 83.

*** *** ***

Membership of the Archives Committee for the past 12 months has been unchanged — David Allan, chairman; Howard Clayton, secretary; Paul Dyson, James Greenfield, Mick Pope, Brian Sanderson, Dennis Smith, David Warner and Roy Wilkinson.

I thank each one of them for their enthusiastic contributions to our deliberations and work, and hope that they have found personal enjoyment in all of this.

During 2013, Yorkshire CCC received about 50 enquiries from general members of the public, including some from overseas, concerning various matters of memorabilia. All were dealt with by members of the Archives Committee.

A considerable number included requests for the identification of autographs and information on deceased players, including Gordon Crofts, Frank Greenwood, Schofield Haigh, Clifford Hare, Bobby Moorhouse, Billy Sutcliffe and Cecil Tyson.

A researcher in India wanted to know what happened when an umpire became injured on the field in a Yorkshire match at Gloucester in 1927; other enquiries concerned the derivation of a pub sign found in a skip in Melbourne; information on Nazim Hafees, who played for the USA against Yorkshire Second Eleven in 2000 and was killed on 9/11 — this research resulted in the game being mentioned in an article by American journalist Peter Della Penna in *The Cricketer* — and details on a wide variety of topics, including certain matches, badges and ties.

Many interesting purchases concerning Len Hutton were made at three separate Knights auctions including:

*About 13 scrapbooks detailing his career from Pudsey St Lawrence through to being captain of England.

*A telegram sent to him in Australia in 1946 congratulating him on scoring two consecutive centuries from Sprotbrough Cricket Club, Wilfred Barber, Cyril Turner, Ellis Robinson and Joe Lumb.

*A photograph of Len Hutton and Arthur Mitchell walking out to open the innings for Yorkshire v. Glamorgan at Hull on June 6, 1934.

*The acquisition of one of Len Hutton's Yorkshire caps.

*A photograph of Yorkshire CCC's tour of Jamaica in 1936.

*A telegram congratulating Hutton on his selection for his first Test match for England against New Zealand from the Mayor of Pudsey.

*About 30 of Len Hutton's ties.

These items were purchased on behalf of the Archives Committee by Brian Sanderson, who also acquired on the Committee's behalf Roy Kilner's birthspoon. We also acquired several items from the estate of the late Don Wilson, including his MCC touring blazer for Australia.

The Committee were joined at their first meeting of 2013 by Danny Reuben, Yorkshire CCC's recently appointed Communications Director, who had been invited to discuss among other things his role and to better understand our work and how this could relate to him. The Committee were also kept informed by Will Saville on progress with the Yorkshire Cricket Federation website, which is now fully functioning.

Ten visits were made to the Yorkshire archives at Morley, Brian Warne supplementing the team on several occasion. One of the tasks undertaken was the sorting of all of the late Tony Woodhouse's photographs. We continued to sort and re-catalogue the collection, together with the initial entries of all new memorabilia received, and we worked with Museum Director David Hall in the public display of our archives in the museum and in the display cabinets of the East Stand Long Room.

Committee members Mick Pope and David Warner generously presented copies of their respective books, *Headingley Ghosts* and *The Sweetest Rose* for the archives, and Warner was congratulated on his election as President of The Cricket Writers' Club in succession to the late Christopher Martin-Jenkins.

A final definition was agreed on the Committee's aims. It read: "The collection, maintenance, cataloguing and display, via the museum and display cabinets, of items relevant to the game of cricket as played in the City of York and the old Ridings of Yorkshire and its grounds, matches thereon and players therein, or anyone associated therewith."

Brian Sanderson travelled to London in March to speak to the

Yorkshire Southern Group about the Archives Committee and its work, and the group donated a cake stand which had belonged to George Hirst.

The Committee organised Open Days at Headingley during the intervals of Championship matches on June 23 and September 18, Brian being on hand to deal with enquiries and also bringing with him items of interest to spectators. Similar events are being planned for 2014.

Yorkshire County Cricket Supporters' Association produced a splendid book outlining all the grounds upon which Yorkshire had played first-class cricket during the Club's 150 years, and several Archives Committee members helped in the provision of details. A copy has been kindly donated to our archive.

HAROLD NORTH
Founder Chairman

Also during the summer Harry Gration interviewed Geoffrey Boycott for a new DVD to add to our series of 12, which became available later in the year.

Before the start of the August meeting Committee members stood in silence in memory of Harold North, who died on April 26, aged 85. He was the founding chairman of the Archives Committee in 2003, and set the tone for the collecting together of the archive and the establishment of an inventory as well as developing the connection with West Yorkshire Archive Service. He resigned as chairman in 2005 due to failing health. His ashes were interred in the Memorial Garden at Headingley in July, and a brass plaque was erected which reads:

> **HAROLD NORTH 1927-2013**
> **President, Yorkshire Cricket Taverners, Club**
> **Founding Chairman of YCCC Archives**
> **Committee Member and past Treasurer of Yorkshire CCC**
> **Charitable Youth Trust**

> * David Allan is Chairman of the Yorkshire
> Foundation Cricket Archives Committee

DIFFERENT PATHS TO FAME
FOR HUTTON AND ROOT

By Martin Howe

Joe Root has been likened to the young Len Hutton.

He has excellent technique, considerable powers of concentration and an equable temperament.

Both had the ambition from a young age to play for Yorkshire and England, and the potential of both was

YOUNG HUTTON　　**YOUNG ROOT**

noted when they were in their early teens. Yet the paths by which Root and Hutton realised their ambitions could hardly have been more different. This is only to say, of course, that vast changes in the way the game is organised and administered have taken place in the last 50 years.

Root was 20 years and four months old when he made his first-class debut for Yorkshire on May 10, 2010, against Loughborough MCCU. His progression to this point had been smooth. He attended King Ecgbert's School in Sheffield, and won a cricket scholarship to Worksop College, where he played for Yorkshire Schools. From the age of 13 he attended the Yorkshire Academy. He left Worksop College with 10 O-Levels to concentrate on a cricket career.

He had joined Sheffield Collegiate Cricket Club, who play in the Yorkshire League, and where he was mentored by Michael Vaughan. Success with Collegiate led to selection for Yorkshire Seconds on July 18, 2007, and he was to play in 12 matches for the Seconds before the match against the MCCU. He played only once more for the first team in 2010, but in the following season he became a fixture. He was awarded his county cap in August 2012, and gained a three-year contract.

Even before this Root was marked down as a Test player: he appeared for England Under-15s in 2006, in the Under-19s Cricket World Cup in 2010, for England Under-19s in 2011 and England Lions in the first of four appearances on August 2, 2011. He was chosen for the tour of India in 2012-13, and was capped for the Fourth Test at Nagpur. He retained his place for the subsequent tour of New Zealand.

By the date of his first Test appearance Root had played in only 36 first-class matches, 28 of them for Yorkshire in the County Championship, half of them in Division Two. By any standard this was very little experience for a Test cricketer, but he had had the advantage of professional coaching and the services of the extensive backroom staff employed nowadays by county clubs and the ECB. He had been as carefully nurtured as a bottle of fine wine.

Len Hutton's career progression was altogether different. He attended Littlemore Council School in Pudsey where cricket "took place in the concrete playground with a shed acting as wicket". He then learned skills needed in the building trade, a fallback should his hopes of being a professional cricketer not materialise. There was none of the security of a three-year contract in Hutton's time. He played for Pudsey St Lawrence Second Eleven when only 12 years old and for the first team at 14. He so impressed that on the recommendation of the Pudsey President, supported by Herbert Sutcliffe, he was invited in February 1930 to the winter nets at Headingley, where he was coached by George Hirst and Bill Bowes. There were further visits to the Headingley nets.

In the summer Hutton played regularly for Pudsey St Lawrence, where Edgar Oldroyd was the professional, in the Bradford League. This was a demanding nursery for any young cricketer, but Hutton did well enough to be selected for Yorkshire Seconds on May 24, 1933. He played 11 matches in the Minor Counties Championship before being called to the first team for the first time on May 2, 1934, against Cambridge University at Fenner's, aged 18 years and 11 months.

It was not until July 1936, when he was awarded his county cap — after which he was entitled to a match fee of £11 with an extra £4 for away games and a £1 win bonus — that Len Hutton could feel that his position as a first-team player was truly established. The competition he had faced had been far keener than anything Root experienced.

It was in his fourth season of first-class cricket that Hutton made his debut for England on June 26 against New Zealand at Lord's. By then he had played in 83 first-class matches, most of them for Yorkshire in the County Championship. There was no intermediate step in the 1930s between a county and the national side. Academies, Under-19s, England Performance Programmes and the like all lay far in the future. Coaching and backroom help was minimal in Hutton's time, but he had the immense advantage from the learning point of view of being a member of one of the most powerful and successful county sides ever.

Just as the paths of Root and Hutton to their first England caps were very different, so were their experiences in the seasons in which they were first capped. In the domestic 2013 season after his overseas tours Root played in only 10 first-class matches. Only two of these were for

Yorkshire, at the beginning of the season. After his appearance at Lord's on May 16, 2013, in the First Test against New Zealand Joe played only international cricket, including one-day internationals and *Twenty20s*, formats unimagined in the 1930s, and the five Tests against Australia.

Hutton played in 37 first-class matches in 1937, the year he was first capped for England, three of them Tests, the others mainly for Yorkshire but including matches for MCC early in the season, for the Players against the Gentlemen at Lord's and for H D G Leveson-Gower's Eleven in the Scarborough Festival.

After his first Test — where he famously made a duck in his first innings, as he had in his first first-class innings for Yorkshire — Hutton trav-

Len Hutton in 1949

elled to Ilford, where two days after the Test he played for Yorkshire against Essex. He turned out 21 times in 1937 after the First Test, including the two further Tests against New Zealand. Test matches interspersed with a full programme of three-day county and other first-class matches was to be the pattern for all of the seasons in Hutton's first-class career.

The contrast in the apprenticeships of these excellent players is obvious. Though younger than Root at the comparable stage of their careers, Hutton had a great deal of top-level experience when he first pulled on his England sweater, and also the benefit of the know-how and wisdom of an exceptional bunch of professionals in the Yorkshire dressing room. Root had virtually nothing of that: instead he could draw on a well-funded and well-organised development programme, backed by a host of specialist coaches and trainers, designed to identify the more promising young players and help them to make the most use of their talent.

It is pointless to speculate which is the better form of apprenticeship. The clock cannot be turned back. But one cannot help thinking that a young player is much more likely to succeed at Test level if he has had more experience of first-class matches than has Root. One would guess that Root himself would have preferred to play more for his county, but his ECB contract pre-empts any choice he or Yorkshire might make.

Yorkshire supporters, while wishing Root well in his international career, will rue the fact that he is not likely to be available to play much first-class cricket for his county in future. By contrast Hutton played 250 times for Yorkshire after the season in which he won his first England cap. Times they are a'changing indeed.

Three years ago professional journalist JOHN FULLER launched Cricket Yorkshire, a website that covers every aspect of the game throughout the White Rose county. He recounts how his project grew into what it is today...

A HOME FOR INTERVIEWS, OPINION AND DEBATE

I can tell you exactly where I was when *Cricket Yorkshire* was born. My wife and I were walking up the steep incline on Dallam Road in Shipley, a stone's throw from the Leeds-Liverpool Canal and the welcome waft of freshly baked bread at Hughes on Hirst Lane.

I had been out of work for a few months and exasperated at a lack of editorial opportunities. It was not quite panic time, but the afternoon walk had been a chance to float any and all ideas. The notion of running my own cricket-related business, so often dismissed, suddenly became exciting, challenging, slightly terrifying but, most crucially of all, possible when simply asked by my better half: "Why Not?"

What would any of us do if the sky was the limit and you could choose your perfect profession? Unemployment suddenly became a springboard, a fresh chapter and a chance to build something in the world of cricket from the ground up. Cricket journalism is in my blood; something I have been doing for 20 years — writing about clubs, leagues and professionals across six counties. Once you decide to forge your own path it's amazing where momentum can take you.

The format came first. It was going to be a cricket magazine distributed to clubhouses all around Yorkshire on a Saturday afternoon so that players could read in their whites while waiting to go in. Logistics, distribution costs and the sheer scale of Yorkshire put paid to that for now.

Creating a website was the logical alternative as a platform, and being a technology geek with a background of setting up sites and a career in both the publishing and digital worlds seemed to tick all the boxes. Choosing a business name felt like a huge decision. The dark arts of search-engine optimisation — put simply, how results are determined when you search for anything online — were a vital consideration.

At some point there was a blank A3 page with a spider diagram and a myriad of options. It's curious to think what might have been, had decisions taken another path. I wanted people to know the essence of what the website covered in an instant. *Cricket Yorkshire* felt concise and refreshingly no-nonsense.

Carving a niche in cricket journalism remains at the heart of everything I try to do. The internet is awash with blogs, websites and writers all vying for your attention and time. I wanted *Cricket Yorkshire* to be distinctive in some way, so the decision to combine professional and amateur coverage in the county was a natural move.

That wasn't enough. There are some superb cricket writers, newspapers and websites covering the game in Yorkshire, and competing directly with them made little sense. Instead, *Cricket Yorkshire's* focus is all on interviews, opinion and debate: no news, results or statistics.

Once the proposition was honed, finding the stories in clubs and leagues and interviewing everyone from the captain of Yorkshire County Cricket Club to the stalwarts in the amateur game fell into place.

If there's one thing we can all be certain of it is that there will never be a shortage of stories, colourful characters and tales from the boundary across Yorkshire cricket. Perhaps the greatest conundrum is picking what to concentrate on, given the astonishing volume of cricket played each and every season.

It has been a whirlwind three or so years, beginning with interviews of "Dickie" Bird about his Foundation and sitting down with Ryan Sidebottom in the indoor Cricket Centre soon after he had rejoined the county. Interviews with most of the Yorkshire first-team squad, and stories of hundreds of clubs and a diverse range of personalities has whistled by quicker than a Moin Ashraf bouncer. Sir Michael Parkinson, Harry Gration, Steven Kirby...all with their own intelligent perspective.

A steely determination to offer something truly unique usually results in a continual bombardment of ideas, often at weird and wonderful times of the night. There's an "on" button when it comes to being submerged in cricket, but I'm yet to discover the "off" switch.

In the past year highlights have included talking to Matt Wood about his Yorkshire career and role with the Professional Cricketers' Association; discussing medium pace with author Harry Pearson, and assessing the next generation of Yorkshire county cricketers with second-team coach Paul Farbrace. From the Bradford University student who signed for Delhi Daredevils to why a yorker is a yorker or Andrew Hodd's superstitions...there are entertaining stories at every turn.

Running a cricket website, there is always the risk that you could spend your life staring at a screen, communicating by e-mail and operating in a world defined by pixels and PDFs. With that in mind, the summer of 2013 represented the chance to pack up the digital camera, clamber on a train and venture out on a tour of Yorkshire clubs.

There were debut visits to a host of grounds from the spectacular arches and first-class clubhouse at Copley in the Halifax League to the hidden gem of Oriel, nestled in the Scarborough backstreets. The weather gods were kind for a hat-trick of cup finals, each with their unique sense of occasion — at Ackworth for the Yorkshire Cricket Council; the

Heavy Woollen at Hanging Heaton and Ossett hosting the Central Yorkshire Cricket League T20 Day.

Sometimes even the best-laid plans can go awry, such as going to Dunnington, hopefully to watch West Indian Collis King, architect of the 1979 World Cup victory over England, rack up a seemingly inevitable century on a June afternoon. As it turned out, Dunnington was a gold-mine of stories, not least the way a young all-rounder called Colin Graves used to deposit balls into the field opposite, but the 62-year-old opener King, in his 18th York & District League season, went cheaply.

Cricket can be delightfully unpredictable, a leveller of even the best. As if to prove it a mere blip Collis scored a hundred on the Sunday in a cup game, and sauntered to his 50th York League hundred in August.

Strategic partnerships played a key role in my efforts to promote both professional and amateur cricket in the county last season. *Cricket Yorkshire* was media partner for Leeds Bradford MCCU, and the students claimed another first-class county scalp at Grace Road.

It was the "year of the yellow" as the Yorkshire-based Centre of Excellence won the treble with the two-day Championship alongside one-day league and cup competitions.

Interviewing Luis Reece on the poignancy of taking over captaincy and an article by seam bowler James Lee on facing his former county at Headingley were particular highlights.

Partnerships with the Yorkshire Cricket Foundation and Yorkshire Cricket Board opened up a wealth of interviews and feature articles, and hopefully promoted the invaluable community work of both to a new, online audience.

Technology inevitably forms the backbone of my work. Social media has been an essential, and sometimes addictive, tool to get word out. Twitter isn't for everyone, and the notion of a limit of 140 characters was initially an anathema. Three years ago my first tweet took 20 minutes to get right, which rather defeats the point of immediacy of the platform.

Since those fumbling first few communications a digital audience of thousands has been carefully nurtured from professional cricketers to governing bodies; from county clubs to a cohort of players and fans. Tweeting as *@cricketyorks* on a daily basis equates to plenty of conversations and making connections.

Whether sharing photography on Facebook, audio interviews on Soundcloud or video on YouTube, these digital channels are only as good as the content — a continual challenge that keeps me on my toes.

Looking forward to the 2014 season? Engaging with those involved in Yorkshire cricket at whatever level, whether interviewing Andrew Gale or a club groundsman, remains key, as does enticing all of you to have a read.

* John Fuller's website is www.cricketyorkshire.com

HOW SPOTLIGHT TURNED ON ALLAN SHACKLETON

By David Swallow

In America they are called Godwinks — the strange set of circumstances which seem to have no rational explanation.

One such is the link between a man who played five times for Yorkshire over 70 years ago, a cricket enthusiast from Harrogate, a one-time Bradford League stalwart and an article I wrote in 2013.

It all began when David Warner, Editor of the YCCC *Yearbook*, asked me to write a piece on Wilfred Rhodes and George Herbert Hirst for the brochure produced to mark the Club's 150th anniversary.

I turned for help to Ron Deaton, Yorkshire member and a man who knows as much as most about the Club's history and players. Among the books he lent me was the classic by A A Thomson on the great pair whose like we shall never see again. It was signed by W A Shackleton, of Birkenshaw, a name I recognised as a friend of a great friend of mine, Geoff Hirst, who scored almost 15,000 runs in the Bradford League with an average of almost 40 over 25 years.

When I spoke to Geoff he could not believe that this important link with his past had come to light. "There will be an inscription from Shack's wife in the front," he said. And there was.

Ron, who scours bookshops and memorabilia sales in his search for something special, had found this treasure in a small shop in York during a lunch break. "I knew the name W A Shackleton as that of a man who had played for Yorkshire a few times, but knew nothing about him except the bare statistics in the *Yearbook*," he said.

Then all was revealed. Geoff, now 87, sent him a picture of himself and Shack, as he was known, going out to bat for Brighouse in 1949. "I had not known either man until then, and was delighted when Geoff, David and I were able to get together for a long walk down memory lane," Ron said. Geoff recalls: "Shack was born in 1908 in Keighley, and became a fine all-rounder. Apart from his appearances with Yorkshire's first team he played for the Colts throughout the 1930s, and wore his *white rosebud* cap with great pride."

Brian Sellers, captain of that star-studded Yorkshire side, also came from Keighley. The two knew each other well, and Sellers called Shack "Double Bounce". Geoff explained: "Allan always denied it but Sellers insisted that he once bowled a delivery which bounced twice before it reached the stump!"

Shack played as a professional in the Bradford League with Keighley, Pudsey St Lawrence, Bowling Old Lane and finally Brighouse.

Geoff was "steeped" in the Brighouse club, where his father was chairman of the committee.

Aged 14, he made a half-century on his debut for the second team, and played for the first team before joining the Fleet Air Arm at the end of the Second World War, spending much of his time playing cricket and rugby for the Air Command.

Throughout the war Allan was employed by a Government Ministry in charge of manufacture and allocation of card clothing, a vital product in the processing of raw wool into yarn.

FLASHBACK: Allan Shackleton, left, going out to open the innings for Brighouse in 1949 with his captain, Geoff Hirst

Despite age difference the two struck up a close friendship, which endured until Shack died in 1971. Geoff succeeded him as captain of Brighouse, and in his 10-year spell the club enjoyed one of the best periods in its history, winning the first division without losing a game.

Geoff spent the last two years of his career at Farsley. Oddly, they and his former club — neither had won the Priestley Cup — met in the semi-final in 1963: "I scored a half-century, which helped win the game, and Farsley went on to take the final at Park Avenue".

Now to his memories and anecdotes about the man who was his mentor and guide: "He had a motto pinned up on the dressing room wall — When You Are Doing Well Keep Quiet, Pick Your Friends When You Are Not Doing So Well."

Like so many Yorkshire players he always stressed the importance of fielding. "A run saved in the field is just as good as one scored at the wicket," was his maxim. And he had a story to illustrate it:

"In 1928 Emmott Robinson took 8-13 against Cambridge University at Fenner's. Shack was fielding at cover when the one bad ball from Emmott was slashed like a bullet to his right. Shack swore to his dying day that he saved a certain four, but did not pick the ball up cleanly.

"The batsmen crossed for a single. At lunchtime scorer Billy Ringrose congratulated Emmott when he announced the figures. With a look of absolute venom the bowler turned to the hapless 20-year-old and said: "Aye, and if it hadn't been for thee it would have been 8-12".

Another story from one of Allan's games with Yorkshire: They were playing Kent at Canterbury with Frank Woolley the man to get out early. Robinson was bowling, with Rhodes at mid-on and Arthur Wood, in one of his first games, keeping wicket.

Woolley went for a drive, but skied the ball. ER: It's mine. WR: I've got it. AW: Right. All three stopped, and the ball dropped in the centre of the triangle. Woolley was still there on his way to a big score. "Total silence reigned over the meal. When they got to the pears and custard, Wilfred said: 'Emmott, when ball goes up air near wickets, whose catch is it?' A short pause until with a look of triumph Robinson replied: 'Man with gloves on' and two pairs of eyes turned on the unfortunate Wood."

In the same game Shack was padded up, feeling apprehensive, when Rhodes put a hand on his shoulder and said: "Nah then, lad, you'll be batting against best leg-spinner in England, Tich Freeman. Only play forward if tha can get right to pitch. If tha can't, play back.

"Remember he bowls leg-spinner, he bowls top-spinner and he bowls googlie." With that he walked away, then turned and said: "But he nob-but bowls 'em one at once!"

Shackleton was a fine cricketer and man. At any other time he would have commanded a regular place in the Yorkshire team. Some thought he would have been captaincy material but for the presence of Sellers.

So this story of coincidence ends. Another Godwink might take me to Albert Cordingley, who once vied for a place in the Yorkshire side with Wilfred Rhodes . He vanished without trace more than a century ago.

Come April

It was (Neville) Cardus who wished all who loved cricket "a good winter's sleep and a quick renewal of life next April." We know the Hambledon men, the gamblers in Dorset Square, the doughty lads of Lascelles Hall, all in their time pondered on the future of cricket. Perhaps all we need to reflect upon is one of the sweetest phrases in the English lexicon: Come April.

The Carnegie History

JOE'S DIARY IS A 'MUST' FOR ALL COUNTY CRICKET FANS

By Graham Hardcastle

ROSE-TINTED SUMMER: The Dressing Room Diary In The 150th Anniversary Year Of Yorkshire County Cricket Club.
Joe Sayers (Great Northern Books, £17.99)

Last year will always be a memorable one for Joe Sayers, the left-handed opening batsman who opted to call time on his professional career after 10 seasons at first-class level with his home county, Yorkshire. There is no doubt that Joe will look back on the summer with regret, because he played in only five LV County Championship matches and scored just 57 runs. He spent most of it doing the hard yards in the Second Eleven, where he did his utmost to move back up a level.

Still, the 30-year-old can be immensely proud of one achievement off the field — that he became a published author of *Rose-Tinted Summer: The Dressing Room Diary of Yorkshire's 150th Anniversary Year*. A graduate from Oxford University with a degree in physics, he was the ideal choice to pen such a diary.

And he did a darned good job! Yes, it was a shame for the purposes of the book that the Leeds-born former England Lion was not around the first team more than he was, but he was able to provide enough behind-the-scenes material to make this a must read for all Yorkshire fans. No, let me rephrase that: to make this a must read for all county cricket fans. Having read Ed Cowan's diary of a season with Tasmania a couple of years ago — ironically, a good mate of Joe's from their university days — I told a number of people that there would be a market for such a book written by an English county player. And this is it.

I was certainly not disappointed. Sayers provides an honest view of a county cricketer's life throughout the year, starting at the Club's Sesquicentennial Soiree at the Crucible Theatre, Sheffield, back in January to their pre-season tour of Barbados and through the hectic nature of the county campaign. He deeply analyses the highs and lows of his form, while mixing it with snippets of dressing-room humour. Adam Lyth is often the butt of the mickey-taking! Sayers reveals plenty of things of interest throughout this enjoyable read. In a pre-season chat with Rich Pyrah he learned that the all-rounder may never again get full feeling back into the two outermost fingers on his left hand after a fielding accident in early 2012.

Sayers also sat down and chatted at length with Joe Root in September about the whirlwind 12 months that had propelled his career in the right direction. Although Joe, who suffered from post-viral-fatigue syndrome ahead of the 2011 season, will not go down as one of Yorkshire's great players, he will certainly go down as one of their great servants. A player who fully subscribed to the theory that there is no "I" in a team. Everybody connected with Yorkshire CCC will wish him well with his future career. *Rose Tinted Summer* is his leaving present to us.

HEADINGLEY GHOSTS: A Collection of Yorkshire Cricket Tragedies. Mick Pope (Scratching Shed Publishing Ltd, £14.99)

An intriguing title, but it got me off on the wrong foot. I half expected stories of spirits strolling — if that's what ghosts do — around the famous village. In fact, it is a collection of Yorkshire cricket tragedies spread over 65 names from George Steer in 1827 to the much-lamented David Bairstow in 1998. It is a masterpiece of the researcher's art, and a great credit to Mick Pope.

It is his sixth book on various aspects of Yorkshire cricket, coming when even the most devoted fanatic of the Club and game might have expected the well to be running dry.

As far as I am concerned there is only one genuine Headingley Ghost, Eric Harris, who came from Australia in 1930 to play on the wing for the Rugby League club, long before they became the *Rhinos*. His last match was in September 1939, the day before war was declared.

In those nine years he scored 392 in 383 matches, and earned the nickname the *Toowoomba Ghost* because of his extraordinary skill in beating defenders. I never saw him, but Ken Dalby wrote of his "extraordinary visitations" being woven into Headingley legend.

Mick Pope's tome is spread over more than 330 pages, and he admits that there is much darkness, with sadness, despair and sorrow the overriding themes. I would have thought there was plenty of those ingredients in the world around us today but admit that the writer has put together an absorbing collection of stories.

My particular interest is in David Bairstow, the incomparable Bluey, and Michael Fearnley whom I played alongside at Farsley as a boy. I was covering Yorkshire cricket for the Bradford paper among others when the young Bairstow was called to the colours from his school examination desk in the city. Over the years we became good pals.

At the start I picked him up at home, and took him around. I had the great pleasure of telling him that Yorkshire had given him his much coveted cap (they do things differently today). I remember going to the opening of his sports-related business in Pudsey, and meeting him on holiday in Tenerife. Happy days, but I can still recall the horror and disbelief when I read of his untimely death and the circumstances surrounding. No-one who knew will ever forget.

Mike Fearnley, known to us as Pop, was a different kind of man. A school teacher with a slightly arrogant air, but a gifted Bradford League bowler and skilful coach. I was on holiday in the Lake District when news came through that he had collapsed and died on July 7, 1979, running into bowl for Farsley at East Bierley. Strange how you can remember where you were when certain events took place! All the details of his distinguished career are here, sympathetically recorded, as are the stories of all the other "victims". Pick where you will, there is a vast variety of anecdotes, many well known, others less so.

And not a hint of a ghost writer in sight!

DAVID SWALLOW

DICKIE BIRD 80 NOT OUT: My Favourite Cricket Memories.
Dickie Bird (Hodder &Stoughton, £20)

Harold "Dickie" Bird, the most famous umpire the game has produced — as well as being Yorkshire CCC's new President — celebrated his 80th birthday on April 19 last year, and the Barnsley-born national treasure wrote a best-selling book to mark the event. It will delight his legion of friends and fans, whether they be avid cricket followers or not.

Dickie loves to regale anyone with his favourite memories from a lifetime in cricket, which began to flower with Barnsley and went on to bloom with Yorkshire and Leicestershire before bursting into full blossom as the greatest umpire on the international scene. After he had made his tearful exit as a Test umpire at Lord's in 1996 Dickie penned his autobiography, which sold three-quarters of a million copies and was among the best-selling sports books ever written. It was crammed with stories from his colourful career, but now Dickie casts a fresh eye over those times as well as coming up with many new tales and observations.

Dickie's love of life has never left him, but he begins by confessing that at one stage he thought he would not make it to his 80th birthday. Early one morning he was hit by a stroke and, in great pain, kept drifting in and out of consciousness. Even though his speech was slurred he eventually managed to summon medical help, and was rushed to Barnsley Hospital. He lost his speech entirely, but that returned, although he admits that the effects of the stroke have slowed him down.

He also has had operations to repair a burst blood vessel and to improve his sight when he was in danger of going blind as a result of standing all those years in some of the hottest countries. Happily, he has recovered from all his afflictions to enjoy life to the full. He is still the master story-teller who quickly casts a spell over his readers, and the book includes many excellent photographs which depict Dickie from his earliest days with Yorkshire to his remarkable life on an off the field.

Dickie was awarded the OBE in 2012 for his services to cricket and charity — he founded The Dickie Bird Foundation, which helps underprivileged young players to gain a foothold in sport. He is an honorary life member of Yorkshire County Cricket Club.

DAVID WARNER

GRAHAM STEVENSON

By David Warner

Graham Stevenson, who died on January 21, aged 58, was an entertainer on a grand scale for Yorkshire with a cavalier approach which went down well with the fans. Born at Ackworth, Graham played in 177 first-class matches for Yorkshire between 1973 and 1986, taking 464 wickets at 28.56, scoring 3,856 runs with two centuries and holding on to 73 catches. He twice played in Test matches for England, and he represented his country in four one-day internationals.

Without doubt Graham was possessed with a rare ability in all aspects of the game. He was a fine seam bowler, who could move the ball both ways, a remarkable late-order batsman who made a habit of hitting good-length deliveries high and hard over extra-cover, and a stunning fielder whose returns from the boundary edge landed in the wicket-keeper's gloves like fire crackers.

He was one of the most popular figures with both teammates and fans ever to wear a Yorkshire sweater, and he was greatly admired by his former captain and friend, Geoffrey Boycott, who was an early mentor and arranged nets for him at Headingley when he was a youth. Geoffrey openly admitted that Graham was one of his favourite cricketers, along with David Bairstow and Ian Botham. He was well-equipped for one-day matches, and played in 216 limited-overs games for Yorkshire, capturing 290 wickets and scoring 1,699 runs.

Graham developed as a first-class cricketer at about the same time as Ian Botham, and there was perhaps little to choose between them so far as raw talent was concerned. Maybe the Yorkshireman could have gone on to achieve even greater things himself with a little more concentration, but then he would not have been the character everyone so loved.

Perhaps, also, he was born a generation too soon: he would have been a huge asset to any side in *Twenty20* cricket, and he would probably have made a big name for himself in the game.

His most important contributions for Yorkshire were generally with the ball, and against Northamptonshire at Headingley in 1980 he grabbed the first eight wickets at a cost of 57. He could well have gone on to bag all 10...but he left the field to change his shirt!

In 1978 he was the scourge of Lancashire, destroying them in their first innings at Headingley with figures of 8-65, Yorkshire going on to win by an innings and 32 runs on the second day. At Old Trafford later in the season Yorkshire were triumphant by 10 wickets, Graham taking 5-61 and 3-57. His new-ball partner, Chris Old, also had a significant say with an unbeaten century and 4-38 and 5-47.

Perhaps one of most headline-grabbing acts was with the bat when he shared a Yorkshire record-breaking last-wicket stand of 149 with Boycott against Warwickshire at Edgbaston.

Going in last, Graham thrashed 115 not out — at the time the highest unbeaten score ever recorded by a No. 11.

Never was the power he wielded with the bat seen to better effect than in a Sunday League match against Somerset at Middlesbrough in 1984, when he lashed 81 not out off 29 deliveries with 10 sixes, several of them straight-drives which put the Press box in danger. One crashed through scorer Ted Lester's window.

Graham's international

GRAHAM STEVENSON: Dashing cavalier of rare all-round talent
(Photo: Yorkshire Post)

debut was in a one-dayer against Australia in Sydney, when he played a big part in England winning the match. He took 4-33, including the wickets of Rod Marsh, Dennis Lillee and Greg Chappell, then strode to the crease to join his Yorkshire teammate and buddy, David Bairstow, at 129-8 with 35 still required. They got there with more than an over to spare, Graham hitting 28 from 18 balls.

Sadly, he had endured much ill-health in recent years, and he died in hospital after suffering a severe stroke 14 weeks earlier. He leaves a widow, Angie, a son, a daughter and two grandsons.

Graham Barry Stevenson
Born: December 16, 1955
Died: January 21, 2014

GRAHAM BARRY STEVENSON

FIRST-CLASS CRICKET FOR YORKSHIRE 1973 TO 1986

Right-hand Batsman.   Right-arm medium-pace bowler
Born: Ackworth   December 16, 1955

Debut: Yorkshire v. Middlesex at Bradford   September 8, 1973
Last played: Yorkshire v. Sussex at Leeds   May 7, 1986
Final First Class: Northamptonshire v. Pakistan at Bletchley   June 13, 1987
Capped: May 28, 1978

FIRST-CLASS MATCHES FOR YORKSHIRE

BATTING AND FIELDING

Season	M	I	NO	Runs	HS	Avge	100s	50s	Ct
1973	1	2	0	8	7	4.00	0	0	1
1974	4	4	0	25	16	6.25	0	0	4
1975	8	8	0	233	63	29.12	0	2	4
1976	11	17	1	442	83	27.62	0	4	10
1977	22	25	4	303	52	14.42	0	1	6
1978	15	18	4	416	70*	29.71	0	1	5
1979	17	20	5	317	73*	21.13	0	1	8
1980	22	29	9	668	111	33.40	1	3	11
1981	20	27	0	355	57	13.14	0	1	8
1982	17	19	4	356	115*	23.73	1	0	6
1983	20	25	1	396	52	16.50	0	2	4
1984	14	16	1	180	27	12.00	0	0	5
1985	4	6	2	99	35*	24.75	0	0	1
1986	2	1	1	58	58*	—	0	1	0
	177	217	32	3856	115*	20.84	2	16	73

BOWLING

Season	Matches	Overs	Mdns	Runs	Wkts	Avge	Best	5wI	10w
1973	1	19	5	50	3	16.66	2-23	0	0
1974	4	29	9	88	2	44.00	2-43	0	0
1975	8	150	28	496	14	35.42	3-31	0	0
1976	11	225.5	43	755	23	32.82	4-25	0	0
1977	22	544.5	122	1772	69	25.68	6-82	2	1
1978	15	331.3	69	1034	42	24.61	8-65	3	0
1979	17	498.3	124	1440	50	28.80	6-14	1	0
1980	22	602.1	164	1669	72	23.18	8-57	5	1
1981	20	537.4	122	1857	61	30.44	7-46	3	0
1982	17	443.4	95	1474	45	32.75	5-72	1	0
1983	20	460.1	103	1400	56	25.00	5-35	2	0
1984	14	262.3	44	892	19	46.94	4-35	0	0
1985	4	72.4	10	252	6	42.00	3-39	0	0
1986	2	29	8	75	2	37.50	2-27	0	0
	177	4206.3	946	13254	464	28.56	8-57	17	2

TEST MATCHES

BATTING AND FIELDING

Season	M	I	NO	Runs	HS	Avge	100s	50s	Ct
1980 & 81	2	2	1	28	27*	28.00	0	0	0

BOWLING

Season	Matches	Overs	Mdns	Runs	Wkts	Avge	Best	5wI	10w
1980 & 81	2	52	7	183	5	36.60	3-111	0	0

v.. India at Bombay on February 15, 1980, and v. West Indies at St John's on March 27, 1981

ALL FIRST-CLASS MATCHES

BATTING AND FIELDING

Matches	Innings	Not Out	Runs	Highest Score	Avge	100s	50s	Ct
188	229	34	3965	115*	20.33	2	16	73

BOWLING

Matches	Overs	Maidens	Runs	Wickets	Average	Best	4wI	10wM
188	4444.4	989	14075	488	28.84	8-57	18	2

DOMESTIC LIST A MATCHES FOR YORKSHIRE 1973 TO 1986

Debut: John Player League v. Northamptonshire at Northampton   June 3, 1973
Last played: John Player Special League v. Gloucestershire at Leeds   June 8, 1986
Final List A: Refuge Assurance League for *Northamptonshire*
v. Lancashire at Tring   July 5, 1987

BATTING AND FIELDING

Season	M	I	NO	Runs	HS	Avge	100s	50s	Ct
1973	5	2	1	12	10	12.00	0	0	2
1974	13	10	2	100	27	12.50	0	0	6
1975	20	12	1	48	18	4.36	0	0	4
1976	18	13	0	143	31	11.00	0	0	4
1977	18	12	2	73	16	7.30	0	0	1
1978	16	13	3	122	33*	12.20	0	0	1
1979	16	9	1	68	15	8.50	0	0	3
1980	23	17	1	168	43	10.50	0	0	6
1981	16	13	2	189	56	17.18	0	1	2
1982	21	18	1	207	43	12.17	0	0	0
1983	19	14	2	176	34	14.66	0	0	3
1984	16	14	4	291	81*	29.10	0	1	2
1985	9	5	0	29	13	5.80	0	0	3
1986	7	6	3	84	27*	28.00	0	0	1
	217	158	23	1710	81*	12.66	0	2	38

BOWLING

Season	Matches	Overs	Mdns	Runs	Wkts	Avge	Best	4wI
1973	5	27	5	111	3	37.00	1-24	0
1974	13	91	7	340	22	15.45	4-57	1
1975	20	169.1	23	622	36	17.27	4-59	1
1976	18	130.1	10	569	23	24.73	5-41	2
1977	18	133.1	10	530	18	29.44	4-20	1
1978	16	111	7	492	27	18.22	5-28	1
1979	16	122	24	448	13	34.46	2-8	0
1980	23	189.4	31	665	28	23.75	3-13	0
1981	16	117.3	11	477	15	31.80	3-23	0
1982	21	159.3	13	768	28	27.42	5-50	1
1983	19	132.1	13	606	28	21.64	5-27	2
1984	16	128.5	6	650	25	26.00	4-29	1
1985	9	68	5	317	15	21.13	4-26	2
1986	7	52	3	225	9	25.00	3-58	0
	217	1631.1	168	6820	290	23.51	5-27	12

INTERNATIONAL MATCHES

BATTING AND FIELDING

Season	M	I	NO	Runs	HS	Avge	100s	50s	Ct
1980 & 81	4	4	3	43	28*	43.00	0	0	2

BOWLING

Season	Matches	Overs	Mdns	Runs	Wkts	Avge	Best	4wI
1980 & 81	4	32	3	125	7	17.85	4-33	1

v. Australia at Sydney on January 14, 1980, v. West Indies at Adelaide, January 16, 1980
v. West Indies at Kingstown on February 4, 1981, v. West Indies at Albion, February 26, 1981

ALL LIST A MATCHES

BATTING AND FIELDING

Matches	Innings	Not Out	Runs	Highest Score	Avge	100s	50s	Ct
225	165	27	1794	81*	13.00	0	2	40

BOWLING

Overs	Maidens	Runs	Wickets	Average	Best	4wI
1698.3	174	7085	307	23.07	5-27	15

CHARLES FENTON OBE

By David Warner

Charles Miller Fenton, a Vice-President of Yorkshire CCC since 1997 and a former chairman of YCCC Charitable Youth Trust, died on August 22, aged 82.

The Charitable Youth Trust started out by acquiring a lease on the old county ground at Bradford Park Avenue, where it gave strong financial support to the *Enjoy Cricket* scheme which began at the ground in 1991 and spread to other centres around the county.

Its aim was to provide facilities, equipment and coaching for young cricketers, particularly those without the opportunity to play at school or at a local club.

For more than 30 years Mr Fenton had been president of Cleckheaton Sports Club, with its rugby, bowls and cricket sections, and he took delight in its ability to field seven junior cricket teams. He

**CHARLES FENTON
Charitable Youth Trust**
(Photo: Yorkshire Post)

remained actively connected with the club as a trustee. He was also president of Craven Gentlemen Cricket Club and Spen Valley Billiards Club, and in 1982 he was made an the OBE for services to the community.

Mr Fenton was the great-grandson of a Scots weaving manager who invented and manufactured a new kind of power-transmission belting. The British Belting Company which he set up to manufacture his invention moved to Cleckheaton — where Mr Charles Fenton was born — and by 1914 was producing 40,000 feet of transmission linings a week for Henry Ford's famous car, the model T.

Mr Fenton worked for the BBA group all his working life, as managing director between 1970 and 1985 and chairman from 1985 to 1989. With numerous overseas subsidiaries, yet retaining its headquarters at the Royds in Cleckheaton, the group was the largest Yorkshire-based company with around 26,000 employees by the time he retired.

Outside his business interests Mr Fenton was actively involved in

95

West Yorkshire life. He was trustee of West Riding Cheshire homes and the AM Fenton Trust, president of Dewsbury & District League of Friendship for Disabled Persons, chairman of Whitcliffe Mount Scholarship Trust, and for 50 years was a governor of Hipperholme Grammar School, remaining governor emeritus. He served as a magistrate on the Dewsbury Bench for 33 years, taking a one-year leave from the bench in 1981 to fulfil his duties as High Sheriff of West Yorkshire.

Mr Fenton is survived by his son, Nigel, who played in eight first-class matches for Cambridge University from 1988 to 1991: against Yorkshire at Fenner's in 1988 he dismissed the first three in the order — Richard Blakey, Ashley Metcalfe and Jim Love — but Yorkshire went on to win by 10 wickets despite a first-innings 75 from the university captain, Michael Atherton.

Garry Keyworth, a devoted Yorkshire fan who travelled the country with his team, died in Rotherham Hospice on February 12 after a long battle with cancer. BBC Radio Leeds cricket commentator Dave Callaghan writes: "Garry was a trustee of the Dickie Bird Foundation, and he loved his visits to Scarborough, where he assisted me at the quiz nights for the Foundation. He often drove Dickie to functions and matches, and the two became good friends. A local umpire, Garry would often take cricket balls on to the pitch at Scarborough when the umpires required a change, and he used to be quite chuffed when the crowd applauded him as he left the field. He had a fine array of cricket shirts from all over the world, but his passion was always with Yorkshire."

Caroline Collinson, a stewarding supervisor at Yorkshire CCC and international matches at Headingley, died in September after being taken ill while stewarding on the first day of Yorkshire's Championship match against Middlesex. She was a popular figure at the ground, and built up a strong rapport with spectators.

Betty Horbury, another well-known figure at Headingley matches, died in October, aged 87. For many years Betty and her husband, Ernest, policed the sightlines behind the bowler's arm, and Ernest used to dash on to the field with a box of balls whenever the match ball went out of shape. They were married in 1946, and celebrated their diamond wedding while on duty during a Yorkshire match, captain David Byas making a presentation to them.

Mick Bourne, a much respected junior coach and Yorkshire CCC member for over 30 years, also died in October. He wrote *Off the Beaten Track* with fellow league watchers Tony Hutton and Brian Senior, and he was going to write a history of the lost cricket grounds of Leeds. In 1993 he became Alwoodley's representative with the Leeds and District Junior Cricket League, and served as League Secretary from 1995 to 2000. He was Booklet Editor for the Northern Cricket Society.

* The obituary of **Harold North** can be found in the Archives Committee section of the *Yearbook*.

The Players

Andrew William GALE
Left-hand batsman
Born: Dewsbury, November 28, 1983

First-Class cricket:
Debut: v. Somerset at Scarborough, 2004
Highest score: 272 v. Nottinghamshire
at Scarborough, 2013
Best bowling: 1-33 v. Loughborough UCCE
at Leeds, 2007

One-Day:
Highest score: 125* v. Essex at Chelmsford, 2010

t20:
Highest score: 91 v. Nottinghamshire
at Leeds, 2009

Timothy Thomas BRESNAN
Right-hand batsman, right-arm medium-fast bowler
Born: Pontefract, February 28, 1985
First-Class cricket:
Debut: v. Northamptonshire at Northampton, 2003
Highest score: 126* for England Lions v. Indians
at Chelmsford, 2007
Highest for Yorkshire: 116 v. Surrey at The Oval, 2007
Best bowling: 5-42 v. Worcestershire at Worcester, 2005
One-Day:
Highest score: 80 for England v. Australia
at Centurion Park, 2009
For Yorkshire: 61 v. Leicestershire at Leeds, 2003
Best bowling: 4-25 v. Somerset at Leeds, 2005
t20:
Highest score: 42 v. Leicestershire at Leeds, 2004
Best bowling: 3-10 England v. Pakistan at Cardiff, 2010
Best bowling for Yorkshire: 3-21 v. Durham
at Chester-le-Street, 2006

Joe Edward ROOT
Right-hand batsman, right-arm off-spin bowler
Born: Sheffield, December 30, 1990
First-Class cricket:
Debut: v. Loughborough MCCU at Leeds, 2010
Highest Score: 236 v. Derbyshire at Leeds, 2013
Best bowling: 3-33 v. Warwickshire
at Birmingham, 2011
One-Day:
Highest Score: 79* for England v. New Zealand
at Napier, 2012/13
Highest for Yorkshire: 63 v. Essex at Leeds, 2009
Best bowling: 2-10 for England Lions v. Bangladesh A
at Sylhet, 2011/12
For Yorkshire: 2-14 v. Kent at Leeds, 2012
t20:
Highest score: 90* for England v. Australia
at Southampton, 2013
For Yorkshire: 65 Worcestershire at Leeds, 2012
Best bowling: 1-12 v.Warwickshire at Leeds, 2011

Jonathan Marc BAIRSTOW

Right-hand batsman, wicket-keeper
Born: Bradford, September 26, 1989
First-Class Cricket:
Debut: v Somerset at Leeds, 2009
Highest score: 205 v. Nottinghamshire
at Nottingham, 2011
One-Day:
Highest score: 114 v. Middlesex at Lord's, 2011
t20:
Highest score: 68* v. Sussex at Cardiff, 2012

Gary Simon BALLANCE

Left-hand batsman, leg-break bowler
Born: Harare, Zimbabwe, November 22, 1989
First-Class Cricket:
Debut: v Kent at Canterbury, 2008
Highest score: 210 for Mid-West Rhinos v.
Southern Rocks at Masvingo, Zimbabwe, 2011-12
For Yorkshire: 148 v Surrey at The Oval, 2013
One-Day:
Highest score: 139 v Unicorns at Leeds, 2013
t20:
Highest score: 68 v Durham
at Chester-le-Street, 2013

Ryan Jay SIDEBOTTOM

Left-hand bat, left-arm fast-medium bowler
Born: Huddersfield, January 15, 1978
First-Class cricket:
Debut: v. Leicestershire at Leicester, 1997
Highest score: 61 v. Worcestershire
at Worcester, 2011
Best bowling: 7-37 v. Somerset at Leeds 2011
One-Day:
Highest score: 32 for Nottinghamshire v. Middlesex
at Nottingham, 2005
Highest score for Yorkshire: 30* v. Glamorgan
at Leeds, 2002
Best bowling: 6-40 v. Glamorgan at Cardiff, 1998
t20:
Highest score for Yorkshire: 16* v. Worcestershire
at Worcester, 2011
Best bowling: 4-25 v. Durham
at Chester-le-Street, 2012

Steven Andrew PATTERSON

Right-hand batsman, right-arm medium-fast bowler
Born: Beverley, October 3, 1983

First-Class cricket:

Debut: v. Bangladesh 'A' at Leeds, 2005
Highest score: 53 v. Sussex at Hove, 2011
Best bowling: 5-43 v. Nottinghamshire
at Nottingham, 2013

One-Day:

Highest score: 25* v. Worcestershire at Leeds, 2006
Best bowling: 6-32 v. Derbyshire at Leeds, 2010

t20:

Highest score: 3* v. Derbyshire at Leeds, 2010
Best bowling: 4-30 v. Lancashire at Leeds, 2010

Andrew John HODD

Right-hand batsman, wicket keeper
Born: Chichester, January 12, 1984
First-Class cricket:
Debut: Sussex v. Zimbabwe at Hove, 2003
Debut for Yorkshire: v. Derbyshire at Leeds, 2012
Highest score: 123 for Sussex v. Yorkshire
at Hove, 2007
Highest score for Yorkshire: 68* v. Somerset
at Taunton, 2013
One-Day:
Highest score: 91 for Sussex v. Lancashire
at Hove, 2010
For Yorkshire: 21 v Middlesex at Radlett, 2013
t20:
Highest score: 26 for Sussex v. Kent at Hove, 2010
For Yorkshire: 11 v Durham
at Chester-le-Street, 2013

Adam LYTH

Left-hand batsman, right-arm medium bowler
Born: Whitby, September 25, 1987

First-Class cricket:

Debut: v. Loughborough UCCE at Leeds, 2007
Highest score: 248* v. Leicestershire
at Leicester, 2012
Best bowling: 2-15 v. Somerset at Taunton, 2013

One-Day:

Highest score: 109* v. Sussex
at Scarborough, 2009
Best bowling: 1-6 v Middlesex at Leeds, 2013

t20:

Highest score: 78 v. Derbyshire at Leeds, 2012
Best bowling: 1-16 v Nottinghamshire
at Nottingham, 2013

Adil Usman RASHID

Right-hand batsman, leg-break bowler
Born: Bradford, February 17, 1988
First-Class cricket:

Debut: v. Warwickshire at Scarborough, 2006
Highest score: 180 v Somerset at Leeds, 2013
Best bowling: 7-107 v. Hampshire
at Southampton, 2008

One-Day:

Highest score: 46* v Middlesex at Radlett, 2013
Best bowling: 4-38 v. Northamptonshire
at Northampton, 2012

t20:

Highest score: 34 v. Worcestershire
at Worcester, 2010
Best bowling: 4-20 v. Leicestershire at Leeds, 2010

Liam Edward PLUNKETT

Right-hand batsman, right-arm fast-medium bowler
Born: Middlesbrough, April 6, 1985
First-Class cricket:
Debut: For Durham v. Durham UCCE at Durham, 2003
Yorkshire Debut: v. Leeds/Bradford MCCU at Leeds, 2013
Highest score: 107* for Durham v. Durham MCCU
at Durham, 2011
For Yorkshire: 68 v. Surrey at Leeds, 2013
Best bowling: 6-33 v. Leeds/Bradford MCCU
at Leeds, 2013
One-Day:
Highest score: 72 for Durham v. Somerset
at Chester-le-Street, 2008
For Yorkshire: 53 v Leicestershire at Scarborough, 2013
Best bowling: 4-15 for Durham v. Essex
at Chester-le-Street, 2007
For Yorkshire: 2-38 v Unicorns at Leeds, 2013
t20:
Highest score: 41 for Durham v. Lancashire
at Manchester, 2011
For Yorkshire: 30 v Durham at Leeds, 2013
Best bowling: 5-31 for Durham v. Lancashire
at Chester-le-Street, 2011
For Yorkshire: 2-20 v Leicestershire at Scarborough, 2013

Richard Michael PYRAH

Right-hand batsman, right-arm medium bowler
Born: Dewsbury, November 1, 1982
First-Class cricket:
Debut: v. Glamorgan at Colwyn Bay, 2004
Highest score: 134* Loughborough v. MCCU
at Leeds, 2010
Best bowling: 5-58 v. Nottinghamshire
at Leeds, 2011
One-Day:
Highest score: 69 v. Netherlands at Leeds, 2011
Best bowling: 5-50 for Yorkshire Cricket Board
v. Somerset at Scarborough, 2002
Best bowling for Yorkshire: 4 for 24 v. Netherlands
at Rotterdam, 2010
t20:
Highest score: 42 v Nottinghamshire
at Nottingham, 2013
Best bowling: 5-16 v. Durham at Scarborough, 2011

Jack Alexander BROOKS
Right-hand batsman, right-arm medium-fast bowler
Born: Oxford, June 4, 1984
First-Class Cricket:
Debut: For Northamptonshire v. Australia
at Northampton, 2009
Debut for Yorkshire: v. Leeds/Bradford MCCU
at Leeds, 2013
Highest score: 53 for Northamptonshire
v. Gloucestershire at Bristol, 2010
For Yorkshire: 33* v Somerset at Leeds, 2013
Best bowling: 5-23 for Northamptonshire
v. Leicestershire at Leicester, 2011
For Yorkshire: 5-40 v Derbyshire at Leeds, 2013
One-Day:
Highest score: 10 for Northamptonshire
v. Middlesex at Uxbridge, 2009
Best bowling: 3-35 for England A
v. Bangladesh A at Sylhet 2011-12
Awaiting Yorkshire debut
t20:
Highest score: 33* for Northamptonshire
v. Warwickshire at Birmingham, 2011
For Yorkshire: Has not batted
Best bowling: 5-21 v Leicestershire at Leeds, 2013

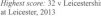

Azeem RAFIQ
Right-hand batsman, off-break bowler
Born: Karachi, Pakistan, February 27, 1991
First-Class Cricket:
Debut: v Sussex at Leeds, 2009
Highest score: 100 v Worcestershire
at Worcester, 2009
Best bowling: 5-50 Essex at Chelmsford, 2012
One-Day:
Highest score: 34* v. Unicorns at Leeds, 2012
Best bowling: 5-30 v Bangladesh A at Leeds, 2013
Domestic: 3-22 v Kent at Leeds, 2012
t20:
Highest score: 21* v Durham at Leeds, 2012
Best bowling: 3-15 v. Lancashire
at Manchester, 2011

Alexander Zak LEES
Left-hand batsman
Born: Halifax, April 14, 1993
First-Class Cricket:
Debut: India A at Leeds, 2010
Highest score: 275* v Derbyshire
at Chesterfield, 2013
Best bowling: 0-14 v. Nottinghamshire
at Scarborough 2013
One-Day:
Highest score: 63 v Unicorns at Leeds, 2013
t20:
Highest score: 32 v Leicestershire
at Leicester, 2013

Kane Stuart WILLIAMSON
Right-hand batsman, right-arm off-break bowler
Born: Tauranga, August 8, 1990
First-Class cricket:
Debut: Northern Districts v. Auckland
at Auckland, 2007/8
Debut for Yorkshire: Nottinghamshire
at Nottingham, 2013
Highest score: 284* for Northern Districts
v. Wellington at Lincoln, 2011/12
For Yorkshire: 97 v. Durham at Scarborough, 2013
Best bowling: 5-75 for Northern Districts
v. Canterbury at Christchurch, 2008-9
For Yorkshire: 2-44 v. Sussex at Hove, 2013
One-Day:
Highest score: 145* for New Zealand
v. South Africa at Kimberley, 2012/13
For Yorkshire: 45 v. Glamorgan at Leeds, 2013
Best bowling: 5-51 for Northern Districts
v. Auckland at Auckland, 2009/10
For Yorkshire: 1-42 v Glamorgan at Leeds, 2013
t20:
Highest score: 52 for Northern Districts
v. Wellington at Wellington, 2011/12
Has not played for Yorkshire
Best bowling: 3-33 for Northern Districts
v. Wellington at Wellington, 2011/12

Daniel Mark HODGSON
Right-hand batsman, wicket-keeper
Born: Northallerton, February 22, 1990
First-Class cricket:
Debut: Leeds MCCU v. Surrey at The Oval, 2012
Awaiting Yorkshire debut
Highest score: 94* for Mountaineers
v Southern Rocks at Mutare, 2012/13
One-Day:
Highest score: 90 v Glamorgan at Leeds, 2013
t20:
Highest score: 52* v Leicestershire at Leeds, 2013

Moin Aqeeb ASHRAF
Left-hand batsman, right-arm fast-medium bowler
Born: Bradford, January 5, 1992
First-Class cricket:
Debut: v. Loughborough MCCU at Leeds, 2010
Highest score: 10 v. Kent at Leeds, 2010
Best bowling: 5-32 v. Kent at Leeds, 2010
One-Day:
Highest Score: 3* v. Kent at Leeds, 2012
Best bowling: 3-38 v Glamorgan at Leeds, 2013
t20:
Highest score: 4 v Leicestershire at Leicester, 2013
Best bowling: 4-18 v. Derbyshire at Derby, 2012

Aaron James FINCH
Right-hand batsman, left-arm medium-pace bowler
Born: Colac, Victoria, November 17, 1986
First-Class cricket:
Debut: Victoria v. Indians at Melbourne, 2007
Highest score: 122 v. Zimbabwe XI at Harare, 2011
One-Day Internationals:
Highest score: 148 v. Scotland at Edinburgh, 2013
International T20s:
Highest score: 156 v. England
at Southampton, 2013
Figures correct to February 15, 2014

Jack Andrew LEANING
Right-hand batsman, right-arm medium
and off-break bowler
Born: Bristol, October 18, 1993
First-Class cricket:
Debut: v. Surrey at Leeds, 2013
Highest score: 0 v Surrey at Leeds, 2013
Best bowling: 0- 4 v Surrey at Leeds, 2013
One-Day:
Highest score: 60 v Somerset at Taunton, 2013
Best bowling: 5-22 v Unicorns at Leeds, 2013
t20:
Highest score: 8 v. Leicestershire at Leicester, 2013
Best bowling: 0-18 v Leicestershire
at Leicester, 2013

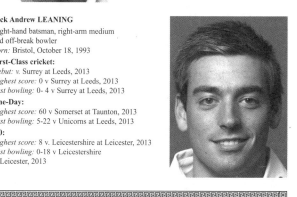

Books raise £4,600

The second-hand bookstall at Headingley Cricket Ground, which is run by Geoff Holmes and Vivien Stone, raised £4,600 for the John Featherstone Foundation during the 2013 season despite the one-day international between England and Australia being wiped out by bad weather. The money went to the Yorkshire Schools' Cricket Association.

YORKSHIRE'S FIRST-CLASS HIGHLIGHTS OF 2013

Wins by an innings (3)

Warwickshire (128 and 140) lost to Yorkshire (407) by an innings and 139 runs at Birmingham

Yorkshire (617-5 dec) defeated Derbyshire (235 and 269) by an innings and 113 runs at Chesterfield

Derbyshire (475 and 163) lost to Yorkshire (677-7 dec) by an innings and 39 runs at Leeds

Wins by 10 wickets (2)

Yorkshire (390 and 7-0) defeated Middlesex (175 and 219) by 10 wickets at Lord's

Yorkshire (407 and 12-0) defeated Nottinghamshire (150 and 266) by 10 wickets at Nottingham

Totals of 400 and over (10)

677-7 dec	v. Derbyshire at Leeds
617-5 dec	v. Derbyshire at Chesterfield
572-8 dec	v. Nottinghamshire at Scarborough
505-9 dec	v. Somerset at Leeds
450-5 dec	v. Somerset at Taunton
434	v. Surrey at The Oval
433-9 dec	v. Surrey at Leeds
419	v. Durham at Scarborough
407	v. Nottinghamshire at Nottingham
407	v. Warwickshire at Birmingham

Century Partnerships (20)

For the 1st wicket (2)

221	A Lyth and A Z Lees	v. Leeds/Bradford MCCU at Leeds
126	A Lyth and J E Root	v. Derbyshire at Leeds

For the 2nd wicket (3)

311	A Z Lees and P A Jaques	v. Derbyshire at Chesterfield
264	P A Jaques and K S Williamson	v. Durham at Scarborough
164	A Lyth and K S Williamson	v. Sussex at Hove

For the 3rd wicket (3)

145	A Z Lees and A W Gale	v. Middlesex at Lord's
138	A Z Lees and A W Gale	v. Derbyshire at Chesterfield
103	A Lyth and A W Gale	v. Somerset at Taunton

For the 4th wicket (4)

231	J E Root and J M Bairstow	v. Derbyshire at Leeds
204	A W Gale and G S Ballance	v. Surrey at Leeds
109	A Z Lees and G S Ballance	v. Derbyshire at Chesterfield
104	K S Williamson and J M Bairstow	v. Durham at Scarborough

For the 5th wicket (4)

297	A W Gale and G S Ballance	v. Nottinghamshire at Scarborough
207	G S Ballance and A U Rashid	v. Somerset at Leeds
117	J M Bairstow and G S Ballance	v. Derbyshire at Leeds
109	A W Gale and A U Rashid	v. Middlesex at Lord's

Century Partnerships *(Continued)*

For the 6th wicket (2)

170*	A U Rashid and A J Hodd	v. Somerset at Taunton
101	J E Root and A U Rashid	v. Durham at Chester-le-Street

For the 7th wicket (1)

121	A W Gale and A J Hodd	v. Nottinghamshire at Scarborough

For the 8th wicket (1)

156	G S Ballance and R J Sidebottom	v. Leeds/Bradford MCCU at Leeds

Centuries (22)

G S Ballance (6)

148	v. Surrey (1st inns) at The Oval
141	v. Nottinghamshire at Scarborough
112	v. Leeds/Bradford MCCU at Leeds
112	v. Warwickshire at Leeds
108 *	v. Surrey (2nd inns) at The Oval
107	v. Somerset at Leeds

A W Gale (3)

272	v. Nottinghamshire at Scarborough
103	v. Middlesex at Lord's
148	v. Surrey at Leeds (consecutive innings)

A Z Lees (3)

275*	v. Derbyshire at Chesterfield
121	v. Leeds/Bradford MCCU at Leeds
100	v. Middlesex at Lord's

A U Rashid (3)

180	v. Somerset at Leeds
110*	v. Warwickshire at Birmingham
103*	v. Somerset at Taunton (consecutive innings)

P A Jaques (2)

152	v. Durham at Scarborough
139	v. Derbyshire at Chesterfield

A Lyth (2)

111	v. Leeds/Bradford MCCU at Leeds
105	v. Somerset at Taunton

J E Root (2)

182	v. Durham at Chester-le-Street
236	v. Derbyshire at Leeds (consecutive innings)

J M Bairstow (1)

186	v. Derbyshire at Leeds

5 wickets in an innings (5)

L E Plunkett (2)

      6 for 33 v. Leeds/Bradford MCCU at Leeds

      5 for 32 v. Warwickshire at Birmingham

J A Brooks (1)

      5 for 40 v. Derbyshire at Leeds

S A Patterson (1)

      5 for 43 v. Nottinghamshire at Nottingham

A U Rashid (1)

      5 for 78 v. Middlesex at Lord's

3 catches in an innings (7)

J M Bairstow (4)

      6   v. Middlesex at Leeds

      4   v. Leeds/Bradford MCCU at Leeds

      3   v. Nottinghamshire (1st inns) at Nottingham

      3   v. Nottinghamshire (2nd inns) at Nottingham

A Lyth (2)

      3   v. Derbyshire at Leeds

      3   v. Warwickshire at Birmingham

A J Hodd (1)

      4   v. Derbyshire at Chesterfield

5 catches in a match (5)

J M Bairstow (3)

      8 (6 + 2) v. Middlesex at Leeds

      6 (4 + 2) v. Leeds/Bradford MCCU at Leeds

      6 (3 + 3) v. Nottinghamshire at Nottingham

A J Hodd (1)

      6 (4 + 2) v. Derbyshire at Chesterfield

A Lyth (1)

      5 (3 + 2) v Warwickshire at Birmingham

Debuts (4)
In first-class cricket for Yorkshire: J A Leaning, J A Brooks, L E Plunkett and K S Williamson

Capped (2)

J A Brooks and L E Plunkett, both on August 2, 2013

LV CHAMPIONSHIP FACTFILE

Compiled by John T Potter

Versus LEEDS/BRADFORD MCCU at Headingley

1. Yorkshire First Class debuts for J A Brooks and L E Plunkett
2. First Class debuts for N R T Gubbins, C A R MacLeod, P Rouse, H L Thompson, W G R Vanderspar and D R Young.
3. D R Young was R J Sidebottom's 250th First Class wicket for Yorkshire.
4. A Z Lees's 122 was his maiden First Class Century.
5. L E Plunkett recorded a career-best with his 6-33.
6. J E Lee had career-best figures with both bat and ball, 34 and 7-45.

Versus SUSSEX at Headingley

1. A Z Lees made his Championship debut.
2. J A Brooks and L E Plunkett made their Yorkshire Championship debuts.
3. Yorkshire's first innings 96 was their lowest Championship total at Headingley since their 93 against Durham in 2003.
4. C J Jordan's 6-48 was his Championship best.

Versus DURHAM at Durham ICG

1. A U Rashid played the 100th First Class match of his career.
2. A W Gale passed the milestone of 5,000 runs in his First Class career runs during his first innings.
3. The opening stand of 123 by M D Stoneman and K K Jennings in Durham's second innings was the county's best against Yorkshire.
4. W R Smith (second innings) was T T Bresnan's 250th First Class wicket for Yorkshire.
5. Yorkshire's 339-6 was the highest successful fourth-innings run chase at Durham ICG (Riverside).
6. Yorkshire's 339-6 was their fourth highest successful run chase.

LV CHAMPIONSHIP FACTFILE *(Continued)*

Versus DERBYSHIRE at Headingley

1. This was the 500th First Class match to be played at Headingley.
2. C F Hughes, with 270* in a first-innings total of 475, carried his bat — the second instance of a Derbyshire player doing so at Headingley. A Hamer, with 147* in a total of 272, did it in 1954. Hughes's score was the fifth highest at Headingley.
3. C F Hughes's 270* — a First Class career best — was the second highest score by any Derbyshire player: he was four short of G A Davidson at Old Trafford, Manchester in 1896.
4. Yorkshire's 677-7 dec equalled their highest First Class total at Headingley against Durham in 2005. It was the highest total against Derbyshire by any team, replacing 662 — also by Yorkshire — at Chesterfield in 1898, and it was Yorkshire's fourth highest in all First Class cricket.
5. J E Root's 236 was his First Class career best.
6. Yorkshire's fourth wicket stand of 231 by J M Bairstow and G S Ballance was their highest against Derbyshire.
7. At 12-49pm on the fourth morning, when C F Hughes was out, he left the field for the first time in the game.
8. J A Brooks with 5-40 recorded his best performance for Yorkshire.

Versus SOMERSET at Headingley

1. Yorkshire's 505-9 dec was only the third instance of them passing 500 against Somerset at Leeds. The other two were 525-4 dec in 1953 and 501-9 dec in 2005.
2. A U Rashid's 180 was his First Class career best
3. Yorkshire's fifth-wicket partnership of 207 between G S Ballance and A U Rashid was their highest against Somerset.
4. It was also the highest by Yorkshire at Leeds and the second highest in Yorkshire — 217 by D B Close and R Illingworth against Warwickshire at Sheffield in 1962 being the highest.

Versus WARWICKSHIRE at Edgbaston

1. Yorkshire's victory by an innings was their first at Edgbaston since 1963.
2. A U Rashid's 110* was his second century in consecutive innings

LV CHAMPIONSHIP FACTFILE *(Continued)*

Versus SOMERSET at Taunton

1. No play on the First Day bwcause of to rain.
2. A U Rashid's 103* was his third century in consecutive innings.
3. Yorkshire's undefeated sixth-wicket partnership of 170 between A U Rashid and A J Hodd was their best against Somerset in Somerset.
4. A J Hodd's 68* was his highest First Class score for Yorkshire.
5. A Lyth's 105 in Yorkshire's first innings was their 900th First Class century to be scored away from Yorkshire.
6. Lyth also passed his milestone of 4,000 First Class runs for Yorkshire during his second innings.

Versus NOTTINGHAMSHIRE at Scarborough

1. M J Lumb became the 10th player to have scored Centuries for and against Yorkshire.
2. Yorkshire's 572-8 dec was their highest total against Nottinghamshire, beating their 562 at Bradford in 1899.
3. It was Yorkshire's third highest total at Scarborough, beaten only by their 600-4 dec against Worcestershire in 1995 and 580-9 dec against Glamorgan in 2001.
4. A W Gale's 272 was his First Class career best. It was also the highest individual Championship score at Scarborough. The only higher score in a First Class match at Scarborough was K R Rutherford's 317 for the New Zealanders v. D B Close's XI in 1986.
5. Yorkshire's fifth-wicket partnership of 297 between A W Gale and G S Ballance was their highest against Nottinghamshire. It was also the highest for this wicket by Yorkshire in Yorkshire. The county's only two higher fifth-wicket partnerships were 340 by E Wainwright and G H Hirst against Surrey at The Oval in 1899 and 329 by F Mitchell and E Wainwright against Leicestershire at Leicester, also in 1899.
6. G S Ballance's 141 was his highest First Class score for Yorkshire.

Versus MIDDLESEX at Lord's

1. This was Yorkshire's first Championship visit to Lord's since 1998.
2. A Z Lees's 100 was his first Championship century for Yorkshire.
3. A W Gale's 103 was his second century in consecutive innings. He passed 5,000 First Class runs for Yorkshire during this innings.
4. This was Yorkshire's first Championship win at Lord's since 1987.
5. Yorkshire's last 10-wicket win against Middlesex was in 1964.
6. This was Middlesex's first loss in a Championship matchat Lord's since May 2011.

Versus SURREY at Headingley

1. A W Gale' s 148 was his third century in consecutive innings.
2. Yorkshire's first-innings fourth-wicket partnership of 204 by A W Gale and G S Ballance was Yorkshire's highest against Surrey in Yorkshire and was three short of being the highest in all matches.
3. J A Leaning made his First Class debut when he replaced G S Ballance on the Third Day.
4. L E Plunkett's 68 was his highest First Class score for Yorkshire.

Versus DERBYSHIRE at Queen's Park, Chesterfield

1. A Z Lees at 20 years and 95 days, with a career-best of 275*, became Yorkshire's youngest player to score a double century. R J Blakey was the previous youngest.
2. It was the third highest individual score against Derbyshire behind 343* by P A Perrin (Essex) in 1904 and 300 by J T Brown (Yorkshire) in 1898.
3. Only two other batsmen have had higher not-out scores for Yorkshire — P Holmes 302* v. Hampshire at Portsmouth in 1920, 277* v. Northamptonshire at Harrogate in 1921 and 315* v. Middlesex at Lord's 1925, and L Hutton 280* v. Hampshire at Sheffield in 1939.
4. Yorkshire's second-wicket partnership of 311 by A Z Lees and P A Jaques was their highest against Derbyshire for this wicket. The only other higher partnership against Derbyshire was in 1898 between J T Brown and J Tunnicliffe — 554 for the first wicket, also at Chesterfield.
5. Yorkshire's total of 617-5 dec was the third highest at the ground behind 662 by Yorkshire in 1898 and 625-6 dec by Durham in 1994.
6. Yorkshire with 677-7 dec at Headingley and 617-5 dec at Chesterfield are the only team to total over 600 twice in their first innings in the same season against Derbyshire.
7. When Yorkshire's total moved to 582 it was the first contribution by a right-handed batsman.
8. The last time Yorkshire did the double over Derbyshire was in 1970.
9. Yorkshire won both 2013 Championship matches against Derbyshire by an innings — the last time they did this was in 1928.
10. A Z Lees spent the whole of the game on the field (1,083 minutes)

LV CHAMPIONSHIP FACTFILE *(Continued)*

Versus WARWICKSHIRE at Headingley

1. K H D Barker took his 100th Championship career wicket when he dismissed L E Plunkett in Yorkshire's second innings.
2. W B Rankin took his 200th First Class career wicket when he dismissed A W Gale in Yorkshire's second innings.

Versus NOTTINGHAMSHIRE at Trent Bridge

1. S A Patterson recorded his First Class career-best of 5-43 in Nottinghamshire's first innings.
2. C M W Read's dismissal by R J Sidebottom took him to 597 First Class career wickets — one more than his father, Arnie.
3. Ryan achieved this feat in his 185th match — 43 fewer than Arnie.
4. Yorkshire defeated Nottinghamshire by 10 wickets for the first time since 1966.

Versus DURHAM at Scarborough

1. Durham's 573 was their highest total against Yorkshire and the fifth highest at Scarborough.
2. M J Richardson scored his maiden First Class century.
3. M D Stoneman's dismissal in Durham's first innings was R J Sidebottom's 600th First Class career wicket.
4. Yorkshire's second-wicket partnership of 264 between P A Jaques and K S Williamson in their second innings was their highest for that wicket against Durham.

Versus SUSSEX at Hove

1. P A Jaques passed the milestone of 15,000 First Class career runs.
2. G S Ballance passed 1,000 First Class runs for Yorkshire in the 2013 season.

Versus MIDDLESEX at Leeds

1. T G Helm made his First Class debut.
2. A W Gale passed 1,000 First Class runs for Yorkshire in the season.
3. S A Patterson and R J Sidebottom both passed 50 First Class wickets for Yorkshire in the season.
4. J A Simpson with six catches in Yorkshire's first innings recorded a Middlesex best against Yorkshire.
5. J M Bairstow with six dismissals in Middlesex's first innings became Yorkshire's eighth wicket-keeper to achieve this feat, and the first against Middlesex. His Father, David, holds the record with seven in an innings. which he achieved in 1982.
6. All 40 wickets fell in a match involving Yorkshire for the first time since the Roses fixture at Headingley in 2011.
7. Yorkshire completed the Championship double over Middlesex for the first time since 1968.

Versus SURREY at The Oval

1. G S Ballance's 148 in Yorkshire's first innings was his First Class best for the county.

2. Surrey's 634-5 dec was their highest total against Yorkshire.

3. D P Sibley's 242 at 18 years and 21 days old made him Surrey's youngest player to score a First Class century, beating a record that had stood since 1905 when J N (Jack) Crawford scored his first century for Surrey at 18 years and 257 days. Sibley became the 13th youngest to score a First Class double-hundred in all cricket.

4. Surrey's third-wicket partnership of 236 between D P Sibley and H M Amla was their best against Yorkshire, removing T W Hayward and C Baldwin — 221 in 1896 at The Oval — from the record books.

5. H M Amla's 151 was the 1,200th First Class century to be scored against Yorkshire.

6. G S Ballance, with 148 and 108*, became Yorkshire's 13th player to score a First Class century in both innings. Younus Khan (106 and 202*) was the last to achieve this feat in 2007 against Hampshire at The Rose Bowl.

7. Ballance's first century of the match came in his 100th First Class career innings.

8. Ballance's second century of the match was Yorkshire's 1,500th to be scored against county opposition.

Thoroughly likeable

There is a saying that nice guys never win anything. One I would dearly like to dispel the myth about is the thoroughly likeable Martyn Moxon. He undoubtedly played a major part in building the Yorkshire team that won the title in 2001 and the Durham team that has struck gold since his return to Headingley.   *Tim Wellock, 2009*

LV Championship
Division 1, 2013

Captain: A W Gale

*Captain

§ Wicket-Keeper

Figures in brackets ( ) indicate position in 2nd Innings batting order,
where different from 1st Innings.

DETAILS OF PLAYERS WHO APPEARED FOR YORKSHIRE IN 2013
(ALL FIRST-CLASS MATCHES)

Player	Date of Birth	Birthplace	First-Class debut for Yorkshire	Date Capped
A W Gale	November 28, 1983	Dewsbury	July 21, 2004	Sept. 18, 2008
A McGrath	October 6, 1975	Bradford	May 18, 1995	July 20, 1999
R J Sidebottom	January 15, 1978	Huddersfield	July 2, 1997	July 23, 2000
P A Jaques	May 3, 1979	Wollongong, Aus	May 12, 2004	April 7, 2005
T T Bresnan	February 28, 1985	Pontefract	May 14, 2003	July 19, 2006
J J Sayers	November 5, 1983	Leeds	August 19, 2004	June 16, 2007
G L Brophy	November 26, 1975	Welkom, S A	April 19, 2006	May 31, 2008
A U Rashid	February 17, 1988	Bradford	July 19, 2006	Sept. 18, 2008
A Shahzad	July 27, 1985	Huddersfield	August 30, 2006	April 8, 2010
A Lyth	September 25, 1987	Whitby	May 16, 2007	Aug. 22, 2010
R M Pyrah	November 1, 1982	Dewsbury	August 24, 2004	Aug. 22, 2010
J M Bairstow	September 26, 1989	Bradford	June 11, 2009	Aug. 17, 2011
S A Patterson	October 3, 1983	Beverley	August 3, 2005	May 16, 2012
G S Ballance	November 22, 1989	Harare, Zim	July 11, 2008	Sept. 4, 2012
J E Root	December 30, 1990	Sheffield	May 10, 2010	Sept. 4, 2012
O J Hannon-Dalby	June 20, 1989	Halifax	May 21, 2008	—
Azeem Rafiq	February 27, 1991	Karachi, Pak	June 5, 2009	—
M A Ashraf	January 5, 1992	Bradford	May 10, 2010	—
I Wardlaw	June 29, 1985	Dewsbury	July 20, 2011	—
M A Starc	January 13, 1990	Sydney, Aus	May 30, 2012	—
S J Harmison	October 23, 1978	Ashington	July 11, 2012	—
A J Hodd	January 12, 1984	Chichester	August 15, 2012	—

Match-By-Match Reports	NIGEL PULLAN
Scorecards	JOHN POTTER
Pictures	SIMON WILKINSON
	VAUGHN RIDLEY
	ALEX WHITEHEAD
	SWpix.com

LV County Championship Division 1
Yorkshire v. Sussex

Played at Headingley, Leeds, on April 10, 11, 12 and 13, 2013
Sussex won by an innings and 12 runs at 11.25am on the Fourth Day

Toss won by Sussex   Sussex 23 points; Yorkshire 3 points

Close of play: First Day, Sussex 104-3 (Joyce 4*, Hamilton-Brown 0*): Second Day, Yorkshire 27-1 (Lyth 8*, Jaques 15*); Third Day, Yorkshire 228-8 (Balance 46*, Brooks 2*)

First Innings	YORKSHIRE		Second Innings	
A Lyth, b Anyon	3		c Brown b Anyon	25
A Z Lees, c Brown b Jordan	6		c Jordan b Magoffin	4
P A Jaques, lbw b Magoffin	2		c Yardy b Magoffin	57
* A W Gale, c Brown b Jordan	2		c Joyce b Anyon	3
§ J M Bairstow, c Brown b Anyon	29		b Jordan	18
G S Ballance, c Brown b Jordan	13		c Brown b Magoffin	63
Azeem Rafiq, c Jordan b Magoffin	23		b Magoffin	0
L E Plunkett, c and b Jordan	5		b Magoffin	5
R J Sidebottom, b Jordan	2		c Jordan b Anyon	48
J A Brooks, b Jordan	2		c Yardy b Jordan	5
S A Patterson, not out	0		not out	0
Extras lb 5, nb 4	9		Extras b 16, lb 4	20
Total	96		Total	248

Bonus points — Sussex 3

FoW: 1-4 (Lyth), 2-9 (Jaques), 3-11 (Gale), 4-18 (Lees), 5-58 · (Bairstow)
1st 6-70 (Ballance), 7-82 (Plunkett), 8-94 (Sidebottom), 9-96 (Brooks), 10-96 (Rafiq)
FoW: 1-4 (Lees), 2-60 (Lyth), 3-64 (Gale), 4-103 (Bairstow), 5-128 (Jaques)
2nd 6-128 (Rafiq), 7-140 (Plunkett), 8-221 (Sidebottom), 9-248 (Brooks), 10-248 (Ballance)

	O	M	R	W		O	M	R	W
Anyon	16	7	24	2	Anyon	15	6	59	3
Magoffin	13.2	5	18	2	Magoffin	21.1	3	51	5
Jordan	15	3	48	6	Jordan	16	4	42	2
Panesar	2	1	1	0	Panesar	24	7	63	0
					Nash	4	2	2	0
					Wells	2	0	11	0

SUSSEX

C D Nash, c Bairstow b Sidebottom	80
L W P Wells, b Sidebottom	2
M H Yardy, c Bairstow b Sidebottom	14
* E C Joyce, c Lyth b Brooks	92
R J Hamilton-Brown, lbw b Plunkett	26
J S Gatting, c Brooks b Azeem Rafiq	20
§ B C Brown, b Brooks	93
C J Jordan, lbw b Brooks	0
S J Magoffin, c Ballance b Brooks	11
J E Anyon, not out	4
M A Panesar, lbw b Sidebottom	1
Extras lb 9, nb 4	13
Total	356

Bonus points — Sussex 4, Yorkshire 3

FoW: 1-11 (Wells), 2-87 (Yardy), 3-104 (Nash), 4-155 (Hamilton-Brown), 5-198 (Gatting)
   6-318 (Joyce), 7-318 (Jordan), 8-342 (Magoffin), 9-355 (Brown), 10-356 (Panesar)

	O	M	R	W
Sidebottom	21.5	6	72	4
Patterson	19	5	66	0
Brooks	13	1	76	4
Plunkett	11	2	53	1
Azeem Rafiq	15	1	70	1
Lyth	1	0	10	0

Umpires: N J Llong and R T Robinson   Scorers: J T Potter and M J Charman

1863 penny drops wrong way

It was a good toss to win, and Sussex put Yorkshire in on a greenish wicket in difficult batting conditions after Gale's 1863 penny came down in their favour.

All three quick bowlers were impressive. Magoffin with his high action, sustained accuracy and notable movement off the pitch

GARY BALLANCE: Reverse-gear on the way to his top-score 63

was excellent in both innings; Anyon was hard-working and consistent, while Jordan increased his speed, and was rewarded with a fine analysis of 6-48 in his first match for Sussex after moving from Surrey.

Some Yorkshire batsmen might be accused of contributing to their misfortune by poor shot selection — Lyth, Gale and Bairstow certainly, although batting is never straightforward at Headingley in early April. Only 40 runs including four overthrows were scored before lunch, but then Nash came in and batted impeccably, making 80 out of 104 with scarcely any misjudgement. Sidebottom took two wickets and added Nash's at the end of the day.

On the second day Sussex ended with a lead of 260 runs. Their captain, Joyce, was the mainstay with a long and valuable innings of 92. Brown looked a very competent cricketer, playing an aggressive innings when it was needed, and he enhanced the good impression given by his wicket-keeping. He perished going for his hundred when Brooks sent his stump cartwheeling. Brooks had not been impressive, but he had the encouragement of four late wickets including that of Joyce. Sidebottom bowled with his usual application, but the other seam bowlers were not incisive enough and Rafiq inaccurate — perhaps it was not a day for spinners in the raw climate of early spring.

All Yorkshire could hope for was to survive over two days, but Magoffin's dismissal of Jaques was a turning point. Again batting indiscretions were evident until resistance came from Ballance, who top-scored with 63, and Sidebottom, who was out for 48 just before the close. On a sunny Saturday morning Yorkshire added only 20 and lost by an innings and 12 runs to start their sesquicentennial programme.

LV County Championship Division 1
Durham v. Yorkshire

Played at Durham ICG, Chester-le-Street, on April 24, 25, 26 and 27, 2013
Yorkshire won by 4 wickets at 5.49pm on the Fourth Day

Toss won by Durham   Yorkshire 19 points, Durham 4 points
Close of play: First Day, Yorkshire 57-3 (Root 30*); Second Day, Yorkshire 177 all out.
Third Day, Yorkshire 17-0 (Lyth 9*, Root 6*)

DURHAM

First Innings						Second Innings	
M D Stoneman, c Plunkett b Sidebottom					6	c Ballance b Plunkett	109
K K Jennings, b Bresnan					0	c Bairstow b Bresnan	48
W R Smith, c Sidebottom b Bresnan					42	c Root b Bresnan	4
D M Benkenstein, c Root b Patterson					40	not out	61
B A Stokes, c Bairstow b Bresnan					2	c Bairstow b Plunkett	7
* P D Collingwood, b Bresnan					0	not out	36
§ P Mustard, b Rashid					70		
S G Borthwick, lbw b Plunkett					1		
C D Thorp, b Rashid					21		
G Onions, run out (Patterson)					27		
C Rushworth, not out					7		
Extras b 3, lb 16, nb 2					21	Extras b 4, lb 6	10
Total					237	Total (4 wkts dec)	275

Bonus points — Durham 1, Yorkshire 3

FoW: 1-2, (Kennings), 2-8 (Stoneman), 3-94 (Smith), 4-96 (Stokes), 5-98 (Benkenstein), 6-104
1st (Collingwood), 7-112 (Borthwick), 8-153 (Thorp), 9-197 (Onions), 10-237 (Mustard)
2nd 1-123 (Jennings), 2-127 (Smith), 3-195 (Stoneman), 4-207 (Stokes)

	O	M	R	W		O	M	R	W
Sidebottom	16	6	27	1	Sidebottom	9	2	23	0
Bresnan	20	6	41	4	Bresnan	16	3	70	2
Plunkett	10	1	67	1	Patterson	10	1	38	0
Patterson	21	7	44	1	Plunkett	16	4	49	2
Rashid	6.4	0	39	2	Rashid	22	1	81	0
					Root	5	2	4	0

YORKSHIRE

First Innings						Second Innings	
A Lyth, b Onions					0	c Mustard b Rushworth	9
J E Root, b Onions					49	b Thorp	182
P A Jaques, run out (Onions)					0	c Mustard b Rushworth	0
* A W Gale, lbw b Onions					25	c Collingwood b Jennings	39
§ J M Bairstow, c Stoneman b Onions					16	c Rushworth b Stokes	26
G S Ballance, c Mustard b Onions					5	c Mustard b Stokes	21
A U Rashid, lbw b Stokes					25	not out	50
T T Bresnan, c Collingwood b Rushworth					10	not out	4
L E Plunkett, not out					25		
R J Sidebottom, c Jennings b Stokes					7		
S A Patterson, b Stokes					7		
Extras lb 6, nb 2					8	Extras nb 8	8
Total					177	Total (6 wkts)	339

Bonus points — Durham 3

FoW: 1-0 (Lyth), 2-13 (Jaques), 3-57 (Gale), 4-96 (Root), 5-97 (Bairstow), 6-107 (Ballance),
1st 7-132 (Rashid), 8-136 (Bresnan), 9-161 (Sidebottom), 10-177 (Patterson)
FoW: 1-23 (Lyth), 2-23 (Jaques), 3-103 (Gale), 4-162 (Bairstow), 5-234 (Ballance),
2nd 6-335 (Root)

	O	M	R	W		O	M	R	W
Onions	19	3	63	5	Onions	20	7	59	0
Rushworth	15	4	49	1	Rushworth	20	7	36	2
Thorp	12	3	33	0	Thorp	15.5	4	38	1
Stokes	9.3	2	26	3	Stokes	20	1	99	2
					Borthwick $	15.4	0	84	0
					Jennings	2	0	5	1
					Smith $	3.2	1	18	0

NOTE Borthwick could not finish his fifth second-innings over. It was completed by Smith

Umpires: J H Evans and A G Wharf   Scorers: J T Potter and B Hunt

Durham v. Yorkshire
Root the 182 match-winner

JOE ROOT: Magnificent in batting dominance

Three days during which Yorkshire were generally inferior to Durham gave way to victory by four wickets after an innings of 182 from Root.

He received good support from the middle-order, especially Rashid, as Yorkshire achieved their fourth-highest winning total. Durham chose to bat first, lost Jennings first ball to Bresnan and Stoneman to Sidebottom, but Smith and Benkenstein took them to respectability at lunch.

Five wickets then fell for 18 runs as Bresnan bowled effectively on his return from an elbow operation, but Mustard refused to submit, so Durham reached 237. By the close Yorkshire were 57-3 with Jaques needlessly run out, and the match was evenly balanced.

Next day after a delayed start, Onions took three more wickets to make his analysis 5-63, and he was well supported by Stokes as Yorkshire fell 60 runs behind. It rained again on Friday, and Yorkshire fared little better as Stoneman hit a sound century and Benkenstein made his usual solid contribution to Durham's cause. Plunkett bowled more economically than in the first innings, and Rashid was unlucky, but Durham had gained a lead of 335 when Collingwood declared, presumably to give them time to bowl Yorkshire out and offer some incentive to them to go for the runs.

Root played a magnificent innings on Saturday. This 182 surpassed in importance his 222 at Southampton last year because it was a match-winner. Had he been out the game would have been lost, yet he had to score at a good rate to maintain the impetus. He is tall and correct, and this season has acquired the assurance and confidence to dominate the bowling as he did here. His success depended on support from Gale, who averted a collapse, Bairstow and Ballance — and Rashid, who made an unbeaten 50. Durham persisted with two young bowlers, Stokes and Borthwick, who were expensive, while Rushworth conceded only 36 runs off 20 overs. Root was bowled by Thorp with a single needed.

117

LV County Championship Division 1
Yorkshire v. Derbyshire

Played at Headingley, Leeds, on April 29 and 30, May 1 and 2, 2013
Yorkshire won by an innings and 39 runs at 4.27pm on the Fourth Day

Toss won by Yorkshire   Yorkshire 21 points, Derbyshire 5 points
Close of play: First Day, Derbyshire 302-4 (Hughes 171*, Redfern 14*); Second Day,
Yorkshire 164-1 (Root 75*, Jaques 15*); Third Day, Yorkshire 597-5 (Ballance 50*, Rashid 0*)

DERBYSHIRE

	First Innings			Second Innings	
B A Godleman, c Root b Bresnan	2		lbw b Bresnan	9
C F Hughes, not out	270		c Ballance b Plunkett	15
* W L Madsen, b Lyth b Patterson	93		lbw b Brooks	52
S Chanderpaul, c Lyth b Rashid	4		c Bairstow b Plunkett	4
W J Durston, c Bresnan b Plunkett	3		c Jaques b Brooks	50
D J Redfern, c Lyth b Bresnan	14		c Bairstow b Brooks	8
D J Wainwright, lbw b Rashid	18		b Rashid	7
J L Clare, lbw b Patterson	5		not out	1
§ T Poynton, b Plunkett	27		lbw b Brooks	0
A P Palladino, b Rashid	18		(11) lbw b Brooks	0
T D Groenewald, lbw b Rashid	0		(10) b Rashid	5
Extras b 16, lb 5	21		Extras b 8, lb 4	12
Total	475		Total	163

Bonus points — Derbyshire 4, Yorkshire 1   110-over score: 354-5

FoW: 1st: 1-10 (Godleman), 2-268 (Madsen), 3-275 (Chanderpaul), 4-279 (Durston), 5-302 (Redfern), 6-383 (Wainwright), 7-388 (Clare), 8-441 (Poyton), 9-474 (Clare), 10-475 (Groenewald)

FoW: 2nd: 1-12 (Godleman), 2-43 (Hughes), 3-47 (Chanderpaul), 4-139 (Durston), 5-150 (Madsen), 6-157 (Wainwright), 7-157 (Redfern), 8-157 (Poynton), 9-162 (Groenewald), 10-163 (Palladino)

	O	M	R	W		O	M	R	W
Bresnan	30	5	103	2	Bresnan	11	3	30	1
Brooks	26	10	63	1	Brooks	14.4	5	40	5
Plunkett	28	5	86	2	Plunkett	7	2	20	2
Patterson	26	6	70	2	Rashid	20	6	61	2
Rashid	30	4	122	3	Root	2	2	0	0
Root	2	0	10	0					

YORKSHIRE

A Lyth, c Redfern b Groenewald		69
J E Root, b Redfern		236
P A Jaques, run out (Madsen/Clare)		39
* A W Gale, c Groenewald b Wainwright		5
§ J M Bairstow, c Groenewald b Durston		186
G S Ballance, c Madsen b Clare		53
A U Rashid, not out		36
T T Bresnan, c Clare b Groenewald		14
L E Plunkett, not out		21
J A Brooks		
S A Patterson	Did not bat	
Extras b 4, lb 8, w 4, nb 2		18
Total (7 wkts dec)		677

Bonus points — Yorkshire 4, Derbyshire 1   110-over score: 381-3

FoW: 1st: 1-126 (Lyth), 2-218 (Jaques), 3-246 (Gale), 4-477 (Root), 5-594 (Bairstow), 6-616 (Ballance), 7-643 (Bresnan)

	O	M	R	W
Groenewald	34	3	142	2
Palladino	10	1	34	0
Wainwright	48	6	169	1
Durston	25	3	127	1
Clare	27	1	145	1
Redfern	7	0	48	1

Umpires: S C Gale and R A Kettleborough   Scorers: J T Potter and J M Brown

Exceptional batsmen point way

A match of high scoring and numerous records saw Yorkshire bowl out Derbyshire on the last day to record a decisive win despite conceding 475 in the visitors' first innings.

Invited to bat first, Derbyshire frustrated the hosts with a partnership of 258 between Madsen and Hughes — who ended the day unbeaten on 171. Next day the tall Anguillan reached an outstanding 270*, carrying his bat but just missing the Derbyshire record individual score.

JOE ROOT: 236 career-best

The outstanding feature was his scintillating cover-driving, but he demonstrated his muscular power with straight sixes, including one to bring up his century and 40 other boundaries. He might have been caught on 70 when the wicket-keeper intercepted and dropped what seemed like a regulation catch to Ballance at first slip.

Wednesday saw a demonstration of immaculate batting in the sunshine by two young players of exceptional ability. Root made his highest score of 236. He appears calm by temperament, usually plays very straight; his shot selection is good, but above all here his timing and placing were impeccable. He is most proficient on the off-side, especially backward of square, but he must watch his running between wickets as Jaques had to sacrifice his own. Bairstow's 186 was equally good and a reassuring reminder of his outstanding qualities: he hits powerfully, even brutally, and has a penchant for the straight six. Derbyshire did miss Palladino, and the wicket offered little assistance.

Yorkshire declared on 677-7. They had to bowl Derbyshire out, and when Madsen and Durston settled in a tedious stalemate was possible. Plunkett had Hughes caught at slip, and took the crucial wicket of Chanderpaul. Now Brooks intervened, first with the fortunate dismissal of Durston to a casual stroke, and then the removal of Madsen, who had seemed so secure. Rashid bowled Wainwright, but it was the hostile, head-banded Brooks who swept away the remaining batsmen.

LV County Championship Division 1
Yorkshire v. Somerset

Played at Headingley, Leeds, on May 7, 8, 9 and 10, 2013

Match drawn at 6.22pm on the Fourth Day

Toss won by Yorkshire

Yorkshire 10 points, Somerset 7 points

Close of play: First Day, Yorkshire 332-5 (Rashid 120*, Hodd 14*); Second Day, Somerset 92-1 (Compton 33*, Leach 2*); Third Day, Somerset 190-5 (Hildreth 31*, Butler 1*)

YORKSHIRE

A Lyth, c Buttler b Trego		0
J J Sayers, c Buttler b Trego		1
P A Jaques, c Trescothick b Kirby		49
* A W Gale, c Buttler b Thomas		17
G S Ballance, lbw b Kirby		107
A U Rashid, c Buttler b Trego		180
§ A J Hodd, c Buttler b Kirby		27
T T Bresnan, lbw b Trego		0
R M Pyrah, b Overton		55
J A Brooks, not out		33
S A Patterson	Did not bat	
Extras b 15, lb 10, nb 11		36
Total (9 wkts dec)		505

Bonus points — Yorkshire 4, Somerset 3

110-over score: 395-7

FoW: 1-0 (Lyth), 2-17 (Sayers), 3-71 (Gale), 4-75 (Jaques), 5-282 (Ballance),
1st   6-370 (Hodd), 7-371 (Bresnan), 8-450 (Pyrah), 9-505 (Rashid)

	O	M	R	W
Trego	33.4	8	107	4
Kirby	30	4	119	3
Thomas	26	3	81	1
Overton	19	0	89	1
Leach	22	3	76	0
Suppiah	5	1	8	0

First Innings	SOMERSET		Second Innings	
* M E Trescothick, lbw b Brooks		53	not out	33
N R D Compton, lbw b Bresnan		33	c Lyth b Brooks	0
M J Leach, b Bresnan		8		
A N Petersen, c Patterson b Rashid		54	(3) c Lyth b Brooks	4
J C Hildreth, c Rashid b Pyrah		39	(4) b Brooks	12
A V Suppiah, c Sayers b Rashid		0	(5) b Brooks	0
§ J C Buttler, c Hodd b Patterson		1	(6) c Ballance b Patterson	7
P D Trego, c Pyrah b Patterson		10	(7) lbw b Patterson	1
A C Thomas, not out		26	(8) not out	5
S P Kirby, c Sayers b Bresnan		15		
J Overton, lbw b Bresnan		0		
Extras b 1, lb 10, nb 2		13		
Total		252	Total (6 wkts)	62

Bonus points — Somerset 2, Yorkshire 3

FoW: 1-90 (Trescothick), 2-92 (Compton), 3-123 (Leach), 4-189 (Petersen), 5-189 (Suppiah),
1st   6-190 (Buttler), 7-200 (Hildreth), 8-222 (Trego), 9-252 (Kirby), 10-252 (Overton)

FoW: 1-6 (Compton), 2-10 (Petersen), 3-30 (Hildreth), 4-32 (Suppiah), 5-46 (Buttler),
2nd   6-48 (Trego)

	O	M	R	W		O	M	R	W
Bresnan	29	8	76	4	Bresnan	11	2	32	0
Brooks	20	6	51	1	Brooks $	5.3	2	22	4
Pyrah	17	5	48	1	Patterson $	4.3	3	4	2
Patterson	22	5	46	2	Rashid	1.3	0	3	0
Rashid	8	2	20	2					

$ Brooks was unable to finish his sixth over in the second innings. It was completed by Patterson

Umpires: M J D Bodenham and G Sharp

Scorers: J T Potter and G A Stickley

Yorkshire v. Somerset
Victory but for the rain

Yorkshire probably would have won if there had not been rain disruptions. The match appeared to be moving to an inevitable draw — but erupted into a dramatic conclusion.

On the first morning Trego struck twice; Jaques and Gale could not consolidate, so Yorkshire subsided to 75-4. An excellent stand of 207 from Rashid and Ballance restored Yorkshire's fortunes.

Rashid, promoted to No. 6, combined scrupulous defence with an array of attacking shots on both sides of the wicket and the occasional hit over the top. He batted into the second day, making his highest score and first century since his 157 in the 2009

ADIL RASHID: Fine array of shots in his career-best 180

Roses match — apart from the one in the *Roses* friendly. Ballance showed that he is an imperturbable and reliable orthodox batsman of genuine quality. Pyrah made a good 50, and then bowled with commendable accuracy. It was good to see Kirby back in Yorkshire after years in the West Country, where he has maintained his commitment but shortened his run.

Somerset enjoyed a solid start on Wednesday evening, but could not save the follow-on despite 50s from Trescothick and Petersen. Yorkshire's steady four-man seam attack was supplemented by Rashid, who dismissed Petersen, century-maker for South Africa in last year's Headingley Test, and then Suppiah first ball. Time was lost to rain and bad light, so it seemed by mid-afternoon that bonus points were the only consideration as Bresnan's two wickets gave Yorkshire their third and Somerset gained a second batting point. Most people went home to the consolation of a warm house as only 23 overs remained.

Then a rampant Brooks removed Compton, Petersen, Hildreth and Suppiah in 5.3 overs before departing with a dislocated thumb, leaving Patterson to dismiss Buttler and Trego. Somerset's consolation was that Trescothick observed this mayhem impassively from the other end, and Thomas stayed with him for the final few overs. It was an exciting finish, but 23 overs were too few in which to bowl out a first-class county.

LV County Championship Division 1
Warwickshire v. Yorkshire

Played at Edgbaston, Birmingham, on May 15, 16 and 17, 2013
Yorkshire won by an innings and 139 runs at 5.03pm on the Third Day

Toss won by Yorkshire   Yorkshire 23 points, Warwickshire 2 points
Close of play: First Day, Yorkshire 11-0 (Lyth 5*, Sayers 4*); Second Day, Yorkshire 318-7 (Rashid 68*, Plunkett 1*)

	First Innings	WARWICKSHIRE		Second Innings	
V Chopra, c Lyth b Sidebottom		4	lbw b Bresnan		0
W T S Porterfield, c Pyrah b Plunkett		14	lbw b Sidebottom		0
* J O Troughton, not out		65	lbw b Sidebottom		37
D L Maddy, lbw b Plunkett		0	c Lyth b Bresnan		5
§ T R Ambrose, c Lyth b Plunkett		0	c Lyth b Sidebottom		22
C R Woakes, b Patterson		1	b Patterson		10
R Clarke, lbw b Sidebottom		13	lbw b Patterson		15
T P Milnes, c Lyth b Patterson		11	c Hodd b Bresnan		18
J S Patel, c Ballance b Patterson		9	c Plunkett b Patterson		6
C J C Wright, c Ballance b Plunkett		0	b Plunkett		11
W B Rankin, c and b Plunkett		0	not out		12
Extras b 4, lb 5, nb 2		11	Extras lb 4		4
Total		128	Total		140

Bonus points — Yorkshire 3

FoW: 1-12 (Chopra), 2-42 (Porterfield), 3-42 (Maddy), 4-46 (Ambrose), 5-55 (Woakes)
1st 6-71 (Clarke), 7-111 (Milnes), 8-127 (Patel), 9-128 (Wright), 10-128 (Rankin)
FoW: 1-0 (Chopra), 2-4 (Porterfield), 3-9 (Maddy), 4-40 (Ambrose), 5-63 (Woakes)
2nd 6-87 (Troughton), 7-89 (Clarke), 8-99 (Patel), 9-112 (Wright), 10-140 (Milnes)

	O	M	R	W		O	M	R	W
Sidebottom	15	5	23	2	Bresnan	13.2	4	41	3
Patterson	17	4	46	3	Sidebottom	14	6	23	3
Plunkett	13.3	6	32	5	Patterson	11	4	19	3
Pyrah	6	1	18	0	Plunkett	10	1	53	1

YORKSHIRE

A Lyth, c Milnes b Rankin	43
J J Sayers, c Ambrose b Rankin	24
P A Jaques, c Ambrose b Patel	25
* A W Gale, c Clarke b Patel	40
G S Ballance, b Patel	52
A U Rashid, not out	110
§ A J Hodd, lbw b Woakes	9
T T Bresnan, c Ambrose b Rankin	38
L E Plunkett, c Ambrose b Wright	9
R J Sidebottom, lbw b Patel	20
S A Patterson, c Milnes b Patel	11
R M Pyrah	
Extras b 1, lb 6, w 1, nb 18	26
Total	407

T T Bresnan replaced R M Pyrah on the Second Day

Bonus points — Yorkshire 5, Warwickshire 2   110-over score: 356-8

FoW: 1-77 (Lyth), 2-80 (Sayers), 3-122 (Jaques), 4-147 (Gale), 5-225 (Ballance), 6-239
1st (Hodd), 7-314 (Bresnan), 8-354 (Plunkett), 9-389 (Sidebottom), 10-407 (Patterson)

	O	M	R	W
Woakes	28	8	76	1
Wright	31	6	102	1
Clarke	13	0	55	0
Patel	24	7	56	5
Rankin	18	2	75	3
Milnes	9	1	36	0

Umpires: M A Gough and T E Jesty   Scorers: J T Potter and M D Smith

Pacemen rout the champions

Overnight rain delayed the start until 2pm, and then Yorkshire exploited the conditions skilfully to dismiss the home side for 128.

Warwickshire captain Troughton displayed his tenacity at No. 3 with an undefeated 65, but received little support.

The bowlers always looked like taking wickets; the catching was good, and Plunkett was rewarded with 5-32, removing Maddy and Ambrose for ducks. Patterson and Sidebottom supported him admirably, but the champions would have been disappointed with their score.

Conditions on Thursday were easier, and Yorkshire took advantage, reaching 318-7 with Rashid unbeaten

LIAM PLUNKETT: Led rampant foursome with first-day 5-32

on 68. Lyth made an attractive 43 and Gale 40, although he was caught just over the boundary by Rankin — if Rankin could not reach it nobody could. Bresnan, released by England from Lord's, joined Ballance, who made a valuable 52 until he was caught off Patel. It was a fine exhibition by the accurate off-spinner, who finished with 5-52. Next morning Yorkshire added 89 runs, led by Rashid in such fine form as he went to his second century of the season: his defence was sound, and his attacking shots a pleasure to watch, thus justifying his promotion in the order.

There was a sensational start to the Warwickshire second innings as both openers were out first ball. Chopra was lbw to Bresnan and Porterfield lbw to Sidebottom at the beginning of the second over, and at lunch Warwickshire were 9-3. Yorkshire's success was a genuine team effort, as the four bowlers all sustained the pressure and the fielding was sharp. Lyth could have caught swallows. Patterson's removal of Woakes's middle stump was perhaps symbolic of Yorkshire's domination in this match. Warwickshire subsided to 140 all out with three wickets apiece for Bresnan, Patterson and Sidebottom.

A good Yorkshire following sampled the newly constructed facilities.

LV County Championship Division 1
Somerset v. Yorkshire

Played at The County Ground, Taunton, on May 28, 29, 30 and 31, 2013
Match drawn at 4.52pm on the Fourth Day

Toss won by Yorkshire   Yorkshire 11 points, Somerset 4 points

Close of play: First Day, no play; Second day, Yorkshire 341-5 (Rashid 47*, Hodd 25*); Third Day, Somerset 232-6 (Hildreth 76*, Meschede 16*)

YORKSHIRE

First Innings		Second Innings	
A Lyth, c Trego b Hussain	105	not out	57
J J Sayers, c Trescothick b Kirby	1	c Trescothick b Kirby	1
P A Jaques, c Barrow b Hussain	26	lbw b Kirby	0
* A W Gale, b Trego	75	lbw b Trego	4
G S Ballance, c Barrow b Dockrell	48	c Kirby b Dockrell	31
A U Rashid, not out	103	not out	5
§ A J Hodd, not out	68		
R M Pyrah			
R J Sidebottom	Did not bat		
S A Patterson			
M A Ashraf			
Extras b 2, lb 13, w 1, nb 8	24	Extras lb 4, nb 2	6
Total (5 wkts dec)	450	Total (4 wkts dec)	104

Bonus points — Yorkshire 5, Somerset 1   110-over score: 400-5

FoW: 1st 1-2 (Sayers), 2-82 (Jaques), 3-185 (Lyth), 4-265 (Ballance), 5-280 (Gale)
2nd 1-14 (Sayers), 2-14 (Jaques), 3-21 (Gale), 4-91 (Ballance)

	O	M	R	W		O	M	R	W
Trego	26	5	87	1	Trego	8	3	22	1
Kirby	25	2	100	1	Kirby	8	2	19	2
Meschede	14	0	75	0	Dockrell	13	4	21	1
Hussain	25	0	106	2	Hussain	8	2	19	0
Dockrell	20.2	5	52	1	Meschede	5	0	19	0
Elgar	6	2	15	0					

SOMERSET

* M E Trescothick, lbw b Pyrah		74
A V Suppiah, lbw b Patterson		5
L Gregory, lbw b Patterson		3
D Elgar, c Rashid b Sidebottom		28
J C Hildreth, b Ashraf		115
§ A W R Barrow, b Lyth		26
P D Trego, c and b Lyth		0
C A J Meschede, c Pyrah b Patterson		32
G Dockrell, b Ashraf		14
S P Kirby, c Ballance b Ashraf		5
G M Hussain, not out		2
Extras b 2, lb 2, nb 2		6
Total		310

Bonus points — Somerset 3, Yorkshire 3

FoW: 1-32 (Suppiah), 2-52 (Gregory), 3-103 (Trescothick), 4-120 (Elgar), 5-172 (Barrow)
6-172 (Trego), 7-272 (Meschede), 8-298 (Hildreth), 9-303 (Dockrell), 10-310 (Kirby)

	O	M	R	W
Sidebottom	23	7	49	1
Patterson	24	6	65	3
Rashid	28	4	72	0
Ashraf	15.3	3	60	3
Pyrah	11	3	45	1
Lyth	3	0	15	2

Umpires: N G B Cook and M J Saggers   Scorers: J T Potter and G A Stickley

Somerset v. Yorkshire
Centuries hat-trick for Rashid

ADAM LYTH: Neat footwork and elegant drives in his top-score 105

Yorkshire declared on 450-5. Somerset were in some danger of following on, but an excellent innings by Hildreth averted that possibility and the best hope of winning the match was lost.

There was no play on the first day, and Yorkshire batted first on Wednesday, making a sound 341-5 led by Lyth, whose 105 was notable for his neat footwork and elegant driving through the covers. It was important that Gale made a valuable 75, while Ballance and Rashid also batted well. Next morning Rashid went on to his third consecutive century and Hodd to an unbeaten 68, having been dropped twice by Trescothick at Kirby's expense, before Yorkshire declared. The small Taunton ground and its placid wicket can be daunting for bowlers, so Kirby, Trego and Hussain had to work hard for any reward, as did Dockrell, an Irish left-arm spinner. Rashid looks a fine batsman at the moment, and his undefeated 103 raised his average to 254.50, including his second innings 5*.

Patterson took two quick wickets for Yorkshire, and by the close six were down, including Trescothick who was dismissed by Pyrah for 74 to add to the 893 he has taken off Yorkshire bowling in his last 10 innings. Lyth took two wickets with consecutive balls at the end of the day, but Hildreth would not concede, and with some assistance from the rest of the Somerset batting he moved towards his match-saving century. Ashraf did bowl Hildreth with three needed to save the follow-on, but only eight wickets were down when Dockrell hit the boundary to pass the 301 target.

On the last morning Ashraf took three wickets on his first Championship appearance of the season, but once the follow-on had been avoided the match had to be a draw. Yorkshire's second innings was not impressive, but it provided some consolation to the industrious Kirby, who took early wickets, as did Trego and Dockrell. Lyth added a half-century to his tally, and stayed resolute until the end.

LV County Championship Division 1
Yorkshire v. Nottinghamshire

Played at North Marine Road, Scarborough on June 5, 6, 7 and 8, 2013
Match drawn at 5pm on the Fourth Day

Toss won by Yorkshire   Yorkshire 8 points; Nottinghamshire 6 points

Close of play: First Day, Nottinghamshire 177-2 (Lumb 116*, Taylor 12*); Second Day, Yorkshire 29-3 (Jaques 19*, Gale 0*); Third Day, Yorkshire 358-4 (Gale 159*, Ballance 103*)

First Innings	NOTTINGHAMSHIRE	Second Innings	
A D Hales, c Hodd b Sidebottom	0	(2) lbw b Patterson	5
E J M Cowan, c Ballance b Patterson	47	(1) not out	53
M J Lumb, c Lyth b Patterson	135	not out	47
J W A Taylor, lbw b Patterson	38		
S R Patel, c Lyth b Ashraf	17		
S J Mullaney, c Lees b Rashid	79		
* § C M W Read, c Hodd b Sidebottom	14		
P J Franks, c Ballance b Rashid	70		
A Shahzad, c Sidebottom b Lyth	12		
L J Fletcher, not out	25		
H F Gurney, c and b Rashid	0		
Extras b 1, lb 3, nb 2	6	Extras	0
Total	443	Total (1 wkt)	105

Bonus points — Nottinghamshire 2, Yorkshire 1   110-over score: 262-5

FoW: 1-0 (Hales), 2-101 (Cowan), 3-210 (Lumb), 4-242 (Patel), 5-242 (Taylor)
1st   6-275 (Read), 7-362 (Mullaney), 8-409 (Franks), 9-437 (Shahzad), 10-443 (Gurney)
2nd: 1-6 (Hales)

	O	M	R	W		O	M	R	W
Sidebottom	28	4	89	2	Sidebottom	6	1	19	0
Patterson	37	12	74	3	Patterson	9	2	42	1
Pyrah	29	8	92	0	Rashid	6	0	17	0
Ashraf	23	10	59	1	Lyth	2	0	13	0
Rashid	29.5	2	98	3	Lees	1	0	14	0
Lyth	6	0	27	1					

YORKSHIRE

A Lyth, c Patel b Gurney		7
A Z Lees, lbw b Fletcher		2
P A Jaques, c Taylor b Patel		51
S A Patterson, c Read b Fletcher		1
* A W Gale, c Read b Patel		272
G S Ballance, c Read b Franks		141
A U Rashid, c Cowan b Fletcher		0
§ A J Hodd, c Gurney b Patel		40
R M Pyrah, not out		14
R J Sidebottom		
M A Ashraf	Did not bat	
Extras b 8, lb 24, nb 12		44
Total (8 wkts dec)		572

Bonus points — Yorkshire 4, Nottinghamshire 1   110-over score: 361-4

FoW: 1-7 (Lyth), 2-17 (Lees), 3-27 (Patterson), 4-121 (Jaques), 5-418 (Ballance)
6-431 (Rashid), 7-552 (Gale), 8-572 (Hodd)

	O	M	R	W
Fletcher	34	9	85	3
Gurney	22	3	93	1
Franks	19	2	77	1
Shahzad	24	3	95	0
Patel	38.1	7	143	3
Mullaney	18	4	47	0

Umpires: N G C Cowley and J W Lloyds   Scorers: J T Potter and I J Smith

Yorkshire v. Nottinghamshire
Out-of-form Gale cracks 272

The Scarborough pitch was too benign to offer any chance of a decisive result, but it encouraged some outstanding batting performances.

Gale had had a run of indifferent form, but now he made a massive 272, the 13th highest score for Yorkshire — Hutton made 269, 270 and 271, but also 280. Ballance played another fine innings, looking a high-quality player, as did Lumb, once with Yorkshire, who made 135 as Nottinghamshire opener.

Yorkshire won the toss and invited Nottinghamshire to bat in bleak conditions, but soon after play had started the sun came out. Lumb and the initially circumspect Australian Test player Cowan made the most of a good wicket after Sidebottom had removed Hales.

Lumb's application and patience established the Nottinghamshire innings, and he reached his century just before the close of a shortened first day. Then Mullaney, who enjoys playing against Yorkshire, and all-rounder Franks both made 70s and ended any prospect of

ANDREW GALE
25 fours, four sixes

defeat for the visitors. On Thursday night Yorkshire lost Lyth, Lees and Patterson, and were in trouble.

The third day saw a transformation as Gale and Ballance added 297 for the fifth wicket. Gale, who had passed 50 when Ballance joined him, ended Friday's play on 159, and he made another 113 on Saturday. He hit 25 fours and four sixes. At first he played with sensible caution, but gradually accelerated, hitting all around the ground. His favourite square-drive and cut backwards of point were much in evidence, and he hit straight or over mid-wicket as he dominated proceedings. He reached his first century of the season with a six which scattered the crowd.

Ballance impressed with a fine 141, but Rashid, in such prolific form and averaging 254.50, failed to score. The hard-working Fletcher was the most effective Nottinghamshire bowler, Patel also taking three wickets, while Shahzad, formerly of Yorkshire, went wicketless. There was insufficient time for Yorkshire to make any inroads, and your correspondent went on to the attractive ground at nearby Ganton.

LV County Championship Division 1
Middlesex v. Yorkshire

Played at Lord's Cricket Ground, London, on June 11, 12, 13 and 14, 2013
Yorkshire won by 10 wickets at 1.01pm on the Fourth Day

Toss won by Yorkshire   Yorkshire 22 points, Middlesex 2 points

Close of play: First Day, Yorkshire 215-2 (Lees 100*, Gale 61*); Second Day, Middlesex 16-1 (Rogers 6*, Denly 0*); Third Day, Middlesex (following on) 137-4 (Dexter 25*, Simpson 20*)

First Innings	YORKSHIRE		Second Innings	
A Lyth, c Dexter b Murtagh	11		not out	4
A Z Lees, c Simpson b Harris	100		not out	0
P A Jaques, c Simpson b Berg	20			
* A W Gale, lbw b Rayner	103			
J J Sayers, lbw b Murtagh	1			
A U Rashid, lbw b Harris	72			
§ A J Hodd, c and b Murtagh	13			
R M Pyrah, c Robson b Harris	1			
L E Plunkett, lbw b Rayner	26			
R J Sidebottom, st Simpson b Rayner	9			
S A Patterson, not out	2			
Extras b 2, lb 19, w 1, nb 10	32		Extras lb 3	3
Total	390		Total (0 wkts)	7

Bonus points — Yorkshire 3, Middlesex 2   110-over score: 345-7

FoW: 1-32 (Lyth), 2-70 (Jaques), 3-215 (Lees), 4-220 (Sayers), 5-329 (Gale)
1st   6-343 (Rashid), 7-345 (Pyrah), 8-361 (Hodd0, 9-387 (Sidebottom), 10-390 (Plunkett)

	O	M	R	W			O	M	R	W
Murtagh $	32.3	3	93	3		Rayner	2	2	0	0
Collymore	19	6	51	0		Denly	1.3	0	4	0
Berg	28	5	103	1						
Harris $	14.3	3	48	3						
Dexter	9	2	23	0						
Rayner	22.1	4	44	3						
Denly	3	0	7	0						

$ Harris was unable to finish his fifth over. It was completed by Murtagh

First Innings	MIDDLESEX		Second Innings	
* C J L Rogers, c Hodd b Plunkett	27		c Hodd b Sidebottom	0
S D Robson, c Lyth b Patterson	5		b Rashid	46
J L Denly, c Sayers b Sidebottom	4		st Hodd b Rashid	31
A B London, c Sayers b Plunkett	28		lbw b Rashid	3
N J Dexter, lbw b Patterson	11		b Sidebottom	36
§ J A Simpson, b Plunkett	9		c Pyrah b Patterson	21
G K Berg, lbw b Patterson	54		c Pyrah b Rashid	38
O P Rayner, lbw b Plunkett	1		lbw b Plunkett	0
J A R Harris, lbw b Sidebottom	5		lbw b Patterson	14
T J Murtagh, not out	18		not out	3
C D Collymore, c Hodd b Patterson	1		c and b Rashid	5
Extras b 1, lb 11, nb 2	14		Extras b 9, lb 13	22
Total	175		Total	219

Bonus points — Yorkshire 3

FoW: 1-12 (Robson), 2-19 (Denly), 3-46 (Rogers), 4-59 (Dexter), 5-84 (Simpson)
1st   6-105 (London), 7-113 (Rayner), 8-141 (Harris), 9-169 (Berg), 10-175 (Collymore)
FoW: 1-0 (Rogers), 2-69 (Denly), 3-90 (Robson), 4-93 (London), 5-143 (Simpson)
2nd   6-155 (Dexter), 7-167 (Rayner), 8-209 (Harris), 9-209 (Berg), 10-219 (Collymore)

	O	M	R	W			O	M	R	W
Sidebottom	15	4	48	2		Sidebottom	11	5	17	2
Patterson	17.2	5	39	4		Patterson	16	6	40	2
Plunkett	15	1	50	4		Plunkett	13	2	46	1
Pyrah	8	1	26	0		Rashid	24.4	3	78	5
						Pyrah	6	1	15	0
						Lyth	1	0	1	0

Umpires: T E Jesty and D J Millns   Scorers: J T Potter and D K Shelley

Lees opens century account

STEVEN PATTERSON
Wickets at important times

It was good to be back at Lord's for a Championship match for the first time since 1998, and for Lady Members to be admitted to the pavilion.

Yorkshire played well in every department, and won convincingly. Occasional drizzle, ominous clouds, indifferent light and, initially at least, punctilious umpiring cost time on the first day.

It was memorable for the first Championship century for Lees, a young man from Halifax, in his third match and his first at Lord's. He had some early good fortune, but settled into a solid, orthodox innings, embellished by attractive straight-driving and notable for his apparent calm assurance and imperturbability.

He managed his hundred just before the close, but was out first ball next morning. Gale played a most valuable captain's innings, taking no risks and giving the batting its backbone. Rashid's entertaining 72 enabled Yorkshire to reach 390. Murtagh bowled straight and looked the best bowler, but Harris and Rayner each collected three wickets as the last six fell for only 61 runs.

Yorkshire's three main seam bowlers, Patterson, Sidebottom and Plunkett, performed with great credit in both innings, while Rashid took five wickets in the second. Fielding and wicket-keeping were of a high standard with Sayers's two catches low and wide in the slips and Hodd's lightning stumping of Denly most memorable. Sidebottom dismissed Rogers in the first over of the second innings with another catch by Hodd. Patterson enhanced his growing reputation with a convincing display at headquarters, taking wickets at important times.

Middlesex did not bat well, as only Berg made much impact in the first innings, although London was adhesive until he was brilliantly caught by Sayers. The hosts followed on, and the Robson-Denly partnership restored some equanimity. Rashid dismissed both, leaving Middlesex 78 behind at the end of the third day. Next morning Sidebottom's yorker disconcerted Dexter, and Berg surrendered his wicket to Rashid, so Yorkshire needed only five to win.

LV County Championship Division 1
Yorkshire v. Surrey

Played at Headingley, Leeds, on June 21, 22, 23 and 24, 2013

Match drawn at 5pm on the Fourth Day

Toss won by Surrey

Surrey 9 points; Yorkshire 8 points

Close of play: First Day, Yorkshire 292-3 (Gale 114*, Hodd 5*); Second Day, Surrey 53-1 (Burns 15*, Linley 0*); Third Day, Yorkshire 52-1 (Lyth 19*, Sayers 5*)

	First Innings	YORKSHIRE		Second Innings	
A Lyth, c Solanki b Tremlett		41	b Keedy		32
A Z Lees, lbw b de Bruyn		15	lbw b Keedy		13
J J Sayers, c de Bruyn b Linley		5	c Keedy b Tremlett		24
* A W Gale, b Keedy		148	c Harinath b Keedy		0
G S Ballance, lbw b Lewis		90			
J A Leaning			c de Bruyn b Keedy		0
A U Rashid, c Solanki b Lewis		1	b Keedy		45
§ A J Hodd, c Burns b Lewis		9	lbw b Linley		16
L E Plunkett, c Davies b Lewis		51	st Davies b Keedy		68
R J Sidebottom, c Pietersen b Linley		26	c de Bruyn b Keedy		4
S A Patterson, not out		11	c and b Linley		7
J A Brooks	Did not bat		not out		1
Extras b 6, lb 13, w 1, nb 16		36	Extras b 4, lb 3, w 1, nb 36		44
Total (9 wkts dec)		433	Total		254

Bonus points — Yorkshire 3, Surrey 2

110-over score: 326-6

G S Ballance joined the England squad after the Second Day. He was replaced by J A Leaning

FoW: 1-62 (Lyth), 2-64 (Lees), 3-77 (Sayers), 4-281 (Ballance), 5-283 (Rashid)
1st 6-304 (Hodd), 7-385 (Gale), 8-391 (Plunkett), 9-433 (Sidebottom)

FoW: 1-42 (Lees), 2-76 (Lyth), 3-86 (Gale), 4-86 (Leaning), 5-114 (Sayers)
2nd 6-160 (Rashid), 7-182 (Hodd), 8-209 (Sidebottom), 9-248 (Patterson), 10-254 (Plunkett)

	O	M	R	W		O	M	R	W
Tremlett	28	5	79	1	Tremlett	20	3	48	1
Lewis	30	6	80	3	Linley	18	3	55	2
Linley	31.5	5	108	3	Keedy	39.1	8	99	7
de Bruyn	18	4	56	1	Lewis	12	3	34	0
Keedy	22	1	73	1	de Bruyn	3	0	6	0
Pietersen	4	1	13	0	Solanki	1	0	5	0
Solanki	2	0	5	0					

	First Innings	SURREY		Second Innings	
R J Burns, lbw b Sidebottom		29	not out		0
A Harinath, c Hodd b Brooks		36	not out		4
T E Linley, c Lyth b Sidebottom		0			
* V S Solanki, c Gale b Brooks		4			
K P Pietersen, not out		177			
Z de Bruyn, c sub (J Wainman) b Brooks		38			
§ S M Davies, c Brooks b Plunkett		44			
G C Wilson, c Plunkett b Lyth		12			
J Lewis, not out		2			
C T Tremlett					
G Keedy	Did not bat				
Extras b 6, lb 3, nb 2		11	Extras		0
Total (7 wkts dec)		353	Total (0 wkts)		4

Bonus points — Surrey 4, Yorkshire 2

FoW: 1-51 (Harinath), 2-53 (Linley), 3-62 (Solanki), 4-76 (Burns), 5-173 (de Bruyn)
1st 6-291 (Davies), 7-329 (Wilson)

	O	M	R	W		O	M	R	W
Sidebottom	21.5	6	84	2	Lyth	1	1	0	0
Brooks	18	1	64	3	Leaning	1	0	4	0
Plunkett	19	2	64	1					
Rashid	19	1	114	0					
Leaning	3	0	18	0					
Lyth	2	2	0	0					

Umpires: N A Mallender and S J O'Shaughnessy

Scorers: J T Potter and K R Booth

Centuries hat-trick for Gale

ANDREW GALE: Sound captain's innings

Yorkshire made 433, but an exceptional innings from Pietersen ensured that Surrey avoided the follow-on.

The match ended in a tame draw.

Yorkshire enjoyed a good start, but were 77-3 after bad light and an early lunch. Gale and Ballance added 204 for the fourth wicket — Gale reaching his third consecutive hundred, including a double, with a sound, responsible captain's innings when it really mattered, and Ballance was equally impressive. Tremlett, beanpole tall, was always dangerous with high bounce, while Lewis and the Yorkshire-born Linley took three wickets apiece. The innings extended over much of a rain disrupted second day.

Sidebottom and Brooks reduced Surrey to 76-4. Pietersen had had a long absence because of a knee injury, and his return was keenly anticipated with the *Ashes* series imminent. Any fears of incapacity were allayed when he eventually appeared on the third day. At his best Pietersen "doth bestride the narrow world like a colossus" especially at Headingley, where this was his fifth century in six games. His straight hitting was devastating, and his pulls and sweeps unstoppable. It is all built on an impregnable defence, so dismissal is usually by inadvertence rather than technical deficiency. Yorkshire did miss two chances, but Pietersen took full control as exemplified by his straight sixes off Rashid and the plundering of Sidebottom for 18 in an over.

Yorkshire's batting on the last day was precarious at first as they faced a long spell from Keedy, who threatened to dismiss them cheaply and give his side a run chase. It was particularly hard on Leaning, deputising for Ballance and making a second-innings debut duck. At 114-5 Yorkshire seemed in imminent danger, but Plunkett, Rashid and Hodd saw time out. Keedy was a pleasure to watch as the experienced orthodox left-arm spinner utilised flight and turn to take 7-99. Patterson broke a toe batting, and as Sidebottom was also handicapped Yorkshire did not feel able to set Surrey a target.

LV County Championship Division 1
Derbyshire v. Yorkshire

Played at Queen's Park, Chesterfield, on July 17, 18 and 19, 2013
Yorkshire won by an innings and 113 runs at 6.12pm on the Third Day

Toss won by Yorkshire   Yorkshire 24 points, Derbyshire 1 point
Close of play: First Day, Yorkshire 367-2 (Lees 171*, Gale 9*); Second Day, Derbyshire 94-5 (Johnson 5*, Turner 4*)

YORKSHIRE

A Lyth, c Poynton b Footitt		10
A Z Lees, not out		275
P A Jaques, c Durston b Groenewald		139
* A W Gale, b Burgoyne		74
G S Ballance, st Poynton b Durston		66
A U Rashid, c Poynton b Footitt		7
§ A J Hodd		
L E Plunkett		
R J Sidebottom	Did not bat	
S A Patterson		
J A Brooks		
Extras b 2, lb 13, w 7, nb 24		46
Total (5 wkts dec)		617

Bonus points — Yorkshire 5. 110-over score: 429-2

FoW: 1-22 (Lyth), 2-333 (Jaques), 3-471 (Gale), 4-580 (Ballance), 5-617 (Rashid)

	O	M	R	W
Footitt	22.3	3	110	2
Groenewald	24	4	112	1
Turner	17	0	128	0
Burgoyne	55	8	149	1
Durston	32	5	94	1
Redfern	2	0	9	0

DERBYSHIRE

First Innings		Second Innings	
B T Slater, c Hodd b Brooks	28	c Hodd b Brooks	1
C F Hughes, lbw b Sidebottom	12	c Ballance b Brooks	16
* W L Madsen, c Hodd b Patterson	17	c and b Plunkett	141
W J Durston, lbw b Patterson	0	b Patterson	2
D J Redfern, c Hood b Brooks	12	c Gale b Plunkett	2
R M Johnson, c Plunkett b Rashid	46	c Hodd b Patterson	23
M L Turner, c Gale b Brooks	8	(10) b Sidebottom	0
P I Burgoyne, c Hodd b Plunkett	15	(7) b Sidebottom	18
§ T Poynton, not out	63	(8) c Plunkett b Patterson	29
T D Groenewald, lbw b Plunkett	6	(9) b Sidebottom	11
M H A Footitt, c Lyth b Rashid	6	not out	0
Extras b 8, lb 1, w 1, nb 8	18	Extras b 16, w 2, nb 8	26
Total	235	Total	269

Bonus points — Derbyshire 1, Yorkshire 3

FoW: 1st 1-17 (Hughes), 2-52 (Madsen), 3-52 (Durston), 4-80 (Redfern), 5-83 (Slater), 6-120 (Turner), 7-146 (Johnson), 8-166 (Burgoyne), 9-202 (Groenewald), 10-235 (Footitt)

FoW: 2nd 1-1 (Slater), 2-29 (Hughes), 3-35 (Durston), 4-38 (Redfern), 5-74 (Johnson), 6-120 (Burgoyne), 7-231 (Poynton), 8-269 (Groenewald), 9-269 (Turner), 10-269 (Madsen)

	O	M	R	W		O	M	R	W
Sidebottom	13	5	31	1	Sidebottom	12	6	27	3
Brooks	16	5	46	3	Brooks	9	2	32	2
Patterson	13	5	35	2	Patterson	13	3	63	3
Plunkett	13	6	33	2	Plunkett	12.2	1	57	2
Rashid	12	1	81	2	Rashid	15	2	54	0
					Lyth	4	1	20	0

Umpires: N G C Cowley and J H Evans   Scorers: J T Potter and J M Brown

Derbyshire v. Yorkshire

Lees the youngest two-tonner

An excellent team performance was enhanced by an
outstanding innings of 275*
from Lees as Yorkshire outplayed Derbyshire in boiling
temperatures.

Well over six feet and
broad of shoulder, Lees plays
straight and has a good temperament. He was undefeated on 171 at the end of the
first day — and went on to
275* to become the youngest
player to make a double-century for Yorkshire.

He hit 38 fours and one
six towards the end of an
exhausting innings. He was
supported by Jaques, who
made 139, a welcome score
after a modest season, then

**ALEX LEES: 38 fours and six
in his exhausting 275 not out**

by Gale with 74 and finally Ballance, who hit four sixes as he accelerated towards a declaration. Derbyshire's attack was limited by injury to
Palladino and the omission of Wainwright, for whom Burgoyne, a young
off-spinning all-rounder from Ilkeston deputised — and bowled Gale for
his first wicket.

Having made a large total on a bland wicket, Yorkshire's task was to
bowl Derbyshire out twice. By the close of the second day they had dismissed five of their batsmen including Hughes, who had made 270 at
Headingley, and were relieved that Chanderpaul was not playing.

The four-man pace combination of Sidebottom, Brooks, Patterson
and Plunkett was able to claim 15 wickets on the third day to complete
the decisive victory. Johnson and Poynton provided some resistance
until Rashid removed Johnson, but no one stayed with the aggressive
Poynton. Following on, Derbyshire lost four quick wickets, but this time
Madsen stayed. He had walked in the first innings when the umpire did
not immediately endorse a thin edge, but now he played a fine captain's
innings before he was last out for 141.

The inexorable four-man attack persisted, and at the end of a long day
Sidebottom took two wickets and Plunkett caught the estimable Madsen
off his own bowling. It was an excellent win, as Yorkshire are now set
to meet some of the stronger sides in the Championship.

LV County Championship Division 1
Yorkshire v. Warwickshire

Played at Headingley, Leeds, on August 2, 3, 4 and 5, 2013
Match drawn at 4.45pm on the Fourth Day

Toss won by Warwickshire

Yorkshire 9 points, Warwickshire 9 points

Close of play: First Day, Yorkshire 294-9 (Patterson 19*, Brooks 12*); Second Day, Warwickshire 221-8 (Barker 12*, Patel 6*); Third Day, Yorkshire 147-7 (Hodd 6*, Sidebottom 0*)

First Innings	YORKSHIRE		Second Innings	
A Lyth, c Clarke b Woakes	11		lbw b Woakes	15
A Z Lees, c Chopra b Woakes	56		c Patel b Woakes	2
* A W Gale, c Ambrose b Barker	0		c Porterfield b Rankin	34
G S Ballance, lbw b Barker	112		b Woakes	45
A U Rashid, c Ambrose b Rankin	7		c Evans b Rankin	0
Azeem Rafiq, c Patel b Clarke	28		c Westwood b Patel	4
§ J A Hodd, b Clarke	21		not out	14
L E Plunkett, lbw b Barker	11		c Ambrose b Woakes	23
R J Sidebottom, c Ambrose b Woakes	4		b Woakes	9
S A Patterson, not out	21		c Westwood b Rankin	10
J A Brooks, c Ambrose b Rankin	18		c Barker b Rankin	0
Extras b 4, lb 8, w 1	13		Extras b 10, lb 10, nb 4	24
Total	302		Total	180

Bonus points — Yorkshire 3, Warwickshire 3

FoW: 1-25 (Lyth), 2-26 (Gale), 3-100 (Lees), 4-123 (Rashid), 5-173 (Rafiq),
1st 6-233 (Hodd), 7-250 (Plunkett), 8-257 (Ballance), 9-267 (Sidebottom), 10-302 (Brooks)
FoW: 1-14 (Lees), 2-19 (Lyth), 3-95 (Gale), 4-95 (Rashid), 5-104 (Rafiq), 6-121 (Ballance)
2nd 7-148 (Plunkett), 8-157 (Sidebottom), 9-180 (Patterson), 10-180 (Brooks)

	O	M	R	W		O	M	R	W
$ Barker	20.5	3	61	3	Barker	14	4	34	0
Woakes	24	0	63	3	Woakes	15	4	42	5
$ Rankin	20.5	1	70	2	Rankin	15	4	29	4
Clarke	18	6	51	2	Clarke	5	1	25	0
Patel	15	4	45	0	Patel	21	7	27	1
					Javid	1	0	3	0

$ Barker was not allowed to finish his 21st over in the first innings after running on the wicket. It was completed by Rankin

First Innings	WARWICKSHIRE		Second Innings	
* V Chopra, lbw b Patterson	23		not out	2
I J Westwood, lbw b Sidebottom	7		not out	0
W T S Porterfield, c Hodd b Plunkett	9			
L J Evans, c Lyth b Plunkett	88			
§ T R Ambrose, c Lyth b Patterson	0			
C R Woakes, c Rashid b Plunkett	21			
R Clarke, lbw b Rashid	24			
A Javid, c Hodd b Plunkett	17			
K H D Barker, run out (Brooks/Hodd)	49			
J S Patel, c Hodd b Sidebottom	63			
W B Rankin, not out	3			
Extras lb 5	5		Extras b 1	1
Total	309		Total (0 wkts)	3

Bonus points — Warwickshire 3, Yorkshire 3

110-over score: 309 all out

FoW: 1-13 (Westwood), 2-36 (Porterfield), 3-50 (Chopra), 4-50 (Ambrose), 5-95 (Woakes),
1st 6-150 (Clarke), 7-182 (Evans), 8-196 (Javid), 9-295 (Barker), 10-309 (Patel)

	O	M	R	W		O	M	R	W
Sidebottom	24	6	66	2	Sidebottom	1	0	2	0
Brooks	13	4	46	0	Brooks	1	1	0	0
Plunkett	24	7	74	4					
Patterson	24	9	50	2					
Azeem Rafiq	1	0	4	0					
Rashid	24	3	64	1					

Umpires: N L Bainton and M R Benson

Scorers: J T Potter and M D Smith

Rain curtain on high drama

GARY BALLANCE: Reached well judged century with a straight six

Invited to bat first, Yorkshire were indebted to Ballance and Lees for laying the foundations of a respectable 302.

Ballance played another excellent innings, combining sensible caution with some well timed scoring strokes against a useful four-man seam attack.

Lyth and Gale soon went, but Lees proved a sound partner until lunch, and then lost his wicket straight afterwards. Test aspirant Woakes bowled well throughout the match; Barker, a former professional goalkeeper, bowled left-arm with an easy fluent action, while Rankin and Clarke also took wickets. Ballance, who reached his hundred with a straight six, received support from the middle-order. He fell to Barker, but Patterson and Brooks saw Yorkshire to a third batting-bonus point.

Warwickshire struggled on the second day, and while Evans played the anchor role he had a certain amount of good fortune as wickets fell around him to Sidebottom, Plunkett — bowling at an impressive pace — and the reliable, economical Patterson. Yorkshire were in a strong position at the end of Saturday's play with the visitors 221-8, still 81 behind.

Last season's champions fought back on Sunday with a ninth-wicket stand of 99 by Patel, who twice was dropped off Rashid, and Barker, who was contentiously run out. Some good bowling from Woakes again, Londonderry-born Rankin, very tall with a good high action achieving steep bounce, and the diligent New Zealand Test off-spinner Patel turned the game further in Warwickshire's favour. Only Ballance again and, to some extent, Gale showed enough application to survive for long, although Hodd remained unbeaten.

Warwickshire needed 174 to win, and it would have been an interesting final session, had not rain intervened in mid-afternoon, with the visitors favourites but Yorkshire's confident seam attack in good form.

LV County Championship Division 1
Nottinghamshire v. Yorkshire

Played at Trent Bridge, Nottingham, on August 21, 22 and 23, 2013
Yorkshire won by 10 wickets at 2.35pm on the Third Day

Toss won by Nottinghamshire   Yorkshire 23 points, Nottinghamshire 2 points
Close of play: First Day, Yorkshire 327-8 (Bairstow 24*, Patterson 8*); Second Day,
Nottinghamshire 2nd Innings 118-4 (Hussey 22*, Wessels 12*)

First Innings	YORKSHIRE		Second Innings	
A Lyth, c Read b Fletcher	95		not out	12
A Z Lees, c Read b Gurney	8		not out	0
P A Jaques, lbw b Fletcher	19			
* A W Gale, c Read b Fletcher	33			
K S Williamson, c Patel b Fletcher	0			
A U Rashid, lbw b Fletcher	78			
L E Plunkett, c Read b Gurney	41			
§ J M Bairstow, b Adams	62			
R J Sidebottom, c Read b Gurney	0			
S A Patterson, c Read b Adams	40			
J A Brooks, not out	2			
$ A J Hodd				
Extras b 4, lb 16, w 1, nb 8	29		Extras	0
Total	407		Total (0 wkts)	12

$ J M Bairstow replaced A J Hodd during the first afternoon

Bonus points — Yorkshire 4, Nottinghamshire 2

FoW: 1-20 (Lees), 2-61 (Jaques), 3-137 (Gale), 4-137 (Williamson), 5-202 (Lyth), 6-281
1st   (Rashid), 7-303 (Plunkett), 8-305 (Sidebottom), 9-396 (Patterson), 10-407 (Bairstow)

110-over score: 383-8

	O	M	R	W		O	M	R	W
$ Fletcher	28.4	6	93	5	Fletcher	0.5	0	12	0
Gurney	18	3	71	3					
$ Adams	24.5	2	95	2					
Mullaney	5	3	14	0					
Shahzad	23	4	68	0					
Patel	14	3	46	0					

$ Fletcher was unable to finish his 25th over. It was completed by Adams

First Innings	NOTTINGHAMSHIRE		Second Innings	
S J Mullaney, c Bairstow b Patterson	13		lbw b Sidebottom	6
A D Hales, c Bairstow b Sidebottom	0		c Bairstow b Brooks	14
M J Lumb, lbw b Sidebottom	0		c and b Plunkett	20
S R Patel, c Jaques b Sidebottom	23		c sub (R M Pyrah) b Plunkett	37
D J Hussey, lbw b Patterson	13		c Bairstow b Sidebottom	24
M H Wessels, c Bairstow b Sidebottom	4		c Lyth b Brooks	22
* § C M W Read, lbw b Patterson	1		c Bairstow b Sidebottom	58
A Shahzad, not out	41		c Williamson b Rashid	19
L J Fletcher, c Rashid b Patterson	0		c Gale b Rashid	19
A R Adams, c Sidebottom b Patterson	39		not out	31
H F Gurney, c Plunkett b Rashid	4		c Jaques b Rashid	0
Extras b 5, lb 5, nb 2	12		Extras b 11, w 1, nb 4	16
Total	150		Total	266

Bonus points — Yorkshire 3

FoW: 1-5 (Hales), 2-9 (Lumb), 3-25 (Mullaney), 4-41 (Patel), 5-57 (Hussey)
1st   6-59 (Wessels), 7-61 (Read), 8-65 (Fletcher), 9-115 (Adams), 10-150 (Gurney)
FoW: 1-22 (Hales), 2-28 (Mullaney), 3-73 (Lumb), 4-102 (Patel), 5-120 (Hussey)
2nd   6-167 (Wessels), 7-209 (Shahzad), 8-218 (Read), 9-252 (Fletcher), 10-266 (Gurney)

	O	M	R	W		O	M	R	W
Sidebottom	14	2	35	4	Sidebottom	17	4	38	3
Brooks	6	0	16	0	Brooks	13	2	68	2
Patterson	11	3	43	5	Plunkett	13	0	70	2
Plunkett	4	0	46	0	Williamson	7	1	24	0
Rashid	0.4	0	0	1	Patterson	13	3	33	0
					Rashid	8.3	1	22	3

Umpires: T E Jesty and G Sharp   Scorers: J T Potter and R Marshall

The pacemen make it quick

RYAN SIDEBOTTOM: Passed his father's first-class tally

Lyth hit 95, and the middle-order made significant contributions to a good first-innings total.

Yorkshire's best bowlers this year, Sidebottom and Patterson, were accurate and incisive as they dismissed Nottinghamshire cheaply, and then the enthusiastic attack ensured that no batsman was able to compile the long innings necessary to save the game.

Nottinghamshire had put Yorkshire in, but had only two wickets by lunchtime. Lyth played his characteristic off-side strokes, but he looked sounder. It was a valuable innings, ending just short of the century he deserved.

Williamson, on debut from New Zealand, was out first ball to a loose shot, but Rashid played well to avert any collapse. How many Yorkshire debutants have been out first ball? Nottingham-born Fletcher, a tall and powerful seam bowler, worked hard to take the top five wickets. Bairstow arrived hotfoot from the Oval Test to emerge at No. 8, and indulged in some vigorous hitting, well supported by Patterson, before he was bowled by the persevering Adams. Read took six catches behind.

Sidebottom struck before lunch, dismissing Hales and Lumb, and despatched two more leading batsmen. Patterson, whose 5-34 was a career-best, claimed Mullaney, the potentially dangerous Hussey who has had a double-century against Yorkshire and skipper Read. Jaques took a fine catch to dismiss Patel. Following on, Nottinghamshire batted with greater resolution but wickets fell regularly, four on Thursday evening. The loss of Hussey in the first over on Friday made defeat inevitable, and Rashid took the last three wickets. Ryan Sidebottom took his 596th first-class wicket to equal the total of his father, Arnie — and surpassed it when he had Read caught by Bairstow.

LV County Championship Division 1
Yorkshire v. Durham

Played at North Marine Road, Scarborough, on August 28, 29, 30 and 31, 2013
Durham won by 7 wickets at 5.46pm on the Fourth Day

Toss won by Durham   Durham 24 points, Yorkshire 4 points

Close of play: First Day, Durham 406-6 (Collingwood 74*, Richardson 3*); Second Day, Yorkshire 182-3 (Williamson 76*, Bairstow 42*); Third Day, Yorkshire 276-1 (Jaques 151*, Williamson 90*)

DURHAM

First Innings		Second Innings	
M D Stoneman, c Bairstow b Sidebottom	122	c Williamson b Sidebottom	0
K K Jennings, lbw b Sidebottom	0	c Jaques b Rashid	17
S G Borthwick, lbw b Sidebottom	0	b Rashid	65
W R Smith, c Williamson b Brooks	20	not out	27
B A Stokes, c Bairstow b Rashid	127	not out	11
* P D Collingwood, lbw b Sidebottom	81		
§ P Mustard, lbw b Williamson	42		
M J Richardson, c Ballance b Williamson	102		
M A Wood, c Brooks b Plunkett	20		
J Harrison, run out (Sidebottom/Bairstow)	35		
C Rushworth, not out	1		
Extras b 4, lb 15, nb 4	23	Extras lb 1, w 1, nb 2	4
Total	573	Total (3 wkts)	124

Bonus points — Durham 5, Yorkshire 2   110-over score: 454-7

FoW: 1-5 (Jennings), 2-5 (Borthwick), 3-67 (Smith), 4-195 (Stoneman), 5-315 (Stokes), 6-403
1st (Mustard), 7-414 (Collingwood), 8-463 (Wood), 9-547 (Harrison), 10-573 (Richardson)
2nd 1-0 (Stoneman), 2-72 (Jennings), 3-103 (Borthwick)

	O	M	R	W		O	M	R	W
Sidebottom	24	4	85	4	Sidebottom	8	0	31	1
Brooks	27	3	111	1	Brooks	2	1	13	0
Patterson	30	8	82	0	Patterson	8	2	19	0
Plunkett	17	1	89	1	Rashid	7	0	47	2
Williamson	15	2	67	2	Williamson	2.4	1	13	0
Rashid	25	3	120	1					

YORKSHIRE

First Innings		Second Innings	
A Lyth, c Stokes b Rushworth	10	lbw b Rushworth	10
P A Jaques, c Smith b Borthwick	36	c Mustard b Stokes	152
K S Williamson, lbw b Stokes	84	c Smith b Stokes	97
* A W Gale, lbw b Harrison	12	c Richardson b Harrison	5
§ J M Bairstow, c and b Borthwick	82	c Richardson b Rushworth	34
G S Ballance, run out (Rushworth/Mustard)	1	c Mustard b Stokes	26
A U Rashid, c Mustard b Harrison	1	c Jennings b Rushworth	1
L E Plunkett, b Wood	10	c Stokes b Borthwick	42
R J Sidebottom, c Mustard b Stokes	5	c Mustard b Borthwick	9
S A Patterson, b Wood	0	not out	4
J A Brooks, not out	14	c Collingwood b Borthwick	0
Extras lb 13, nb 6	19	Extras b 9, lb 19, w 1, nb 10	39
Total	274	Total	419

Bonus points — Yorkshire 2, Durham 3

FoW: 1-18 (Lyth), 2-72 (Jaques), 3-107 (Gale), 4-211 (Williamson), 5-212 (Ballance), 6-219
1st (Rashid), 7-253 (Bairstow), 8-257 (Plunkett), 9-257 (Patterson), 10-274 Sidebottom)
FoW: 1-19 (Lyth), 2-283 (Williamson), 3-284 (Jaques), 4-313 (Gale), 5-349 (Bairstow),
2nd 6-351 (Rashid), 7-357 (Balance), 8-410 (Sidebottom), 9-419 (Plunkett), 10-419 (Brooks)

	O	M	R	W		O	M	R	W
Rushworth	14	1	52	1	Harrison	18	2	59	1
Harrison	19	6	66	2	Rushworth	24	7	72	3
Wood	14	3	32	2	Stokes	33	5	108	3
Stokes	17	3	54	2	Borthwick	38.2	7	134	3
Borthwick	19	4	57	2	Smith	7	2	17	0
					Collingwood	3	2	1	0

Umpires: M J D Bodenham and R A Kettleborough   Scorers: J T Potter and B Hunt

138

Yorkshire v. Durham

Stoking up a Test career...

Four full days in the Scarborough sun saw Durham win a match in which they had been much the better side.

They had three centurians in a vast first-innings total, but after a reasonable start Yorkshire suffered a first-innings collapse.

Yorkshire staged an admirable fight-back in the second innings, but further batting inadequacies left the visitors with a straightfor-

JONATHAN BAIRSTOW: A fine-form 82

ward task. Sidebottom won lbw decisions against Jennings and Borthwick to reduce Durham to 5-2, and Smith was brilliantly caught low and wide to his right by Williamson. Stoneman and Stokes found numerous gaps in the field to score with considerable rapidity: Stoneman played a fine opener's innings, while Stokes's elegance, timing and power should presage an international career. Having removed these two, Yorkshire were unable to make further inroads. Only Sidebottom, who took his 600th wicket, impressed. Collingwood made 81 and Richardson a career-best 102 as Durham reached a mighty 573.

Yorkshire had to survive for two and a half days. Onions was absent injured, and Wood suffered a side strain, but the Durham seam attack, assisted by the eager Borthwick, was equal to its task. Williamson played with patience and a straight bat, and Bairstow looked in good form, but Yorkshire lost seven wickets for 63 to finish 299 behind. The running-out of Ballance was a serious error when survival was paramount. Jaques and Williamson put on 264 for the second wicket in the follow-on, but both fell to Stokes on Saturday morning before they took the lead. A second batting failure made defeat inevitable, and Borthwick saw Durham home. Stokes looked a good all-rounder with a high action and admirable stamina, while Borthwick got plenty of turn for his leg-breaks, and was rewarded with the last three wickets. Victorious Durham were now 5.5 points behind Yorkshire with a game in hand.

LV County Championship Division 1
Sussex v. Yorkshire

Played at The County Ground, Hove, on September 11, 12, 13 and 14, 2013
Match drawn at 3.30pm on the Fourth Day

Toss won by Yorkshire Yorkshire 9 points, Sussex 7 points

Close of play: First Day, Sussex 276-9 (Brown 78*, Hatchett 11*); Second Day, Yorkshire 246-4 (Williamson 80*, Patterson 2*); Third Day, Sussex 48-2 (Nash 21*, Joyce 4*)

SUSSEX

	First Innings			Second Innings	
C D Nash, c Bairstow b Plunkett	35		(2) not out		167
L W P Wells, c Lyth b Brooks	10		(1) b Sidebottom		0
M H Yardy, b Plunkett	29		c Jaques b Plunkett		15
* E C Joyce, b Sidebottom	3		c Brooks b Jaques		14
M J Prior, b Patterson	23				
R J Hamilton-Brown, b Williamson	20		(5) not out		126
§ B C Brown, not out	84				
A Zaidi, lbw b Sidebottom	17				
S J Magoffin, c Bairstow b Sidebottom	26				
J E Anyon, b Williamson	6				
L J Hatchett, c Lyth b Sidebottom	21				
Extras b 4, lb 8, nb 6	18		Extras b 8, lb 3		11
Total	292		Total (3 wkts dec)		333

Bonus points — Sussex 2, Yorkshire 3

FoW: 1st 1-24 (Wells), 2-58 (Nash), 3-79 (Yardy), 4-83 (Joyce), 5-114 (Hamilton-Brown), 6-137 (Prior), 7-164 (Zaidi), 8-238 (Magoffin), 9-254 (Anyon), 10-292 (Hatchett)
2nd 1-4 (Wells), 2-33 (Yardy), 3-73 (Joyce)

	O	M	R	W		O	M	R	W
Sidebottom	15.5	5	50	4	Sidebottom	5	1	11	1
Brooks	13	2	42	1	Brooks	4	0	17	0
Patterson	14	4	59	1	Plunkett	1	0	1	1
Plunkett	14	0	54	2	Rashid	3	0	7	0
Williamson	9	2	44	2	Williamson	2	0	4	0
Rashid	14	0	31	0	Jaques	6	0	75	1
					Gale	9	0	94	0
					Ballance	12	0	88	0
					Lyth	5	0	25	0

YORKSHIRE

	First Innings			Second Innings	
A Lyth, c Prior b Zaidi	93		not out		40
P A Jaques, lbw b Magoffin	21		(3) lbw b Zaidi		23
K S Williamson, lbw b Anyon	80		(4) not out		5
* A W Gale, c Brown b Anyon	28				
§ J M Bairstow, b Anyon	8				
S A Patterson, c Brown b Magoffin	11				
G S Ballance, c Prior b Zaidi	19				
A U Rashid, c Magoffin b Zaidi	13				
L E Plunkett, st Brown b Zaidi	27		(2) c Joyce b Hatchett		11
R J Sidebottom, b Hatchett	5				
J A Brooks, not out	0				
Extras b 6, lb 7, nb 8	21		Extras nb 2		2
Total	326		Total (2 wkts)		81

Bonus points — Yorkshire 3, Sussex 2

110-over score: 303-7

FoW: 1st 1-25 (Jaques), 2-189 (Lyth), 3-234 (Gale), 4-243 (Bairstow), 5-250 (Williamson), 6-276 (Patterson), 7-284 (Ballance), 8-313 (Rashid), 9-320 (Sidebottom), 10-326 (Plunkett)
2nd 1-22 (Plunkett), 2-64 (Jaques)

	O	M	R	W		O	M	R	W
Magoffin	37	18	59	2	Magoffin	5	0	22	0
Hatchett	19	5	71	1	Hatchett	5	1	17	1
Zaidi	23.2	3	57	4	Nash	4	0	14	0
Anyon	29	4	107	3	Zaidi	5	0	24	1
Nash	7	0	19	0	Anyon	1	0	4	0

Umpires: M R Benson and S J O'Shaughnessy Scorers: J T Potter and M J Charman

Embarrassment washed away

Any prospect of an exciting finish after last-day calculations was washed away by intermittent showers, and Yorkshire had to settle for a draw while Championship rivals Durham defeated Derbyshire.

Yorkshire asked Sussex to bat in blustery conditions and dismissed seven batsmen for 164, but a resolute Brown, twice dropped, produced an undefeated 84. The quick bowlers impressed as Patterson dismantled Prior's off-stump and Plunkett despatched Nash with a fine ball, but the late batsmen solidly supported Brown, and they reached a commendable 292.

Yorkshire were in a strong position at the close on Thursday with 246-4. Lyth played a responsible innings with good concentration and self-discipline, and he was unfortunate to be caught at slip by Prior for 93. He was well supported by Williamson, quietly orthodox and correct. As at Headingley, Magoffin bowled with great skill and economy.

On the third day Yorkshire were unable to make the large total that would have regained the initiative in a match they had to win. They lost six wickets for 83, and Williamson was out soon after play resumed in the afternoon. Zaidi, a left-arm spinner on debut, took three more wickets.

There were further weather disruptions, and it was decided that Yorkshire

KANE WILLIAMSON
Orthodox and correct

would be set 300. A large number of cheap runs were conceded, mostly to Nash and Hamilton-Brown, so each had first-class centuries to their name. Arguably, it is justifiable to make such arrangements to avoid a dull draw, but it makes embarrassing viewing. An alternative approach would have been to attempt to bowl Sussex out on an overcast morning, utilising the four seamers in favourable conditions. The assumption seemed to be that batting might win the match, but bowling could not. The weather decided.

LV County Championship Division 1
Yorkshire v. Middlesex

Played at Headingley, Leeds, on September 17, 18, 19 and 20, 2013
Yorkshire won by 80 runs at 4.21pm on the Fourth Day

Toss won by Middlesex

Yorkshire 20 points, Middlesex 3 points

Close of play: First Day, Yorkshire 109-3 (Williamson 34*, Bairstow 1*); Second Day, Yorkshire 4-0 (Lyth 0*, Jaques 3*); Third Day, Yorkshire 130-5 (Ballance 53*, Rashid 0*)

First Innings	YORKSHIRE		Second Innings	
A Lyth, lbw b Collymore	0		lbw b Collymore	0
P A Jaques, c Simpson b Murtagh	3		c Malan b Murtagh	21
K S Williams, c Simpson b Helm	52		b Murtagh	2
* A W Gale, c Simpson b Collymore	66		lbw b Helm	40
§ J M Bairstow, c Malan b Murtagh	5		b Collymore	3
G S Ballance, c Simpson b Berg	12		c Malan b Helm	90
A U Rashid, c Simpson b Helm	19		c Malan b Murtagh	21
L E Plunkett, c Rayner b Berg	18		c Dexter b Helm	1
R J Sidebottom, c Rayner b Murtagh	1		c Rayner b Berg	0
S A Patterson, c Simpson b Collymore	16		not out	1
J A Brooks, not out	4		c Robson b Berg	0
Extras b 4, lb 8, n b4	16		Extras lb 12, w 1, nb 2	15
Total	210		Total	194

Bonus points — Yorkshire 1, Middlesex 3

FoW: 1-1 (Lyth), 2-1 (Jaques), 3-98 (Gale), 4-117 (Bairstow), 5-142 (Ballance), 6-166
1st (Rashid), 7-187 (Williamson), 8-189 (Plunkett), 9-204 (Sidebottom), 10-110 (Patterson)
FoW: 1-4 (Lyth), 2-7 (Williamson), 3-40 (Jaques), 4-50 (Bairstow), 5-129 (Gale)
2nd 6-166 (Rashid), 7-178 (Plunkett), 8-179 (Sidebottom), 9-193 (Ballance), 10-194 (Brooks)

	O	M	R	W		O	M	R	W
Murtagh	28	9	49	3	Murtagh	18	3	74	3
Collymore	22.5	8	38	3	Berg	8.2	0	27	2
Berg	12	2	44	2	Collymore	13	4	25	2
Helm	9	0	32	2	Helm	9	0	46	3
Dexter	8	2	35	0	Rayner	5	0	10	0

First Innings	MIDDLESEX		Second Innings	
* C J L Rogers, c Rashid b Patterson	8		(2) c Bairstow b Patterson	65
S D Robson, c Bairstow b Brooks	45		(1) c Lyth b Patterson	3
J L Denly, c Lyth b Patterson	2		b Sidebottom	12
D J Malan, c Bairstow b Patterson	15		lbw b Plunkett	31
N J Dexter, c Bairstow b Sidebottom	12		c Williamson b Brooks	8
§ J A Simpson, lbw b Brooks	14		c Lyth b Patterson	9
G K Berg, c Bairstow b Sidebottom	8		c Bairstow b Patterson	6
O P Rayner, c Brooks b Sidebottom	2		c Patterson b Brooks	25
T G Helm, c Bairstow b Brooks	4		lbw b Brooks	18
T J Murtagh, c Bairstow b Sidebottom	0		c Ballance b Brooks	0
C D Collymore, not out	0		not out	0
Extras b 1, lb 1, nb 4	6		Extras lb 8, w 1, nb 10	19
Total	128		Total	196

Bonus points — Yorkshire 3

FoW: 1-9 (Rogers), 2-21 (Denly), 3-45 (Malan), 4-86 (Robson), 5-92 (Dexter)
1st 6-106 (Berg), 7-110 (Simpson), 8-114 (Helm), 9-115 (Murtagh), 10-128 (Collymore)
FoW: 1-9 (Robson), 2-34 (Denly), 3-90 (Malan), 4-103 (Dexter), 5-134 (Rogers)
2nd 6-138 (Simpson), 7-149 (Berg), 8-185 (Helm), 9-185 (Murtagh), 10-196 (Rayner)

	O	M	R	W		O	M	R	W
Sidebottom	16	7	27	4	Sidebottom	12	1	49	1
Patterson	12	4	44	3	Patterson	15	4	50	2
Plunkett	5	0	21	0	Plunkett	13	1	55	2
Brooks	8	0	34	3	Brooks	7.5	0	33	4
					Williamson	2	1	1	0

Umpires: N J Llong and M J Saggers

Scorers: J T Potter and D K Shelley

Yorkshire take silver medal...

JACK BROOKS: Seven wickets in the match

Yorkshire won this match on a lively pitch with superior batting — but principally because their four-man seam attack twice dismissed Middlesex cheaply.

Murtagh and Collymore bowled well in Yorkshire's first innings: Murtagh, tall and accurate, with a straight, smooth run-up, and Collymore moving the ball significantly. It was to the credit of Gale and Williamson that they provided the backbone of the Yorkshire innings that had begun precariously at one run for two wickets.

Williamson was sound and very patient, batting for four and a half hours, whereas Gale was more combative. The value of their contribution was demonstrated when Middlesex collapsed in a disastrous first innings.

Sidebottom and Patterson have both had outstanding seasons. Sidebottom took four wickets and Patterson the top three, including Rogers, the captain, with only Robson surviving for very long.

Ballance's durability was seen in Yorkshire's second innings through an excellent innings of 90, which ended when he pulled debutant Helm to Malan on the fine-leg boundary. Helm, a tall young bowler from Buckinghamshire, took five wickets in the match. Gale reached his 1,000 runs for the season, but the rest succumbed too easily.

Yorkshire's lead of 276 proved unassailable, despite Rogers's contribution, which was ended with a debatable dismissal. This time all four bowlers shared the wickets, and Brooks demolished the tail in one of his characteristic bursts of energy. It was notable that in the first innings both wicket-keepers took six catches, as Bairstow emulated Simpson's achievement. Almost all the catches were taken behind square, and three were outstanding: Raynor with left hand outstretched in a 6ft 5in man's dive at slip; Williamson with wonderful anticipation, also at slip, and not least Malan, turning and running with the ball behind him...then diving forward to catch Rashid. Yorkshire confirmed second place, and were warmly applauded as they left the field after a very good season.

LV County Championship Division 1
Surrey v. Yorkshire

Played at The Oval, London, on September 24, 25, 26 and 27, 2013
Match drawn at 4.41pm on the Fourth Day

Toss won by Yorkshire   Surrey 8 points, Yorkshire 7 points
Close of play: First Day, Yorkshire 316-6 (Ballance 72*, Rashid 14*); Second Day, Surrey 172-1 (Sibley 81*, Linley 0*); Third Day, Surrey 572-4 (Sibley 220*, Davies 25*)

YORKSHIRE

	First Innings		Second Innings	
A Lyth, c Davies b Dunn	24		c Solanki b Linley	4
A Z Lees, c Davies b Dunn	8		c Davies b Linley	11
P A Jaques, c Batty b Ansari	88		b Dunn	1
K S Williamson, b Ansari	23		c Solanki b Batty	60
§ J M Bairstow, lbw b Jewell	24		lbw b Linley	35
G S Ballance, c Wilson b Ansari	148		not out	108
* A W Gale, c Solanki b Jewell	29		c Wilson b Ansari	13
A U Rashid, lbw b Jewell	43		not out	8
R J Sidebottom, c Davies b Dunn	6			
S A Patterson, not out	5			
J A Brooks, c Davies b Ansari	0			
Extras b 13, lb 8, w 7, nb 8	36		Extras b 13, lb 8, nb 4	25
Total	434		Total (6 wkts)	265

Bonus points — Yorkshire 4, Surrey 2   110 over score: 368-7

FoW: 1-22 (Lees), 2-58 (Lyth), 3-146 (Williamson), 4-169 (Jaques), 5-227 (Bairstow)
1st 6-296 (Gale), 7-368 (Rashid), 8-402 (Sidebottom), 9-434 (Ballance), 10-434 (Brooks)
FoW: 1-4 (Lyth), 2-11 (Jaques), 3-21 (Lees), 4-84 (Bairstow), 5-133 (Williamson)
2nd 6-198 (Gale)

	O	M	R	W		O	M	R	W
Linley	27	5	100	0	Linley	10	3	33	3
Dunn	25	1	97	3	Dunn	10	1	36	1
Jewell	25	4	100	3	Jewell	8	1	47	0
Batty	20	4	46	0	Ansari	24	4	79	1
Ansari	27.5	7	70	4	Batty	18	4	45	1
					Sibley	1	0	4	0

SURREY

R J Burns, c Bairstow b Patterson		82
D P Sibley, b Sidebottom		242
T E Linley, lbw b Rashid		12
H M Amla, c Bairstow b Sidebottom		151
V S Solanki, c Ballance b Rashid		51
§ S M Davies, not out		46
G C Wilson, not out		15
Z S Ansari		
* G J Batty	Did not bat	
T M Jewell		
M P Dunn		
Extras b 13, lb 10, w 2, nb 10		35
Total (5 wkt dec)		634

Bonus points — Surrey 3   110-over score 303-2

FoW: 1st 1-171 (Burns), 2-190)Linley, 3-426 (Amla), 4-502 (Solanki), 5-596 (Sibley)

	O	M	R	W
Sidebottom	26.4	7	69	2
Patterson	27	8	82	1
Brooks	24	4	85	0
Rashid	55	6	227	2
Williamson	28	6	94	0
Lyth	11	0	44	0
Ballance	2	0	10	0

Umpires: I J Gould and M J Saggers   Scorers: J T Potter and K R Booth

England calls two-ton Ballance

It was the last match of the season, and Yorkshire could not catch Durham while Surrey would be relegated.

Yet it was distinguished by a remarkable innings of 242 from a Surrey schoolboy, a hundred from Amla and two centuries for Yorkshire from Ballance.

Dominic Sibley, taking A-levels at Whitgift School, Croydon, had been the out-standing player in the 2011 Under-15 Bunbury Festival and was playing his third Championship match.

A tall right-hander with good orthodox technique and considerable patience, he put on 171 with Burns. who was out for 82 just before the close of the second day.

Then when he hit a full

GARY BALLANCE: Best batsman saved Yorkshire's day

toss for four he became Surrey's youngest first-class century maker, surpassing J N Crawford and Graham Thorpe. His total of 242 including 24 fours and two sixes was made in a minute under 10 hours. At 18 years and 21 days he was the youngest double-century-maker since W G Grace made 224 for England against Surrey, also at The Oval, on July 31, 1866, aged 18 years and 13 days. He even overshadowed Amla's 151, but must have benefited by batting alongside him. Surrey reached 634-5, and Rashid conceded 227 runs, another record.

Ballance's two centuries crowned a season in which he had been Yorkshire's best batsman and which culminated in his selection for England's *Ashes* tour. His first-innings 148, along with Jaques's 88, was the basis of a total of 434 as Surrey's young bowlers, Jewell, Dunn and slow left-armer Ansari shared the wickets. Surrey led by 138, and Yorkshire were in trouble in their second innings after losing their fifth wicket at 133. Ballance's second century was a match-saving one, and was invaluable as Batty was getting some turn. Jaques announced that he would be leaving Yorkshire, and Williamson was given a contract. It had been a very good first-class season for Yorkshire, a clear second.

LV COUNTY CHAMPIONSHIP 2013

DIVISION 1

	P	W	L	D	**BAT**	**BOWL**	Pen.	Points
						Bonus Points		
1 Durham (Div 1, 6) * *	16	10	4	2	36	46	2.5	245.5
2 Yorkshire (Div 2, 2)	**16**	**7**	**2**	**7**	**49**	**39**	**0.0**	**221.0**
3 Sussex (Div 1, 4)	16	5	3	8	45	39	0.0	188.0
4 Warwickshire (Div 1, 1)	16	5	2	9	37	42	0.0	186.0
5 Middlesex (Div 1, 3)	16	6	5	5	32	39	0.0	182.0
6 Somerset (Div 1, 2)	16	3	5	8	33	41	0.0	146.0
7 Nottinghamshire (Div 1, 6)	16	2	5	9	47	40	0.0	146.0
8 Derbyshire (Div 2, 1) *	16	3	10	3	31	34	0.0	122.0
9 Surrey (Div 1, 7) *	16	1	6	9	36	37	0.0	116.0

Pen. 1 point deducted for each over short in a match based on a rate of 16 overs per hour

* Relegated to Division 2 for 2014

* * Deducted 2.5 points for breach of salary cap in 2012

DIVISION 2

	P	W	L	D	**BAT**	**BOWL**	Pen.	Points
						Bonus Points		
1 Lancashire (Div 1, 8) *	16	8	1	7	45	45	1.0	238.0
2 Northamptonshire (Div 2, 8) *	16	5	3	8	55	43	0.0	202.0
3 Essex (Div 2, 5)	16	5	4	7	43	41	3.0	182.0
4 Hampshire (Div 2, 4)	16	4	3	9	45	35	0.0	171.0
5 Worcestershire (Div 1, 9)	16	5	6	5	29	43	0.0	167.0
6 Gloucestershire (Div 2, 9)	16	4	4	8	43	36	0.0	167.0
7 Kent (Div 2, 3)	16	3	2	11	39	31	0.0	151.0
8 Glamorgan (Div 2, 6)	16	3	6	7	41	39	0.0	149.0
9 Leicestershire (Div 2, 7)	16	0	8	8	23	32	0.0	79.0

Pen. 1 point deducted for each over short in a match based on a rate of 16 overs per hour

* Promoted to Division 1 for 2013.

(2012 positions in brackets)

YORKSHIRE AVERAGES 2013

LV COUNTY CHAMPIONSHIP

Played 16   Won 7   Lost 2   Drawn 7

BATTING AND FIELDING

(Qualification 10 completed innings)

Player	M.	I.	N.O.	Runs	H.S.	Avge	100s	50s	ct/st
G S Ballance	14	21	1	1251	148	62.55	5	6	13
A U Rashid	15	22	6	825	180	51.56	3	3	7
A Z Lees	8	14	3	500	275*	45.45	2	1	1
A W Gale	16	24	0	1067	272	44.45	3	3	4
J M Bairstow	8	13	0	528	186	40.61	1	2	27/0
P A Jaques	14	21	0	770	152	36.66	2	3	5
A Lyth	16	27	4	730	105	31.73	1	4	25
L E Plunkett	12	17	2	394	68	26.26	0	2	9
R J Sidebottom	14	16	0	155	48	9.68	0	0	3
Also played									
J E Root	2	3	0	467	236	155.66	2	0	3
K S Williamson	5	9	1	403	97	50.37	0	5	4
R M Pyrah	5	3	1	70	55	35.00	0	1	5
A J Hodd	9	9	2	217	68*	31.00	0	1	17/1
T T Bresnan	4	5	1	66	38	16.50	0	0	1
Azeem Rafiq	2	4	0	55	28	13.75	0	0	0
J A Brooks	11	13	6	79	33*	11.28	0	0	5
S A Patterson	16	17	8	147	40	16.33	0	0	2
J J Sayers	5	7	0	57	24	8.14	0	0	4
J A Leaning	1	1	0	0	0	0.00	0	0	0
M A Ashraf	2	0	0	0	—	—	0	0	0

BOWLING

(Qualification 10 wickets)

Player	Overs	Mdns	Runs	Wkts	Avge	Best	5wI	10wM
R J Sidebottom	369.1	100	995	49	20.30	4-27	0	0
T T Bresnan	130.2	31	393	16	24.56	4-41	0	0
S A Patterson	413.5	119	1153	46	25.06	5-43	1	0
J A Brooks	241	49	859	34	25.26	5-40	1	0
L E Plunkett	258.5	42	1020	36	28.33	5-32	1	0
A U Rashid	359.5	39	1358	29	46.82	5-78	1	0
Also bowled								
M A Ashraf	38.3	13	119	4	29.75	3-60	0	0
A Lyth	36	4	155	4	38.75	2-15	0	0
K S Williamson	65.4	13	247	4	61.75	2-44	0	0
Azeem Rafiq	16	1	74	1	74.00	1-70	0	0
P A Jaques	6	0	75	1	75.00	1-75	0	0
R M Pyrah	77	19	244	2	122.00	1-45	0	0
G S Ballance	14	0	98	0	—	0-10	0	0
J E Root	9	4	14	0	—	0-0	0	0
A W Gale	9	0	94	0	—	0-94	0	0
J A Leaning	4	0	22	0	—	0-4	0	0
A Z Lees	1	0	14	0	—	0-14	0	0

MCC University Match (First-Class)
Yorkshire v. Leeds/Bradford MCCU

Played at Headingley, Leeds, on April 5, 6 and 7, 2013
Yorkshire won by 294 runs at 5.33pm on the Third Day
Toss won by Leeds/Bradford MCCU

Close of play: First Day, Leeds/Bradford 40-3 (Thompson 14*, MacLeod 2*); Second Day, Yorkshire 192-0 (Lyth 93*, Lees 86*)

First Innings	YORKSHIRE		Second Innings	
A Lyth, c Young b Thomas	9		c Vanderspar b MacQueen	111
A Z Lees, c Reece b Lee	0		b Rouse	121
J J Sayers, c Gubbins b Lee	1		not out	25
* A W Gale, lbw b Lee	0		not out	9
§ J M Bairstow, c MacLeod b Reece	20			
G S Ballance, c MacLeod b Lee	112			
Azeem Rafiq, c Webb b Lee	3			
L E Plunkett, lbw b Lee	0			
R J Sidebottom, b Vanderspar	40			
J A Brooks, not out	21			
S A Patterson, b Lee	0			
Extras b 11, lb 9, w 8, nb 10	38		Extras b 10, lb 3, w6, nb4	23
Total	244		Total (2 wkts dec)	289

FoW: 1-9 (Lyth), 2-9 (Lees), 3-9 (Gale), 4-10 (Sayers), 5-59 (Bairstow), 6-65 (Rafiq),
1st 7-65 (Plunkett), 8-221 (Sidebottom), 9-244 (Ballance), 10-244 (Patterson)
2nd 1-221 (Lyth), 2-272 (Lees)

	O	M	R	W		O	M	R	W
Lee	14.3	1	45	7	Lee	15	3	30	0
Thomas	15	3	52	1	Thomas	20	4	52	0
Rouse	12	3	41	0	Rouse	18	1	64	1
Reece	16	3	34	0	Reece	24	2	68	0
Vanderspar	7	1	26	1	MacQueen	18	6	45	1
MacQueen	19	6	26	0	Thompson	2	1	6	0
Thompson	1	1	0	0	Vanderspar	3	0	9	0
					Young	1	0	2	0

First Innings	LEEDS/BRADFORD MCCU	Second innings	
H L Thompson, lbw b Patterson	15	c Bairstow b Plunkett	2
N R T Gubbins, c Bairstow b Brooks	14	c Bairstow b Patterson	8
J P Webb, b Brooks	0	c Gale b Plunkett	0
D R Young, c Bairstow b Sidebottom	5	lbw b Patterson	0
§ C A R MacLeod, c Lyth b Patterson	4	(10) c Lees b Plunkett	0
* L M Reece, c Bairstow b Sidebottom	0	(5) c Brooks b Plunkett	6
W G R Vanderspar, c Bairstow b Patterson	4	(6) b Plunkett	37
H P Rouse, c Lyth b Azeem Rafiq	14	(7) b Azeem Rafiq	15
A MacQueen, lbw b Sidebottom	2	(8) lbw b Sidebottom	30
J E Lee, b Brooks	34	(9) c Sidebottom b Plunkett	20
I A A Thomas, not out	10	not out	1
Extras b 4, lb 11, w 1	16	Extras lb 2	2
Total	118	Total	121

FoW: 1-22 (Gubbins), 2-22 (Webb), 3-33 (Young), 4-41 (MacLeod), 5-42 (Reece)
1st 6-42 (Thompson), 7-53 (Vanderspar), 8-60 (MacQueen), 9-88 (Rouse), 10-118 (Lee)
FoW: 1-7 (Thompson), 2-11 (Gubbins), 3-11 (Webb), 4-15 (Young), 5-17 (Reece)
2nd 6-38 (Rouse), 7-81 (MacQueen), 8-104 (Vanderspar), 9-104 (MacLeod), 10-121 (Lee)

	O	M	R	W		O	M	R	W
Patterson	16	7	39	3	Patterson	6	4	5	2
Brooks	13.2	5	26	3	Plunkett	11.5	4	33	6
Sidebottom	11	5	9	3	Azeem Rafiq	18	7	50	1
Plunkett	8	3	12	0	Brooks	7	1	23	0
Azeem Rafiq	6	1	17	1	Sidebottom	5	2	8	1

Umpires: P J Hartley and P R Pollard   Scorers: J T Potter and H Claydon

Lethal Lee rocks his county

JONATHAN BAIRSTOW: Catches van der Spar, one of his six victims

Liam Plunkett, from Durham, and Jack Brooks, from Northamptonshire, made their Yorkshire debuts in this early April curtain-raiser.

But it was a former *White Rose* player, James Lee, who attracted all the attention on the first day.

The Sheffield-born seamer, who was with Yorkshire from 2006 to 2009 and took part in two first-class matches, scythed his way through the home team on his way to a career-best 7-45.

Lee soon proved to be virtually unplayable, grabbing three wickets in 13 balls as Yorkshire slumped to 10-4 in 4.2 overs. They were still very much under the cosh at 65-7, but were spared further embarrassment by Ballance and Sidebottom, who added 156 for the eighth wicket before Sidebottom departed for a tenacious 40 from 175 balls with five boundaries. Most of the scoring was done by Ballance, and when he fell during another lethal burst from Lee he had 112 off 227 deliveries with 14 fours and a six.

Patterson, Brooks and Sidebottom each captured three wickets as their young opponents fell apart, and they would have been well short of three figures had not Lee also shown his prowess with the bat. Going in at 60-8, he played some fine attacking strokes before being last out at 118, bowled by Brooks for a plucky 34 from 91 balls with six fours.

With the pressure off, Lyth and Lees then wore down the attack with an opening stand of 221. Lyth was a shade quicker than his up-and-coming partner with 111 to Lees's 97 when he was caught after receiving 223 balls and striking 13 boundaries. Lees completed his maiden century off 232 balls with 12 fours, and was finally bowled by Rouse for 121. Sayers and Gale spent some time in the middle before the declaration at 289-2, and it was Plunkett who wrecked Leeds/Bradford second time around with a career-best 6-33 as they were routed for 121.

YORKSHIRE AVERAGES 2013

ALL FIRST-CLASS MATCHES

Played 17   Won 8   Lost 2   Drawn 7

BATTING AND FIELDING

(Qualification 10 completed innings)

Player	M.	I.	N.O.	Runs	H.S.	Avge	100s	50s	ct/st
G S Ballance	15	22	1	1363	148	64.90	6	6	13
A U Rashid	15	22	6	825	180	51.56	3	3	7
A Z Lees	9	16	3	621	275*	47.76	3	1	2
A W Gale	17	26	1	1076	272	43.04	3	3	5
J M Bairstow	9	14	0	548	186	39.14	1	2	33
P A Jaques	14	21	0	770	152	36.66	2	3	5
A Lyth	17	29	4	850	111	34.00	2	4	27
L E Plunkett	13	18	2	394	68	24.62	0	2	9
S A Patterson	17	18	8	147	40	14.70	0	0	2
R J Sidebottom	15	17	0	195	48	11.47	0	0	4
Also played									
J E Root	2	3	0	467	236	155.66	2	0	3
K S Williamson	5	9	1	403	97	50.37	0	5	4
R M Pyrah	5	3	1	70	55	35.00	0	1	5
A J Hodd	9	9	2	217	68*	31.00	0	1	17/1
T T Bresnan	4	5	1	66	38	16.50	0	0	1
J A Brooks	12	14	7	100	33*	14.28	0	0	6
Azeem Rafiq	3	5	0	58	28	11.60	0	0	0
J J Sayers	6	9	1	83	25*	10.37	0	0	4
J A Leaning	1	1	0	0	0	0.00	0	0	0
M A Ashraf	2	0	0	0	—	—	0	0	0

BOWLING

(Qualification 10 wickets)

Player	Overs	Mdns	Runs	Wkts	Avge	Best	5wI	10wM
R J Sidebottom	385.1	107	1012	53	19.09	4-27	0	0
S A Patterson	435.5	130	1197	51	23.47	5-43	1	0
J A Brooks	261.2	55	908	37	24.54	5-40	1	0
T T Bresnan	130.2	31	393	16	24.56	4-41	0	0
L E Plunkett	278.4	49	1065	42	25.35	6-33	2	0
A U Rashid	359.5	39	1358	29	46.82	5-78	1	0
Also bowled								
M A Ashraf	38.3	13	119	4	29.75	3-60	0	0
A Lyth	36	4	155	4	38.75	2-15	0	0
Azeem Rafiq	40	9	141	3	47.00	1-17	0	0
K S Williamson	65.4	13	247	4	61.75	2-44	0	0
P A Jaques	6	0	75	1	75.00	1-75	0	0
R M Pyrah	77	19	244	2	122.00	1-45	0	0
G S Ballance	14	0	98	0	—	0-10	0	0
J E Root	9	4	14	0	—	0-4	0	0
A W Gale	9	0	94	0	—	0-94	0	0
J A Leaning	4	0	22	0	—	0-4	0	0
A Z Lees	1	0	14	0	—	0-14	0	0

Second Investec Test Match
England v. New Zealand

Played at Headingley, Leeds, on May 24, 25, 26, 27 and 28, 2013
England won by 247 runs at 3.39pm on the Fifth Day

Toss won by England

Close of play: First Day, no play; Second Day, England 337-7 (Prior 38*, Swann 21*); Third Day, England 116-1 (Cook 88*, Trott 11*); Fourth Day, New Zealand 158-6 (McCullum 9*, Southee 4*)

First Innings	ENGLAND	Second innings	
* A N Cook, c Brownlie b Bracewell	34	c Southee b Williamson	130
N R D Compton, c Brownlie b Southee	1	c Rutherford b Williamson	7
I J L Trott, c McCullum b Wagner	28	c McCullum b Wagner	76
I R Bell, c McCullum b Williamson	30	c Guptill b Williamson	6
J E Root, c McCullum b Boult	104	c Guptill b Wagner	28
J M Bairstow, c McCullum b Boult	64	not out	26
§ M J Prior, c Taylor b Southee	39	not out	4
S C J Broad, c McCullum b Boult	0		
G P Swann, not out	26		
S T Finn, b Boult	0		
J M Anderson, c and b Boult	0		
Extras b 9, lb 7, w 5, nb 1	22	Extras b 8, lb 1, w 1	10
Total	354	Total (5 wkts dec)	287

FoW: 1st: 1-11 (Compton), 2-67 (Trott), 3-67 (Cook), 4-146 (Bell), 5-270 (Root), 6-279 (Bairstow), 7-286 (Broad), 8-345 (Prior), 9-354 (Finn), 10-354 (Anderson)
2nd: 1-72 (Compton), 2-206 (Cook), 3-214 (Bell), 4-249 (Trott), 5-268 (Root)

	O	M	R	W		O	M	R	W
Boult	22	4	57	5	Boult	2	1	2	0
Southee	26	6	76	2	Southee	15	4	51	0
Wagner	23	4	73	1	Wagner	17	3	67	2
Bracewell	19	3	83	1	Williamson	24	4	68	3
Williamson	9	0	49	1	Bracewell	13	3	49	0
					Guptill	5	0	41	0

First Innings	NEW ZEALAND	Second innings	
P G Fulton, c and b Finn	28	c Bell b Broad	5
H D Rutherford, c Bell b Finn	27	c Root b Swann	42
K S Williamson, lbw b Swann	13	lbw b Swann	3
L R P L Taylor, b Finn	6	b Swann	70
D G Brownlie, b Swann	1	c Bell b Finn	25
M J Guptill, b Swann	1	c Trott b Swann	3
* § B B McCullum, c Prior b Broad	20	c and b Broad	1
T G Southee, lbw b Broad	19	c Trott b Swann	38
D A J Bracewell, c Bell b Swann	4	c Bell b Swann	19
N Wagner, b Anderson	27	not out	0
T A Boult, not out	24	c Prior b Anderson	0
Extras lb 5, w 1	6	Extras b 2, lb 11, w 1	14
Total	174	Total	220

FoW: 1st: 1-55 (Fulton), 2-62 (Rutherford), 3-72 (Taylor), 4-79 (Brownlie), 5-81 (Guptill), 6-82 (Williamson), 7-119 (Southee), 8-122 (Bracewell), 9-122 (McCullum), 10-174 (Wagner)
2nd: 1-21 (Fulton), 2-40 (Williamson), 3-65 (Rutherford), 4-144 (Brownlie), 5-153 (Guptill), 6-154 (Taylor), 7-162 (McCullum), 8-218 (Southee), 9-220 (Bracewell), 10-220 (Boult)

	O	M	R	W		O	M	R	W
Anderson	7.4	2	34	1	Anderson	11.3	4	28	1
Broad	15	2	57	2	Broad	11	3	26	2
Finn	12	3	36	3	Swann	32	12	90	6
Swann	9	1	42	4	Finn	19	5	62	1
					Root	3	2	1	0

Man of the Match: G P Swann

Umpires: S J Davis and M Erasmus   Scorers: J T Potter and H D Galley
Third Umpire: Aleem Dar   Fourth Umpire: D J Millns   Referee: D C Boon

YORKSHIRE BANK 40
HIGHLIGHTS OF 2013

Totals of 250 and over (4)

266-6	v. Unicorns at Leeds (won)
261-8	v. Somerset at Taunton (lost)
258-9	v. Leicestershire at Scarborough (lost)
257	v. Glamorgan at Colwyn Bay (lost)

Match aggregates of 450 and over (8)

545	Somerset (338-5) defeated Yorkshire (207) by 131 runs at Leeds
542	Glamorgan (285-7) defeated Yorkshire (257) by 28 runs at Colwyn Bay
523	Yorkshire (261-8) lost to Somerset (262-7) by 3 wickets at Taunton
518	Yorkshire (258-9) lost to Leicestershire (260-7) by 3 wickets at Scarborough
500	Yorkshire (266-6) defeated Unicorns (234) by 32 runs at Leeds
483	Yorkshire (240-6) lost to Gloucestershire (243-5) by 5 wickets at Leeds
473	Yorkshire (236-8) lost to Middlesex (237-4) by 6 wickets at Radlett
460	Yorkshire (228-7) lost to Leicestershire (232-7) by 3 wickets at Leicester

Century Partnerships (3)

For the 3rd wicket (3)

134	A Z Lees and G S Ballance	v. Unicorns at Leeds
118	A Z Lees and A Lyth	v. Somerset at Taunton
100	D M Hodgson and A Lyth	v. Glamorgan at Leeds

Century (1)

G S Ballance (1)

139	v. Unicorns at Leeds

4 wickets in an innings (2)

J A Leaning (1)

5 for 22	v. Unicorns at Leeds

R M Pyrah (1)

4 for 43	v. Glamorgan at Colwyn Bay

3 catches in an innings (4)

A J Hodd (1)

3	v. Leicestershire at Scarborough

D M Hodgson (1)

3	v. Unicorns at Leeds

J A Leaning (1)

3	v. Somerset at Taunton

O E Robinson (1)

3	v. Glamorgan at Leeds

Debuts (9)

List A cricket: B O Coad, M D Fisher, R Gibson, O E Robinson, W M H Rhodes and J A Tattersall

For Yorkshire: A J Hodd, L E Plunkett and K S Williamson

Yorkshire Bank 40 Matches Played by Yorkshire in 2013

WINNERS
NOTTINGHAMSHIRE, who defeated Glamorgan by 87 runs

PREVIOUS WINNERS		*Yorkshire's Position*
2010	**Warwickshire**	1st Group B
2011	**Surrey**	6th Group A
2012	Hampshire	5th Group C

NATIONAL LEAGUE

1999	**Lancashire**	5th Div 1
2000	**Gloucestershire**	2nd Div 1
2001	**Kent**	6th Div 1
2002	**Glamorgan**	4th Div 1
2003	**Surrey**	8th Div 1
2004	**Glamorgan**	4th Div 2
2005	**Essex**	8th Div 2
2006	**Essex**	9th Div 2
2007	**Worcestershire**	6th Div 2
2008	**Sussex**	2nd Div2
2009	**Sussex**	7th Div1

SUNDAY LEAGUE

PREVIOUS WINNERS		*Yorkshire's Position*	PREVIOUS WINNERS		*Yorkshire's Position*
1969	**Lancashire**	8th	1984	**Essex**	=13th
1970	**Lancashire**	14th	1985	**Essex**	6th
1971	**Worcestershire**	15th	1986	**Hampshire**	8th
1972	**Kent**	4th	1987	**Worcestershire**	=13th
1973	**Kent**	2nd	1988	**Worcestershire**	8th
1974	**Leicestershire**	=6th	1989	**Lancashire**	11th
1975	**Hampshire**	=5th	1990	**Derbyshire**	6th
1976	**Kent**	15th	1991	**Nottinghamshire**	7th
1977	**Leicestershire**	=13th	1992	**Middlesex**	15th
1978	**Hampshire**	7th	1993	**Glamorgan**	9th
1979	**Somerset**	=4th	1994	**Warwickshire**	5th
1980	**Warwickshire**	=14th	1995	**Kent**	12th
1981	**Essex**	=7th	1996	**Surrey**	3rd
1982	**Sussex**	16th	1997	**Warwickshire**	10th
1983	**Yorkshire**	1st	1998	**Lancashire**	9th

Match-By-Match Reports	**DAVE CALDWELL**
Scorecards	**JOHN POTTER**
Pictures	**SIMON WILKINSON**
	VAUGHN RIDLEY
	ALEX WHITEHEAD
	SWpix.com

Yorkshire Bank 40 — Group C
Glamorgan v. Yorkshire

Played at Rhos-on-Sea Cricket Club, Colwyn Bay, on May 5, 2013
Glamorgan won by 28 runs

Toss won by Glamorgan   Glamorgan 2 points, Yorkshire 0 points

GLAMORGAN

W D Bragg, b Pyrah		50
§ M A Wallace, b Patterson		10
C B Cooke, c and b Patterson		58
* M J North, c and b Pyrah		68
J Allenby, c Root b Rhodes		14
M W Goodwin, c Rhodes b Pyrah		45
G G Wagg, lbw b Pyrah		3
W T Owen, not out		11
D A Cosker, not out		7
M G Hogan		
M T Reed	Did not bat	
Extras b 1, lb 10, w 4, nb 4		19
Total (7 wkts, 40 overs)		285

FoW:-1-49 (Wallace), 2-105 (Bragg), 3-151 (Cooke), 4-190 (Allenby), 5-245 (North)
6-267 (Goodwin), 7-267 (Wagg)

	O	M	R	W
Wardlaw	5	0	41	0
Patterson	8	0	48	2
Root	2	0	18	0
Ashraf	8	0	58	0
Rashid	4	0	33	0
Pyrah	8	1	43	4
Rhodes	5	0	33	1

YORKSHIRE

* A W Gale, lbw b Cosker		65
P A Jaques, b Wagg		0
J E Root, c Cooke b Wagg		0
G S Ballance, st Wallace b Cosker		50
§ J M Bairstow, c Owen b Hogan		53
R M Pyrah, c sub (B J Wright) b Cosker		9
A U Rashid, not out		42
W M H Rhodes, b Owen		18
S A Patterson, c Cooke b Hogan		5
I Wardlaw, c Allenby b Owen		2
M A Ashraf, lbw b Hogan		0
Extras b 4, lb 3, w 4, nb 2		13
Total (38.2 overs)		257

FoW:-1-1 (Jaques), 2-1 (Root), 3-93 (Ballance), 4-159 (Gale), 5-181 (Pyrah), 6-186
(Bairstow), 7-222 (Rhodes) 8-235 (Patterson), 9-255 (Wardlaw), 10-257 (Ashraf)

	O	M	R	W
Wagg	7	0	59	2
Hogan	7.2	1	29	3
Reed	6	0	41	0
Allenby	6	0	30	0
Owen	6	0	55	2
Cosker	6	0	36	3

Umpires: R T Robinson and M J Saggers   Scorers: J T Potter and A K Hignell

Glamorgan v. Yorkshire

Run tide drowns the Vikings

OWZTHAT? Yorkshire's Richard Pyrah celebrates his fourth wicket as Graham Wagg is lbw

A much changed Vikings gave a debut to Will Rhodes, 17, who had impressed for the Seconds at Northop Hall earlier that week.

There were also starts for Ashraf and Wardlaw as Yorkshire opted to rest some of their front-line bowling resources.

Glamorgan chose to bat, and were soon making hay while the sun shone. Patterson, Ashraf, Root and Rashid all struggled to contain the top order, and 49 were scored before Wallace was bowled trying to cut Patterson.

Bragg and Cooke took up the mantle, and runs continued to flow as Yorkshire's fielding became more ragged. It was only when Pyrah was introduced that a modicum of control was obtained, his first over bringing the wicket of Bragg, who played round a straight ball, for a finely constructed 50. The Dragons' Australian skipper, North, continued the good work, but Patterson took Cooke neatly off his own bowling for 58. The run rate never abated, despite an encouraging debut from Rhodes, whose five overs cost 33 runs and a first wicket of Allenby, caught at long-on by Root. Pyrah was pick of the attack with 4-43 from his eight overs, including a return catch to send back top-scorer North for 68.

Faced with Glamorgan's 285-7, the strong-looking Vikings needed a positive start: they lost two wickets in Wagg's first over without a run on the board. Jaques was bowled playing an indeterminate shot, and Root skied a mistimed pull. Gale and Ballance started to open their shoulders, and the score had reached 93 when Ballance was neatly stumped off Cosker's first ball for 50. Skipper Gale brought up his half-century in 55 balls before perishing on the sweep for 65. Bairstow was hitting the ball all over the park; his 50 duly arrived, but he mistimed to wide mid-on, and Yorkshire's hopes departed with him. A breezy 18 from Rhodes and an unbeaten 42 from Rashid took Yorkshire to within 29 of the target.

Yorkshire Bank 40 — Group C
Yorkshire v. Somerset

Played at Headingley, Leeds, on May 11, 2013
Somerset won by 131 runs

Toss won by Yorkshire   Somerset 2 points, Yorkshire 0 points

SOMERSET

* M E Trescothick, run out (Sidebottom)	37
P D Trego, b Moin Ashraf	58
A V Suppiah, c Lyth b Sidebottom	4
A N Petersen, c Hodd b Rhodes	42
J C Hildreth, not out	96
§ J C Buttler, c Rhodes b Sidebottom	89
L Gregory, not out	1
A C Thomas	
M T C Waller	
C A J Meschede Did not bat	
S P Kirby	
Extras lb 4, w 5, nb 2	11
Total (5 wkts, 40 overs)	338

FoW: 1-96 (Trescothick), 2-99 (Trego), 3-114 (Suppiah), 4-181 (Petersen), 5-310 (Buttler)

	O	M	R	W
Sidebottom	8	0	77	2
Patterson	8	0	62	0
Pyrah	5	0	40	0
Ashraf	8	0	80	1
Rashid	7	0	48	0
Rhodes	4	0	27	1

YORKSHIRE

* A W Gale, b Kirby	28
R M Pyrah, c Waller b Trego	6
P A Jaques, c Buttler b Thomas	16
G S Ballance, c Buttler b Thomas	60
A Lyth, c Petersen b Thomas	39
A U Rashid, c and b Thomas	0
§ A J Hodd, lbw b Kirby	15
W M H Rhodes, c Trescothick b Meschede	5
R J Sidebottom, run out (sub J Overton/Buttler)	10
S A Patterson, c Gregory b Meschede	12
M A Ashraf, not out	0
Extras lb 1, w 11, nb 4	16
Total (30 overs)	207

FoW:- 1-10 (Pyrah), 2-42 (Gale), 3-64 (Jaques), 4-134 (Lyth), 5-135 (Rashid), 6-167 (Hodd), 7-179 (Ballance), 8-192 (Sidebottom), 9-202 (Rhodes), 10-207 (Patterson)

	O	M	R	W
Trego	4	0	25	1
Kirby	6	0	49	2
Thomas	6	0	41	4
Meschede	6	0	37	2
Waller	3	0	26	0
Gregory	5	0	28	0

TV Man of the Match: J C Buttler

Umpires: S J O'Shaughnessy and G Sharp   Scorers: J T Potter and G A Stickley
Third Umpire: M J D Bodenham

Yorkshire put to the sword

Yorkshire found themselves on the receiving end of a 131-run thrashing after putting their opponents in.

Trescothick and Trego cut loose from the off, putting on 96 runs in the first 10 overs.

The Somerset captain had a life on 15 as Ballance spilled a difficult chance at slip, but

GARY BALLANCE: Cuts hard on the way to his top-score run-a-ball 60

at 96 Trescothick was run out unluckily at the non-striker's end while backing up, having made 37 from 27 balls. Trego fell three balls later, bowled by the erratic Ashraf for a 33-ball 58, and Suppiah soon followed, taken by Lyth at lip off Sidebottom for four. The Yorkshire tails were up...but never again in this match.

Petersen joined Hildreth in a 13-over partnership of 67 before Rhodes had Petersen smartly pouched by Hodd standing up to the stumps, and Buttler proved his credentials in tandem with Hildreth as a stand of 129 in 14 overs blew the Vikings away. Hildreth came agonisingly close to a century, but he lost the strike in the final over, finishing on 96 from 84 balls. Buttler fell in the last-but-one over for 89 from a mere 51 balls.

Somerset's 338-5 was the highest total conceded at Headingley by Yorkshire, and their fourth largest in all List A fixtures. The bowlers toiled, but were left with some astonishing figures: Ashraf conceded 80 in his eight overs, with Sidebottom not far behind at 77 and Patterson 62. Somerset struck an astonishing 31 fours and 10 sixes, and Yorkshire's chances at the half-way stage seemed remote.

The mountain to climb looked even higher with the early departure of Pyrah, and after an early escape Gale was bowled by former Yorkshire paceman Kirby for 28. Jaques was caught behind at 64, but a tidy enough stand of 70 between Lyth and Ballance briefly offered some respite. Two wickets in two balls for Thomas accounted for Lyth, 39, and Rashid, and from then on it was simply a matter of how severe the beating would be. Ballance went on to a near run-a-ball 60, but Yorkshire still subsided meekly to 207 all out with 10 overs left.

Yorkshire Bank 40 — Group C
Unicorns v. Yorkshire

Played at Queen's Park, Chesterfield, on May 19, 2013
Yorkshire won by 5 wickets

Toss won by Unicorns   Yorkshire 2 points, Unicorns 0 points

UNICORNS

T J Lancefield, c Hodd b Patterson	....	15
§ T J New, b Patterson	....	6
M P O'Shea, c Ballance b Pyrah	....	26
G T Park, b Pyrah	....	13
S L Elstone, c Gale b Rashid	....	16
* K A Parsons, run out (Lyth/Hodd)	....	28
V Tripathi, b Rashid	....	0
R G Querl, b Sidebottom	....	23
A J Norman, not out	....	38
W W Lee, c Patterson b Pyrah	....	6
L E Beaven, not out	....	0
Extras b 9, lb 2, w 5, nb 2	....	18
Total (9 wkts, 40 overs)	....	189

FoW:-1-21 (New), 2-22 (Lancefield), 3-64 (Park), 4-65 (O'Shea), 5-103 (Elstone)
6-103 (Tripathi), 7-118 (Parsons), 8-155 (Querl), 9-179 (Lee)

	O	M	R	W
Patterson	8	0	35	2
Sidebottom	8	0	37	1
Plunkett	8	0	45	0
Rashid	8	0	27	2
Pyrah	8	0	34	3

YORKSHIRE

* A W Gale, lbw b Lee	....	8
R M Pyrah, b Lee	....	6
P A Jaques, c Parsons b Norman	....	25
G S Ballance, b Beaven	....	44
A Lyth, not out	....	58
A U Rashid, c O'Shea b Beaven	....	32
§ A J Hodd, not out	....	11
L E Plunkett		
R J Sidebottom	Did not bat	
W M H Rhodes		
S A Patterson		
Extras b 1, lb 1, w 5	....	7
Total (5 wkts, 38.5 overs)	....	191

FoW:-1-16 (Pyrah), 2-24 (Gale), 3-80 (Jaques), 4-88 (Ballance), 5-143 (Rashid)

	O	M	R	W
Querl	8	0	40	0
Lee	5	0	31	2
O'Shea	8	0	21	0
Norman	6.5	0	39	1
Beaven	8	1	29	2
Tripathi	3	0	29	0

Umpires: N G B Cook and R K Illingworth   Scorers: J T Potter and K B O'Connell

Livewire Lyth the saviour

ADAM LYTH: Smashed his way to Vikings' first points

First points at last in this campaign...but the Vikings were made to work incredibly hard.

Only an unbeaten half-century from Lyth, assisted by an in-form Rashid, saved Yorkshire from a potentially perilous position at 88-4 in the 22nd over chasing a combative Unicorns total of 189.

Unicorns opted to bat, but struggled initially as Patterson removed both openers in the seventh over after a circumspect 22 runs had been compiled. O'Shea and Park took the total to 64 before Pyrah dismissed both in the same over.

Rashid, who bowled beautifully, claimed two wickets in two balls as Unicorns slipped to 103-6, but Parsons added a patient 28 until he was run out by livewire Lyth. It was Norman who propelled the total to a competitive level, finishing unbeaten on 38 from 26 balls. Rashid was the pick of Yorkshire's attack with 2-27, and Pyrah also bowled admirably to claim 3-34.

The experiment with Pyrah opening the innings as pinch-hitter again failed as he was bowled by Lee for six. Gale fell in the bowler's next over, trapped in front for a painstaking eight runs, and Yorkshire needed a period of consolidation. A stand of 56 between Jaques and Ballance threatened to take the game away from the Unicorns, but the curse of the two quick wickets struck again: Jaques was caught behind for 25 from 39 balls, and Ballance went eight runs later for 44 in 58 balls, just as he looked to be settled for the duration.

Rashid and Lyth circumspectly added a further 55 runs before Rashid was caught for 32. Hodd made a positive start until Lyth, who up to that point had struggled, assumed control. With only 24 from his previous 46 deliveries, Lyth smashed 34 from his next 11 balls to take the Vikings into harbour with seven balls remaining.

Yorkshire Bank 40 — Group C
Middlesex v. Yorkshire

Played at Radlett Cricket Club on May 27, 2013
Middlesex won by 6 wickets

Toss won by Yorkshire   Middlesex 2 points, Yorkshire 0 points

YORKSHIRE

* A W Gale, c Morgan b Roland-Jones	....	11
R M Pyrah, c Denly b Roland-Jones	....	6
P A Jaques, c Morgan b Harris	....	81
G S Ballance, c Stirling b Berg	....	40
A Lyth, c Rossington b Harris	....	14
A U Rashid, not out	....	46
§ A J Hodd, b Roland-Jones	....	21
T T Bresnan, c Stirling b Harris	....	0
W M H Rhodes, c Dexter b Roland-Jones	....	10
I D Wardlaw, not out	....	0
M A Ashraf	Did not bat	
Extras lb 3, w 4		7
Total (8 wkts, 40 overs)	....	236

FoW: 1-12 (Gale), 2-18 (Pyrah), 3-103 (Ballance), 4-153 (Lyth), 5-154 (Jaques)
6-206 (Hodd), 7-207 (Bresnan), 8-233 (Rhodes)

	O	M	R	W
Roland-Jones	8	1	44	4
Rayner	8	0	39	0
Harris	8	0	54	3
Stirling	3	0	16	0
Murtagh	4	0	27	0
Berg	4	0	29	1
Dexter	5	0	24	0

MIDDLESEX

P R Stirling, b Wardlaw	....	0
D J Malan, c Hodd b Bresnan	....	96
J L Denly, b Pyrah	....	38
E J G Morgan, lbw b Rashid	....	0
§ A M Rossington, not out	....	79
* N J Dexter, not out	....	15
G K Berg		
O P Rayner		
J A R Harris	Did not bat	
T S Roland-Jones		
T J Murtagh		
Extras lb 6, w 1, nb 2		9
Total (4 wkts, 35.4 overs)	....	237

FoW: 1-0 (Stirling), 2-65 (Denly), 3-66 (Morgan), 4-201 (Malan)

	O	M	R	W
Wardlaw	7	0	39	1
Bresnan	7	0	45	1
Ashraf	3.4	0	22	0
Pyrah	6	0	42	1
Rashid	8	0	49	1
Lyth	2	0	16	0
Rhodes	2	0	18	0

Umpires: R J Bailey and S A Garratt   Scorers: M S Fryer and D K Shelley

Yorkshire's sniff snuffed out

PHIL JAQUES: Gave hope with his excellent 81

Yorkshire opted for first use on winning the toss in front of a sun-basking capacity Bank Holiday crowd, and were soon cursing the soft dismissals of Gale and Pyrah, both giving simple catches off the imposing Roland-Jones.

Ballance and Jaques made a cautious start, but then opened up, and the run rate began to creep over five an over.

Ballance struck the off-spin of Berg straight to mid-on to end a partnership of 85 and his own innings of 40 from 42 balls, and his dismissal put a serious dent in the Vikings' chances of a competitive total.

The onus was very much on Jaques to bat through, which, in company with the industrious Lyth looked feasible. They had added 50 when Lyth was caught at the wicket for 14, and Jaques met his downfall almost immediately, miscuing a leg-side shot to Morgan.

Jaques's excellent 81 from 86 deliveries with 10 boundaries had given Yorkshire hope, but despite a breezy unbeaten 46 from Rashid their total of 236 looked at least 30 short. Roland-Jones collected four wickets in two probing spells for the Panthers, pacemen Harris adding three scalps.

Yorkshire's bowlers got off to the perfect start: Wardlaw hit Stirling in the abdominal area first ball, and followed up with a yorker that tore out his off-stump. Malan, in tandem with Denly, counter-attacked, adding 50 in quick time, but at 65 Denly played all round a straight one from Pyrah, and Morgan was trapped in front attempting a reverse-sweep first ball to Rashid. Yorkshire sniffed a chance at 66-3, but Malan, strong on both sides of the wicket, took the game away with 96 from 88 balls with 10 boundaries, and by the time he was caught behind off Bresnan it was over. Rossington, who partnered Malan in a stand of 135, remained unbeaten on 79, his highest limited-overs contribution.

Yorkshire Bank 40 — Group C
Yorkshire v. Gloucestershire

Played at Headingley, Leeds, on June 2, 2013
Gloucestershire won by 5 wickets

Toss won by Yorkshire

Gloucestershire 2 points, Yorkshire 0 points

YORKSHIRE

* A W Gale, c Gidman b Payne		26
R M Pyrah, c Howell b McCarter		2
P A Jaques, b Gidman		70
G S Ballance, c Dent b Hammond		37
A Lyth, b Gidman		30
A U Rashid, not out		43
§ A J Hodd, c Klinger b Payne		4
W M H Rhodes, not out		19
I Wardlaw		
B O Coad	Did not bat	
M A Ashraf		
Extras lb 3, w 4, nb 2		9
Total (6 wkts, 40 overs)		240

FoW:-1-4 (Pyrah), 2-56 (Gale), 3-119 (Ballance), 4-164 (Lyth), 5-183 (Jaques) 6-188 (Hodd)

	O	M	R	W
Fuller	8	0	47	0
McCarter	6	0	32	1
Payne	8	0	49	2
Howell	7	0	32	0
Hammond	8	0	50	1
Gidman	3	0	27	2

GLOUCESTERSHIRE

H J H Marshall, c Wardlaw b Coad		44
* M Klinger, c Balance b Ashraf		96
§ G H Roderick, c Hodd b Wardlaw		63
A P R Gidman, b Pyrah		5
B A C Howell, c Coad b Pyrah		8
I A Cobain, not out		16
J K Fuller, not out		7
C D J Dent		
D A Payne	Did not bat	
G J McCarter		
M A H Hammond		
Extras lb 1, w 1, nb 2		4
Total (5 wkts, 38.1 overs)		243

FoW:-1-74 (Marshall), 2-193 (Roderick), 3-206 (Gidman), 4-216 (Howell), 5-226 (Klinger)

	O	M	R	W
Wardlaw	7	0	41	1
Lyth	1	0	11	0
Ashraf	5.1	0	39	1
Pyrah	7	0	48	2
Coad	8	0	42	1
Rashid	8	0	46	0
Rhodes	2	0	15	0

Umpires: N A Mallender and A G Wharf

Scorers: J T Potter and A J Bull

Vikings blood paceman Coad

A debut for Harrogate-born Ben Coad, 19, as Yorkshire continued to try out youth on a lovely, sunny Sunday at Headingley before a good crowd.

Yorkshire won the toss, elected to bat, and soon found themselves a wicket down, Pyrah playing a tame cover-drive straight to Howell off McCarter. Gale and Jaques took up the mantle, and the skipper was looking well set until he fetched Payne's slow bouncer from outside off-stump to Gidman at mid-wicket for 26.

Ballance and Jaques added 63 for the third wicket before Ballance slog-swept promising off-spinner Miles Hammond straight to deep-square-leg for 37. Lyth entered the fray, and looked in splendid touch as he reached 30 with a glorious off-drive before playing on next ball, the score having advanced to 164.

Jaques reached his half-century from 66 balls and the onus was again on him to take Yorkshire to 250-plus. On reaching 70 he was bowled trying a paddle-sweep off Gidman, his innings spanning 86 deliveries with seven boundaries.

Hodd was caught in the slips for four, so it was then up to Rashid to take charge. Despite some tight bowling he and the promising Rhodes added 50 in an unbro-

BEN COAD: His first senior wicket

ken stand of 45 balls, Rashid closing on 43 and Vikings reaching 240.

From the outset the visitors put themselves in pole position with the run-a-ball rate easily surpassed. The naturally attacking Marshall looked in fine fettle, the first 10 overs yielding 73 runs before he provided Coad with his first senior wicket, courtesy of a diving catch by Wardlaw at short-fine-leg. Klinger kept the runs ticking over with wicket-keeper Roderick: they took the total to 100 in 17 overs and the landmarks kept coming — Klinger's 50 from 57 balls, the 100 partnership in 98 balls and Roderick's half-century from 55 balls. The partnership of 119 was broken by Wardlaw, who had Roderick caught for a career-best 63. Pyrah cleaned up Gidman, and Howell and Klinger followed, the skipper for 96 in 98 deliveries, but Gloucester cruised home.

Coad's brisk medium-pace earned him 1-42. He looks a fine prospect.

Yorkshire Bank 40 — Group C
Yorkshire v. Leicestershire

Played at North Marine Road, Scarborough, on June 9, 2013
Leicestershire won by 3 wickets

Toss won by Yorkshire

Leicestershire 2 points, Yorkshire 0 points

YORKSHIRE

* A W Gale, c O'Brien b Naik		44
P A Jaques, b Taylor		19
A Lyth, c O'Brien b Naik		39
J J Sayers, c Taylor b Thakor		58
A U Rashid, b Taylor		15
§ A J Hodd, c and b Thakor		3
L E Plunkett, c Buck b Williams		53
W H M Rhodes, c O'Brien b Thakor		0
R Gibson, not out		4
M D Fisher, run out (O'Brien/Taylor)		10
B O Coad	Did not bat	
Extras lb 2, w 7, nb 4		13
Total (9 wkts, 40 overs)		258

FoW: 1-61 (Jaques), 2-82 (Gale), 3-147 (Lyth), 4-186 (Sayers), 5-187 (Rashid)
6-197 (Hodd), 7-197 (Rhodes), 8-244 (Plunkett), 9-258 Fisher)

	O	M	R	W
Williams	7	0	48	1
Buck	8	0	65	0
Taylor	8	1	40	2
Thakor	5	0	39	3
Naik	8	0	34	2
Cobb	4	0	30	0

LEICESTERSHIRE

* J J Cobb, c Lyth b Rashid		26
§ N J O'Brien, c Coad b Plunkett		5
G P Smith, c Hodd b Rhodes		58
E J H Eckersley, c Lyth b Rhodes		24
M A G Boyce, c Hodd b Plunkett		42
M A Thornely, c Hodd b Gibson		21
R M L Taylor, not out		48
S J Thakor, lbw b Fisher		0
J K H Naik, not out		22
N L Buck		
R E M Williams	Did not bat	
Extras b 1, lb 6, w 3, nb 4		14
Total (7 wkts, 39.1 overs)		260

FoW:-1-16 (O'Brien), 2-55 (Cobb), 3-117 (Smith), 4-124 (Eckersley), 5-184 (Boyce)
6-188 (Thornely), 7-189 (Thakor)

	O	M	R	W
Coad	7.1	1	69	0
Plunkett	8	1	47	2
Rashid	8	0	47	1
Fisher	7	0	40	1
Rhodes	6	0	26	2
Gibson	3	0	24	1

Umpires: J H Evans and J W Lloyds

Scorers: J T Potter and P J Rogers

Debut for the youngest of all

Matthew Fisher at 15 years and 212 days became the youngest player in a competitive county match as injury-ravaged Yorkshire went in with four teenage seam bowlers — and ran their opponents close in a high-scoring affair.

Fisher was joined by another debutant, Ryan Gibson, 17, the pair complementing Coad and Rhodes in an all-star Academy attack.

Yorkshire made a brisk start in front of a typically healthy Scarborough crowd, Gale and Jaques to 61 within 10 overs before Jaques was bowled by Taylor for 19.

Gale followed for 44 after looking in good touch, taken at the wicket aiming to cut Naik's spin.

MATTHEW FISHER: First blood and not yet 16

An excellent stand between Lyth and Sayers added 65 in 12 overs. Lyth fell in similar fashion to his skipper for 39, but Sayers continued to a faultless 58 from 63 deliveries before being taken on the boundary by Taylor. Plunkett added gusto to the final overs with a half-century from 24 balls, contributing all but a single to his partnership of 47 with Gibson. There were further cheers in the last over as Fisher opened his account with two thick edges to the third-man boundary off successive balls, and Vikings closed on a highly respectable 258-9.

Plunkett and Rashid took the first two Leicestershire wickets before the much anticipated introduction of Fisher at 56-2. The Sheriff Hutton Bridge seamer bowled with admirable control in his first four-over spell, conceding only 18 runs before Rhodes claimed two vital wickets in two overs — the dangerous Smith caught behind for 58 and Eckersley pouched comfortably in the deep by Lyth: 123-4 and Yorkshire's young chargers scenting victory. Plunkett dismissed Boyce, and Gibson added the scalp of Thornely, while Fisher trapped Thakor in front for a duck. The Foxes were in the mire at 189-7 with eight overs remaining.

The game took a decisive swing towards the visitors as Taylor and Naik counter-attacked, and there was to be no fairytale ending for Fisher and his young cohorts. With 14 needed in 12 balls nerves got the better of Fisher — a leg-side wide, a no-ball and a boundary coming in the last-but-one over. Naik and Taylor crossed the line with an unbeaten 71.

Yorkshire Bank 40 — Group C
Gloucestershire v. Yorkshire

Played at The County Ground, Bristol, on June 16, 2013
Gloucestershire won by 36 runs

Toss won by Yorkshire   Gloucestershire 2 points, Yorkshire 0 points

GLOUCESTERSHIRE

H J H Marshall, st Hodd b Rashid		27
* M Klinger, b Wardlaw		45
C D J Dent, c Pyrah b Plunkett		56
I A Cockbain, not out		46
A P R Gidman, c Gale b Coad		0
B A C Howell, b Wardlaw		32
J K Fuller, b Wardlaw		6
§ G H Roderick, not out		1
D A Payne		
M A H Hammond	Did not bat	
W R S Gidman		
Extras b 5, lb 8, w 1, nb 2		16
Total (6 wkts, 27 overs)		229

FoW: 1-52 (Marshall), 2-110 (Klinger), 3-159 (Dent), 4-165 (APR Gidman), 5-215 (Howell), 6-221 (Fuller)

	O	M	R	W
Plunkett	6	0	44	1
Wardlaw	4	0	44	3
Coad	5	0	34	1
Pyrah	5	0	38	0
Rashid	6	1	42	1
Rhodes	1	0	14	0

YORKSHIRE

* A W Gale, c Payne b W R S Gidman		2
A Lyth, c Roderick b Payne		27
D M Hodgson, st Roderick b Hammond		76
J J Sayers, c A P R Gidman b Howell		20
A U Rashid, c Dent b Hammond		5
R M Pyrah, c Howell b Payne		34
L E Plunkett, c Klinger b Payne		7
§ A J Hodd, c W R S Gidman b Fuller		2
W M H Rhodes, c Roderick b Payne		1
I Wardlaw, c Roderick b Fuller		8
B O Coad, not out		0
Extras b 1, lb 3, w 3, nb 4		11
Total (26.3 overs)		193

FoW: 1-8 (Gale), 2-68 (Lyth), 3-129 (Sayers), 4-138 (Hodgson), 5-145 (Rashid), 6-166 (Plunkett), 7-175 (Hodd), 8-177 (Rhodes), 9-185 (Pyrah), 10-193 (Wardlaw)

	O	M	R	W
W R S Gidman	5	0	33	1
Fuller	5.3	0	48	2
Payne	5	0	44	4
Howell	6	0	35	1
Hammond	5	0	29	2

Umpires: M J D Bodenham and J W Lloyds   Scorers: J T Potter and A J Bull

March of the Gladiators

DAN HODGSON: Valiant and swashbuckling 76

Yorkshire gave a spirited performance in a rain-shortened match against their second-placed opponents. The game was trimmed to 27 overs a side after a long delay.

The Vikings elected to field, and their relatively inexperienced attack was taught some severe lessons in one-day strokeplay.

Marshall and Klinger set off at *t20* pace, and rattled up 50 before Marshall charged Rashid in the seventh over and was stumped by the swift work of Hodd for 27.

Klinger showed his credentials, striking a lusty 45 from 30 balls, Coad taking the brunt of the Australian's savagery.

A trademark fast yorker from Wardlaw ripped out the skipper's middle-stump at 110 in the 14th over, but Dent and Cockbain continued Klinger's good work before Dent holed out on the leg-side to a full toss for a splendid 56.

Gidman fell early, but Cockbain powered his way through the rest of the innings to an unbeaten 46 in the Gladiators' total of 229-6. Wardlaw picked up three victims, but at a cost of 11 runs per over.

Much depended on Gale, but he left early, leaving Hodgson and Lyth to regroup: they combined in a fine partnership of 60 in six overs before Lyth, 27, pulled a short one from Payne high in the air to be brilliantly caught by wicket-keeper Roderick. Hodgson continued merrily on his way, bringing up his first List A 50 while adding 61 with Sayers, who then found the waiting hands of Gidman at short-third-man. Nine runs later at 138 Hodgson was lured down the track by young spinner Hammond, Roderick completing the formalities, to end his swashbuckling innings of 76 from 55 balls with nine fours and two sixes. A breezy 34 from Pyrah apart, Yorkshire lost wickets regularly in pursuit of the impossible.

Yorkshire Bank 40 — Group C
Yorkshire v. Middlesex

Played at Headingley, Leeds, on June 20, 2013
Yorkshire won by 17 runs D/L method

Toss won by Yorkshire   Yorkshire 2 points, Middlesex 0 points

MIDDLESEX

P R Stirling, b Wardlaw		32
D L Malan, c Hodd b Wardlaw		14
J L Denly, b Wardlaw		7
S D Robson, b Gibson		1
§ A M Rossington, c and b Lyth		42
* N J Dexter, c Rashid b Pyrah		22
G K Berg, b Pyrah		43
O P Rayner, not out		22
T S Roland-Jones, b Pyrah		13
T J Murtagh, not out		3
T G Helm	Did not bat	
Extras b 5, w 13		18
Total (8 wkts, 40 overs)		217

FoW: 1-42 (Stirling), 2-54 (Denly), 3-55 (Robson), 4-65 (Malan), 5-105 (Dexter)
6-166 (Rossington), 7-178 (Berg), 8-214 (Roland-Jones)

	O	M	R	W
Wardlaw	8	0	39	3
Fisher	7	0	45	0
Gibson	7	0	53	1
Rashid	8	0	36	0
Pyrah	8	0	33	3
Lyth	2	0	6	1

YORKSHIRE

* A W Gale, not out		34
A Lyth, not out		38
D M Hodgson		
G S Ballance		
J J Sayers		
A U Rashid		
R M Pyrah	Did not bat	
§ A J Hodd		
R Gibson		
M D Fisher		
I Wardlaw		
Extras b 4, lb 1, nb 4		9
Total (0 wkts, 17.2 overs)		81

D/L par score 64-0

	O	M	R	W
Murtagh	5	0	18	0
Roland-Jones	4	0	28	0
Berg	4.2	0	19	0
Rayner	4	1	11	0

Umpires: N A Mallender and S J O'Shaughnessy   Scorers: J T Potter and D K Shelley

First 2013 win over a county

This was the first Vikings victory over a county in the 2013 competition.

It was gained through disciplined bowling, an excellent opening partnership between Gale and Lyth and, most tellingly, the rain.

Yorkshire were able to bat for only 17.2 overs, and the 17-run win was calculated by Duckworth and Lewis.

Under threatening skies Yorkshire chose to field first, and were rewarded as Wardlaw steamed in to take three of the first four wickets to fall in an all-action

VICTORY IN VIEW: Vikings skipper Andrew Gale goes for the sweep

opening eight overs. Sterling opened for the Panthers in positive fashion, tucking in to Wardlaw and Fisher with zest until a Wardlaw yorker sent him back for a blistering 32 from 20 balls. Denly played on to the same bowler before Gibson's nip-backer took Robson's inside edge and cannoned into his stumps. Middlesex were soon four down as a nervy Malan's wild cut at Wardlaw allowed Hodd a simple catch behind.

Dexter and Rossington engineered a partnership of 40 to bring some solidity to the Panthers before Pyrah achieved the breakthrough, and a lower-order riposte from Rossington, 42, and Berg, 43, ensured a total of some respectability. Pyrah and Wardlaw were in good form with three wickets apiece, and Rashid impressed with a tight spell.

Set a target of under 5.5 an over, Vikings skipper Gale and opening partner Lyth set about their task with the minimum of fuss. They always looked within touching distance of the required rate, and as they progressed the shackles were visibly lifted. The gathering gloom brought the first spots of rain, and at 54-0 from 13 overs there was a 26-minute break. The pace picked up rapidly on the restart, and Yorkshire had reached 81-0 after 17.2 overs when the rain resumed and play was abandoned, leaving them comfortably ahead of the D/L requirement.

Yorkshire Bank 40 — Group C
Leicestershire v. Yorkshire

Played at Grace Road, Leicester, on August 11, 2013
Leicestershire won by 3 wickets

Toss won by Yorkshire   Leicestershire 2 points, Yorkshire 0 points

YORKSHIRE

* A W Gale, b Taylor	....	31
§ D M Hodgson, b Williams	....	8
A Z Lees, b Sykes	....	28
G S Ballance, c Smith b Taylor	....	56
A Lyth, c Taylor b Williams	....	36
Azeem Rafiq, b Cobb	....	18
L E Plunkett, b Thakor	....	4
R M Pyrah, not out	....	15
O E Robinson, not out	....	12
I Wardlaw		
M A Ashraf	Did not bat	
Extras b 4, lb 2, w 8, nb 6	....	20
Total (7 wkts, 40 overs)	....	228

FoW:-1-40 (Hodgson), 2-56 (Gale), 3-90 (Lees), 4-170 (Lyth), 5-173 (Ballance) 6-178 (Plunkett), 7-200 (Rafiq)

	O	M	R	W
Williams	8	0	35	2
Ireland	6	0	48	0
Taylor	8	0	37	2
Cobb	8	0	40	1
Sykes	4	0	26	1
Thornely	3	0	19	0
Thakor	3	0	17	1

LEICESTERSHIRE

* J J Cobb, c Plunkett b Azeem Rafiq	....	45
§ N J O'Brien, c Hodgson b Plunkett	....	5
G P Smith, b Plunkett	....	0
E J H Eckersley, c Plunkett b Ashraf	....	108
M A G Boyce, b Wardlaw	....	37
S J Thakor, c Hodgson b Ashraf	....	3
M A Thornely, c Lyth b Wardlaw	....	6
R M L Taylor, not out	....	12
A J Ireland, not out	....	6
J S Sykes		
R E M Williams	Did not bat	
Extras lb 5, w 1, nb 4	....	10
Total (7 wkts, 39.5 overs)	....	232

FoW:-1-21 (O'Brien), 2-21 (Smith), 3-55 (Cobb), 4-158 (Boyce), 5-168 (Thakor) 6-213 (Thornely), 7-217 (Eckersley)

	O	M	R	W
Ashraf	8	1	45	2
Wardlaw	7.5	0	43	2
Plunkett	8	1	47	2
Pyrah	7	1	27	0
Azeem Rafiq	4	0	36	1
Robinson	3	0	17	0
Lyth	2	0	12	0

Umpires: S J O'Shaughnessy and R T Robinson   Scorers: J T Potter and P J Rogers

Six fells Yorkshire at the wire

OLIVER ROBINSON: Young all-rounder blooded in nailbiter

The latest List A debutant was Yorkshire all-rounder Oliver Robinson, who had impressed for the Seconds in recent weeks.

Yet it was to be Eckersley's day as his maiden one-day century steered the Foxes to victory with one ball remaining.

Chasing 229 to win, Leicestershire lost O'Brien, caught at the wicket off an excellent Plunkett delivery for five, and in the same over Plunkett bowled the dangerous Smith for a duck.

At 21-2 Yorkshire were in control. The grip tightened as an explosive 45 from Cobb ended with off-spinner Rafiq luring the lusty opener into the waiting hands of Plunkett at mid-off.

From 55-3 in the 12th over Foxes seized control through a near faultless part-nership between Eckersley and Boyce. Eckersley went to his 50 from 62 balls before accelerating markedly, but Boyce dropped anchor as his partner gave Rafiq short shrift — despatching him for two maximums and a four in one over. The pair had added 103 in 16 overs when Wardlaw crashed through Boyce's defences.

Thakor fell 10 runs later, but Eckersley took it away from Vikings, 40 runs coming from the batting power-play and his century in 98 balls. Ashraf got his man in the 38th over, with Leicestershire needing 12, but only one more came in Ashraf's excellent over. Only six were scrambled in the 39th, leaving Wardlaw to restrict the Foxes to less than five: it came down to three from two balls before Taylor struck a six to settle it.

Yorkshire's inning was a stop-start affair with the usual mid-innings lull and clutter of wickets. Ballance top-scored with 56 in 60 balls as he featured in a fourth-wicket stand of 80 with Lyth. Only a late rally from Rafiq, Pyrah and Robinson took the score to a competitive level. At least Robinson reached double figures, and had his first three-over spell.

Yorkshire Bank 40 — Group C
Yorkshire v. Unicorns

Played at Headingley, Leeds, on August 13, 2013
Yorkshire won by 32 runs

Toss won by Unicorns   Yorkshire 2 points, Unicorns 0 points

YORKSHIRE

* A W Gale, c Lineker b Reed	....	6
§ D M Hodgson, c Parsons b Skidmore	....	9
A Z Lees, lbw b Park	....	63
G S Ballance, c Park b Beaven	....	139
A Lyth, b Park	....	14
J A Leaning, b Norman	....	1
L E Plunkett, not out	....	25
R M Pyrah, not out	....	4
O E Robinson		
B O Coad	Did not bat	
M A Ashraf		
Extras lb 2, w 1, nb 2	....	5
Total (6 wkts, 40 overs)	....	266

FoW: 1-10 (Gale), 2-16 (Hodgson), 3-150 (Lees), 4-182 (Lyth), 5-185 (Leaning)
6-261 (Ballance)

	O	M	R	W
Read	7	0	63	1
Skidmore	8	0	40	1
Poysden	4	0	26	0
Norman	8	0	53	1
Beaven	5	0	40	1
Park	8	0	42	2

UNICORNS

T J Lancefield, c Hodgson b Plunkett	....	39
M S Lineker, lbw b Leaning	....	107
M P O'Shea, c Robinson b Coad	....	7
G T Park, c Hodgson b Ashraf	....	6
§ P J Hill, c Coad b Plunkett	....	17
* K A Parsons, c Hodgson b Leaning	....	31
A J Norman, c Plunkett b Leaning	....	4
L E Beaven, b Leaning	....	8
D T Reed, c Ashraf b Leaning	....	2
C J Skidmore, not out	....	0
J E Poysden, b Ashraf	....	2
Extras lb 4, w 5, nb 2	....	11
Total (38.2 overs)	....	234

FoW: 1-77 (Lancefield), 2-116 (O'Shea), 3-147 (Park), 4-175 (Hill), 5-202 (Lineker)
6-221 (Parsons), 7-229 (Beaven), 8-232 (Norman), 9-232 (Reed), 10-234 (Poysden)

	O	M	R	W
Coad	6	0	48	1
Ashraf	7.2	0	36	2
Robinson	5	0	34	0
Lyth	2	0	12	0
Plunkett	8	1	38	2
Pyrah	6	0	40	0
Leaning	4	0	22	5

Umpires: N G C Cowley and P J Hartley   Scorers: J T Potter and K B O'Connell

Yorkshire v. Unicorns

Savage century for Ballance

JACK LEANING: Yorkshire's best analysis of the season with 5-22

Ballance gave the England selectors yet more food for thought as he prepared for Lions duty with a career-best 139 to help Vikings to a less than convincing win.

The hosts, who were asked to bat, soon lost Gale and Hodgson — the skipper taken at second slip to a circumspect prod, while his partner sent a thick edge to Parsons from another indeterminate stroke.

Yorkshire needed a rebuild at 16-2, and Lees and Ballance provided the perfect platform with 134 for the third wicket. Both reached their half-centuries in the same over at a shade over a run a ball. Lees was lbw trying a reverse-sweep for 63, closely followed by Lyth and Leaning as Yorkshire's customary mid-innings wobble took shape.

Ballance was in no mood for buckling as he strode to a near faultless century from 98 balls. Plunkett very much played second fiddle in a savage partnership that took the total from 185-5 in the 34th over to 261 before Ballance was caught on the long-on fence with two balls remaining for a 113-ball 139 with 15 fours and three sixes. Plunkett came in with an unbeaten 25 as Yorkshire posted their highest total this year.

The run chase was always going to be hard, but an opening stand of 77 between Lancefield and Lineker in 14 overs gave the nomadic visitors a whiff of victory. A wild swipe at Plunkett saw Lancefield caught behind for 39, but Lineker continued unruffled: he brought up his 50 in sumptuous fashion off 56 balls, and with 10 overs remaining despite the loss of three more wickets Unicorns needed 91.

Plunkett removed Hill, and Lineker's excellent innings ended on 107 from 105 balls as he swept Leaning's off-spin. Leaning cleaned up the tail to finish with Yorkshire's best analysis in 2013 of 5-22 from four overs as Yorkshire claimed only their third victory of the campaign.

Yorkshire Bank 40 — Group C
Somerset v. Yorkshire

Played at The County Ground, Taunton, on August 15, 2013
Somerset won by 3 wickets

Toss won by Somerset   Somerset 2 points, Yorkshire 0 points

YORKSHIRE

* A W Gale, c Overton b Dibble	....	17
§ D M Hodgson, c Overton b Thomas	....	14
A Z Lees, b Thomas	....	62
A Lyth, c Thomas b Waller	....	58
J A Leaning, c Waller b Dibble	....	60
Azeem Rafiq, c Trego b Thomas	....	12
R Gibson, b Dibble	....	6
R M Pyrah, c Buttler b Dibble	....	1
I Wardlaw, not out	....	17
B O Coad, not out	....	1
M A Ashraf	Did not bat	
Extras lb 5, w 4, nb 4	....	13
Total (8 wkts, 40 overs)	....	261

FoW: 1-28 (Gale), 2-39 (Hodgson), 3-157 (Lees), 4-164 (Lyth), 5-207 (Rafiq), 6-214 (Gibson), 7-216 (Pyrah), 8-248 (Leaning)

	O	M	R	W
Dibble	7	0	52	4
Trego	7	0	40	0
Thomas	8	0	49	3
Meschede	8	0	35	0
Waller	7	0	52	1
Petersen	1	0	9	0
Overton	2	0	19	0

SOMERSET

* M E Trescothick, c Lees b Wardlaw	....	10
C Kieswetter, c Leaning b Gibson	....	40
P D Trego, not out	....	140
A N Petersen, c Leaning b Pyrah	....	51
§ J C Buttler, b Pyrah	....	0
J C Hildreth, c Leaning b Wardlaw	....	11
C A J Meschede, c Lyth b Ashraf	....	0
A C Thomas, b Wardlaw	....	0
A Dibble, not out	....	0
J Overton		
M T C Waller	Did not bat	
Extras b 4, lb 4, w 2	....	10
Total (7 wkts, 39.1 overs)	....	262

FoW: 1-10 (Trescothick), 2-113 (Kieswetter), 3-209 (Petersen), 4-209 (Buttler), 5-237 (Hildreth), 6-253 (Meschede), 7-258 (Thomas)

	O	M	R	W
Wardlaw	7	0	55	3
Ashraf	8	0	48	1
Pyrah	8	1	50	2
Lyth	4	0	29	0
Coad	4.1	0	30	0
Gibson	4	0	21	1
Leaning	4	0	21	0

Umpires: R J Bailey and P Willey   Scorers: J T Potter and G A Stickley

One more defeat at the wire

IAIN WARDLAW: Three-wicket haul

Yorkshire produced another spirited but ultimately fruitless performance in a typically high-scoring affair at The County Ground.

Somerset won the toss, chose to field and after a positive start the Vikings were two wickets down in the seventh over.

Gale and Hodgson were dismissed by Dibble and Thomas, but Lees and Lyth seized the initiative with a stand of 118 in 20 overs, allowing a platform for late-innings fireworks.

Both completed half-centuries at close to a run a ball, but with 157 on the board in the 27th over Lees received a nigh on unplayable yorker from the impressive Thomas, and so Lightcliffe's finest graduate departed for 62 in 66 balls. As is often the case in Yorkshire's *YB40* campaign another wicket fell swiftly: Lyth had made 58 from 60 balls when he picked out Thomas at long-on. Leaning produced a gem of an innings before falling to a full ball from Dibble. His 60 from 49 balls showed maturity and authority beyond his years.

In reply to Yorkshire's 261-8 Somerset saw skipper Trescothick throw his wicket away with a poor shot off Wardlaw to mid-off. The powerful combination of Trego and Kieswetter combined effortlessly to add 103 in 14 overs to wrest the game from Yorkshire. Gibson claimed the prize scalp of Kieswetter, taken by Leaning at mid-off for 40, but Trego charged along with Petersen for company. With the match seemingly heading for an inevitable home win Petersen, 51, was sent back by Pyrah at 209. Pyrah bowled Buttler first ball, and all eyes were on Trego.

Wickets fell in the 37th, 38th and 39th overs, but Trego, who by this point had sailed past his century, stood firm and led his side to victory with five balls remaining and three wickets in hand. Trego's 140 not out came from 103 balls, with 88 in boundaries.

Yorkshire Bank 40 — Group C
Yorkshire v. Glamorgan

Played at Headingley, Leeds, on August 26, 2013
Glamorgan won by 4 wickets

Toss won by Yorkshire

Glamorgan 2 points, Yorkshire 0 points

YORKSHIRE

J A Tattersall, b Hogan	0
§ D M Hodgson, c Cosker b Wagg	90
A Z Lees, run out (Salter)	2
K S Williamson, c Jones b Allenby	45
A Lyth, b Hogan	44
J A Leaning, not out	24
O E Robinson, not out	4
M A Ashraf	
* R M Pyrah Did not bat	
B O Coad	
I Wardlaw	
Extras b 1, lb 1, w 4	6
Total (5 wkts, 40 overs)	215

FoW: 1-3 (Tattersall), 2-7 (Lees), 3-107 (Williamson), 4-162 (Hodgson), 5-208 (Lyth)

	O	M	R	W
Hogan	8	0	43	2
Allenby	7	1	23	1
Jones	2	0	14	0
Cosker	8	0	48	0
Salter	8	0	34	0
Wagg	7	0	51	1

GLAMORGAN

G P Rees, c Robinson b Wardlaw	3
§ M A Wallace, c Robinson b Ashraf	7
C B Cooke, c Robinson b Leaning	84
J Allenby, b Williamson	40
* M J North, b Ashraf	25
M W Goodwin, not out	22
G G Wagg, c Wardlaw b Ashraf	31
A G Salter, not out	1
S P Jones	
D A Cosker Did not bat	
M G Hogan	
Extras lb 1, w 2	3
Total (6 wkts, 38.5 overs)	216

FoW: 1-8 (Rees), 2-33 (Wallace), 3-113 (Allenby), 4-160 (Cooke), 5-174 (North), 6-210 (Wagg)

	O	M	R	W
Wardlaw	6.5	1	31	1
Ashraf	7	0	38	3
Coad	5	0	21	0
Pyrah	7	0	51	0
Williamson	8	0	42	1
Robinson	2	0	15	0
Leaning	3	0	17	1

Umpires: T E Jesty and P Willey

Scorers: J T Potter and A K Hignell

Yorkshire v. Glamorgan

Dragons devour the Vikings

DAN HODGSON: Caught out 10 runs short of his century

Yet another debut was handed to an up-and-coming Yorkshire Colt as Jonathan Tattersall had his first limited-overs outing.

Asked to open the batting with Hodgson, he was bowled by Hogan's second legitimate delivery for a duck after the bowler had started with three wides.

Lees was soon back in the shed after an ill-judged single saw him short of his ground, and New Zealand import Williamson arrived at the crease after a scoreless County Championship debut for Yorkshire.

He displayed good technique and seemed odds-on for a sizeable score until he drove uppishly to be caught for 45 from 69 balls to end the third-wicket stand of exactly 100.

Meanwhile, Hodgson had reached his 50 in 63 balls. He was joined by Lyth, and they enjoyed an excellent partnership of 55 before Hodgson got out on 90 slashing into the grateful hands of Cosker. Hogan bowled Lyth for a sprightly 44, but a breezy unbeaten 24 from Leaning took Yorkshire to 214.

A fine new-ball spell from Ashraf and Wardlaw gave Yorkshire some hope. Openers Wallace and Rees offered identical catches to deep-square-leg Robinson, but from 33-2 Glamorgan grabbed a vital foothold as Cooke and Allenby profited from some good fortune. Their 50 stand came with a huge six by Allenby from Williamson's off-spin, but when Allenby tried to repeat the feat at 113 Williamson rearranged the furniture to end his innings of 40 in 44 balls. North joined Cooke, and the game started to drift away from Yorkshire — not helped by Leaning dropping a caught-and-bowled chance when Cooke was on 77. Cooke fell for 84 off Leaning, Robinson holding his third catch, and North was bowled at 174, but Wagg's 31 off 17 balls brought Dragons the spoils.

Yorkshire Bank 40

FINAL TABLES 2013

GROUP A

		P	W	L	T	NR/A	PTS	NRR
1	Nottinghamshire Outlaws (B4) *	12	9	3	0	0	18.00	0.457
2	Northamptonshire Steelbacks (C6)	12	8	3	0	1	17.00	0.392
3	Sussex Sharks (C1)	12	6	4	0	2	14.00	0.464
4	Kent Spitfires (C3)	12	6	6	0	0	12.00	0.229
5	Worcestershire Royals (A7)	12	5	7	0	0	10.00	0.249
6	Netherlands (A4)	12	2	7	0	3	7.00	-1.157
7	Warwickshire Bears (C2)	12	2	8	0	2	6.00	-0.929

GROUP B

		P	W	L	T	NR/A	PTS	NRR
1	Hampshire Royals (B1) *	12	9	3	0	0	18.00	0.734
2	Essex Eagles (A5)	12	8	4	0	0	16.00	0.972
3	Lancashire Lightning (A1)	12	7	4	0	1	15.00	-0.023
4	Durham Dynamos (B5) * *	12	7	4	0	1	14.75	0.657
5	Surrey (B2)	12	4	6	0	2	10.00	-0.524
6	Derbyshire Falcons (C4)	12	3	6	0	3	9.00	0.250
7	Scotland (B7)	12	0	11	0	1	1.00	-1.940

GROUP C

		P	W	L	T	NR/A	PTS	NRR
1	Somerset (B3) *	12	8	3	0	1	17.00	1.006
2	Glamorgan (B6) *	12	8	3	0	1	17.00	0.576
3	Middlesex Panthers (A2)	12	7	4	0	1	15.00	0.315
4	Gloucestershire (A3)	12	7	4	0	1	15.00	0.163
5	Leicestershire Foxes (A6)	12	5	7	0	0	10.00	-0.353
6	**Yorkshire Vikings (C5)**	**12**	**3**	**9**	**0**	**0**	**6.00**	**-0.468**
7	Unicorns (C7)	12	1	9	0	2	4.00	-1.196

* Qualified for Semi-Finals

* * Deducted 0.25 points for breach of salary cap in 2012

(2012 group positions in brackets)

YORKSHIRE AVERAGES 2013

YORKSHIRE BANK 40

Played 12   Won 3   Lost 9

BATTING AND FIELDING
(Qualification 4 completed innings)

Player	M.	I.	N.O.	Runs	H.S.	Avge	100s	50s	ct/st
G S Ballance	8	7	0	426	139	60.85	1	3	2
A U Rashid	8	7	3	183	46*	45.75	0	0	1
A Lyth	11	11	2	397	58*	44.11	0	2	6
D M Hodgson	6	5	0	197	90	39.40	0	2	5/0
A Z Lees	4	4	0	155	63	38.75	0	2	1
P A Jaques	6	6	0	211	81	35.16	0	2	0
A W Gale	11	11	1	272	65	27.20	0	1	2
R M Pyrah	11	9	2	83	34	11.85	0	0	2
A J Hodd	7	6	1	56	21	11.20	0	0	8/1
W M H Rhodes	7	6	1	53	19*	10.60	0	0	2
Also played									
J M Bairstow	1	1	0	53	53	53.00	0	1	0/0
K S Williamson	1	1	0	45	45	45.00	0	0	0
J A Leaning	3	3	1	85	60	42.50	0	1	3
J J Sayers	3	2	0	78	58	39.00	0	1	0
L E Plunkett	5	4	1	89	53	29.66	0	1	3
Azeem Rafiq	2	2	0	30	18	15.00	0	0	0
I Wardlaw	8	4	2	27	17*	13.50	0	0	2
R J Sidebottom	2	1	0	10	10	10.00	0	0	0
M D Fisher	2	1	0	10	10	10.00	0	0	0
R Gibson	3	2	1	10	6	10.00	0	0	0
S A Patterson	3	2	0	17	12	8.50	0	0	2
M A Ashraf	8	2	1	0	0*	0.00	0	0	1
T T Bresnan	1	1	0	0	0	0.00	0	0	0
J E Root	1	1	0	0	0	0.00	0	0	1
J A Tattersall	1	1	0	0	0	0.00	0	0	0
O E Robinson	3	2	2	16	12*	—	0	0	4
B O Coad	6	2	2	1	1*	—	0	0	3

BOWLING
(Qualification 4 wickets)

Player	Overs	Mdns	Runs	Wkts	Avge	Best	4wI	RPO
J A Leaning	11	0	60	6	10.00	5-22	1	5.45
I Wardlaw	52.4	1	333	14	23.78	3-39	1	6.32
R M Pyrah	75	3	446	15	29.73	4-43	1	5.94
L E Plunkett	38	3	221	7	31.57	2-38	0	5.81
W M H Rhodes	20	0	133	4	33.25	2-26	0	6.65
S A Patterson	24	0	145	4	36.25	2-35	0	6.04
M A Ashraf	55.1	1	366	10	36.60	3-38	0	6.63
A U Rashid	57	1	328	5	65.60	2-27	0	5.75
Also bowled								
R Gibson	14	0	98	3	32.66	1-21	0	7.00
Azeem Rafiq	4	0	36	1	36.00	1-36	0	9.00
R J Sidebottom	16	0	114	3	38.00	2-77	0	7.12
K S Williamson	8	0	42	1	42.00	1-42	0	5.25
T T Bresnan	7	0	45	1	45.00	1-45	0	6.42
B O Coad	35.2	1	244	3	81.33	1-34	0	6.90
M D Fisher	14	0	85	1	85.00	1-40	0	6.07
A Lyth	13	0	86	1	86.00	1-6	0	6.61
O E Robinson	10	0	66	0	—	0-17	0	6.60
J E Root	2	0	18	0	—	0-18	0	9.00

Tourist Match — List A
Yorkshire v. Bangladesh A

Played at Headingley, Leeds, on August 9, 2013

Yorkshire won by 7 runs

Toss won by Yorkshire

YORKSHIRE

* A W Gale, c Anamul b Al Amin	4
§ D M Hodgson, b Robiul	5
A Z Lees, st Anamul b Sunny	39
A Lyth, c Anamul b Sunny	45
J A Leaning, st Anamul b Mominul	18
R Gibson, lbw b Farhad	0
Azeem Rafiq, b Mominul	5
R M Pyrah, lbw b Sunny	7
L E Plunkett, not out	47
I Wardlaw, c Anamul b Robiul	18
M A Ashraf, run out (Raqibul/Farhad)	0
Extras lb 2, w 8	10
Total (47.4 overs)	198

FoW: 1-9 (Hodgson), 2-11 (Gale), 3-99 (Lees), 4-104 (Lyth), 5-105 (Gibson)
6-122 (Leaning), 7-126 (Rafiq), 8-148 (Pyrah), 9-197 (Wardlaw), 10-198 (Ashraf)

	O	M	R	W
Robiul Islam	8	0	35	2
Al Amin Hossain	7	0	33	1
Farhad Reza	6.4	0	32	1
Sohag Gazi	10	0	49	0
Elias Sunny	10	1	25	3
Mominul Haque	6	0	22	2

BANGLADESH A

§ Anamul Haque, b Azeem Rafiq	69
Shamsur Rahman, lbw b Wardlaw	4
* Jahural Islam, run out (Lees/Hodgson)	11
Mominul Haque, c Gibson b Azeem Rafiq	31
Marshall Ayub, b Gibson	1
Raqibul Hasan, b Plunkett	24
Farhad Reza, st Hodgson b Azeem Rafiq	22
Sohag Gazi, c Ashraf b Azeem Rafiq	4
Elias Sunny, lbw b Azeem Rafiq	2
Robiul Islam, lbw b Wardlaw	19
Al Amin Hossain, not out	0
Extras w 3, nb 1	4
Total (44.1 overs)	191

FoW: 1-17 (Shamsur), 2-42 (Jahural), 3-116 (Mominul), 4-119 (Marshall), 5-119 (Anamul)
6-147 (Farhad), 7-153 (Sohag), 8-163 (Sunny), 9-191 (Robiul), 10-191 (Raqibul)

	O	M	R	W
Ashraf	7	0	38	0
Wardlaw	5	0	27	2
Pyrah	7	0	35	0
Plunkett	7.1	0	28	1
Leaning	2	0	16	0
Azeem Rafiq	10	2	30	5
Gibson	6	2	17	1

Umpires: M A Eggleston and S C Gale   Scorers: J T Potter and H Clayton

First NatWest Series One-Day International
England v. Australia

At Headingley, Leeds, on September 6, 2013
Match abandoned without a ball bowled

Umpires: Aleem Dar and R K Illingworth   Scorers: J T Potter and H Clayton
Third Umpire: S Ravi   Fourth Umpire: R J Bailey   Match Referee: J J Crowe

Finch and Dawson boost

Yorkshire showed their determination to succeed in the 2014 season by making two significant signings in February to their playing and coaching staff.

They gained the services of one of cricket's most spectacular and hard-hitting batsmen with the signing of 27-year-old Victoria-born Aaron James Finch, whose blistering 156 for Australia against England at the Ageas Bowl, Southampton, last year, was the highest International Twenty20 score ever recorded. His innings also included a world record 14 sixes. Although Finch misses the start of the Yorkshire season he will be available for all competitions upon his arrival.

Just before Yorkshire broke the news on Finch they announced that their former off-spinner, Richard Dawson, was returning to Headingley as Second Eleven coach in place of Paul Farbrace, who is now in charge of the Sri Lanka national side.

Dawson, 33, played in 72 First-Class matches for Yorkshire between 2001 and 2006, and enjoyed a significant role in helping them to clinch the Championship title in 2001 for the first time in 33 years. He also played in seven Tests for England.

After leaving Yorkshire, Dawson had spells with Northamptonshire and Gloucestershire, where he has spent the last four years as the county's specialist spin bowling and one-day cricket coach.

FRIENDS LIFE t20
HIGHLIGHTS OF 2013

Totals of 150 and over (1)

   152-6   v. Lancashire at Leeds (tied)

Match aggregates of 350 and over (1)

   354   Durham (215-6) defeated Yorkshire (139-8) by 76 runs at Chester-le-Street

4 wickets in an innings (2)

   J A Brooks (2)

     5 for 21 v. Leicestershire at Leeds
     4 for 21 v. Derbyshire at Leeds

Debuts (6)

t20 cricket: J A Leaning, A Z Lees and W M H Rhodes
For Yorkshire: J A Brooks, A J Hodd and L E Plunkett

Tour De Yorkshire

Yorkshire County Cricket Supporters' Association found a novel way of marking the Club's 150th anniversary last year — and boosting their own funds in the process.

On June 18, after weeks of careful planning, six sponsored cars left Headingley with the task of visiting and photographing each of the 20 grounds upon which Yorkshire have played first-class cricket during their long and eventful history.

Between them the drivers visited grounds or former grounds in Hull (2), Savile Town, Dewsbury; Thrum Hall, Halifax; Fartown, Huddersfield; St George's Road, Harrogate; Middlesbrough (3); Wiggington Road, York; North Marine Road, Scarborough; College Grove, Wakefield; Bramall Lane and Abbeydale Park, Sheffield; Horsforth, Holbeck, Hunslet, and Park Avenue and Great Horton Road, Bradford.

The event was a huge success, and the Association brought out a splendid book, *150 Not Out, Yorkshire's Home Grounds 1863-2013* which proved to be a big seller.

The vehicles were kindly supplied by Evans Halshaw, Clifton Moor Gate, York; Evans Halshaw, Roseville Road, Leeds; Holmfirth Garage, Huddersfield Road, Holmfirth; JCT600, Europa Link, Sheffield, and JCT Mazda, Ring Road, Leeds.

Friends Life t20 in 2013

Northamptonshire, who beat Surrey by 102 runs *(D/L method)*

PREVIOUS WINNERS

2003 **Surrey,** who beat Warwickshire by 9 wickets
2004 **Leicestershire,** who beat Surrey by 7 wickets
2005 **Somerset,** who beat Lancashire by 7 wickets
2006 **Leicestershire,** who beat Nottinghamshire by 4 runs
2007 **Kent,** who beat Gloucestershire by 4 wickets
2008 **Middlesex,** who beat Kent by 3 run
2009 **Sussex,** who beat Somerset by 64 runs
2010 **Hampshire,** who beat Somerset by losing fewer wickets
    with the scores level
2011 **Leicestershire,** who beat Somerset by 18 runs
2012 **Hampshire,** who beat Yorkshire by 10 runs

NORTH GROUP

		P	W	L	T	NR/A	PTS	NRR
1	Nottinghamshire Outlaws (N 2) *	10	7	3	0	0	14.00	1.009
2	Lancashire Lightning (N 4) *	10	5	3	2	0	12.00	0.177
3	Durham Dynamos (N 3) * $$	10	6	4	0	0	11.75	0.317
4	Leicestershire Foxes (N 6)	10	4	5	1	0	9.00	0.417
5	Derbyshire Falcons (N 5)	10	4	6	0	0	8.00	-0.604
6	**Yorkshire Vikings (N 1)**	10	2	7	1	0	5.00	-1.223

SOUTH GROUP

		P	W	L	T	NR/A	PTS	NRR
1	Hampshire Royals (S 2) *	10	8	1	0	1	17.00	0.810
2	Surrey (S 6) *	10	7	3	0	0	14.00	0.915
3	Essex Eagles (S 3) *	10	5	4	0	1	11.00	-0.040
4	Middlesex Panthers (S 5)	10	5	5	0	0	10.00	-0.194
5	Kent Spitfires (S 4)	10	3	7	0	0	6.00	-0.941
6	Sussex Sharks (S 1)	10	1	9	0	0	2.00	-0.520

MIDLAND/WALES and WEST GROUP

		P	W	L	T	NR/A	PTS	NRR
1	Northamptonshire Steelbacks (M 6) *	10	7	3	0	0	14.00	0.329
2	Somerset (M 1) *	10	6	4	0	0	12.00	0.841
3	Glamorgan (M 5)	10	5	5	0	0	10.00	-0.168
4	Warwickshire Bears (M 4)	10	5	5	0	0	10.00	-0.410
5	Worcestershire Royals (M 3)	10	4	6	0	0	8.00	-0.327
6	Gloucestershire (M 2)	10	3	7	0	0	6.00	-0.245

* Qualified for the Quarter-Finals
$$ Deducted 0.25 points for breach of salary cap in 2012

(2012 group positions in brackets)

Match-By-Match Reports **Scorecards** **Pictures**	**DAVE CALDWELL** **JOHN POTTER** **SIMON WILKINSON** **VAUGHN RIDLEY** **ALEX WHITEHEAD** *SWpix.com*

Friends Life t20 — North Group
Yorkshire v. Derbyshire

Played at Headingley, Leeds, on June 28, 2013
Derbyshire won by 2 wickets

Toss won by Derbyshire

Derbyshire 2 points, Yorkshire 0 points

YORKSHIRE

* A W Gale, c Durston Morkel		5
A Lyth, c Poynton b Morkel		5
D M Hodgson, run out (Redfern)		17
§ J M Bairstow, c Groenewald b Footitt		12
G S Ballance, c Redfern b Footitt		44
A U Rashid, c Poynton b Footitt		4
R M Pyrah, b Wainwright		7
L E Plunkett, run out (Madsen)		2
Azeem Rafiq, not out		14
R J Sidebottom, not out		5
J A Brooks	Did not bat	
Extras lb 1, w 3		4
Total (8 wkts, 20 overs)		119

FoW: 1-5 (Gale), 2-26 (Lyth), 3-27 (Hodgson), 4-41 (Bairstow), 5-54 (Rashid) 6-82 (Pyrah), 7-85 (Plunkett), 8-105 (Ballance)

	O	M	R	W
Durston	4	0	19	0
Morkel	3	0	9	2
Groenewald	4	0	31	0
Footitt	3	0	22	3
Clare	1	0	5	0
Wainwright	4	0	22	1
Redfern	1	0	10	0

DERBYSHIRE

C F Hughes, b Brooks		36
W J Durston, c Rafiq b Pyrah		14
S Chanderpaul, c Bairstow b Pyrah		5
* W L Madsen, c Bairstow b Brooks		7
D J Redfern, c Rafiq b Brooks		4
J A Morkel, c Lyth b Azeem Rafiq		1
§ T Poynton, c Hodgson b Brooks		0
J L Clare, not out		35
D J Wainwright, lbw b Azeem Rafiq		7
T D Groenewald, not out		7
M H A Footitt	Did not bat	
Extras w 4		4
Total (8 wkts, 19.3 overs)		120

FoW: 1-40 (Durston), 2-56 (Chanderpaul), 3-62 (Hughes), 4-65 (Madsen), 5-69 (Redfern) 6-70 (Poynton), 7-70 (Morkel), 8-92 (Wainwright)

	O	M	R	W
Sidebottom	4	0	20	0
Brooks	4	0	21	4
Plunkett	3.3	0	32	0
Pyrah	4	1	18	2
Rashid	1	0	11	0
Azeem Rafiq	3	0	18	2

Man of the Match: J L Clare

Umpires: P J Hartley and M J Saggers

Scorers: J T Potter and J M Brown

Woeful batting costs Yorkshire

A woefully inadequate batting display proved to be the Vikings' downfall.

Despite a fine bowling and fielding effort a total of 119 was nigh on impossible to defend after Derbyshire had opted to bowl first under murky skies.

The Falcons were soon in pole position as Morkel tore into the top order, removing Gale and Lyth in the first three overs. 26-2, and one run later a breezy 17 in 12 balls from Hodgson ended when Redfern ran him out with a fine piece of work.

GARY BALLANCE: His 44 the only Yorkshire innings of note

Wickets continued to fall, and only a patient but none-too-fluent 44 from Ballance provided Yorkshire with a total of any substance. Derbyshire's bowling squeezed the life out of the batsmen, with Morkel's 2-9 in three overs outstanding.

Yorkshire seemed to turn the game back in their favour, restricting the Falcons to 70-7 inside 13 overs after Hughes and Durston had opened up with 40. Pyrah, as is often the case, provided the breakthrough, having Durston caught in the gully and Chanderpaul at the wicket. Brooks seized the initiative, forcing Hughes to play on for 36 and having Madsen caught behind. The headband warrior continued his good work in his next over with Redfern taken brilliantly by Rafiq in the gully and Poynton holing out in the deep, Brooks returning career-best figures of 4-21.

Rafiq added the wicket of Morkel, but a minor recovery was led by Clare and Wainwright until the off-spinner trapped Wainwright in front. Derbyshire were now 92-8 with the game hugely in the balance. Partnered by Groenewald, Clare finished unbeaten on 35 as the Falcons inched home with three balls remaining. The deciding factor was Plunkett's last-but-one over, which yielded 12 runs. The ninth-wicket pair added 28 to see their side home with three balls to spare in front of a tense Headingley crowd. Pyrah and Rafiq both impressed along with Brooks as Yorkshire were left cursing their poor batting.

Friends Life t20 — North Group
Yorkshire v. Durham

Played at North Marine Road, Scarborough, on June 30, 2013
Durham won by 4 wickets

Toss won by Durham   Durham 2 points, Yorkshire 0 points

YORKSHIRE

*A W Gale, b Pringle		34
A Lyth, b Pringle		21
D M Hodgson, c and b Collingwood		7
G S Ballance, b Smith		19
A U Rashid, c Pringle b Stokes		10
R M Pyrah, b Wood		7
L W Plunkett, run out (Richardson)		30
§ A J Hodd, not out		8
Azeem Rafiq, not out		4
R J Sidebottom		
J A Brooks	Did not bat	
Extras lb 5, w 1		6
Total (7 wkts, 20 overs)		146

FoW: 1-51 (Gale), 2-62 (Lyth), 3-68 (Hodgson), 4-94 (Ballance), 5-101 (Pyrah)
6-103 (Rashid), 7-142 (Plunkett)

	O	M	R	W
Smith	2	0	12	1
Rushworth	4	0	40	0
Stokes	4	0	32	1
Wood	3	0	20	1
Pringle	4	0	13	2
Collingwood	2	0	13	1
Borthwick	1	0	11	0

DURHAM

M D Stoneman, c Hodd b Brooks		3
§ P Mustard, c Rashid b Plunkett		59
S G Borthwick, c Hodgson b Brooks		12
W R Smith, c Brooks b Sidebottom		14
B A Stokes, st Hodd b Azeem Rafiq		0
G J Muchall, not out		44
R D Pringle, run out (Rashid/Hodd)		5
M J Richardson, not out		5
* P D Collingwood		
M A Wood	Did not bat	
C Rushworth		
Extras lb 2, w 3		5
Total (6 wkts, 19.5 overs)		147

FoW: 1-4 (Stoneman), 2-25 (Borthwick), 3-64 (Smith), 4-65 (Stokes), 5-110 (Mustard)
6-142 (Pringle)

	O	M	R	W
Brooks	4	1	13	2
Sidebottom	3.5	0	30	1
Plunkett	4	0	32	1
Pyrah	4	0	27	0
Azeem Rafiq	4	0	43	1

Man of the Match: G J Muchall

Umpires: N G B Cook and J H Evans   Scorers: J T Potter and B Hunt

Sorry Plunkett loses his radar

ANDY HODD: Enhanced his growing reputation with this fine dive to stop a wayward return

The Vikings were left to rue the last-but-one over from former Durham star Plunkett as Dynamos recovered from 110-5 with four overs left to snatch victory in front of the 4,500 seaside crowd.

Yorkshire had got off to a positive start with Gale and Lyth bringing up 50 in the seventh over, but as in the previous match the middle-order was found wanting and the Vikings slipped to 103-6.

Gale reached 34 from 25 deliveries with seven boundaries before he was bowled by Ryan Pringle, playing in his second *t20* match. Lyth fell in near-identical fashion fell for 21, again to Pringle, and when Hodgson sent a stinging return catch to Collingwood the hosts had slumped to 68-3 in the 10th over. Collingwood left the field with a damaged finger, and there was concern as to whether he would bat.

The pitch appeared slower than the standard North Marine Road surface, and it suited the Durham bowlers. Ballance, Pyrah and Rashid all struggled to time the ball, and boundaries became elusive. A total over 125 looked unlikely until Plunkett plundered an unbeaten 30 from 16 balls as Yorkshire managed 39 from the last three overs to reach 146.

Yorkshire were going to need an excellent bowling and fielding performance to defend that total, but Brooks proved the man for the occasion as he captured Stoneman early on and completed his four-over allocation for a miserly 13 runs. He added Borthwick, caught in the deep, to his bag as Dynamos struggled to power their way free of the shackles.

Smith fell in the 12th over to a great catch by Brooks off Sidebottom. 64-3. Stokes was stumped brilliantly by Hodd off a wide from the wayward Rafiq for a duck, but Mustard reached his half-century. "Colonel's" demise at 110 seemed to confirm a home win, but the experienced Muchall tore into Plunkett, and with 25 needed in two overs 16 came as the all-rounder's radar failed and leg-stump full-tosses and half-trackers became easy pickings. Muchall finished with 44 from 27 balls.

187

Friends Life t20 — North Group
Yorkshire v. Lancashire

Played at Headingley, Leeds, on July 5, 2013
Match tied

Toss won by Lancashire   Yorkshire 1 point, Lancashire 1 point

YORKSHIRE

* A W Gale, c Cross b Smith		18
P A Jaques, not out		66
D M Hodgson, c Katich b Parry		13
A U Rashid, lbw b Lilley		16
G S Ballance, c Brown b Croft		11
L E Plunkett, c Croft b Kabir Ali		12
R M Pyrah, run out (Cross)		4
§ A J Hodd, not out		4
Azeem Rafiq		
R J Sidebottom	Did not bat	
J A Brooks		
Extras b 3, lb 1, w 2, nb 2		8
Total (6 wkts, 20 overs)		152

FoW: 1-32 (Gale), 2-59 (Hodgson), 3-89 (Rashid), 4-108 (Ballance), 5-123 (Plunkett)
6-148 (Pyrah)

	O	M	R	W
Croft	2	0	15	1
Chapple	3	0	25	0
McClenaghan	3	0	26	0
Smith	2	0	13	1
Parry	4	0	21	1
Lilley	4	0	22	1
Kabir Ali	2	0	26	1

LANCASHIRE

S C Moore, c Ballance b Plunkett		12
T C Smith, c Plunkett b Pyrah		35
K R Brown, b Pyrah		25
S M Katich, b Pyrah		18
S J Croft, not out		42
§ G D Cross, b Plunkett		8
Kabir Ali, not out		8
A M Lilley		
* G Chapple	Did not bat	
S D Parry		
M J McClenaghan		
Extras b 1, lb 1, w 2		4
Total (5 wkts, 20 overs)		152

FoW: 1-46 (Moore), 2-48 (Smith), 3-92 (Katich), 4-97 (Brown), 5-118 (Cross)

	O	M	R	W
Sidebottom	4	0	30	0
Brooks	4	0	47	0
Plunkett	3	0	21	2
Pyrah	4	0	15	3
Azeem Rafiq	2	0	21	0
Rashid	3	0	16	0

Man of the Match: R M Pyrah

Umpires: R J Bailey and N L Bainton   Scorers: J T Potter and A West
Third Umpire: G Sharp

Yorkshire v. Lancashire
Tight bowlers tie up *Roses*

PHIL JAQUES: Unbeaten top-scorer

A full house on a glorious day saw Gale and Jaques run up 32 in the first four overs before Smith had the skipper chasing a wide one to feather a catch to wicket-keeper Cross.

Hodgson arrived in confident mood, and Vikings sailed past 50 in the seventh over. This platform floundered as Hodgson struck the ball high but not very far, and was pouched by Katich for 13. Huddersfield League all-rounder Aaron Lilley, making his Lancashire debut, accounted for Rashid with his tidy off-spin, and his four overs cost a miserly 22 runs. Ballance on 11 was caught in the deep from a big drive, but Jaques continued to his 50 at nearly a run a ball, with boundaries hard to come by. Croft dropped Plunkett over the boundary for six — but made no mistake two balls later: 123-5. Jaques remained unbeaten on 66 as 15 were plundered in the last over, Yorkshire closing on a respectable 152.

Three tight overs from Yorkshire's opening attack yielded 18 before Smith struck Brooks for 24 runs. Plunkett brought Vikings back into the game, Moore picking out the bucket-like hands of Ballance at mid-off. The game then turned as Smith, who had had made 35 from 20 balls, drilled Pyrah low to wide mid-off where Plunkett took a superb catch.

Yorkshire kept it tight as 85-2 at 10 overs dipped to 98-4 after 14. Rashid and Pyrah bowled beautifully in tandem, Pyrah claiming three wickets for 15 as the runs dried up. At 118-5 in 17.3 overs Plunkett bowled Cross with a deceptive, slow full-toss, the batsmen thinking that no-ball should have been called. While Croft was there the *Red Rose* could hope — and 14 came in the 19th over off Plunkett.

Lancashire needed 10 off the last over: the first ball was edged just wide of Hodd to the boundary, but Sidebottom's outstanding death bowling pegged them back. Last ball...three runs needed...Croft squeezed the yorker-length delivery to deep point and the batsmen scrambled two, leaving the match tied in breath-taking fashion.

Friends Life t20 — North Group
Yorkshire v. Leicestershire

Played at Headingley, Leeds, on July 9, 2013
Yorkshire won by 7 wickets

Toss won by Yorkshire   Yorkshire 2 points, Leicestershire 0 points

LEICESTERSHIRE

* J J Cobb, c Ballance b Brooks	....	17
G P Smith, c and b Brooks	....	0
J A Burns, c Plunkett b Brooks	....	4
Shakib al Hasan, c Sayers b Brooks	....	14
M A G Boyce, b Brooks	....	0
§ E J H Eckersley, b Plunkett	....	26
M A Thorneley, c Hodgson b Azeem Rafiq	....	1
R M L Taylor, b Rashid	....	16
A J Ireland, c Pyrah b Plunkett	....	23
J K H Naik, not out	....	6
M J Hoggard, not out	....	3
Extras w 1, nb 2		3
Total (9 wkts, 20 overs)	....	113

FoW: 1-1 (Smith), 2-19 (Cobb), 3-33 (Shakib), 4-33 (Boyce), 5-38 (Burns)
6-45 (Thorneley), 7-67 (Taylor), 8-104 (Ireland), 9-104 (Eckersley)

	O	M	R	W
Sidebottom	3	0	18	0
Brooks	4	0	21	5
Plunkett	4	0	20	2
Azeem Rafiq	4	0	20	1
Pyrah	2	0	10	0
Rashid	3	0	24	1

YORKSHIRE

P A Jaques, c Taylor b Ireland	....	9
J J Sayers, c Cobb b Naik	....	28
D M Hodgson, not out	....	52
A U Rashid, lbw b Naik	....	4
G S Ballance, not out	....	21
L E Plunkett		
R M Pyrah		
§ A J Hodd	Did not bat	
* Azeem Rafiq		
R J Sidebottom		
J A Brooks		
Extras w 3	....	3
Total (3 wkts, 16.5 overs)	....	117

FoW: 1-9 (Jaques), 2-50 (Sayers), 3-54 (Rashid)

	O	M	R	W
Hoggard	3	0	18	0
Ireland	2.5	0	28	1
Taylor	2	0	15	0
Shakib al Hasan	4	0	18	0
Naik	4	0	25	2
Cobb	1	0	13	0

Man of the Match: J A Brooks

Umpires: N L Bainton and D J Millns   Scorers: J T Potter and P J Rogers
Third Umpire: G D Lloyd

Paceman Brooks no argument

A game Yorkshire coach Jason Gillespie described as a "must win" began with the news that skipper Gale would miss at least two fixtures with a broken hand.

Brooks recorded his and Yorkshire's best *t20* bowling analysis, the effervescent pace bowler claiming 5-21 to help his side to their first victory of the 2013 campaign.

Tearing in from the Kirkstall Lane end, Brooks took a return catch to despatch Smith for a duck before a remarkable take on the run by Ballance accounted for Cobb: the ball was soaring high over his shoulder at deep extra-cover as Ballance set off in what seemed a forlorn hope.

DANCE OF TRIUMPH: Joe Sayers congratulates the headbanded Jack Brooks

Ballance dived to take a full-length one-handed catch to the delight of the home crowd, and from this point the Vikings seldom looked troubled. Brooks bagged three more wickets before his pace partner, Plunkett, got in on the act by bowling Eckersley. Plunkett, too, was bowling with zest — often in excess of 85mph. The Foxes had slumped to 45-6, and only a late surge led by Ireland, who crashed 23 from 15 balls with three huge sixes, took them passed 100. Leicestershire's total was their lowest against Yorkshire.

The Vikings' reply was positive, but swiftly hit problems as Jaques picked out cover from an Ireland long-hop and was on his way back for nine. Sayers, who curiously had been given the nod over Lyth, was in uncompromising mood — the highlight of his 23-ball 28 was a lovely six straight over the bowler's head.

Sayers holed out at extra-cover; Rashid departed soon afterwards, and Yorkshire's fragile batting looked shaky again. No such issues worried Hodgson, who went on to record his highest *t20* score, the wristy Academy graduate finishing unbeaten on 52 from 46 balls. Hodgson struck seven boundaries while showing an excellent range of shots, especially the sweep, which he played with real panache.

Ballance added the calming influence, also unbeaten as he contributed 21, and Yorkshire cruised over the line with 19 balls to spare.

Friends Life t20 — North Group
Durham v. Yorkshire

Played at Durham ICG, Chester-le-Street, on July 12, 2013
Durham won by 76 runs

Toss won by Yorkshire   Durham 2 points, Yorkshire 0 points

DURHAM

* M D Stoneman, c Brooks b Pyrah	....	12
§ P Mustard, b Brooks	....	91
S G Borthwick, c Sidebottom b Pyrah	....	35
B A Stokes, c Sayers b Sidebottom	....	23
G J Muchall, not out	....	27
G R Breese, c Sayers b Azeem Rafiq	....	12
W R Smith, run out (Balance/Plunkett)	....	6
R D Pringle, not out	....	0
M J Richardson		
M A Wood	Did not bat	
C Rushworth		
Extras b 3, lb 2, w 2, nb 2	....	9
Total (6 wkts, 20 overs)	....	215

FoW: 1-62 (Stoneman), 2-145 (Mustard), 3-151 (Borthwick), 4-171 (Stokes), 5-189 (Breese), 6-204 (Smith)

	O	M	R	W
Sidebottom	4	0	29	1
Brooks	3	0	45	1
Plunkett	4	0	43	0
Pyrah	4	0	37	2
Rashid	2	0	23	0
Azeem Rafiq	3	0	33	1

YORKSHIRE

P A Jaques, c Borthwick b Rushworth	....	2
J J Sayers, b Stokes	....	1
D M Hodgson, c Breese b Rushworth	....	2
§ A J Hodd, b Breese	....	11
G S Ballance, c Stoneman b Breese	....	68
A U Rashid, st Mustard b Pringle	....	11
L E Plunkett, c Richardson b Smith	....	9
R M Pyrah, c Stoneman b Smith	....	1
* Azeem Rafiq, not out	....	15
R J Sidebottom, not out	....	5
J A Brooks	Did not bat	
Extras b 4, lb 1, w 9	....	14
Total (8 wkts, 20 overs)	....	139

FoW: 1-9 (Jaques), 2-12 (Sayers), 3-22 (Hodgson), 4-51 (Hodd), 5-101 (Ballance), 6-110 (Rashid), 7-111 (Pyrah), 8-130 (Plunkett)

	O	M	R	W
Smith	4	0	25	2
Rushworth	4	0	13	2
Stokes	2	0	4	1
Breese	4	0	31	2
Pringle	4	0	29	1
Wood	2	0	32	0

Man of the Match: P Mustard

Umpires: S C Gale and J W Lloyds   Scorers: J T Potter and B Hunt

Mustard powers the Dynamos

Vikings found themselves on the receiving end of a serious lesson from their North Eastern counterparts, with Mustard the headmaster stroking a scintillating 91 from 52 balls.

The wicket-keeper's breathtaking scamper set a record as the highest individual score in this form of the game for his side.

He and Stoneman raced to 62 inside the power-play overs — a feat even more remarkable after only 18 runs had come from the first three overs.

Mustard smashed 27 in the fourth from Brooks, and although Stoneman was caught on the leg side off Pyrah for 12 it was very much the "Colonel" Mustard show from then on, with Borthwick, Stokes

GARY BALLANCE: Restored pride with his quickfire 68

and Muchall all playing second fiddle to the dashing left-hander. Plunkett was smacked off line in his next two spells — four successive boundaries for Muchall and 17 off the last over ruining his figures against his former employers. None of the bowlers came away with dignity intact, Brooks taking the brunt of Mustard's violence as his three overs cost 45 runs. The partnership of the innings came from Borthwick and Mustard, 83 runs from the middle overs giving the crowd real entertainment as Durham reached 215-6.

Yorkshire's reply soon hit the buffers with Jaques, Sayers and Hodgson all gone for 22 by the fourth over. The game looked played out, although Ballance hit a fine 68 in 39 balls to restore some pride. He was caught at extra-cover off Breese after at least ensuring that the visitors reached three figures. All of the Durham bowlers impressed, none more so than Rushworth, the burly seamer who showed accuracy with good pace and excellent variation in a wonderful 2-13 from his four overs.

193

Friends Life t20 — North Group
Derbyshire v. Yorkshire

Played at Queen's Park, Chesterfield, on July 14, 2013
Yorkshire won by 6 runs

Toss won by Derbyshire

Yorkshire 2 points, Derbyshire 0 points

YORKSHIRE

P A Jaques, b Redfern	22
J J Sayers, c Godleman b Morkel	11
D M Hodgson, c Durston b Morkel	31
G S Ballance, c Godleman b Morkel	28
§ A J Hodd, b Morkel	0
A U Rashid, c Groenewald b Turner	11
L E Plunkett, c Groenewald b Turner	15
R M Pyrah, b Turner	6
* Azeem Rafiq, not out	2
R J Sidebottom, c Hughes b Groenewald	3
J A Brooks	Did not bat
Extras b 1, lb 3, w 5, nb 4	13
Total (9 wkts, 20 overs)	142

FoW: 1-21 (Sayers), 2-70 (Jaques), 3-81 (Hodgson), 4-81 (Hodd), 5-114 (Ballance), 6-117 (Rashid), 7-136 (Pyrah), 8-137 (Plunkett), 9-142 (Sidebottom)

	O	M	R	W
Durston	3	0	17	0
Morkel	4	0	25	4
Redfern	2	0	12	1
Groenewald	4	0	34	1
Turner	4	0	21	3
Wainwright	2	0	16	0
Clare	1	0	13	0

DERBYSHIRE

C F Hughes, c Pyrah b Azeem Rafiq	21
W J Durston, retired hurt	8
* W L Madsen, run out (Jaques/Rafiq)	19
D J Redfern, c Pyrah b Azeem Rafiq	9
B A Godleman, c Jaques b Azeem Rafiq	8
J A Morkel, not out	51
§ T Poynton, c Ballance b Pyrah	15
J L Clare, not out	3
D J Wainwright	
T D Groenewald	Did not bat
M L Turner	
Extras w 2	2
Total (5 wkts, 20 overs)	136

FoW: 0-14 (Durston retired hurt), 1-49 (Madsen), 2-49 (Hughes), 3-64 (Redfern), 4-67 (Godleman), 5-102 (Poynton)

	O	M	R	W
Sidebottom	4	0	27	0
Brooks	1	0	7	0
Pyrah	4	0	24	1
Plunkett	3	0	35	0
Rashid	4	0	21	0
Azeem Rafiq	4	0	22	3

Man of the Match: J A Morkel

Umpires: R K Illingworth and D J Millns

Scorers: J T Potter and J M Brown

Plunkett finds radar in time

Three late wickets and a run-out by off-spinning all-rounder Rafiq helped Yorkshire home.

Jaques and Sayers put on 21 in the first four overs for the Vikings before Sayers pulled high and long to be taken with a fine diving catch by Godleman at deep backward-square-leg.

Hodgson and Jaques added 49 for the second wicket before Redfern bowled Jaques for 22. Hodgson made a fluent 31, but he picked out Durston at deep mid-off, and two balls later Hodd played round one.

Ballance and Rashid enjoyed a bright partnership until Ballance on 28 skied to deep mid-wicket to give Morkel his fourth victim, but from here Vikings lost wickets regularly, only 18 runs coming in the last four overs.

Misfortune swooped on the Falcons in the third over as Durston retired hurt. They progressed to 49 in the eighth over, but a huge mixup between Hughes and Madsen left the skipper 21 yards short.

Hughes drove Rafiq to extra-cover where Pyrah took a stunning diving catch, and Rafiq and Pyrah did it again as Redfern

AZEEM RAFIQ: Three key wickets and a run-out

mistimed his cut: 64-3 after 10 overs. Three runs later Godleman reverse-swept Rafiq to the diving Jaques, but Morkel and Poynton battled on with a stand of 35. Ballance caught Poynton superbly at long-off, and with three overs left Falcons needed 40. Plunkett and Sidebottom bowled two overs for eight runs, leaving 32 to get in six balls. Enter Morkel. Plunkett's first six deliveries including a wide yielded 25 as full toss followed full toss. Morkel hit the last-but-one out of the ground to bring up his half-century from 30 balls, and a six would tie the match: Plunkett's yorker-length delivery whistled past Morkel's outside edge.

Yorkshire v. Nottinghamshire

Played at Headingley, Leeds, on July 21, 2013
Nottinghamshire won by 25 runs

Toss won by Yorkshire   Nottinghamshire 2 points, Yorkshire 0 points

NOTTINGHAMSHIRE

M J Lumb, c Hodd b Sidebottom	6
A D Hales, b Plunkett	5
S R Patel, c Plunkett b Azeem Rafiq	46
J W A Taylor, c Rashid b Plunkett	8
* D J Hussey, not out	52
S J Mullaney, c Hodgson b Pyrah	3
§ C M W Read, c Hodgson b Azeem Rafiq	2
I G Butler, run out (Lyth/Rafiq)	18
G G White, run out (Ballance/Plunkett)	0
A Shahzad	
H F Gurney	Did not bat
Extras b 6, lb 3, w 4, nb 2	15
Total (8 wkts, 20 overs)	155

FoW: 1-7 (Lumb), 2-33 (Hales), 3-57 (Taylor), 4-99 (Patel), 5-105 (Mullaney)
6-110 (Read), 7-141 (Butler), 8-155 (White)

	O	M	R	W
Sidebottom	3	0	31	1
Rashid	3	0	22	0
Brooks	2	0	24	0
Plunkett	4	0	26	2
Pyrah	4	0	14	1
Azeem Rafiq	4	0	29	2

YORKSHIRE

A Lyth, c Patel b Gurney	8
J J Sayers, c Mullaney b Patel	38
D M Hodgson, st Read b White	32
G S Ballance, c White b Patel	18
§ A J Hodd, lbw b White	6
L E Plunkett, c Patel b Butler	12
R M Pyrah, not out	11
A U Rashid, not out	1
* Azeem Rafiq	
R J Sidebottom	Did not bat
J A Brooks	
Extras lb 3, w 1	4
Total (6 wkts, 20 overs)	130

FoW: 1-8 (Lyth), 2-75 (Sayers), 3-90 (Hodgson), 4-104 (Hodd), 5-104 (Ballance)
6-124 (Plunkett)

	O	M	R	W
Gurney	4	0	29	1
Shahzad	2	0	17	0
Butler	4	0	30	1
Patel	4	0	19	2
White	4	0	18	2
Hussey	1	0	8	0
Mullaney	1	0	6	0

Man of the Match: S R Patel

Umpires: S A Garratt and P Willey   Scorers: J T Potter and R Marshall

Outlaw arrows pierce batting

Yorkshire's dwindling hopes of a quarter-final spot were in tatters after a disappointing chase of a gettable 156.

With Gale rested after his return from injury Lyth was recalled, but was to fall early. Opening partner Sayers and No.3 Hodgson gave the hosts more than a whiff of victory with a 67-run partnership in 10 overs.

Momentum shifted to the Outlaws as Sayers found the safe hands of Mullaney at long-on off Patel for a well-crafted 38 from 30 deliveries.

The third wicket fell at 90 as White lured Hodgson from his crease, leaving Read to complete the formalities behind. Hodgson impressed again with his 32, but the need was for him to see the job through after the loss of Sayers.

As was so often the case in this 2013 tournament the boundaries dried up. The batting became more desperate with wickets falling regularly, including the prized scalp of Ballance, who was taken in spectacular fashion by White off Patel on the leg-side boundary for 18.

The run chase was effectively over,

DAN HODGSON: Gave side more than a whiff

Yorkshire finishing 25 runs adrift for the loss of six wickets.

Nottinghamshire had been inserted under leaden skies, Sidebottom gaining instant reward with the wicket of Lumb in the first over. Hales departing at 33 in the fifth, Plunkett producing a ripper to remove the England *T20* man's off-stump in unceremonious fashion. Danger man Taylor also departed cheaply before two superb innings from Patel and David Hussey took the Outlaws to a respectable total.

Patel struck the ball cleanly for a 37-ball 46, assisted in a more restrained fashion by his Australian teammate who contributed an unbeaten half century. Yorkshire had bowled and fielded well in equal measure but, alas, the batting again was to be the difference.

Friends Life t20 — North Group
Lancashire v. Yorkshire

Played at Old Trafford, Manchester, on July 24, 2013
Lancashire won by 8 wickets

Toss won by Yorkshire   Lancashire 2 points, Yorkshire 0 points

YORKSHIRE

A Lyth, c Prince b Smith		32
J J Sayers, c Kerrigan b Smith		3
§ D M Hodgson, c Kerrigan b McClenaghan		4
G S Ballance, c Croft b Lilley		28
J A Leaning, b Kerrigan		2
A U Rashid, run out (Smith/Kerrigan)		19
L E Plunkett, c Croft b McClenaghan		10
R M Pyrah, not out		20
* Azeem Rafiq, run out (Cross/Kabir Ali)		0
R J Sidebottom, not out		1
I Wardlaw Did not bat		
Extras lb 4, w 1		5
Total (8 wkts, 20 overs)		124

FoW: 1-15 (Sayers), 2-20 (Hodgson), 3-53 (Lyth), 4-57 (Leaning), 5-81 (Rashid)
6-96 (Ballance), 7-112 (Plunkett), 8-122 (Rafiq)

	O	M	R	W
Croft	2	0	13	0
Kabir Ali	4	0	23	0
McClenaghan	4	0	19	2
Smith	4	0	21	2
Lilley	2	0	22	1
Kerrigan	4	0	22	1

LANCASHIRE

S C Moore, not out		66
T C Smith, st Hodgson b Azeem Rafiq		42
A G Prince, c Lyth b Azeem Rafiq		0
K R Brown, not out		19
S M Katich		
* S J Croft		
§ G D Cross		
M J McClenaghan Did not bat		
A M Lilley		
S C Kerrigan		
Kabir Ali		
Extras		0
Total (2 wkts, 11 overs)		127

FoW: 1-88 (Smith), 2-88 (Prince)

	O	M	R	W
Sidebottom	2	0	15	0
Wardlaw	1	0	10	0
Pyrah	1	0	14	0
Rashid	3	0	39	0
Plunkett	1	0	17	0
Azeem Rafiq	2	0	14	2
Leaning	1	0	18	0

Man of the Match: T C Smith

Umpires: S C Gale and P J Hartley   Scorers: J T Potter and A West
Third Umpire: I Dawood

Vikings struck by Lightning

A 12,000-strong crowd roared the *Red Rose* hosts to a resounding victory which all but guaranteed them a place in the knockout stages.

The match very nearly failed to get under way because of a power cut which caused some floodlights to go out as well as lights in the dressing rooms. Step forward Jimmy Anderson — the electrician, not the England seam bowler — who sorted the problem shortly before the start of play.

The game was a formality: an almost second-string Yorkshire without Bairstow, Bresnan, Root, Jaques and Gale to name but a few were blown away with minimal fuss by a fiercely competitive Lightning.

Having won the toss, the Vikings' 124-8 was never going to be enough. They limped apologetically through the power-play overs to 20-2, and only a partnership of 33 from 27 balls between Lyth and Ballance offered any resistance as Lightning's out-cricket reached to new highs.

Lyth was dismissed trying a paddle over fine-leg for a top-score 32, while Ballance was superbly taken in the deep by a diving Croft for 28. From there the runs dried up.

Lancashire's reply was swift, brutal and calculated. Smith and Moore cracked on to 88 in just short of eight overs before Rafiq had Smith stumped by Hodgson for 42. The lusty left-hander's innings had

ADAM LYTH: Fought back with top-score 32

spanned a mere 22 balls, and contained three fours and three sixes. Prince fell two balls later, Lyth taking the catch expertly at cover, but Moore went on to an unbeaten 66 from 35 balls, and Brown finished with 19 not out. Lancashire were home with nine overs remaining, consigning arch-rivals Yorkshire to a humiliating eight-wicket defeat.

Friends Life t20 — North Group
Nottinghamshire v. Yorkshire

Played at Trent Bridge, Nottingham, on July 26, 2013
Nottinghamshire won by 6 wickets

Toss won by Yorkshire   Nottinghamshire 2 points, Yorkshire 0 points

YORKSHIRE

A Lyth, b Ball	23
A Z Lees, b Patel	1
§ D M Hodgson, c White b Patel	8
G S Ballance, c Patel b White	30
J A Leaning, run out (Hussey/Read)	4
W M H Rhodes, b Gurney	13
R M Pyrah, c Mullaney b Patel	42
L E Plunkett, not out	4
* Azeem Rafiq, not out	0
J A Brooks	
I Wardlaw	
Extras lb 4, w 3	7
Total (7 wkts, 20 overs)	132

FoW: 1-3 (Lees), 2-17 (Hodgson), 3-63 (Ballance), 4-66 (Lyth), 5-71 (Leaning)
6-108 (Rhodes), 7-131 (Pyrah)

	O	M	R	W
Gurney	4	0	27	1
Patel	4	0	17	3
Ball	4	0	30	1
Butler	4	0	37	0
White	4	0	17	1

NOTTINGHAMSHIRE

A D Hales, c Ballance b Azeem Rafiq	62
M J Lumb, c Pyrah b Lyth	6
S R Patel, c Pyrah b Brooks	2
* D J Hussey, b Plunkett	28
M H Wessels, not out	18
§ C M W Read, not out	9
S J Mullaney	
G G White	
I G Butler	Did not bat
J T Ball	
H F Gurney	
Extras lb 2, w 6	8
Total (4 wkts, 16.1 overs)	133

FoW: 1-14 (Lumb), 2-23 (Patel), 3-85 (Hales), 4-111 (Hussey)

	O	M	R	W
Lyth	2	0	16	1
Brooks	3	0	11	1
Wardlaw	1.1	0	22	0
Plunkett	3	0	25	1
Pyrah	3	0	25	0
Azeem Rafiq	4	0	32	1

Man of the Match: A D Hales

Umpires: T E Jesty and S J O'Shaughnessy   Scorers: J T Potter and R Marshall

Nottinghamshire v. Yorkshire

Hales rains winning blows

Outlaws booked a quarter-final berth with another emphatic win over Vikings.

Yorkshire won the toss and decided to bat, but *t20* debutant Lees left in the second over, bowled by Patel, and Hodgson was to fall victim to the same bowler.

Vikings were in the mire at 17-2 in the fourth over, but a stand between left-handers Ballance and Lyth added 46 before Patel neatly pouched Ballance in the deep off White for 30 at

RICHARD PYRAH: Only his lusty 42 gave Yorkshire a score of any worth

the halfway stage. As has been so often the case in the Vikings' campaign, two more wickets fell swiftly: Lyth played on to Ball for a painstaking 23, and Leaning run out by Hussey for four. *T20* debutant Rhodes reached 13 before left-arm seamer Gurney castled him, but only a lusty 42 from the dependable Pyrah ensured that Yorkshire would post a score of any worth — six fours and a six in his innings of 42 from 25 balls propelling the total to an unlikely 132-7.

The Outlaws ran straight into the buffers as the unlikely opening bowling pairing of Lyth and Brooks claimed a victim apiece, Patel and Lumb both gone with only 23 runs on the board in the fourth over. From this point on Hales took on the role of chief enforcer as the *t20* specialist smashed the ball to all parts. Wardlaw in particular was at the sharp end of vicious treatment, his seven balls costing 22 runs. Hales had amassed 62 of the 85 scored before he was taken in the deep by Ballance off Rafiq when eyeing up his third consecutive maximum. His innings spanning 38 balls had included four fours and five sixes.

The Outlaws lost Hussey for 28, but Read and Wessels calmly completed the task, remaining unbeaten as the hosts strolled over the line with 23 balls to spare. Brooks was the only Yorkshire bowler to impress with 1-11 from his three overs.

Friends Life t20 — North Group
Leicestershire v. Yorkshire

Played at Grace Road, Leicester, on July 28, 2013
Leicestershire won by 10 wickets

Toss won by Yorkshire

Leicestershire 2 points, Yorkshire 0 points

YORKSHIRE

A Lyth, c Taylor b Ireland	12
A Z Lees, run out (Eckersley/Cobb)	32
§ D M Hodgson, c Wells b Taylor	11
G S Ballance, b Cobb	2
J A Leaning, c Wells b Cobb	8
W M H Rhodes, b Cobb	0
R M Pyrah, b Shakib al Hasan	6
L E Plunkett, b Thakor	7
* Azeem Rafiq, c Wells b Taylor	12
I Wardlaw, not out	1
M A Ashraf, b Shakib al Hasan	4
Extras lb 6, w 4	10
Total (17.2 overs)	105

FoW: 1-23 (Lyth), 2-51 (Hodgson), 3-55 (Ballance), 4-67 (Lees), 5-68 (Rhodes) 6-75 (Pyrah), 7-77 (Leaning), 8-91 (Rafiq), 9-95 (Plunkett), 10-105 (Ashraf)

	O	M	R	W
Cobb	4	0	9	3
Ireland	3	0	15	1
Buck	2	0	19	0
Taylor	4	0	24	2
Shakib al Hasan	3.2	0	26	2
Thakor	1	0	6	1

LEICESTERSHIRE

* J J Cobb, not out		52
G P Smith, not out		39
E J H Eckersley		
Shakib al Hasan		
§ N J O'Brien		
T J Wells		
R M L Taylor	Did not bat	
S J Thakor		
M A Thornely		
A J Ireland		
N L Buck		
Extras lb 1, w 12, nb 2		15
Total (0 wkts, 12.1 overs)		106

	O	M	R	W
Plunkett	4	0	26	0
Wardlaw	2	0	14	0
Ashraf	2	0	28	0
Azeem Rafiq	1	0	15	0
Pyrah	2	0	8	0
Rhodes	1.1	0	14	0

Man of the Match: J J Cobb

Umpires: M R Benson and P Willey

Scorers: J T Potter and P J Rogers

Leicestershire v. Yorkshire

Lees stands above wreckage

ALEX LEES: Catastrophic mixup

Yorkshire's dismal *t20* campaign ended with the young side unceremoniously trounced by 10 wickets as just under eight overs remained.

Their 105 all out from 17.2 overs was as inept a batting display as we had seen all summer — with the notable exception of Lees, who contributed 32 from 32 deliveries with five pleasing fours.

The Vikings reached 23 without loss in the fourth over, but Lyth fell to Ireland for 12. Wickets then fell at an alarming rate as the Foxes' modest attack turned the screw on a visibly beaten side. Leicestershire skipper Cobb bowled his four overs for only nine runs, collecting three wickets, the hapless batsmen offering themselves in almost apologetic fashion. The innings was typified by the comical run-out of Lees in a catastrophic mixup with Leaning as they attempted a single off a wide. Yorkshire's final wicket fell to almost silence as the contest already appeared to be over at the half-way stage.

Cobb and Smith made light work of the Vikings attack, and only Pyrah offered any modicum of control, his two overs costing eight runs. Yorkshire were in charitable mood in the field as Cobb was dropped by Lyth in the covers on 13 and Smith put down by Wardlaw at third-man on seven. These misdemeanors were incidental in the final analysis, but they served as a reminder of the unforgiving nature of this form of the game. Both batsmen continued along their merry way with Ashraf, Wardlaw and Rafiq all receiving stern treatment. Cobb finished unbeaten on 52 from 44 balls and Smith on 39 from 30 as the Foxes ran out easy winners to consign Yorkshire to the bottom of the North Division.

A few players may look back on the experiences of 2012 with fond memories, but those happy days could not be further from the minds of the many disgruntled supporters who will be demanding answers to an insipid campaign that will do little for the confidence of the young players as they seek vital experience.

FRIENDS LIFE t20

Played 10   Won 2   Lost 7   Tied 1

BATTING AND FIELDING

(Qualification 4 completed innings)

Player	M.	I.	N.O.	Runs	H.S.	Avge	100s	50s	ct/st
G S Ballance	10	10	1	269	68	29.88	0	1	4
D M Hodgson	10	10	1	177	52*	19.66	0	1	5/1
A Lyth	6	6	0	101	32	16.83	0	0	2
J J Sayers	5	5	0	81	38	16.20	0	0	3
R M Pyrah	10	9	2	104	42	14.85	0	0	5
L E Plunkett	10	9	1	101	30	12.62	0	0	3
A U Rashid	8	8	1	76	19	10.85	0	0	2
Also played									
P A Jaques	4	4	1	99	66*	33.00	0	1	1
Azeem Rafiq	10	7	5	47	15*	23.50	0	0	2
A W Gale	3	3	0	57	34	19.00	0	0	0
A Z Lees	2	2	0	33	32	16.50	0	0	0
R J Sidebottom	8	4	3	14	5*	14.00	0	0	1
J M Bairstow	1	1	0	12	12	12.00	0	0	2/0
A J Hodd	6	5	2	29	11	9.66	0	0	2/1
W M H Rhodes	2	2	0	13	13	6.50	0	0	0
J A Leaning	3	3	0	14	8	4.66	0	0	0
M A Ashraf	1	1	0	4	4	4.00	0	0	0
I Wardlaw	3	1	1	1	1*	—	0	0	0
J A Brooks	8	0	0	0	—	—	0	0	3

BOWLING

(Qualification 4 wickets)

Player	Overs	Mdns	Runs	Wkts	Avge	Best	4wI	RPO
J A Brooks	25	1	189	13	14.53	5-21	2	7.56
Azeem Rafiq	31	0	247	13	19.00	3-22	0	7.96
R M Pyrah	32	1	192	9	21.33	3-15	0	6.00
L E Plunkett	33.3	0	277	8	34.62	2-20	0	8.26
Also bowled								
A Lyth	2	0	16	1	16.00	1-16	0	8.00
R J Sidebottom	27.5	0	200	3	66.66	1-29	0	7.18
A U Rashid	19	0	156	1	156.00	1-24	0	8.21
I Wardlaw	4.1	0	46	0	—	0-10	0	11.04
M A Ashraf	2	0	28	0	—	0-28	0	14.00
W M H Rhodes	1.1	0	14	0	—	0-14	0	12.00
I Wardlaw	2	0	22	0	—	0-22	0	11.00
J A Leaning	1	0	18	0	—	0-18	0	18.00

THE MAGNIFICENT SEVEN

T20 SEASON TICKET

SEE IT
TO BELIEVE IT

IN 2014
HEADINGLEY CRICKET GROUND PRESENTS
7 HOME NATWEST T20 BLAST FIXTURES STARRING...

FRI 27 JUNE
LANCASHIRE

FRI 16 MAY
NORTHAMPTONSHIRE

FRI 30 MAY
DERBYSHIRE

TUE 1 JULY
LEICESTERSHIRE

WED 2 JULY
DURHAM

FRI 18 JULY
BIRMINGHAM

FRI 25 JULY
NOTTINGHAMSHIRE

£70 FOR 7

BOOK YOUR TICKET TODAY
YORKSHIRECCC.COM
0843 504 3099

Calls are charged between 1p and 13p per minute for landline customers.
Calls from mobile phones may vary

Second Eleven 2013

Player	Date of Birth	Birthplace	Type
M A Ashraf *	January 5, 1992	Bradford	RHB/RF
A Z Lees *	April 14, 1993	Halifax	LHB/LB
D M Hodgson *	February 26, 1990	Northallerton	RHB/WK
A J Hodd *	January 12, 1984	Chichester, W Sussex	RHB/WK
Azeem Rafiq *	February 27, 1991	Karachi, Pakistan	RHB/OB
G S Randhawa *	January 25, 1992	Huddersfield	LHB/SLA
I Wardlaw *	June 29, 1985	Dewsbury	RHB/RMF
J W P Brown	March 27, 1998	Sheffield	LHB/LM
K Carver	March 26, 1996	Northallerton	LHB/SLA
E Callis	November 8, 1994	Doncaster	RHB
B O Coad	January 10, 1994	Harrogate	RHB/RM
M D Fisher	November 9, 1997	York	RHB/RMF
B P Gibson	March 31, 1996	Leeds	RHB/WK
R Gibson	January 22, 1996	Middlesbrough	RHB/RM
M Hussain	March 27, 1997	Leeds	RHB/RM
J P Inglis	March 4, 1995	Leeds	RHB/WK
A R Laws	September 21, 1991	Reigate, Surrey	RHB/OB
J A Leaning	October 18, 1993	Bristol	RHB/OB
J J Moxon	May 6, 1993	Harrogate	LHB/RM
W M H Rhodes	March 2, 1995	Nottingham	LHB/RM
O E Robinson	December 1, 1993	Margate, Kent	RHB/RM
C G Roebuck	August 14, 1991	Huddersfield	RHB/RM
W T Root	August 5, 1992	Sheffield	LHB/OB
J Shaw	January 3, 1996	Wakefield	RHB/RMF
L R Stabler	September 18, 1994	Darlington	RHB/LMF
J A Tattersall	December 15, 1994	Knaresborough	RHB/LB
J A Thompson	October 9, 1996	Leeds	LHB/RMF
J C Wainman	January 25, 1993	Harrogate	RHB/LM
G P Whiles	October 14, 1993	Harrogate	LHB/RMF
E Wilson	July 7, 1994	Huddersfield	LHB/WK

* Second Eleven cap

SECOND ELEVEN HIGHLIGHTS OF 2013

CHAMPIONSHIP

Century partnerships (5)

For the 2nd wicket (2)

| 176 | J A Tattersall and D M Hodgson | v. Leicestershire at Market Harborough |
| 131 | A Z Lees and J A Leaning | v. MCC YC at Stamford Bridge |

For the 4th wicket (3)

211	J A Leaning and W M H Rhodes	v. Leicestershire at Market Harborough
147	A Z Lees and A J Hodd	v. Nottinghamshire at York
143	J A Tattersall and J A Leaning	v. Derbyshire at Stamford Bridge

Centuries (4)

A Z Lees (2)

   102 v. MCC YC at Stamford Bridge
   100 v. Nottinghamshire at York

W M H Rhodes (1)

   126 v. Leicestershire at Market Harborough

E Callis (1)

   100 v. Lancashire at Todmorden

Four wickets in an innings (5)

S A Patterson (1)

   5 for 24 v. Durham at South Northumberland

J A Brooks (1)

   5 for 40 v. Durham at South Northumberland

I Wardlaw (1)

   4 for 15 v. Derbyshire at Stamford Bridge

M A Ashraf (1)

   4 for 36 Worcestershire at Barnt Green

R J Sidebottom (1)

   4 for 42 Durham at South Northumberland

Three victims in an innings (2)

J A Leaning (1)

   3 (3ct) v. Worcestershire at Barnt Green

B P Gibson (1)

   3 (3ct) v. Durham at South Northumberland.

Records and personal milestones

Alex Lees and Jack Leaning each passed the 1,000-run mark in the competition. Steven Patterson achieved his best bowling figures in the Championship of 5-24 v. Durham at South Northumberland CC. Iain Wardlaw achieved his best bowling figures of 4-15 v. Derbyshire at Stamford Bridge. A 10th-wicket parternership record against Warwickshire of 76 was set by O E Robinson and M A Ashraf at Coventry and North Warwickshire CC.

TROPHY

Century Partnerships (1)

For the 2nd wicket (1)

| 103 | J J Sayers and D M Hodgson | v. Leicestershire at Grace Road |

Centuries (2)

P A Jaques (1)

    105   v. Nottinghamshire at Barnsley

A Lyth (1)

    102   v MCC YC at Weetwood

4 wickets in an innings (1)

M D Fisher (1)

    6 for 25   v. Leicestershire at Grace Road

Four victims in an innings (1)

D M Hodgson (1)

    4 (4ct)   v. Nottinghamshire at Barnsley

Records and personal milestones

Richard Pyrah passed the 1000-run mark in the competition. Moin Ashraf achieved his best competition figures of 3-24 v. Glamorgan at Pudsey Congs CC. Adam Lyth took his first wickets in the competition with 2-30 v. MCC Young Cricketers at Weetwood. Matthew Fisher's 6-25 v. Leicestershire at Grace Road was the second-best analysis ever for Yorkshire in the competiton, beaten only by Paul Booth's 6-21 v. Nottinghamshire in 1986. It was the second-best return nationally in 2013. A first-wicket record v. Warwickshire of 73 was set by A W Gale and D M Hodgson at Rugby School. A fifth-wicket record v. Durham of 53 was set by R Gibson and J C Wainman at South Northumberland CC.

T20 COMPETITION

No century partnerships were compiled for Yorkshire in 2013. The best performance was the 77 by Azeem Rafiq and J A Leaning for the fourth wicket v. Nottinghamshire at Headingley, Yorkshire's first match of the competition. No individual centuries were recorded for Yorkshire in the competition, the highest score being O E Robinson's 53 v. England Under-19s at Loughborough University. D M Hodgson reached 111 not out in the second game of two in a pre-competition warm-up fixture v. Durham at York.

Azeem Rafiq returned Yorkshire's best bowling figures in the competition with 4-11 v. Derbyshire at Denby (second match), which were also the best-ever figures in the competition for Yorkshire and sixth-best nationally for 2013).

A fifth-wicket partnership record of 58 was set for Yorkshire by J A Leaning and W M H Rhodes v. Lancashire at Marske-by-the-Sea, and a sixth-wicket record of 33 was set by W M H Rhodes and G S Randhawa v. England Ungland-19s at Loughborough University (second match) An eighth-wicket record of 25 was set by L R Stabler and J W P Brown v. Lancashire at Marske-by-the-Sea (second match), and a ninth-wicket partnership record of 32 was set by I Wardlaw and B O Coad v. England Under-19s at Loughborough University (second match).

4 wickets in an innings (1)

Azeem Rafiq (1)

    4 for 11   v. Derbyshire at Denby (second match)

Three victims in an innings (1)

R Gibson (1)

    3 (3ct)   v. England Under-19s at Loughborough (first match).

Debuts (9)

J W P Brown, E Callis, M D Fisher, B P Gibson, J P Inglis, A R Laws, J J Moxon, O E Robinson and J A Thompson.

Second Eleven Championship
Yorkshire v Derbyshire

Played at Stamford Bridge CC on May 29, 30 and 31, 2013

Match drawn at 6.03pm on the Third Day

Toss won by Yorkshire   Yorkshire 5 points, Derbyshire 7 points

Close of play: First Day, Yorkshire (1) 43-2 (Lees 28, Tattersall 1) 14 overs. Second day, no play Derbyshire forfeited their first innings and Yorkshire their second.

YORKSHIRE (1)

*A Z Lees, c Poynton b Evans	28
E Callis, lbw b Harding	0
§ D M Hodgson, c Poynton b Higginbottom	6
J A Tattersall, run out (Higginbottom)	65
J A Leaning, c Cotton b Higginbottom	63
W M H Rhodes, st Poynton b Knight	8
M Hussain, c Borrington b Knight	6
G S Randhawa, c Fletcher b Higginbottom	0
J Shaw, lbw b Higginbottom	0
M D Fisher, not out	0
I Wardlaw, c Poynton b Higginbottom	0
L R Stabler Did not bat	
Extras (b 4, lb 14, w 1, nb 14)	33
Total (55.5 overs)	209

FoW: 1-10 (Callis), 2-29 (Hodgson), 3-43 (Lees), 4-186 (Tattersall), 5-195 (Leaning) 6-205 (Hussain), 7-209 (Randhawa), 8-209 (Rhodes), 9-209 (Shaw), 10-209 (Wardlaw)

	O	M	R	W
Higginbottom	19.5	7	54	5
Harding	13	1	47	1
Cotton	5	1	13	0
Evans	4	0	17	1
Cork	4	0	29	0
Knight	9	2	31	2
Redfern	1	1	0	0

DERBYSHIRE (2)

P M Borrington, c Leaning b Fisher	3
M Fletcher, lbw b Fisher	28
* D J Redfern, lbw b Fisher	9
§ T Poynton, c Lees b Leaning	22
C M Durham, lbw b Wardlaw	5
H R Hosein, lbw b Wardlaw	0
G T G Cork, lbw b Wardlaw	1
M Higginbottom, c Leaning b Wardlaw	24
T C Knight, c Hodgson b Leaning	32
B D Cotton, not out	4
C T Harding, not out	0
A C Evans Did not bat	
Extras (b 1, lb 2, nb 8)	11
Total (9 wkts, 56 overs)	139

FoW: 1-23 (Borrington), 2-43 (Redfern), 3-48 (Fletcher), 4-55 (Durham), 5-55 (Hosein) 6-65 (Cork), 7-97 (Poynton), 8-121 (Higginbottom), 9-139 (Knight)

	O	M	R	W
Wardlaw	14	8	15	4
Shaw	7	0	24	0
Fisher	7	1	31	3
Stabler	5	0	20	0
Randhawa	16	5	32	0
Leaning	6	3	6	2
Tattersall	1	0	8	0

Umpires: S J Malone and P R Pollard   Scorers: H Clayton and T M Cottam

Second Eleven Championship
Leicestershire v. Yorkshire

Played at Market Harborough on June 5, 6 and 7, 2013

Yorkshire won by an innings and 39 runs at 5.53pm on the Third Day

Toss won by Leicestershire   Leicestershire 5 points; Yorkshire 24 points

Close of play: First Day, Yorkshire 10-0 (Tattersall 4, Sayers 6); 5 overs. Second Day, Yorkshire 358-3 (Leaning 66, Rhodes 85); 109 overs.

LEICESTERSHIRE

Batsman	First Innings		Second Innings	
A J Robson	lbw b R Gibson	51	(8) c Rhodes b Randhawa	0
*M A Thornely	c Hodgson b Rhodes	22	(1) c Rhodes b Coad	0
J J Cobb	c Coad b R Gibson	16	c Hodgson b R Gibson	6
H Bush	lbw b Randhawa	46	b Shaw	0
R M L Taylor	c Leaning b Shaw	28		
T J Wells	lbw b R Gibson	29	(5) lbw b Leaning	52
S B Patel	c Hodgson b Randhawa	7	(6) run out (Leaning)	14
B A Raine	c Hodgson b Shaw	63	(4) run out (Hodgson)	4
§ S F G Bullen	c Fisher b Carver	0	(7) c and b Carver	4
A J Ireland	c B P Gibson b Rhodes	39	(9) c Leaning b Randhawa	8
A C F Wyatt	not out	19	lbw b Randhawa	0
J S Sykes	Did not bat		not out	2
Extras	(b 3, lb 10, w 1, nb 2)	16	(b 4, lb 11)	15
Total	(99.2 overs)	336	(62.4 overs)	105

FoW 1st: 1-51 (Thornely), 2-84 (Cobb), 3-101 (Robson), 4-155 (Taylor), 5-196 (Bush), 6-204 (Wells), 7-210 (Patel), 8-221 (Bullen), 9-301 (Ireland), 10-336 (Raine)

FoW 2nd: 1-0 (Bush), 2-2 (Thornely), 3-10 (Raine), 4-32 (Cobb), 5-69 (Patel), 6-84 (Bullen), 7-85 (Robson), 8-95 (Wells), 9-103 (Ireland), 10-105 (Wyatt)

Bowler	O	M	R	W		O	M	R	W
Coad	10	1	31	0		5	2	4	1
Shaw	11.2	1	55	2		7	1	15	1
Rhodes	7	3	25	2	R Gibson	8	2	23	1
Fisher	11	2	40	0		5	0	21	0
Randhawa	27	8	81	2		21.4	12	20	3
R Gibson	16	6	35	3	Carver	10	8	5	1
Carver	13	3	43	1	Leaning	6	4	2	1
Leaning	4	1	13	0					

YORKSHIRE

Batsman	First Innings	
J A Tattersall	c Thornely b Bush	84
J J Sayers	c Bullen b Wyatt	13
§ D M Hodgson	b Bush	93
J A Leaning	c Raiine b Sykes	78
*W M H Rhodes	lbw b Taylor	126
R Gibson	c Raine b Sykes	4
G S Randhawa	c Raine b Taylor	25
B P Gibson	c Ireland b Sykes	17
M D Fisher	lbw b Sykes	9
J Shaw	c Robson b Raine	3
B O Coad	not out	6
K Carver	Did not bat	
Extras	(b 5, lb 11, w 2, nb 4)	22
Total	(140.3 overs)	480

FoW: 1-20 (Sayers), 2-196 (Hodgson), 3-199 (Tattersall), 4-410 (Leaning), 5-416 (R Gibson), 6-418 (Rhodes), 7-449 (Randhawa), 8-467 (B P Gibson), 9-470 (Fisher), 10-480 (Shaw)

Bowler	O	M	R	W
Ireland	24	5	63	0
Wyatt	26	3	90	1
Taylor	20	3	78	2
Sykes	40	8	131	4
Bush	7	0	32	2
Cobb	8	2	20	0
Raine	7.3	2	20	1
Wells	6	0	24	0
Thornely	2	0	6	0

Umpires: B J Debenham and R J Warren   Scorers: P N Johnson and H Clayton

NOTE: R M L Taylor was given permission to miss the Leicestershire second innings, and the designated non-batsman, J S Sykes, was given permission to take his place.

Second Eleven Championship
Yorkshire v. MCC Young Cricketers

Played at Stamford Bridge CC on July 9, 10 and 11, 2013

MCC Young Cricketers won by 112 runs at 5.15pm on the Third Day

Toss won by MCC Young Cricketers   Yorkshire 8 points; MCC Young Cricketers 22 points

Close of play: First day, Yorkshire 32-0 (Lees 13, Tattersall 15); Second Day, MCC Young Cricketers 21-1 (Piesley 10, Gough 6)

First Innings   MCC YOUNG CRICKETERS   Second Innings

	First Innings		Second Innings	
W T Root, c Wilson b Wainman	45	lbw b Ashraf	2
C D Piesley, c Wilson b Rhodes	41	c Robinson b Leaning	120
L J Gough, c Wilson b Moxon	1	c Wilson b Patterson	6
G Clark, lbw b Ashraf	19	c Wilson b Coad	14
* § S W Poynter, lbw b Patterson	25	b Robinson	18
S S McKechnie, c Lees b Leaning	50	lbw b Patterson	34
N B Budayair, c Moxon b Patterson	31	c Patterson b Robinson	0
D O D Hampton, c Robinson b Rhodes	37	c Lees b Wainman	39
Z Shahzad, c Patterson b Robinson	14		
J G Hoddle, c Wilson b Moxon	4	(9) lbw b Shaw	8
Mohammed Abid, not out	9	(10) not out	13
J A Porter	Did not bat		
Extras (lb 6, w 2, nb 14)	22	Extras (b15, lb1, w1, nb6)	23
Total (89.3 overs)	298	Total (9 wkts dec, 73 overs)	277

FoW: 1-66 (Root), 2-79 (Gough), 3-110 (Clark), 4-116 (Piesley), 5-164 (Poynter)
1st 6-203 (McKechnie), 7-266 (Budayair), 8-284 (Hampton), 9-284 (Hoddle), 10-298 (Shahzad)
FoW: 1-2 (Root), 2-31 (Gough), 3-62 (9Clark), 4-100 (Poynter), 5-158 (McKechnie)
2nd 6-161 (Budayair), 7-227 (Hampton), 8-251 (Hoddle), 9-277 (Piesley)

	O	M	R	W		O	M	R	W
Ashraf	14	6	39	1	Ashraf	12	4	29	1
Shaw	8	2	35	0	Wainman	7	2	28	1
Patterson	15	5	47	2	Shaw	10	2	41	1
Coad	9	3	16	0	Coad	6	1	14	1
Wainman	9	1	26	1	Patterson	12	1	40	2
Rhodes	13	6	30	2	Robinson	16	2	66	2
Moxon	7	2	29	2	Rhodes	9	1	43	0
Leaning	8	1	54	1	Leaning	1	1	0	1
Robinson	5.3	1	15	1					
Tattersall	1	0	1	0					

First Innings   YORKSHIRE   Second Innings

	First Innings		Second Innings	
A Z Lees, run out (	McKechnie)	102	c Clark b Mohammed Abid	0
J A Tattersall, c Gough b Porter	15	(5) c Piesley b Root	0
J A Leaning, c Poynter b Hoddle	43	(6) b Hoddle	66
W M H Rhodes, lbw b Root	27	(7) c Budayair b Root	10
O E Robinson, lbw b Piesley	45	(8) c Piesley b Hoddle	34
§ E Wilson, c McKechnie b Mohammed Abid	0	(2) c Clark b Root	10
J Shaw, b Piesley	47	(3) c Porter b Mohammed Abid	15
*S A Patterson, c Budayair b Piesley	23	(9) b Hoddle	1
J C Wainman, c Hoddle b Piesley	11	(4) run out (Poynter)	1
M A Ashraf, not out	11	st Poynter b Piesley	0
B O Coad, not out	0	not out	0
J J Moxon	Did not bat		
Extras (b 1, lb 3, w 3, nb 2)	9	Extras (lb 1, nb 2)	3
Total (9 wkts dec; 103 overs)	323	Total (20.4 overs)	140

FoW: 1-35 (Tattersall), 2-166 (Leaning), 3-166 (Lees), 4-217 (Rhodes), 5-218 (Wilson)
1st 6-254 (Robinson), 7-310 (Patterson), 8-311 (Shaw) 9-312 (Wainman)
FoW: 1-0 (Lees), 2-16 (Wilson), 3-17 (Wainman), 4-27 (Shaw), 5-27 (Tattersall)
2nd 6-51 (Rhodes), 7-120 (Robinson), 8-133 (Patterson), 9-138 (Ashraf), 10-140 (Leaning)

	O	M	R	W		O	M	R	W
Potter	19	9	49	1	Mohammed Abid	5	0	39	2
Hoddle	17	5	53	1	Root	7	1	47	3
Shahzad	3	1	6	0	Clark	2	0	20	0
Mohammed Abid	22	6	53	1	Hoddle	3.4	0	20	3
Hampton	14	0	71	0	Piesely	3	0	13	1
Clark	3	0	19	0					
Root	13	3	48	1					
Piesley	12	5	20	4					

Umpires: I Dawood and G Parker   Scorers: H Clayton and A P Scarlett

Played at Headingley, Leeds, on July 16, 17 and 18, 2013
Yorkshire won by 78 runs at 4.06pm on the Third Day

Toss won by Yorkshire   Yorkshire 23 points, Glamorgan 5 points
Close of play: First Day, Glamorgan 39-0 (Walters 16, James 22); Second Day, Yorkshire 101-8 (Pyrah 37, Coad 0)

First Innings	YORKSHIRE		Second Innings	
J A Tattersall, lbw b Smith	60		c Wright b Reed	6
§ D M Hodgson, c Smith b Murphy	13		c Baker b Reed	27
J A Leaning, lbw b Murphy	77		lbw b Smith	1
W M H Rhodes, c Baker b Murphy	89		b Reed	1
* R M Pyrah, c Baker b Smith	10		c Walters b James	71
O E Robinson, lbw b Murphy	26		c Walters b Reed	6
I Wardlaw, lbw b Murphy	0		lbw b Murphy	3
J C Wainman, not out	0		c Baker b Bull	13
M A Ashraf			c Baker b Bull	2
K Carver	Did not bat		not out	2
B O Coad			lbw b James	17
Extras (b 12, lb 17)	29		Extras (b 10, lb 2)	12
Total (6 wkts dec; 97 overs)	304		Total (50.2 overs)	161

FoW: 1-34 (Hodgson), 2-118 (Tattersall), 3-205 (Leaning), 4-229 (Pyrah), 5-301 (Rhodes)
1st   6-301 (Wardlaw)
FoW: 1-23 (Tattersall), 2-24 (Leaning), 3-31 (Rhodes), 4-36 (Hodgson), 5-46 (Robinson)
2nd   6-49 (Wardlaw), 7-81 (Wainman), 8-93 (Ashraf), 9-154 (Prrah), 10-161 (Coad)

	O	M	R	W		O	M	R	W
Smith	21	6	60	2	Smith	14	2	49	1
Reed	18	5	42	0	Reed	13	1	46	4
Murphy	16	0	50	4	Murphy	6	2	13	1
James	23	3	62	0	Bull	10	2	24	2
Bull	19	2	61	0	Lawlor	3	0	14	0
					James	4.2	2	3	2

First Innings	GLAMORGAN		Second Innings	
* S J Walters, lbw b Carver	45		lbw b Ashraf	6
N A James, c Robinson b Pyrah	48		lbw b Carver	36
T J Lancefield, not out	98		b Ashraf	0
B J Wright, lbw b Ashraf	10		c Hodgson b Wardlaw	16
A H T Donald, c Rhodes b Coad	9		c Leaning b Pyrah	3
J L Lawlor, b Robinson	10		c and b Carver	12
R A J Smith, c and b Carver	5		c Robinson b Pyrah	20
S W Griffiths, c Hodgson b Wainman	23		c Leaning b Pyrah	0
§ T J Baker			not out	10
J R Murphy			c Hodgson b Wardlaw	11
D T Reed	Did not bat		c and b Wardlaw	0
K A Bull				
Extras (b 4, lb 5, nb 2)	11		Extras (b 4, lb 6, w 2, nb 2)	14
Total (7 wkts dec, 79.4 overs)	259		Total (38.5 overs)	128

FoW: 1-80 (James), 2-116 (Walters), 3-148 (Wright), 4-161 (Donald), 5-180 (Lawlor)
1st   6-214 (Smith), 7-259 (Griffiths)
FoW: 1-11 (Walters), 2-15 (Lancefield), 3-50 (Wright), 4-56 (Donald), 5-80 (James)
2nd   6-105 (Smith), 7-108 (Griffiths), 8-106 (Lawlor), 9-128 (Murphy), 10-128 (Reed)

	O	M	R	W		O	M	R	W
Wardlaw	14	5	39	0	Wardlaw	9.5	2	30	3
Coad	10	2	34	1	Ashraf	9	4	23	2
Wainman	8.4	2	30	1	Robinson	4	1	8	0
Pyrah	16	4	42	1	Pyrah	7	2	29	3
Robinson	10	3	25	1	Carver	8	3	25	2
Carver	16	2	66	2	Leaning	1	0	3	0
Ashraf	5	1	14	1					

Umpires: M A Eggleston and H Fidler   Scorers: H Clayton and G Watkins

Second Eleven Championship
Warwickshire v. Yorkshire

Played at Coventry and North Warwickshire CC on August 1, 2, and 3, 2013

Match drawn at 6.01pm on the Third Day

Toss won by Yorkshire   Warwickshire 8 points, Yorkshire 9 points

Close of play: First Day, no play. Second Day, Warwickshire 83-6 (Lewis 11)

First Innings		YORKSHIRE	Second Innings	
E Callis, c McKay b Ali	5		b Allin	10
C G Roebuck, b Milnes	6		lbw b Haque	36
§ D M Hodgson, b Milnes	12		b Haque	16
J A Leaning, b Piolet	21		lbw b Haque	1
O E Robinson, not out	90		not out	30
E Wilson, c Hain b Ali	3		c and b Haque	5
J P Inglis, c McKay b Ali	22		not out	24
J C Wainman, b Gordon	4			
I Wardlaw, lbw b Ali	8			
B O Coad, b Ali	0			
* M A Ashraf, lbw b Haque	12			
G P Whiles	Did not bat			
Extras (b 6, lb 6, w 2, nb 12)	26		Extras (b 2, lb 3, w 1)	6
Total (66.3 overs)	209		Total (5 wkts dec, 32.3 overs)	173

FoW: 1-11 (Callis), 2-19 (Roebuck), 3-44 (Hodgson), 4-72 (Leaning), 5-77 (Wilson)

1st   6-111 (Inglis), 7-116 (Wainman), 8-133 (Wardlaw), 9-133 (Coad), 10-209 (Ashraf)

FoW: 1-21 (Callis), 2-102 (Hodgson), 3-108 (Leaning), 4-111 (Roebuck), 5-125 (Wilson)

	O	M	R	W		O	M	R	W
Milnes	16	3	54	2	Ali	6	0	21	0
Ali	20	6	61	5	Allin	5	0	26	1
Piolet	12	3	27	1	Gordon	4	1	18	0
Gordon	10	0	30	1	Enamul Haque	10.3	0	63	4
Enamul Haque	8.3	2	25	1	Piolet	4	1	7	0
					Webb	3	0	33	0

First Innings		WARWICKSHIRE	Second Innings	
F R J Coleman, c Leaning b Wainman	25		c Hodgson b Coad	23
J O Troughton, lbw b Ashraf	0			
* P M Best, b Wainman	11		(2) c Hodgson b Robinson	48
T P Lewis, c Hodgson b Wardlaw	37		(3) c Whiles b Coad	3
S R Hain, c Hodgson b Robinson	13		c Wainman b Robinson	2
R O Gordon, b Robinson	0			
J P Webb, c Hodgson b Ashraf	5		(6) not out	8
S A Piolet, c Wilson b Ashraf	62		(4) not out	11
T W Allin, c Leaning b Wardlaw	0			
§ P J McKay, c Callis b Robinson	1			
Enamul Haque, not out	11			
T P Milnes				
S A Ali	Did not bat			
Extras (lb 15, nb 18)	33		Extras	0
Total (73.5 overs)	198		Total (4 wkts; 20 overs)	95

FoW: 1-10 (Troughton), 2-43 (Coleman), 3-46 (Best), 4-73 (Hain), 5-73 (Gordon)

1st   6-83 (Webb), 7-138 (Lewis), 8-138 (Allin), 9-164 (McKay), 10-198 (Piolet)

FoW: 1-61 (Coleman), 2-73 (Lewis), 3-74 (Best), 4-84 (Hain)

	O	M	R	W		O	M	R	W
Wardlaw	13	3	43	2	Wardlaw	6	0	30	0
Ashraf	15.5	4	40	3	Ashraf	2	0	24	0
Coad	13	7	14	0	Coad	6	0	29	2
Wainman	12	1	34	2	Robinson	4	2	7	2
Robinson	10	6	14	3	Leaning	2	1	5	0
Whiles	7	2	22	0					
Leaning	3	2	16	0					

Umpires: M J D Bodenham and M Qureshi   Scorers: S Smith and H Clayton

NOTE: J O Troughton and T P Milnes were called to first-team duty at the end of the First Day.

Second Eleven Championship
Worcestershire v. Yorkshire

Played at Barnt Green CC on August 6, 7 and 8, 2013

Worcestershire won by an innings and 121 runs at 1.44pm on the Second Day

Toss won by Yorkshire   Worcestershire 23 points, Yorkshire 4 points

Close of play: First Day, Worcestershire 242-9 (Rhodes 76, Denning 8)

First Innings	YORKSHIRE		Second Innings	
C G Roebuck, lbw b Lucas	8		c Johnson b Lucas	4
* J J Sayers, lbw b Morris	23		c D'Oliveira b Morris	0
§ D M Hodgson, b Choudhry	14		c Johnson b Lucas	0
J A Leaning, lbw b Morris	0		c Johnson b Morris	5
O E Robinson, b Morris	0		c Kohler-Cadmore b Choudhry	31
M Hussain, c Kohler-Cadmore b D'Oliveira	17		c D'Oliveira b Denning	0
R Gibson, c and b Choudhry	0		c Johnson b Choudhry	7
J C Wainman, c Whiteley b Choudhry	0		lbw b D'Oliveira	6
I Wardlaw, c Denning b Choudhry	2		c Kohler-Cadmore b D'Oliveira	14
M A Ashraf, c Kohler-Cadmore b Choudhry	0		c Kervezee b D'Oliveira	0
G P Whiles, not out	0		not out	0
Extras (w 2, nb 2)	4		Extras	6
Total (28.1 overs)	68		Total (41.1 overs)	7

FoW: 1-20 (Roebuck), 2-34 (Sayers), 3-34 (Leaning), 4-38 (Robinson), 5-63 (Hodgson),
1st 6-64 (Gibson), 7-64 (Wainman), 8-68 (Wardlaw), 9-68 (Hussain), 10-68 (Ashraf)
FoW: 1-4 (Roebuck), 2-4 (Sayers), 3-4 (Hodgson), 4-30 (Leaning), 5-36 (Hussain),
2nd 6-40 (Robinson), 7-49 (Gibson), 8-64 (Wardlaw), 9-64 (Ashraf), 10-67 (Wainman)

	O	M	R	W		O	M	R	W
Lucas	6	0	36	1	Lucas	6	3	16	2
Morris	7	1	14	3	Morris	7	5	13	2
Denning	5	1	5	0	Choudhry	15	7	20	2
Whiteley	5	2	9	0	Denning	4	3	1	1
Choudhry	3.1	2	2	5	D'Oliveira	9.1	4	17	3
D'Oliveira	2	1	2	1					

WORCESTERSHIRE

T Kohler-Cadmore, lbw b Ashraf		14
* § M A Johnson, c Leaning b Ashraf		5
A N Kervezee, c Whiles b Gibson		42
R A Whiteley, b Ashraf		0
S H Choudhry, c Leaning b Gibson		21
B L D'Oliveira, c Hodgson b Gibson		1
A Hepburn, c Hussain b Wainman		56
G H Rhodes, c Leaning b Wainman		81
D S Lucas, c Hodgson b Wainman		1
C A J Morris, b Robinson		4
J S T Denning, not out		13
A Rashid	Did not bat	
Extras (b 1, lb 7, nb 10)		18
Total (75.1)		256

FoW: 1-14 (Johnson), 2-21 (Kohler-Cadmore), 3-27 (Whiteley), 4-78 (Choudhry), 5-80 (D'Oliveira)
6-93 (Kervezee), 7-208 (Hepburn), 8-212 (Lucas), 9-225 (Morris), 10-256 (Rhodes)

	O	M	R	W
Wardlaw	10	1	47	0
Ashraf	14.1	6	36	4
Wainman	12	3	42	2
Robinson	11	4	34	1
Gibson	12	3	28	3
Leaning	9	3	11	0
Whiles	7	0	30	0

Umpires: A C Harris and P R Pollard   Scorers- P M Mellish and H Clayton

Second Eleven Championship
Durham v Yorkshire

Played at South Northumberland CC on August 13, 14 and 15, 2013

Yorkshire won by 165 runs at 12.49pm on the Third Day

Toss won by Yorkshire   Durham 4 points, Yorkshire 21 points

Close of play: First Day, Durham (1) 96-6 (Coughlin 19); Second Day, Durham (2) 49-3 (Singh 11, Foster 7)

First Innings	YORKSHIRE				Second Innings				
E Callis, c Coughlin b Bousfield	4				b Bousfield				4
C G Roebuck, c Coughlin b Main	7				c Singh b Bousfield				0
§ A J Hodd, c J Clark b Morley	34				c Singh b Arshad				54
A U Rashid, lbw b Buckley	85				run out (Main)				1
Azeem Rafiq, c and b Morley									
E Wilson, c G Clark b Arshad	4				(5) c Jennings b Main				9
J P Inglis, c G Clark b Arshad	1				(6) c Coughlin b Buckley				23
* S A Patterson, c Buckley b Bousfield	6				(8) c and b Buckley				36
J A Brooks, c Singh b Jennings	37				(9) c G Clark b Buckley				57
J C Wainman, c Buckley b Main	2				(10) lbw b Foster				6
B P Gibson, not out	3				(11) not out				0
R J Sidebottom					(7) lbw b Jennings				5
G P Whiles	Did not bat								
Extras (lb 5, w 3. nb 2)	10				Extras (b 1, lb 4, w 3. nb 2)				1 4
Total (72.4 overs)	188				Total (72.5 overs)				2 0 9

FoW: 1-10 (Callis), 2-21 (Roebuck), 3-72 (Hodd), 4-86 (Azeem Rafiq), 5-93 (Wilson),
1st 6-97 (Inglis), 7-101 (Patterson), 8-172 (Brooks), 9-184 (Rashid), 10-188 (Wainman)
FoW: 1-1 (Roebuck), 2-10 (Callis), 3-11 (Rashid), 4-36 (Wilson), 5-93 (Inglis),
2nd 6-97 (Hodd), 7-111 (Sidebottom), 8-202 (Patterson), 9-207 (Brooks), 10-209 (Wainman)

	O	M	R	W		O	M	R	W
Bousfield	13	2	20	2	Bousfield	14	6	33	3
Arshad	14	5	32	2	Arshad	15	6	23	1
Jennings	17	4	30	1	Main	9	1	40	1
Main	7.4	0	29	2	Jennings	14	1	40	1
Buckley	8	1	29	1	Morley	1	0	5	0
Morley	9	2	27	2	Buckley	11	3	41	2
Foster	4	0	16	0	Foster	8.5	1	18	1

First Innings	DURHAM				Second Innings				
J Clark, c Rashid b Brooks	0				lbw b Brooks				2
K K Jennings, lbw b Patterson	15				lbw b Sidebottom				14
* R Singh, c Gibcon b Patterson	17				b Sidebottom				14
G Clark, b Hodd b Patterson	21				b Patterson				11
U Arshad, lbw b Brooks	46				(7) c Gibson b Sidebottom				0
P Coughlin, lbw b Brooks	26				(6) lbw b Patterson				10
§ S W Poynter, b Brooks	0				(8) c Gibson b Patterson				22
R S Buckley, c Callis b Brooks	0				(9) c Gibson b Patterson				8
J P Bousfield, lbw b Sidebottom	19				(10) c Hodd b Patterson				3
D W Foster, b Sidebottom	0				(5) lbw b Sidebottom				11
M G Morley, not out	0				(11) not out				3
G T Main	Did not bat								
Extras (lb 11)	11				Extras (b 2, lb 4, w 1)				7
Total (39.2 overs)	129				Total (45.5 overs)				1 0 5

FoW: 1-0 (J Clark), 2-28 (Jennings), 3-45 (Singh), 4-66 (G Clark), 5-88 (Arshad),
1st 6-96 (Poynter), 7-96 (Buckley), 8-127 (Bousfield), 9-127 (Coughlin), 10-129 (Foster)
FoW: 1-3 (J Clark), 2-28 (Jennings), 3-39 (G Clark), 4-53 (Foster), 5-56 (Singh),
2nd 6-58 (U Arshad), 7-89 (Coughlin), 8-90 (Poynter), 9-98 (Bousfield), 10-105 (Buckley)

	O	M	R	W		O	M	R	W
Brooks	12	2	40	5	Sidebottom	14	3	42	4
Patterson	10	3	28	3	Brooks	12	6	14	1
Wainman	6	2	18	0	Patterson	11.5	3	24	5
Whiles	5	1	17	0	Rashid	8	2	19	0
Rashid	2	1	1	0					
Sidebottom	4.2	1	12	2					

Umpires: B V Taylor and P Gardener   Scorers: R V Hilton and H Clayton

NOTE: R J Sidebottom replaced Azeem Rafiq at the end of the First Day.
A J Hodd kept wicket in Durham's first innings and B P Gibson in their second innings

Second Eleven Championship
Yorkshire v. Lancashire

Played at Todmorden CC on August 21, 22 and 23, 2013
Lancashire won by 10 wickets at 6.13pm on the Second Day

Toss won by Yorkshire — Yorkshire 5 points, Lancashire 24 points
Close of play: First Day, Lancashire 252-7 (Steele 33, Griffiths 3)

	YORKSHIRE	First Innings		Second Innings	
E Callis	b Griffiths	2	b Livingstone		100
J A Tattersall	lbw b Bailey	4	c Davies b Bailey		1
§ D M Hodgson	lbw b Clark	53	c Davies b Bailey		26
J A Leaning	b Bailey	0	c Brown b Ghaus		15
* W M H Rhodes	c Davies b Bailey	1	c Davies b Ghaus		3
O E Robinson	lbw b Croft	32	c Davies b Ghaus		1
E Wilson	lbw b Croft	6	lbw b Bailey		15
M D Fisher	c Croft b Clark	5	c Clark b Bailey		9
I Wardlaw	b Clark	0	b Livingstone		30
M A Ashraf	c Brown b Clark	18	not out		1
B O Coad	not out	5	b Griffiths		0
K Carver	Did not bat				
Extras	(b 4, lb 6, nb 16)	26	(b 2, lb 10, nb 12)		24
Total	(42.1 overs)	152	(60.5 overs)		225

FoW: 1-7 (Callis), 2-13 (Tattersall), 3-13 (Leaning), 4-37 (Rhodes), 5-98 (Robinson)
1st 6-116 (Wilson), 7-118 (Hodgson), 8-122 (Wardlaw), 9-127 (Fisher), 10-152 (Ashraf)
FoW: 1-5 (Tattersall), 2-59 (Hodgson), 3-93 (Leaning), 4-103 (Rhodes), 5-111 (Robinson)
2nd 6-163 (Wilson), 7-177 (Fisher), 8-215 (Callis), 9-224 (Wardlaw), 10-225 (Coad)

	O	M	R	W		O	M	R	W
Bailey	9	3	24	3	Bailey	18	2	68	4
Griffiths	6	0	27	1	Griffiths	9.5	1	24	1
Adnan Guaus	5	0	21	0	Clark	4	0	19	0
Clark	13.1	5	31	4	Adnan Ghaus	10	1	36	3
Croft	5	1	20	2	Croft	8	0	34	0
Mohammed Anid	4	0	19	0	Parkinson	8	2	24	0
					Livingstone	3	1	8	2

	LANCASHIRE	First Innings		Second Innings	
§ A L Davies	lbw b Robinson	23	not out		22
K R Brown	lbw b Coad	57	not out		26
* S J Croft	lbw b Robinson	0			
J Clark	c Fisher b Robinson	2			
L S Livingstone	c Coad b Wardlaw	101			
R P Zelem	c Hodgson b Rhodes	25			
T E Bailey	c Wilson b Carver	1			
T A Steele	c Hodgson b Fisher	39			
G T Griffiths	b Wardlaw	15			
Mohammed Abid	lbw b Carver	44			
Adnan Ghaus	not out	10			
M W Parkinson	Did not bat				
Extras	(b 4, lb 7, nb 2)	13	Extras		0
Total	(82.1 overs)	330	Total	(0 wkts; 5.4 overs)	48

FoW: 1-52 (Davies), 2-52 (Croft), 3-82 (Clark), 4-82 (Brown), 5-155 (Zelem), 6-156 (Bailey)
7-242 (Livingstone), 8-261 (Steele), 9-282 (Griffiths), 10-330 (Mohammed Abid)

	O	M	R	W		O	M	R	W
Wardlaw	16	5	62	2	Wardlaw	3	1	9	0
Ashraf	15	3	49	0	Ashraf	2	0	26	0
Robinson	16	6	43	3	Fisher	0.4	0	13	0
Coad	9	2	40	1					
Fisher	12	2	38	1					
Rhodes	4	0	16	1					
Carver	8.1	1	47	2					
Leaning	2	0	24	0					

Umpires : G D Lloyd and H Evans — Scorers: D M White and H Clayton

Second Eleven Championship
Yorkshire v. Nottinghamshire

Played at York CC on August 28, 29 and 30, 2013
Nottinghamshire won by 7 wickets at 5.46pm on the Third Day

Toss won by Yorkshire   Yorkshire 7 points, Nottinghamshire 21 points
Close of play: First Day, Yorkshire 335-6 (Robinson 23, Leaning 7); Second Day, Yorkshire 23-1 (Callis 15, Hodgson 1)

	First Innings	YORKSHIRE		Second Innings	
E Callis, lbw b Ball		29	(2) c White b Ball		54
W M H Rhodes, c Franks b Hutton		7	(7) c Wood b White		12
§ D M Hodgson, c Cross b Ball		43	(3) c Cross b Bacon		37
A Z Lees, c Kelsall b Ball		100	(1) lbw b Ball		0
A J Hodd, run out (Ball)		93	(5) st Cross b White		11
* R M Pyrah, c Cross b Bacon		19	(4) c Kelsall b Bacon		0
O E Robinson, c Bacon b Ball		23	(6) c Franks b White		12
J A Leaning, c Cross b Hutton		10	(8) c Cross b Bacon		11
B O Coad, c Kelsall b Hutton		4	(9) not out		0
M A Ashraf, c Hutton b Ball		3			
G P Whiles, not out		0			
K Carver	Did not bat				
Extras (b 3, lb 6, w 2, nb 4)		15	Extras (b 5, lb 1, w 1, nb 2)		9
Total (110 overs)		346	Total (8 wkts dec, 26.5 overs)		146

FoW: 1-14 (Rhodes), 2-81 (Callis), 3-112 (Hodgson), 4-259 (Lees), 5-287 (Hodd)
1st 6-312 (Pyrah), 7-335 (Robinson), 8-341 (Coad), 9-344 (Ashraf), 10-346 (Leaning)
FoW: 1-21 (Lees), 2-67 (Hodgson), 3-67 (Pyrah), 4-110 (Callis), 5-123 (Robinson)
2nd 6-124 (Hodd), 7-137 (Rhodes), 8-146 (Leaning)

	O	M	R	W		O	M	R	W
Ball	25	11	67	5	Ball	8	2	25	1
Hutton	24	7	57	3	Hutton	10	1	41	0
Franks	15	3	42	0	Bacon	5.5	0	43	4
Bacon	19	2	78	1	White	3	0	31	3
White	18	3	47	0					
Wood	3	0	25	0					
Dal	2	0	11	0					
Tillcock	4	1	10	0					

	First Innings	NOTTINGHAMSHIRE		Second Innings	
Hassan Azad, not out		122	not out		97
S Kelsall, b Whiles		0	c Carver b Coad		15
S K W Wood, c Hodgson b Robinson		43	st Hodd b Carver		33
A Dal, b Carver		33	c Hodd b Pyrah		66
A D Tillcock, c Whiles b Leaning		2	not out		22
§ M H Cross, c Robinson b Carver		0			
* P J Franks, b Leaning		0			
G G White, c Robinson b Leaning		0			
B A Hutton, lbw b Robinson		36			
G P W Bacon, not out		9			
J T Ball	Did not bat				
Extras (lb 6, nb 2)		8	Extras (b 1, lb 7)		8
Total (8 wkts dec, 89 overs)		253	Total (3 wkts, 64 overs)		241

FoW: 1-6 (Kelsall), 2-72 (Wood), 3-148 (Dal), 4-151 (Tillcock), 5-151 (Cross)
1st 6-158 (Franks), 7-158 (White), 8-225 (Hutton)
2nd 1-22 (Kelsall), 2-92 (Wood), 3-194 (Dal)

	O	M	R	W		O	M	R	W
Ashraf	12	8	15	0	Ashraf	12	5	15	0
Whiles	8	2	30	1	Whiles	6	1	24	0
Pyrah	16	7	31	0	Coad	9	1	37	1
Coad	10	2	35	0	Pyrah	9	0	50	1
Robinson	11	3	51	2	Carver	14	2	50	1
Carver	21	8	57	2	Robinson	4	1	11	0
Leaning	11	2	28	3	Leaning	4	0	22	0
					Rhodes	6	0	24	0

Umpires: G Sharp and H Fidler   Scorers: H Clayton and Mrs A Cusworth

SECOND ELEVEN CHAMPIONSHIP 2013

FINAL

Lancashire (113-2) drew with **Middlesex** (Did not bat) — *Title shared*

NORTHERN GROUP FINAL TABLE

	P	W	L	D	Tied	Aban.	Bat	Bowl	Pen.	Points
1 Lancashire (3)	9	6	0	3	0	0	32	33	0	170
2 Derbyshire (7)	9	5	0	4	0	0	22	28	0	142
3 Worcestershire (5)	9	4	4	1	0	0	22	35	0	124
4 Yorkshire (9)	**9**	**3**	**4**	**2**	**0**	**0**	**22**	**30**	**0**	**106**
5 Glamorgan (-)	9	3	2	4	0	0	17	28	0	105
6 Nottinghamshire (10) ...	9	2	2	5	0	0	16	29	0	92
7 MCC Young Cricketers (-)	9	1	4	4	0	0	22	26	0	76
8 Warwickshire (8)	9	1	3	5	0	0	16	27	6.5	67.5
9 Leicestershire (1)	9	0	3	6	0	0	25	24	0	67
10 Durham (2)	9	1	4	4	0	0	17	21	0	66

SOUTHERN GROUP FINAL TABLE

	P	W	L	D	Tied	Aban.	Bat	Bowl	Pen.	Points
1 Middlesex (4)	9	5	1	3	0	0	25	35	0	149
2 Essex (6)	9	5	3	1	0	0	21	34	0	138
3 Gloucestershire (10)	9	4	1	4	0	0	24	24	0	124
4 Kent (1)	9	3	2	4	0	0	30	33	0	123
5 Somerset (9)	9	3	2	4	0	0	25	31	6.5	109.5
6 Northamptonshire (-) ...	9	3	1	5	0	0	24	19	0	106
7 Surrey (2)	9	3	4	2	0	0	18	30	4.5	97.5
8 Hampshire (5)	9	1	4	4	0	0	20	29	3	74
9 Sussex (7)	9	0	5	4	0	0	24	27	0	63
10 MCC Universities (-) ...	9	0	4	5	0	0	23	24	0	62

(2012 group positions in brackets)

SECOND ELEVEN CHAMPIONS

(In the seasons in which Yorkshire have competed. The Championship has been split into two groups since 2009, the group winners playing off for the Championship. These groups were deemed North and South for the 2012 season.)

Season	Champions	Yorkshire's Position	Season	Champions	Yorkshire's Position
1959	Gloucestershire	7th	1994	Somerset	2nd
1960	Northamptonshire	14th	1995	Hampshire	5th
1961	Kent	11th	1996	Warwickshire	4th
1975	Surrey	4th	1997	Lancashire	2nd
1976	Kent	5th	1998	Northamptonshire	9th
1977	**Yorkshire**	**1st**	1999	Middlesex	14th
1978	Sussex	5th	2000	Middlesex	5th
1979	Warwickshire	3rd	2001	Hampshire	2nd
1980	Glamorgan	5th	2002	Kent	3rd
1981	Hampshire	11th	**2003**	**Yorkshire**	**1st**
1982	Worcestershire	14th	2004	Somerset	8th
1983	Leicestershire	2nd	2005	Kent	10th
1984	**Yorkshire**	**1st**	2006	Kent	3rd
1985	Nottinghamshire	12th	2007	Sussex	10th
1986	Lancashire	5th	2008	Durham	5th
1987	**Yorkshire** and Kent	**1st**	2009	Surrey	A 2nd
1988	Surrey	9th	2010	Surrey	A 8th
1989	Middlesex	9th	2011	Warwickshire	A 10th
1990	Sussex	17th	2012	Kent	North 9th
1991	**Yorkshire**	**1st**	2013	Lancashire & Middlesex	
1992	Surrey	5th			(North) 4th
1993	Middlesex	3rd			

SECOND ELEVEN CHAMPIONSHIP
AVERAGES 2013

Played 9   Won 3   Lost 4   Drawn 2

BATTING AND FIELDING

(Qualification 5 innings)

Player	M.	I.	N.O.	Runs	H.S.	Avge	100s	50s	ct/st
A Z Lees	3	5	0	230	102	46.00	2	0	3
O E Robinson	6	12	3	329	90*	36.55	0	1	4
D M Hodgson	7	12	0	385	93	32.08	0	3	11
J A Tattersall	5	8	0	235	84	29.37	0	3	0
W M H Rhodes	6	10	0	284	126	28.40	1	1	3
J A Leaning	8	14	0	391	78	27.92	0	4	7
E Callis	5	9	0	208	100	23.11	1	1	2
C G Roebuck	3	6	0	61	36	10.16	0	0	0
B O Coad	6	9	5	32	12	8.00	0	0	0
I Wardlaw	4	7	0	49	30	7.00	0	0	1
M A Ashraf	6	9	2	47	18	6.71	0	0	0
E Wilson	4	8	0	52	15	6.50	0	0	7
J C Wainman	5	9	1	33	13	5.50	0	0	2
Also played									
A J Hodd	2	4	0	192	93	48.00	0	2	3/1
J A Brooks	1	2	0	94	57	47.00	0	1	0
A U Rashid	1	2	0	86	85	42.50	0	1	1
J P Inglis	2	4	1	70	24*	23.34	0	0	0
R M Pyrah	2	4	0	90	71	22.50	0	0	0
B P Gibson	3	3	0	20	17	20.00	0	0	4
J Shaw	2	4	2	65	47	16.25	0	0	0
S A Patterson	2	4	0	60	36	15.00	0	0	2
G S Randhawa	2	2	0	25	25	12.50	0	0	0
J J Sayers	2	3	0	36	23	12.00	0	0	0
M Hussain	2	3	0	23	17	7.66	0	0	0
M D Fisher	3	4	1	23	9	7.66	0	0	0
R J Sidebottom	1	1	0	5	5	5.00	0	0	0
R Gibson	2	3	0	11	7	3.66	0	0	0
Azeem Rafiq	1	1	0	1	1	1.00	0	0	0
K Carver	4	1	1	2	2*	—	0	0	4
G P Whiles	5	3	3	0	0*	—	0	0	0
J J Moxon	1	0	0	0	—	—	0	0	2
L R Stabler	1	0	0	0	—	—	0	0	0

BOWLING

(Qualification 10 wickets)

Player	Overs	Mdns	Runs	Wkts	Avge	Best	5wI	10wM
S A Patterson	48.5	13	139	11	12.63	5-24	1	0
O E Robinson	91.3	29	274	15	18.26	3-14	0	0
I Wardlaw	86.4	25	274	11	24.90	4-15	0	0
M A Ashraf	113	41	310	12	25.83	4-36	0	0
K Carver	90.3	27	293	11	26.63	2-25	0	0

Also bowled

Player	Overs	Mdns	Runs	Wkts	Avge	Best	5wI	10wM
J A Brooks	24	8	54	6	9.00	5-40	1	0
R J Sidebottom	18.2	4	54	6	9.00	4-42	0	0
R Gibson	36	11	85	7	12.14	3-28	0	0
J J Moxon	7	2	29	2	14.50	2-29	0	0
J C Wainman	55.2	12	178	7	25.42	3-22	0	0
J A Leaning	57	18	204	8	25.50	3-57	0	0
G S Randhawa	64.4	25	133	5	26.60	3-20	0	0
W M H Rhodes	39	10	138	5	27.60	2-25	0	0
R M Pyrah	48	13	152	5	30.40	3-29	0	0
M D Fisher	35.4	5	143	4	35.75	3-31	0	0
B O Coad	71	21	253	7	36.14	2-29	0	0
J Shaw	43.2	6	171	4	42.75	2-55	0	0
G P Whiles	13	6	123	1	123.00	1-30	0	0
A U Rashid	10	3	20	0	—	—	0	0
L R Stabler	5	0	20	0	—	—	0	0
J A Tattersall	1	0	8	0	—	—	0	0

Second Eleven Trophy
Yorkshire v. Derbyshire

Played at Stamford Bridge on May 28, 2013
Derbyshire won by 6 wickets at 4.46pm

Toss won by Yorkshire   Yorkshire 0 points, Derbyshire 2 points

YORKSHIRE

*A Z Lees, lbw b Burgoyne	54
E Callis, lbw b Knight	19
§ D M Hodgson, c and b Burgoyne	4
J A Leaning, not out	58
M Hussain, c Burgoyne b Hiogginbottom	29
R Gibson, c Burgoyne b Hiogginbottom	8
J Shaw, lbw b Redfern	5
M D Fisher, lbw b Redfern	0
L R Stabler, b Redfern	0
I Wardlaw, c and b Durston	11
K Carver, lbw b Redfern	1
Extras (b 1, lb 3, w 5, nb 4)	13
Total (39 overs)	202

FoW: 1-82 (Lees), 2-82 (Callis), 3-92 (Hodgson), 4-134 (Hussain), 5-149 (Gibson), 6-165 (Shaw), 7-165 (Fisher), 8-165 (Stabler), 9-179 (Wardlaw), 10-202 (Carver)

D J Redfern did the hat-trick, dismissing Shaw, Fisher and Stabler in the 33rd over

	O	M	R	W
Higginbottom	8	0	48	2
Cotton	6	0	32	0
Harding	3	0	21	0
Burgoyne	6	0	31	2
Knight	6	0	14	1
Durston	5	0	23	1
Redfern	5	0	29	4

DERBYSHIRE

B T Slater, not out	112
D J Redfern, c and b Leaning	25
* W J Durston, st Hodgson b Leaning	2
§ T Poynton, c Stabler b Shaw	50
C M Durham, lbw b Wardlaw	4
M Fletcher, not out	4
P I Burgoyne	
M Higginbottom	
T C Knight	Did not bat
B D Cotton	
C T Harding	
Extras (lb 4, nb 2)	6
Total (4 wkts, 37.2 overs)	203

FoW: 1-79 (Redfern), 2-83 (Durston), 3-183 (Poynton), 4-190 (Durham)

	O	M	R	W
Shaw	7	0	46	1
Wardlaw	6.2	0	36	1
Fisher	4	0	22	0
Stabler	4	0	20	0
Leaning	8	1	35	2
Carver	8	0	40	0

Umpires: P R Pollard and S J Malone   Scorers: C N Rawson and T M Cottam

Second Eleven Trophy
Leicestershire v. Yorkshire

Played at Grace Road, Leicester, on June 4, 2013
Yorkshire won by 57 runs at 5.31pm

Toss won by Yorkshire   Leicestershire 0 points, Yorkshire 2 points

YORKSHIRE

J A Tattersall, c Bush b Taylor	....	33
J J Sayers, run out (Bush)	....	91
§ D M Hodgson, c Bush b Thornely	....	53
J A Leaning, b Hoggard	....	7
* W M H Rhodes, not out	....	12
R Gibson, c Buck b Ireland	....	21
G S Randhawa, not out	....	13
M D Fisher		
J Shaw	Did not bat	
B O Coad		
K Carver		
Extras (b 1, lb 4, w 7, pen 6)	....	18
Total (5 wkts, 40 overs)	....	248

Six penalty runs were awarded against Leicestershire for failing to bowl their 40 overs in the stipulated time

FoW: 1-83 (Tattersall), 2-186 (Hodgson), 3-190 (Sayers), 4-196 (Leaning), 5-226 (Gibson)

	O	M	R	W
Hoggard	8	0	34	1
Buck	8	1	50	0
Ireland	6	0	31	1
Wyatt	2	0	25	0
Taylor	7	0	56	1
Thornely	7	0	31	1
Bush	2	0	20	0

LEICESTERSHIRE

A J Robson, c Hodgson b Fisher	....	28
* M A Thornely, c Randhawa b Shaw	....	10
H Bush, lbw b Fisher	....	12
R M L Taylor, c Leaning b Gibson	....	35
T J Wells, lbw b Fisher	....	0
B A Raine, st Hodgson b Randhawa	....	62
§ S F G Bullen, b Fisher	....	12
A J Ireland, b Randhawa	....	5
N L Buck, b Fisher	....	15
A C F Wyatt, not out	....	1
M Hoggard, b Fisher	....	4
Extras (lb 1, w 6)	....	7
Total (38 overs)	....	191

FoW: 1-25 (Thornely), 2-48 (Bush), 3-55 (Robson), 4-55 (Wells), 5-151 (Raine), 6-151 (Taylor), 7-157 (Ireland), 8-185 (Bullen), 9-186 (Buck), 10-191 (Hoggard)

	O	M	R	W
Tattersall	1	0	8	0
Coad	6	0	24	0
Shaw	5	0	25	1
Fisher	7	1	25	6
Rhodes	5	0	33	0
Carver	5	0	19	0
Leaning	2	0	14	0
Randhawa	4	0	26	2
Gibson	3	0	16	1

Umpires: B J Debenham and A Payne   Scorers: P N Johnson and H Clayton

Second Eleven Trophy
Yorkshire v. MCC Young Cricketers

Played at Weetwood, Leeds, on July 8, 2013
Match tied at 5.32pm

Toss won by Yorkshire   Yorkshire 1 point, MCC Young Cricketers 1 point

YORKSHIRE

A Lyth, lbw b M Abid	....	102
A Z Lees, run out (McKechnie)	....	30
J J Sayers, run out (McKechnie)	....	21
§ D M Hodgson, b M Abid	....	43
* Azeem Rafiq, c Budhayer b Piesley		35
J A Leaning, st McKechnie b M Abid		9
W M H Rhodes, c McKechnie b Shahzad	....	14
O E Robinson, b Shahzad	....	3
I Wardlaw, not out	....	4
J Shaw, b Piesley	....	4
B O Coad, not out	....	6
Extras (lb 1, w 5, nb 2)		8
Total (9 wkts, 40 overs)	....	279

FoW: 1-61 (Lees), 2-96 (Sayers), 3-191 (Hodgson), 4-208 (Lyth), 5-234 (Leaning)
6-257 (Rhodes), 7-265 (Robinson), 8-267 (Rafiq), 9-272 (Shaw)

	O	M	R	W
Shahzad	8	0	44	2
Getkate	4	0	38	0
W T Root	7	0	54	0
Mohammed Abid	8	0	47	3
Piesley	8	0	58	2
Clark	5	0	37	0

MCC YOUNG CRICKETERS

* S W Poynter, c and b Rafiq	....	51
C D Piesley, c Hodgson b Rafiq		56
S C Getkate, b Rhodes		40
W T Root, b Rafiq		25
G Clark, lbw b Robinson	....	36
§ S S McKechnie, c Robinson b Rafiq		2
J N J Rollings, c Hodgson b Lyth		0
R M Pulami, b Lyth		0
N B Budhayer, lbw b Robinson		9
Z Shahzad, c Sayers b Wardlaw		39
Mohammed Abid, not out	....	11
Extras (lb 2, w 4, nb 4)		10
Total (39.3 overs)	....	279

FoW: 1-95 (Poynter), 2-124 (Piesley), 3-170 (Root), 4-182 (Getkate), 5-189 (McKechnie)
6-190 (Rollings), 7-190 (Pulami), 8-206 (Budhayer), 9-237 (Clark), 10-279 (Shahzad)

	O	M	R	W
Wardlaw	7.3	0	52	1
Coad	2	0	19	0
Robinson	7	0	63	2
Lyth	6	0	30	2
Rafiq	8	0	45	4
Leaning	2	0	14	0
Sayers	2	0	19	0
Rhodes	5	0	35	0

Umpires: N L Bainton and G Parker   Scorers: H Clayton and A P Scarlett

Second Eleven Trophy
Yorkshire v. Glamorgan

Played at Pudsey Congs CC on July 19, 2013
Yorkshire won by 5 wickets at 3.43pm

Toss won by Glamorgan

Yorkshire 2 points, Glamorgan 0 points

GLAMORGAN

*S J Walters, lbw b Wardlaw	.....	0
S W Griffiths, c Hodgson b Ashraf	.....	0
T J Lancefield, b Rafiq	.....	80
A H T Donald, c Hodgson b Ashraf	.....	4
J L Lawlor, st Hodgson b Rafiq	.....	17
R A J Smith, c Wainman b Rafiq	.....	3
§ T J Baker, c Wainman b Leaning	.....	31
J R Murphy, c Coad b Ashraf	.....	33
K A Bull, lbw b Leaning	.....	0
D Penrhyn-Jones, c and b Wardlaw	.....	8
H W Powell, not out	.....	1
Extras (lb 1, w 5, nb 2)	.....	8
Total (37.5 overs)	.....	185

FoW: 1-1 (Griffiths), 2-5 (Walters), 3-14 (Donald), 4-77 (Lawlor), 5-83 (Smith), 6-132 (Lancefield), 7-144 (Baker), 8-144 (Bull), 9-183 (Penrhyn-Jones), 10-185 (Murphy)

	O	M	R	W
Wardlaw	6	2	20	2
Ashraf	6.5	1	24	3
Pyrah	2	0	17	0
Coad	4	0	25	0
Rafiq	8	1	35	3
Carver	5	0	38	0
Leaning	6	1	25	2

YORKSHIRE

§ D M Hodgson, c Baker b Powell	.....	21
J J Sayers, b Powell	.....	13
J A Leaning, c Baker b Penrhyn-Jones	.....	14
A Rafiq, c Lancefield b Penrhyn-Jones	.....	80
* R M Pyrah, c Walters b Bull	.....	7
W M H Rhodes, not out	.....	33
I Wardlaw, not out	.....	7
J C Wainman		
M A Ashraf	Did not bat	
B O Coad		
K Carver		
Extras (lb 2, w 10, nb 4)	.....	16
Total (5 wkts, 28.1 overs)	.....	191

FoW: 1-27 (Hodgson), 2-48 (Sayers), 3-93 (Leaning), 4-103 (Pyrah), 5-184 (Rafiq)

	O	M	R	W
Smith	3	0	28	0
Powell	6	0	38	2
Murphy	2	0	16	0
Penrhyn-Jones	6	0	37	2
Bull	6	1	37	1
Lawlor	2	0	13	0
Lancefield	3	0	20	0

Umpires: M A Eggleston and S J Malone

Scorers: H Clayton and G Watkins

Second Eleven Trophy
Warwickshire v. Yorkshire

Played at Rugby School on July 30, 2013
Yorkshire won by 8 wickets at 3.33pm

Toss won by Warwickshire   Warwickshire 0 points, Yorkshire 2 points

WARWICKSHIRE

T P Lewis, lbw b Sidebottom	0
* P M Best, c Hodd b Sidebottom	1
J P Webb, b Patterson	2
S R Hain, c Hodd b Sidebottom	8
B Zaman, lbw b Patterson	0
§ J Middleton, b Ashraf	13
T P Milnes, c Hodd b Coad	29
T W Allin, c Robinson b Coad	36
S A Ali, c Wardlaw b Rafiq	1
Enamul Haque, c Patterson b Coad	1
R O Gordon, not out	0
Extras (b 1, lb 1, w 2)	4
Total (27.2 overs)	95

FoW: 1-0 (Lewis), 2-3 (Best), 3-11 (Webb), 4-12 (Hain), 5-12 (Zaman)
6-40 (Middleton), 7-88 (Allin), 8-92 (Milnes), 9-95 (Enamul Haque), 10-95 (Ali)

	O	M	R	W
Sidebottom	6	1	14	3
Patterson	6	2	14	2
Ashraf	5	1	23	1
Wardlaw	3	0	13	0
Rafiq	4.2	0	24	1
Coad	3	1	5	3

YORKSHIRE

A W Gale, b Gordon		40
D M Hodgson, run out (Webb)		38
§ A J Hodd, not out		5
A Rafiq, not out		12
J A Leaning		
O E Robinson		
R J Sidebottom		
*S A Patterson	Did not bat	
I Wardlaw		
M A Ashraf		
B O Coad		
Extras (w 3)		3
Total (2 wkts, 17.4 overs)		98

FoW: 1-73 (Hodgson), 2-80 (Gale)

	O	M	R	W
Milnes	4	0	26	0
Ali	4	1	24	0
Gordon	5	0	28	1
Enamul Haque	4.4	1	20	0

Umpires: M J D Bodenham and M A Gumbley   Scorers: S Smith and H Clayton

Second Eleven Trophy
Worcestershire v. Yorkshire

At Barnt Green CC on August 5, 2013
No result. Match abandoned without a ball bowled at 2.30pm

No toss

Umpires: P R Pollard and W Smith

Worcestershire 1 point; Yorkshire 1 point

Scorers: Mrs S M Drinkwater and H Clayton

Durham v. Yorkshire

Played at South Northumberland CC, Gosforth, on August 12, 2013
No result. Match abandoned because of rain at 3.07pm

Toss won by Durham

Durham 1 point, Yorkshire 1 point

YORKSHIRE

E Callis, b Buckley		24
C G Roebuck, c Poynter b Arshad		27
A J Hodd, c Poynter b Buckley		6
* A Rafiq, c Poynter b Jennings		11
E Wilson, b Arshad		3
R Gibson, not out		78
§ J P Inglis, b Jennings		12
A R Laws, lbw b Morley		2
J C Wainman, b Brathwaite		14
L R Stabler, b Arshad		6
G P Whiles, not out		7
Extras (lb 4, w 8)		12
Total (9 wkts, 40 overs)		202

FoW: 1-51 (Roebuck), 2-63 (Hodd), 3-69 (Callis), 4-72 (Wilson), 5-84 (Azeem Rafiq)
6-98 (Inglis), 7-111 (Laws), 8-164 Wainman, 9-176 (Stabler)

	O	M	R	W
Brathwaite	8	0	46	1
Main	3	0	24	0
Morley	8	0	37	1
Buckley	7	0	25	2
Arshad	6	0	29	3
Jennings	8	2	37	2

DURHAM

R Singh
K K Jennings
J Clark
G Clark
§ S W Poynter
R S Buckley   Did not bat
* U Arshad
C J Pearce
R M R Brathwaite
M G Morley
G T Main

Umpires: B V Taylor and A Clark

Scorers: R V Hilton and H Clayton

Second Eleven Trophy
Yorkshire v. Nottinghamshire

Played at Barnsley CC on August 19, 2013
Yorkshire won by 21 runs at 5.47pm

Toss won by Nottinghamshhire   Yorkshire 2 points, Nottinghamshire 0 points

YORKSHIRE

E Callis, c Bacon b L Wood		44
P A Jaques, c and b S K W Wood		105
§ D M Hodgson, c White b Franks		35
J A Leaning, c Cross b Franks		3
* R M Pyrah, b S K W Wood		17
O E Robinson, not out		14
I Wardlaw, b Hutton		6
J C Wainman, not out		3
M A Ashraf		
B O Coad	Did not bat	
G P Whiles		
Extras (b 4, b 9, w 12)		25
Total (6 wkts, 40 overs)		252

FoW: 1-99 (Callis), 2-172 (Hodgson), 3-186 (Leaning), 4-212 (Jaques) 5-227 (Pyrah) 6-234 (Wardlaw)

	O	M	R	W
Hutton	6	0	46	1
Bacon	4	1	24	0
L Wood	6	0	22	1
White	8	0	49	3
Franks	8	0	50	0
S K W Wood	8	1	48	1

NOTTINGHAMSHIRE

* S Kelsall, c Hodgson b Wardlaw	7
§ M H Cross, c Hodgson b Ashraf	0
T C Rowe, c Hodgson b Coad	25
S K W Wood, b Coad	5
A D Tillock, run out (Robinson)	1
P J Franks, c Pyrah b Robinson	11
G G White, c Hodgson b Robinson	27
B A Hutton, c Whiles b Ashraf	64
G P W Bacon, c Leaning b Ashraf	58
I Woodlbw b Ashraf	1
B M Kitt, not out	7
Extras (b 8, lb 3, w 13)	24
Total (38.4 overs)	231

FoW: 1-7 (Cross), 2-15 (Kelsall), 3-26 (S K W Wood), 4-36 (Tillock), 5-50 (Rowe) 6-88 (Franks), 7-89 (White), 8-216 Hutton), 9-224 (Bacon), 10-231 (L Wood)

	O	M	R	W
Ashraf	7.4	0	36	3
Wardlaw	7	0	32	2
Coad	8	1	37	2
Pyrah	7	0	56	0
Leaning	3	0	23	0
Robinson	6	0	36	2

Umpires: A G Wharf and W B Jones   Scorers: H Clayton and Mrs A Cusworth

Second Eleven Trophy
Yorkshire v.Lancashire

Played at Centre Vale, Todmorden, on August 20, 2013
Lancashire won by 5 wickets at 4.58pm

Toss won by Yorkshire   Yorkshire 0 points, Lancashire 2 points

YORKSHIRE

E Callis, lbw b Newby	....	3
J A Tattersall, lbw b Bailey	....	5
§ D M Hodgson, c Livingstone b McKiernan	....	43
O E Robinson, c Davies b Newby	....	0
J A Leaning, c Ghaus b McKiernan	....	47
W M H Rhodes, c Davies b Bailey	....	42
I Wardlaw, st Davies b McKiernan	....	1
J A Wainman, not out	....	22
M A Ashraf, not out	....	4
B O Coad		
K Carver	Did not bat	
Extras (b 1, lb 3, w 9)		13
Total (7 wkts, 40 overs)	....	180

FoW: 1-10 (Tattersall), 2-10 (Callis), 3-10 (Robinson), 4-96 (Hodgson), 5-132 (Leaning)
6-138 (Wardlaw), 7-157 (Rhodes)

	O	M	R	W
Newby	8	1	38	2
Bailey	8	1	28	2
Griffiths	4	0	14	0
White	6	0	33	0
McKiernan	6	0	33	2
Agathangelou	6	0	27	0

LANCASHIRE

* L M Reece, c Hodgson b Ashraf	....	7
§ A L Davies, c Tattersall b Ashraf	....	0
A P Agathangelou, run out (Robinson)	....	11
L S Livingstone, not out	....	121
W A White, lbw b Leaning	....	28
O J Newby, lbw b Leaning	....	1
R P Zelem, not out	....	1
T E Bailey		
M H McKiernan	Did not bat	
G T Griffiths		
Adnan Ghaus		
Extras (b 5, lb 7, w 1)	....	13
Total (5 wkts, 30.2 overs)	....	182

FoW: 1-2 (Davies), 2-15 (Reece), 3-45 (Agathangelou), 4-150 (White), 5-158 (Newby)

	O	M	R	W
Ashraf	5	0	20	2
Wardlaw	6.2	0	36	0
Robinson	6	1	22	0
Coad	3	0	15	0
Carver	3	0	30	0
Leaning	5	1	26	2
Wainman	2	0	21	0

Umpires: A G Wharf and H Evans   Scorers: H Clayton and D M White

SECOND ELEVEN TROPHY 2013

NORTHERN GROUP – FINAL TABLE *(2012 in brackets)*

		P	W	L	Tie	No result	Aban.	Net run rate	Points
1	Lancashire (2)	9	7	2	0	0	0	-0.013	14
2	Nottinghamshire (7)	9	6	3	0	0	0	0.035	12
3	Glamorgan (-)	9	5	3	0	1	0	0.473	11
4	**Yorkshire (6) ....**	**9**	**4**	**2**	**1**	**1**	**1**	**0.707**	**11**
5	MCC Young Cricketers (-)	9	3	4	0	1	0	-0.350	8
6	Durham (1)	9	3	4	0	2	0	-0.350	8
7	Derbyshire (8)	9	3	5	0	0	1	-0.387	7
8	Warwickshire (4)	9	3	5	0	0	1	-0.645	7
9	Leicestershire (5)	9	2	5	0	2	0	-0.065	6
10	Worcestershire (3)	9	2	5	0	1	1	-0.34	6

SOUTHERN GROUP – FINAL TABLE *(2012 in brackets)*

		P	W	L	Tie	No result	Aban.	Net run rate	Points
1	Middlesex (1)	9	7	2	0	0	0	0.362	14
2	Unicorns A (-)	9	5	3	0	0	1	-0.326	11
3	Surrey (4)	9	4	3	0	0	2	0.613	10
4	Gloucestershire (6)	9	3	2	0	1	3	1.272	10
5	Northamptonshire (-)	9	4	4	0	0	1	-0.482	9
6	Sussex (2)	9	4	5	0	0	0	0.124	8
7	Kent (8)	9	4	5	0	0	0	0.077	8
8	Essex (3)	9	3	4	0	1	1	0.348	8
9	Somerset (7)	9	3	5	0	0	1	-0.700	7
10	Hampshire (10)	9	2	6	0	0	1	-0.843	5

SEMI-FINALS

Unicorns A (94) lost to Lancashire (95-5) by 5 wickets
Nottinghamshire (252-4) beat Middlesex (228) by 24 runs.

FINAL

Lancashire (259-8) beat Nottinghamshire (183) by 76 runs

SECOND ELEVEN TROPHY
AVERAGES 2013

Played 9   Won 4   Lost 2   Tied 1   Abandoned 2

BATTING AND FIELDING

(Qualification 3 innings)

Player	M.	I.	N.O.	Runs	H.S.	Avge	100s	50s	ct/st
R Gibson	3	3	1	107	78*	53.50	0	1	0
Azeem Rafiq	4	4	1	138	80	46.00	0	1	1
J J Sayers	3	3	0	125	91	41.66	0	1	1
J C Wainman	4	3	2	39	22*	39.00	0	0	2
D M Hodgson	7	7	0	237	53	33.85	0	1	10/3
W M H Rhodes	4	4	1	101	42	33.66	0	0	0
J A Leaning	7	6	1	138	58*	27.60	0	1	3
E Callis	4	4	0	90	44	22.50	0	0	0
I Wardlaw	6	5	2	29	11	9.66	0	0	1
O E Robinson	4	3	1	17	14*	8.50	0	0	2
Also played									
P A Jaques	1	1	0	105	105	105.00	1	0	0
A Lyth	1	1	0	102	102	102.00	1	0	0
A Z Lees	2	2	0	84	54	42.00	0	1	0
A W Gale	1	1	0	40	40	40.00	0	0	0
M Hussain	1	1	0	29	29	29.00	0	0	0
C G Roebuck	1	1	0	27	27	27.00	0	0	0
J A Tattersall	2	2	0	38	33	19.00	0	0	1
J P Inglis	1	1	0	12	12	12.00	0	0	0
R M Pyrah	2	2	0	24	17	12.00	0	0	1
A J Hodd	2	2	1	11	6	11.00	0	0	3
J Shaw	2	2	0	8	5	4.00	0	0	0
E Wilson	1	1	0	3	3	3.00	0	0	0
L R Stabler	2	2	0	6	6	3.00	0	0	1
A R Laws	1	1	0	2	2	2.00	0	0	0
K Carver	4	1	0	1	1	1.00	0	0	0
B O Coad	6	1	1	6	6*	—	0	0	0
M A Ashraf	4	1	1	4	4*	—	0	0	0
G P Whiles	2	1	1	7	7*	—	0	0	1
G S Randhawa	1	1	1	13	13*	—	0	0	1
M D Fisher	1	1	0	0	0	—	0	0	0
R J Sidebottom	1	0	0	0	—	—	0	0	0
S A Patterson	1	0	0	0	—	—	0	0	0

BOWLING
(Qualification 5 wickets)

Player	Overs	Mdns	Runs	Wkts	Avge	Best	4wI
M D Fisher	11	1	47	6	7.83	6-25	1
M A Ashraf	24.3	2	103	9	11.44	3-24	0
Azeem Rafiq	18.2	1	103	8	12.87	4-45	1
J A Leaning	26	3	137	6	22.83	2-25	0
B O Coad	26	2	125	5	25.00	3-5	0
I Wardlaw	36	2	189	6	31.50	2-20	0
Also bowled							
R J Sidebottom	6	1	14	3	4.66	3-14	0
S A Patterson	6	2	14	2	7.00	2-14	0
G S Randhawa	4	0	26	2	13.00	2-26	0
A Lyth	6	0	30	2	15.00	2-30	0
R Gibson	3	0	16	1	16.00	1-16	0
O E Robinson	19	1	121	4	30.25	2-36	0
J Shaw	12	0	71	2	35.50	1-25	0
W M H Rhodes	10	0	68	1	68.00	1-35	0
K Carver	21	0	121	0	—	—	0
R M Pyrah	9	0	73	0	—	—	0
L R Stabler	4	0	20	0	—	—	0
J C Wainman	2	0	21	0	—	—	0
J J Sayers	2	0	19	0	—	—	0
J A Tattersall	1	0	8	0	—	—	0

Second Eleven Twenty20
Yorkshire v. Nottinghamshire

Played at Headingley, Leeds, on June 14, 2013
Yorkshire won by 4 wickets at 2pm

Toss won by Yorkshire

Yorkshire 2 points, Nottinghamshire 0 points

NOTTINGHAMSHIRE

S Kelsall, c Stabler b Gibson		65
§ M H Cross, b Whiles		0
S K W Wood, b Whiles		7
G G White, run out (Gibson)		45
T C Rowe, c Shaw b Rhodes		3
A D Tilcock, c Fisher b Gibson		5
* B A Hutton, not out		2
Hassan Azad, not out		5
G P W Bacon		
B M Kitt	Did not bat	
L Wood		
Extras (b 4, lb 5, w 8)		17
Total (6 wkts, 20 overs)		149

FoW: 1-6 (Cross), 2-20 (S K W Wood), 3-125 (Kelsall), 4-135 (White), 5-142 (Tillcock) 6-143 (Rowe)

	O	M	R	W
Stabler	2	0	15	0
Whiles	3	0	10	2
Fisher	2	1	6	0
Shaw	2	0	20	0
Azeem Rafiq	4	0	35	0
Randhawa	1	0	10	0
Rhodes	4	0	32	1
Gibson	2	0	12	2

YORKSHIRE

§ D M Hodgson, c Rowe b S K W Wood		19
R Gibson, c Rowe b Bacon		14
E Wilson, run out (Rowe)		7
* Azeem Rafiq, c Cross b Bacon		49
J A Leaning, c Kelsall b Bacon		26
W M H Rhodes, c Cross b Kitt		7
G S Randhawa, run out		18
M D Fisher, not out		4
J Shaw		
L R Stabler	Did not bat	
G P Whiles		
Extras (lb 2, w 5)		7
Total (6 wkts, 17.1 overs)		151

FoW: 1-25 (Gibson), 2-39 (Wilson), 3-43 (Hodgson), 4-120 (Leaning), 5-121 (Azeem Rafiq), 6-143 (Rhodes)

	O	M	R	W
Hutton	2	0	29	0
L Wood	2	0	21	0
Bacon	3	0	14	3
S K W Wood	4	0	31	1
White	4	0	29	0
Kitt	2	0	21	1
Tillcock	0.1	0	4	0

Umpires: A G Wharf and H Fidler

Scorers: H Clayton and Mrs A Cusworth

Second Eleven Twenty20
Yorkshire v. Nottinghamshire

Played at Headingley, Leeds, on June 14, 2013
No result. Match abandoned at 5.07pm (rain)

Toss won by Yorkshire

Yorkshire 1 point, Nottinghamshire 1 point

NOTTINGHAMSHIRE

H Azad, c Gibson b Stabler	19
§ M H Cross, c Wilson b Shaw	1
T C Rowe, b Carver	34
S K W Wood, c Wilson b Carver	28
A D Tilcock, not out	39
S Kelksall, not out	39
* B A Hutton	
G G White	
G P W Bacon	Did not bat
B M Kitt	
L Wood	
Extras (lb 5, w 1)	6
Total (4 wkts, 19 overs)	166

FoW: 1-3 (Cross), 2-37 (Hassan Azad), 3-71 (Rowe), 4-86 (S K W Wood)

	O	M	R	W
Shaw	3	0	17	1
Whiles	2	1	19	0
Stabler	2	0	23	1
Carver	4	0	32	2
Fisher	1	0	14	0
Leaning	2	0	20	0
Rhodes	2	0	14	0
Gibson	3	0	22	0

YORKSHIRE

§ D M Hodgson	
R Gibson	
E Wilson	
M Hussain	
J A Leaning	
* W M H Rhodes	Did not bat
M D Fisher	
J Shaw	
L R Stabler	
K Carver	
G P Whiles	

Umpires: A G Wharf and H Fidler

Scorers: H Clayton and Mrs A Cusworth

Second Eleven Twenty20
Yorkshire v. Lancashire

Played at Marske-by-the-Sea CC on June 20, 2013
Lancashire won by 15 runs at 2.18 pm

Toss won by Yorkshire

Yorkshire 0 points, Lancashire 2 points

LANCASHIRE

S C Moore, b Stabler	6
§ A L Davies, c Gibson b Stabler	7
* K R Brown, not out	101
J Clark, c Lees b Rhodes	61
L S Livingstone, c Robinson b Stabler	16
A M Lilley, not out	1
H Hameed	
M H McKiernan	
G T Griffiths	Did not bat
Adnan Ghaus	
L J Hurt	
Extras (lb 5, nb 4; w 2)	11
Total (4 wkts, 20 overs)	203

FoW: 1-15 (Davies), 2-16 (Moore), 3-159 (Clark), 4-183 (Livingstone)

	O	M	R	W
Stabler	4	0	40	3
Robinson	4	1	33	0
Rhodes	2.4	0	33	1
Carver	4	0	27	0
Azeem Rafiq	1	0	16	0
Leaning	1	0	8	0
Wainman	3.2	0	41	0

YORKSHIRE

A Z Lees, c Lilley b Griffiths	20
W T Root, c Adnan Ghaus b Clark	20
E Wilson, c and b Clark	13
* Azeem Rafiq, c Livingstone b Lilley	17
J A Leaning, c Livingstone b Hurt	21
W M H Rhodes, run out (Hameed)	15
O E Robinson, lbw b McKiernan	25
J C Wainman, not out	8
L R Stabler, not out	7
K Carver	
§ B P Gibson	Did not bat
Extras (b 3; lb 3, nb 3; w 3)	12
Total (7 wkts, 20 overs)	188

FoW: 1-43 (Lees), 2-49 (Root), 3-65 (Wilson), 4-77 (Azeem Rafiq), 5-135 (Rhodes)
6-159 (Leaning), 7-173 (Robinson)

	O	M	R	W
Adnan Ghaus	2	0	35	0
Griffiths	3	0	23	1
Clark	4	0	32	2
Lilley	4	0	37	1
Hurt	4	0	37	1
McKiernan	3	0	18	1

Umpires: B J Debenham and S J Malone   Scorers: H Clayton and D M White

Second Eleven Twenty20
Yorkshire v. Lancashire

Played at Marske-by-the-Sea CC on June 20, 2013
Lancashire won by 58 runs at 5.48pm

Toss won by Lancashire   Yorkshire 0 points, Lancashire 2 points

LANCASHIRE

S C Moore, c Robinson b Rhodes		22
§ A L Davies, c Leaning b Azeem Rafiq		56
L S Livingstone, c Leaning b Brown		100
J Clark, c and b Stabler		13
* K R Brown, not out		16
A M Lilley, not out		3
D J Lamb		
M H McKiernan		
G T Griffiths	Did not bat	
Adnan Ghaus		
L J Hurt		
Extras (lb 2, nb 8; w 4)		14
Total (4 wkts, 20 overs)		224

FoW: 1-60 (Moore), 2-114 (Davies), 3-197 (Clark), 4-207 (Livingstone)

	O	M	R	W
Leaning	2	0	23	0
Robinson	3	0	40	0
Stabler	3	0	25	1
Rhodes	2	0	33	1
Carver	3	0	28	0
Azeem Rafiq	4	0	42	1
Brown	3	0	30	1

YORKSHIRE

A Z Lees, c Lilley b Clark		17
E Wilson, c Livingstone b Clark		39
W T Root, c Davies b Hurt		8
* Azeem Rafiq, b Hurt		6
J A Leaning, c Clark b Lilley		0
W M H Rhodes, c Clark b McKiernan		38
O E Robinson, c Clark b Lilley		10
§ B P Gibson, run out (McKiernan)		9
L R Stabler, run out (Clark)		9
J P W Brown, not out		7
K Carver, not out		3
Extras (b5; lb 2, nb 12; w 1)		20
Total (9 wkts, 20 overs)		166

FoW: 1-44 (Lees), 2-59 (Root), 3-75 (Azeem Rafiq), 4-80 (Leaning), 5-83 (Wilson)
6-111 (Robinson), 7-126 (Gibson), 8-151 (Stabler), 9-159 (Rhodes)

	O	M	R	W
Adnan Ghaus	2	0	20	0
Griffiths	3	0	15	0
Clark	4	0	30	1
Hurt	4	0	41	3
Lilley	4	0	30	2
McKiernan	3	0	23	1

Umpires: B J Debenham and S J Malone   Scorers: H Clayton and D M White

Second Eleven Twenty20
England Under-19s v. Yorkshire

Played at the Haslegrave Ground, Loughborough University, on June 21, 2013
Yorkshire won by 54 runs at 2.08pm

Toss won by Yorkshire   England Under-19s 0 points, Yorkshire 2 points

YORKSHIRE

§ D M Hodgson, c Hudson-Prentice b Sayer	9
R Gibson, c Clark b Higgins	30
M Hussain, c Shaw b Pickering	13
* Azeem Rafiq, c Sibley b Higgins	7
O E Robinson, run out (Tattersall)	53
W M H Rhodes, run out (Shaw)	5
G S Randhawa, b Jones	13
M D Fisher, c Jackson b Jones	15
J C Wainman, not out	6
I Wardlaw, not out	8
B O Coad	Did not bat
Extras (b 1; lb 3, w 5)	9
Total (8 wkts, 20 overs)	168

FoW: 1-16 (Hodgson), 2-52 (Gibson), 3-62 (Azeem Rafiq), 4-90 (Hussain), 5-115 (Rhodes), 6-131 (Robinson), 7-145 (Randhawa), 8-160 (Fisher)

	O	M	R	W
Shaw	3	0	18	0
Sayer	4	0	42	1
Ireland	1	0	22	0
Higgins	4	0	22	2
Pickering	4	0	32	1
Jones	4	0	28	2

ENGLAND UNDER-19s

R F Higgins, b Robinson	3
J Clark, run out (Coad)	3
* J A Tattersall, c Gibson b Wainman	12
R Jones, c Fisher b Robinson	3
D P Sibley, c and b Randhawa	34
F J Hudson-Prentice, c Wainman b Azeem Rafiq	8
§ C F Jackson, c and b Azeem Rafiq	0
P J Sayer, c Wardlaw b Randhawa	1
J Shaw, c Gibson b Fisher	25
A W Ireland, c Gibson b Coad	9
H T Pickering, not out	1
Extras (b 1; lb 4, w 10)	15
Total (18.4 overs)	114

FoW: 1-6 (Higgins), 2-19 (Clark), 3-23 (Jones), 4-38 (Tattersall), 5-57 (Hudson-Prentice), 6-58 (Jackson), 7-67 (Sayer), 8-77 (Sibley), 9-113 (Shaw), 10-114 (Ireland)

	O	M	R	W
Wardlaw	4	0	19	0
Robinson	2	0	10	2
Coad	1.4	0	8	1
Wainman	1	0	7	1
Randhawa	4	0	33	2
Azeem Rafiq	4	0	20	2
Fisher	2	0	12	1

Umpires: M A Eggleston and T Lungley   Scorers: Mrs S M Drinkwater and H Clayton

Second Eleven Twenty20
England Under-19s v. Yorkshire

Played at the Haslegrave Ground, Loughborough University, on June 21, 2013
Yorkshire won by 22 runs at 5.23pm

Toss won by Yorkshire   England Under-19s 0 points, Yorkshire 2 points

YORKSHIRE

§ D M Hodgson, b Ireland	28
R Gibson, c Clark b Shaw	0
M Hussain, c Jones b Ireland	30
* Azeem Rafiq, c Clark b Pickering	6
O E Robinson, c Higgins b Pickering	15
W M H Rhodes, run out (Ireland)	36
G S Randhawa, c Pickering b Sibley	7
M D Fisher, c Clark b Sibley	3
I Wardlaw, c Tattersall b Shaw	33
B O Coad, c Higgins b Sibley	1
K Carver, not out	0
Extras (b 1, lb 3, nb 4; w 2)	10
Total (18.2 overs)	169

FoW: 1-2 (Gibson), 2-42 (Hussain), 3-70 (Hodgson), 4-79 (Azeem Rafiq), 5-93 (Robinson) 6-126 (Randhawa), 7-133 (Fisher), 8-136 (Rhodes), 9-168 (Coad); 10-169 (Wardlaw)

	O	M	R	W
Shaw	3	0	47	2
Sayer	2	0	12	0
Ireland	4	0	26	2
Dal	1	0	21	0
Pickering	3	0	33	2
Higgins	2	0	10	0
Sibley	3	0	16	3

ENGLAND UNDER-19s

R F Higgins, c Robinson b Rhodes	38
J Clark, run out (Rhodes)	29
* J A Tattersall, c Rhodes b Azeem Rafiq	9
R Jones, run out (Hussain)	14
D P Sibley, not out	30
A Dal, b Randhawa	4
§ C F Jackson, b Wardlaw	7
P J Sayer, c Hodgson b Gibson	6
J Shaw, not out	3
A W Ireland	
H T Pickering Did not bat	
Extras (b 1; lb 3, w 3)	7
Total (7 wkts, 20 overs)	147

FoW: 1-54 (Higgins), 2-74 (Tattersall), 3-92 (Clark), 4-102 (Jones), 5-122 (Dal) 6-137 (Jackson), 7-144 (Sayer)

	O	M	R	W
Wardlaw	3	0	14	1
Fisher	1	0	19	0
Gibson	2	0	24	1
Coad	1	0	7	0
Rhodes	1	0	9	1
Randhawa	4	0	25	1
Azeem Rafiq	4	0	18	1
Carver	4	0	27	0

Umpires: M A Eggleston and T Lungley   Scorers: Mrs S M Drinkwater and H Clayton

Second Eleven Twenty20
Derbyshire v. Yorkshire

Played at the Copper Yard, Denby, on June 24, 2013
Derbyshire won by 6 wkts at 1.40pm

Toss won by Derbyshire   Derbyshire 2 points, Yorkshire 0 points

YORKSHIRE

§ D M Hodgson, b Burgoyne	22
E Wilson, c Burgoyne b Wheatcroft	12
Azeem Rafiq, c Lezar b Taylor	6
* R M Pyrah, c Lezar b Burgoyne	6
O E Robinson, c Taylor b Burgoyne	8
M Hussain, c Bird b Cork	5
I Wardlaw, c Bird b Burgoyne	8
G S Randhawa, run out (Elstone)	1
M D Fisher, not out	7
J C \Wainman, run out (Elstone)	0
B O Coad, c Redfern b Cork	0
Extras (lb 2, nb 2; w 2)	6
Total (14.5 overs)	81

FoW: 1-23 (Wilson), 2-42 (Azeem Rafiq), 3-45 (Hodgson), 4-58 (Pyrah), 5-59 (Robinson)
6-71 (Hussain), 7-72 (Randhawa), 8-74 (Wardlaw), 9-81 (Wainman), 10-81 (Coad)

	O	M	R	W
Wheatcroft	3	0	26	1
Lezar	3	0	15	0
Taylor	2	0	6	1
Burgoyne	4	0	23	4
Cork	3	0	9	2

DERBYSHIRE

* D J Redfern, st Hodgson b Azeem Rafiq		28
§ T Poynton, c Fisher b Wardlaw		1
P M Borrington, not out		37
P I Burgoyne, c and b Azeem Rafiq		1
S L Elstone, st Hodgson b Randhawa		8
G T G Cork, not out		3
T S I Hamilton		
T A I Taylor		
M J K Bird	Did not bat	
W Lezar		
MA Wheatcroft		
Extras (lb 5, w 3)		8
Total (4 wkts; 16.4 overs)		86

FoW: 1-3 (Poynton), 2-53 (Redfern), 3-57 (Burgoyne), 4-74 (Elstone)

	O	M	R	W
Wardlaw	3	0	15	1
Coad	2	1	2	0
Fisher	1	0	12	0
Azeem Rafiq	4	0	23	2
Pyrah	4	0	13	0
Randhawa	1.4	0	14	1
Robinson	1	0	2	0

Umpires: M A Eggleston and T Lungley   Scorers: T M Cottam and H Clayton

Second Eleven Twenty20
Derbyshire v. Yorkshire

Played at the Copper Yard, Denby, on June 24, 2013
Yorkshire won by 6 wkts at 4.44pm

Toss won by Yorkshire

Derbyshire 0 points, Yorkshire 2 points

DERBYSHIRE

* D J Redfern, c Wardlaw b Azeem Rafiq	29
P I Burgoyne, c Wainman b Wardlaw	1
S L Elstone, c Fisher b Coad	1
P M Borrington, b Azeem Rafiq	16
§ T Poynton, c Azeem Rafiq b Pyrah	14
G T G Cork, b Pyrah	6
T S I Hamilton, run out (Robinson)	9
M J K Bird, not out	13
T A I Taylor, st Hodgson b Azeem Rafiq	5
W Lezar, c Wardlaw b Azeem Rafiq	0
MA Wheatcroft, not out	2
Extras (nb 2, w 1)	3
Total (9 wkts; 20 overs)	99

FoW: 1-15 (Burgoyne), 2-19 (Elstone), 3-43 (Borrington), 4-50 (Redfern), 5-62 (Cork)
6-76 (Hamilton), 7-80 (Poynton), 8-90 (Taylor), 9-90 (Lezar)

	O	M	R	W
Wardlaw	4	0	29	1
Coad	2	0	11	1
Pyrah	4	0	25	2
Wainman	2	0	9	0
Azeem Rafiq	4	0	11	4
Randhawa	4	0	14	0

YORKSHIRE

§ D M Hodgson, c Cork b Redfern		9
E Wilson, c Taylor b Wheatcroft		9
Azeem Rafiq, c Elstone b Burgoyne		33
* R M Pyrah, run out (Taylor)		24
O E Robinson, not out		9
I Wardlaw, not out		16
M Hussain		
G S Randhawa		
M D Fisher	Did not bat	
J C Wainman		
B O Coad		
Extras (lb 2, w 2)		4
Total (4 wkts; 13.3 overs)		104

FoW: 1-14 (Hodgson), 2-19 (Wilson), 3-56 (Pyrah), 4-86 (Azeem Rafiq)

	O	M	R	W
Redfern	4	0	14	1
Wheatcroft	4	0	38	1
Birgoyne	3	0	21	1
Taylor	2	0	13	0
Lezar	0.3	0	16	0

Umpires: M A Eggleston and T Lungley   Scorers: T M Cottam and H Clayton

SECOND ELEVEN
TWENTY20 2013

*(Two matches played against the same opponents
at the same venue on the same day)*

GROUP A – FINAL TABLE

		P	W	L	Tie	No result	Aban.	Net run rate	Points
1	Durham (3)	8	7	1	0	0	0	1.229	14
2	Lancashire (2)	8	7	1	0	0	0	1.159	14
3	**Yorkshire (6)**	**8**	**4**	**3**	**0**	**1**	**0**	**0.382**	**9**
4	Derbyshire (4)	8	2	6	0	0	0	-0.684	4
5	England Under-19s (1)	8	2	6	0	0	0	-1.084	4
6	Nottinghamshire (5)	8	1	6	0	1	0	-0.965	3

GROUP B – FINAL TABLE

		P	W	L	Tie	No result	Aban.	Net run rate	Points
1	Gloucestershire (4)	8	6	2	0	0	0	1.570	12
2	Somerset (2)	8	6	2	0	0	0	1.163	12
3	Worcestershire (1)	8	3	3	0	0	2	-1.147	8
4	Glamorgan (3)	8	2	4	0	0	2	-1.324	6
5	Warwickshire (5)	8	1	7	0	0	0	-0.776	2

GROUP C – FINAL TABLE

		P	W	L	Tie	No result	Aban.	Net run rate	Points
1	Middleesex (2)	8	5	2	0	1	0	0.827	11
2	Unicorns A (3)	8	4	2	0	2	0	0.131	10
3	Essex (1)	8	4	3	0	1	0	0.912	9
4	Northamptonshire (4)	8	3	5	0	0	0	-0.739	6
5	Leicestershire (5)	8	2	6	0	0	0	-0.858	4

GROUP D – FINAL TABLE

		P	W	L	Tie	No result	Aban.	Net run rate	Points
1	Surrey (3)	8	5	1	0	0	2	1.509	12
2	Kent (2)	8	4	3	0	0	1	1.137	9
3	Sussex (1)	8	3	4	0	0	1	-0.465	7
4	MCC Young Cricketers (5)	8	3	5	0	0	0	-0.751	6
5	Hampshire (4)	8	3	5	0	0	0	-1.012	6

(2012 positions in brackets)

SEMI-FINALS

Middlesex (164-7) beat Durham (135-9) by 29 runs

Surrey (168-6) beat Gloucestershire (83) by 85 runs

FINAL

Surrey (169-8) beat Middlesex (163-8) by six runs

PREVIOUS WINNERS

2011   **Sussex**, who beat Durham by 24 runs

2012   **England Under-19s**, who beat Sussex by 8 wkts

SECOND ELEVEN TWENTY20
AVERAGES 2013

Played 8   Won 4   Lost 3   Abandoned 1

BATTING AND FIELDING

(Qualification 3 innings)

Player	M.	I.	N.O.	Runs	H.S.	Avge	100s	50s	ct/st
I Wardlaw	4	4	2	65	33	32.50	0	0	0
O E Robinson	5	5	1	123	53	30.75	0	1	2
J A Leaning	4	3	0	79	54	26.33	0	1	2
W M H Rhodes	6	5	0	101	38	20.20	0	0	0
Azeem Rafiq	7	7	0	124	49	17.71	0	0	3
D M Hodgson	6	5	0	87	28	17.10	0	0	0/3
E Wilson	6	5	0	81	39	16.20	0	0	2
M Hussain	5	3	0	48	30	16.00	0	0	0
R Gibson	4	3	0	44	30	14.55	0	0	6
M D Fisher	6	4	2	29	15	14.50	0	0	4
J C Wainman	4	3	2	14	8*	14.00	0	0	2
G S Randhawa	5	4	1	39	18*	13.00	0	0	1

Also batted

Player	M.	I.	N.O.	Runs	H.S.	Avge	100s	50s	ct/st
L R Stabler	4	2	1	16	9	16.00	0	0	3
R.M Pyrah	2	2	0	30	21	15.00	0	0	0
W T Root	2	2	0	28	20	14.00	0	0	0
B P Gibson	2	1	0	9	9	9.00	0	0	0
B O Coad	4	2	0	1	1	0.50	0	0	0
J W P Brown	1	1	1	7	7*	—	0	0	0
K Carver	4	2	2	3	3*	—	0	0	0

BOWLING

(Qualification 5 wickets)

Player	Overs	Mdns	Runs	Wkts	Avge	Best	4wI
Azeem Rafiq	25	0	165	10	16.50	4-11	1
L R Stabler	15	0	179	6	29.83	3-40	0

Also bowled

Player	Overs	Mdns	Runs	Wkts	Avge	Best	4wI
B O Coad	6.4	1	28	2	14.00	1-8	0
G R Whiles	5	1	29	2	14.50	2-10	0
R M Pyrah	8	0	38	2	19.00	2-25	0
R Gibson	7	0	58	3	19.33	2-12	0
G S Randhawa	10.4	0	71	3	23.66	2-33	0
I Wardlaw	14	0	77	3	25.66	1-14	0
J W P Brown	3	0	30	1	30.00	1-30	0
W M H Rhodes	11.4	0	121	4	30.25	1-9	0
J Shaw	5	0	37	1	37.00	1-17	0
O E Robinson	12	1	85	2	42.50	2-10	0
K Carver	15	0	114	2	57.00	2-32	0
J C Wainman	6.2	0	57	1	57.00	1-7	0
M D Fisher	7	1	63	1	63.00	1-12	0
J A Leaning	5	0	51	0	—	—	0

Other Second Eleven Match
Durham v. Yorkshire

Played at Hartlepool CC on April 16, 17 and 18, 2013
Match drawn at 6.23pm on the Third Day
Toss won by Yorkshire

Close of play: First Day, Yorkshire 6-0 (Lees 1, Sayers 5); Second Day, Durham 110-3 (Pringle 35*, Wood 4*)

DURHAM

First Innings			Second Innings	
R Singh, b Pyrah	31		lbw b Pyrah	50
J A Thompson, lbw b Shaw	27			
* G J Muchall, c Lees b Ashraf	25		(2) c Hodd b Ashraf	1
R D Pringle, c Sayers b Pyrah	44		(4) c Leaning b Wardlaw	54
G R Breese, c and b Randhawa	108		(6) lbw b Pyrah	1
U Arshad, c Hodd b Ashraf	15			
§ C J Pearce, c Lees b Wardlaw	27		(7) c Shaw b Wardlaw	5
A W Ireland, not out	5		(8) lbw b Ashraf	32
J P Bousfield	Did not bat		(9) c Lees b Ashraf	9
M E Claydon			(10) not out	33
R M R Brathwaite				
J Harrison				
M J Richardson			(3) lbw b Wardlaw	6
M A Wood			(5) lbw b Pyrah	23
Extras (b 10, lb 7, nb 4)	21		Extras (b 1, lb 8)	9
Total (7 wkts dec; 93.5 overs)	303		Total (9 wkts dec, 52.2 overs)	232

FoW: 1-48 (Singh), 2-78 (Thompson), 3-92 (Muchall), 4-149 (Pringle), 5-175 (Arshad)
1st 6-291 (Pearce), 7-303 (Breese)

FoW: 1-2 (Muchall), 2-29 (Richardson), 3-103 (Singh), 4-143 (Pringle), 5-149 (Wood)
2nd 6-150 (Breese), 7-158 (Pearce), 8-183 (Bousfield), 9-216 (Ireland)

	O	M	R	W		O	M	R	W
Wardlaw	13	4	36	1	Wardlaw	17	5	51	3
Ashraf	16	7	33	2	Ashraf	12	5	50	3
Pyrah	13	3	32	2	Pyrah	14	4	58	3
Coad	15	3	55	0	Coad	9	1	52	0
Shaw	8	0	30	1	Shaw	0.2	0	12	0
Randhawa	23.5	4	77	1					
Tattersall	5	0	23	0					

YORKSHIRE

First Innings			Second Innings	
A Z Lees, lbw b Bousfield	18		lbw b Pringle	62
J J Sayers, not out	100		c Breese b Pringle	21
* D M Hodgson, b Wood	50		(6) c Richardson b Harrison	13
§ A J Hodd, c Singh b Pringle	35		(5) c Singh b Harrison	61
R M Pyrah, b Pringle	0		(3) b Bousfield	1
J A Leaning, not out	0		(4) lbw b Wood	25
I Wardlaw				
J A Tattersall	Did not bat		(7) not out	20
M A Ashraf				
G S Randhawa			(8) not out	21
B O Coad				
J Shaw				
Extras (lb 11, w 1, nb 14)	26		Extras (lb 9, nb 2)	11
Total (4 wkts dec, 82.5 overs)	229		Total (6 wkts, 60.2 overs)	235

FoW: 1-33 (Lees), 2-144 (Hodgson), 3-210 (Hodd), 4-226 (Pyrah)
2nd: 1-69 (Sayers), 2-70 (Pyrah), 3-94 (Lees), 4-142 (Leaning), 5-176 (Hodgson), 6-199 (Hodd)

	O	M	R	W		O	M	R	W
Claydon	14	3	22	0	Wood	10	2	31	1
Brathwaite	13	5	30	0	Harrison	11	1	23	2
Bousfield	5.5	0	21	1	Brathwaite	5	0	22	0
Harrison	10	0	45	0	Claydon	5	1	19	0
Breese	15	5	29	0	Pringle	14.2	1	66	2
Ireland	10	1	46	0	Bousfield	6	2	13	1
Pringle	9	2	19	2	Breese	9	2	52	0
Wood	5	4	6	1					

Umpires: P K Baldwin and I A Ward   Scorers: R V Hilton and H Clayton

NOTE:M J Richardson and M A Wood returned from First Eleven duty in time for the Second Day

Other Second Eleven Match
Yorkshire v. Lancashire

Played at Scarborough on April 23, 24 and 25, 2013
Match drawn at 3.22pm on the Third Day (rain)
Toss won by Yorkshire

Close of play: First Day, Lanacshire 161-1 (Davies 79, Agathangelou 23); Second Day, Yorkshire 36-0 (Lees 9, Sayers 16)

First Innings	YORKSHIRE		Second Innings	
A Z Lees, lbw b Newby	0		not out	121
J J Sayers, b Parry	91		run out (Newby)	25
*D M Hodgson, c Davies b Clark	26		c Moore b Clark	26
§ A J Hodd, c Davies b Clark	1		not out	4
R M Pyrah, c Jones b Clark	5			
J A Leaning, c Lilley b Ghaus	52			
G S Randhawa, c Moore b Newby	27			
J Shaw, c Hameed b Ghaus	0			
I Wardlaw, run out (Hameed)	0			
M A Ashraf, c Bailey b Ghaus	3			
B O Coad, not out	18			
W M H Rhodes	Did Not Bat			
Extras (b 5, lb 3, w 1, nb 16)	25		Extras (b 4, lb 3, nb 5)	12
Total (71.2 overs)	248		Total (2 wkts; 53.1 overs)	188

FoW: 1-0 (Lees), 2-46 (Hodgson), 3-50 (Hodd); 4-63 (Pyrah); 5-198 (Sayers)
1st 6-198 (Leaning), 7-198 (Shaw), 8-198 (Wardlaw), 9-201 (Ashraf), 10-248 (Randhawa)
2nd 1-79 (Sayers), 2-157 (Hodgson)

	O	M	R	W		O	M	R	W
Newby	14.2	4	42	2	Newby	16	4	54	0
Bailey	15	3	47	0	Adnan Ghaus	11	3	44	0
Clark	13	1	65	3	Clark	6.1	1	16	1
Adnan Ghaus	13	3	60	3	Lilley	10	1	36	0
Parry	15	4	25	1	Parry	3	0	8	0
Lilley	1	0	1	0	Bailey	7	1	23	0

LANCASHIRE

S C Moore, lbw b Pyrah		58
§ A L Davies, c Hodd b Randhawa		119
A P Agathangelou, c Hodd b Ashraf		30
J Clark, b Shaw		102
* S D Parry, b Randhawa		0
L S Livingstone, c Hodd b Shaw		27
O J Newby, lbw b Shaw		20
H Hameed, not out		43
A M Lilley, c Hodd b Rhodes		2
R Jones, b Rhodes		40
T E Bailey		
Adnan Ghaus	Did not bat	
Extras (lb 8, nb 6)		14
Total (9 wkts dec, 116.5 overs)		455

FoW: 1-107 (Moore), 2-184 (Agathangelou), 3-239 (Davies), 4-239 (Parry), 5-311 (Livingstone) 6-360 (Clark), 7-367 (Newby), 8-372 (Lilley), 9-455 (Jones)

	O	M	R	W
Wardlaw	17	3	68	0
Ashraf	19	2	97	1
Coad	13	2	50	0
Pyrah	23	3	70	1
Shaw	17	5	65	3
Randhawa	21	7	75	2
Rhodes	6.5	1	22	2

Umpires: R J Bailey and H Fidler   Scorers: H Clayton and D M White
NOTE: Jordan Clark, of Lancashire, hit six sixes from Gurham Randhawa's 13th over

244

Other Second Eleven Match
Lancashire v. Yorkshire

Played at Northop Hall CC, Flintshire, on April 30 and May 1 and 2, 2013
Yorkshire won by 5 wickets at 5.23pm on the Third Day

Toss won by Lancashire

Close of play: First Day, Yorkshire 25-1 (Sayers 16, Hodgson 3); Second Day, Lancashire 147-4 (White 39, Parry 15)

LANCASHIRE

First Innings		Second Innings	
T C Smith, c Hodd b Ashraf	89	c Hodgson b Wardlaw	13
§ A L Davies, c Leaning b Ashraf	0	c Sayers b Pyrah	31
A P Agathangelou, c Hodd b Pyrah	40	lbw b Pyrah	21
J Clark, lbw b Pyrah	20	lbw b Randhawa	24
W A White, c Rhodes b Wardlaw	67	not out	70
* S D Parry, c Hodd b Ashraf	2	c Hodd b Ashraf	27
O J Newby, b Wardlaw	31	c and b Pyrah	0
L S Llivingstone, c Hodd b Rhodes	35	not out	15
A M Lilley, not out	28		
T E Bailey, not out	0		
Mohammed Abid			
B Roberts	Did not bat		
Extras (b 1, lb 4, w 2, nb 10)	17	Extras (b 2, lb 2)	4
Total (8 wkts dec, 96 overs)	329	Total (6 wkts dec, 56 overs)	209

FoW: 1-0 (Davies), 2-91 (Agathangelou), 3-117 (Clark), 4-194 (Smith), 5-196 (Parry)
1st 6-246 (Newby), 7-277 (White), 8-321 (Livingstone)
FoW: 1-26 (Smith), 2-68 (Agathangelou), 3-69 (Davies), 4-99 (Clark), 5-163 (Parry)
2nd 6-186 (Newby)

	O	M	R	W		O	M	R	W
Wardlaw	16	3	60	2	Wardlaw	6	1	19	1
Ashraf	16	4	40	3	Ashraf	14	3	57	1
Pyrah	15	5	30	2	Randhawa	18	3	59	1
Coad	12	5	28	0	Leaning	5	0	17	0
Randhawa	23	5	95	0	Pyrah	13	4	53	3
Rhodes	5	0	29	1					
Leaning	5	0	26	0					
Stabler	4	0	16	0					

YORKSHIRE

First Innings		Second Innings	
A Z Lees, c Agathangelou b Newby	0	lbw b Smith	54
J J Sayers, lbw b White	29	c Agathangelou b Smith	35
D M Hodgson, c Davies b White	21	c Davies b White	87
§ A J Hodd, c Davies b White	18	b Lilley	74
* R M Pyrah, lbw b White	0	c and b Parry	41
J A Leaning, c Smith b Clark	0	not out	40
W M H Rhodes, lbw b Lilley	41	not out	9
G S Randhawa, b Parry	21		
B O Coad, lbw b Parry	4		
I Wardlaw, lbw b Parry	9		
M A Ashraf, not out	10		
L R Stabler	Did not bat		
Extras (b 14, lb 11, w 1, nb 6)	32	Extras (b 4, lb 8, w 1, nb 2)	15
Total (62.1 overs)	185	Total (5 wkts, 81.2 overs)	355

FoW: 1-0 (Lees), 2-59 (Sayers), 3-78 (Hodgson), 4-78 (Pyrah), 5-81 (Leaning)
1st 6-112 (Hodd), 7-150 (Rhodes), 8-159 (Coad), 9-166 (Randhawa), 10-185 (Wardlaw)
FoW: 1-93 (Lees), 2-94 (Sayers), 3-229 (Hodd), 4-282 (Pyrah), 5-324 (Hodgson)

	O	M	R	W		O	M	R	W
Newby	13	9	14	1	Newby	10	1	50	0
Bailey	3	0	18	0	Lilley	18	2	87	1
Smith	11	3	31	0	Smith	6.3	2	19	2
Clark	7	3	17	1	White	15.2	3	57	1
White	11	3	41	4	Parry	22.3	6	81	1
Parry	9.1	4	15	3	Clark	3	0	20	0
Lilley	8	2	24	1	Mohammed Abid	6	0	29	0

Umpires: R J Evans and B Parker   Scorers: D M White and Sarah R Smith

Other Second Eleven Match
Kent and Surrey v. Yorkshire

Played at the County Ground, Canterbury, on May 6, 7, 8 and 9, 2013
Match drawn at 4.55pm on the Fourth Day
Toss won by Kent and Surrey

Close of play: First Day, Kent and Surrey 299-8 (Hampton 8, Shinwari 10); Second Day, Yorkshire 250-2 (Hodgson 114, Leaning 54); Third Day, Kent and Surrey 28-0 (Bell-Drummond 7, Patel 19)

KENT AND SURREY

	First Innings		Second Innings	
* D J Bell-Drummond, lbw b Coad	25	c Hodgson b Wardlaw	9
A Patel, lbw b Wardlaw	72	c Coad b Randhawa	55
B A Raine, c and b Randhawa	0	b Ashraf	35
A J Blake, c Coad b Shaw	69	lbw b Ashraf	162
O E Robinson, c Hodgson b Wardlaw	28	c Leaning b Wardlaw	27
§ M G K Burgess, b Fisher	39	c Ashraf b Randhawa	2
G A Edwards, c Lees b Randhawa	24		
M P Dunn, c Hussain b Randhawa	2	(8) c Callis b Coad	4
T R G Hampton, lbw b Wardlaw	30	(9) not out	1
A Shinwari, c Hodgson b Coad	62	(10) not out	0
H T Pickering, not out	1		
J R Winslade	*Did not bat*	(7) c Fisher b Ashraf	37
Extras (b 4, lb 9. w 1, nb 16)	30	Extras (b 6, lb 10, w 1, nb 6)	23
Total (113.4 overs)	382	Total (8 wkts, 84 overs)	355

FoW: 1-67 (Bell-Drummond), 2-68 (Raine), 3-146 (Patel), 4-188 (Blake),5-209 (Robinson)
1st 6-279 (Burgess), 7-279 (Edwards), 8-282 (Dunn), 9-340 (Hampton), 10-382 (Shinwari)
FoW: 1-30 (Bell-Drummond), 2-90 (Patel), 3-114 (Raine), 4-208 (Robinson), 5-225 (Burgess)
2nd 6-336 (Winslade), 7-352 (Blake), 8-354 (Dunn)

	O	M	R	W		O	M	R	W
Wardlaw	27	7	98	3	Wardlaw	16	5	44	2
Ashraf	24	6	80	0	Ashraf	18	3	62	3
Shaw	10	1	47	1	Randhawa	20	5	112	2
Coad	19.4	6	66	2	Coad	12	3	35	1
Randhawa	20	6	49	3	Shaw	5	0	20	0
Fisher	12	2	28	1	Leaning	8	0	47	0
Leaning	1	0	1	0	Fisher	5	0	19	0

YORKSHIRE

A Z Lees, c Shinwari b Hampton	23
E Callis, c Burgess b Bell-Drummond	25
§ D M Hodgson, c Burgess b Hampton	115
J A Leaning, c Burgess b Winslade	57
M Hussain, c Pickering b Hampton	97
E Wilson, b Dunn	43
G S Randhawa, lbw b Robinson	45
M D Fisher, lbw b Patel	5
J Shaw, run out (Hampton)	3
I Wardlaw, b Shinwari	19
* M A Ashraf, not out	0
B O Coad	*Did not bat*
Extras (lb 17, w 2, nb 34)	53
Total (148.5 overs)	485

FoW: 1-44 (Lees), 2-90 (Callis), 3-251 (Hodgson), 4-263 (Leaning), 5-351 (Wilson)
6-453 (Hussain), 7-456 (Randhawa), 8-464 (Fisher), 9-485 (Wardlaw), 10-485 (Shaw)

	O	M	R	W
Dunn	28	7	65	1
Edwards	0.3	0	4	0
Hampton	27.3	3	94	3
Shinwari	17	2	55	1
Robinson	17	4	48	1
Bell-Drummond	17	5	43	1
Pickering	12	0	44	0
Raine	3	0	29	0
Patel	14.5	0	43	1
Winslade	12	1	43	1

G A Edwards (Surrey) broke down after three deliveries. He was replaced by J R Winslade (Surrey)

Umpires: G D Lloyd and R L Collins   Scorers: A L Bateup and H Clayton

Other Second Eleven Match
Lancashire v. Yorkshire

Played at Aigburth, Liverpool, on May 13, 2013 (40-over match)

Lancashire won by 7 wickets at 5.27pm

Toss won by Lancashire

YORKSHIRE

* A W Gale, lbw b Lilley		60
A Z Lees, st Davies b Lilley		35
§ D M Hodgson, b Lilley		0
J A Tattersall, c Horton b Lilley		0
J A Leaning, c Horton b Procter		31
L E Plunkett, not out		27
E Wilson, b Reece		8
G S Randhawa, c Davies b Procter		15
M D Fisher, b Adnan Ghaus		1
J Shaw, not out		0
B O Coad		
M A Ashraf	Did not bat	
Extras (b 1, lb 4, w 9, nb 10)		24
Total (8 wkts, 40 overs)		201

FoW: 1-64 (Lees), 2-64 (Hodgson), 3-64 (Tattersall), 4-139 (Leaning), 5-143 (Gale) 6-156 (Wilson), 7-195 (Randhawa), 8-201 (Fisher)

	O	M	R	W
Griffiths	6	0	41	0
Adnan Ghaus	4	0	35	1
Ali	5	1	10	0
Lilley	8	2	28	4
Agathangelou	8	0	45	0
Procter	7	0	31	2
Reece	2	0	6	1

LANCASHIRE

T C Smith, b Coad		30
§ A L Davies, b Coad		38
A P Agathangelou, b Coad		55
* P J Horton, not out		70
L A Procter, not out		5
L M Reece		
L S Livingstone		
K Ali		
A M Lilley	Did not bat	
T E Bailey		
Adnan Ghaus		
G T Griffiths		
Extras (w 4)		4
Total (3 wkts, 35 overs)		202

FoW: 1-67 (Davies), 2-74 (Smith), 3-171 (Agathangelou)

	O	M	R	W
Shaw	2	0	34	0
Ashraf	5	0	27	0
Coad	8	0	31	3
Plunkett	5	0	27	0
Leaning	3	0	14	0
Randhawa	4	0	26	0
Fisher	4	0	24	0
Tattersall	4	0	19	0

Umpires: M Burns and H Evans   Scorers: D M White and C N Rawson

Other Second Eleven Match
Lancashire v. Yorkshire

Played at Aigburth, Liverpool, on May 14, 15 and 16, 2013
Lancashire won by 144 runs at 4.07pm on the Third Day
Yorkshire forfeited their first innings and Lancashire their second

Toss won by Lancashire

Close of play: First Day, Lancashire 320-4 (Agathangelou 135, Smith 1); Second Day, no play

LANCASHIRE

* P J Horton, lbw b Shaw	....	10
S C Moore, lbw b Fisher	....	134
A P Agathangelou, not out	....	135
L A Procter, b Coad	....	17
S J Croft, c Tattersall b Whiles	....	15
T C Smith		
J Clark		
§ A L Davies		
K Ali	Did not bat	
O J Newby		
A M Lilley		
G T Griffiths		
Extras (lb 5, w 1, nb 2)	....	8
Total (4 wkts dec, 70 overs)	....	320

FoW: 1-29 (Horton), 2-231 (Moore), 3-284 (Procter), 4-313 (Croft)

	O	M	R	W
Coad	14	6	37	1
Shaw	11	1	66	1
Whiles	10	1	52	1
Stabler	12	4	43	0
Fisher	11	1	54	1
Randhawa	9	2	45	0
Tattersall	3	1	18	0

YORKSHIRE

* A Z Lees, c Smith b Newby	....	17
E Callis, c Horton b Lilley	....	50
§ D M Hodgson, c Croft b Newby	....	0
J A Tattersall, b Ali	....	0
J A Leaning, c Smith b Ali	....	0
E Wilson, c Moore b Lilley	....	22
G S Randhawa, lbw b Lilley	....	4
M D Fisher, c Davies b Croft	....	30
J Shaw, c Davies b Croft	....	19
B O Coad, b Croft	....	5
G P Whiles, not out	....	0
L R Stabler	Did not bat	
Extras (b 9, lb 6, nb 14)	....	29
Total (63.4 overs)	....	176

FoW: 1-31 (Lees), 2-31 (Hodgson), 3-36 (Tattersall), 4-38 (Leaning), 5-85 (Wilson)
6-94 (Randhawa), 7-115 (Callis), 8-164 (Shaw), 9-165 (Fisher), 10-176 (Coad)

	O	M	R	W
Ali	11	0	35	2
Newby	7	2	19	2
Smith	3	1	3	0
Griffiths	8	0	40	0
Procter	6	0	15	0
Lilley	16	4	28	3
Clark	7	1	18	0
Croft	5.4	3	3	3

Umpires: M Burns and H Evans   Scorers: D M White and C N Rawson

Other Second Eleven Match
Yorkshire v. Durham

Played at York CC on June 12, 2013 (20-over match)
Yorkshire won by 3 wickets at 2.15pm
Toss won by Yorkshire

DURHAM

R.Singh, c Randhawa b Whiles		12
T.W.M.Latham, c Hussain b Stabler		105
* G.J.Muchall, c Shaw b Stabler		49
G.Clark, not out		23
U.Arshad, not out		1
A.W.Ireland		
§ C.D.Wallace		
J.Harrison	Did not bat	
J.P.Bousfield		
R.M.R.Brathwaite		
M.G.Morley		
Extras (lb 2, w 3)		5
Total (3 wkts, 20 overs)		195

FoW: 1-30 (Singh), 2-170 (Muchall), 3-193 (Latham)

	O	M	R	W
Shaw	2	0	17	0
Whiles	3	0	26	1
Fisher	2	0	23	0
Randhawa	4	0	32	0
Azeem Rafiq	4	0	42	0
Stabler	3	0	32	2
Rhodes	2	0	21	0

YORKSHIRE

§ D.M.Hodgson, b Harrison		2
G.S.Randhawa, c Singh b Ireland		7
E.Wilson, c Muchaell b Harrison		10
*Azeem Rafiq, c Singh b Harrison		19
W.M.H.Rhodes, st Wallace b Morley		40
J.A Leaning, not out		69
M.Hussain, run out		9
M.D.Fisher, st Wallace b Clark		20
J.Shaw, not out		7
G.P.Whiles		
L.R.Stabler	Did not bat	
Extras (lb 4, w 10)		14
Total (7 wkts, 19 overs)		197

FoW: 1-2 (Hodgson), 2-21 (Wilson), 3-40 (Azeem Rafiq), 4-45 (Randhawa), 5-118
(Rhodes), 6-138 (Hussain), 7-165 (Fisher)

	O	M	R	W
Harrison	4	0	24	3
Brathwaite	3	0	41	0
Ireland	4	0	37	1
Morley	4	0	30	1
Bousfield	3	0	42	0
Clark	1	0	19	1

Umpires: H Fidler and P J Hartley   Scorers: Sarah R Smith and R.V.Hilton

Other Second Eleven Match
Yorkshire v. Durham

Played at York CC on June 12, 2013 (20-over match)
Durham won by 7 wickets at 5.23pm
Toss won by Durham

YORKSHIRE

§ D.M.Hodgson, not out	111
M Hussain, c Singh b Morley	48
E Wilson, lbw b Muchall	9
J A Leaning, not out	55
* W M H Rhodes	
G S Randhawa	
M D Fisher	
J Shaw	
L R Stabler	
K Carver	
G P Whiles	
Extras (b 4, lb 2, nb 4, w 4)	14
Total (2 wkts, 20 overs)	237

J Shaw, L R Stabler, K Carver, G P Whiles — Did not bat

FoW: 1-97 (Hussain), 2-131 (Wilson)

	O	M	R	W
Harrison	4	0	59	0
Brathwaite	4	0	39	0
Ireland	4	0	52	0
Ashford	2	0	31	0
Morley	4	0	31	1
Muchall	2	0	19	1

DURHAM

R Singh, c Whiles b Rhodes	93
G Clark, st Hodgson b Leaning	0
U Arshad, c Wilson b Carver	56
* G.J.Muchall, not out	66
§ C.D.Wallace, not out	19
T M W Latham	
A| W Ireland	
J Harrison	
R M R Brathwaite	
M G Morley	
O J Ashford	
Extras (lb 1, w 5)	6
Total (3 wkts, 19.3 Overs)	240

T M W Latham, A| W Ireland, J Harrison, R M R Brathwaite, M G Morley, O J Ashford — Did not bat

FoW: 1-3 (Clark), 2-128 (Arshad), 3-199 (Singh)

	O	M	R	W
Leaning	2	0	22	1
Whiles	3	0	43	0
Shaw	2	0	24	0
Fisher	1	0	23	0
Stabler	2.3	0	36	0
Randhawa	3	0	36	0
Carver	3	0	27	1
Rhodes	3	0	29	1

Umpires: H Fidler and P J Hartley   Scorers: Sarah R Smith and R.V.Hilton

Other Second Eleven Match
Middlesex v. Yorkshire

Played at Merchant Taylors School, Northwood, on September 9, 10 and 11, 2013
Yorkshire won by 93 runs at 5.14pm on the Third Day
Middlesex forfeited their first innings and Yorkshire their second
Toss won by Middlesex
Close of play: First Day, Yorkshire 291-4 (Rhodes 23, Azeem Rafiq 6); Second Day, no play

YORKSHIRE

J A Tattersall, c Eskinazi b Podmore		18
§ A J Hodd, b Fairhead		165
D M Hodgson, c Podmore b Arif		57
J A Leaning, c London b Fairhead		6
* W M H Rhodes, b Fairhead		30
Azeem Rafiq, b Fairhead		23
O E Robinson, b Kulkarni		10
J Shaw, b Fairhead		1
J A Thompson, not out		1
M A Ashraf		
B O Coad	Did not bat	
K Carver		
Extras (b 1, lb 2, nb 16)		19
Total (8 wkts dec, 87.1 overs)		330

FoW: 1-59 (Tattersall), 2-217 (Hodgson), 3-233 (Leaning), 4-276 (Hodd), 5-303 (Rhodes)
6-324 (Azeem Rafiq), 7-326 (Robinson), 8-330 (Shaw)

	O	M	R	W
Sandhu	7	1	19	0
Helm	7	2	16	0
Wilkin	5	2	13	0
Podmore	15	1	62	1
Usman Arif	11	1	39	1
Fairhead	18.1	4	77	5
London	15	1	63	0
Higgins	5	0	20	0
Kulkarni	4	1	18	1

MIDDLESEX

N R T Gubbins, c Rhodes b Carver		72
A B London, c Hodgson b Ashraf		7
§ S S Eskinazi, c Coad b Carver		68
* A M Rossington, c Coad b Carver		20
R F Higgins, lbw b Thompson		26
C F Wakefield, b Carver		0
O Wilkin, run out (Hodd)		16
F J B Fairhead, c Rafiq b Carver		1
H W Podmore, c Robinson b Carver		0
Usman Arif, b Rafiq		1
A S Kulkarni, not out		5
T G Helm	Did not bat	
G S Sandhu		
Extras (b 2, lb 9)		11
Total (95.3 overs)		237

FoW: 1-9 (London), 2-148 (Gubbins), 3-173 (Eskinazi), 4-180 (Rossington), 5-180 (Wakefield)
6-204 (Wilkin), 7-230 (Fairhead), 8-230 (Podmore), 9-232 (Higgins), 10-237 (Usman Arif)

	O	M	R	W
Ashraf	12	5	17	1
Coad	11	2	26	0
Azeem Rafiq	9.3	1	39	1
Shaw	4	1	13	0
Rhodes	6	0	21	0
Robinson	9	1	23	0
Carver	26	9	43	6
Leaning	12	2	37	0
Thompson	6	4	7	1

Umpires: G D Lloyd and A J Salkeld　　　　　　　Scorers: M S Fryer and H Clayton

NOTE: T G Helm and G S Sandhu were called to First Eleven duty at the end of the First Day, and were replaced by A S Kulkarni

Other Second Eleven Match
Yorkshire v. Durham

Played at Weetwood, Leeds, on September 17, 18 and 19, 2013

Match drawn at 6pm on the Second Day. Rain prevented any play on the Third Day

Toss won by Yorkshire

Close of play: First Day, Yorkshire (1) 68-3 (Rhodes 21, Pyrah 26); Second Day, Yorkshire (2) 33-1 (Lees 5, Hodgson 0)

First Innings		YORKSHIRE		Second Innings	
A Z Lees, lbw b Ireland			4	not out	5
§ A J Hodd, c Pringle b Milnes			0	b Milnes	24
D M Hodgson, c Poynter b Milnes			6	not out	0
W M H Rhodes, c Clark b Ireland			23		
* R M Pyrah b Chase			51		
Azeem Rafiq, c Thompson b Chase			9		
J A Leaning, c Pringle b Buckley			42		
O E Robinson, c Clark b Milnes			10		
J Shaw, not out			31		
K Carver, not out			5		
M A Ashraf					
B O Coad		Did not bat			
Extras (lb 13, nb 12)			25	Extras (b 4)	4
Total (8 wkts dec, 52 overs)			206	Total (1 wkt; 7 overs)	33

FoW: 1-4 (Lees), 2-6 (Hodd), 3-21 (Hodgson), 4-75 (Rhodes), 5-94 (Azeem Rafiq)
1st 6-117 (Pyrah), 7-138 (Robinson), 8-182 (Leaning)
2nd: 1-30 (Hodd)

	O	M	R	W		O	M	R	W
Ireland	14	2	59	2	Ireland	3	0	17	0
Milnes	10	3	37	3	Milnes	3	1	12	1
Chase	11	2	40	2	Pringle	1	1	0	0
Carr	1	0	5	0					
Buckley	10	1	37	1					
Foster	6	0	15	0					

DURHAM

J Clark lbw b Azeem Rafiq		40
J A Thompson, lbw b Carver		26
R Carr, not out		37
* R D Pringle, b Carver		43
G Clark, c Hodgson b Carver		3
§ S W Poynter, not out		17
P Coughlin		
A W Ireland		
R S Buckley	Did not bat	
D W Foster		
M E Milnes		
P K D Chase		
Extras (b 3, lb 5, w 1, nb 2)		11
Total (4 wkts dec, 54 overs)		177

FoW: 1-69 (Thompson), 2-77 (J Clark), 3-140 (Pringle), 4-144 (G Clark)

	O	M	R	W
Ashraf	6	4	7	0
Coad	6	1	8	0
Pyrah	5	0	16	0
Robinson	4	0	17	0
Carver	17	2	69	3
Shaw	4	2	4	0
Azeem Rafiq	12	1	48	1

Umpires: I Dawood and N R Roper   Scorers: H Clayton and R V Hilton

YORKSHIRE ECB COUNTY PREMIER LEAGUE 2013

*	P	CW	IW1	IW2	IW3	IL1	IL2	IL3	CL	T	C	A	Points
York (1)	26	16	1	0	4	0	0	0	2	0	1	2	167
Yorkshire Acad.(4)	**26**	**13**	**1**	**2**	**4**	**0**	**1**	**0**	**2**	**0**	**2**	**1**	**156**
Harrogate (2)	26	12	1	1	2	0	0	2	4	0	1	3	132
Scarborough (7) ...	26	6	2	1	5	2	0	3	2	1	2	2	116
Doncaster Town (11)	26	10	0	1	3	1	0	2	7	0	0	2	112
Driffield Town (6) .	26	7	0	2	6	1	0	1	8	0	0	1	109
Sheffield Coll. (14)	26	9	1	1	3	1	0	0	11	0	0	0	104
Barnsley (3)	26	7	1	0	2	1	1	4	8	0	1	1	83
Cleethorpes (8) ...	26	6	0	1	2	0	0	6	7	0	1	3	78
Appleby Frod. (13)	26	4	1	0	5	0	0	0	14	1	0	1	75
Rotherham Town (5)	26	4	1	1	2	0	0	4	11	0	1	2	65
Hull (9)	26	4	1	0	1	0	2	7	8	0	1	2	55
Castleford (12)	26	2	1	0	2	0	2	6	10	0	2	1	45
Sheffield United (10)	26	2	0	0	0	5	4	6	8	0	0	1	33

* P = Played; CW = Complete win (8 points); IW1 = Incomplete win (6 points); IW2 = Incomplete win (6 points); IW3 = Incomplete win (6 points); IL1 = Incomplete loss (2 points); IL2 = Incomplete loss 1 (1 point); IL3 = Incomplete loss (0 points); CL = Complete loss (0 points); T = Tied (4 points); C = Cancelled no play (3 points); A = Abandoned incomplete (3 points)

(2012 positions in brackets)

Yorkshire League Cup: Winners: **Driffield Town.** Runners-up: York

YORKSHIRE ACADEMY BATTING IN ECB LEAGUE AND CUP

Player	M.	I.	N.O.	Runs	H.S.	Avge	100s	50s	4s	6s	ct/st
A Lees	12	12	3	715	163*	79.44	2	5	88	10	10
J Warner	12	3	2	75	41	75.00	0	0	2	0	3
Y Imtiaz (J)	4	2	0	143	81	71.50	0	2	19	2	0
W Rhodes	13	11	2	462	121	51.33	1	2	43	2	5
M Hussain	21	20	7	629	69*	48.38	0	5	56	1	6
J Shaw	17	12	4	342	78*	42.75	0	2	30	3	4
E Callis	9	9	0	383	168	42.56	1	2	44	9	5
J Tattersall	17	16	3	517	85*	39.77	0	2	55	0	5
R Gibson	9	7	0	276	139	39.43	1	0	33	3	2
S Patterson	2	2	0	56	56	28.00	0	1	8	0	1
J Thompson	7	6	1	131	95	26.20	0	1	8	6	2
E Wilson	7	7	1	126	45	21.00	0	0	10	0	3/2
M Fisher	16	12	5	135	44	19.29	0	0	9	1	11
B Gibson	23	17	2	284	74*	18.93	0	2	30	0	27/3
L Stabler	16	10	2	140	27*	17.50	0	0	8	3	2
J Wainman	14	10	0	137	38	13.70	0	0	10	3	6
J Brown	9	6	2	47	19	11.75	0	0	2	1	2
M Waite	3	2	1	8	4*	8.00	0	0	1	0	0
E Barnes	2	1	1	22	22*	—	0	0	3	0	0
K Carver	19	6	4	15	5*	7.50	0	0	1	0	5
B Coad	19	6	4	14	6*	5.00	0	0	0	0	4
M Fraine	2	2	0	11	6	5.50	0	0	2	0	0
A Leyshon	9	2	1	4	2*	4.00	0	0	0	0	2
A Rafiq	3	1	0	3	3	3.00	0	0	0	0	2
P Farbrace	1	1	1	0	0*	—	0	0	0	0	0

YORKSHIRE ACADEMY BOWLING IN ECB LEAGUE AND CUP

Player	M	Overs	Mdns	Runs	Wkts	Avge	Econ.	5wh	Best
E Callis	7	3	0	19	2	9.50	6.33	0	2-19
A Rafiq	3	36.5	8	124	9	13.78	3.37	0	4-45
B Coad	19	146.5	35	420	25	16.80	2.86	1	5-27
J Tattersall	17	59.3	9	207	12	17.25	3.48	0	3-4
R Gibson	9	34	6	129	7	18.43	3.79	0	3-9
J Brown	9	29	5	116	6	19.33	4.00	0	2-25
M Fisher	16	97.2	15	370	18	20.56	3.80	0	3-37
A Leyshon	9	61.3	9	268	12	22.33	4.36	0	4-50
A Robinson	6	8	1	26	1	26.00	3.25	0	1-16
M Waite	3	21	3	90	4	22.50	4.29	0	3-14
S Patterson	2	22	6	69	3	23.00	3.14	0	3-42
J Warner	12	57.2	7	260	11	23.64	4.53	0	3-28
K Carver	19	234	50	740	30	24.67	3.16	1	5-29
W Rhodes	13	60.1	6	232	9	25.78	3.86	0	3-23
J Shaw	17	122.1	14	527	19	27.74	4.31	0	3-33
J Thompson	7	28	3	139	5	27.80	4.96	0	2-14
L Stabler	16	87.1	17	337	12	28.08	3.87	1	5-20
J Wainman	14	64	11	219	7	31.29	3.42	0	2-21
E Barnes	2	12	2	47	1	47.00	3.92	0	1-16
D Cross (J)	1	15	1	58	0	—	3.87	0	0-58
M Rafique (J)	1	3	0	12	0	—	4.00	0	0-12

Cricket, we love it

SAMOA: The game seems to have been introduced here by HMS Diamond in about the year 1884, and the natives, who took to it readily, at once saw that there was much room for improvement. Matches of 200 a side took place, with four or five umpires and three batsmen at each end, the contests lasting for weeks. Work was neglected, and steps had to be taken to compel the natives to return to reason. Men who played were expelled from the church, and the King had to issue a special decree.

Cricketer Annual 1922-23

In the Beginning

So another attempt was made to launch a county club, and on January 8, 1863, it was resolved "that a county club be formed"; the membership unlimited, the minimum subscription ten shillings and sixpence (55p). The stated object was the playing of first-class matches "either in Sheffield or any other towns of the county according as arrangments may be made".

The Carnegie History

RECORDS SECTION

(All records in this section relate to First-Class Yorkshire matches only — except where otherwise stated)

HONOURS

County Champions (32)
1867, 1870, 1893, 1896, 1898, 1900, 1901, 1902, 1905, 1908, 1912, 1919, 1922, 1923, 1924, 1925, 1931, 1932, 1933, 1935, 1937, 1938, 1939, 1946, 1959, 1960, 1962, 1963, 1966, 1967, 1968, 2001.

Joint Champions (2)
1869, 1949

Promoted to Division 1
2005
2012

Gillette Cup Winners (2)
1965, 1969

Cheltenham & Gloucester Trophy (1)
2002

Benson & Hedges Cup Winners (1)
1987

John Player Special League Winners (1)
1983

Fenner Trophy Winners (3)
1972, 1974, 1981

Asda Challenge Winners (1)
1987

Ward Knockout Cup (1)
1989

Joshua Tetley Festival Trophy (7)
1991, 1992 (Joint), 1993, 1994, 1996, 1997 and 1998

Tilcon Trophy Winners (2)
1978 and 1988

Pro-Arch Trophy (1)
2007-08

Second Eleven Champions (4)
1977, 1984, 1991, 2003

Joint Champions (1)
1987

Minor Counties Champions (5)
1947, 1957, 1958, 1968, 1971

Under-25 Competition Winners (3)
1976, 1978, 1987

Bain Clarkson Trophy Winners (2)
1988 and 1994

Second Eleven Trophy (1)
2009

YORKSHIRE'S CHAMPIONSHIP CAPTAINS

1867 to 2001

R Iddison (2)	1867, 1870
Lord Hawke (8)	1893, 1896, 1898, 1900, 1901, 1902, 1905, 1908
Sir Archibald White (1)	1912
D C F Burton (1)	1919
G Wilson (3)	1922, 1923, 1924
A W Lupton (1)	1925
F E Greenwood (2)	1931, 1932
A B Sellers (6)	1933, 1935, 1937, 1938, 1939, 1946
J R Burnet (1)	1959
J V Wilson (2)	1960, 1962
D B Close (4)	1963, 1966, 1967, 1968
D Byas (1)	2001

Joint Champions

R Iddison (1)	1869
N W D Yardley (1)	1949

GALE FORCE DESTRUCTION: Yorkshire captain Andrew Gale returned to his best form with a vengeance against Nottinghamshire at Scarborough in June by thrashing 272. He followed up with further centuries in the next two Championship matches to put his side on course for the title until they were pipped at the post by Durham.

MINSTER OVATION FOR 150 YEARS

PACKED ENCLOSURE: The congregation settles itself for the special York Minster service in June to celebrate the 150th anniversary of Yorkshire County Cricket Club. **BELOW:** Chairman Colin Graves, left, arrives with Board member Robin Smith and Club chaplain Canon Max Wigley, who took part in the service.

MINSTER OVATION FOR 150 YEARS

PEWS NEWS: Dickie Bird, who was elected Yorkshire President at the Club's 2014 annual meeting, outside the Minster with BBC Television's Harry Gration, who is now on the Yorkshire Board of Directors. **BELOW:** Former Yorkshire and England captain, Brian Close, with his former Yorkshire and England team-mate, Philip Sharpe. *(Yorkshire Post Picture Feature By Gary Longbottom)*

PRESIDENT'S MEDALS: Yorkshire Supporters and Kabin stalwart Joan Pickering is honoured by Geoffrey Boycott in recognition of her outstanding work for the Club and, below, the President also catches up with lifelong archivist Ron Deaton, who is pictured with his wife, Pam.

SILVER SERVICE: Tony Loffill with his wife, Maureen, after Yorkshire CCC had presented him with an inscribed silver tray to mark his retirement after 15 years of service as public-address announcer.

CAP THAT: Yorkshire captain Andrew Gale, centre, presents first-team caps to new signings Liam Plunkett, left, and Jack Brooks ahead of the Championship match against Warwickshire at Headingley in August.

SACHIN FLASHBACK: Indian batting maestro Sachin Tendulkar retired from first-class cricket last year. Our picture shows former Yorkshire Chief Executive Chris Hassell signing up Sachin for the 1992 season, when the teenage batting sensation became Yorkshire's first overseas player. Chris travelled to Mumbai in the April to clinch the deal.

PLAYERS' PRESIDENT: Retiring Yorkshire CCC Players' Association President Jim Love, left, hands over to Peter Chadwick.

BOBBY PEEL REMEMBERED: Yorkshire CCC chaplain Max Wigley dedicates the newly erected headstone on the grave of former Yorkshire and England all-rounder Bobby Peel at Morley Cemetery. Also, from left, are Yorkshire Members' Committee chairman Stephen Mann, Players' Association secretary Geoff Cope, Yorkshire Board member Robin Smith, and Peel descendant Robin Barron. **BELOW:** Robin Smith joins relatives at the headstone. *(Photos: Mike Cowling)*

THEN AND NOW: Bryan Stott, left, and Doug Padgett going out to bat at Scarborough. Near the end of 1959 their dashing third-wicket stand of 141 against Sussex at Hove raced Yorkshire towards the Championship title. They were able to reminisce about that match in January at the Players' Association lunch at Fulford Golf Club, right.

ONWARD CRICKETING SOLDIERS: The Leeds Pals gather for training in the autumn of 1914 at Colsterdale, North Yorkshire. Major Booth is standing in the back row, third from the right, and Roy Kilner is sitting in the middle of the front row. Second Lieutenant Booth died on July 1, 1916, the first day of the Battle of the Somme. Kilner was wounded but survived the war, playing in nine Test matches and continuing his Yorkshire career until his death from enteric fever in 1928 when he was 37. **(Photo: www.adelphiarchive.co.uk)**

RECORDS SECTION INDEX

The County Championship

The County Championship was officially constituted in 1890, and before that Yorkshire were generally considered Champions by the Press in 1867 and 1870, and equal top in 1869. From 1873 the list was generally accepted in the form as it is today.

		Yorkshire's Position
1873	{ Gloucestershire / Nottinghamshire	.........7th
1874	Gloucestershire	...........4th
1875	Nottinghamshire	...........4th
1876	Gloucestershire	...........3rd
1877	Gloucestershire	...........7th
1878	Middlesex	...............6th
1879	Nottinghamshire/Lancashire	..6th
1880	Nottinghamshire	...........5th
1881	Lancashire	...............3rd
1882	Nottinghamshire/Lancashire	.3rd
1883	Nottinghamshire	...........2nd
1884	Nottinghamshire	...........3rd
1885	Nottinghamshire	...........2nd
1886	Nottinghamshire	...........4th
1887	Surrey	...................3rd
1888	Surrey	...................2nd
1889	{ Surrey/Lancashire / Nottinghamshire	.........7th
1890	Surrey	...................3rd
1891	Surrey	...................8th
1892	Surrey	...................6th
1893	**Yorkshire**	**................1st**
1894	Surrey	...................2nd
1895	Surrey	...................3rd
1896	**Yorkshire**	**................1st**
1897	Lancashire	...............4th
1898	**Yorkshire**	**................1st**
1899	Surrey	...................3rd
1900	**Yorkshire**	**................1st**
1901	**Yorkshire**	**................1st**
1902	**Yorkshire**	**................1st**
1903	Middlesex	................3rd
1904	Lancashire	...............2nd
1905	**Yorkshire**	**................1st**
1906	Kent	.....................2nd
1907	Nottinghamshire	...........2nd
1908	**Yorkshire**	**................1st**

		Yorkshire's Position
1909	Kent	.....................3rd
1910	Kent	.....................8th
1911	Warwickshire	.............7th
1912	**Yorkshire**	**................1st**
1913	Kent	.....................2nd
1914	Surrey	...................4th
1919	**Yorkshire**	**................1st**
1920	Middlesex	................4th
1921	Middlesex	................3rd
1922	**Yorkshire**	**................1st**
1923	**Yorkshire**	**................1st**
1924	**Yorkshire**	**................1st**
1925	**Yorkshire**	**................1st**
1926	Lancashire	...............2nd
1927	Lancashire	...............3rd
1928	Lancashire	...............4th
1929	Nottinghamshire	...........2nd
1930	Lancashire	...............3rd
1931	**Yorkshire**	**................1st**
1932	**Yorkshire**	**................1st**
1933	**Yorkshire**	**................1st**
1934	Lancashire	...............5th
1935	**Yorkshire**	**................1st**
1936	Derbyshire	...............3rd
1937	**Yorkshire**	**................1st**
1938	**Yorkshire**	**................1st**
1939	**Yorkshire**	**................1st**
1946	**Yorkshire**	**................1st**
1947	Middlesex	................7th
1948	Glamorgan	................4th
1949	**Yorkshire/Middlesex**	**.......1st**
1950	Lancashire/Surrey	........3rd
1951	Warwickshire	.............2nd
1952	Surrey	...................2nd
1953	Surrey	...................12th
1954	Surrey	...................2nd
1955	Surrey	...................2nd
1956	Surrey	...................7th
1957	Surrey	...................3rd

		Yorkshire's Position			Yorkshire's Position
1958	Surrey	11th	1986	Essex	10th
1959	**Yorkshire**	**1st**	1987	Nottinghamshire	8th
1960	**Yorkshire**	**1st**	1988	Worcestershire	13th
1961	Hampshire	2nd	1989	Worcestershire	16th
1962	**Yorkshire**	**1st**	1990	Middlesex	10th
1963	**Yorkshire**	**1st**	1991	Essex	14th
1964	Worcestershire	5th	1992	Essex	16th
1965	Worcestershire	4th	1993	Middlesex	12th
1966	**Yorkshire**	**1st**	1994	Warwickshire	13th
1967	**Yorkshire**	**1st**	1995	Warwickshire	8th
1968	**Yorkshire**	**1st**	1996	Leicestershire	6th
1969	Glamorgan	13th	1997	Glamorgan	6th
1970	Kent	4th	1998	Leicestershire	3rd
1971	Surrey	13th	1999	Surrey	6th
1972	Warwickshire	10th	2000	Surrey	3rd
1973	Hampshire	14th	**2001**	**Yorkshire**	**1st**
1974	Worcestershire	11th	2002	Surrey	9th
1975	Leicestershire	2nd	2003	Sussex	Div 2, 4th
1976	Middlesex	8th	2004	Warwickshire	Div 2, 7th
1977	Kent/Middlesex	12th	2005	Nottinghamshire	Div 2, 3rd
1978	Kent	4th	2006	Sussex	Div 1, 6th
1979	Essex	7th	2007	Sussex	Div 1, 6th
1980	Middlesex	6th	2008	Durham	Div 1, 7th
1981	Nottinghamshire	10th	2009	Durham	Div 1, 7th
1982	Middlesex	10th	2010	Nottinghamshire	Div 1, 3rd
1983	Essex	17th	2011	Lancashire	Div 1, 8th
1984	Essex	14th	2012	Warwickshire	Div 2, 2nd
1985	Middlesex	11th	2013	Durham	Div 1, 2nd

If the time should come

If the time should come when, almost universally, white flannels are exchanged for tracksuits of many colours, synthetic pitches are delivered each evening to floodlit arenas and computerised robots take the place of umpires and scorers — then the image of Broad Halfpenny Down will fade away under the arc lights, and the ghosts of John Nyren and Silver Billy Beldham will return to the village green, which is cricket's natural setting.

Blackwood's Magazine 1978

SEASON-BY-SEASON RECORD OF ALL FIRST-CLASS MATCHES PLAYED BY YORKSHIRE 1863-2013

Season	Played	Won	Lost	Drawn	Abd§	Season	Played	Won	Lost	Drawn	Abd§
1863	4	2	1	1		1921	30	17	5	8	
1864	7	2	4	1		1922	33	20	2	11	
1865	9	—	7	2		1923	35	26	1	8	
1866	3	—	2	1		1924	35	18	4	13	
1867	7	7	—	—		1925	36	22	—	14	
1868	7	4	3	—		1926	35	14	—	21	1
1869	5	4	1	—		1927	34	11	3	20	1
1870	7	6	—	1		1928	32	9	—	23	
1871	7	3	3	1		1929	35	11	2	22	
1872	10	2	7	1		1930	34	13	3	18	2
1873	13	7	5	1		1931	33	17	1	15	1
1874	14	10	3	1		1932	32	21	2	9	2
1875	12	6	4	2		1933	36	21	5	10	
1876	12	5	3	4		1934	35	14	7	14	
1877	14	2	7	5		1935	36	24	2	10	
1878	20	10	7	3		1935-6	3	1	—	2	
1879	17	7	5	5		1936	35	14	2	19	
1880	20	6	8	6		1937	34	22	3	9	1
1881	20	11	6	3		1938	36	22	2	12	
1882	24	11	9	4		1939	34	23	4	7	1
1883	19	10	2	7		1945	2	—	—	2	
1884	20	10	6	4		1946	31	20	1	10	
1885	21	8	3	10		1947	32	10	9	13	
1886	21	5	8	8		1948	31	11	6	14	
1887	20	6	5	9		1949	33	16	3	14	
1888	20	7	7	6		1950	34	16	6	12	1
1889	16	3	11	2	1	1951	35	14	3	18	
1890	20	10	4	6		1952	34	17	3	14	
1891	17	5	11	1	2	1953	35	7	7	21	
1892	19	6	6	7		1954	35	16	3	16*	
1893	23	15	5	3		1955	33	23	6	4	
1894	28	18	6	4	1	1956	35	11	7	17	
1895	31	15	10	6		1957	34	16	5	13	1
1896	32	17	6	9		1958	33	10	8	15	2
1897	30	14	7	9		1959	35	18	8	9	
1898	30	18	3	9		1960	38	19	7	24	
1899	34	17	4	13		1961	39	19	5	15	
1900	32	19	1	12		1962	37	16	5	16	
1901	35	23	2	10	1	1963	33	14	4	15	
1902	31	15	3	13	1	1964	33	12	4	17	
1903	31	16	5	10		1965	33	12	4	17	
1904	32	10	2	20	1	1966	32	16	6	10	1
1905	33	21	4	8		1967	31	16	5	10	2
1906	33	19	6	8		1968	32	13	4	15	
1907	31	14	5	12	2	1969	29	4	7	18	
1908	33	19	—	14		1970	26	10	5	11	
1909	30	12	5	13		1971	27	5	8	14	
1910	31	11	8	12		1972	21	4	5	12	1
1911	32	16	9	7		1973	22	3	5	14*	
1912	35	14	3	18	1	1974	22	6	7	9	1
1913	32	16	5	11		1975	21	11	1	9	
1914	31	16	4	11	2	1976	22	7	7	8	
1919	31	12	5	14		1977	23	7	5	11	1
1920	30	17	6	7		1978	24	10	3	11	1

Season	Played	Won	Lost	Drawn	Abd§	Season	Played	Won	Lost	Drawn	Abd§
1979	22	6	3	13	1	1996	19	8	5	6	
1980	24	5	4	15		1997	20	7	4	9	
1981	24	5	9	10		1998	19	9	3	7	
1982	22	5	1	16	1	1999	17	8	6	3	
1983	23	1	5	17	1	2000	18	7	4	7	
1984	24	5	4	15		2001	16	9	3	4	
1985	25	3	4	18	1	2002	16	2	8	6	
1986	25	4	6	15		2003	17	4	5	8	
1986-7	1	—	—	1		2004	16	3	4	9	
1987	24	7	4	13	1	2005	17	6	1	10	
1988	24	5	6	13		2006	16	3	6	7	
1989	22	3	9	10		2007	17	5	4	8	
1990	24	5	9	10		2008	16	2	5	9	
1991	24	4	6	14		2009	17	2	2	13	
1991-2	1	—	1	—		2010	18	6	2	10	
1992	22	4	6	12	1	2011	17	4	6	7	
1992-3	1	—	—	1		2012	17	5	0	12	
1993	19	6	4	9		2013	17	8	2	7	
1994	20	7	6	7			3549	1491	647	1411	38
1995	20	8	8	4							
1995-6	2	2	—	—		*Includes one tie in each season.					

§ All these matches were abandoned without a ball being bowled, except Yorkshire v Kent at Harrogate, 1904, which was abandoned under Law 9. The two in 1914 and the one in 1939 were abandoned because of war. All these matches are excluded from the total played.

Of the 1,491 matches won, 510 have been by an innings margin, 83 by 200 runs or more, and 132 by 10 wickets. Of the 647 matches lost, 109 have been by an innings margin, 12 by 200 runs or more and 34 by 10 wickets.

ANALYSIS OF RESULTS VERSUS ALL FIRST-CLASS
TEAMS 1863-2013

COUNTY CHAMPIONSHIP

Opponents	Played	Won	Lost	Drawn	Tied
Derbyshire	205	103	19	83	—
Durham	30	13	8	9	—
Essex	160	84	25	51	—
Glamorgan	111	53	13	45	—
Gloucestershire	200	102	43	55	—
Hampshire	165	72	19	74	—
Kent	200	84	39	77	—
Lancashire	253	74	52	127	—
Leicestershire	166	84	15	66	1
Middlesex	227	80	54	92	1
Northamptonshire	140	65	26	49	—
Nottinghamshire	248	88	47	113	—
Somerset	167	89	22	56	—
Surrey	240	85	67	88	—
Sussex	195	83	33	79	—
Warwickshire	184	81	31	72	—
Worcestershire	138	68	21	49	—
Cambridgeshire	8	3	4	1	—
Total	3037	1311	538	1186	2

ANALYSIS OF RESULTS VERSUS ALL FIRST-CLASS
TEAMS 1863-2013 *(continued.)*

OTHER FIRST-CLASS MATCHES

Opponents	Played	Won	Lost	Drawn	Tied
Derbyshire	2	1	1	0	—
Essex	2	2	0	0	—
Hampshire	1	0	0	1	—
Lancashire	12	5	3	4	—
Leicestershire	2	1	1	0	—
Middlesex	1	1	0	0	—
Nottinghamshire	2	1	1	0	—
Surrey	1	0	0	1	—
Sussex	2	0	0	2	—
Warwickshire	2	0	0	2	—
Totals	27	11	6	10	—
Australians	55	6	19	30	—
Indians	14	5	1	8	—
New Zealanders	10	2	0	8	—
Pakistanis	4	1	0	3	—
South Africans	17	1	3	13	—
Sri Lankans	3	0	0	3	—
West Indians	17	3	7	7	—
Zimbabweans	2	0	1	1	—
Bangladesh A	1	1	0	0	—
India A	2	0	0	2	—
Pakistan A	1	1	0	0	—
South Africa A	1	0	0	1	—
Totals	127	20	31	76	—
Cambridge University/U C C E	88	42	17	29	—
Canadians	1	1	0	0	—
Combined Services	1	0	0	1	—
Durham MCCU	1	1	0	0	—
England XI's	6	1	2	3	—
Hon. M.B. Hawke's XI	1	0	1	0	—
International XI	1	1	0	0	—
Ireland	3	3	0	0	—
Jamaica	3	1	0	2	—
Leeds/Bradford MCCU	2	1	0	1	—
Liverpool and District*	3	2	1	0	—
Loughborough UCCE	2	1	0	1	—
MCC	153	54	39	60	—
Mashonaland	1	1	0	0	—
Matebeleland	1	1	0	0	—
Minor Counties	1	1	0	0	—
Oxford University	44	21	3	20	—
Philadelphians	1	0	0	1	—
Rest of England	16	4	5	7	—
Royal Air Force	1	0	0	1	—
Scotland**	11	7	0	4	—
South of England	2	1	0	1	—
C. I. Thornton's XI	5	2	0	3	—
United South of England	1	1	0	0	—
Western Province	2	0	1	1	—
Windward Islands	1	0	0	1	—
I Zingari	6	2	3	1	—
Totals	358	149	72	137	0
Grand Totals	3549	1491	647	1409	2

*Matches played in 1889, 1891, 1892 and 1893 are excluded. **Match played in 1878 is included

HIGHEST MATCH AGGREGATES – OVER 1350 RUNS

Runs	Wkts	
1665	33	Yorkshire (351 and 481) lost to Warwickshire (601:9 dec and 232:4) by 6 wkts at Birmingham, 2002
1606	31	Yorkshire (438 and 363:5 dec) lost to Somerset (326 and 479:6) by 4 wkts at Taunton, 2009
1479	28	Yorkshire (405 and 333:4 dec) lost to Somerset (377 and 364:4) by 6 wkts at Taunton , 2010
1473	17	Yorkshire (600:4 dec. and 231:3 dec.) drew with Worcestershire (453:5 dec. and 189:5) at Scarborough, 1995.
1442	29	Yorkshire (501:6 dec. and 244:6 dec.) beat Lancashire (403:7 dec. and 294) by 48 runs at Scarborough, 1991.
1439	32	Yorkshire (536:8 dec. and 205:7 dec.) beat Glamorgan (482: 7 dec. and 216) by 43 runs at Cardiff, 1996.
1431	32	Yorkshire (388 and 312:6) drew with Sussex (398 and 333:6 dec) at Scarborough, 2011
1417	33	Yorkshire (422 and 193:7) drew with Glamorgan (466 and 336:6 dec) at Colwyn Bay, 2003
1406	37	Yorkshire (354 and 341:8) drew with Derbyshire (406 and 305:9 dec) at Derby, 2004
1400	32	Yorkshire (299 and 439: 4 dec.) drew with Hampshire (296 and 366:8) at Southampton, 2007
1393	35	Yorkshire (331 and 278) lost to Kent (377 and 407:5 dec) by 175 runs at Maidstone, 1994.
1390	34	Yorkshire (431:8 dec and 265:7) beat Hampshire (429 and 265) by 3 wkts at Southampton, 1995.
1390	33	Durham (573 and 124-3) beat Yorkahire (274 and 419) by 7 wkts at Scarborough, 2013.
1376	33	Yorkshire (531 and 158:3) beat Lancashire (373 and 314) by 7 wkts at Leeds, 2001
1376	20	Yorkshire (677: 7 dec.) drew with Durham (518 and 181:3 dec.) at Leeds, 2006
1374	36	Yorkshire (594: 9 dec. and 266:7 dec.) beat Surrey (344 and 170) by 346 runs at The Oval, 2007
1373	36	Yorkshire (520 and 114:6) drew with Derbyshire (216 and 523) at Derby, 2005
1364	35	Yorkshire (216 and 433) lost to Warwickshire (316 and 399:5 dec.) by 66 runs at Birmingham, 2006
1359	25	Yorkshire (561 and 138:3 dec.) drew with Derbyshire (412:4 dec. and 248:8) at Sheffield, 1996.
1359	30	Yorkshire (358 and 321) lost to Somerset (452 and 228:0) by 10 wickets at Taunton, 2011
1353	18	Yorkshire (377:2 dec. and 300:6) beat Derbyshire (475:7 dec. and 201:3 dec.) by 4 wkts at Scarborough, 1990.

LOWEST MATCH AGGREGATES – UNDER 225 RUNS
IN A COMPLETED MATCH

Runs	Wkts	
165	30	Yorkshire (46 and 37:0) beat Nottinghamshire (24 and 58) by 10 wkts at Sheffield, 1888.
175	29	Yorkshire (104) beat Essex (30 and 41) by an innings and 33 runs at Leyton, 1901.
182	15	Yorkshire (4:0 dec. and 88.5) beat Northamptonshire (4:0 dec. and 86) by 5 wkts at Bradford, 1931.
193	29	Yorkshire (99) beat Worcestershire (43 and 51) by an innings and 5 runs at Bradford, 1900.
219	30	Yorkshire (113) beat Nottinghamshire (71 and 35) by an innings and 7 runs at Nottingham, 1881.
222	32	Yorkshire (98 and 14:2) beat Gloucestershire (68 and 42) by 8 wkts at Gloucester, 1924.
223	40	Yorkshire (58 and 51) lost to Lancashire (64 and 50) by 5 runs at Manchester, 1893.

LOWEST MATCH AGGREGATES – UNDER 325 RUNS
IN A MATCH IN WHICH ALL 40 WICKETS FELL

Runs	Wkts	
223	40	Yorkshire (58 and 51) lost to Lancashire (64 and 50) by 5 runs at Manchester, 1893.
288	40	Yorkshire (55 and 68) lost to Lancashire (89 and 76) by 42 runs at Sheffield, 1872.
295	40	Yorkshire (71 and 63) lost to Surrey (56 and 105) by 27 runs at The Oval, 1886.
303	40	Yorkshire (109 and 77) beat Middlesex (63 and 54) by 69 runs at Lord's, 1891.
318	40	Yorkshire (96 and 96) beat Lancashire (39 and 87) by 66 runs at Manchester, 1874.
318	40	Yorkshire (94 and 104) beat Northamptonshire (61 and 59) by 78 runs at Bradford, 1955.
319	40	Yorkshire (84 and 72) lost to Derbyshire (106 and 57) by 7 runs at Derby, 1878.
320	40	Yorkshire (98 and 91) beat Surrey (72 and 59) by 58 runs at Sheffield, 1893.
321	40	Yorkshire (88 and 37) lost to I Zingari (103 and 93) by 71 runs at Scarborough, 1877.
321	40	Yorkshire (80 and 67) lost to Derbyshire (129 and 45) by 27 runs at Sheffield, 1879.

LARGE MARGINS OF VICTORY – BY AN INNINGS
AND OVER 250 RUNS

Inns and 397 runs	Yorkshire (548:4 dec.) beat Northamptonshire (58 and 93) at Harrogate, 1921.
Inns and 387 runs	Yorkshire (662) beat Derbyshire (118 and 157) at Chesterfield, 1898.
Inns and 343 runs	Yorkshire (673:8 dec) beat Northamptonshire (184 and 146) at Leeds, 2003.
Inns and 321 runs	Yorkshire (437) beat Leicestershire (58 and 58) at Leicester, 1908.
Inns and 314 runs	Yorkshire (356:8 dec) beat Northamptonshire (27 and 15) at Northampton, 1908. (Yorkshire's first match v. Northamptonshire).
Inns and 313 runs	Yorkshire (555:1 dec) beat Essex (78 and 164) at Leyton, 1932.
Inns and 307 runs	Yorkshire (681:5 dec.) beat Sussex (164 and 210) at Sheffield, 1897.
Inns and 302 runs	Yorkshire (660) beat Leicestershire (165 and 193) at Leicester, 1896.
Inns and 301 runs	Yorkshire (499) beat Somerset (125 and 73) at Bath, 1899.
Inns and 294 runs	Yorkshire (425:7 dec.) beat Gloucestershire (47 and 84) at Bristol, 1964.

LARGE MARGINS OF VICTORY – BY AN INNINGS
AND OVER 250 RUNS *(Continued)*

Inns and 284 runs	Yorkshire (467:7 dec) beat Leicestershire (111 and 72) at Bradford, 1932.
Inns and 282 runs	Yorkshire (481:8 dec) beat Derbyshire (106 and 93) at Huddersfield, 1901.
Inns and 280 runs	Yorkshire (562) beat Leicestershire (164 and 118) at Dewsbury, 1903.
Inns and 271 runs	Yorkshire (460) beat Hampshire (128 and 61) at Hull, 1900.
Inns and 271 runs	Yorkshire (495:5 dec) beat Warwickshire (99 and 125) at Huddersfield, 1922.
Inns and 266 runs	Yorkshire (352) beat Cambridgeshire (40 and 46) at Hunslet, 1869.
Inns and 260 runs	Yorkshire (521: 7dec.) beat Worcestershire (129 and 132) at Leeds, 2007.
Inns and 258 runs	Yorkshire (404:2 dec) beat Glamorgan (78 and 68) at Cardiff, 1922. (Yorkshire's first match v. Glamorgan).
Inns and 256 runs	Yorkshire (486) beat Leicestershire (137 and 93) at Sheffield, 1895.
Inns and 251 runs	Yorkshire (550) beat Leicestershire (154 and 145) at Leicester, 1933.

LARGE MARGINS OF VICTORY – BY OVER 300 RUNS

389 runs	Yorkshire (368 and 280:1 dec) beat Somerset (125 and 134) at Bath, 1906.
370 runs	Yorkshire (194 and 274) beat Hampshire (62 and 36) at Leeds, 1904.
351 runs	Yorkshire (280 and 331) beat Northamptonshire (146 and 114) at Northampton, 1947.
346 runs	Yorkshire (594: 9 dec. and 266: 7 dec.) beat Surrey (344 and 179) at The Oval, 2007.
328 runs	Yorkshire (186 and 318:1 dec) beat Somerset (43 and 133) at Bradford, 1930.
328 runs	Yorkshire (280 and 277:7 dec) beat Glamorgan (104 and 105) at Swansea, 2001
320 runs	Yorkshire (331 and 353:9 dec) beat Durham (150 and 214) at Chester-le-Street, 2004
308 runs	Yorkshire (89 and 420) beat Warwickshire (72 and 129) at Birmingham, 1921.

LARGE MARGINS OF VICTORY – BY 10 WICKETS
(WITH OVER 100 RUNS SCORED IN THE 4th INNINGS)

4th Innings

167:0 wkt	Yorkshire (247 and 167:0) beat Northamptonshire 233 and 180) at Huddersfield, 1948.
147:0 wkt	Yorkshire (381 and 147:0) beat Middlesex (384 and 142) at Lord's, 1896.
142:0 wkt	Yorkshire (304 and 142:0) beat Sussex (254 and 188) at Bradford, 1887.
139:0 wkt	Yorkshire (163:9 dec and 139:0) beat Nottinghamshire (234 and 67) at Leeds, 1932.
138:0 wkt	Yorkshire (293 and 138:0) beat Hampshire (251 and 179) at Southampton, 1897.
132:0 wkt	Yorkshire (328 and 132:0) beat Northamptonshire (281 and 175) at Leeds, 2005.
129:0 wkt	Yorkshire (355 and 129:0) beat Durham MCCU (196 and 287) at Durham, 2011
127:0 wkt	Yorkshire (258 and 127:0) beat Cambridge University (127 and 257) at Cambridge, 1930.
119:0 wkt	Yorkshire (109 and 119:0) beat Essex (108 and 119) at Leeds, 1931.
118:0 wkt	Yorkshire (121 and 118:0) beat MCC (125 and 113) at Lord's, 1883.
116:0 wkt	Yorkshire (147 and 116:0) beat Hampshire (141 and 120) at Bournemouth, 1930.
114:0 wkt	Yorkshire (135 and 114:0) beat Hampshire (71 and 176) at Bournemouth, 1948.

HEAVY DEFEATS – BY AN INNINGS
AND OVER 250 RUNS

Inns and 272 runs	Yorkshire (78 and 186) lost to Surrey (536) at The Oval, 1898.
Inns and 261 runs	Yorkshire (247 and 89) lost to Sussex (597: 8 dec.) at Hove, 2007.
Inns and 255 runs	Yorkshire (125 and 144) lost to All England XI (524) at Sheffield, 1865.

HEAVY DEFEATS – BY OVER 300 RUNS

324 runs	Yorkshire (247 and 204) lost to Gloucestershire (291 and 484) at Cheltenham, 1994.
305 runs	Yorkshire (119 and 51) lost to Cambridge University (312 and 163) at Cambridge, 1906.

HEAVY DEFEATS – BY 10 WICKETS
(WITH OVER 100 RUNS SCORED IN THE 4th INNINGS)

4th Innings

228:0 wkt   Yorkshire (358 and 321) lost to Somerset (452 and 228:0)
        at Taunton, 2011

148:0 wkt   Yorkshire (83 and 216) lost to Lancashire (154 and 148:0)
        at Manchester, 1875.

119:0 wkt   Yorkshire (92 and 109) lost to Nottinghamshire (86 and 119:0 wkt)
        at Leeds, 1989.

108:0 wkt   Yorkshire (236 and 107) lost to Hampshire (236 and 108:0 wkt)
        at Southampton, 2008

100:0 wkt   Yorkshire (95 and 91) lost to Gloucestershire (88 and 100:0)
        at Bristol, 1956.

NARROW VICTORIES – BY 1 WICKET

Yorkshire (70 and 91:9) beat Cambridgeshire (86 and 74) at Wisbech, 1867.
Yorkshire (91 and 145:9) beat MCC (73 and 161) at Lord's, 1870.
Yorkshire (265 and 154:9) beat Derbyshire (234 and 184) at Derby, 1897.
Yorkshire (177 and 197:9) beat MCC (188 and 185) at Lord's, 1899.
Yorkshire (391 and 241:9) beat Somerset (349 and 281) at Taunton, 1901.
Yorkshire (239 and 168:9) beat MCC (179 and 226) at Scarborough, 1935.
Yorkshire (152 and 90:9) beat Worcestershire (119 and 121) at Leeds, 1946.
Yorkshire (229 and 175:9) beat Glamorgan (194 and 207) at Bradford, 1960.
Yorkshire (265.9 dec and 191:9) beat Worcestershire (227 and 227) at Worcester, 1961.
Yorkshire (329:6 dec and 167:9) beat Essex (339.9 dec and 154) at Scarborough, 1979.
Yorkshire (Innings forfeited and 251:9 beat Sussex (195 and 55.1 dec) at Leeds, 1986.
Yorkshire (314 and 150:9) beat Essex (200 and 261) at Scarborough, 1998.

NARROW VICTORIES – BY 5 RUNS OR LESS

By 1 run   Yorkshire (228 and 214) beat Middlesex (206 and 235) at Bradford, 1976.
By 1 run   Yorkshire (383 and inns forfeited) beat Loughborough UCCE (93: 3 dec.
        and 289) at Leeds, 2007.
By 2 runs   Yorkshire (108 and 122) beat Nottinghamshire (56 and 172)
        at Nottingham, 1870.
By 2 runs   Yorkshire (304:9 dec and 135) beat Middlesex (225:2 dec and 212)
        at Leeds, 1985.
By 3 runs   Yorkshire (446:9 dec and 172:4 dec) beat Essex (300:3 dec and 315)
        at Colchester, 1991.
By 5 runs   Yorkshire (271 and 147:6 dec) beat Surrey (198 and 215) at Sheffield, 1950.
By 5 runs   Yorkshire (151 and 176) beat Hampshire (165 and 157) at Bradford, 1962.
By 5 runs   Yorkshire (376:4 and 106) beat Middlesex (325:8 and 152) at Lord's, 1975
By 5 runs   Yorkshire (323:5 dec and inns forfeited) beat Somerset (inns forfeited
        and 318) at Taunton, 1986.

NARROW DEFEATS – BY 1 WICKET

Yorkshire (224 and 210) lost to Australian Imperial Forces XI (265 and 170:9)
    at Leeds, 1985.
Yorkshire (101 and 159) lost to Warwickshire (45 and 216:9) at Scarborough, 1934.
Yorkshire (239 and 184:9 dec.) lost to Warwickshire (125 and 302:9)
    at Birmingham, 1983.
Yorkshire (289 and 153) lost to Surrey (250:2 dec and 193:9) at Guildford, 1991.
Yorkshire (341 and Inns forfeited) lost to Surrey (39:1 dec and 306:9) at Bradford, 1992.

NARROW DEFEATS – BY 5 RUNS OR LESS

By 1 run	Yorkshire (135 and 297) lost to Essex (139 and 294) at Huddersfield, 1897.
By 1 run	Yorkshire (159 and 232) lost to Gloucestershire (164 and 228) at Bristol, 1906.
By 1 run	Yorkshire (126 and 137) lost to Worcestershire (101 and 163) at Worcester, 1968.
By 1 run	Yorkshire (366 and 217) lost to Surrey (409 and 175) at The Oval, 1995.
By 2 runs	Yorkshire (172 and 107) lost to Gloucestershire (157 and 124) at Sheffield, 1913.
By 2 runs	Yorkshire (179:9 dec and 144) lost to MCC (109 and 216) at Lord's, 1957.
By 3 runs	Yorkshire (126 and 181) lost to Sussex (182 and 128) at Sheffield, 1883.
By 3 runs	Yorkshire (160 and 71) lost to Lancashire (81 and 153) at Huddersfield, 1889.
By 3 runs	Yorkshire (134 and 158) lost to Nottinghamshire (200 and 95) at Leeds, 1923.
By 4 runs	Yorkshire (169 and 193) lost to Middlesex (105 and 261) at Bradford, 1920.
By 5 runs	Yorkshire (58 and 51) lost to Lancashire (64 and 50) at Manchester, 1893.
By 5 runs	Yorkshire (119 and 115) lost to Warwickshire (167 and 72) at Bradford, 1969.

HIGH FOURTH INNINGS SCORES – 300 AND OVER

By Yorkshire

To Win:	406:4	beat Leicestershire by 6 wkts at Leicester, 2005
	402:6	beat Gloucestershire by 4 wkts at Bristol, 2012
	400:4	beat Leicestershire by 6 wkts at Scarborough, 2005
	339:6	beat Durham by 4 wickets at Chester-le-Street, 2013
	331:8	beat Middlesex by 2 wkts at Lord's, 1910.
	327:6	beat Nottinghamshire by 4 wkts at Nottingham, 1990.*
	323:5	beat Nottinghamshire by 5 wkts at Nottingham, 1977.
	318:3	beat Glamorgan by 7 wkts at Middlesbrough, 1976.
	316:8	beat Gloucestershire by 2 wkts at Scarborough, 2012
	309:7	beat Somerset by 3 wkts at Taunton, 1984.
	305:8	beat Nottinghamshire by 2 wkts at Worksop, 1982.
	305:3	beat Lancashire by 7 wickets at Manchester, 1994.
	304:4	beat Derbyshire by 6 wkts at Chesterfield, 1959.
	300:4	beat Derbyshire by 6 wkts at Chesterfield, 1981.
	300:6	beat Derbyshire by 4 wkts at Scarborough, 1990.*
To Draw:	341:8	(set 358) drew with Derbyshire at Derby, 2004.
	333:7	(set 369) drew with Essex at Chelmsford, 2010
	316:6	(set 326) drew with Oxford University at Oxford, 1948.
	312:6	(set 344) drew with Sussex at Scarborough 2011
	316:7	(set 320) drew with Somerset at Scarborough, 1990.
	300:5	(set 392) drew with Kent at Canterbury, 2010
To Lose:	433	(set 500) lost to Warwickshire by 66 runs at Birmingham, 2006
	380	(set 406) lost to MCC. by 25 runs at Lord's, 1937.
	343	(set 490) lost to Durham by 146 runs at Leeds 2011
	324	(set 485) lost to Northamptonshire by 160 runs at Luton, 1994.
	322	(set 344) lost to Middlesex by 21 runs at Lord's, 1996.
	309	(set 400) lost to Middlesex by 90 runs at Lord's 1878.

*Consecutive matches

By Opponents:

To Win:	479:6	Somerset won by 4 wkts at Taunton, 2009
	404:5	Hampshire won by 5 wkts at Leeds, 2006
	392:4	Gloucestershire won by 6 wkts at Bristol, 1948.
	364:4	Somerset won by 6 wickets at Taunton, 2010
	354:5	Nottinghamshire won by 5 wkts at Scarborough, 1990.
	337:4	Worcestershire won by 6 wkts at Kidderminster, 2007.
	334:6	Glamorgan won by 4 wkts at Harrogate, 1955.
	329:5	Worcestershire won by 5 wkts at Worcester, 1979.
	306:9	Surrey won by 1 wkt at Bradford, 1992.
	305:7	Lancashire won by 3 wkts at Manchester, 1980.
	302:9	Warwickshire won by 1 wkt at Birmingham, 1983

HIGH FOURTH INNINGS SCORES – 300 AND OVER *(Continued)*

By Opponents:

To Draw:

366:8	(set 443) Hampshire drew at Southampton, 2007.
334:7	(set 339) MCC. drew at Scarborough, 1911.
322:9	(set 334) Middlesex drew at Leeds, 1988.
317:6	(set 355) Nottinghamshire drew at Nottingham, 1910.
300:9	(set 314) Northamptonshire drew at Northampton, 1990.

To Lose:

370	(set 539) Leicestershire lost by 168 runs at Leicester, 2001
319	(set 364) Gloucestershire lost by 44 runs at Leeds, 1987.
318	(set 324) Somerset lost by 5 runs at Taunton, 1986.
315	(set 319) Essex lost by 3 runs at Colchester, 1991.
314	(set 334) Lancashire lost by 19 runs at Manchester, 1993.
310	(set 417) Warwickshire lost by 106 runs at Scarborough, 1939.
306	(set 413) Kent lost by 106 runs at Leeds, 1952.
300	(set 330) Middlesex lost by 29 runs at Sheffield, 1930.

TIE MATCHES

Yorkshire (351:4 dec and 113) tied with Leicestershire (328 and 136) at Huddersfield, 1954.
Yorkshire (106:9 dec and 207) tied with Middlesex (102 and 211) at Bradford, 1973.

HIGHEST SCORES BY AND AGAINST YORKSHIRE

Yorkshire versus: —

Derbyshire:

	By Yorkshire:	**Against Yorkshire:**
In Yorkshire:	677:7 dec at Leeds 2013	491 at Bradford, 1949
Away:	662 at Chesterfield, 1898	523 at Derby, 2005

Durham:

In Yorkshire:	677:7 dec. at Leeds, 2006	573 at Scarborough, 2013
Away:	448 at Chester-le-Street, 2003	481 at Chester-le-Street, 2007

Essex:

In Yorkshire:	516 at Scarborough, 2010	622:8 dec. at Leeds, 2005
Away:	555:1 dec. at Leyton, 1932	521 at Leyton, 1905

Glamorgan:

In Yorkshire:	580:9 dec at Scarborough, 2001	498 at Leeds, 1999
Away:	536:8 dec. at Cardiff, 1996	482:7 dec. at Cardiff, 1996

Gloucestershire:

In Yorkshire:	504:7 dec. at Bradford, 1905	411 at Leeds, 1992
Away:	494 at Bristol, 1897	574 at Cheltenham, 1990

Hampshire:

In Yorkshire:	493:1 dec. at Sheffield, 1939	498:6 dec at Scarborough, 2010
Away	585:3 dec at Portsmouth 1920	599:3 at Southampton, 2011

Kent:

In Yorkshire	550:9 at Scarborough, 1995	537:9 dec at Leeds, 2012
Away:	559 at Canterbury, 1887	580: 9 dec. at Maidstone, 1998

Lancashire:

In Yorkshire:	590 at Bradford, 1887	517 at Leeds, 2007.
Away:	528:8 dec. at Manchester, 1939	537 at Manchester, 2005

Leicestershire:

In Yorkshire	562 { at Scarborough, 1901 at Dewsbury, 1903	681:7 dec. at Bradford, 1996
Away:	660 at Leicester, 1896	425 at Leicester, 1906

Yorkshire versus: —

Middlesex:	**By Yorkshire:**	**Against Yorkshire:**
In Yorkshire:	575:7 dec. at Bradford, 1899	527 at Huddersfield, 1887
Away:	538:6 dec. at Lord's, 1925	488 at Lord's, 1899

Northamptonshire:
In Yorkshire:	673:8 dec. at Leeds, 2003	517:7 dec. at Scarborough, 1999
Away:	523:8 dec. at Wellingborough, 1949	531:4 at Northampton, 1996

Nottinghamshire:
In Yorkshire:	572:8 dec at Scarborough, 2013	545:7 dec at Leeds, 2010
Away	534:9 dec at Nottingham, 2011	490 at Nottingham, 1897

Somerset:
In Yorkshire:	525:4 dec. at Leeds, 1953	630 at Leeds, 1901
Away:	589:5 dec at Bath, 2001	592 at Taunton, 1892

Surrey:
In Yorkshire:	582:7 dec. at Sheffield, 1935	510 at Leeds, 2002
Away:	704 at The Oval, 1899	634:5 dec at The Oval, 2013

Sussex:
In Yorkshire:	681:5 dec. at Sheffield, 1897	566 at Sheffield, 1937
Away:	522:7 dec. at Hastings, 1911	597:8 dec. at Hove, 2007

Warwickshire:
In Yorkshire	561:7 dec at Scarborough 2007	482 at Leeds, 2011
Away:	887 at Birmingham, 1896	601:9 dec. at Birmingham, 2002
	(Highest score by a First-Class county)	

Worcestershire:
In Yorkshire:	600: 4 dec. at Scarborough, 1995	453:5 dec. at Scarborough, 1995
Away:	560:6 dec. at Worcester, 1928	456:8 at Worcester, 1904

Australians:
In Yorkshire:	377 at Sheffield, 1953	470 at Bradford, 1893

Indians:
In Yorkshire:	385 at Hull, 1911	490:5 dec. at Sheffield, 1946

New Zealanders:
In Yorkshire:	419 at Bradford, 1965	370:7 dec. at Bradford, 1949

Pakistanis:
In Yorkshire:	433:9 dec. at Sheffield, 1954	356 at Sheffield, 1954

South Africans:
In Yorkshire:	579 at Sheffield, 1951	454:8 dec at Sheffield, 1951

Sri Lankans:
In Yorkshire:	314:8 dec. at Leeds, 1991	422:8 dec. at Leeds, 1991

West Indians:
In Yorkshire:	312:5 dec. at Scarborough, 1973	426 at Scarborough, 1995

Zimbabweans:
In Yorkshire:	298:9 dec at Leeds, 1990	235 at Leeds, 2000

Cambridge University:
In Yorkshire:	359 at Scarborough, 1967	366 at Leeds, 1998
Away:	540 at Cambridge, 1938	425:7 at Cambridge, 1929

Durham MCCU:
Away:	355 at Durham, 2011	287 at Durham, 2011

Leeds/Bradford MCCU:
In Yorkshire	289:2 dec at Leeds, 2013	211 at Leeds, 2012

Loughborough MCCU:
In Yorkshire:	383:6 dec at Leeds, 2007	289 at Leeds, 2007

Yorkshire versus: —

MCC:	By Yorkshire:	Against Yorkshire:
In Yorkshire:	557:8 dec. at Scarborough, 1933	478:8 at Scarborough, 1904
Away:	528:8 dec. at Lord's, 1919	488 at Lord's, 1919

Oxford University:

In Yorkshire:	173 at Harrogate, 1972	190:6 dec at Harrogate, 1972
Away:	468:6 dec. at Oxford, 1978	422:9 dec. at Oxford, 1953

LOWEST SCORES BY AND AGAINST YORKSHIRE

Yorkshire versus:

Derbyshire: By Yorkshire: Against Yorkshire:
In Yorkshire: 50 at Sheffield, 1894 — 20 at Sheffield, 1939
Away: 44 at Chesterfield, 1948 — 26 at Derby, 1880

Durham:
In Yorkshire: 93 at Leeds, 2003 — 125 at Harrogate, 1995
Away: 108 at Durham, 1992 — 74 at Chester-le-Street, 1998

Essex:
In Yorkshire: 31 at Huddersfield, 1935 — 52 at Harrogate, 1900
Away: 98 at Leyton, 1905 — 30 at Leyton, 1901

Glamorgan:
In Yorkshire: 83 at Sheffield, 1946 — 52 at Hull, 1926
Away: 92 at Swansea, 1956 — 48 at Cardiff, 1924

Gloucestershire:
In Yorkshire: 61 at Leeds, 1894 — 36 at Sheffield, 1903
Away: 35 at Bristol, 1959 — 42 at Gloucester, 1924

Hampshire:
In Yorkshire: 23 at Middlesbrough, 1965 — 36 at Leeds, 1904
Away: 96 at Bournemouth, 1971 — 36 at Southampton, 1898

Kent:
In Yorkshire: 30 at Sheffield, 1865 — 39 { at Sheffield, 1882 / at Sheffield, 1936

Away: 62 at Maidstone, 1889 — 63 at Canterbury, 1901

Lancashire:
In Yorkshire: 33 at Leeds, 1924 — 30 at Holbeck, 1868
Away: 51 { at Manchester, 1888 / at Manchester, 1893 — 39 at Manchester, 1874

Leicestershire: By Yorkshire: Against Yorkshire:
In Yorkshire: 93 at Leeds, 1935 — 34 at Leeds, 1906
Away: 47 at Leicester, 1911 — 57 at Leicester, 1898

Middlesex:
In Yorkshire: 45 at Leeds, 1898 — 45 at Huddersfield, 1879
Away: 43 at Lord's, 1888 — 49 at Lord's in 1890

Northamptonshire:
In Yorkshire: 85 at Sheffield, 1919 — 51 at Bradford, 1920
Away 64 at Northampton, 1959 — 15 at Northampton, 1908
(and 27 in first innings)

Nottinghamshire:
In Yorkshire: 32 at Sheffield, 1876 — 24 at Sheffield, 1888
Away: 43 at Nottingham, 1869 — 13 at Nottingham, 1901
(second smallest total
by a First-Class county)

Yorkshire versus:

Somerset:	By Yorkshire:	Against Yorkshire:
In Yorkshire:	73 at Leeds, 1895	43 at Bradford, 1930
Away:	83 at Wells, 1949	35 at Bath, 1898

Surrey:

In Yorkshire:	54 at Sheffield, 1873	31 at Holbeck, 1883
Away:	26 at The Oval, 1909	44 at The Oval, 1935

Sussex:

In Yorkshire:	61 at Dewsbury, 1891	20 at Hull, 1922
Away:	42 at Hove, 1922	24 at Hove, 1878

Warwickshire:

In Yorkshire:	49 at Huddersfield, 1951	35 at Sheffield, 1979
Away:	54 at Birmingham, 1964	35 at Birmingham, 1963

Worcestershire:

In Yorkshire:	62 at Bradford, 1907	24 at Huddersfield, 1903
Away:	72 at Worcester, 1977	65 at Worcester, 1925

Australians:

In Yorkshire:	48 at Leeds, 1893	23 at Leeds, 1902

Indians:

In Yorkshire:	146 at Bradford, 1959	66 at Harrogate, 1932

New Zealanders:

In Yorkshire:	189 at Harrogate, 1931	134 at Bradford, 1965

Pakistanis:

In Yorkshire:	137 at Bradford, 1962	150 at Leeds, 1967

South Africans:

In Yorkshire:	113 at Bradford, 1907	76 at Bradford, 1951

Sri Lankans:

In Yorkshire:	Have not been dismissed. Lowest is 184:1 dec at Leeds, 1991	287:5 dec at Leeds, 1988

West Indians:

In Yorkshire:	50 at Harrogate, 1906	58 at Leeds, 1928

Zimbabweans:

In Yorkshire:	124 at Leeds, 2000	68 at Leeds, 2000

Cambridge University:

In Yorkshire:	110 at Sheffield, 1903	39 at Sheffield, 1903
Away:	51 at Cambridge, 1906	30 at Cambridge, 1928

Durham MCCU:

Away:	355 at Durham, 2011	196 at Durham, 2011

Loughborough MCCU:

In Yorkshire	348:5 dec at Leeds, 2010	289 at Leeds, 2007

MCC:

In Yorkshire:	46 { at Scarborough, 1876 / at Scarborough, 1877	31 at Scarborough, 1877
Away:	44 at Lord's, 1880	27 at Lord's, 1902

Oxford University:

In Yorkshire:	Have not been dismissed. Lowest is 115:8 at Harrogate, 1972	133 at Harrogate, 1972
Away:	141 at Oxford, 1949	46 at Oxford, 1956

INDIVIDUAL INNINGS OF 150 AND OVER

**A complete list of all First-class Centuries up to and including 2007
is to be found in the 2008 edition**

J M BAIRSTOW (3)

205	v. Nottinghamshire	Nottingham	2011
182	v. Leicestershire	Scarborough	2012
186	v. Derbyshire	Leeds	2013

W BARBER (7)

162	v. Middlesex	Sheffield	1932
168	v. MCC	Lord's	1934
248	v. Kent	Leeds	1934
191	v. Sussex	Leeds	1935
255	v. Surrey	Sheffield	1935
158	v. Kent	Sheffield	1936
157	v. Surrey	Sheffield	1938

M G BEVAN (2)

153*	v. Surrey	The Oval	1995
160*	v. Surrey	Middlesbrough	1996

H D BIRD (1)

181*	v. Glamorgan	Bradford	1959

R J BLAKEY (3)

204*	v. Gloucestershire	Leeds	1987
196	v. Oxford University	Oxford	1991
223*	v. Northamptonshire	Leeds	2003

G BLEWETT (1)

190	v. Northamptonshire	Scarborough	1999

M W BOOTH (1)

210	v. Worcestershire	Worcester	1911

G BOYCOTT (32)

165*	v. Leicestershire	Scarborough	1963
151	v. Middlesex	Leeds	1964
151*	v. Leicestershire	Leicester	1964
177	v. Gloucestershire	Bristol	1964
164	v. Sussex	Hove	1966
220*	v. Northamptonshire	Sheffield	1967
180*	v. Warwickshire	Middlesbrough	1968
260*	v. Essex	Colchester (Garrison Ground)	1970
169	v. Nottinghamshire	Leeds	1971
233	v. Essex	Colchester (Garrison Ground)	1971
182*	v. Middlesex	Lord's	1971
169	v. Lancashire	Sheffield	1971
151	v. Leicestershire	Bradford	1971
204*	v. Leicestershire	Leicester	1972
152*	v. Worcestershire	Worcester	1975
175*	v. Middlesex	Scarborough	1975
201*	v. Middlesex	Lord's	1975
161*	v. Gloucestershire	Leeds	1976
207*	v. Cambridge University	Cambridge	1976
156*	v. Glamorgan	Middlesbrough	1976

273

G BOYCOTT *(Continued)*

154	v Nottinghamshire	Nottingham	1977
151*	v Derbyshire	Leeds	1979
167	v Derbyshire	Chesterfield	1979
175*	v Nottinghamshire	Worksop	1979
154*	v Derbyshire	Scarborough	1980
159	v Worcestershire	Sheffield (Abbeydale Park)	1982
152*	v Warwickshire	Leeds	1982
214*	v Nottinghamshire	Worksop	1983
163	v Nottinghamshire	Bradford	1983
169*	v Derbyshire	Chesterfield	1983
153*	v Derbyshire	Harrogate	1984
184	v Worcestershire	Worcester	1985

G L BROPHY *(1)*

177*	v Worcestershire	Worcester	2011

J T BROWN *(8)*

168*	v Sussex	Huddersfield	1895
203	v Middlesex	Lord's	1896
311	v Sussex	Sheffield	1897
300	v Derbyshire	Chesterfield	1898
150	v Sussex	Hove	1898
168	v Cambridge University	Cambridge	1899
167	v Australians	Bradford	1899
192	v Derbyshire	Derby	1899

D BYAS *(5)*

153	v Nottinghamshire	Worksop	1991
156	v Essex	Chelmsford	1993
181	v Cambridge University	Cambridge	1995
193	v Lancashire	Leeds	1995
213	v Worcestershire	Scarborough	1995

D B CLOSE *(5)*

164	v Combined Services	Harrogate	1954
154	v Nottinghamshire	Nottingham	1959
198	v Surrey	The Oval	1960
184	v Nottinghamshire	Scarborough	1960
161	v Northamptonshire	Northampton	1963

D DENTON *(11)*

153*	v Australians	Bradford	1905
165	v Hampshire	Bournemouth	1905
172	v Gloucestershire	Bradford	1905
184	v Nottinghamshire	Nottingham	1909
182	v Derbyshire	Chesterfield	1910
200*	v Warwickshire	Birmingham	1912
182	v Gloucestershire	Bristol	1912
221	v Kent	Tunbridge Wells	1912
191	v Hampshire	Southampton	1912
168*	v Hampshire	Southampton	1914
209*	v Worcestershire	Worcester	1920

A W GALE (3)

150	v. Surrey	The Oval	2008
151*	v. Nottinghamshire	Nottingham	2010
272	v. Nottinghamshire	Scarborough	2013

P A GIBB (1)

157*	v. Nottinghamshire	Sheffield	1935

S HAIGH (1)

159	v. Nottinghamshire	Sheffield	1901

L HALL (1)

160	v. Lancashire	Bradford	1887

J H HAMPSHIRE (5)

150	v. Leicestershire	Bradford	1964
183*	v. Sussex	Hove	1971
157*	v. Nottinghamshire	Worksop	1974
158	v. Gloucestershire	Harrogate	1974
155*	v. Gloucestershire	Leeds	1976

I J HARVEY (1)

209*	v. Somerset	Leeds	2005

LORD HAWKE (1)

166	v. Warwickshire	Birmingham	1896

G H HIRST (15)

186	v. Surrey	The Oval	1899
155	v. Nottinghamshire	Scarborough	1900
214	v. Worcestershire	Worcester	1901
153	v. Leicestershire	Dewsbury	1903
153	v. Oxford University	Oxford	1904
152	v. Hampshire	Portsmouth	1904
157	v. Kent	Tunbridge Wells	1904
341	v. Leicestershire	Leicester (Aylestone Road)	1905
232*	v. Surrey	The Oval	1905
169	v. Oxford University	Oxford	1906
158	v. Cambridge University	Cambridge	1910
156	v. Lancashire	Manchester	1911
218	v. Sussex	Hastings	1911
166*	v. Sussex	Hastings	1913
180*	v. MCC	Lord's	1919

P HOLMES (16)

302*	v. Hampshire	Portsmouth	1920
150	v. Derbyshire	Chesterfield	1921
277*	v. Northamptonshire	Harrogate	1921
209	v. Warwickshire	Birmingham	1922
220*	v. Warwickshire	Huddersfield	1922
199	v. Somerset	Hull	1923
315*	v. Middlesex	Lord's	1925
194	v. Leicestershire	Hull	1925
159	v. Hampshire	Southampton	1925
180	v. Gloucestershire	Gloucester	1927
175*	v. New Zealanders	Bradford	1927
179*	v. Middlesex	Leeds	1928

P HOLMES *(Continued)*

275	v. Warwickshire	Bradford	1928
285	v. Nottinghamshire	Nottingham	1929
250	v. Warwickshire	Birmingham	1931
224*	v. Essex	Leyton	1932

L HUTTON *(31)*

196	v. Worcestershire	Worcester	1934
163	v. Surrey	Leeds	1936
161	v. MCC	Lord's	1937
271*	v. Derbyshire	Sheffield	1937
153	v. Leicestershire	Hull	1937
180	v. Cambridge University	Cambridge	1938
158	v. Warwickshire	Birmingham	1939
280*	v. Hampshire	Sheffield	1939
151	v. Surrey	Leeds	1939
177	v. Sussex	Scarborough	1939
183*	v. Indians	Bradford	1946
171*	v. Northamptonshire	Hull	1946
197	v. Glamorgan	Swansea	1947
197	v. Essex	Southend-on-Sea	1947
270*	v. Hampshire	Bournemouth	1947
176*	v. Sussex	Sheffield	1948
155	v. Sussex	Hove	1948
167	v. New Zealanders	Bradford	1949
201	v. Lancashire	Manchester	1949
165	v. Sussex	Hove	1949
269*	v. Northamptonshire	Wellingborough	1949
156	v. Essex	Colchester (Castle Park)	1950
153	v. Nottinghamshire	Nottingham	1950
156	v. South Africans	Sheffield	1951
151	v. Surrey	The Oval	1951
194*	v. Nottinghamshire	Nottingham	1951
152	v. Lancashire	Leeds	1952
189	v. Kent	Leeds	1952
178	v. Somerset	Leeds	1953
163	v. Combined Services	Harrogate	1954
194	v. Nottinghamshire	Nottingham	1955

R A HUTTON *(1)*

189	v. Pakistanis	Bradford	1971

R ILLINGWORTH *(2)*

150	v. Essex	Colchester (Castle Park)	1959
162	v. Indians	Sheffield	1959

Hon F S JACKSON *(3)*

160	v. Gloucestershire	Sheffield	1898
155	v. Middlesex	Bradford	1899
158	v. Surrey	Bradford	1904

P A JAQUES *(7)*

243	v. Hampshire	Southampton (Rose Bowl)	2004
173	v. Glamorgan	Leeds	2004
176	v. Northamptonshire	Leeds	2005
219	v. Derbyshire	Leeds	2005
172	v. Durham	Scarborough	2005
160	v. Gloucestershire	Bristol	2012
152	v. Durham	Scarborough	2013

R KILNER (5)

169	v. Gloucestershire	Bristol	1914
206*	v. Derbyshire	Sheffield	1920
166	v. Northamptonshire	Northampton	1921
150	v. Northamptonshire	Harrogate	1921
150	v. Middlesex	Lord's	1926

F LEE (1)

165	v. Lancashire	Bradford	1887

A Z LEES (1)

275*	v. Derbyshire	Chesterfield	2013

D S LEHMANN (13)

177	v. Somerset	Taunton	1997
163*	v. Leicestershire	Leicester	1997
182	v. Hampshire	Portsmouth	1997
200	v. Worcestershire	Worcester	1998
187*	v. Somerset	Bath	2001
252	v. Lancashire	Leeds	2001
193	v. Leicestershire	Leicester	2001
216	v. Sussex	Arundel	2002
187	v. Lancashire	Leeds	2002
150	v. Warwickshire	Birmingham	2006
193	v. Kent	Canterbury	2006
172	v. Kent	Leeds	2006
339	v. Durham	Leeds	2006

E I LESTER (5)

186	v. Warwickshire	Scarborough	1949
178	v. Nottinghamshire	Nottingham	1952
157	v. Cambridge University	Hull	1953
150	v. Oxford University	Oxford	1954
163	v. Essex	Romford	1954

M LEYLAND (17)

191	v. Glamorgan	Swansea	1926
204*	v. Middlesex	Sheffield	1927
247	v. Worcestershire	Worcester	1928
189*	v. Glamorgan	Huddersfield	1928
211*	v. Lancashire	Leeds	1930
172	v. Middlesex	Sheffield	1930
186	v. Derbyshire	Leeds	1930
189	v. Middlesex	Sheffield	1932
153	v. Leicestershire	Leicester (Aylestone Road)	1932
166	v. Leicestershire	Bradford	1932
153*	v. Hampshire	Bournemouth	1932
192	v. Northamptonshire	Leeds	1933
210*	v. Kent	Dover	1933
263	v. Essex	Hull	1936
163*	v. Surrey	Leeds	1936
167	v. Worcestershire	Stourbridge	1937
180*	v. Middlesex	Lord's	1939

E LOCKWOOD (1)

208	v. Kent	Gravesend	1883

INDIVIDUAL INNINGS OF 150 AND OVER *(Continued)*

J D LOVE (4)

163	v. Nottinghamshire	Bradford	1976
170*	v. Worcestershire	Worcester	1979
161	v. Warwickshire	Birmingham	1981
154	v. Lancashire	Manchester	1981

F A LOWSON (10)

155	v. Kent	Maidstone	1951
155	v. Worcestershire	Bradford	1952
166	v. Scotland	Glasgow	1953
259*	v. Worcestershire	Worcester	1953
165	v. Sussex	Hove	1954
164	v. Essex	Scarborough	1954
150*	v. Kent	Dover	1954
183*	v. Oxford University	Oxford	1956
154	v. Somerset	Taunton	1956
154	v. Cambridge University	Cambridge	1957

R G LUMB (2)

159	v. Somerset	Harrogate	1979
165*	v. Gloucestershire	Bradford	1984

A LYTH (1)

248 *	v. Leicestershire	Leicester	2012

A McGRATH (7)

165	v. Lancashire	Leeds	2002
174	v. Derbyshire	Derby	2004
165*	v. Leicestershire	Leicester	2005
173*	v. Worcestershire	Leeds	2005
158	v. Derbyshire	Derby	2005
188*	v. Warwickshire	Birmingham	2007
211	v. Warwickshire	Birmingham	2009

D R MARTYN (1)

238	v. Gloucestershire	Leeds	2003

A A METCALFE (7)

151	v. Northamptonshire	Luton	1986
151	v. Lancashire	Manchester	1986
152	v. MCC	Scarborough	1987
216*	v. Middlesex	Leeds	1988
162	v. Gloucestershire	Cheltenham	1990
150*	v. Derbyshire	Scarborough	1990
194*	v. Nottinghamshire	Nottingham	1990

A MITCHELL (7)

189	v. Northamptonshire	Northampton	1926
176	v. Nottinghamshire	Bradford	1930
177*	v. Gloucestershire	Bradford	1932
150*	v. Worcestershire	Worcester	1933
158	v. MCC	Scarborough	1933
152	v. Hampshire	Bradford	1934
181	v. Surrey	Bradford	1934

F MITCHELL (2)

194	v. Leicestershire	Leicester	1899
162*	v. Warwickshire	Birmingham	1901

M D MOXON (14)

153	v. Lancashire	Leeds	1983
153	v. Somerset	Leeds	1985
168	v. Worcestershire	Worcester	1985
191	v. Northamptonshire	Scarborough	1989
162*	v. Surrey	The Oval	1989
218*	v. Sussex	Eastbourne	1990
200	v. Essex	Colchester (Castle Park)	1991
183	v. Gloucestershire	Cheltenham	1992
171*	v. Kent	Leeds	1993
161*	v. Lancashire	Manchester	1994
274*	v. Worcestershire	Worcester	1994
203*	v. Kent	Leeds	1995
213	v. Glamorgan	Cardiff (Sophia Gardens)	1996
155	v. Pakistan 'A'	Leeds	1997

E OLDROYD (5)

151*	v. Glamorgan	Cardiff	1922
194	v. Worcestershire	Worcester	1923
162*	v. Glamorgan	Swansea	1928
168	v. Glamorgan	Hull	1929
164*	v. Somerset	Bath	1930

D E V PADGETT (1)

161*	v. Oxford University	Oxford	1959

R PEEL (2)

158	v. Middlesex	Lord's	1889
210*	v. Warwickshire	Birmingham	1896

A U RASHID (2)

157*	v. Lancashire	Leeds	2009
180	v. Somerset	Leeds	2013

W RHODES (8)

196	v. Worcestershire	Worcester	1904
201	v. Somerset	Taunton	1905
199	v. Sussex	Hove	1909
176	v. Nottinghamshire	Harrogate	1912
152	v. Leicestershire	Leicester (Aylestone Road)	1913
167*	v. Nottinghamshire	Leeds	1920
267*	v. Leicestershire	Leeds	1921
157	v. Derbyshire	Leeds	1925

P E ROBINSON (2)

150*	v. Derbyshire	Scarborough	1990
189	v. Lancashire	Scarborough	1991

J E ROOT (4)

160	v. Sussex	Scarborough	2011
222 *	v. Hampshire	Southampton (West End)	2012
182	v. Durham	Chester-le-Street	2013
236	v. Derbyshire	Leeds	2013

2013 innings consecutive

J W ROTHERY (1)

161	v. Kent	Dover	1908

J A RUDOLPH (5)

220	v. Warwickshire	Scarborough	2007
155	v. Somerset	Taunton	2008
198	v. Worcestershire	Leeds	2009
191	v. Somerset	Taunton	2009
228*	v. Durham	Leeds	2010

H RUDSTON (1)

164	v. Leicestershire	Leicester (Aylestone Rd)	1904

J J SAYERS (3)

187	v. Kent	Tunbridge Wells	2007
173	v. Warwickshire	Birmingham	2009
152	v. Somerset	Taunton	2009

A B SELLERS (1)

204	v. Cambridge University	Cambridge	1936

K SHARP (2)

173	v. Derbyshire	Chesterfield	1984
181	v. Gloucestershire	Harrogate	1986

P J SHARPE (4)

203*	v. Cambridge University	Cambridge	1960
152	v. Kent	Sheffield	1960
197	v. Pakistanis	Leeds	1967
172*	v. Glamorgan	Swansea	1971

G A SMITHSON (1)

169	v. Leicestershire	Leicester	1947

W B STOTT (2)

181	v. Essex	Sheffield	1957
186	v. Warwickshire	Birmingham	1960

H SUTCLIFFE (39)

174	v. Kent	Dover	1919
232	v. Surrey	The Oval	1922
213	v. Somerset	Dewsbury	1924
160	v. Sussex	Sheffield	1924
255*	v. Essex	Southend-on-Sea	1924
235	v. Middlesex	Leeds	1925
206	v. Warwickshire	Dewsbury	1925
171	v. MCC	Scarborough	1925
200	v. Leicestershire	Leicester (Aylestone Road)	1926
176	v. Surrey	Leeds	1927
169	v. Nottinghamshire	Bradford	1927
228	v. Sussex	Eastbourne	1928
150	v. Northamptonshire	Northampton	1929
150*	v. Essex	Dewsbury	1930
173	v. Sussex	Hove	1930
173*	v. Cambridge University	Cambridge	1931
230	v. Kent	Folkestone	1931
183	v. Somerset	Dewsbury	1931
195	v. Lancashire	Sheffield	1931
187	v. Leicestershire	Leicester (Aylestone Road)	1931
153*	v. Warwickshire	Hull	1932
313	v. Essex	Leyton	1932
270	v. Sussex	Leeds	1932

H SUTCLIFFE (Continued)

182	v. Derbyshire	Leeds	1932
194	v. Essex	Scarborough	1932
205	v. Warwickshire	Birmingham	1933
177	v. Middlesex	Bradford	1933
174	v. Leicestershire	Leicester (Aylestone Road)	1933
152	v. Cambridge University	Cambridge	1934
166	v. Essex	Hull	1934
203	v. Surrey	The Oval	1934
187*	v. Worcestershire	Bradford	1934
200*	v. Worcestershire	Sheffield	1935
212	v. Leicestershire	Leicester (Aylestone Road)	1935
202	v. Middlesex	Scarborough	1936
189	v. Leicestershire	Hull	1937
165	v. Lancashire	Manchester	1939
234*	v. Leicestershire	Hull	1939
175	v. Middlesex	Lord's	1939

W H SUTCLIFFE (3)

171*	v. Worcestershire	Worcester	1952
181	v. Kent	Canterbury	1952
161*	v. Glamorgan	Harrogate	1955

K TAYLOR (8)

168*	v. Nottinghamshire	Nottingham	1956
159	v. Leicestershire	Sheffield	1961
203*	v. Warwickshire	Birmingham	1961
178*	v. Oxford University	Oxford	1962
163	v. Nottinghamshire	Leeds	1962
153	v. Lancashire	Manchester	1964
160	v. Australians	Sheffield	1964
162	v. Worcestershire	Kidderminster	1967

T L TAYLOR (1)

156	v. Hampshire	Harrogate	1901

J TUNNICLIFFE (2)

243	v. Derbyshire	Chesterfield	1898
158	v. Worcestershire	Worcester	1900

G ULYETT (1)

199*	v. Derbyshire	Sheffield	1887

M P VAUGHAN (7)

183	v. Glamorgan	Cardiff (Sophia Gardens)	1996
183	v. Northamptonshire	Northampton	1996
161	v. Essex	Ilford	1997
177	v. Durham	Chester-le-Street	1998
151	v. Essex	Chelmsford	1999
153	v. Kent	Scarborough	1999
155*	v. Derbyshire	Leeds	2000

E WAINWRIGHT (3)

171	v. Middlesex	Lord's	1897
153	v. Leicestershire	Leicester	1899
228	v. Surrey	The Oval	1899

W WATSON (7)

153*	v. Surrey	The Oval	1947
172	v. Derbyshire	Scarborough	1948
162*	v. Somerset	Leeds	1953
163	v. Sussex	Sheffield	1955
174	v. Lancashire	Sheffield	1955
214*	v. Worcestershire	Worcester	1955
162	v. Northamptonshire	Harrogate	1957

C WHITE (6)

181	v. Lancashire	Leeds	1996
172*	v. Worcestershire	Leeds	1997
186	v. Lancashire	Manchester	2001
183	v. Glamorgan	Scarborough	2001
161	v. Leicestershire	Scarborough	2002
173*	v. Derbyshire	Derby	2003

B B WILSON (2)

150	v. Warwickshire	Birmingham	1912
208	v. Sussex	Bradford	1914

J V WILSON (7)

157*	v. Sussex	Leeds	1949
157	v. Essex	Sheffield	1950
166*	v. Sussex	Hull	1951
223*	v. Scotland	Scarborough	1951
154	v. Oxford University	Oxford	1952
230	v. Derbyshire	Sheffield	1952
165	v. Oxford University	Oxford	1956

M J WOOD (5)

200*	v. Warwickshire	Leeds	1998
157	v. Northamptonshire	Leeds	2003
207	v. Somerset	Taunton	2003
155	v. Hampshire	Scarborough	2003
202*	v. Bangladesh 'A'	Leeds	2005

N W D YARDLEY (2)

177	v. Derbyshire	Scarborough	1947
183*	v. Hampshire	Leeds	1951

YOUNUS KHAN (2)

202*	v. Hampshire	Southampton (Rose Bowl)	2007
217*	v. Kent	Scarborough	2007

CENTURIES BY CURRENT PLAYERS

A complete list of all First-class Centuries up to and including 2007 is to be found in the 2008 edition

AZEEM RAFIQ (1)

100	v Worcestershire	Worcester	2009

J M BAIRSTOW (6)

205	v. Nottinghamshire	Nottingham	2011
136	v. Somerset	Taunton	2011
182	v. Leicestershire	Scarborough	2012
118	v. Leicestershire	Leicester	2012
107	v. Kent	Leeds	2012
186	v. Derbyshire	Leeds	2013

G S BALLANCE (8)

111	v. Warwickshire	Birmingham	2011
121*	v. Gloucestershire	Bristol	2012
112	v. Leeds/Bradford MCCU	Leeds	2013
107	v. Somerset	Leeds	2013
141	v. Nottinghamshire	Scarborough	2013
112	v. Warwickshire	Leeds	2013
148	v. Surrey 1st inns	The Oval	2013
108*	v. Surrey 2nd inns	The Oval	2013

T T BRESNAN (2)

116	v. Surrey	The Oval	2007
101*	v. Warwickshire	Scarborough	2007

A W GALE (14)

149	v. Warwickshire	Scarborough	2006
138	v. Hampshire	Leeds	2008
150	v. Surrey	The Oval	2008
136	v. Lancashire	Manchester	2008
101	v. Worcestershire	Worcester	2009
121	v. Lancashire	Manchester	2009
101	v. Somerset	Leeds	2010
135	v. Essex	Scarborough	2010
151*	v. Nottinghamshire	Nottingham	2010
145*	v. Nottinghamshire	Leeds	2011
101*	v. Durham	Chester-le-Street	2011
272	v. Nottinghamshire	Scarborough	2013
103	v. Middlesex	Lord's	2013
148	v. Surrey	Leeds	2013

(2013 consecutive innings)

P A JAQUES (11)

115	v. Essex	Chelmsford	2004
243	v. Hampshire	Southampton (Rose Bowl)	2004
173	v. Glamorgan	Leeds	2004
176	v. Northamptonshire	Leeds	2005
219	v. Derbyshire	Leeds	2005
106	v. Somerset	Taunton	2005
172	v. Durham	Scarborough	2005
126	v. Essex	Leeds	2012
160	v. Gloucestershire	Bristol	2012
139	v. Derbyshire	Chesterfield	2013
152	v. Durham	Scarborough	2013

A Z LEES (3)

121	v. Leeds/Bradford MCCU	Leeds	2013
100	v. Middlesex	Lord's	2013
275*	v. Derbyshire	Chesterfield	2013

A LYTH (7)

132	v. Nottinghamshire	Nottingham	2008
142	v. Somerset	Taunton	2010
133	v. Hampshire	Southampton	2010
100	v. Lancashire	Manchester	2010
248*	v. Leicestershire	Leicester	2012
111	v. Leeds/Bradford	Leeds	2013
105	v. Somerset	Taunton	2013

R M PYRAH (3)

106	v. Loughborough UCCE	Leeds	2007
134*	v. Loughborough MCCU	Leeds	2010
117	v. Lancashire	Leeds	2011

A U RASHID (7)

108	v. Worcestershire	Kidderminster	2007
111	v. Sussex	Hove	2008
117*	v. Hampshire	Basingstoke	2009
157*	v. Lancashire	Leeds	2009
180	v. Somerset	Leeds	2013
110*	v. Warwickshire	Birmingham	2013
103	v. Somerset	Taunton	2013

(2013 consecutive innings)

J E ROOT (5)

160	v. Sussex	Scarborough	2011
222 *	v. Hampshire	Southampton (West End)	2012
125	v. Northamptonshire	Leeds	2012
182	v. Durham	Chester-le-Street	2013
236	v. Derbyshire	Leeds	2013

J J SAYERS (9)

104	v. Leicestershire	Scarborough	2005
115	v. Bangladesh 'A'	Leeds	2005
122*	v. Middlesex	Scarborough	2006
149*	v. Durham	Leeds	2007
123	v. Worcestershire	Leeds	2007
187	v. Kent	Tunbridge Wells	2007
173	v. Warwickshire	Birmingham	2009
152	v. Somerset	Taunton	2009
139	v. Durham MCCU	Durham	2011

CENTURIES

(Including highest score)

112	H Sutcliffe	313	v Essex	at Leyton	1932
103	G Boycott	260*	v Essex	at Colchester (Garrison Gd)	1970
85	L Hutton	280*	v Hampshire	at Sheffield	1939
62	M Leyland	263	v Essex	at Hull	1936
61	D Denton	221	v Kent	at Tunbridge Wells	1912
60	P Holmes	315*	v Middlesex	at Lord's	1925
56	G H Hirst	341	v Leicestershire	at Leicester (Aylestone Rd)	1905
46	W Rhodes	267*	v Leicestershire	at Leeds	1921
41	M D Moxon	274*	v Worcestershire	at Worcester	1994

CENTURIES (Including highest score) *(Continued)*

39	A Mitchell	189	v Northamptonshire	at Northampton	1926
37	E Oldroyd	194	v Worcestershire	at Worcester	1923
34	J H Hampshire	183*	v Sussex	at Hove	1971
34	A McGrath	211	v Warwickshire	at Birmingham	2009
33	D B Close	198	v Surrey	at The Oval	1960
30	F A Lowson	259*	v Worcestershire	at Worcester	1953
29	D E V Padgett	161*	v Oxford University	at Oxford	1959
29	J V Wilson	230	v Derbyshire	at Sheffield	1952
28	D Byas	213	v Worcestershire	at Scarborough	1995
27	W Barber	255	v Surrey	at Sheffield	1935
26	D S Lehmann	339	v Durham	at Leeds	2006
26	W Watson	214*	v Worcestershire	at Worcester	1955
25	A A Metcalfe	216*	v Middlesex	at Leeds	1988
24	E I Lester	186	v Warwickshire	at Scarborough	1949
23	J T Brown	311	v Sussex	at Sheffield	1897
23	P J Sharpe	203*	v Cambridge University	at Cambridge	1960
22	R J Lumb	165*	v Gloucestershire	at Bradford	1984
22	J Tunnicliffe	243	v Derbyshire	at Chesterfield	1898
21	Hon F S Jackson	160	v Gloucestershire	at Sheffield	1898
20	M P Vaughan	183	v Glamorgan	at Cardiff (Sophia Gardens)	1996
	and	183	v Northamptonshire	at Northampton	1996
19	C White	186	v Lancashire	at Manchester	2001
18	J A Rudolph	228*	v Durham	at Leeds	2010
18	E Wainwright	228	v Surrey	at The Oval	1899
17	W B Stott	186	v Warwickshire	at Birmingham	1960
17	N W D Yardley	183*	v Hampshire	at Leeds	1951
16	K Taylor	203*	v Warwickshire	at Birmingham	1961
16	M J Wood	207	v Somerset	at Taunton	2003
15	R Kilner	206*	v Derbyshire	at Sheffield	1920
15	G Ulyett	199*	v Derbyshire	at Sheffield	1887
15	B B Wilson	208	v Sussex	at Bradford	1914
14	A W Gale	272	v. Nottinghamshire	at Scarborough	2013
14	R Illingworth	162	v Indians	at Sheffield	1959
13	J D Love	170*	v Worcestershire	at Worcester	1979
12	R J Blakey	223*	v Northamptonshire	at Leeds	2003
12	H Halliday	144	v Derbyshire	at Chesterfield	1950
11	P A Jaques	243	v. Hampshire	at Southampton (Rose Bowl)	2004
11	K Sharp	181	v Gloucestershire	at Harrogate	1986
10	C W J Athey	134	v Derbyshire	at Derby	1982
10	Lord Hawke	166	v Warwickshire	at Birmingham	1896
10	F Mitchell	194	v Leicestershire	at Leicester	1899
9	D L Bairstow	145	v Middlesex	at Scarborough	1980
9	M G Bevan	160*	v Surrey	at Middlesbrough	1996
9	L Hall	160	v Lancashire	at Bradford	1887
9	J J Sayers	187	v Kent	at Tunbridge Wells	2007
8	G S Ballance	148	v. Surrey	at The Oval	2013
8	W Bates	136	v Sussex	at Hove	1886
8	M J Lumb	144	v Middlesex	at Southgate	2006
7	T L Taylor	156	v Hampshire	at Harrogate	1901
7	J B Bolus	146*	v Hampshire	at Portsmouth	1960
7	A Lyth	248*	v. Leicestershire	at Leicester	2012
7	A U Rashid	180	v. Somerset	at Leeds	2013
7	E Robinson	135*	v Leicestershire	at Leicester (Aylestone Rd)	1921
7	P E Robinson	189	v Lancashire	at Scarborough	1991
6	J M Bairstow	205	v. Nottinghamshire	at Nottingham	2011
6	E Lockwood	208	v Kent	at Gravesend	1883

6	R Peel	210*	v Warwickshire	at Birmingham	1896
6	W H H Sutcliffe	181	v Kent	at Canterbury	1952
5	C M Old	116	v Indians	at Bradford	1974
5	J E Root	236	v. Derbyshire	at Leeds	2013
4	I Grimshaw	129*	v Cambridge University	at Sheffield	1885
4	S Haigh	159	v Nottinghamshire	at Sheffield	1901
4	S N Hartley	114	v Gloucestershire	at Bradford	1982
4	R A Hutton	189	v Pakistanis	at Bradford	1971
4	A B Sellers	204	v Cambridge University	at Cambridge	1936
3	G L Brophy	177*	v Worcestershire	at Worcester	2011
3	P Carrick	131*	v Northamptonshire	at Northampton	1980
3	A J Dalton	128	v Middlesex	at Leeds	1972
3	A Drake	147*	v Derbyshire	at Chesterfield	1911
3	F Lee	165	v Lancashire	at Bradford	1887
3	A Z Lees	275*	v. Derbyshire	at Chesterfield	2013
3	G G Macaulay	125*	v Nottinghamshire	at Nottingham	1921
3	R Moorhouse	113	v Somerset	at Taunton	1896
3	R M Pyrah	134*	v Loughborough MCCU	at Leeds	2010
3	J W Rothery	161	v Kent	at Dover	1908
3	J Rowbotham	113	v Surrey	at The Oval	1873
3	T F Smailes	117	v Glamorgan	at Cardiff	1938
3	Younus Khan	217*	v Kent	at Scarborough	2007
2	M W Booth	210	v Worcestershire	at Worcester	1911
2	T T Bresnan	116	v Surrey	at The Oval	2007
2	D C F Burton	142*	v Hampshire	at Dewsbury	1919
2	K R Davidson	128	v Kent	at Maidstone	1934
2	P A Gibb	157*	v Nottinghamshire	at Sheffield	1935
2	P J Hartley	127*	v Lancashire	at Manchester	1988
2	I J Harvey	209*	v Somerset	at Leeds	2005
2	C Johnson	107	v Somerset	at Sheffield	1973
2	S A Kellett	125*	v Derbyshire	at Chesterfield	1991
2	N Kilner	112	v Leicestershire	at Leeds	1921
2	B Parker	138*	v Oxford University	at Oxford	1997
2	A Sellers	105	v Middlesex	at Lord's	1893
2	E Smith (Morley)	129	v Hampshire	at Bradford	1899
2	G A Smithson	169	v Leicestershire	at Leicester	1947
2	G B Stevenson	115*	v Warwickshire	at Birmingham	1982
2	F S Trueman	104	v Northamptonshire	at Northampton	1963
2	C Turner	130	v Somerset	at Sheffield	1936
2	D J Wainwright	104*	v Sussex	at Hove	2008
2	T A Wardall	106	v Gloucestershire	at Gloucester (Spa Ground)	1892
1	Azeem Rafiq	100	v Worcestershire	at Worcester	2009
1	A T Barber	100	v England XI	at Sheffield	1929
1	H D Bird	181*	v Glamorgan	at Bradford	1959
1	T J D Birtles	104	v Lancashire	at Sheffield	1914
1	G S Blewett	190	v Northamptonshire	at Scarborough	1999
1	M T G Elliott	127	v Warwickshire	at Birmingham	2002
1	T Emmett	104	v Gloucestershire	at Clifton	1873
1	G M Fellows	109	v Lancashire	at Manchester	2002
1	J N Gillespie	123*	v Surrey	at The Oval	2007
1	D Gough	121	v Warwickshire	at Leeds	1996
1	A K D Gray	104	v Somerset	at Taunton	2003
1	A P Grayson	100	v Worcestershire	at Worcester	1994
1	F E Greenwood	104*	v Glamorgan	at Hull	1929
1	G M Hamilton	125	v Hampshire	at Leeds	2000
1	W E Harbord	109	v Oxford University	at Oxford	1930

1	R Iddison	112	v Cambridgeshire	at Hunslet	1869
1	W G Keighley	110	v Surrey	at Leeds	1951
1	R A Kettleborough				
		108	v Essex	at Leeds	1996
1	B Leadbeater	140*	v Hampshire	at Portsmouth	1976
1	D R Martyn	238	v Gloucestershire	at Leeds	2003
1	J T Newstead	100*	v Nottinghamshire	at Nottingham	1908
1	R B Richardson	112	v Warwickshire	at Birmingham	1993
1	H Rudston	164	v Leicestershire	at Leicester (Aylestone Road)	1904
1	A Sidebottom	124	v Glamorgan	at Cardiff (Sophia Gardens)	1977
1	I G Swallow	114	v MCC	at Scarborough	1987
1	S R Tendulkar	100	v Durham	at Durham	1992
1	J Thewlis	108	v Surrey	at The Oval	1868
1	C T Tyson	100*	v Hampshire	at Southampton	1921
1	H Verity	101	v Jamaica	at Kingston (Sabina Park)	1935/36
1	A Waddington	114	v Worcestershire	at Leeds	1927
1	W A I Washington				
		100*	v Surrey	at Leeds	1902
1	H Wilkinson	113	v MCC	at Scarborough	1904
1	W H Wilkinson	103	v Sussex	at Sheffield	1909
1	E R Wilson	104*	v Essex	at Bradford	1913
1	A Wood	123*	v Worcestershire	at Sheffield	1935
1	J D Woodford	101	v Warwickshire	at Middlesbrough	1971

SUMMARY OF CENTURIES
FOR AND AGAINST YORKSHIRE 1863-2013

FOR YORKSHIRE				AGAINST YORKSHIRE		
Total	In Yorkshire	Away		Total	In Yorkshire	Away
110	65	45	Derbyshire	57	27	30
22	10	12	Durham	20	13	7
75	34	41	Essex	46	21	25
68	38	30	Glamorgan	23	13	10
87	41	46	Gloucestershire	53	27	26
88	36	52	Hampshire	56	25	31
81	37	44	Kent	60	29	31
109	56	53	Lancashire	112	58	54
97	52	45	Leicestershire	46	23	23
91	45	46	Middlesex	84	36	48
78	34	44	Northamptonshire	53	25	28
120	57	63	Nottinghamshire	82	33	49
97	49	48	Somerset	57	20	37
114	48	66	Surrey	107	38	69
87	41	46	Sussex	72	31	41
103	36	67	Warwickshire	71	27	44
72	30	42	Worcestershire	40	14	26
1	1	—	Cambridgeshire	—	—	—
1500	710	790	Totals	1039	460	579
9	9	—	Australians	16	16	—
9	9	—	Indians	7	7	—
8	8	—	New Zealanders	3	3	—
5	5	—	Pakistanis	1	1	—
9	9	—	South Africans	7	7	—
5	5	—	Sri Lankans	1	1	—
5	5	—	West Indians	6	6	—
1	1	—	Zimbabweans	—	—	—
3	3	—	Bangladesh 'A'	1	1	—
—	—	—	India 'A'	1	1	—
1	1	—	Pakistan 'A'	1	1	—
45	1	44	Cambridge University	20	2	18
2	2	—	Combined Services	—	—	—
1	—	1	Durham MCCU	1	—	1
4	3	1	England XI's	3	2	1
—	—	—	International XI	1	1	—
1	—	1	Ireland	—	—	—
3	—	3	Jamaica	3	—	3
3	3	—	Leeds/Bradford MCCU	—	—	—
1	—	1	Liverpool & District	—	—	—
2	2	—	Loughborough MCCU	1	1	—
1	—	1	Mashonaland	—	—	—
2	—	2	Matebeleland	1	—	1
52	38	14	MCC	52	34	18
39	—	39	Oxford University	11	—	11
6	—	6	Rest of England	15	—	15
9	5	4	Scotland	1	—	1
3	3	—	C I Thornton's XI	4	4	—
—	—	—	Western Province	1	—	1
1	1	—	I Zingari	1	1	—
230	113	117	Totals	161	91	70
1730	823	907	Grand Totals	1200	551	649

FOUR CENTURIES IN ONE INNINGS

			F S Jackson	117
			E Wainwright	126
1896	v.	Warwickshire	Lord Hawke	166
		at Birmingham	R Peel	*210

(First instance in First-Class cricket)

THREE CENTURIES IN ONE INNINGS

			L Hall	116
1884	v.	Cambridge University	W Bates	133
		at Cambridge	I Grimshaw	115
			G Ulyett	124
1887	v.	Kent	L Hall	110
		at Canterbury	F Lee	119
			J T Brown	311
1897	v.	Sussex	J Tunnicliffe	147
		at Sheffield	E Wainwright	*104
			F S Jackson	155
1899	v.	Middlesex	D Denton	113
		at Bradford	F Mitchell	121
			D Denton	105
1904	v.	Surrey	G H Hirst	104
		at The Oval	J Tunnicliffe	*139
			H Sutcliffe	118
1919	v.	Gloucestershire	D Denton	122
		at Leeds	R Kilner	*115
			P Holmes	130
1925	v.	Glamorgan	H Sutcliffe	121
		at Huddersfield	E Robinson	*108
			P Holmes	105
1928	v.	Middlesex	E Oldroyd	108
		at Lord's	A Mitchell	105
			H Sutcliffe	129
1928	v.	Essex	P Holmes	136
		at Leyton	M Leyland	*133
			E Oldroyd	168
1929	v.	Glamorgan	W Barber	114
		at Hull	F E Greenwood	*104
			H Sutcliffe	107
1933	v.	MCC	A Mitchell	158
		at Scarborough	M Leyland	133
			H Sutcliffe	129
1936	v.	Surrey	L Hutton	163
		at Leeds	M Leyland	*163
			H Sutcliffe	189
1937	v.	Leicestershire	L Hutton	153
		at Hull	M Leyland	*118
			L Hutton	137
1947	v.	Leicestershire	N W D Yardley	100
		at Leicester	G.A Smithson	169
			J H Hampshire	*116
1971	v.	Oxford University	R A Hutton	101
		at Oxford	A J Dalton	111

THREE CENTURIES IN ONE INNINGS *(Continued)*

			G Boycott	141
1975	v.	Gloucestershire	R G Lumb	101
		at Bristol	J H Hampshire	*106
			M D Moxon	130
1995	v.	Cambridge University	D Byas	181
		at Cambridge	M G Bevan	*113
			M J Wood	102
2001	v.	Leicestershire	M J Lumb	122
		at Leeds	D S Lehmann	104
			C White	183
2001	v.	Glamorgan	M J Wood	124
		at Scarborough	D Byas	104
			J A Rudolph	122
2007	v.	Surrey	T T Bresnan	116
		at The Oval	J N Gillespie	*123

CENTURY IN EACH INNINGS

D Denton	107 and 109*	v. Nottinghamshire at Nottingham, 1906
G H Hirst	111 and 117*	v. Somerset at Bath, 1906
D Denton	133 and 121	v. MCC at Scarborough, 1908
W Rhodes	128 and 115	v. MCC at Scarborough, 1911
P Holmes	126 and 111*	v. Lancashire at Manchester, 1920
H Sutcliffe	107 and 109*	v. MCC at Scarborough, 1926
H Sutcliffe	111 and 100*	v. Nottinghamshire at Nottingham, 1928
E I Lester	126 and 142	v. Northamptonshire at Northampton, 1947
L Hutton	197 and 104	v. Essex at Southend, 1947
E I Lester	125* and 132	v. Lancashire at Manchester, 1948
L Hutton	165 and 100	v. Sussex at Hove, 1949
L Hutton	103 and 137	v. MCC at Scarborough, 1952
G Boycott	103 and 105	v. Nottinghamshire at Sheffield, 1966
G Boycott	163 and 141*	v. Nottinghamshire at Bradford, 1983
M D Moxon	123 and 112*	v. Indians at Scarborough, 1986
A A Metcalfe	194* and 107	v. Nottinghamshire at Nottingham, 1990
M P Vaughan	100 and 151	v. Essex at Chelmsford, 1999
Younus Khan	106 and 202*	v. Hampshire at Southampton, 2007
G S Ballance	148 and 108*	v. Surrey at The Oval, 2013

HIGHEST INDIVIDUAL SCORES
FOR AND AGAINST YORKSHIRE

Highest For Yorkshire:
341 G H Hirst v. Leicestershire at Leicester, 1905

Highest Against Yorkshire:
318* W G Grace for Gloucestershire at Cheltenham, 1876

Yorkshire versus:

Derbyshire	*For Yorkshire:*	300 — J T Brown at Chesterfield, 1898
	Against:	270* — C F Hughes at Leeds, 2013
Most Centuries	*For Yorkshire:*	G Boycott 9
	Against:	K J Barnett and W Storer 4 each
Durham	*For Yorkshire:*	339 — D S Lehmann at Leeds, 2006
	Against:	184 — M J di Venuto at Chester-le-Street, 2008
Most Centuries	*For Yorkshire:*	A McGrath 5
	Against:	M J Di Venuto 4

Yorkshire versus

Essex
For Yorkshire:	313 — H Sutcliffe at Leyton, 1932
Against:	219* — D J Insole at Colchester, 1949
Most Centuries *For Yorkshire:*	H Sutcliffe 9
Against:	F L Fane, K W R Fletcher, G A Gooch and D J Insole 3 each

Glamorgan
For Yorkshire:	213 — M D Moxon at Cardiff, 1996
Against:	202* — H Morris at Cardiff, 1996
Most Centuries *For Yorkshire:*	G Boycott, P Holmes and H Sutcliffe 5 each
Against:	H Morris 5

Gloucestershire
For Yorkshire:	238 — D R Martyn at Leeds, 2003
Against:	318* — W G Grace at Cheltenham, 1876
Most Centuries *For Yorkshire:*	G Boycott 6
Against:	W G Grace 9

Hampshire
For Yorkshire:	302* — P Holmes at Portsmouth, 1920
Against:	300* — M A Carberry at Southampton, 2011
Most Centuries *For Yorkshire:*	H Sutcliffe 6
Against:	C P Mead 10

Kent
For Yorkshire:	248 — W Barber at Leeds, 1934.
Against:	207 — D P Fulton at Maidstone, 1998
Most Centuries *For Yorkshire:*	A McGrath 6
Against:	F E Woolley 5

Lancashire
For Yorkshire:	252 — D S Lehmann at Leeds, 2001
	225 — G D Lloyd at Leeds, 1997 (Non-Championship)
	206 — S G Law at Leeds, 2007
Most Centuries *For Yorkshire:*	G Boycott and H Sutcliffe 9 each
Against:	M A Atherton and C H Lloyd 6 each.

Leicestershire
For Yorkshire:	341 — G H Hirst at Leicester, 1905
Against:	218 — J J Whitaker at Bradford, 1996
Most Centuries *For Yorkshire:*	H Sutcliffe 10
Against:	J J Whitaker and C J B Wood 5 each

Middlesex
For Yorkshire:	315* — P Holmes at Lord's, 1925
Against:	243* — A J Webbe at Huddersfield, 1887
Most Centuries *For Yorkshire:*	P Holmes and H Sutcliffe 7 each
Against:	M W Gatting 8

Northamptonshire
For Yorkshire:	277* — P Holmes at Harrogate, 1921
Against:	235 — A J Lamb at Leeds, 1990
Most Centuries *For Yorkshire:*	H Sutcliffe 5
Against:	W Larkins 5

Nottinghamshire
For Yorkshire:	285 — P Holmes at Nottingham, 1929
Against:	251* — D J Hussey at Leeds, 2010
Most Centuries *For Yorkshire:*	G Boycott 15
Against:	R T Robinson 6

Somerset
For Yorkshire:	213 — H Sutcliffe at Dewsbury, 1924
Against:	297 — M J Wood at Taunton, 2005
Most Centuries *For Yorkshire:*	G Boycott 6
Against:	L C H Palairet, IVA. Richards, M E Trescothick 5 each

Surrey
For Yorkshire:	255 — W Barber at Sheffield, 1935
Against:	273 — T W Hayward at The Oval, 1899
Most Centuries *For Yorkshire:*	H Sutcliffe 9
Against:	J B Hobbs 8

Yorkshire versus

Sussex

	For Yorkshire:	311 — J T Brown at Sheffield, 1897
	Against:	274* — M W Goodwin at Hove, 2011
Most Centuries	*For Yorkshire:*	L Hutton 8
	Against:	C B Fry 7

Warwickshire

	For Yorkshire:	275 — P Holmes at Bradford, 1928
	Against:	225 — D P Ostler at Birmingham, 2002
Most Centuries	*For Yorkshire:*	G Boycott and H Sutcliffe 8 each
	Against:	D L Amiss, H E Dollery, R B Khanhai and W G Quaife 4 each.

Worcestershire

	For Yorkshire:	274* — M D Moxon at Worcester, 1994
	Against:	259 — D Kenyon at Kidderminster, 1956
Most Centuries	*For Yorkshire:*	M Leyland 6
	Against:	D Kenyon and G M Turner 5 each

Australians

	For Yorkshire:	167 — J T Brown at Bradford, 1899
	Against:	193* — B C Booth at Bradford, 1964
Most Centuries	*For Yorkshire:*	G Boycott and D Denton 2 each
	Against:	N C O'Neill 2

Indians

	For Yorkshire:	183* — L Hutton at Bradford, 1946
	Against:	244* — V S Hazare at Sheffield, 1946
Most Centuries	*For Yorkshire:*	M D Moxon 2
	Against:	V S Hazare, V Mankad, P R Umrigar D K Gaekwad, G A Parkar and R Lamba 1 each

New Zealanders

	For Yorkshire:	175 — P Holmes at Bradford, 1927
	Against:	126 — W M Wallace at Bradford, 1949
Most Centuries	*For Yorkshire:*	L Hutton and D B Close 2 each
	Against:	H G Vivian, W M Wallace and J G Wright 1 each

Pakistanis

	For Yorkshire:	197 — P J Sharpe at Leeds, 1967
	Against:	139 — A H Kardar at Sheffield, 1954
Most Centuries	*For Yorkshire:*	P J Sharpe 2
	Against:	A H Kardar 1

South Africans

	For Yorkshire:	156 — L Hutton at Sheffield, 1951
	Against:	168 — I J Seidle at Sheffield, 1929
Most Centuries	*For Yorkshire:*	L Hutton 2
	Against:	H B Cameron, J D Lindsay, B Mitchell, D P B Morkel, I J Seidle, L J Tancred, C B van Ryneveld 1 each

Sri Lankans

	For Yorkshire:	132 — M D Moxon at Leeds, 1988
	Against:	112 — S A R Silva at Leeds, 1988
Most Centuries	*For Yorkshire:*	K Sharp 2
	Against:	S A R Silva 1

West Indians

	For Yorkshire:	112* — D Denton at Harrogate, 1906
	Against:	164 — S F A Bacchus at Leeds, 1980
Most Centuries	*For Yorkshire:*	M G Bevan, D Denton, L Hutton, R G Lumb and A A Metcalfe 1 each
	Against:	S F A Bacchus, C O Browne, S Chanderpaul P A Goodman, C L Hooper and G St A Sobers 1 each

Yorkshire versus

Zimbabweans	*For Yorkshire:*	113 — M D Moxon at Leeds, 1990
	Against:	89 — G J Whittall at Leeds, 2000
Most Centuries	*For Yorkshire:*	M D Moxon 1
	Against:	None
Cambridge University	*For Yorkshire:*	207* — G Boycott at Cambridge, 1976
	Against:	171* — G L Jessop at Cambridge, 1899
		171 — P B H May at Cambridge, 1952
Most Centuries	*For Yorkshire:*	H Sutcliffe 4
	Against:	G M Kemp 2
Durham MCCU	*For Yorkshire:*	139 — J J Sayers at Durham, 2011
	Against:	127 — T Westley at Durham, 2011
Most Centuries	*For Yorkshire:*	J J Sayers 1
	Against:	T Westley 1
Leeds Bradford MCCU	*For Yorkshire:*	121 — A Z Lees at Leeds, 2013
	Against:	69 — A MacQueen at Leeds, 2012
Most Centuries	*For Yorkshire:*	J M Bairstow, A Z Lees and A Lyth 1 each
Loughborough MCCU	*For Yorkshire:*	134* — R M Pyrah at Leeds, 2010
	Against:	107 — C P Murtagh at Leeds, 2007
Most Centuries	*For Yorkshire:*	R M Pyrah 2
	Against:	C P Murtagh 1
MCC	*For Yorkshire:*	180* — G H Hirst at Lord's, 1919
	Against:	214 — E H Hendren at Lord's, 1919
Most Centuries	*For Yorkshire:*	L Hutton 8
	Against:	R E S Wyatt 5
Oxford University	*For Yorkshire:*	196 — R J Blakey at Oxford, 1991
	Against:	201— J E Raphael at Oxford, 1904
Most Centuries	*For Yorkshire:*	M Leyland 4
	Against:	A A Baig and Nawab of Pataudi (Jun.) 2 each

J B Hobbs scored 11 centuries against Yorkshire – the highest by any individual (8 for Surrey and 3 for the Rest of England).

Three players have scored 10 centuries against Yorkshire – W G Grace (9 for Gloucestershire and 1 for MCC). E H Hendren (6 for Middlesex, 3 for MCC and 1 for the Rest of England) and C P Mead (all 10 for Hampshire).

CARRYING BAT THROUGH A COMPLETED INNINGS

Batsman	Score	Total	Against	Season
G R Atkinson	30*	73	Nottinghamshire at Bradford	1865
L Hall	31*	94	Sussex at Hove	1878
L Hall	124*	331	Sussex at Hove	1883
L Hall	128*	285	Sussex at Huddersfield	1884
L Hall	32*	81	Kent at Sheffield	1885
L Hall	79*	285	Surrey at Sheffield	1885
L Hall	37*	96	Derbyshire at Derby	1885
L Hall	50*	173	Sussex at Huddersfield	1886
L Hall	74*	172	Kent at Canterbury	1886
G Ulyett	199*	399	Derbyshire at Sheffield	1887
L Hall	119*	334	Gloucestershire at Dewsbury	1887
L Hall	82*	218	Sussex at Hove	1887
L Hall	34*	104	Surrey at The Oval	1888
L Hall	129*	461	Gloucestershire at Clifton	1888
L Hall	85*	259	Middlesex at Lord's	1889
L Hall	41*	106	Nottinghamshire at Sheffield	1891
W Rhodes	98*	184	MCC at Lord's	1903
W Rhodes	85*	152	Essex at Leyton	1910
P Holmes	145*	270	Northamptonshire at Northampton	1920
H Sutcliffe	125*	307	Essex at Southend	1920
P Holmes	175*	377	New Zealanders at Bradford	1927
P Holmes	110*	219	Northamptonshire at Bradford	1929
H Sutcliffe	104*	170	Hampshire at Leeds	1932
H Sutcliffe	114*	202	Rest of England at The Oval	1933
H Sutcliffe	187*	401	Worcestershire at Bradford	1934
H Sutcliffe	135*	262	Glamorgan at Neath	1935
H Sutcliffe	125*	322	Oxford University at Oxford	1939
L Hutton	99*	200	Leicestershire at Sheffield	1948
L Hutton	78*	153	Worcestershire at Sheffield	1949
F A Lowson	76*	218	MCC at Lord's	1951
W B Stott	144*	262	Worcestershire at Worcester	1959
D E V Padgett	115*	230	Gloucestershire at Bristol	1962
G Boycott	114*	297	Leicestershire at Sheffield	1968
G Boycott	53*	119	Warwickshire at Bradford	1969
G Boycott	182*	320	Middlesex at Lord's	1971
G Boycott	138*	232	Warwickshire at Birmingham	1971
G Boycott	175*	360	Nottinghamshire at Worksop	1979
G Boycott	112*	233	Derbyshire at Sheffield	1983
G Boycott	55*	183	Warwickshire at Leeds	1984
G Boycott	55*	131	Surrey at Sheffield	1985
M J Wood	60*	160	Somerset at Scarborough	2004
J J Sayers	122*	326	Middlesex at Scarborough	2006
J J Sayers	149*	414	Durham at Leeds	2007
A Lyth	248*	486	Leicestershire at Leicester	2012

44 instances, of which L Hall (14 times), G Boycott (8) and H Sutcliffe (6) account for 28 between them.

The highest percentage of an innings total is 61.17 by H. Sutcliffe (104* v. Hampshire at Leeds in 1932) but P Holmes was absent ill, so only nine wickets fell.

Other contributions exceeding 55% are:

59.48%	G Boycott	(138* v. Warwickshire at Birmingham, 1971)
56.87%	G Boycott	(182* v. Middlesex at Lord's, 1971)
56.43%	H Sutcliffe	(114* v. Rest of England at The Oval, 1933)
55.92%	W Rhodes	(85* v. Essex at Leyton, 1910)

2,000 RUNS IN A SEASON

Batsman	Season	M	I	NO	Runs	HS	Avge	100s
G H Hirst	1904	32	44	3	2257	157	55.04	8
D Denton	1905	33	52	2	2258	172	45.16	8
G H Hirst	1906	32	53	6	2164	169	46.04	6
D Denton	1911	32	55	4	2161	137*	42.37	6
D Denton	1912	36	51	4	2088	221	44.23	6
P Holmes	1920	30	45	6	2144	302*	54.97	7
P Holmes	1925	35	49	9	2351	315*	58.77	6
H Sutcliffe	1925	34	48	8	2236	235	55.90	7
H Sutcliffe	1928	27	35	5	2418	228	80.60	11
P Holmes	1928	31	40	4	2093	275	58.13	6
H Sutcliffe	1931	28	33	8	2351	230	94.04	9
H Sutcliffe	1932	29	41	5	2883	313	80.08	12
M Leyland	1933	31	44	4	2196	210*	54.90	7
A Mitchell	1933	34	49	10	2100	158	53.84	6
H Sutcliffe	1935	32	47	3	2183	212	49.61	8
L Hutton	1937	28	45	6	2448	271*	62.76	8
H Sutcliffe	1937	32	52	5	2054	189	43.70	4
L Hutton	1939	29	44	5	2316	280*	59.38	10
L Hutton	1947	19	31	2	2068	270*	71.31	10
L Hutton	1949	26	44	6	2640	269*	69.47	9
F A Lowson	1950	31	54	5	2067	141*	42.18	5
D E V Padgett	1959	35	60	8	2158	161*	41.50	4
W B Stott	1959	32	56	2	2034	144*	37.66	3
P J Sharpe	1962	36	62	8	2201	138	40.75	7
G Boycott	1971	18	25	4	2221	233	105.76	11
A A Metcalfe	1990	23	44	4	2047	194*	51.17	6

1,000 RUNS IN A SEASON

Batsman		Runs scored	Runs scored	Runs scored
C W J Athey	(2)	1113 in 1980	1339 in 1982	—
D L Bairstow	(3)	1083 in 1981	1102 in 1983	1163 in 1985
J M Bairstow	(1)	1015 in 2011	—	—
G S Ballance	(1)	1363 in 2013	—	—
W Barber	(8)	1000 in 1932	1595 in 1933	1930 in 1934
		1958 in 1935	1466 in 1937	1455 in 1938
		1501 in 1939	1170 in 1946	—
M G Bevan	(2)	1598 in 1995	1225 in 1996	—
R J Blakey	(5)	1361 in 1987	1159 in 1989	1065 in 1992
		1236 in 1994	1041 in 2002	—
J B Bolus	(2)	1245 in 1960	1970 in 1961	—
M W Booth	(2)	1189 in 1911	1076 in 1913	—
G Boycott	(19)	1628 in 1963	1639 in 1964	1215 in 1965
		1388 in 1966	1530 in 1967	1004 in 1968
		1558 in 1970	2221 in 1971	1156 in 1972
		1478 in 1974	1915 in 1975	1288 in 1976
		1259 in 1977	1074 in 1978	1160 in 1979
		1913 in 1982	1941 in 1983	1567 in 1984
		1657 in 1985	—	—
J T Brown	(9)	1196 in 1894	1260 in 1895	1755 in 1896
		1634 in 1897	1641 in 1898	1375 in 1899
		1181 in 1900	1627 in 1901	1291 in 1903
D Byas	(5)	1557 in 1991	1073 in 1993	1297 in 1994
		1913 in 1995	1319 in 1997	—

1,000 RUNS IN A SEASON *(Continued)*

Batsman		Runs scored	Runs scored	Runs scored
D B Close	(13)	1192 in 1952	1287 in 1954	1131 in 1955
		1315 in 1957	1335 in 1958	1740 in 1959
		1699 in 1960	1821 in 1961	1438 in 1962
		1145 in 1963	1281 in 1964	1127 in 1965
		1259 in 1966	—	—
K R Davidson	(1)	1241 in 1934	—	—
D Denton	(20)	1028 in 1896	1357 in 1897	1595 in 1899
		1378 in 1900	1400 in 1901	1191 in 1902
		1562 in 1903	1919 in 1904	2258 in 1905
		1905 in 1906	1128 in 1907	1852 in 1908
		1765 in 1909	1106 in 1910	2161 in 1911
		2088 in 1912	1364 in 1913	1799 in 1914
		1213 in 1919	1324 in 1920	—
A Drake	(2)	1487 in 1911	1029 in 1913	—
A W Gale	(1)	1076 in 2013	—	—
A P Grayson	(1)	1046 in 1994	—	—
S Haigh	(1)	1031 in 1904	—	—
L Hall	(1)	1120 in 1887	—	—
H Halliday	(4)	1357 in 1948	1484 in 1950	1351 in 1952
		1461 in 1953	—	—
J H Hampshire	(12)	1236 in 1963	1280 in 1964	1424 in 1965
		1105 in 1966	1244 in 1967	1133 in 1968
		1079 in 1970	1259 in 1971	1124 in 1975
		1303 in 1976	1596 in 1978	1425 in 1981
Lord Hawke	(1)	1005 in 1895	—	—
G H Hirst	(19)	1110 in 1896	1248 in 1897	1546 in 1899
		1752 in 1900	1669 in 1901	1113 in 1902
		1535 in 1903	2257 in 1904	1972 in 1905
		2164 in 1906	1167 in 1907	1513 in 1908
		1151 in 1909	1679 in 1910	1639 in 1911
		1119 in 1912	1431 in 1913	1655 in 1914
		1312 in 1919	—	—
P Holmes	(14)	1876 in 1919	2144 in 1920	1458 in 1921
		1614 in 1922	1884 in 1923	1610 in 1924
		2351 in 1925	1792 in 1926	1774 in 1927
		2093 in 1928	1724 in 1929	1957 in 1930
		1431 in 1931	1191 in 1932	—
L Hutton	(12)	1282 in 1936	2448 in 1937	1171 in 1938
		2316 in 1939	1322 in 1946	2068 in 1947
		1792 in 1948	2640 in 1949	1581 in 1950
		1554 in 1951	1956 in 1952	1532 in 1953
R Illingworth	(5)	1193 in 1957	1490 in 1959	1029 in 1961
		1610 in 1962	1301 in 1964	—
F S Jackson	(4)	1211 in 1896	1300 in 1897	1442 in 1898
		1468 in 1899	—	—
P A Jaques	(2)	1118 in 2004	1359 in 2005	—
S A Kellett	(2)	1266 in 1991	1326 in 1992	—
R Kilner	(10)	1586 in 1913	1329 in 1914	1135 in 1919
		1240 in 1920	1137 in 1921	1132 in 1922
		1265 in 1923	1002 in 1925	1021 in 1926
		1004 in 1927	—	—
D S Lehmann	(5)	1575 in 1997	1477 in 2000	1416 in 2001
		1136 in 2002	1706 in 2006	—

1,000 RUNS IN A SEASON *(Continued)*

Batsman		Runs scored	Runs scored	Runs scored
E I Lester	(6)	1256 in 1948	1774 in 1949	1015 in 1950
		1786 in 1952	1380 in 1953	1330 in 1954
M Leyland	(17)	1088 in 1923	1203 in 1924	1560 in 1925
		1561 in 1926	1478 in 1927	1554 in 1928
		1407 in 1929	1814 in 1930	1127 in 1931
		1821 in 1932	2196 in 1933	1228 in 1934
		1366 in 1935	1621 in 1936	1120 in 1937
		1640 in 1938	1238 in 1939	
J D Love	(2)	1161 in 1981	1020 in 1983	—
F A Lowson	(8)	1678 in 1949	2067 in 1950	1607 in 1951
		1562 in 1952	1586 in 1953	1719 in 1954
		1082 in 1955	1428 in 1956	—
M J Lumb	(1)	1038 in 2003	—	—
R G Lumb	(5)	1002 in 1973	1437 in 1975	1070 in 1978
		1465 in 1979	1223 in 1980	—
A Lyth	(1)	1509 in 2010	—	—
A McGrath	(3)	1425 in 2005	1293 in 2006	1219 in 2010
A A Metcalfe	(6)	1674 in 1986	1162 in 1987	1320 in 1988
		1230 in 1989	2047 in 1990	1210 in 1991
A Mitchell	(10)	1320 in 1928	1633 in 1930	1351 in 1932
		2100 in 1933	1854 in 1934	1530 in 1935
		1095 in 1936	1602 in 1937	1305 in 1938
		1219 in 1939	—	—
F Mitchell	(2)	1678 in 1899	1801 in 1901	
R Moorhouse	(1)	1096 in 1895		
M D Moxon	(11)	1016 in 1984	1256 in 1985	1298 in 1987
		1430 in 1988	1156 in 1989	1621 in 1990
		1669 in 1991	1314 in 1992	1251 in 1993
		1458 in 1994	1145 in 1995	—
E Oldroyd	(10)	1473 in 1921	1690 in 1922	1349 in 1923
		1607 in 1924	1262 in 1925	1197 in 1926
		1390 in 1927	1304 in 1928	1474 in 1929
		1285 in 1930	—	—
D E V Padgett	(12)	1046 in 1956	2158 in 1959	1574 in 1960
		1856 in 1961	1750 in 1962	1380 in 1964
		1220 in 1965	1194 in 1966	1284 in 1967
		1163 in 1968	1078 in 1969	1042 in 1970
R Peel	(1)	1193 in 1896	—	—
W Rhodes	(17)	1251 in 1904	1353 in 1905	1618 in 1906
		1574 in 1908	1663 in 1909	1355 in 1910
		1961 in 1911	1030 in 1912	1805 in 1913
		1325 in 1914	1138 in 1919	1329 in 1921
		1368 in 1922	1168 in 1923	1030 in 1924
		1256 in 1925	1071 in 1926	—
E Robinson	(2)	1104 in 1921	1097 in 1929	—
P E Robinson	(3)	1173 in 1988	1402 in 1990	1293 in 1991
J A Rudolph	(4)	1078 in 2007	1292 in 2008	1366 in 2009
		1375 in 2010	—	—
J J Sayers	(1)	1150 in 2009	—	—
A B Sellers	(1)	1109 in 1938	—	—
K Sharp	(1)	1445 in 1984	—	—

1,000 RUNS IN A SEASON *(Continued)*

Batsman		*Runs scored*	*Runs scored*	*Runs scored*
P J Sharpe	(10)	1039 in 1960	1240 in 1961	2201 in 1962
		1273 in 1964	1091 in 1965	1352 in 1967
		1256 in 1968	1012 in 1969	1149 in 1970
		1320 in 1973	—	—
W B Stott	(5)	1362 in 1957	1036 in 1958	2034 in 1959
		1790 in 1960	1409 in 1961	—
H Sutcliffe	(21)	†1839 in 1919	1393 in 1920	1235 in 1921
		1909 in 1922	1773 in 1923	1720 in 1924
		2236 in 1925	1672 in 1926	1814 in 1927
		2418 in 1928	1485 in 1929	1636 in 1930
		2351 in 1931	2883 in 1932	1986 in 1933
		1511 in 1934	2183 in 1935	1295 in 1936
		2054 in 1937	1660 in 1938	1416 in 1939

† First season in First-Class cricket – The record for a debut season.

Batsman		*Runs scored*	*Runs scored*	*Runs scored*
W H H Sutcliffe	(1)	1193 in 1955	—	—
K Taylor	(6)	1306 in 1959	1107 in 1960	1494 in 1961
		1372 in 1962	1149 in 1964	1044 in 1966
T L Taylor	(2)	1236 in 1901	1373 in 1902	—
S R Tendulkar	(1)	1070 in 1992	—	—
J Tunnicliffe	(12)	1333 in 1895	1368 in 1896	1208 in 1897
		1713 in 1898	1434 in 1899	1496 in 1900
		1295 in 1901	1274 in 1902	1650 in 1904
		1096 in 1905	1232 in 1906	1195 in 1907
C Turner	(1)	1153 in 1934	—	—
G Ulyett	(4)	1083 in 1878	1158 in 1882	1024 in 1885
		1285 in 1887	—	—
M P Vaughan	(4)	1066 in 1994	1235 in 1995	1161 in 1996
		1161 in 1998	—	—
E Wainwright	(3)	1492 in 1897	1479 in 1899	1044 in 1901
W A I Washington	(1)	1022 in 1902	—	—
W Watson	(8)	1331 in 1947	1352 in 1948	1586 in 1952
		1350 in 1953	1347 in 1954	1564 in 1955
		1378 in 1956	1455 in 1957	—
W H Wilkinson	(1)	1282 in 1908	—	—
B B Wilson	(5)	1054 in 1909	1455 in 1911	1453 in 1912
		1533 in 1913	1632 in 1914	—
J V Wilson	(12)	1460 in 1949	1548 in 1950	1985 in 1951
		1349 in 1952	1531 in 1953	1713 in 1954
		1799 in 1955	1602 in 1956	1287 in 1957
		1064 in 1960	1018 in 1961	1226 in 1962
A Wood	(1)	1237 in 1935	—	—
M J Wood	(4)	1080 in 1998	1060 in 2001	1432 in 2003
		1005 in 2005	—	—
N W D Yardley	(4)	1028 in 1939	1299 in 1947	1413 in 1949
		1031 in 1950	—	—

PLAYERS WHO HAVE SCORED CENTURIES
FOR AND AGAINST YORKSHIRE

Player		For	Venue	Season
C W J Athey (5)	114*	Gloucestershire	Bradford	1984
(10 for Yorkshire)	101	Gloucestershire	Gloucester	1985
	101*	Gloucestershire	Leeds	1987
	112	Sussex	Scarborough	1993
	100	Sussex	Eastbourne	1996
M G Bevan (1)	142	Leicestershire	Leicester	2002
(9 for Yorkshire)				
J B Bolus (2)	114	Nottinghamshire	Bradford	1963
(7 for Yorkshire)	138	Derbyshire	Sheffield	1973
D B Close (1)	102	Somerset	Taunton	1971
(33 for Yorkshire)				
M T G Elliott (1)	125	Glamorgan	Leeds	2004
(1 for Yorkshire)				
P A Gibb (1)	107	Essex	Brentwood	1951
(2 for Yorkshire)				
P A Jaques (1)	222	Northamptonshire	Northampton	2003
(11 for Yorkshire)				
N Kilner (2)	119	Warwickshire	Hull	1932
(2 for Yorkshire)	197	Warwickshire	Birmingham	1933
M J Lumb (1)	135	Nottinghamshire	Scarborough	2013
(8 for Yorkshire)				
P J Sharpe (1)	126	Derbyshire	Chesterfield	1976
(23 for Yorkshire)				

BATSMEN WHO HAVE SCORED OVER 10,000 RUNS

Player	M	I	NO	Runs	HS	Av'ge	100s
H Sutcliffe	602	864	96	38558	313	50.20	112
D Denton	676	1058	61	33282	221	33.38	61
G Boycott	414	674	111	32570	260*	57.85	103
G H Hirst	717	1050	128	32024	341	34.73	56
W Rhodes	883	1195	162	31075	267*	30.08	46
P Holmes	485	699	74	26220	315*	41.95	60
M Leyland	548	720	82	26180	263	41.03	62
L Hutton	341	527	62	24807	280*	53.34	85
D B Close	536	811	102	22650	198	31.94	33
J H Hampshire	456	724	89	21979	183*	34.61	34
J V Wilson	477	724	75	20548	230	31.66	29
D E V Padgett	487	774	63	20306	161*	28.55	29
J Tunnicliffe	472	768	57	19435	243	27.33	22
M D Moxon	277	476	42	18973	274*	43.71	41
A Mitchell	401	550	69	18189	189	37.81	39
P J Sharpe	411	666	71	17685	203*	29.72	23
E Oldroyd	383	509	58	15891	194	35.23	37
J T Brown	345	567	41	15694	311	29.83	23
W Barber	354	495	48	15315	255	34.26	27
R Illingworth	496	668	131	14986	162	27.90	14
D Byas	268	449	42	14398	213	35.37	28
G Ulyett	355	618	31	14157	199*	24.11	15
R J Blakey	339	541	84	14150	223*	30.96	12
A McGrath	242	405	29	14091	211	37.47	34
W Watson	283	430	65	13953	214*	38.22	26
F A Lowson	252	404	31	13897	259*	37.25	30
Lord Hawke	510	739	91	13133	166	20.26	10
R Kilner	365	478	46	13018	206*	30.13	15
D L Bairstow	429	601	113	12985	145	26.60	9
K Taylor	303	505	35	12864	203*	27.37	16
N W D Yardley	302	420	56	11632	183*	31.95	17
R G Lumb	239	395	30	11525	165*	31.57	22
E Wainwright	352	545	30	11092	228	21.53	18
S Haigh	513	687	110	10993	159	19.05	4
E I Lester	228	339	27	10616	186	34.02	24
A A Metcalfe	184	317	19	10465	216*	35.11	25
C White	221	350	45	10376	186	34.01	19
Hon F S Jackson	207	328	22	10371	160	33.89	21
J D Love	247	388	58	10263	170*	31.10	13

RECORD PARTNERSHIPS FOR YORKSHIRE

1st wkt	555	P Holmes (224*) and H Sutcliffe (313) v. Essex at Leyton, 1932
2nd wkt	346	W Barber (162) and M Leyland (189) v. Middlesex at Sheffield, 1932
3rd wkt	346	J J Sayers (173) and A McGrath (211) v. Warwickshire at Birmingham, 2009
4th wkt	358	D S Lehmann (339) and M J Lumb (98) v. Durham at Leeds, 2006
5th wkt	340	E Wainwright (228) and G H Hirst (186) v. Surrey at The Oval, 1899
6th wkt	276	M Leyland (191) and E Robinson (124*) v. Glamorgan at Swansea, 1926
7th wkt	254	W Rhodes (135) and D C F Burton (142*) v. Hampshire at Dewsbury, 1919
8th wkt	292	R Peel (210*) and Lord Hawke (166) v. Warwickshire at Birmingham, 1896
9th wkt	246	T T Bresnan (116) and J N Gillespie (123*) v. Surrey at The Oval, 2007
10th wkt	149	G Boycott (79) and G B Stevenson (115*) v. Warwickshire at Birmingham, 1982

RECORD PARTNERSHIPS AGAINST YORKSHIRE

1st wkt	372	R R Montgomerie (127) and M B Loye (205) for Northamptonshire at Northampton, 1996
2nd wkt	417	K J Barnett (210*) and TA Tweats (189) for Derbyshire at Derby, 1997
3rd wkt	523	M A Carberry (300*) and N D McKenzie (237) for Hampshire at Southampton, 2011
4th wkt	447	R Abel (193) and T Hayward (273) for Surrey at The Oval, 1899
5th wkt	261	W G Grace (318*) and W O Moberley (103) for Gloucestershire at Cheltenham, 1876
6th wkt	294	D R Jardine (157) and P G H Fender (177) for Surrey at Bradford, 1928
7th wkt	315	D M Benkenstein (151) and O D Gibson (155) for Durham at Leeds, 2006
8th wkt	178	A P Wells (253*) and B T P Donelan (59) for Sussex at Middlesbrough, 1991
9th wkt	233	I J L Trott (161*) and J S Patel (120) for Warwickshire at Birmingham, 2009
10th wkt	132	A Hill (172*) and M Jean-Jacques (73) for Derbyshire at Sheffield, 1986

CENTURY PARTNERSHIPS FOR THE FIRST WICKET IN BOTH INNINGS

128	108	G Ulyett (82 and 91) and L Hall (87 and 37) v. Sussex at Hove, 1885 (First instance in First-Class cricket)
138	147*	J T Brown (203 and 81*) and J Tunnicliffe (62 and 63*) v. Middlesex at Lord's, 1896 (Second instance in First-class cricket)
105	265*	P Holmes (51 and 127*) and H Sutcliffe (71 and 131*) v. Surrey at The Oval, 1926
184	210*	P Holmes (83 and 101*) and H Sutcliffe (111 and 100*) v. Nottinghamshire at Nottingham, 1928
110	117	L Hutton (95 and 86) and W Watson (34 and 57) v. Lancashire at Manchester, 1947
122	230	W B Stott (50 and 114) and K Taylor (79 and 140) v. Nottinghamshire at Nottingham, 1957
136	138	J B Bolus (108 and 71) and K Taylor (89 and 75) v. Cambridge University at Cambridge, 1962
105	105	G Boycott (38 and 64) and K Taylor (85 and 49) v. Leicestershire at Leicester, 1963
116	112*	K Taylor (45 and 68) and J H Hampshire (68 and 67*) v. Oxford University at Oxford, 1964
104	104	G Boycott (117 and 49*) and R G Lumb (47 and 57) v. Sussex at Leeds, 1974
134	185*	M D Moxon (57 and 89*) and A A Metcalfe (216* and 78*) v. Middlesex at Leeds, 1988
118	129*	G S Ballance (72 and 73*) and J J Sayers (139 and 53*) v. Durham MCCU at Durham, 2011

CENTURY PARTNERSHIPS FOR THE FIRST WICKET
IN BOTH INNINGS BUT WITH CHANGE OF PARTNER

109		W H H Sutcliffe (82) and F A Lowson (46)
	143	W H H Sutcliffe (88) and W Watson (52) v. Canadians at Scarborough, 1954
109		G Boycott (70) and R G Lumb (44)
	135	G Boycott (74) and JH Hampshire (58) v. Northamptonshire at Bradford, 1977

CENTURY PARTNERSHIPS

FIRST WICKET (Qualification 200 runs)

555	P Holmes (224*) and H Sutcliffe (313) v. Essex at Leyton, 1932
554	J T Brown (300) and J Tunnicliffe (243) v. Derbyshire at Chesterfield, 1898
378	J T Brown (311) and J Tunnicliffe (147) v. Sussex at Sheffield, 1897
362	M D Moxon (213) and M P Vaughan (183) v. Glamorgan at Cardiff, 1996
351	G Boycott (184) and M D Moxon (168) v. Worcestershire at Worcester, 1985
347	P Holmes (302*) and H Sutcliffe (131) v. Hampshire at Portsmouth, 1920
323	P Holmes (125) and H Sutcliffe (195) v. Lancashire at Sheffield, 1931
315	H Sutcliffe (189) and L Hutton (153) v. Leicestershire at Hull, 1937
315	H Sutcliffe (116) and L Hutton (280*) v. Hampshire at Sheffield, 1939
309	P Holmes (250) and H Sutcliffe (129) v. Warwickshire at Birmingham, 1931
309	C White (186) and M J Wood (115) v. Lancashire at Manchester, 2001
290	P Holmes (179*) and H Sutcliffe (104) v. Middlesex at Leeds, 1928
288	G Boycott (130*) and R G Lumb (159) v. Somerset at Harrogate, 1979
286	L Hutton (156) and F A Lowson (115) v. South Africans at Sheffield, 1951
282	M D Moxon (147) and A A Metcalfe (151) v. Lancashire at Manchester, 1986
281*	W B Stott (138*) and K Taylor (130*) v. Sussex at Hove, 1960
279	P Holmes (133) and H Sutcliffe (145) v. Northamptonshire at Northampton, 1919
274	P.Holmes (199) and H Sutcliffe (139) v. Somerset at Hull, 1923
274	P Holmes (180) and H Sutcliffe (134) v. Gloucestershire at Gloucester, 1927
272	P Holmes (194) and H Sutcliffe (129) v. Leicestershire at Hull, 1925
272	M J Wood (202*) and J J Sayers (115) v. Bangladesh 'A' at Leeds, 2005
268	P Holmes (136) and H Sutcliffe (129) v. Essex at Leyton, 1928
267	W Barber (248) and L Hutton (70) v. Kent at Leeds, 1934
265*	P Holmes (127*) and H Sutcliffe (131*) v. Surrey at The Oval, 1926
264	G Boycott (161*) and R G Lumb (132) v. Gloucestershire at Leeds, 1976
253	P Holmes (123) and H Sutcliffe (132) v. Lancashire at Sheffield, 1919
248	G Boycott (163) and A A Metcalfe (122) v. Nottinghamshire at Bradford, 1983
245	L Hutton (153) and F A Lowson (120) v. Lancashire at Leeds, 1952
244	J A Rudolph (149) and J J Sayers (86) v Nottinghamshire at Nottingham, 2009
241	P Holmes (142) and H Sutcliffe (123*) v. Surrey at The Oval, 1929
240	G Boycott (233) and P J Sharpe (92) v. Essex at Colchester, 1971
238*	P Holmes (126*) and H Sutcliffe (105*) v. Cambridge University at Cambridge, 1923
236	G Boycott (131) and K Taylor (153) v. Lancashire at Manchester, 1964
235	P Holmes (130) and H Sutcliffe (132*) v. Glamorgan at Sheffield, 1930
233	G Boycott (141*) and R G Lumb (90) v. Cambridge University at Cambridge, 1973
233	H Halliday (116) and W Watson (108) v. Northamptonshire at Northampton, 1948
231	M P Vaughan (151) and D Byas (90) v. Essex at Chelmsford, 1999
230	H Sutcliffe (129) and L Hutton (163) v. Surrey at Leeds, 1936
230	W B Stott (114) and K Taylor (140*) v. Nottinghamshire at Nottingham, 1957
228	H Halliday (90) and J V Wilson (223*) v. Scotland at Scarborough, 1951
228	G Boycott (141) and R G Lumb (101) v. Gloucestershire at Bristol, 1975
227	P Holmes (110) and H Sutcliffe (119) v. Leicestershire at Leicester, 1928
225	R G Lumb (101) and C W J Athey (125*) v. Gloucestershire at Sheffield, 1980
224	C W J Athey (114) and J D Love (104) v. Warwickshire at Birmingham, 1980

222	W B Stott (141) and K Taylor (90) v. Sussex at Bradford, 1958
221	P Holmes (130) and H Sutcliffe (121) v. Glamorgan at Huddersfield, 1925
221	M D Moxon (141) and A A Metcalfe (73) v. Surrey at The Oval, 1992
221	A Lyth (111) and A Z Lees (121) v. Leeds/Bradford MCCU at Leeds, 2013
219	P Holmes (102) and A Mitchell (130*) v. Somerset at Bradford, 1930
218	M Leyland (110) and H Sutcliffe (235) v. Middlesex at Leeds, 1925
218	R G Lumb (145) and M D Moxon (111) v. Derbyshire at Sheffield, 1981
210*	P Holmes (101*) and H Sutcliffe (100*) v. Nottinghamshire at Nottingham, 1928
210	G Boycott (128) and P J Sharpe (197) v. Pakistanis at Leeds, 1967
209	F A Lowson (115) and D E V Padgett (107) v. Scotland at Hull, 1956
208	A Mitchell (85) and E Oldroyd (111) v. Cambridge University at Cambridge, 1929
207	A Mitchell (90) and W Barber (107) v. Middlesex at Lord's, 1935
206	G Boycott (118) and R G Lumb (87) v. Glamorgan at Sheffield, 1978
204	M D Moxon (66) and A A Metcalfe (162) v. Gloucestershire at Cheltenham, 1990
203	L Hutton (119) and F A Lowson (83) v. Somerset at Huddersfield, 1952
203	M D Moxon (117) and S A Kellett (87) v. Somerset at Middlesbrough, 1992
203	M D Moxon (134) and M P Vaughan (106) v. Matebeleland at Bulawayo, 1996
200*	P Holmes (107*) and H Sutcliffe (80*) v. Oxford University at Oxford, 1930

Note: P Holmes and H Sutcliffe shared 69 century opening partnerships for Yorkshire;
G Boycott and R G Lumb 29; L Hutton and F A Lowson 22; M D Moxon and A A Metcalfe 21;
J T Brown and J Tunnicliffe 19; H Sutcliffe and L Hutton 15, and L Hall and G Ulyett 12.

SECOND WICKET (Qualification 200 runs)

346	W Barber (162) and M Leyland (189) v. Middlesex at Sheffield, 1932
343	F A Lowson (183*) and J V Wilson (165) v. Oxford University at Oxford, 1956
333	P Holmes (209) and E Oldroyd (138*) v. Warwickshire at Birmingham, 1922
314	H Sutcliffe (255*) and E Oldroyd (138) v. Essex at Southend-on-Sea, 1924
311	A Z Lees (275*) and P A Jaques (139) v. Derbyshire at Chesterfield, 2013
305	J W.Rothery (134) and D Denton (182) v. Derbyshire at Chesterfield, 1910
302	W Watson (172) and J V Wilson (140) v. Derbyshire at Scarborough, 1948
301	P J Sharpe (172*) and D E V Padgett (133) v. Glamorgan at Swansea, 1971
288	H Sutcliffe (165) and A Mitchell (136) v. Lancashire at Manchester, 1939
280	L Hall (160) and F Lee (165) v. Lancashire at Bradford, 1887
266*	K Taylor (178*) and D E V Padgett (107*) v. Oxford University at Oxford, 1962
264	P A Jaques (152) and K S Williamson (97) v. Durham at Scarborough, 2013
261*	L Hutton (146*) and J V Wilson (110*) v. Scotland at Hull, 1949
260	R G Lumb (144) and K Sharp (132) v. Glamorgan at Cardiff, 1984
258	H Sutcliffe (230) and E Oldroyd (93) v. Kent at Folkestone, 1931
253	B B Wilson (150) and D Denton (200*) v. Warwickshire at Birmingham, 1912
248	H Sutcliffe (200) and M. Leyland (116) v. Leicestershire at Leicester, 1926
244	P. Holmes (138) and E Oldroyd (151*) v. Glamorgan at Cardiff, 1922
243	G Boycott (141) and J D Love (163) v. Nottinghamshire at Bradford, 1976
243	C White (183) and M J Wood (124) v. Glamorgan at Scarborough, 2001
237	H Sutcliffe (118) and D Denton (122) v. Gloucestershire at Leeds, 1919
237	M D Moxon (132) and K Sharp (128) v. Sri Lankans at Leeds, 1988
236	F A Lowson (112) and J V Wilson (157) v. Essex at Leeds, 1950
235	M D Moxon (130) and D Byas (181) v. Cambridge University at Cambridge, 1995
230	L Hutton (180) and A Mitchell (100) v. Cambridge University at Cambridge, 1938
230	M P Vaughan (109) and B Parker (138*) v. Oxford University at Oxford, 1997.
227	M J Wood (102) and M J Lumb (122) v. Leicestershire at Leeds, 2001
225	H Sutcliffe (138) and E Oldroyd (97) v. Derbyshire at Dewsbury, 1928
223	M D Moxon (153) and R J Blakey (90) v. Somerset at Leeds, 1985
222	H Sutcliffe (174) and D Denton (114) v. Kent at Dover, 1919
219	F S Jackson (155) and D Denton (113) v. Middlesex at Bradford, 1899
217	R G Lumb (107) and J D Love (107) v. Oxford University at Oxford, 1978
216	M P Vaughan (105) and D Byas (102) v. Somerset at Bradford, 1994

215	A W Gale (136) and A McGrath (99) v. Lancashire at Manchester, 2008
211	J A Rudolph (141) and A McGrath (80) v Nottinghamshire at Leeds, 2010
207	P A Jaques (115) and A McGrath (93) v. Essex at Chelmsford, 2004
206	J Tunnicliffe (102) and F S Jackson (134*) v. Lancashire at Sheffield, 1898
206	H Sutcliffe (187) and M Leyland (90) v. Leicestershire at Leicester, 1931
205	H Sutcliffe (174) and A Mitchell (95) v. Leicestershire at Leicester, 1933
205	G Boycott (148) and P J Sharpe (108) v. Kent at Sheffield, 1970
203	A T Barber (100) and E Oldroyd (143) v. An England XI at Sheffield, 1929
203	J J Sayers (187) and A McGrath (100) v. Kent at Tunbridge Wells, 2007
202*	W Rhodes (115*) and G H Hirst (117*) v. Somerset at Bath, 1906
202	G Boycott (113) and C W J Athey (114) v. Northamptonshire at Northampton, 1978

THIRD WICKET (Qualification 200 runs)

346	J J Sayers (173) and A McGrath (211) v. Warwickshire at Birmingham, 2009
323*	H Sutcliffe (147*) and M Leyland (189*) v. Glamorgan at Huddersfield, 1928
317	A McGrath (165) and D S Lehmann (187) v. Lancashire at Leeds, 2002
310	A McGrath (134) and P A Jaques (219) v. Derbyshire at Leeds, 2005
301	H Sutcliffe (175) and M Leyland (180*) v. Middlesex at Lord's, 1939
293*	A A Metcalfe (150*) and P E Robinson (150*) v. Derbyshire at Scarborough, 1990
269	D Byas (101) and R J Blakey (196) v. Oxford University at Oxford, 1991
258*	J T Brown (134*) and F Mitchell (116*) v. Warwickshire at Bradford, 1901
252	D E V Padgett (139*) and D B Close (154) v. Nottinghamshire at Nottingham, 1959
249	D E V Padgett (95) and D B Close (184) v. Nottinghamshire at Scarborough, 1960
248	C Johnson (102) and J H Hampshire (155*) v. Gloucestershire at Leeds, 1976
247	P Holmes (175*) and M Leyland (118) v. New Zealanders at Bradford, 1927
244	D E V Padgett (161*) and D B Close (144) v. Oxford University at Oxford, 1959
240	L Hutton (151) and M Leyland (95) v. Surrey at Leeds, 1939
237	J A Rudolph (198) and A McGrath (120) v. Worcestershire at Leeds, 2009
236	H Sutcliffe (107) and R Kilner (137) v. Nottinghamshire at Nottingham, 1920
236	M J Wood (94) and D S Lehmann (200) v. Worcestershire at Worcester, 1998
234*	D Byas (126*) and A McGrath (105*) v. Oxford University at Oxford, 1997.
233	L Hutton (101) and M Leyland (167) v. Worcestershire at Stourbridge, 1937
230	D Byas (103) and M J Wood (103) v. Derbyshire at Leeds, 1998
229	L Hall (86) and R Peel (158) v. Middlesex at Lord's, 1889
228	A Mitchell (142) and M Leyland (133) v. Worcestershire at Sheffield, 1933
228	W Barber (141) and M Leyland (114) v. Surrey at The Oval, 1939
228	J V Wilson (132*) and D E V Padgett (115) v. Warwickshire at Birmingham, 1955
226	D E V Padgett (117) and D B Close (198) v. Surrey at The Oval, 1955
224	J V Wilson (110) and D B Close (114) v. Cambridge University at Cambridge, 1955
224	G Boycott (140*) and K Sharp (121) v. Gloucestershire at Cheltenham, 1983
221	A Mitchell (138) and M Leyland (134) v. Nottinghamshire at Bradford, 1933
219	L Hall (116) and W Bates (133) v. Cambridge University at Cambridge, 1884
218	J A Rudolph (127) and A W Gale (121) v. Lancashire at Manchester, 2009
217	A McGrath (144) and J A Rudolph (129) v. Kent at Canterbury, 2008
216	R G Lumb (118) and J H Hampshire (127) v. Surrey at The Oval, 1975
215	A Mitchell (73) and M Leyland (139) v. Surrey at Bradford, 1928
213	E Oldroyd (168) and W Barber (114) v. Glamorgan at Hull, 1929
208	J V Wilson (157*) and E I Lester (112) v. Sussex at Leeds, 1949
206	A McGrath (105) and J A Rudolph (228*) v Durham at Leeds, 2010
205*	E Oldroyd (122*) and M Leyland (100*) v. Hampshire at Harrogate, 1924
205	F S Jackson (124) and D Denton (112) v. Somerset at Taunton, 1897
205	D E V Padgett (83) and D B Close (128) v. Somerset at Bath, 1959
204	M P Vaughan (113) and A McGrath (70) v. Essex at Scarborough, 2001
203	D Denton (132) and J Tunnicliffe (102) v. Warwickshire at Birmingham, 1905
203	A A Metcalfe (216*) and P E Robinson (88) v. Middlesex at Leeds, 1988
201	J Tunnicliffe (101) and T L Taylor (147) v. Surrey at The Oval, 1900

CENTURY PARTNERSHIPS *(Continued)*

THIRD WICKET (Qualification 200 runs) *(Continued)*

201	H Sutcliffe (87) and W Barber (130) v. Leicestershire at Leicester, 1938
200	M D Moxon (274*) and A P Grayson (100) v. Worcestershire at Worcester, 1994

FOURTH WICKET (Qualification 175 runs)

358   D S Lehmann (339) and M J Lumb (98) v. Durham at Leeds, 2006
330   M J Wood (116) and D R Martyn (238) v. Gloucestershire at Leeds, 2003
312   D Denton (168*) and G H Hirst (146) v. Hampshire at Southampton, 1914
299   P Holmes (277*) and R Kilner (150) v. Northamptonshire at Harrogate, 1921
272   D Byas (138) and A McGrath (137) v. Hampshire at Harrogate, 1996
271   B B Wilson (208) and W Rhodes (113) v. Sussex at Bradford, 1914
259   A Drake (115) and G H Hirst (218) v. Sussex at Hastings, 1911
258   J Tunnicliffe (128) and G H Hirst (152) v. Hampshire at Portsmouth, 1904
258   P E Robinson (147) and D Byas (117) v. Kent at Scarborough, 1989
249   W B Stott (143) and G Boycott (145) v. Lancashire at Sheffield, 1963
247*   R G Lumb (165*) and S N Hartley (104*) v. Gloucestershire at Bradford, 1984
247   M Leyland (263) and L Hutton (83) v. Essex at Hull, 1936
238   D S Lehmann (216) and M J Lumb (92) v. Susex at Arundel, 2002
233   D Byas (120) and P E Robinson (189) v. Lancashire at Scarborough, 1991
231   J E Root (236) and J M Bairstow (186) v. Derbyshire at Leeds, 2013
226   W H Wilkinson (89) and G H Hirst (140) v. Northamptonshire at Hull, 1909
225   C H Grimshaw (85) and G H Hirst (169) v. Oxford University at Oxford, 1906
212   B B Wilson (108) and G H Hirst (166*) v. Sussex at Hastings, 1913
212   B Boycott (260*) and J H Hampshire (80) v. Essex at Colchester, 1970
211   J V Wilson (120) and W Watson (108) v. Derbyshire at Harrogate, 1951
210*   A Mitchell (150*) and M Leyland (117*) v. Worcestershire at Worcester, 1933
210   E I. Lester (178) and W Watson (97) v. Nottinghamshire at Nottingham, 1952
207   D Byas (213) and C White (107*) v. Worcestershire at Scarborough, 1995
206   J A Rudolph (121) and A W Gale (150) v. Surrey at The Oval, 2008
205*   G Boycott (151*) and P J Sharpe (79*) v. Leicestershire at Leicester, 1964
205   E Oldroyd (121) and R Kilner (117) v. Worcestershire at Dudley, 1922
205   W Watson (162*) and E I Lester (98) v. Somerset at Leeds, 1953
204   A W Gale (148) and G S Ballance (90) v. Surrey at Leeds, 2013
201*   J H Hampshire (105*) and D B Close (101*) v. Surrey at Bradford, 1965
203   P A Jaques (160) and G S Ballance (121*) v. Gloucestershire at Bristol, 2012
201   W H H Sutcliffe (181) and L Hutton (120) v. Kent at Canterbury, 1952
200   J V Wilson (92) and W Watson (102) v. Somerset at Taunton, 1950
198   A A Metcalfe (138) and D Byas (95) v. Warwickshire at Leeds, 1989
197   N W D Yardley (177) and A Coxon (58) v. Derbyshire at Scarborough, 1947
197   A Lyth (248*) and J M Bairstow (118) v. Leicestershire at Leicester, 2012
196   M D Moxon (130) and D L Bairstow (104) v. Derbyshire at Harrogate, 1987
193   A Drake (85) and G H Hirst (156) v. Lancashire at Manchester, 1911
192   J V Wilson (132) and W Watson (105) v. Essex at Bradford, 1955
191   M Leyland (114) and C Turner (63) v. Essex at Ilford, 1938
188   H Myers (60) and G H Hirst (158) v. Cambridge University at Cambridge, 1910
187   E Oldroyd (168) and F E Greenwood (104*) v. Glamorgan at Hull, 1929
187   K Taylor (203*) and W B Stott (57) v. Warwickshire at Birmingham, 1961
186   D S Lehmann (193) and D Byas (100) v. Leicestershire at Leicester, 2001
184   J H Hampshire (96) and R Illingworth (100*) v. Leicestershire at Sheffield, 1968
182*   E I Lester (101*) and M Watson (103*) v. Nottinghamshire at Bradford, 1952
180*   G Boycott (207*) and B Leadbeater (50*) v. Cambridge University
        at Cambridge, 1976
180   J Tunnicliffe (139*) and G H Hirst (108) v. Surrey at The Oval, 1904
179   J H Hampshire (179) and S N Hartley (63) v. Surrey at Harrogate, 1981
179   M D Moxon (171*) and R J Blakey (71) v. Kent at Leeds, 1993
178   E I Lester (186) and J V Wilson (71) v. Warwickshiire at Scarborough, 1949
177   J D Love (105*) and J H Hampshire (89) v. Lancashire at Manchester, 1980
175   L Hutton (177) and W Barber (84) v. Sussex at Scarborough, 1939
175   A McGrath (188*) and J A Rudolph (82) v. Warwickshire at Birmingham, 2007

FIFTH WICKET (Qualification 150 runs)

340	E Wainwright (228) and G H Hirst (186) v. Surrey at The Oval, 1899
329	F Mitchell (194) and E Wainwright (153) v. Leicestershire at Leicester, 1899
297	A W Gale (272) and G S Ballance (141) v. Nottinghamshire at Scarborough, 2013
276	W Rhodes (104*) and R Kilner (166) v. Northamptonshire at Northampton, 1921
273	L Hutton (270*) and N W D Yardley (136) v. Hampshire at Bournemouth, 1947
245*	H Sutcliffe (107*) and W Barber (128*) v. Northamptonshire at Northampton, 1939
229	D S Lehmann (193) and C White (79) v. Kent at Canterbury, 2006
217	D B Close (140*) and R Illingworth (107) v. Warwickshire at Sheffield, 1962
207	G S Ballance (107) and A U Rashid (180) v. Somerset at Leeds, 2013
198	E Wainwright (145) and R Peel (111) v. Sussex at Bradford, 1896
198	W Barber (168) and K R Davidson (101*) v. MCC at Lord's, 1934
196*	R Kilner (115*) and G H Hirst (82*) v. Gloucestershire at Leeds, 1919
195	M J Lumb (93) and C White (173*) v. Derbyshire at Derby, 2003
194*	Younus Khan (202*) and G L Brophy (100*) v. Hampshire at Southampton, 2007
193	A Mitchell (189) and W Rhodes (88) v. Northamptonshire at Northampton, 1926
193	J D Love (106) and S N Hartley (108) v. Oxford University at Oxford, 1985
192	C W J Athey (114*) and J D Love (123) v. Surrey at The Oval, 1982
191*	L Hutton (271*) and C Turner (81*) v. Derbyshire at Sheffield, 1937
191	M G Bevan (105) and A A Metcalfe (100) v. West Indians at Scarborough, 1995
190*	R J Blakey (204*) and J D Love (79*) v. Gloucestershire at Leeds, 1987
189	J E Root (160) and G S Ballance (87) v. Sussex at Scarborough 2011
188	D E V Padgett (146) and J V Wilson (72) v. Sussex at Middlesbrough, 1960
187	J V Wilson (230) and H Halliday (74) v. Derbyshire at Sheffield, 1952
185	G Boycott (104*) and K Sharp (99) v. Kent at Tunbridge Wells, 1984
182	E Lockwood (208) and E Lumb (40) v. Kent at Gravesend, 1882
182	B B Wilson (109) and W Rhodes (111) v. Sussex at Hove, 1910
182	D B Close (164) and J V Wilson (55) v. Combined Services at Harrogate, 1954
181	A A Metcalfe (149) and J D Love (88) v. Glamorgan at Leeds, 1986
177	Hon F S Jackson (87) and G H Hirst (232*) v. Surrey at The Oval, 1905
176	L Hutton (176*) and A Coxon (72) v. Sussex at Sheffield, 1948
175	A Drake (108) and R Kilner (77) v. Cambridge University at Cambridge, 1913
173	H Sutcliffe (206) and R Kilner (124) v. Warwickshire at Dewsbury, 1925
170	W Rhodes (157) and R Kilner (87) v. Derbyshire at Leeds, 1925
170	J V Wilson (130*) and N W D Yardley (67) v. Lancashire at Manchester, 1954
169	W Watson (147) and A B Sellers (92) v. Worcestershire at Worcester, 1947
168	A T Barber (63) and A Mitchell (122*) v. Worcestershire at Worcester, 1929
167	J M Bairstow (136) and G S Ballance (61) v. Somerset at Taunton 2011
165	E Oldroyd (143) and W Rhodes (110) v. Glamorgan at Leeds, 1922
165	K Sharp (100*) and P Carrick (73) v. Middlesex at Lord's, 1980
164	A A Metcalfe (151) and D L Bairstow (88) v. Northamptonshire at Luton, 1986
159*	J D Love (170*) and D L Bairstow (52*) v. Worcestershire at Worcester, 1979
159	D B Close (128) and R Illingworth (74) v. Lancashire at Sheffield, 1959
159	J H Hampshire (183*) and C Johnson (53) v. Sussex at Hove, 1971
158*	G Boycott (153*) and P E Robinson (74*) v. Derbyshire at Harrogate, 1984
157	T L Taylor (135*) and G H Hirst (72) v. An England XI at Hastings, 1901
157	G H Hirst (142) and F Smith (51) v. Somerset at Bradford, 1903
157	W Barber (87) and N W D Yardley (101) v. Surrey at The Oval, 1937
156	A McGrath (158) and I J Harvey (103) v. Derbyshire at Derby, 2005
153	S N Hartley (87) and M D Moxon (112*) v. Indians at Scarborough, 1986
152	J H Hampshire (83) and S N Hartley (106) v. Nottinghamshire at Nottingham, 1981
151*	G H Hirst (102*) and R Kilner (50*) v. Kent at Bradford, 1913
151	G H Hirst (120) and F Smith (55) v. Kent at Leeds, 1903
151	W Rhodes (57) and R Kilner (90) v. Nottinghamshire at Nottingham, 1925

CENTURY PARTNERSHIPS *(Continued)*

SIXTH WICKET (Qualification 150 runs)

276	M Leyland (191) and E Robinson (124*) v. Glamorgan at Swansea, 1926	
252	C White (181) and R J Blakey (109*) v. Lancashire at Leeds, 1996	
233	M W Booth (210) and G H Hirst (100) v. Worcestershire at Worcester, 1911	
229	W Rhodes (267*) and N Kilner (112) v. Leicestershire at Leeds, 1921	
225	E Wainwright (91) and Lord Hawke (127) v. Hampshire at Southampton, 1899	
217*	H Sutcliffe (200*) and A Wood (123*) v. Worcestershire at Sheffield, 1935	
214	W Watson (214*) and N W D Yardley (76) v. Worcestershire at Worcester, 1955	
205	G H Hirst (125) and S Haigh (159) v. Nottinghamshire at Sheffield, 1901	
200	D Denton (127) and G H Hirst (134) v. Essex at Bradford, 1902	
198	M Leyland (247) and W Rhodes (100*) v. Worcestershire at Worcester, 1928	
190	W Rhodes (126) and M Leyland (79) v. Middlesex at Bradford, 1923	
190	J A Rudolph (122) and A U Rashid (86) v. Surrey at The Oval, 2007	
188	W Watson (174) and R Illingworth (53) v. Lancashire at Sheffield, 1955	
188	M P Vaughan (161) and R J Blakey (92) v. Essex at Ilford, 1997.	
188	G S Ballance (111) and A U Rashid (82) v. Warwickshire at Birmingham 2011	
184	R Kilner (104) and M W Booth (79) v. Leicestershire at Leeds, 1913	
183	G H Hirst (131) and E Smith (129) v. Hampshire at Bradford, 1899	
183	W Watson (139*) and R Illingworth (78) v. Somerset at Harrogate, 1956	
178*	D Denton (108*) and G H Hirst (112*) v. Lancashire at Manchester, 1902	
178*	N W D Yardley (100*) and R Illingworth (71*) v. Gloucestershire at Bristol, 1955	
178	E Robinson (100) and D C F Burton (83) v. Derbyshire at Hull, 1921	
178	H Sutcliffe (135) and P A Gibb (157*) v. Nottinghamshire at Sheffield, 1935	
175	G M Fellows (88) and R J Blakey (103) v. Warwickshire at Birmingham, 2002	
174	D S Lehmann (136) and G M Hamilton (73) v. Kent at Maidstone, 1998	
172	A J Dalton (119*) and D L Bairstow (62) v. Worcestershire at Dudley, 1971	
170*	A U Rashid 103* and A J Hodd (68*) v. Somerset at Taunton, 2013	
170	A W Gale (101) and T T Bresnan (97) v. Worcestershire at Worcester, 2009	
169	W Barber (124) and H Verity (78*) v. Warwickshire at Birmingham, 1933	
169	R Illingworth (162) and J Birkenshaw (37) v. Indians at Sheffield, 1959	
166	E Wainwright (116) and E Smith (61) v. Kent at Catford, 1900	
166	D B Close (161) and F S Trueman (104) v. Northamptonshire at Northampton, 1963	
162*	G Boycott (220*) and J G Binks (70*) v. Northamptonshire at Sheffield, 1967	
161*	D L Bairstow (100*) and P Carrick (57*) v. Middlesex at Leeds, 1983	
159*	D S Lehmann (187*) and R J Blakey (78*) v. Somerset at Bath, 2001	
159	J M Bairstow (182) and A McGrath (90) v. Leicestershire at Scarborough, 2012	
156	W Rhodes (82*) and E Robinson (94) v. Derbyshire at Chesterfield, 1919	
154	C Turner (84) and A Wood (79) v. Glamorgan at Swansea, 1936	
153*	J A Rudolph (92*) and A U Rashid (73*) v. Worcestershire at Kidderminster, 2007	
153	J A Rudolph (69*) and J M Bairstow (81) v. Warwickshire at Birmingham, 2010	
151	D Denton (91) and W Rhodes (76) v. Middlesex at Sheffield, 1904	
151	G Boycott (152*) and P Carrick (75) v. Warwickshire at Leeds, 1982	
150	G Ulyett (199*) and J M Preston (93) v. Derbyshire at Sheffield, 1887	

SEVENTH WICKET (Qualification 125 runs)

254	W Rhodes (135) and D C F Burton (142*) v. Hampshire at Dewsbury, 1919	
247	P Holmes (285) and W Rhodes (79) v. Nottinghamshire at Nottingham, 1929	
215	E Robinson (135*) and D C F Burton (110) v. Leicestershire at Leicester, 1921	
185	E Wainwright (100) and G H Hirst (134) v. Gloucestershire at Bristol, 1897	
183	G H Hirst (341) and H Myers (57) v. Leicestershire at Leicester, 1905	
183	J A Rudolph (220) and T T Bresnan (101*) v. Warwickshire at Scarborough, 2007	
180	C Turner (130) and A Wood (97) v. Somerset at Sheffield, 1936	
168	G L Brophy (99) and A U Rashid (73*) v. Lancashire at Leeds, 2009	
170	G S Blewett (190) and G M Hamilton (84*) v. Northamptonshire at Scarborough, 1999	
166	R Peel (55) and I Grimshaw (122*) v. Derbyshire at Holbeck, 1886	
162	E Wainwright (109) and S Haigh (73) v. Somerset at Taunton, 1900	
162	R J Blakey (90) and R K J Dawson (87) v. Kent at Canterbury, 2002	
162	A W Gale (149) and G L Brophy (97) v. Warwickshire at Scarborough, 2006	

161	R G Lumb (118) and C M Old (89) v. Worcestershire at Bradford, 1980
160	J Tunnicliffe (158) and D Hunter (58*) v. Worcestershire at Worcester, 1900
157*	F A Lowson (259*) and R Booth (53*) v. Worcestershire at Worcester, 1953
155	D Byas (122*) and P Carrick (61) v. Leicestershire at Leicester.1991.
154*	G H Hirst (76*) and J T Newstead (100*) v. Nottinghamshire at Nottingham, 1908
148	J Rowbotham (113) and J Thewlis (50) v. Surrey at The Oval, 1873
147	E Wainwright (78) and G Ulyett (73) v. Somerset at Taunton, 1893
147	M P Vaughan (153) and R J Harden (64) v. Kent at Scarborough, 1999
143	C White (135*) and A K D Gray (60) v. Durham at Chester-le-Street, 2003
141	G H Hirst (108*) and S Haigh (48) v. Worcestershire at Worcester, 1905
141	J H Hampshire (149*) and J G Binks (72) v. MCC at Scarborough, 1965
140	E Wainwright (117) and S Haigh (54) v. CI Thornton's XI at Scarborough, 1900
140	D Byas (67) and P J Hartley (75) v. Derbyshire at Chesterfield, 1990
138	D Denton (78) and G H Hirst (103*) v. Sussex at Leeds, 1905
136	GH Hirst (93) and S Haigh (138) v. Warwickshire at Birmingham, 1904
136	E Robinson (77*) and A Wood (65) v. Glamorgan at Scarborough, 1931
133*	W Rhodes (267*) and M Leyland (52*) v. Leicestershire at Leeds, 1921
133*	E I Lester (86*) and A B Sellers (73*) v. Northamptonshire at Northampton, 1948
133	D Byas (100) and P W Jarvis (80) v. Northamptonshire at Scarborough, 1992
132	W Rhodes (196) and S Haigh (59*) v. Worcestershire at Worcester, 1904
131*	D L Bairstow (79*) and A Sidebottom (52*) v. Oxford University at Oxford, 1981
130	P J Sharpe (64) and J V Wilson (134) v. Warwickshire at Birmingham, 1962
128	W Barber (66) and T F Smailes (86) v. Cambridge University at Cambridge, 1938
128	D B Close (88*) and A Coxon (59) v. Essex at Leeds, 1949
126	E Wainwright (171) and R Peel (46) v. Middlesex at Lord's, 1897
126	W Rhodes (91) and G G Macaulay (63) v. Hampshire at Hull, 1925
126	J C Balderstone (58) and J G Binks (95) v. Middlesex at Lord's, 1964
126	J M Bairstow (70) and A U Rashid (59) v. Kent at Canterbury, 2010
125	A B Sellers (109) and T F Smailes (65) v. Kent at Bradford, 1937

EIGHTH WICKET (Qualification 125 runs)

292	R Peel (210*) and Lord Hawke (166) v. Warwickshire at Birmingham, 1896
238	I J Harvey (209*) and T T Bresnan (74) v. Somerset at Leeds, 2005
192*	W Rhodes (108*) and G G Macaulay (101*) v. Essex at Harrogate, 1922
192	A U Rashid (117*) and A Shahzad (78) v. Hampshire at Basingstoke, 2009
180	W Barber (191) and T F Smailes (89) v. Sussex at Leeds, 1935
165	S Haigh (62) and Lord Hawke (126) v. Surrey at The Oval, 1902
163	G G Macaulay (67) and A Waddington (114) v. Worcestershire at Leeds, 1927
159	E Smith (95) and W Rhodes (105) v. MCC at Scarborough, 1901
157	A Shahzad (88) and D J Wainwright (85*) v. Sussex at Hove, 2009
156	G S Ballance (112) and R J Sidebottom (40) v. Leeds/Bradford MCCU at Leeds, 2013
152	W Rhodes (98) and J W Rothery (70) v. Hampshire at Portsmouth, 1904
151	W Rhodes (201) and Lord Hawke (51) v. Somerset at Taunton, 1905
151	R J Blakey (80*) and P J Hartley (89) v. Sussex at Eastbourne, 1996
149	G L Brophy (177*) and R J Sidebottom (61) v. Worcestershire at Worcester 2011
147	J P G Chadwick (59) and F S Trueman (101) v. Middlesex at Scarborough, 1965
146	S Haigh (159) and Lord Hawke (89) v. Nottinghamshire at Sheffield, 1901
144	G L Brophy (85) and D J Wainwright (102*) v. Warwickshire at Scarborough, 2009
138	E Wainwright (100) and Lord Hawke (81) v. Kent at Tonbridge, 1899
137	E Wainwright (171) and Lord Hawke (75) v. Middlesex at Lord's, 1897
135	P W Jarvis (55) and P J Hartley (69) v. Nottinghamshire at Scarborough, 1992
133	R Illingworth (61) and F S Trueman (74) v. Leicestershire at Leicester, 1955
132	G H Hirst (103) and E Smith (59) v. Middlesex at Sheffield, 1904
132	W Watson (119) and J H Wardle (65) v. Leicestershire at Leicester, 1949
131	P E Robinson (85) and P Carrick (64) v. Surrey at Harrogate, 1990
130	E Smith (98) and Lord Hawke (54) v. Lancashire at Leeds, 1904
128	H Verity (96*) and T F Smailes (77) v. Indians at Bradford, 1936
128	D L Bairstow (145) and G B Stevenson (11) v. Middlesex at Scarborough, 1980

CENTURY PARTNERSHIPS (Continued)

127	E Robinson (70*) and A Wood (62) v. Middlesex at Leeds, 1928
126	R Peel (74) and E Peate (61) v. Gloucestershire at Bradford, 1883
126	M W Booth (56) and E R Wilson (104*) v. Essex at Bradford, 1913
126	J D Middlebrook (84) and C E W Silverwood (70) v. Essex at Chelmsford, 2001
126	M J Lumb (115*) and D Gough (72) v. Hampshire at Southampton, 2003

NINTH WICKET (Qualification 100 runs)

246	T T Bresnan (116) and J N Gillespie (123*) v. Surrey at The Oval, 2007
192	G H Hirst (130*) and S Haigh (85) v. Surrey at Bradford, 1898
179	R A Hutton (189) and G A Cope (30*) v. Pakistanis at Bradford, 1971
176*	R Moorhouse (59*) and G H Hirst (115*) v. Gloucestershire at Bristol, 1894
173	S Haigh (85) and W Rhodes (92*) v. Sussex at Hove, 1902
167	H Verity (89) and T F Smailes (80) v. Somerset at Bath, 1936
162	W Rhodes (94*) and S Haigh (84) v. Lancashire at Manchester, 1904
161	E Smith (116*) and W Rhodes (79) v. Sussex at Sheffield, 1900
154	R M Pyrah (117) and R J Sidebottom (52) v.Lancashire at Leeds 2011
151	J M Bairstow (205) and R J Sidebottom (45*) v. Nottinghamshire at Nottingham 2011
150	Azeem Rafiq (100) and M J Hoggard (56*) v. Worcestershire at Worcester, 2009
149*	R J Blakey (63*) and A K D Gray (74*) v. Leicestershire at Scarborough, 2002
149	G H Hirst (232*) and D Hunter (40) v. Surrey at The Oval, 1905
146	G H Hirst (214) and W Rhodes (53) v. Worcestershire at Worcester, 1901
144	T T Bresnan (91) and J N Gillespie (44) v. Hampshire at Leeds, 2006
140	A U Rashid (111) and D J Wainwright (104) v. Sussex at Hove, 2008
136	R Peel (210*) and G H Hirst (85) v. Warwickshire at Birmingham, 1896
125*	L Hutton (269*) and A Coxon (65*) v. Northamptonshire at Wellingborough, 1949
124	P J Hartley (87*) and P W Jarvis (47) v. Essex at Chelmsford, 1986
120	G H Hirst (138) and W Rhodes (38) v. Nottinghamshire at Nottingham, 1899
119	A B Sellers (80*) and E P Robinson (66) v. Warwickshire at Birmingham, 1938
118	S Haigh (96) and W Rhodes (44) v. Somerset at Leeds, 1901
114	E Oldroyd (194) and A Dolphin (47) v. Worcestershire at Worcester, 1923
114	N Kilner (102*) and G G Macaulay (60) v. Gloucestershire at Bristol, 1923
113	G G Macaulay (125*) and A Waddington (44) v. Nottinghamshire at Nottingham, 1921
113	A Wood (69) and H.Verity (45*) v. MCC at Lord's, 1938
112	G H Hirst (78) and Lord Hawke (61*) v. Essex at Leyton, 1907
109	Lees Whitehead (60) and W Rhodes (81*) v. Sussex at Harrogate, 1899
108	A McGrath (133*) and C E W Silverwood (80) v. Durham at Chester-le-Street, 2005
105	J V Wilson (134) and A G Nicholson (20*) v. Nottinghamshire at Leeds, 1962
105	C M Old (100*) and H P Cooper (30) v. Lancashire at Manchester, 1978
105	C White (74*) and J D Batty (50) v. Gloucestershire at Sheffield, 1993
104	L Hall (129*) and R Moorhouse (86) v. Gloucestershire at Clifton, 1888
100	G Pollitt (51) and Lees Whitehead (54) v. Hampshire at Bradford, 1899

TENTH WICKET (Qualification 100 runs)

149	G Boycott (79) and G B Stevenson (115*) v. Warwickshire at Birmingham, 1982
148	Lord Hawke (107*) and D Hunter (47) v. Kent at Sheffield, 1898
144	A Sidebottom (124) and A L Robinson (30*) v. Glamorgan at Cardiff, 1977
121	J T Brown (141) and D Hunter (25*) v. Liverpool & District at Liverpool, 1894
118	Lord Hawke (110*) and D Hunter (41) v. Kent at Leeds, 1896
113	P J Hartley (88*) and R D Stemp (22) v. Middlesex at Lord's, 1996
110	C E W Silverwood (45*) and R D Stemp (65) v. Durham at Chester-le-Street, 1996
109	A Shahzad (70) and R J Sidebottom (28*) v. Worcestershire at Scarborough, 2011
108	Lord Hawke (79) and Lees Whitehead (45*) v. Lancashire at Manchester, 1903
108	G Boycott (129) and M K Bore (37*) v. Nottinghamshire at Bradford, 1973
106	A B Sellers (79) and D V Brennan (30) v. Worcestershire at Worcester, 1948
103	A Dolphin (62*) and E Smith (49) v. Essex at Leyton, 1919
102	D Denton (77*) and D Hunter (45) v. Cambridge University at Cambridge, 1895

FIFTEEN WICKETS OR MORE IN A MATCH

A complete list of 12, 13 and 14 wickets in a match up to and including 2007 is to be found in the 2008 edition

W E BOWES (1)

16 for 35 (8 for 18 and 8 for 17) v. Northamptonshire at Kettering, 1935

A DRAKE (1)

15 for 51 (5 for 16 and 10 for 35) v. Somerset at Weston-super-Mare, 1914

T EMMETT (1)

16 for 38 (7 for 15 and 9 for 23) v. Cambridgeshire at Hunslet, 1869

G H HIRST (1)

15 for 63 (8 for 25 and 7 for 38) v. Leicestershire at Hull, 1907

R ILLINGWORTH (1)

15 for 123 (8 for 70 and 7 for 53) v. Glamorgan at Swansea, 1960

R PEEL (1)

15 for 50 (9 for 22 and 6 for 28) v. Somerset at Leeds, 1895

W RHODES (1)

15 for 56 (9 for 28 and 6 for 28) v. Essex at Leyton, 1899

H VERITY (4)

17 for 91 (8 for 47 and 9 for 44) v. Essex at Leyton, 1933
15 for 129 (8 for 56 and 7 for 73) v. Oxford University at Oxford, 1936
15 for 38 (6 for 26 and 9 for 12) v. Kent at Sheffield, 1936
15 for 100 (6 for 52 and 9 for 48) v. Essex at Westcliffe-on-Sea, 1936

J H WARDLE (1)

16 for 112 (9 for 48 and 7 for 64) v. Sussex at Hull, 1954

TEN WICKETS IN A MATCH

(including best analysis)

61	W Rhodes	15 for	56	v Essex	at Leyton	1899
48	H Verity	17 for	91	v Essex	at Leyton	1933
40	G H Hirst	15 for	63	v Leicestershire	at Hull	1907
31	G G Macaulay	14 for	92	v Gloucestershire	at Bristol	1926
28	S Haigh	14 for	43	v Hampshire	at Southampton	1898
27	R Peel	14 for	33	v Nottinghamshire	at Sheffield	1888
25	W E Bowes	16 for	35	v Northamptonshire	at Kettering	1935
25	J H Wardle	16 for	112	v Sussex	at Hull	1954
22	E Peate	14 for	77	v Surrey	at Huddersfield	1881
20	F S Trueman	14 for	123	v Surrey	at The Oval	1960
19	T Emmett	16 for	38	v Cambridgeshire	at Hunslet	1869
17	R Appleyard	12 for	43	v Essex	at Bradford	1951
15	E Wainwright	14 for	77	v Essex	at Bradford	1896
11	R Illingworth	15 for	123	v Glamorgan	at Swansea	1960
10	A Waddington	13 for	48	v Northamptonshire	at Northampton	1920
9	M W Booth	14 for	160	v Essex	at Leyton	1914
9	R Kilner	12 for	55	v Sussex	at Hove	1924
8	W Bates	11 for	47	v Nottinghamshire	at Nottingham	1881
8	G Freeman	13 for	60	v Surrey	at Sheffield	1869
7	E P Robinson	13 for	115	v Lancashire	at Leeds	1939
7	D Wilson	13 for	52	v Warwickshire	at Middlesbrough	1967

6 G A Cope	12 for 116	v Glamorgan	at Cardiff (Sophia Gardens)	1968
6 A Hill	12 for 59	v Surrey	at The Oval	1871
6 T F Smailes	14 for 58	v Derbyshire	at Sheffield	1939
5 P Carrick	12 for 89	v Derbyshire	at Sheffield (Abbeydale Pk)	1983
5 J M Preston	13 for 63	v MCC	at Scarborough	1888
5 E Robinson	12 for 95	v Northamptonshire	at Huddersfield	1927
4 J T Newstead	11 for 72	v Worcestershire	at Bradford	1907
3 T W Foster	11 for 93	v Liverpool & District	at Liverpool	1894
3 G P Harrison	11 for 76	v Kent	at Dewsbury	1883
3 F S Jackson	12 for 80	v Hampshire	at Southampton	1897
3 P W Jarvis	11 for 92	v Middlesex	at Lord's	1986
3 S P Kirby	13 for 154	v Somerset	at Taunton	2003
3 A G Nicholson	12 for 73	v Glamorgan	at Leeds	1964
3 R K Platt	10 for 87	v Surrey	at The Oval	1959
3 A Sidebottom	11 for 64	v Kent	at Sheffield (Abbeydale Pk)	1980
3 G Ulyett	12 for 102	v Lancashire	at Huddersfield	1889
2 T Armitage	13 for 46	v Surrey	at Sheffield	1876
2 R Aspinall	14 for 65	v Northamptonshire	at Northampton	1947
2 J T Brown (Darfield)	12 for 109	v Gloucestershire	at Huddersfield	1899
2 R O Clayton	12 for 104	v Lancashire	at Manchester	1877
2 D B Close	11 for 116	v Kent	at Gillingham	1965
2 M J Cowan	12 for 87	v Warwickshire	at Birmingham	1960
2 A Coxon	10 for 57	v Derbyshire	at Chesterfield	1949
2 D Gough	10 for 80	v Lancashire	at Leeds	1995
2 G M Hamilton	11 for 72	v Surrey	at Leeds	1998
2 P J Hartley	11 for 68	v Derbyshire	at Chesterfield	1995
2 R A Hutton	11 for 62	v Lancashire	at Manchester	1971
2 E Leadbeater	11 for 162	v Nottinghamshire	at Nottingham	1950
2 M A Robinson	12 for 124	v Northamptonshire	at Harrogate	1993
2 M Ryan	10 for 77	v Leicestershire	at Bradford	1962
2 E Smith (Morley)	10 for 97	v MCC	at Scarborough	1893
2 R J Sidebottom	11 for 43	v Kent	at Leeds	2000
2 G B Stevenson	11 for 74	v Nottinghamshire	at Nottingham	1980
2 S Wade	11 for 56	v Gloucestershire	at Cheltenham	1886
2 E R Wilson	11 for 109	v Sussex	at Hove	1921
1 A B Bainbridge	12 for 111	v Essex	at Harrogate	1961
1 J Birkenshaw	11 for 134	v Middlesex	at Leeds	1960
1 A Booth	10 for 91	v Indians	at Bradford	1946
1 H P Cooper	11 for 96	v Northamptonshire	at Northampton	1976
1 A Drake	15 for 51	v Somerset	at Weston-Super-Mare	1914
1 L Greenwood	11 for 71	v Surrey	at The Oval	1867
1 P M Hutchison	11 for 102	v Pakistan 'A'	at Leeds	1997
1 L Hutton	10 for 101	v Leicestershire	at Leicester (Aylestone Rd)	1937
1 R Iddison	10 for 68	v Surrey	at Sheffield	1864
1 M Leyland	10 for 94	v Leicestershire	at Leicester (Aylestone Rd)	1933
1 J D Middlebrook	10 for 170	v Hampshire	at Southampton	2000
1 F W Milligan	12 for 110	v Sussex	at Sheffield	1897
1 H Myers	12 for 192	v Gloucestershire	at Dewsbury	1904
1 C M Old	11 for 46	v Gloucestershire	at Middlesbrough	1969
1 D Pickles	12 for 133	v Somerset	at Taunton	1957
1 A U Rashid	11 for 114	v Worcestershire	at Worcester	2011
1 W Ringrose	11 for 135	v Australians	at Bradford	1905
1 C E W Silverwood	12 for 148	v Kent	at Leeds	1997
1 W Slinn	12 for 53	v Nottinghamshire	at Nottingham	1864
1 J Waring	10 for 63	v Lancashire	at Leeds	1966
1 F Wilkinson	10 for 129	v Hampshire	at Bournemouth	1938
1 A C Williams	10 for 66	v Hampshire	at Dewsbury	1919

TEN WICKETS IN AN INNINGS

*Includes the hat trick.

EIGHT WICKETS OR MORE IN AN INNINGS

(Ten wickets in an innings also listed above)

**A complete list of seven wickets in an innings up to and including 2007
is to be found in the 2008 edition**

R APPLEYARD (1)

8 for 76 v. MCC at Scarborough, 1951

R ASPINALL (1)

8 for 42 v. Northamptonshire at Northampton, 1947

W BATES (2)

8 for 45 v. Lancashire at Huddersfield, 1878
8 for 21 v. Surrey at The Oval, 1879

M W BOOTH (4)

8 for 52 v. Leicestershire at Sheffield, 1912
8 for 47 v. Middlesex at Leeds, 1912
8 for 86 v. Middlesex at Sheffield, 1913
8 for 64 v. Essex at Leyton, 1914

W E BOWES (9)

8 for 77 v. Leicestershire at Dewsbury, 1929
8 for 69 v. Middlesex at Bradford, 1930
9 for 121 v. Essex at Scarborough, 1932
8 for 62 v. Sussex at Hove, 1932
8 for 69 v. Gloucestershire at Gloucester, 1933
8 for 40 v. Worcestershire at Sheffield, 1935
8 for 18 v. Northamptonshire at Kettering, 1935
8 for 17 v. Northamptonshire at Kettering, 1935
8 for 56 v. Leicestershire at Scarborough, 1936

J T BROWN (Darfield) (1)

8 for 40 v. Gloucestershire at Huddersfield, 1899

P CARRICK (2)

8 for 33 v. Cambridge University at Cambridge, 1973
8 for 72 v. Derbyshire at Scarborough, 1975

R O CLAYTON (1)

8 for 66 v. Lancashire at Manchester, 1877

D B CLOSE (2)

8 for 41 v. Kent at Leeds, 1959
8 for 43 v. Essex at Leeds, 1960

H P COOPER (1)

8 for 62 v. Glamorgan at Cardiff, 1975

G A COPE (1)

8 for 73 v. Gloucestershire at Bristol, 1975

M J COWAN (1)

9 for 43 v. Warwickshire at Birmingham, 1960

A COXON (1)

8 for 31 v. Worcestershire at Leeds, 1946

A DRAKE (2)

8 for 59 v. Gloucestershire at Sheffield, 1913
10 for 35 v. Somerset at Weston-super-Mare, 1914

T EMMETT (8)

9 for 34 v. Nottinghamshire at Dewsbury, 1868
9 for 23 v. Cambridgeshire at Hunslet, 1869
8 for 31 v. Nottinghamshire at Sheffield, 1871
8 for 46 v. Gloucestershire at Clifton, 1877
8 for 16 v. MCC at Scarborough, 1877
8 for 22 v. Surrey at The Oval, 1881
8 for 52 v. MCC at Scarborough, 1882
8 for 32 v. Sussex at Huddersfield, 1884

S D FLETCHER (1)

8 for 58 v. Essex at Sheffield, 1988

T W FOSTER (1)

9 for 59 v. MCC at Lord's, 1894

G FREEMAN (2)

8 for 11 v. Lancashire at Holbeck, 1868
8 for 29 v. Surrey at Sheffield, 1869

L GREENWOOD (1)

8 for 35 v. Cambridgeshire at Dewsbury, 1867

S HAIGH (5)

8 for 78 v. Australians at Bradford, 1896
8 for 35 v. Hampshire at Harrogate, 1896
8 for 21 v. Hampshire at Southampton, 1898
8 for 33 v. Warwickshire at Scarborough, 1899
9 for 25 v. Gloucestershire at Leeds, 1912

P J HARTLEY (2)

8 for 111 v. Sussex at Hove, 1992
9 for 41 v. Derbyshire at Chesterfield, 1995

G H HIRST (8)

8 for 59 v. Warwickshire at Birmingham, 1896
8 for 48 v. Australians at Bradford, 1899
8 for 25 v. Leicestershire at Hull, 1907
9 for 45 v. Middlesex at Sheffield, 1907
9 for 23 v. Lancashire at Leeds, 1910
8 for 80 v. Somerset at Sheffield, 1910
9 for 41 v. Worcestershire at Worcester, 1911
9 for 69 v. MCC at Lord's, 1912

EIGHT WICKETS OR MORE IN AN INNINGS *(Continued)*

R ILLINGWORTH (5)

8 for 69 v. Surrey at The Oval, 1954
9 for 42 v. Worcestershire at Worcester, 1957
8 for 70 v. Glamorgan at Swansea, 1960
8 for 50 v. Lancashire at Manchester, 1961
8 for 20 v. Worcestershire at Leeds, 1965

R KILNER (2)

8 for 26 v. Glamorgan at Cardiff, 1923
8 for 40 v. Middlesex at Bradford, 1926

S P KIRBY (1)

8 for 80 v. Somerset at Taunton, 2003

E LEADBEATER (1)

8 for 83 v. Worcestershire at Worcester, 1950

M LEYLAND (1)

8 for 63 v. Hampshire at Huddersfield, 1938

G G MACAULAY (3)

8 for 43 v. Gloucestershire at Bristol, 1926
8 for 37 v. Derbyshire at Hull, 1927
8 for 21 v. Indians at Harrogate, 1932

H MYERS (1)

8 for 81 v. Gloucestershire at Dewsbury, 1904

A G NICHOLSON (2)

9 for 62 v. Sussex at Eastbourne, 1967
8 for 22 v. Kent at Canterbury, 1968

E PEATE (6)

8 for 24 v. Lancashire at Manchester, 1880
8 for 30 v. Surrey at Huddersfield, 1881
8 for 69 v. Sussex at Hove, 1881
8 for 32 v. Middlesex at Sheffield, 1882
8 for 5 v. Surrey at Holbeck, 1883
8 for 63 v. Kent at Gravesend, 1884

R PEEL (6)

8 for 12 v. Nottinghamshire at Sheffield, 1888
8 for 60 v. Surrey at Sheffield, 1890
8 for 54 v. Cambridge University at Cambridge, 1893
9 for 22 v. Somerset at Leeds, 1895
8 for 27 v. South of England XI at Scarborough, 1896
8 for 53 v. Kent at Halifax, 1897

J M PRESTON (2)

8 for 27 v. Sussex at Hove, 1888
9 for 28 v. MCC at Scarborough, 1888

EIGHT WICKETS OR MORE IN AN INNINGS *(Continued)*

W RHODES (18)

9 for 28 v. Essex at Leyton, 1899
8 for 38 v. Nottinghamshire at Nottingham, 1899
8 for 68 v. Cambridge University at Cambridge, 1900
8 for 43 v. Lancashire at Bradford, 1900
8 for 23 v. Hampshire at Hull, 1900
8 for 72 v. Gloucestershire at Bradford, 1900
8 for 28 v. Essex at Harrogate, 1900
8 for 53 v. Middlesex at Lord's, 1901
8 for 55 v. Kent at Canterbury, 1901
8 for 26 v. Kent at Catford, 1902
8 for 87 v. Worcestershire at Worcester, 1903
8 for 61 v. Lancashire at Bradford, 1903
8 for 90 v. Warwickshire at Birmingham, 1905
8 for 92 v. Northamptonshire at Northampton, 1911
8 for 44 v. Warwickshire at Bradford, 1919
8 for 39 v. Sussex at Leeds, 1920
8 for 48 v. Somerset at Huddersfield, 1926
9 for 39 v. Essex at Leyton, 1929

W RINGROSE (1)

9 for 76 v. Australians at Bradford, 1905

E ROBINSON (3)

9 for 36 v. Lancashire at Bradford, 1920
8 for 32 v. Northamptonshire at Huddersfield, 1927
8 for 13 v. Cambridge University at Cambridge, 1928

E P ROBINSON (2)

8 for 35 v. Lancashire at Leeds, 1939
8 for 76 v. Surrey at The Oval, 1946

M A ROBINSON (1)

9 for 37 v. Northamptonshire at Harrogate, 1993

A SIDEBOTTOM (1)

8 for 72 v. Leicestershire at Middlesbrough, 1986

T F SMAILES (2)

8 for 68 v. Glamorgan at Hull, 1938
10 for 47 v. Derbyshire at Sheffield, 1939

G B STEVENSON (2)

8 for 65 v. Lancashire at Leeds, 1978
8 for 57 v. Northamptonshire at Leeds, 1980

F S TRUEMAN (8)

8 for 70 v. Minor Counties at Lord's, 1949
8 for 68 v. Nottinghamshire at Sheffield, 1951
8 for 53 v. Nottinghamshire at Nottingham, 1951
8 for 28 v. Kent at Dover, 1954
8 for 84 v. Nottinghamshire at Worksop, 1962
8 for 45 v. Gloucestershire at Bradford, 1963
8 for 36 v. Sussex at Hove, 1965
8 for 37 v. Essex at Bradford, 1966

H VERITY (20)

9 for 60 v. Glamorgan at Swansea, 1930
10 for 36 v. Warwickshire at Leeds, 1931
8 for 33 v. Glamorgan at Swansea, 1931
8 for 107 v. Lancashire at Bradford, 1932
8 for 39 v. Northamptonshire at Northampton, 1932
10 for 10 v. Nottinghamshire at Leeds, 1932
8 for 47 v. Essex at Leyton, 1933
9 for 44 v. Essex at Leyton, 1933
9 for 59 v. Kent at Dover, 1933
8 for 28 v. Leicestershire at Leeds, 1935
8 for 56 v. Oxford University at Oxford, 1936
8 for 40 v. Worcestershire at Stourbridge, 1936
9 for 12 v. Kent at Sheffield, 1936
9 for 48 v. Essex at Westcliff-on-Sea, 1936
8 for 42 v. Nottinghamshire at Bradford, 1936
9 for 43 v. Warwickshire at Leeds, 1937
8 for 80 v. Sussex at Eastbourne, 1937
8 for 43 v. Middlesex at The Oval, 1937
9 for 62 v. MCC at Lord's, 1939
8 for 38 v. Leicestershire at Hull, 1939

A WADDINGTON (3)

8 for 34 v. Northamptonshire at Leeds, 1922
8 for 39 v. Kent at Leeds, 1922
8 for 35 v. Hampshire at Bradford, 1922

E WAINWRIGHT (3)

8 for 49 v. Middlesex at Sheffield, 1891
9 for 66 v. Middlesex at Sheffield, 1894
8 for 34 v. Essex at Bradford, 1896

J H WARDLE (4)

8 for 87 v. Derbyshire at Chesterfield, 1948
8 for 26 v. Middlesex at Lord's, 1950
9 for 48 v. Sussex at Hull, 1954
9 for 25 v. Lancashire at Manchester, 1954

C WHITE (1)

8 for 55 v. Gloucestershire at Gloucester, 1998

A C WILLIAMS (1)

9 for 29 v. Hampshire at Dewsbury, 1919

R WOOD (1)

8 for 45 v. Scotland at Glasgow, 1952

SIX WICKETS IN AN INNINGS AT LESS THAN FOUR RUNS EACH

A complete list of 5 wickets at less than 4 runs each up to and including 2007 is to be found in the 2008 edition

R APPLEYARD (2)

6 for 17 v. Essex at Bradford, 1951
6 for 12 v. Hampshire at Bournemouth, 1954

T ARMITAGE (1)

6 for 20 v. Surrey at Sheffield, 1876

R ASPINALL (1)

6 for 23 v. Northamptonshire at Northampton, 1947

W BATES (5)

6 for 11 v. Middlesex at Huddersfield, 1879
6 for 22 v. Kent at Bradford, 1881
6 for 17 v. Nottinghamshire at Nottingham, 1881
6 for 12 v. Kent at Sheffield, 1882
6 for 19 v. Lancashire at Dewsbury, 1886

A BOOTH (1)

6 for 21 v. Warwickshire at Birmingham, 1946

W E BOWES (4)

6 for 17 v. Middlesex at Lord's, 1934
6 for 16 v. Lancashire at Bradford, 1935
6 for 20 v. Gloucestershire at Sheffield, 1936
6 for 23 v. Warwickshire at Birmingham, 1947

J T BROWN (Darfield) (1)

6 for 19 v. Worcestershire at Worcester, 1899

R.O CLAYTON (1)

6 for 20 v. Nottinghamshire at Sheffield, 1876

A COXON (1)

6 for 17 v. Surrey at Sheffield, 1948

T EMMETT (6)

6 for 7 v. Surrey at Sheffield, 1867
6 for 13 v. Lancashire at Holbeck, 1868
6 for 21 v. Middlesex at Scarborough, 1874
6 for 12 v. Derbyshire at Sheffield, 1878
6 for 19 v. Derbyshire at Bradford, 1881
6 for 22 v. Australians at Bradford, 1882

H FISHER (1)

6 for 11 v. Leicestershire at Bradford, 1932

SIX WICKETS IN AN INNINGS AT LESS THAN FOUR
RUNS EACH *(Continued)*

S HAIGH (10)

6 for 18 v. Derbyshire at Bradford, 1897
6 for 22 v. Hampshire at Southampton, 1898
6 for 21 v. Surrey at The Oval, 1900
6 for 23 v. Cambridge University at Cambridge, 1902
6 for 19 v. Somerset at Sheffield, 1902
6 for 22 v. Cambridge University at Sheffield, 1903
6 for 21 v. Hampshire at Leeds, 1904
6 for 21 v. Nottinghamshire at Sheffield, 1905
6 for 13 v. Surrey at Leeds, 1908
6 for 14 v. Australians at Bradford, 1912

A HILL (2)

6 for 9 v. United South of England XI at Bradford, 1874
6 for 18 v. MCC at Lord's, 1881

G H HIRST (7)

6 for 23 v. MCC at Lord's, 1893
6 for 20 v. Lancashire at Leeds, 1906
6 for 12 v. Northamptonshire at Northampton, 1908
6 for 7 v. Northamptonshire at Northampton, 1908
6 for 23 v. Surrey at Leeds, 1908
6 for 23 v. Lancashire at Manchester, 1909
6 for 20 v. Surrey at Sheffield, 1909

R ILLINGWORTH (2)

6 for 15 v. Scotland at Hull, 1956
6 for 13 v. Leicestershire at Leicester, 1963

F S JACKSON (1)

6 for 19 v. Hampshire at Southampton, 1897

R KILNER (5)

6 for 22 v. Essex at Harrogate, 1922
6 for 13 v. Hampshire at Bournemouth, 1922
6 for 14 v. Middlesex at Bradford, 1923
6 for 22 v. Surrey at Sheffield, 1923
6 for 15 v. Hampshire at Portsmouth, 1924

G G MACAULAY (10)

6 for 10 v. Warwickshire at Birmingham, 1921
6 for 3 v. Derbyshire at Hull, 1921
6 for 8 v. Northamptonshire at Northampton, 1922
6 for 12 v. Glamorgan at Cardiff, 1922
6 for 18 v. Northamptonshire at Bradford, 1923
6 for 19 v. Northamptonshire at Northampton, 1925
6 for 22 v. Leicestershire at Leeds, 1926
6 for 11 v. Leicestershire at Hull, 1930
6 for 22 v. Leicestershire at Bradford, 1933
6 for 22 v. Middlesex at Leeds, 1934

SIX WICKETS IN AN INNINGS AT LESS THAN FOUR
RUNS EACH *(Continued)*

E PEATE (5)

6 for 14 v. Middlesex at Huddersfield, 1879
6 for 12 v. Derbyshire at Derby, 1882
6 for 13 v. Gloucestershire at Moreton-in-Marsh, 1884
6 for 16 v. Sussex at Huddersfield, 1886
6 for 16 v. Cambridge University at Sheffield, 1886

R PEEL (4)

6 for 21 v. Nottinghamshire at Sheffield, 1888
6 for 19 v. Australians at Huddersfield, 1888
6 for 22 v. Gloucestershire at Bristol, 1891
6 for 19 v. Leicestershire at Scarborough, 1896

A C RHODES (1)

6 for 19 v. Cambridge University at Cambridge, 1932

W RHODES (12)

6 for 21 v. Somerset at Bath, 1898
6 for 16 v. Gloucestershire at Bristol, 1899
6 for 4 v. Nottinghamshire at Nottingham, 1901
6 for 15 v. MCC at Lord's, 1902
6 for 16 v. Cambridge University at Cambridge, 1905
6 for 9 v. Essex at Huddersfield, 1905
6 for 22 v. Derbyshire at Glossop, 1907
6 for 17 v. Leicestershire at Leicester, 1908
6 for 13 v. Sussex at Hove, 1922
6 for 23 v. Nottinghamshire at Leeds, 1923
6 for 22 v. Cambridge University at Cambridge, 1924
6 for 20 v. Gloucestershire at Dewsbury, 1927

W RINGROSE (1)

6 for 20 v. Leicestershire at Dewsbury, 1903

R J SIDEBOTTOM (1)

6 for 16 v. Kent at Leeds, 2000

W SLINN (1)

6 for 19 v. Nottinghamshire at Nottingham, 1864

G B STEVENSON(1)

6 for 14 v. Warwickshire at Sheffield, 1979

F S TRUEMAN (4)

6 for 23 v. Oxford University at Oxford, 1955
6 for 23 v. Oxford University at Oxford, 1958
6 for 18 v. Warwickshire at Birmingham, 1963
6 for 20 v. Leicestershire at Sheffield, 1968

H VERITY (5)

6 for 11 v. Surrey at Bradford, 1931
6 for 21 v. Glamorgan at Swansea, 1931
6 for 12 v. Derbyshire at Hull, 1933
6 for 10 v. Essex at Ilford, 1937
6 for 22 v. Hampshire at Bournemouth, 1939

SIX WICKETS IN AN INNINGS AT LESS THAN FOUR
RUNS EACH *(Continued)*

A WADDINGTON (2)

6 for 21 v. Northamptonshire at Harrogate, 1921
6 for 21 v. Northamptonshire at Northampton, 1923

S WADE (1)

6 for 18 v. Gloucestershire at Dewsbury, 1887

E WAINWRIGHT (4)

6 for 16 v. Sussex at Leeds, 1893
6 for 23 v. Sussex at Hove, 1893
6 for 18 v. Sussex at Dewsbury, 1894
6 for 22 v. MCC at Scarborough, 1894

J H WARDLE (8)

6 for 17 v. Sussex at Sheffield, 1948
6 for 10 v. Scotland at Edinburgh, 1950
6 for 12 v. Gloucestershire at Hull, 1950
6 for 20 v. Kent at Scarborough, 1950
6 for 23 v. Somerset at Sheffield, 1951
6 for 21 v. Glamorgan at Leeds, 1951
6 for 18 v. Gloucestershire at Bristol, 1951
6 for 6 v. Gloucestershire at Bristol, 1955

D WILSON (3)

6 for 22 v. Sussex at Bradford, 1963
6 for 15 v. Gloucestershire at Middlesbrough, 1966
6 for 22 v. Middlesex at Sheffield, 1966

FOUR WICKETS IN FOUR BALLS

A Drake v. Derbyshire at Chesterfield, 1914

FOUR WICKETS IN FIVE BALLS

F S Jackson v. Australians at Leeds, 1902
A Waddington v. Northamptonshire at Northampton, 1920
G G Macaulay v. Lancashire at Manchester, 1933
P J Hartley v. Derbyshire at Chesterfield, 1995
D Gough v. Kent at Leeds, 1995
J D Middlebrook v. Hampshire at Southampton, 2000

BEST BOWLING ANALYSES IN A MATCH
FOR AND AGAINST YORKSHIRE

Best For Yorkshire:
17 for 91 (8 for 47 and 9 for 44) H Verity v Essex at Leyton, 1933

Against Yorkshire:
17 for 91 (9 for 62 and 8 for 29) H Dean for Lancashire at Liverpool, 1913
(non-championship)

County Championship
16 for 114 (8 for 48 and 8 for 66) G Burton for Middlesex at Sheffield, 1888

Yorkshire versus:

Derbyshire	*For Yorkshire:*	14 for 58 (4 for 11 and 10 for 47) T F Smailes at Sheffield, 1939
	Against:	13 for 65 (7 for 33 and 6 for 32) W Mycroft at Sheffield, 1879
Most 10 wickets in a match	*For Yorkshire:*	P Carrick and E Peate 4 each
	Against:	W Mycroft 3
Durham	*For Yorkshire:*	10 for 101 (6 for 57 and 4 for 44) M A Robinson at Durham, 1992
	Against:	10 for 144 (7 for 81 and 3 for 63) O D Gibson at Chester-le-Street, 2007
Most 10 wickets in a match	*For Yorkshire:*	M A Robinson 1
	Against:	G R Breese and O D Gibson 1 each
Essex	*For Yorkshire:*	17 for 91 (8 for 47 and 9 for 44) H Verity at Leyton, 1933
	Against:	14 for 127 (7 for 37 and 7 for 90) W Mead at Leyton, 1899
Most 10 wickets in a match	*For Yorkshire:*	W Rhodes 7
	Against:	J K Lever, W Mead 2 each
Glamorgan	*For Yorkshire:*	15 for 123 (8 for 70 and 7 for 53) R Illingworth at Swansea. 1960
	Against:	12 for 76 (7 for 30 and 5 for 46) D J Shepherd at Cardiff, 1957
Most 10 wickets in a match	*For Yorkshire:*	H Verity 5
	Against:	D J Shepherd, J S Pressdee 1 each
Gloucestershire	*For Yorkshire:*	14 for 64 (7 for 58 and 7 for 6) R Illingworth at Harrogate, 1967
	Against:	15 for 79 (8 for 33 and 7 for 46) W G Grace at Sheffield, 1872
Most 10 wickets in a match	*For Yorkshire:*	W Rhodes 8
	Against:	E G Dennett 5
Hampshire	*For Yorkshire:*	14 for 43 (8 for 21 and 6 for 22) S Haigh at Southampton, 1898
	Against:	12 for 145 (7 for 78 and 5 for 67) D Shackleton at Bradford, 1962
Most 10 wickets in a match	*For Yorkshire:*	W Rhodes, E Robinson, H Verity 3 each
	Against:	A S Kennedy 3

Yorkshire versus

Kent
	For Yorkshire:	15 for 38 (6 for 26 and 9 for 12)
		H Verity at Sheffield, 1936
	Against:	13 for 48 (5 for 13 and 8 for 35)
		A Hearne at Sheffield, 1885

Most 10 wickets in a match — For Yorkshire: E Peate and J H Wardle 4 each

Against: C Blythe 6

Lancashire
	For Yorkshire:	14 for 80 (6 for 56 and 8 for 24)
		E Peate at Manchester, 1880
	Against:	17 for 91 (9 for 62 and 8 for 29)
		H Dean at Liverpool, 1913 (non-championship)
		14 for 90 (6 for 47 and 8 for 43)
		R Tattersall at Leeds, 1956 (championship)

Most 10 wickets in a match — For Yorkshire: T Emmett 5

Against: J Briggs 8

Leicestershire
	For Yorkshire:	15 for 63 (8 for 25 and 7 for 38)
		G H Hirst at Hull, 1907
	Against:	12 for 139 (8 for 85 and 4 for 54)
		A D Pougher at Leicester, 1895

Most 10 wickets in a match — For Yorkshire: G H Hirst 5

Against: A D Pougher 2

Middlesex
	For Yorkshire:	13 for 94 (6 for 61 and 7 for 33)
		S Haigh at Leeds, 1900
	Against:	16 for 114 (8 for 48 and 8 for 66)
		G Burton at Sheffield, 1888

Most 10 wickets in a match — For Yorkshire: W Rhodes 5

Against: J T Hearne 7

Northamptonshire
	For Yorkshire:	16 for 35 (8 for 18 and 8 for 17)
		W E Bowes at Kettering, 1935
	Against:	15 for 31 (7 for 22 and 8 for 9)
		G E Tribe at Northampton, 1958

Most 10 wickets in a match — For Yorkshire: W E Bowes, G G Macaulay, H Verity, A Waddington 3 each

Against: G E Tribe 3

Nottinghamshire
	For Yorkshire:	14 for 33 (8 for 12 and 6 for 21)
		R Peel at Sheffield, 1888
	Against:	14 for 94 (8 for 38 and 6 for 56)
		F Morley at Nottingham, 1878

Most 10 wickets in a match — For Yorkshire: G H Hirst 5

Against: F Morley, J C Shaw 4 each

Somerset
	For Yorkshire:	15 for 50 (9 for 22 and 6 for 28)
		R Peel at Leeds, 1895
	Against:	15 for 71 (6 for 30 and 9 for 41)
		L C Braund at Sheffield, 1902

Most 10 wickets in a match — For Yorkshire: G H Hirst 7

Against: L C Braund 3

Yorkshire versus

Surrey	*For Yorkshire:*	14 for 77 (6 for 47 and 8 for 30) E Peate at Huddersfield, 1881
	Against:	15 for 154 (7 for 55 and 8 for 99) T Richardson at Leeds, 1897
Most 10 wickets *in a match*	*For Yorkshire:* *Against:*	W Rhodes 7 G A Lohmann, T Richardson 6 each
Sussex	*For Yorkshire:*	16 for 112 (9 for 48 and 7 for 64) J H Wardle at Hull, 1954
	Against:	12 for 110 (6 for 71 and 6 for 39) G R Cox at Sheffield, 1907
Most 10 wickets *in a match*	*For Yorkshire:* *Against:*	R Peel, E Wainwright 3 each Twelve players 1 each
Warwickshire	*For Yorkshire:*	14 for 92 (9 for 43 and 5 for 49) H Verity at Leeds, 1937
	Against:	12 for 55 (5 for 21 and 7 for 34) T W Cartwright at Bradford, 1969
Most 10 wickets *in a match*	*For Yorkshire:* *Against:*	S Haigh 4 E F Field 4
Worcestershire	*For Yorkshire:*	14 for 211 (8 for 87 and 6 for 124) W Rhodes at Worcester, 1903
	Against:	13 for 76 (4 for 38 and 9 for 38) J A Cuffe at Bradford, 1907
Most 10 wickets *in a match*	*For Yorkshire:* *Against:*	S Haigh, G G Macaulay 4 each N Gifford 2
Australians	*For Yorkshire:*	13 for 149 (8 for 48 and 5 for 101) G H Hirst at Bradford, 1899
	Against:	13 for 170 (6 for 91 and 7 for 79) J M Gregory at Sheffield, 1919
Most 10 wickets *in a match*	*For Yorkshire:* *Against:*	S Haigh 2 C V Grimmett, F R Spofforth, C T B Turner, H Trumble 2 each

BEST BOWLING ANALYSES IN AN INNINGS
FOR AND AGAINST YORKSHIRE

Best For Yorkshire:
10 for 10 H Verity v Nottinghamshire at Leeds, 1932

Against Yorkshire:
10 for 37 C V Grimmett for Australians at Sheffield, 1930
(non-championship)

County Championship
10 for 51 H Howell for Warwickshire at Birmingham, 1923

Yorkshire versus:

Derbyshire	*For Yorkshire:*	10 for 47	T F Smailes at Sheffield, 1939
	Against:	9 for 27	J J Hulme at Sheffield, 1894
Most 5 wickets *in an innings*	*For Yorkshire:* *Against:*	S Haigh, E Peat, W Rhodes 11 each W Mycroft 10	

Yorkshire versus

Durham | *For Yorkshire:* | 6 for 37 | R D Stemp at Durham, 1994
| | 6 for 37 | J N Gillespie at Chester-le-Street, 2006
| *Against:* | 7 for 58 | J Wood at Leeds, 1999
Most 5 wickets | *For Yorkshire:* | D Gough and M J Hoggard 2 each
in an innings | *Against:* | G R Breese, S J E Brown, S J Harmison
| | and G Onions 2 each

Essex | *For Yorkshire:* | 9 for 28 | W Rhodes at Leyton, 1899
| *Against:* | 8 for 44 | F G Bull at Bradford, 1896
Most 5 wickets | *For Yorkshire:* | W Rhodes 18
in an innings | *Against:* | W Mead 14

Glamorgan | *For Yorkshire:* | 9 for 60 | H Verity at Swansea, 1930
| *Against:* | 9 for 43 | J S Pressdee at Swansea, 1965
Most 5 wickets | *For Yorkshire:* | H Verity 12
in an innings | *Against:* | D J Shepherd 6

Gloucestershire | *For Yorkshire:* | 9 for 25 | S Haigh at Leeds, 1912
| *Against:* | 9 for 36 | C W L Parker at Bristol, 1922
Most 5 wickets | *For Yorkshire:* | W Rhodes 22
in an innings | *Against:* | T W J Goddard 17

Hampshire | *For Yorkshire:* | 9 for 29 | A C Williams at Dewsbury, 1919
| *Against:* | 8 for 49 | O W Herman at Bournemouth, 1930
Most 5 wickets | *For Yorkshire:* | G H Hirst 10
in an innings | *Against:* | A S Kennedy 10

Kent | *For Yorkshire:* | 9 for 12 | H Verity at Sheffield, 1936
| *Against:* | 8 for 35 | A Hearne at Sheffield, 1885
Most 5 wickets | *For Yorkshire:* | W Rhodes 12
in an innings | *Against:* | A P Freeman 14

Lancashire | *For Yorkshire:* | 9 for 23 | G H Hirst at Leeds, 1910
| *Against:* | 9 for 41 | A Mold at Huddersfield, 1890
Most 5 wickets | *For Yorkshire:* | T Emmett 16
in an innings | *Against:* | J Briggs 19

Leicestershire | *For Yorkshire:* | 8 for 25 | G H Hirst at Hull, 1907
| *Against:* | 9 for 63 | C T Spencer at Huddersfield, 1954
Most 5 wickets | *For Yorkshire:* | G H Hirst 15
in an innings | *Against:* | H A Smith 7

Middlesex | *For Yorkshire:* | 9 for 45 | G H Hirst at Sheffield 1907
| *Against:* | 9 for 57 | F A Tarrant at Leeds, 1906
Most 5 wickets | *For Yorkshire:* | W Rhodes 18
in an innings | *Against:* | J T Hearne 21

Northamptonshire | *For Yorkshire:* | 9 for 37 | M A Robinson at Harrogate, 1993
| *Against:* | 9 for 30 | A E Thomas at Bradford, 1920
Most 5 wickets | *For Yorkshire:* | G G Macaulay 14
in an innings | *Against:* | G E Tribe, W Wells 7 each

Nottinghamshire | *For Yorkshire:* | 10 for 10 | H Verity at Leeds, 1932
| *Against:* | 8 for 32 | J C Shaw at Nottingham, 1865
Most 5 wickets | *For Yorkshire:* | W Rhodes 17
in an innings | *Against:* | F Morley 17

BEST BOWLING ANALYSES IN AN INNINGS
FOR AND AGAINST YORKSHIRE *(continued)*

Yorkshire versus

Somerset	*For Yorkshire:*	10 for 35	A Drake at Weston-super-Mare, 1914
	Against:	9 for 41	L C Braund at Sheffield, 1902
Most 5 wickets	*For Yorkshire:*	G H Hirst 16	
in an innings	*Against:*	E J Tyler 8	
Surrey	*For Yorkshire:*	8 for 5	E Peate at Holbeck, 1883
	Against:	9 for 47	T Richardson at Sheffield, 1893
Most 5 wickets	*For Yorkshire:*	W Rhodes 17	
in an innings	*Against:*	W Southerton 19	
Sussex	*For Yorkshire:*	9 for 48	J H Wardle at Hull, 1954
	Against:	9 for 34	James Langridge at Sheffield, 1934
Most 5 wickets	*For Yorkshire:*	W Rhodes 14	
in an innings	*Against:*	G R Cox, J A Snow 6 each	
Warwickshire	*For Yorkshire:*	10 for 36	H Verity at Leeds, 1930
	Against:	10 for 51	H Howell at Birmingham, 1923
Most 5 wickets	*For Yorkshire:*	W Rhodes 18	
in an innings	*Against:*	E F Field, W E Hollies 7 each	
Worcestershire	*For Yorkshire:*	9 for 41	G H Hirst at Worcester, 1911
	Against:	9 for 38	J A Cuffe at Bradford, 1907
Most 5 wickets	*For Yorkshire:*	S Haigh, W Rhodes 11 each	
in an innings	*Against:*	R T D Perks 7	
Australians	*For Yorkshire:*	9 for 76	W Ringrose at Bradford, 1905
	Against:	10 for 37	C V Grimmett at Sheffield, 1930
Most 5 wickets	*For Yorkshire:*	R Peel 7	
in an innings	*Against:*	F R Spofforth 7	

HAT-TRICKS

G Freeman v. Lancashire at Holbeck, 1868
G Freeman v. Middlesex at Sheffield, 1868
A Hill v. United South of England XI at Bradford, 1874
A Hill v. Surrey at The Oval, 1880
E Peate v. Kent at Sheffield, 1882
G Ulyett v. Lancashire at Sheffield, 1883
E Peate v. Gloucestershire at Moreton-in-Marsh, 1884
W Fletcher v. MCC at Lord's, 1892
E Wainwright v. Sussex at Dewsbury, 1894
G H Hirst v. Leicestershire at Leicester, 1895
J T Brown v. Derbyshire at Derby, 1896
R Peel v. Kent at Halifax, 1897
S Haigh v. Derbyshire at Bradford, 1897
W Rhodes v. Kent at Canterbury, 1901
S Haigh v. Somerset at Sheffield, 1902
H A Sedgwick v. Worcestershire at Hull, 1906
G Deyes v. Gentlemen of Ireland at Bray, 1907
G H Hirst v. Leicestershire at Hull, 1907
J T Newstead v. Worcestershire at Bradford, 1907
S Haigh v. Lancashire at Manchester, 1909
M W Booth v. Worcestershire at Bradford, 1911
A Drake v. Essex at Huddersfield, 1912

HAT-TRICKS *(Continued)*

M W Booth v. Essex at Leyton, 1912
A Drake v. Derbyshire at Chesterfield, 1914 (4 in 4)
W Rhodes v. Derbyshire at Derby, 1920
A Waddington v. Northamptonshire at Northampton, 1920 (4 in 5)
G G Macaulay v. Warwickshire at Birmingham, 1923
E Robinson v. Sussex at Hull, 1928
G G Macaulay v. Leicestershire at Hull, 1930
E Robinson v. Kent at Gravesend, 1930
H Verity v. Nottinghamshire at Leeds, 1932
H Fisher v. Somerset at Sheffield, 1932 (all lbw)
G G Macaulay v. Glamorgan at Cardiff, 1933
G G Macaulay v. Lancashire at Manchester, 1933 (4 in 5)
M.Leyland v. Surrey at Sheffield, 1935
E Robinson v. Kent at Leeds, 1939
A Coxon v. Worcestershire at Leeds, 1946
F S Trueman v. Nottinghamshire at Nottingham, 1951
F S Trueman v. Nottinghamshire at Scarborough, 1955
R Appleyard v. Gloucestershire at Sheffield, 1956
F S.Trueman v. MCC at Lord's, 1958
D Wilson v. Nottinghamshire at Middlesbrough, 1959
F S Trueman v. Nottinghamshire at Bradford, 1963
D Wilson v. Nottinghamshire at Worksop, 1966
D Wilson v. Kent at Harrogate, 1966
G A Cope v. Essex at Colchester, 1970
A L Robinson v. Nottinghamshire at Worksop, 1974
P W Jarvis v. Derbyshire at Chesterfield, 1985
P J Hartley v. Derbyshire at Chesterfield, 1995 (4 in 5)
D Gough v. Kent at Leeds, 1995 (4 in 5)
C White v. Gloucestershire at Gloucester, 1998
M J Hoggard v. Sussex at Hove, 2009

52 Hat-Tricks: G G Macaulay and F S Trueman took four each, S Haigh and D Wilson three each. There have been seven hat-tricks versus Kent and Nottinghamshire, and six versus Derbyshire.

200 WICKETS IN A SEASON

Bowler	Season	Overs	Maidens	Runs	Wickets	Average
W Rhodes	1900	1366.4	411	3054	240	12.72
W Rhodes	1901	1455.3	474	3497	233	15.00
G H Hirst	1906	1111.1	262	3089	201	15.36
G G Macaulay	1925	1241.2	291	2986	200	14.93
R Appleyard†	1951	1323.2	394	2829	200	14.14

† First full season in First-Class cricket.

100 WICKETS IN A SEASON

Bowler		Wickets taken	Wickets taken	Wickets taken
R Appleyard	(3)	200 in 1951	141 in 1954	110 in 1956
A Booth	(1)	111 in 1946	—	—
M W Booth	(3)	104 in 1912	167 in 1913	155 in 1914
W E Bowes	(8)	117 in 1931	168 in 1932	130 in 1933
		109 in 1934	154 in 1935	113 in 1936
		106 in 1938	107 in 1939	—

100 WICKETS IN A SEASON *(Continued)*

Bowler		*Wickets taken*	*Wickets taken*	*Wickets taken*
D B Close	(2)	105 in 1949	114 in 1952	—
A Coxon	(2)	101 in 1949	129 in 1950	—
A Drake	(2)	115 in 1913	158 in 1914	—
T Emmett	(1)	112 in 1886	—	—
S Haigh	(10)	100 in 1898	160 in 1900	154 in 1902
		102 in 1903	118 in 1904	118 in 1905
		161 in 1906	120 in 1909	100 in 1911
		125 in 1912	—	—
G H Hirst	(12)	150 in 1895	171 in 1901	121 in 1903
		114 in 1904	100 in 1905	201 in 1906
		169 in 1907	164 in 1908	138 in 1910
		130 in 1911	113 in 1912	100 in 1913
R Illingworth	(5)	103 in 1956	120 in 1961	116 in 1962
		122 in 1964	105 in 1968	—
R Kilner	(4)	107 in 1922	143 in 1923	134 in 1924
		123 in 1925	—	—
G G Macaulay	(10)	101 in 1921	130 in 1922	163 in 1923
		184 in 1924	200 in 1925	133 in 1926
		130 in 1927	117 in 1928	102 in 1929
		141 in 1933	—	—
J T Newstead	(1)	131 in 1908	—	—
A G Nicholson	(2)	113 in 1966	101 in 1967	—
E Peate	(3)	131 in 1880	133 in 1881	165 in 1882
R Peel	(6)	118 in 1888	132 in 1890	106 in 1892
		134 in 1894	155 in 1895	108 in 1896
W Rhodes	(22)	141 in 1898	153 in 1899	240 in 1900
		233 in 1901	174 in 1902	169 in 1903
		118 in 1904	158 in 1905	113 in 1906
		164 in 1907	100 in 1908	115 in 1909
		105 in 1911	117 in 1914	155 in 1919
		156 in 1920	128 in 1921	100 in 1922
		127 in 1923	102 in 1926	111 in 1928
		100 in 1929	—	—
E Robinson	(1)	111 in 1928	—	—
E P Robinson	(4)	104 in 1938	120 in 1939	149 in 1946
		108 in 1947	—	—
T F Smailes	(4)	105 in 1934	125 in 1936	120 in 1937
		104 in 1938	—	—
F S Trueman	(8)	129 in 1954	140 in 1955	104 in 1959
		150 in 1960	124 in 1961	122 in 1962
		121 in 1965	107 in 1966	—
H Verity	(9)	169 in 1931	146 in 1932	168 in 1933
		100 in 1934	199 in 1935	185 in 1936
		185 in 1937	137 in 1938	189 in 1939
A Waddington	(5)	100 in 1919	140 in 1920	105 in 1921
		132 in 1922	105 in 1925	—
E Wainwright	(3)	114 in 1893	157 in 1894	102 in 1896
J H Wardle	(10)	148 in 1948	100 in 1949	172 in 1950
		122 in 1951	169 in 1952	126 in 1953
		122 in 1954	159 in 1955	146 in 1956
		106 in 1957	—	—
D Wilson	(3)	100 in 1966	107 in 1968	101 in 1969

BOWLERS WHO HAVE TAKEN OVER 500 WICKETS

Player	M	Runs	Wkts	Av'ge	Best
W Rhodes	883	57634	3598	16.01	9 for 28
G H Hirst	717	44716	2481	18.02	9 for 23
S Haigh	513	29289	1876	15.61	9 for 25
G G Macaulay	445	30554	1774	17.22	8 for 21
F S Trueman	459	29890	1745	17.12	8 for 28
H Verity	278	21353	1558	13.70	10 for 10
J H Wardle	330	27917	1539	18.13	9 for 25
R Illingworth	496	26806	1431	18.73	9 for 42
W E Bowes	301	21227	1351	15.71	9 for 121
R Peel	318	20638	1311	15.74	9 for 22
T Emmett	299	15465	1216	12.71	9 for 23
D Wilson	392	22626	1104	20.49	7 for 19
P Carrick	425	30530	1018	29.99	8 for 33
E Wainwright	352	17744	998	17.77	9 for 66
D B Close	536	23489	967	24.29	8 for 41
Emmott Robinson	413	19645	893	21.99	9 for 36
A G Nicholson	282	17296	876	19.74	9 for 62
R Kilner	365	14855	857	17.33	8 for 26
A Waddington	255	16203	835	19.40	8 for 34
T F Smailes	262	16593	802	20.68	10 for 47
E Peate	154	9986	794	12.57	8 for 5
Ellis P Robinson	208	15141	735	20.60	8 for 35
C M Old	222	13409	647	20.72	7 for 20
R Appleyard	133	9903	642	15.42	8 for 76
W Bates	202	10692	637	16.78	8 for 21
G A Cope	230	15627	630	24.80	8 for 73
P J Hartley	195	17438	579	30.11	9 for 41
A Sidebottom	216	13852	558	24.82	8 for 72
M W Booth	144	11017	557	19.17	8 for 47
A Hill	140	7002	542	12.91	7 for 14
Hon F S Jackson	207	9690	506	19.15	7 for 42

BOWLERS UNCHANGED IN A MATCH

(IN WHICH THE OPPONENTS WERE DISMISSED TWICE)

**There have been 31 instances. The first and most recent are listed below.
A complete list is to be found in the 2008 edition.**

First: L Greenwood (11 for 71) and G Freeman (8 for 73) v. Surrey
at The Oval, 1867
Yorkshire won by an innings and 111 runs

Most Recent: E Robinson (8 for 65) and G G Macaulay (12 for 50) v. Worcestershire
at Leeds, 1927
Yorkshire won by an innings and 106 runs

FIELDERS (IN MATCHES FOR YORKSHIRE)

MOST CATCHES IN AN INNINGS

6	E P Robinson v. Leicestershire at Bradford, 1938
5	J Tunnicliffe v. Leicestershire at Leeds, 1897
5	J Tunnicliffe v. Leicestershire at Leicester, 1900
5	J Tunnicliffe v. Leicestershire at Scarborough, 1901
5	A B Sellers v. Essex at Leyton, 1933
5	D Wilson v. Surrey at The Oval, 1969
5	R G Lumb v. Gloucestershire at Middlesbrough, 1972

MOST CATCHES IN A MATCH

7	J Tunnicliffe v. Leicestershire at Leeds, 1897
7	J Tunnicliffe v. Leicestershire at Leicester, 1900
7	A B Sellers v Essex at Leyton, 1933
7	E P Robinson v. Leicestershire at Bradford, 1938

MOST CATCHES IN A SEASON

70	J Tunnicliffe in 1901
70	P J Sharpe in 1962
61	J Tunnicliffe in 1895
60	J Tunnicliffe in 1904
59	J Tunnicliffe in 1896
57	J V Wilson in 1955
54	J V Wilson in 1961
53	J V Wilson in 1957
51	J V Wilson in 1951

MOST CATCHES IN A CAREER

665	J Tunnicliffe (1.40 per match)
586	W Rhodes (0.66 per match)
564	D B Close (1.05 per match)
525	P J Sharpe (1.27 per match)
520	J V Wilson (1.09 per match)
518	G H Hirst (0.72 per match)

WICKET-KEEPERS IN MATCHES FOR YORKSHIRE

MOST DISMISSALS IN AN INNINGS

7	(7ct)	D L Bairstow v. Derbyshire at Scarborough, 1982
6	(6ct)	J Hunter v. Gloucestershire at Gloucester, 1887
6	(5ct,1st)	D Hunter v. Surrey at Sheffield, 1891
6	(6ct)	D Hunter v. Middlesex at Leeds, 1909
6	(2ct,4st)	W R Allen v. Sussex at Hove, 1921
6	(5ct,1st)	J G Binks v. Lancashire at Leeds, 1962
6	(6ct)	D L Bairstow v. Lancashire at Manchester, 1971
6	(6ct)	D L Bairstow v. Warwickshire at Bradford, 1978
6	(5ct,1st)	D L Bairstow v. Lancashire at Leeds, 1980
6	(6ct)	D L Bairstow v. Derbyshire at Chesterfield, 1984
6	(6ct)	R J Blakey v. Sussex at Eastbourne, 1990
6	(5ct,1st)	R J Blakey v. Gloucestershire at Cheltenham, 1992
6	(5ct,1st)	R J Blakey v. Glamorgan at Cardiff, 1994
6	(6ct)	R J Blakey v. Glamorgan at Leeds, 2003
6	(6ct)	G L Brophy v. Durham at Chester-le-Street, 2009
6	(6ct)	J M Bairstow v. Middlesex at Leeds, 2013

MOST DISMISSALS IN A MATCH

11	(11ct)	D L Bairstow v. Derbyshire at Scarborough, 1982
		(Equalled World Record)
9	(9ct)	J.Hunter v. Gloucestershire at Gloucester, 1887
9	(8ct,1st)	A Dolphin v. Derbyshire at Bradford, 1919
9	(9ct)	D L Bairstow v. Lancashire at Manchester, 1971
9	(9ct)	R J Blakey v. Sussex at Eastbourne, 1990
8	(2ct,6st)	G Pinder v. Lancashire at Sheffield, 1872
8	(2ct,6st)	D Hunter v. Surrey at Bradford, 1898
8	(7ct,1st)	A Bairstow v. Cambridge University at Cambridge, 1899
8	(8ct)	A Wood v. Northamptonshire at Huddersfield, 1932
8	(8ct)	D L Bairstow v. Lancashire at Leeds, 1978
8	(7ct,1st)	D L Bairstow v. Derbyshire at Chesterfield, 1984
8	(6ct,2st)	D L Bairstow v. Derbyshire at Chesterfield, 1985
8	(8ct)	R J Blakey v. Hampshire at Southampton, 1989
8	(8ct)	R J Blakey v. Northamptonshire at Harrogate, 1993
8	(8ct)	A J Hodd v. Glamorgan at Leeds, 2012
8	(8ct)	J M Bairstow v. Middlesex at Leed, 2013

MOST DISMISSALS IN A SEASON MOST DISMISSALS IN A CAREER

107	(96ct,11st)	J G Binks, 1960	1186	(863ct,323st) D Hunter (2.29 per match)
94	(81ct,13st)	JG Binks, 1961	1044	(872ct,172st) J G Binks (2.12 per match)
89	(75ct,14st)	A Wood, 1934	1038	(907ct,131st) D L Bairstow (2.41 per match)
88	(80ct,8st)	J G Binks, 1963	855	(612ct,243st) A Wood (2.09 per match)
86	(70ct,16st)	J G Binks, 1962	829	(569ct,260st) A Dolphin (1.94 per match)
82	(52ct,30st)	A Dolphin, 1919	824	(768ct, 56st) R J Blakey (2.43 per match)
80	(57ct,23st)	A. Wood, 1935		

YORKSHIRE PLAYERS WHO HAVE COMPLETED THE "DOUBLE"

(all First-Class matches)

Player	Year	Runs	Average	Wickets	Average
M W Booth (1)	1913	1,228	27.28	181	18.46
D B Close (2)	†1949	1,098	27.45	113	27.87
	1952	1,192	33.11	114	24.08
A Drake (1)	1913	1,056	23.46	116	16.93
S Haigh (1)	1904	1,055	26.37	121	19.85
G H Hirst (14)	1896	1,122	28.20	104	21.64
	1897	1,535	35.69	101	23.22
	1901	1,950	42.39	183	16.38
	1903	1,844	47.28	128	14.94
	1904	2,501	54.36	132	21.09
	1905	2,266	53.95	110	19.94
	††1906	2,385	45.86	208	16.50
	1907	1,344	28.38	188	15.20
	1908	1,598	38.97	114	14.05
	1909	1,256	27.30	115	20.05
	1910	1,840	32.85	164	14.79
	1911	1,789	33.12	137	20.40
	1912	1,133	25.75	118	17.37
	1913	1,540	35.81	101	20.13
R Illingworth (6)	1957	1,213	28.20	106	18.40
	1959	1,726	46.64	110	21.46
	1960	1,006	25.79	109	17.55
	1961	1,153	24.53	128	17.90
	1962	1,612	34.29	117	19.45
	1964	1,301	37.17	122	17.45
F S Jackson (1)	1898	1,566	41.21	104	15.67
R Kilner (4)	1922	1,198	27.22	122	14.73
	1923	1,404	32.24	158	12.91
	1925	1,068	30.51	131	17.92
	1926	1,187	37.09	107	22.52
R Peel (1)	1896	1,206	30.15	128	17.50
W Rhodes (16)	1903	1,137	27.07	193	14.57
	1904	1,537	35.74	131	21.59
	1905	1,581	35.93	182	16.95
	1906	1,721	29.16	128	23.57
	1907	1,055	22.93	177	15.57
	1908	1,673	31.56	115	16.13
	1909	2,094	40.26	141	15.89
	1911	2,261	38.32	117	24.07
	1914	1,377	29.29	118	18.27
	1919	1,237	34.36	164	14.42
	1920	1,123	28.07	161	13.18
	1921	1,474	39.83	141	13.27
	1922	1,511	39.76	119	12.19
	1923	1.321	33.02	134	11.54
	1924	1,126	26.18	109	14.46
	1926	1,132	34.30	115	14.86
T F Smailes (1)	1938	1,002	25.05	113	20.84
E Wainwright (1)	1897	1,612	35.82	101	23.06

† First season in First-Class cricket.
†† The only instance in First-Class cricket of 2,000 runs and 200 wickets in a season.

H Sutcliffe (194) and M Leyland (45) hit 102 off six consecutive overs for Yorkshire v. Essex at Scarborough in 1932.

From 1898 to 1930 inclusive, Wilfred Rhodes took no less than 4,187 wickets, and scored 39,969 runs in First-Class cricket at home and abroad, a remarkable record. He also took 100 wickets and scored 1,000 in a season 16 times, and G H Hirst 14 times.

Of players with a qualification of not less than 50 wickets, Wilfred Rhodes was first in bowling in First-Class cricket in 1900, 1901, 1919, 1920, 1922, 1923 and 1926; Schofield Haigh in 1902, 1905, 1908 and 1909; Mr E R Wilson in 1921; G G Macaulay in 1924; H Verity in 1930, 1933, 1935, 1937 and 1939; W E Bowes in 1938; A Booth in 1946; R Appleyard in 1951 and 1955, and F S Trueman in 1952 and 1963.

The highest aggregate of runs made in one season in First-Class cricket by a Yorkshire player is 3,429 by L Hutton in 1949. This total has been exceeded three times, viz: D C S Compton 3,816 and W J Edrich 3,539 in 1947, and 3,518 by T Hayward in 1906. H Sutcliffe scored 3,336 in 1932.

Three players have taken all 10 Yorkshire wickets in an innings. G Wootton, playing for All England XI at Sheffield in 1865, took all 10 wickets for 54 runs. H Howell performed the feat for Warwickshire at Edgbaston in 1923 at a cost of 51 runs; and C V Grimmett, Australia, took all 10 wickets for 37 runs at Sheffield in 1930.

The match against Sussex at Dewsbury on June 7th and 8th, 1894, was brought to a summary conclusion by a remarkable bowling performance on the part of Edward Wainwright. In the second innings of Sussex, he took the last five wickets in seven balls, including the "hat trick". In the whole match he obtained 13 wickets for only 38 runs.

M D Moxon has the unique distinction of scoring a century in each of his first two First-Class matches in Yorkshire — 116 (2nd inns.) v. Essex at Leeds and 111 (1st inns.) v. Derbyshire at Sheffield, June 1981).

In the Yorkshire v. Norfolk match — played on the Hyde Park Ground, Sheffield, on July 14th to 18th, 1834 — 851 runs were scored in the four innings, of which no fewer than 128 were extras: 75 byes and 53 wides. At that time wides were not run out, so that every wide included in the above total represents a wide actually bowled. This particular achievement has never been surpassed in the annals of county cricket.

L Hutton reached his 1,000 runs in First-Class cricket in 1949 as early as June 9th.

W Barber reached his 1,000 runs in 1934 on June 13th. P Holmes reached his 1,000 in 1925 on June 16th, as also did H Sutcliffe in 1932. J T Brown reached his 1,000 in 1899 on June 22nd. In 1905, D Denton reached his 1,000 runs on June 26th; and in 1906 G H Hirst gained the same total on June 27th.

In 1912, D Denton scored over 1,000 runs during July, while M Leyland and H Sutcliffe both scored over 1,000 runs in August 1932.

L Hutton scored over 1,000 in June and over 1,000 runs in August in 1949.

H Verity took his 100th wicket in First-Class cricket as early as June 19th in 1936 and on June 27th in 1935. In 1900, W Rhodes obtained his 100th wicket on June 21st, and again on the same date in 1901, while G H Hirst obtained his 100th wicket on June 28th, 1906.

In 1930, Yorkshiremen (H Sutcliffe and H Verity) occupied the first places by English players in the batting and the bowling averages of First-Class cricket, which is a record without precedent. H Sutcliffe was also first in the batting averages in 1931 and 1932.

G Boycott was the first player to have achieved an average of over 100 in each of two English seasons. In 1971, he scored 2,503 runs for an average of 100.12, and in 1979 he scored 1,538 runs for an average of 102.53.

FIRST-CLASS MATCHES BEGUN AND FINISHED IN ONE DAY

Yorkshire v. Somerset, at Huddersfield, July 9th, 1894.
Yorkshire v. Hampshire, at Southampton, May 27th, 1898
Yorkshire v. Worcestershire, at Bradford, May 7th, 1900

YORKSHIRE TEST CRICKETERS 1877-2014 (Correct to January 6, 2014)

Player	M.	I	NO	Runs	HS.	Av'ge.	100s	50s	Balls	R	W	Av'ge	Best	5wI	10wM	c/st
APPLEYARD, R ..1954-56	9	9	6	51	19*	17.00	—	—	1,596	554	31	17.87	5-51	1	—	4
ARMITAGE, T 1877	2	3	0	33	21	11.00	—	—	12	15	0	—	—	—	—	0
ATHEY, C W J ..1980-88	23	41	1	919	123	22.97	1	4	—	—	—	—	—	—	—	13
BAIRSTOW, D L ..1979-81	4	7	1	125	59	20.83	—	1	—	—	—	—	—	—	—	12/1
BAIRSTOW, J M .2012-13/14	14	24	2	593	95	26.95	—	4	—	—	—	—	—	—	—	16
BALLANCE, G S ...2013/14	1	2	0	25	18	12.50	—	—	—	—	—	—	—	—	—	0
BARBER, W 1935	2	4	0	83	44	20.75	—	—	2	0	1	0.00	1-0	—	—	1
BATES, W 1881-87	15	26	2	656	64	27.33	—	5	2,364	821	50	16.42	7-28	4	1	9
BINKS, J G 1964	2	4	0	91	55	22.75	—	1	—	—	—	—	—	—	—	8/0
BLAKEY, R J 1993	2	4	0	7	6	1.75	—	—	—	—	—	—	—	—	—	2/0
BOOTH, M W ...1913-14	2	2	0	46	32	23.00	—	—	312	130	7	18.57	4-49	—	—	0
BOWES, W E ...1932-46	15	11	5	28	10*	4.66	—	—	3,655	1,519	68	22.33	6-33	6	—	2
†BOYCOTT, G 1964-82	108	193	23	8,114	246*	47.72	22	42	944	382	7	54.57	3-47	—	—	33
BRENNAN, D V 1951	2	2	0	16	16	8.00	—	—	—	—	—	—	—	—	—	0/1
BRESNAN, T T ..2009-13/14	23	26	4	575	91	26.13	—	3	4,674	2,357	72	32.73	5-48	1	—	8
BROWN, J T 1894-99	8	16	3	470	140	36.15	1	1	35	22	0	—	—	—	—	7
†CLOSE, D B 1949-76	22	37	2	887	70	25.34	—	4	1,212	532	18	29.55	4-35	—	—	24
COPE, G A 1977-78	3	3	0	40	22	13.33	—	—	864	277	8	34.62	3-102	—	—	1
COXON, A 1948	1	2	0	19	19	9.50	—	—	378	172	3	57.33	2-90	—	—	0
DAWSON, R K J ..2002-03	7	13	3	114	19*	11.40	—	—	1,116	677	11	61.54	4-134	—	—	3
DENTON, D 1905-10	11	22	1	424	104	20.19	1	1	—	—	—	—	—	—	—	8
DOLPHIN, A 1921	1	2	0	1	1	0.50	—	—	—	—	—	—	—	—	—	1/0
EMMETT, T 1877-82	7	13	1	160	48	13.33	—	—	728	284	9	31.55	7-68	1	—	9
GIBB, P A 1938-46	8	13	0	581	120	44.69	2	3	—	—	—	—	—	—	—	3/1
GOUGH, D ...1994-2003	58	86	18	855	65	12.57	—	2	11,821	6,503	229	28.39	6-42	9	—	13

333

For England

YORKSHIRE TEST CRICKETERS 1877-2014 (Continued)

Player	M.	I	NO	Runs	HS.	Av'ge.	100s	50s	Balls	R	W	Av'ge	Best	5wI	10wM	c/st
GREENWOOD, A 1877	2	4	0	77	49	19.25	—	—	—	—	—	—	—	—	—	2
HAIGH, S 1899-1912	11	18	3	113	25	7.53	—	—	1,294	622	24	25.91	6-11	1	—	8
HAMILTON, G.M. 1999	1	2	1	0	0	0.00	—	—	90	63	0	—	—	—	—	0
HAMPSHIRE, J H ...1969-75	8	16	1	403	107	26.86	1	2	—	—	—	—	—	—	—	9
†HAWKE, LORD ...1896-99	5	8	4	55	30	7.85	—	—	—	—	—	—	—	—	—	3
HILL, A 1877	2	4	2	101	49	50.50	—	—	340	130	7	18.57	4-27	—	—	1
HIRST, G H 1897-1909	24	38	3	790	85	22.57	—	5	3,967	1,770	59	30.00	5-48	3	—	18
HOGGARD, M J ..2000-2008	67	92	27	473	38	7.27	—	—	13,909	7,564	248	30.50	7-61	7	1	24
HOLMES, P 1921-32	7	14	1	357	88	27.46	—	4	—	—	—	—	—	—	—	3
HUNTER, J 1884-85	5	7	2	93	39*	18.60	—	—	—	—	—	—	—	—	—	8/3
†HUTTON, L 1937-55	79	138	15	6,971	364	56.67	19	33	260	232	3	77.33	1-2	—	—	57
HUTTON, R A 1971	5	8	2	219	81	36.50	—	2	738	257	9	28.55	3-72	—	—	9
†ILLINGWORTH, R .1958-73	61	90	11	1,836	113	23.24	2	5	11,934	3,807	122	31.20	6-29	3	—	45
†JACKSON, Hon F S1893-1905	20	33	4	1,415	144*	48.79	5	6	1,587	799	24	33.29	5-52	1	—	10
JARVIS, P W 1988-93	9	15	2	132	29*	10.15	—	—	1,912	965	21	45.95	4-107	—	—	2
KILNER, R 1924-26	9	8	1	233	74	33.28	—	2	2,368	734	24	30.58	4-51	—	—	6
LEADBEATER, E ..1951-52	2	2	0	40	38	20.00	—	—	289	218	2	109.00	1-38	—	—	3
LEYLAND, M 1928-38	41	65	5	2,764	187	46.06	9	10	1,103	585	6	97.50	3-91	—	—	13
LOWSON, F A ...1951-55	7	13	1	245	68	18.84	—	2	—	—	—	—	—	—	—	5
McGRATH, A 2003	4	5	0	201	81	40.20	—	2	102	56	4	14.00	3-16	—	—	3
MACAULAY, G G ..1923-33	8	10	4	112	76	18.66	—	1	1,701	662	24	27.58	5-64	1	—	5
MILLIGAN, F W 1899	2	4	0	58	38	14.50	—	—	45	29	0	—	—	—	—	1
MITCHELL, A ...1933-36	6	10	0	298	72	29.80	—	2	6	4	0	—	—	—	—	9
*MITCHELL, F 1899	2	4	0	88	41	22.00	—	—	—	—	—	—	—	—	—	2
MOXON, M D ...1986-89	10	17	1	455	99	28.43	—	3	48	30	0	—	—	—	—	10

For England

YORKSHIRE TEST CRICKETERS 1877-2014 (Continued)

Player	M.	I	NO	Runs	HS.	Av'ge.	100s	50s	Balls	R	W	Av'ge	Best	5wI	10wM	c/st
OLD, CM 1972-81	46	66	9	845	65	14.82	—	2	8,858	4,020	143	28.11	7-50	4	—	22
PADGETT, D E V ...1960	2	4	0	51	31	12.75	—	—	12	8	0	—	—	—	—	0
PEATE, E 1881-86	9	14	8	70	13	11.66	—	—	2,096	682	31	22.00	6-85	2	—	2
PEEL, R 1884-96	20	33	4	427	83	14.72	—	3	5,216	1,715	101	16.98	7-31	5	1	17
RHODES, W ...1899-1930	58	98	21	2,325	179	30.19	2	11	8,231	3,425	127	26.96	8-68	6	1	60
ROOT, J E ...2012-13/14	15	29	3	955	180	36.73	2	4	372	169	3	56.33	2-9	—	—	8
SHARPE, P J 1963-69	12	21	4	786	111	46.23	1	4	—	—	—	—	—	—	—	17
SHAHZAD, A 2010	1	1	0	5	5	5.00	—	—	102	63	4	15.75	3-45	—	—	2
SIDEBOTTOM, A 1985	1	1	0	2	2	2.00	—	—	112	65	1	65.00	1-65	—	—	0
SIDEBOTTOM, R J .2001-10	22	31	11	313	31	15.65	—	—	4,812	2,231	79	28.24	7-47	5	1	5
SILVERWOOD, CEW1997-2003	6	7	3	29	10	7.25	—	—	828	444	11	40.36	5-91	1	—	2
SMAILES, T F 1946	1	1	0	25	25	25.00	—	—	120	62	3	20.66	3-44	—	—	0
SMITHSON, G A 1948	2	3	0	70	35	23.33	—	—	—	—	—	—	—	—	—	0
†STANYFORTH, R T 1927-28	4	6	1	13	6*	2.60	—	—	—	—	—	—	—	—	—	7/2
STEVENSON, G B .1980-81	2	2	1	28	27*	28.00	—	—	312	183	5	36.60	3-111	—	—	0
SUTCLIFFE, H .1924-35	54	84	9	4,555	194	60.73	16	23	—	—	—	—	—	—	—	23
TAYLOR, K ...1959-64	3	5	0	57	24	11.40	—	—	12	6	0	—	—	—	—	1
TRUEMAN, F S ...1952-65	67	85	14	981	39*	13.81	—	7	15,178	6,625	307	21.57	8-31	17	3	64
ULYETT, G 1877-90	25	39	0	949	149	24.33	1	7	2,627	1,020	50	20.40	7-36	1	—	19
†VAUGHAN M P .1999-2008	82	147	9	5,719	197	41.44	18	18	978	561	6	93.50	2-71	—	—	44
VERITY, H 1931-39	40	44	12	669	66*	20.90	—	3	11,173	3,510	144	24.37	8-43	5	2	30
WADDINGTON, A ...1920-21	2	4	0	16	7	4.00	—	—	276	119	1	119.00	1-35	—	—	1
WAINWRIGHT, E ..1893-98	5	9	0	132	49	14.66	—	—	127	73	0	—	—	—	—	2
WARDLE, J H 1948-57	28	41	8	653	66	19.78	—	2	6,597	2,080	102	20.39	7-36	5	1	12
WATSON, W 1951-59	23	37	3	879	116	25.85	2	3	—	—	—	—	—	—	—	8
WHITE, C 1994-2002	30	50	7	1,052	121	24.46	1	5	3,959	2,220	59	37.62	5-32	3	—	14

For England

Player	M.	I	NO	Runs	HS.	Av'ge.	100s	50s	Balls	R	W	Av'ge	Best	5wI	10wM	c/st
WILSON, C E M 1899	2	4	1	42	18	14.00	—	—	—	—	—	—	—	—	—	0
WILSON, D 1964-71	6	7	1	75	42	12.50	—	—	1,472	466	11	42.36	2-17	—	—	1
WILSON, E R 1921	1	2	0	10	5	5.00	—	—	123	36	3	12.00	2-28	—	—	0
WOOD, A 1938-39	4	5	1	80	53	20.00	—	1	—	—	—	—	—	—	—	10/1
†YARDLEY, N W D ...1938-50	20	34	2	812	99	25.37	—	4	1,662	707	21	33.66	3-67	—	—	14

*Also represented and captained South Africa

For South Africa

Player	M.	I	NO	Runs	HS.	Av'ge.	100s	50s	Balls	R	W	Av'ge	Best	5wI	10wM	c/st
†MITCHELL, F 1912	3	6	0	28	12	4.66	—	—	—	—	—	—	—	—	—	0

†Captained South Africa

Overseas Players

(Qualification: 20 first-class matches for Yorkshire)

For Australia

Player	M.	I	NO	Runs	HS.	Av'ge.	100s	50s	Balls	R	W	Av'ge	Best	5wI	10wM	c/st
BEVAN, M G 1994-98	18	30	3	785	91	29.07	—	6	1,285	703	29	24.24	6-82	1	1	8
GILLESPIE, J N ...1996-2006	71	93	28	1,218	201*	18.73	1	2	14,234	6,770	259	26.13	7-37	8	—	27
JAQUES, P A 2005-2008	11	19	0	902	150	47.47	3	6	—	—	—	—	—	—	—	7
LEHMANN, D S ...1999-2004	27	42	2	1,798	177	44.95	5	10	974	412	15	27.46	3-42	—	—	11

For South Africa

Player	M.	I	NO	Runs	HS.	Av'ge.	100s	50s	Balls	R	W	Av'ge	Best	5wI	10wM	c/st
RUDOLPH, J A 2003-12/13	48	83	9	2,622	222*	35.43	6	11	664	432	4	108.00	1-1	—	—	29

For West Indies

Player	M.	I	NO	Runs	HS.	Av'ge.	100s	50s	Balls	R	W	Av'ge	Best	5wI	10wM	c/st
RICHARDSON, R B 1983-84/95	86	146	12	5,949	194	44.39	16	27	66	18	0	—	—	—	—	90

CENTURIES FOR ENGLAND

C W J ATHEY (1)
123 v Pakistan at Lord's, 1987

G BOYCOTT (22)

113	v. Australia at The Oval, 1964	112	v West Indies at Port-of-Spain, 1974
117	v. South Africa at Port Elizabeth, 1965	107	v. Australia at Nottingham, 1977
246*	v. India at Leeds, 1967	191	v. Australia at Leeds, 1977
116	v. West Indies at Georgetown, 1968	100*	v. Pakistan at Hyderabad, 1978
128	v. West Indies at Manchester, 1969	131	v. New Zealand at Nottingham, 1978
106	v. West Indies at Lord's, 1969	155	v. India at Birmingham, 1979
142*	v. Australia at Sydney, 1971	125	v. India at The Oval, 1979
119*	v. Australia at Adelaide, 1971	128*	v. Australia at Lord's, 1980
121*	v. Pakistan at Lord's, 1971	104*	v. West Indies at St John's, 1981
112	v. Pakistan at Leeds, 1971	137	v. Australia at The Oval, 1981
115	v. New Zealand at Leeds, 1973	105	v. India at Delhi, 1981

J T BROWN (1)
140 v. Australia at Melbourne, 1895

D DENTON (1)
104 v. South Africa at Old Wanderers, Johannesburg, 1910

P A GIBB (2)
106 v. South Africa at Old Wanderers, Johannesburg, 1938
120 v. South Africa at Kingsmead, Durban, 1939

J H HAMPSHIRE (1)
107 v. West Indies at Lord's, 1969

L HUTTON (19)

100	v. New Zealand at Manchester, 1937	206	v. New Zealand at The Oval, 1949
100	v. Australia at Nottingham, 1938	202*	v. West Indies at The Oval, 1950
364	v. Australia at The Oval, 1938	156*	v. Australia at Adeladide, 1951
196	v. West Indies at Lord's, 1939	100	v. South Africa at Leeds, 1951
165*	v. West Indies at The Oval, 1939	150	v. India at Lord's, 1952
122*	v. Australia at Sydney, 1947	104	v. India at Manchester, 1952
100	v. South Africa at Leeds, 1947	145	v. Australia at Lord's, 1953
158	v. South Africa at Ellis Park, J'b'rg, 1948	169	v. West Indies at Georgetown, 1954
123	v. South Africa at Ellis Park, J'b'rg, 1949	205	v. West Indies at Kingston, 1954
101	v. New Zealand at Leeds, 1949		

R ILLINGWORTH (2)
113 v. West Indies at Lord's, 1969
107 v. India at Manchester, 1971

Hon. F S JACKSON (5)

103	v. Australia at The Oval, 1893	144*	v. Australia at Leeds, 1905
118	v. Australia at The Oval, 1899	113	v. Australia at Manchester, 1905
128	v. Australia at Manchester, 1902		

M LEYLAND (9)

137	v. Australia at Melbourne, 1929	161	v. South Africa at The Oval, 1935
102	v. South Africa at Lord's, 1929	126	v. Australia at Woolloongabba, Brisbane, 1936
109	v. Australia at Lord's, 1934		
153	v. Australia at Manchester, 1934	111*	v. Australia at Melbourne, 1937
110	v. Australia at The Oval, 1934	187	v. Australia at The Oval, 1938

CENTURIES FOR ENGLAND

W RHODES (2)
179 v. Australia at Melbourne, 1912
152 v. South Africa at Old Wanderers, Johannesburg, 1913

P J SHARPE (1)
111 v. New Zealand at Nottingham, 1969

H SUTCLIFFE (16)

122	v. South Africa at Lord's, 1924	114	v. South Africa at Birmingham, 1929
115	v. Australia at Sydney, 1924	100	v. South Africa at Lord's, 1929
176	v. Australia at Melbourne, 1925 (1st Inns)	104	v. South Africa at The Oval, 1929 (1st inns)
127	v. Australia at Melbourne, 1925 (2nd Inns)	109*	v. South Africa at The Oval, 1929 (2nd inns)
143	v. Australia at Melbourne, 1925	161	v. Australia at The Oval, 1930
161	v. Australia at The Oval, 1926	117	v. New Zealand at The Oval, 1931
102	v. South Africa at Old Wanderers, Jbg.1927	109*	v. New Zealand at Manchester, 1931
135	v. Australia at Melbourne, 1929	194	v. Australia at Sydney, 1932

G ULYETT (1)
149 v. Australia at Melbourne, 1882

M P VAUGHAN (18)

120	v. Pakistan at Manchester, 2001	105	v. Sri Lanka at Kandy, 2003
115	v. Sri Lanka at Lord's, 2002	140	v. West Indies at Antigua, 2004
100	v. India at Lord's, 2002	103	v. West Indies at Lord's (1st inns) 2004
197	v. India at Nottingham, 2002	101*	v. West Indies at Lord's (2nd inns) 2004
195	v. India at The Oval, 2002	120	v. Bangladesh at Lord's, 2005
177	v. Australia at Adelaide, 2002	166	v. Australia at Manchester,2005
145	v. Australia at Melbourne, 2002	103	v. West Indies at Leeds, 2007
183	v. Australia at Sydney, 2003	124	v. India at Nottingham, 2007
156	v. South Africa at Birmingham, 2003	106	v. New Zealand at Lord's, 2008

W WATSON (2)
109 v. Australia at Lord's, 1953   116 v. West Indies at Kingston, 1954

C WHITE (1)
121 v. India at Ahmedabad, 2001

Summary of the Centuries

versus	Total	In England	Away
Australia	40	21	19
Bangladesh	1	1	0
India	12	10	2
New Zealand	9	9	—
Pakistan	5	4	1
South Africa	18	10	8
Sri Lanka	2	1	1
West Indies	17	10	7
Totals	104	66	38

For Australia

J N GILLESPIE (1)
201* v. Bangladesh at Chittagong, 2006

P A JAQUES (3)
100 v. Sri Lanka at Brisbane, 2007   108 v. West Indies at Bridgetown, 2008
150 v. Sri Lanka at Hobart, 2007

D S LEHMANN (5)

160	v. West Indies at Port of Spain, 2003	129	v. Sri Lanka at Galle, 2004
110	v. Bangladesh at Darwin, 2003	153	v. Sri Lanka at Columbo, 2004
177	v. Bangladesh at Cairns, 2003		

10 WICKETS IN A MATCH FOR ENGLAND

W BATES (1)
14 for 102 (7 for 28 and 7 for 74) v. Australia at Melbourne, 1882

M J HOGGARD (1)
12 for 205 (5 for 144 and 7 for 61) v. South Africa at Johannesburg, 2005

R PEEL (1)
11 for 68 (7 for 31 and 4 for 37) v. Australia at Mancester, 1888

Note: The scorebook for the Australia v. England Test match at Sydney in February 1888
shows that the final wicket to fall was taken by W Attewell, and not by Peel
Peel therefore took 9, and not 10 wickets, in the match
His career totals have been amended to take account of this alteration

W RHODES (1)
15 for 124 (7 for 56 and 8 for 68) v. Australia at Melbourne, 1904

R J SIDEBOTTOM (1)
10 for 139 (4 for 90 and 6 for 49) v. New Zealand at Hamilton, 2008

F S TRUEMAN (3)
11 for 88 (5 for 58 and 6 for 30) v. Australia at Leeds, 1961
11 for 152 (6 for 100 and 5 for 52) v. West Indies at Lord's, 1963*
12 for 119 (5 for 75 and 7 for 44) v. West Indies at Birmingham, 1963*
consecutive Tests

H VERITY (2)
11 for 153 (7 for 49 and 4 for 104) v. India at Chepauk, Madras, 1934
15 for 104 (7 for 61 and 8 for 43) v. Australia at Lord's, 1934

J H WARDLE (1)
12 for 89 (5 for 53 and 7 for 36) v. South Africa at Cape Town, 1957

Summary of Ten Wickets in a Match

versus	Total	In England	Away
Australia	5	3	2
India	1	—	1
New Zealand	1	—	1
Pakistan	—	—	—
South Africa	2	—	2
Sri Lanka	—	—	—
West Indies	2	2	—
Totals	11	5	6

For Australia

M G BEVAN (1)
10 for 113 (4 for 31and 6 for 82) v. West Indies at Adelaide, 1997

5 WICKETS IN AN INNINGS FOR ENGLAND

R APPLEYARD (1)
5 for 51 v. Pakistan at Nottingham, 1954

W BATES (4)
7 for 28 v. Australia at Melbourne, 1882   5 for 31 v. Australia at Adelaide, 1884
7 for 74 v. Australia at Melbourne, 1882   5 for 24 v. Australia at Sydney, 1885

5 WICKETS IN AN INNINGS FOR ENGLAND *(Continued)*

W E BOWES (6)

6 for 34	v. New Zealand at Auckland, 1933	5 for 100	v. South Africa at Manchester, 1935
6 for 142	v. Australia at Leeds, 1934*	5 for 49	v. Australia at The Oval, 1938
5 for 55	v. Australia at The Oval, 1934*	6 for 33	v. West Indies at Manchester, 1939

*consecutive Test matches

T T BRESNAN (1))

5 for 48 v. India at Nottingham, 2011

T EMMETT (1)

7 for 68 v. Australia at Melbourne, 1879

D GOUGH (9)

6 for 49	v. Australia at Sydney, 1995	5 for 70	v. South Africa at Johannesburg, 1999
5 for 40	v.New Zealand at Wellington, 1997	5 for 109	v. West Indies at Birmingham, 2000
5 for 149	v. Australia at Leeds, 1997	5 for 61	v. Pakistan at Lord's, 2001
6 for 42	v.South Africa at Leeds, 1998	5 for 103	v. Australia at Leeds, 2001
5 for 96	v. Australia at Melbourne, 1998		

S HAIGH (1)

6 for 11 v. South Africa at Cape Town, 1909

G H HIRST (3)

5 for 77	v. Australia at The Oval, 1902	5 for 58	v. Australia at Birmingham, 1909
5 for 48	v. Australia at Melbourne, 1904		

M J HOGGARD (7)

7 for 63	v. New Zealand at Christchurch, 2002	5 for 73	v. Bangladesh at Chester-le-Street, 2005
5 for 92	v. Sri Lanka at Birmingham, 2002	6 for 57	v. India at Nagpur, 2006
5 for 144	v. South Africa at Johannesburg, 2005*	7 for 109	v. Australia at Adelaide, 2006
7 for 61	v. South Africa at Johannesburg, 2005*		

*Consecutive Test innings

R ILLINGWORTH (3)

6 for 29	v. India at Lord's, 1967	5 for 70	v. India at The Oval, 1971
6 for 87	v. Australia at Leeds, 1968		

Hon F S JACKSON (1)

5 for 52 v. Australia at Nottingham, 1905

G G MACAULAY (1)

5 for 64 v. South Africa at Cape Town, 1923

C M OLD (4)

5 for 113	v. New Zealand at Lord's, 1973	6 for 54	v. New Zealand at Wellington, 1978
5 for 21	v. India at Lord's, 1974	7 for 50	v. Pakistan at Birmingham, 1978

E PEATE (2)

5 for 43 v. Australia at Sydney, 1882   6 for 85 v. Australia at Lord's, 1884

R PEEL (5)

5 for 51 v. Australia at Adelaide, 1884		6 for 67 v. Australia at Sydney, 1894
5 for 18 v. Australia at Sydney, 1888		6 for 23 v. Australia at The Oval, 1896
7 for 31 v. Australia at Manchester, 1888		

W RHODES (6)

7 for 17 v. Australia at Birmingham, 1902	7 for 56 v. Australia at Melbourne, 1904*
5 for 63 v. Australia at Sheffield, 1902	8 for 68 v. Australia at Melbourne, 1904*
5 for 94 v. Australia at Sydney, 1903*	5 for 83 v. Australia at Manchester, 1909

*consecutive Test innings

5 WICKETS IN AN INNINGS FOR ENGLAND *(Continued)*

C E W SILVERWOOD (1)

5 for 91 v. South Africa, at Cape Town, 2000

R J SIDEBOTTOM (5)

5 for 88	v. West Indies at Chester-le-Street, 2007	7 for 47	v. New Zealand at Napier, 2008
6 for 49	v. New Zealand at Hamilton, 2008	6 for 47	v. New Zealand at Nottingham, 2008
5 for 105	v. New Zealand at Wellington, 2008		

F S TRUEMAN (17)

8 for 31	v. India at Manchester, 1952	6 for 31	v. Pakistan at Lord's, 1962
5 for 48	v. India at The Oval, 1952	5 for 62	v. Australia at Melbourne, 1963
5 for 90	v. Australia at Lord's, 1956	7 for 75	v. New Zealand at Christchurch, 1963
5 for 63	v. West Indies at Nottingham, 1957	6 for 100	v. West Indies at Lord's, 1963*
5 for 31	v. New Zealand at Birmingham, 1958	5 for 52	v. West Indies at Lord's, 1963*
5 for 35	v. West Indies at Port-of-Spain, 1960	5 for 75	v. West Indies at Birmingham, 1963*
5 for 27	v. South Africa at Nottingham, 1960	7 for 44	v. West Indies at Birmingham, 1963*
5 for 58	v. Australia at Leeds, 1961*	5 for 48	v. Australia at Lord's, 1964
6 for 30	v. Australia at Leeds, 1961*		

G ULYETT (1)

7 for 36 v. Australia at Lord's, 1884

H VERITY (5)

5 for 33	v. Australia at Sydney, 1933	8 for 43	v. Australia at Lord's, 1934*
7 for 49	v. India at Chepauk, Madras, 1934	5 for 70	v. South Africa at Cape Town, 1939
7 for 61	v. Australia at Lord's, 1934*		

J H WARDLE (5)

7 for 56	v. Pakistan at The Oval, 1954	7 for 36	v. South Africa at Cape Town, 1957*
5 for 79	v. Australia at Sydney, 1955	5 for 61	v. South Africa at Kingsmead,
5 for 53	v. South Africa at Cape Town, 1957*		Durban, 1957*

C WHITE (3)

5 for 57	v. West Indies at Leeds, 2000	5 for 32	v. West Indies at The Oval, 2000
	5 for 127 v. Australia at Perth, 2002		

*consecutive Test innings

Summary of Five Wickets in an Innings

versus	Total	In England	Away
Australia	42	22	20
Bangladesh	1	1	—
India	7	5	2
India	8	6	2
New Zealand	11	3	8
Pakistan	5	5	—
South Africa	13	3	10
Sri Lanka	1	1	—
West Indies	11	10	1
Totals	92	51	41

For Australia

M G BEVAN (1)

6 for 82 v. West Indies at Adelaide, 1997

5 WICKETS IN AN INNINGS

J N GILLESPIE (8)

5 for 54	v.	South Africa at Port Elizabeth, 1997
7 for 37	v.	England at Leeds, 1997
5 for 88	v.	England at Perth, 1998
5 for 89	v.	West Indies at Adelaide, 2000
6 for 40	v.	West Indies at Melbourne, 2000
5 for 53	v.	England at Lord's, 2001
5 for 39	v.	West Indies at Georgetown, 2003
5 for 56	v.	India at Nagpur, 2004

HAT-TRICKS

W Bates v. Australia at Melbourne, 1882
D Gough v. Australia at Sydney, 1998
M J Hoggard v. West Indies at Bridgetown, 2004
R J Sidebottom v. New Zealand at Hamilton, 2008

FOUR WICKETS IN FIVE BALLS

C M Old v. Pakistan at Birmingham, 1978

THREE WICKETS IN FOUR BALLS

R Appleyard v. New Zealand at Auckland, 1955
D Gough v. Pakistan at Lord's, 2001

YORKSHIRE PLAYERS WHO PLAYED ALL THEIR TEST CRICKET AFTER LEAVING YORKSHIRE

For England

Player	M.	I	NO	Runs	HS.	Av'ge.	100s	50s	Balls	R	W	Av'ge	Best	5wI	10wM	c/st
BALDERSTONE, J C 1976	2	4	0	39	35	9.75	—	—	96	80	1	80.00	1:80	—	—	1
BATTY, G J 2003	4	7	1	136	38	22.66	—	—	992	504	8	63.00	3:55	—	—	0
BIRKENSHAW, J ...1973-74	5	7	1	148	64	21.14	—	1	1,017	469	13	36.07	5:57	1	—	3
BOLUS, J B 1963-64	7	12	0	496	88	41.33	—	4	18	16	0	—	—	—	—	2
†PARKIN, C H 1920-24	10	16	3	160	36	12.30	—	—	2,095	1,128	32	35.25	5:38	2	—	3
RHODES, S J 1994-95	11	17	5	294	65*	24.50	—	1	—	—	—	—	—	—	—	46/3
†SUGG, F H 1888	2	2	0	55	31	27.50	—	—	—	—	—	—	—	—	—	0
WARD, A 1893-95	7	13	0	487	117	37.46	1	3	98	50	0	—	—	—	—	1
WOOD, B 1972-78	12	21	0	454	90	21.61	—	2	—	—	—	—	—	—	—	6

For South Africa

Player	M.	I	NO	Runs	HS.	Av'ge.	100s	50s	Balls	R	W	Av'ge	Best	5wI	10wM	c/st
THORNTON, P G 1902	1	1	1	1	1*	—	—	—	24	20	1	20.00	1:20	—	—	1

†Born outside Yorkshire

CENTURIES FOR ENGLAND

A WARD (1)
117 v. Australia at Sydney, 1894

5 WICKETS IN AN INNINGS FOR ENGLAND

J BIRKENSHAW (1)
5 : 57 v. Pakistan at Karachi, 1973

C H PARKIN (2)
5 : 60 v. Australia at Adelaide, 1921
5 : 38 v. Australia at Manchester, 1921

343

YORKSHIRE'S TEST CRICKET RECORDS

R APPLEYARD

Auckland 1954-55: took 3 wickets in 4 balls as New Zealand were dismissed for the lowest total in Test history (26).

C W J ATHEY

Perth 1986-87: shared an opening stand of 223 with B C Broad – England's highest for any wicket at the WACA Ground.

W BATES

Melbourne 1882-83 (Second Test): achieved the first hat-trick for England when he dismissed P S McDonnell, G Giffen and G J Bonnor in Australia's first innings. Later in the match, he became the first player to score a fifty (55) and take 10 or more wickets (14 for 102) in the same Test.

W E BOWES

Melbourne 1932-33: enjoyed the unique satisfaction of bowling D G Bradman first ball in a Test match (his first ball to him in Test cricket).

G BOYCOTT

Leeds 1967: scored 246 not out off 555 balls in 573 minutes to establish the record England score against India. His first 100 took 341 minutes (316 balls) and he was excluded from the next Test as a disciplinary measure; shared in hundred partnerships for three successive wickets.

Adelaide 1970-71: with J H Edrich, became the third opening pair to share hundred partnerships in both innings of a Test against Australia.

Port-of-Spain 1973-74: first to score 99 and a hundred in the same Test.

Nottingham 1977: with A P E Knott, equalled England v. Australia sixth-wicket partnership record of 215 – the only England v. Australia stand to be equalled or broken since 1938. Batted on each day of the five-day Test (second after M L Jaisimha to achieve this feat).

Leeds 1977: first to score his 100th First Class hundred in a Test; became the fourth England player to be on the field for an entire Test.

Perth: 1978-79: eighth to score 2,000 runs for England against Australia.

Birmingham 1979: emulated K F Barrington by scoring hundreds on each of England's six current home grounds.

Perth: 1979-80: fourth to carry his bat through a completed England.

innings (third v. Australia) and the first to do so without scoring 100; first to score 99 not out in a Test.

Lord's 1981: 100th Test for England – second after M C Cowdrey (1968).

The Oval, 1981: second after Hon F S Jackson to score five hundreds v. Australia in England.

Gained three Test records from M C Cowdrey: exceeded England aggregate of 7,624 runs in 11 fewer Tests (Manchester 1981); 61st fifty – world record (The Oval 1981); 189th innings – world record (Bangalore 1981-82).

Delhi, 4.23p.m. on 23 December 1981: passed G St.A Sobers's world Test record of 8,032 runs, having played 30 more innings and batted over 451 hours (cf. 15 complete five-day Tests); his 22nd hundred equalled the England record.

J T BROWN

Melbourne 1894-95: his 28-minute fifty remains the fastest in Test cricket, and his 95-minute hundred was a record until 1897-98; his third-wicket stand of 210 with A Ward set a Test record for any wicket.

YORKSHIRE'S TEST CRICKET RECORDS *(Continued)*

D B CLOSE

Manchester 1949: at 18 years 149 days he became – and remains – the youngest to represent England.

Melbourne 1950-51: became the youngest (19 years 301 days) to represent England against Australia.

T EMMETT

Melbourne 1878-79: first England bowler to take seven wickets in a Test innings.

P A GIBB

Johannesburg 1938-39: enjoyed a record England debut, scoring 93 and 106 as well as sharing second-wicket stands of 184 and 168 with E Paynter.

Durban 1938-39: shared record England v. South Africa second-wicket stand of 280 with W J Edrich, his 120 in 451 minutes including only two boundaries.

D GOUGH

Sydney 1998-99: achieved the 23rd hat-trick in Test cricket (ninth for England and first for England v. Australia since 1899).

Lord's 2001: took 3 wickets in 4 balls v. Pakistan.

S HAIGH

Cape Town 1898-99: bowled unchanged through the second innings with A E Trott, taking 6 for 11 as South Africa were dismissed for 35 in the space of 114 balls.

J H HAMPSHIRE

Lord's 1969: became the first England player to score 100 at Lord's on his debut in Tests.

A HILL

Melbourne 1876-77: took the first wicket to fall in Test cricket when he bowled N Thompson, and held the first catch when he dismissed T P Horan.

G H HIRST

The Oval 1902: helped to score the last 15 runs in a match-winning tenth-wicket partnership with W Rhodes.

Birmingham 1909: shared all 20 Australian wickets with fellow left-arm spinner C Blythe (11 for 102).

M J HOGGARD

Bridgetown 2004: became the third Yorkshire player to take a hat-trick in Test cricket (see W Bates and D Gough). It was the 10th hat-trick for England and the third for England versus West Indies.

L HUTTON

Nottingham 1938: scored 100 in his first Test against Australia.

The Oval 1938: his score (364) and batting time (13 hours 17 minutes – the longest innings in English First-Class cricket) remain England records, and were world Test records until 1958. It remains the highest Test score at The Oval. His stand of 382 with M Leyland is the England second-wicket record in all Tests and the highest for any wicket against Australia. He also shared a record England v. Australia sixth-wicket stand of 216 with J Hardstaff Jr. – the first instance of a batsman sharing in two stands of 200 in the same Test innings. 770 runs were scored during his innings (Test record) which was England's 100th century against Australia, and contained 35 fours. England's total of 903 for 7 declared remains the Ashes Test record.

Lord's 1939: added 248 for the fourth wicket with D C S Compton in 140 minutes.

YORKSHIRE'S TEST CRICKET RECORDS *(Continued)*

L HUTTON *(Continued)*

The Oval 1939: shared (then) world-record third-wicket stand of 264 with W R Hammond, which remains the record for England v. West Indies. Hutton's last eight Tests had brought him 1,109 runs.

The Oval 1948: last out in the first innings, he was on the field for all but the final 57 minutes of the match.

Johannesburg 1948-49: shared (then) world-record first-wicket stand of 359 in 310 minutes with C Washbrook on the opening day of Test cricket at Ellis Park; it remains England's highest opening stand in all Tests.

The Oval 1950: scored England's first 200 in a home Test v. West Indies, and remains alone in carrying his bat for England against them; his 202 not out (in 470 minutes) is the highest score by an England batsman achieving this feat.

Adelaide 1950-51: only England batsman to carry his bat throughout a complete Test innings twice, and second after R Abel (1891-92) to do so for any country against Australia.

Manchester 1951: scored 98 not out, just failing to become the first to score his 100th First Class hundred in a Test match.

The Oval 1951: became the only batsman to be out 'obstructing the field' in Test cricket.

1952: first professional to be appointed captain of England in the 20th Century.

The Oval 1953: first captain to win a rubber after losing the toss in all five Tests.

Kingston 1953-54: scored the first 200 by an England captain in a Test overseas.

R ILLINGWORTH

Manchester 1971: shared record England v. India eighth-wicket stand of 168 with P. Lever.

Hon. F S JACKSON

The Oval 1893: his 100 took 135 minutes, and was the first in a Test in England to be completed with a hit over the boundary (then worth only four runs).

The Oval 1899: his stand of 185 with T W Hayward was then England's highest for any wicket in England, and the record opening partnership by either side in England v. Australia Tests.

Nottingham 1905: dismissed M A Noble, C Hill and J Darling in one over (W01W0W).

Leeds 1905: batted 268 minutes for 144 not out – the third hundred in a Headingley Test.

Manchester 1905: first to score five Test hundreds in England.

The Oval 1905: first captain to win every toss in a five-match rubber.

M LEYLAND

Melbourne 1928-29: scored 137 in his first innings against Australia.

1934: first to score three hundreds in a rubber against Australia in England.

Brisbane 1936-37: scored England's only 100 at 'The Gabba' before 1974-75.

The Oval 1938: contributed 187 in 381 minutes to the record Test total of 903 for 7 declared, sharing in England's highest stand against Australia (all wickets) and record second-wicket stand in all Tests: 382 with L Hutton. First to score hundreds in his first and last innings against Australia.

G G MACAULAY

Cape Town 1922-23: fourth bowler (third for England) to take a wicket (G A L Hearne) with his first ball in Test cricket. Made the winning hit in the fourth of only six Tests to be decided by a one-wicket margin.

Leeds 1926: shared a match-saving ninth-wicket stand of 108 with G Geary.

C M OLD

Birmingham 1978: took 4 wickets in 5 balls in his 19th over (0WW no-ball WW1) to emulate the feat of M J C Allom.

R PEEL

Took his 50th wicket in his ninth Test and his 100th in his 20th Test – all against Australia.

W RHODES

Birmingham 1902: his first-innings analysis of 7 for 17 remains the record for all Tests at Edgbaston.

The Oval 1902: helped to score the last 15 runs in a match-winning tenth-wicket partnership with G H Hirst.

Sydney 1903-04: shared record England v. Australia tenth-wicket stand of 130 in 66 minutes with R E Foster.

Melbourne 1903-04: first to take 15 wickets in England v. Australia Tests; his match analysis of 15 for 124 remains the record for all Tests at Melbourne.

Melbourne 1911-12: shared record England v. Australia first-wicket stand of 323 in 268 minutes with J B Hobbs.

Johannesburg 1913-14: took his 100th wicket and completed the first 'double' for England (in 44 matches).

Sydney 1920-21: first to score 2,000 runs and take 100 wickets in Test cricket.

Adelaide 1920-21: third bowler to take 100 wickets against Australia.

The Oval 1926: set (then) record of 109 wickets against Australia.

Kingston 1929-30: ended the world's longest Test career (30 years 315 days) as the oldest Test cricketer (52 years 165 days).

H SUTCLIFFE

Birmingham 1924: shared the first of 15 three-figure partnerships with J B Hobbs at the first attempt.

Lord's 1924: shared stand of 268 with J B Hobbs, which remains the first-wicket record for all Lord's Tests, and was then the England v. South Africa record.

Sydney 1924-25: his first opening stands against Australia with J B Hobbs realised 157 and 110.

Melbourne 1924-25 (Second Test): with J B Hobbs achieved the first instance of a batting partnership enduring throughout a full day's Test match play; they remain the only England pair to achieve this feat, and their stand of 283 in 289 minutes remains the longest for the first wicket in this series. Became the first to score 100 in each innings of a Test against Australia, and the first Englishman to score three successive hundreds in Test cricket.

Melbourne 1924-25 (Fourth Test): first to score four hundreds in one rubber of Test matches; it was his third 100 in successive Test innings at Melbourne. Completed 1,000 runs in fewest Test innings (12) – since equalled.

Sydney 1924-25: his aggregate of 734 runs was the record for any rubber until 1928-29.

The Oval 1926: shared first-wicket stand of 172 with J B Hobbs on a rain-affected pitch.

The Oval 1929: first to score hundreds in each innings of a Test twice; only England batsman to score four hundreds in a rubber twice.

Sydney 1932-33: his highest England innings of 194 overtook J B Hobbs's world record of 15 Test hundreds.

F S TRUEMAN

Leeds 1952: reduced India to 0 for 4 in their second innings by taking 3 wickets in 8 balls on his debut.

Manchester 1952: achieved record England v. India innings analysis of 8 for 31.

The Oval 1952: set England v. India series record with 29 wickets.

F S TRUEMAN *(Continued)*

Leeds 1961: took 5 for 0 with 24 off-cutters at a reduced pace v. Australia.

Lord's 1962: shared record England v. Pakistan ninth-wicket stand of 76 with T W Graveney.

Christchurch 1962-63: passed J B Statham's world Test record of 242 wickets; his analysis of 7 for 75 remains the record for Lancaster Park Tests and for England in New Zealand.

Birmingham 1963: returned record match analysis (12 for 119) against West Indies in England and for any Birmingham Test, ending with a 6 for 4 spell from 24 balls.

The Oval 1963: set England v. West Indies series record with 34 wickets.

The Oval 1964: first to take 300 wickets in Tests.

G ULYETT

Sydney 1881-82: with R G Barlow shared the first century opening partnership in Test cricket (122).

Melbourne 1881-82: his 149 was the first Test hundred for England in Australia, and the highest score for England on the first day of a Test in Australia until 1965-66.

M P VAUGHAN

Scored 1481 runs in 2002 – more than any other England player in a calendar year, surpassing the 1379 scored by D L Amiss in 1979. It was the fourth highest in a calendar year.

Scored 633 runs in the 2002-3 series versus Australia – surpassed for England in a five Test series versus Australia only by W R Hammond, who scored 905 runs in 1928-29, H Sutcliffe (734 in 1924-25), J B Hobbs (662 in 1911-12) and G Boycott (657 in 1970-71), when he played in five of the six Tests.

Scored six Test Match centuries in 2002 to equal the record set for England by D C S Compton in 1947.

Lord's 2004: scored a century in each innings (103 and 101*) versus West Indies and so became the third player (after G A Headley and G A Gooch) to score a century in each innings of a Test match at Lord's.

Lord's 2005: only the second player (J B Hobbs is the other) to have scored centuries in three consecutive Test match innings at Lord's. Scored the 100th century for England by a Yorkshire player.

H VERITY

Lord's 1934: took 14 for 80 on the third day (six of them in the final hour) to secure England's first win against Australia at Lord's since 1896. It remains the most wickets to fall to one bowler in a day of Test cricket in England. His match analysis of 15 for 104 was then the England v. Australia record, and has been surpassed only by J C Laker.

W WATSON

Lord's 1953: scored 109 in 346 minutes in his first Test against Australia.

N W D YARDLEY

Melbourne 1946-47: dismissed D G Bradman for the third consecutive innings without assistance from the field. Became the first to score a fifty in each innings for England and take five wickets in the same match.

Nottingham 1947: shared record England v. South Africa fifth-wicket stand of 237 with D C S Compton.

* * *

Facts adapted by Bill Frindall from his *England Test Cricketers – The Complete Record from 1877* (Collins Willow, 1989). With later additions.

TEST MATCHES AT HEADINGLEY, LEEDS 1899-2013

1899 **Australia 172** (J Worrall 76) and **224** (H Trumble 56, J T Hearne hat-trick). **England 220** (A F A Lilley 55, H Trumble 5 for 60) and **19 for 0 wkt**.
Match drawn
Toss: Australia

1905 **England 301** (Hon F S Jackson 144*) and **295 for 5 wkts dec** (J T Tyldesley 100, T W Hayward 60, W W Armstrong 5 for 122). **Australia 195** (W W Armstrong 66, A R Warren 5 for 57) and **224 for 7 wkts** (M A Noble 62).
Match drawn
Toss: England

1907 **England 76** (G A Faulkner 6 for 17) and **162** (C B Fry 54). **South Africa 110** (C Blythe 8 for 59) and **75** (C Blythe 7 for 40).
England won by 53 runs
Toss: England

1909 **Australia 188** and **207** (S F Barnes 6 for 63). **England 182** (J Sharp 61, J T Tyldesley 55, C G Macartney 7 for 58) and **87** (A Cotter 5 for 38).
Australia won by 126 runs
Toss: Australia

1912 **England 242** (F E Woolley 57) and **238** (R H Spooner 82, J B Hobbs 55). **South Africa 147** (S F Barnes 6 for 52) and **159**.
England won by 174 runs
Toss: England

1921 **Australia 407** (C G Macartney 115, W W Armstrong 77, C E Pellew 52, J M Taylor 50) and **273 for 7 wkts dec** (T J E Andrew 92). **England 259** (J W H T Douglas 75, Hon L H Tennyson 63, G Brown 57) and **202**.
Australia won by 219 runs
Toss: Australia

1924 **England 396** (E H Hendren 132, H Sutcliffe 83) and **60 for 1 wkt**. **South Africa 132** (H W Taylor 59*, M W Tate 6 for 42) and **323** (H W Taylor 56, R H Catterall 56).
England won by 9 wickets
Toss: England

1926 **Australia 494** (C G Macartney 151, W M Woodfull 141, A J Richardson 100). **England 294** (G G Macaulay 76, C V Grimmett 5 for 88) and **254 for 3 wkts** (H Sutcliffe 94, J B Hobbs 88).
Match drawn
Toss: England

1929 **South Africa 236** (R H Catterall 74, C L Vincent 60, A P Freeman 7 for 115) and **275** (H G Owen-Smith 129). **England 328** (F E Woolley 83, W R Hammond 65, N A Quinn 6 for 92) and **186 for 5 wkts** (F E Woolley 95*).
England won by 5 wickets
Toss: South Africa

1930 **Australia 566** (D G Bradman 334, A F Kippax 77, W M Woodfull 50, M W Tate 5 for 124). **England 391** (W R Hammond 113, C V Grimmett 5 for 135) and **95 for 3 wkts**.
Match drawn
Toss: Australia

1934 **England 200** and **229 for 6 wkts**. **Australia 584** (D G Bradman 304, W H Ponsford 181, W E Bowes 6 for 142).
Match drawn
Toss: England

1935 **England 216** (W R Hammond 63, A Mitchell 58) and **294 for 7 wkts dec** (W R Hammond 87*, A Mitchell 72, D Smith 57). **South Africa 171** (E A B Rowan 62) and **194 for 5 wkts** (B Mitchell 58).
Match drawn
Toss: England

1938 **England 223** (W R Hammond 76, W J O'Reilly 5 for 66) and **123** (.W J O'Reilly 5 for 56). **Australia 242** (D G Bradman 103, B A Barnett 57) and **107 for 5 wkts**.
Australia won by 5 wickets
Toss: England

1947 **South Africa 175** (B Mitchell 53, A Nourse 51) and **184** (A D Nourse 57). **England 317 for 7 wkts dec** (L Hutton 100, C Washbrook 75) and **47 for 0 wkt**.
England won by 10 wickets
Toss: South Africa

1948 **England 496** (C Washbrook 143, W J Edrich 111, L Hutton 81, A V Bedser 79) and **365 for 8 wkts dec** (D C S. Compton 66, C Washbrook 65, L Hutton 57, W J Edrich 54). **Australia 458** (R N Harvey 112, S J E Loxton 93, R R Lindwall 77, K R Miller 58) and **404 for 3 wkts** (A R Morris 182, D G Bradman 173*).
Australia won by 7 wickets
Toss: England

1949 **England 372** (D C S Compton 114, L Hutton 101, T B Burtt 5 for 97, J Cowie 5 for 127) and **267 for 4 wkts dec** (C Washbrook 103*, W J Edrich 70). **New Zealand 341** (F B Smith 96, M P Donnelly 64, T E Bailey 6 for 118) and **195 for 2 wkts** (B Sutcliffe 82, F Smith 54*).
Match drawn   Toss: England

1951 **South Africa 538** (E A B Rowan 236, P N F Mansell 90, C B. van Ryneveld 83, R A McLean 67) and **87 for 0 wkt** (E A B Rowan 60*). **England 505** (P B H May 138, L Hutton 100, T E Bailey 95, F A Lowson 58, A M B Rowan 5 for 174).
Match drawn   Toss: South Africa

1952 **India 293** (V L Manjrekar 133, V S Hazare 89) and 165 (D G Phadkar 64, V S Hazare 56). **England 334** (T W Graveney 71, T G Evans 66, Ghulam Ahmed 5 for 100) and **128 for 3 wkts** (R T Simpson 51).
England won by 7 wickets   Toss: India

1953 **England 167** (T W Graveney 55, R R Lindwall 5 for 54) and **275** (W J Edrich 64, D C S Compton 61). **Australia 266** (R N Harvey 71, G B Hole 53, A V Bedser 6 for 95) and **147 for 4 wkts.**
Match drawn   Toss: Australia

1955 **South Africa 171** and **500** (D J McGlew 133, W R Endean 116*, T L Goddard 74, H J Keith 73). **England 191** (D C S Compton 61) and **256** (P B H May 97, T L Goddard 5 for 69, H J Tayfield 5 for 94).
South Africa won by 224 runs   Toss: South Africa

1956 **England 325** (P B H May 101, C Washbrook 98). **Australia 143** (J C Laker 5 for 58) and **140** (R N Harvey 69, J C Laker 5 for 55).
England won by an innings and 42 runs   Toss: England

1957 **West Indies 142** (P J Loader 6 for 36, including hat-trick) and **132.** **England 279** (P B H May 69, M C Cowdrey 68, Rev D S Sheppard 68, F M M Worrell 7 for 70).
England won by an innings and 5 runs   Toss: West Indies

1958 **New Zealand 67** (J C Laker 5 for 17) and **129** (G A R Lock 7 for 51). **England 267 for 2 wkts dec** (P B H May 113*, C A Milton 104*).
England won by an innings and 71 runs   Toss: New Zealand

1959 **India 161** and **149.** **England 483 for 8 wkts dec** (M C Cowdrey 160, K F Barrington 80, W G A Parkhouse 78, G Pullar 75).
England won by an innings and 173 runs   Toss: India

1961 **Australia 237** (R N Harvey 73, C C McDonald 54, F S Trueman 5 for 58) and **120** (R N Harvey 53, F S Trueman 6 for 30); **England 299** (M C Cowdrey 93, G Pullar 53, A K Davidson 5 for 63) and **62 for 2 wkts.**
England won by 8 wickets   Toss: Australia

1962 **England 428** (P H Parfitt 119, M J Stewart 86, D A Allen 62, Munir Malik 5 for 128). **Pakistan 131** (Alimuddin 50) and **180** (Alimuddin 60, Saeed Ahmed 54).
England won by an innings and 117 runs   Toss: Pakistan

1963 **West Indies 397** (G St A Sobers 102, R B Kanhai 92, J S Solomon 62) and **229** (B F Butcher 78, G St.A Sobers 52). **England 174** (G A R Lock 53, C C Griffith 6 for 36) and **231** (J M Parks 57, D B Close 56).
West Indies won by 221 runs   Toss: West Indies

1964 **England 268** (J M Parks 64, E R Dexter 66, N J N Hawke 5 for 75) and 229 (K F Barrington 85). **Australia 389** (P J P Burge 160, W M Lawry 78) and **111 for 3 wkts** (I R Redpath 58*).
Australia won by 7 wickets   Toss: England

1965 **England 546 for 4 wkts dec** (J H Edrich 310*, K F Barrington 163). **New Zealand 193** (J R Reid 54) and **166** (V Pollard 53, F J Titmus 5 for 19).
England won by an innings and 7 runs   Toss: England

1966 **West Indies 500 for 9 wkts dec** (G.St.A Sobers 174, S M Nurse 137). **England 240** (B L D'Oliveira 88, G.St.A Sobers 5 for 41) and **205** (R W Barber 55, L R Gibbs 6 for 39).
West Indies won by an innings and 55 runs   Toss: West Indies

1967 **England 550 for 4 wkts dec** (G Boycott 246*, B L D'Oliveira 109, K F Barrington 93, T W Graveney 59) and **126 for 4 wkts**. **India 164** (Nawab of Pataudi jnr 64) and **510** (Nawab of Pataudi jnr 148, A L Wadekar 91, F M Engineer 87, Hanumant Singh 73).
England won by 6 wickets   Toss: England

1968 **Australia 315** (I R Redpath 92, I M Chappell 65) and **312** (I M Chappell 81, K D Walters 56, R Illingworth 6 for 87). **England 302** (R M Prideaux 64, J H Edrich 62, A N Connolly 5 for 72) and **230 for 4 wkts** (J H Edrich 65).
Match drawn   Toss: Australia

1969 **England 223** (J H Edrich 79) and **240** (G.St A Sobers 5 for 42). **West Indies 161** and **272** (B F Butcher 91, G S Camacho 71).
England won by 30 runs   Toss: England

1971 **England 316** (G Boycott 112, B L D'Oliveira 74) and **264** (B L D'Oliveira 72, D L Amiss 50). **Pakistan 350** (Zaheer Abbas 72, Wasim Bari 63, Mushtaq Mohammad 57) and **205** (Sadiq Mohammad 91).
England won by 25 runs   Toss: England

1972 **Australia 146** (K R Stackpole 52) and **136** (D L Underwood 6 for 45). **England 263** (R Illingworth 57, A A Mallett 5 for 114) and **21 for 1 wkt**.
England won by 9 wickets   Toss: Australia

1973 **New Zealand 276** (M G Burgess 87, V Pollard 62) and **142** (G M Turner 81, G G Arnold 5 for 27). **England 419** (G Boycott 115, K W R Fletcher 81, R Illingworth 65, RO Collinge 5 for 74).
England won by an innings and 1 run   Toss: New Zealand

1974 **Pakistan 285** (Majid Khan 75, Safraz Nawaz 53) and **179**. **England 183** and **238 for 6 wkts** (J H Edrich 70, K W R Fletcher 67*).
Match drawn   Toss: Pakistan

1975 **England 288** (D S Steele 73, J H Edrich 62, A W Greig 51, G J Gilmour 6 for 85) and **291** (D S Steele 92). **Australia 135** (P H Edmonds 5 for 28) and **220 for 3 wkts** (R B McCosker 95*, I M Chappell 62).
Match drawn   Toss: England

1976 **West Indies 450** (C G Greenidge 115, R C Fredericks 109, I V A Richards 66, L G Rowe 50) and **196** (C L King 58, R G D Willis 5 for 42). **England 387** (A W Greig 116, A P E Knott 116) and **204** (A W Greig 76*).
West Indies won by 55 runs   Toss: West Indies

1977 **England 436** (G Boycott 191, A P E Knott 57). **Australia 103** (I T Botham 5 for 21) and **248** (R W Marsh 63).
England won by an innings and 85 runs   Toss: England

1978 **Pakistan 201** (Sadiq Mohammad 97). **England 119 for 7 wkts** (Safraz Nawaz 5 for 39).
Match drawn   Toss: Pakistan

1979 **England 270** (I T Botham 137). **India 223 for 6 wkts** (S M Gavaskar 78, D B Vengsarkar 65*).
Match drawn   Toss: England

1980 **England 143 and 227 for 6 wkts dec** (G A Gooch 55). **West Indies 245**.
Match drawn   Toss: West Indies

1981 **Australia 401 for 9 wkts dec** (J Dyson 102, K J Hughes 89, G N Yallop 58, I T Botham 6 for 95) and **111** (R G D Willis 8 for 43). **England 174** (I T Botham 50) and **356** (I T Botham 149*, G R Dilley 56, T M Alderman 6 for 135).
England won by 18 runs   Toss: Australia

1982 **Pakistan 275** (Imran Khan 67*, Mudassar Nazar 65, Javed Miandad 54) and **199** (Javed Miandad 52, I T Botham 5 for 74). **England 256** (D I Gower 74, I T Botham 57, Imran Khan 5 for 49) and **219 for 7 wkts** (G Fowler 86).
England won by 3 wickets   Toss: Pakistan

1983 **England 225** (C J Tavaré 69, A J Lamb 58, B L Cairns 7 for 74) and **252** (D I Gower 112*, E J Chatfield 5 for 95). **New Zealand 377** (J G Wright 93, B A Edgar 84, R J Hadlee 75) and **103 for 5 wkts** (R G D Willis 5 for 35).
New Zealand won by 5 wickets   Toss: New Zealand

1984 **England 270** (A J Lamb 100) and **159** (G Fowler 50, M D Marshall 7 for 53). **West Indies 302** (H A Gomes 104*, M A Holding 59, P J W Allott 6 for 61) and **131 for 2 wkts.**
West Indies won by 8 wickets   Toss: England

1985 **Australia 331** (A M J Hilditch 119) and **324** (W B Phillips 91, A M J Hilditch 80, K C Wessels 64, J E Emburey 5 for 82). **England 533** (R T Robinson 175, I T Botham 60, P R Downton 54, M W Gatting 53) and **123 for 5 wkts.**
England won by 5 wickets   Toss: Australia

1986 **India 272** (D B Vengsarkar 61) and **237** (D B Vengsarkar 102*). **England 102** (R M H Binny 5 for 40) and **128.**
India won by 279 runs   Toss: India

1987 **England 136** (D J Capel 53) and **199** (D I Gower 55, Imran Khan 7 for 40). **Pakistan 353** (Salim Malik 99, Ijaz Ahmed 50, N A Foster 8 for 107).
Pakistan won by an innings and 18 runs   Toss: England

1988 **England 201** (A J Lamb 64*) and **138** (G A Gooch 50). **West Indies 275** (R A Harper 56, D L Haynes 54, D R Pringle 5 for 95) and **67 for 0 wkt.**
West Indies won by 10 wickets   Toss: West Indies

1989 **Australia 601 for 7 wkts dec** (S R Waugh 177*, M A Taylor 136, D M Jones 79, M G Hughes 71, A R Border 66) and **230 for 3 wkts dec** (M A Taylor 60, A R Border 60*). **England 430** (A J Lamb 125, K J Barnett 80, R A Smith 66, T M Alderman 5 for 107) and **191.** (G A Gooch 68, T M Alderman 5 for 44).
Australia won by 210 runs   Toss: England

1991 **England 198** (R A Smith 54) and **252** (G A Gooch 154*, C E L Ambrose 6 for 52). **West Indies 173** (I V A Richards 73) and **162** (R B Richardson 68).
England won by 115 runs   Toss: West Indies

1992 **Pakistan 197** (Salim Malik 82*) and **221** (Salim Malik 84*, Ramiz Raja 63, N A Mallinder 5 for 50). **England 320** (G A Gooch 135, M A Atherton 76, Waqar Younis 5 for 117) and **99 for 4 wkts.**
England won by 6 wickets   Toss: Pakistan

1993 **Australia 653 for 4 wkts dec** (A R Border 200*, S R Waugh 157*, D C Boon 107, M J Slater 67, M E Waugh 52). **England 200** (G A Gooch 59, M A Atherton 55, P R Reiffel 5 for 65) and **305** (A J Stewart 78, M A Atherton 63).
Australia won by an innings and 148 runs   Toss: Australia

1994 **England 477 for 9 wkts dec** (M A Atherton 99, A J Stewart 89, G P Thorpe 72, S J Rhodes 65*) and **267 for 5 wkts dec** (G A Hick 110, G P Thorpe 73). **South Africa 447** (P N Kirsten 104, B M McMillan 78, C R Matthews 62*) and **116 for 3 wkts** (G Kirsten 65).
Match drawn   Toss: England

1995 **England 199** (M A Atherton 81, I R Bishop 5 for 32) and **208** (G P Thorpe 61). **West Indies 282** (S L Campbell 69, J C Adams 58, B C Lara 53) and **129 for 1 wkt** (C L Hooper 73*).
West Indies won by 9 wickets   Toss: West Indies

1996 **Pakistan 448** (Ijaz Ahmed 141, Mohin Khan 105, Salim Malik 55, Asif Mujtaba 51, D G Cork 5 for 113) and **242 for 7 wkts dec** (Inzamam-ul-Haq 65, Ijaz Ahmed sen 52) **England 501** (A J Stewart 170, N V Knight 113, J P Crawley 53).
Match drawn   Toss: England

1997 **England 172** (J N. Gillespie 7 for 37) and **268** (N Hussain 105, J P Crawley 72, P R Reiffel 5 for 49). **Australia 501 for 9 wkts dec** (M T G Elliott 199, R T Ponting 127, P R Reiffel 54*, D Gough 5 for 149).
Australia won by an innings and 61 runs   Toss: Australia

1998 **England 230** (M A Butcher 116) and **240** (N Hussain 94, S M Pollock 5 for 53, A A Donald 5 for 71). **South Africa 252** (W J. Cronje 57, A R C Fraser 5 for 42) and **195** (J N Rhodes 85, B M McMillan 54, D Gough 6 for 42).
England won by 23 runs   Toss: England

2000 **West Indies 172** (R R Sarwan 59*, C White 5 for 57) and **61** (A R Caddick 5 for 14). **England 272** (M P Vaughan 76, G A Hick 59).
England won by an innings and 39 runs   Toss: West Indies

2001 **Australia 447** (R T Ponting 144, D R Martyn 118, M E Waugh 72, D Gough 5 for 103) and **176 for 4 wkts dec** (R T Ponting 72). **England 309** (A J Stewart 76*, G D McGrath 7 for 76) and **315 for 4 wkts** (M A Butcher 173*, N Hussain 55).
England won by 6 wickets Toss: Australia

2002 **India 628 for 8 wkts dec** (S R Tendulkar 193, R S Dravid 148, S C Ganguly 128, S B Bangar 68). **England 273** (A J Stewart 78*, M P Vaughan 61) and **309** (N Hussain 110.)
India won by an innings and 46 runs Toss: India

2003 **South Africa 342** (G Kirsten 130, M Zondeki 59, J A Rudolph 55) and **365** (A J Hall 99*, G Kirsten 60). **England 307** (M A Butcher 77, M E Trescothick 59, A Flintoff 55) and **209** (M A Butcher 61, A Flintoff 50, J H Kallis 6 for 54.)
South Africa won by 191 runs Toss: South Africa

2004 **New Zealand 409** (S P Fleming 97, M H W Papps 86, B B McCullum 54) and **161.** **England 526** (M E Trescothick 132, G O Jones 100, A Flintoff 94, A J Strauss 62) and **45 for 1 wkt**
England won by 9 wickets Toss: England

2006 **England 515** (K P Pietersen 135, I R Bell 119, Umar Gul 5 for 123) and **345** (A J Strauss 116, M E Trescothick 58, C M W Reid 55). **Pakistan 538** (Mohammad Yousuf 192, Younis Khan 173) and **155**.
England won by 167 runs Toss: England

2007 **England 570 for 7 wkts dec** (K P Pietersen 226, M P Vaughan 103, M J Prior 75). **West Indies 146** and **141** (D J Bravo 52).
England won by an innings and 283 runs Toss: England

2008 **England 203** and **327** (S C J Broad 67*, A N Cook 60). **South Africa 522** (A B de Villiers 174, A G Prince 149) and **9 for 0 wkt**.
South Africa won by 10 wickets Toss: South Africa

2009 **England 102** (P M Siddle 5 for 21) and **263** (G P Swann 62, S C J Broad 61, M G Johnson 5 for 69). **Australia 445** (M J North 110, M J Clarke 93, R T Ponting 78, S R Watson 51, S C J Broad 6 for 91).
Australia won by an innings and 80 runs Toss: England

2010 **Australia 88** and **349** (R T Ponting 66, M J Clarke 77, S P D Smith 77). **Pakistan 258** (S R Watson 6-33) and **180-7** (Imran Farhat 67, Azhar Ali 51).
Pakistan won by 3 wickets Toss: Australia
(This was a Home Test Match for Pakistan)

2012 **South Africa 419** (A N Petersen 182, G C Smith 52) and **258-9 dec** (J A Rudolph 69, GC Smith 52, S C J Broad 5-69). **England 425** (K P Pietersen 149, M J Prior 68) and **130-4**.
Match drawn Toss: England

2013 **England 354** (J E Root 104, J M Bairstow 64, T M Boult 5-57) and **287-5 dec** (A N Cook 130, I J L Trott 76). **New Zealand 174** and **220** (L R P L Taylor 70, G P Swann 6-90).
England won by 247 runs Toss: England

SUMMARY OF RESULTS

ENGLAND	First played	Last played	Played	Won	Lost	Drawn
v. Australia	1899	2009	24	7	9	8
v. India	1952	2002	6	3	2	1
v. New Zealand	1949	2013	7	5	1	1
v. Pakistan	1962	2006	9	5	1	3
v. South Africa	1907	2012	13	6	3	4
v. West Indies	1957	2007	12	5	6	1
Totals	1899	2013	71	31	22	18

CENTURY PARTNERSHIPS

For England
(six highest)
For the 1st wicket

168	L Hutton (81) and C Washbrook (143) v. Australia, 1948 (1st inns)
168	G A Gooch (135) and M A Atherton (76) v. Pakistan, 1992
158	M E Trescothick (58) and A J Strauss (116) v. Pakistan, 2006
156	J B Hobbs (88) and H Sutcliffe (94) v. Australia, 1926
153	M E Trescothick (132) and A J Strauss (62) v. New Zealand, 2004
146	W G A Parkhouse (78) and G Pullar (75) v. India, 1959

For all other wickets

369	(2nd wkt) J H Edrich (310*) and K F Barrington (163) v. New Zealand, 1965
252	(4th wkt) G Boycott (246*) and B L D'Oliveira (109) v. India, 1967
194*	(3rd wkt) C A Milton (104*) and P B H May (113*) v. New Zealand, 1958
193	(4th wkt) M C Cowdrey (160) and K F Barrington (80) v. India, 1959
187	(4th wkt) P B H May (101) and C Washbrook (98) v. Australia, 1956
181	(3rd wkt) M A Butcher (173*) and N Hussain (55) v. Australia, 2001

For Australia
(six highest)
For the 1st wkt – none
For all other wickets

388	(4th wkt) W H Ponsford (181) and D G Bradman (304), 1934
332*	(5th wkt) A R Border (200*) and S R Waugh (157*), 1993
301	(2nd wkt) A R Morris (182) and D G Bradman (173*), 1948
268	(5th wkt) M T G Elliott (199) and R T Ponting (127), 1997
235	(2nd wkt) W M Woodfull (141) and C G Macartney (151), 1926
229	(3rd wkt) D G Bradman (334) and A F Kippax (77), 1930

For other countries in total

India

249	(4th wkt) S R Tendulkar (193) and S C Ganguly (128), 2002
222	(4th wkt) V S Hazare (89) and V L Manjrekar (133), 1952
170	(2nd wkt) S B Bangar (68) and R S Dravid (148), 2002
168	(2nd wkt) F M Engineer (87) and A L Wadekar (91), 1967
150	(3rd wkt) R S Dravid (148) and S R Tendulkar (193), 2002
134	(5th wkt) Hanumant Singh (73) and Nawab of Pataudi jnr (148), 1967
105	(6th wkt) V S Hazare (56) and D G Phadkar (64), 1952

New Zealand

169	(2nd wkt) M H W Papps (86) and S P Fleming (97), 2004
120	(5th wkt) M P Donnelly (64) and F B Smith (96), 1949
116	(2nd wkt) J G Wright (93) and M D Crowe (37), 1983
112	(1st wkt) B Sutcliffe (82) and V J Scott (43), 1949
106	(5th wkt) M G Burgess (87) and V Pollard (62), 1973

Pakistan

363	(3rd wkt) Younis Khan (173) and Mohammad Yousuf (192), 2006
130	(4th wkt) Ijaz Ahmed (141) and Salim Malik (55), 1996
129	(3rd wkt) Zaheer Abbas (72) and Mushtaq Mohammed (57), 1971
112	(7th wkt) Asif Mujtaba (51) and Moin Khan (105), 1996
110	(2nd wkt) Imran Farhat (67) and Azhar Ali (51), 2010 v. Australia
100	(3rd wkt) Mudassar Nazar (65) and Javed Miandad (54), 1982
100	(4th wkt) Majid Khan (75) and Zaheer Abbas (48), 1974

CENTURY PARTNERSHIPS *(Continued)*

South Africa

212	(5th wkt) A G Prince (149) and A B de Villiers (174), 2008	
198	(2nd wkt) E A B Rowan (236) C B van Ryneveld (83), 1951	
176	(1st wkt) D J McGlew (133) and T L Goddard (74), 1955	
150	(8th wkt) G Kirsten (130) and M Zondeki (59), 2003	
120	(1st wkt) A N Petersen (182) and G C Smith (52), 2012	
120	(1st wkt) J A Rudolph (69) and G C Smith (52), 2012	
117	(6th wkt) J N Rhodes (85) and B M McMillan (54), 1998	
115	(7th wicket) P N Kirsten (104) and B M McMillan (78), 1994	
108	(5th wkt) E A B Rowan (236) and R A McLean (67), 1951	
103	(10th wkt) H G Owen-Smith (129) and A J Bell (26*), 1929	

West Indies

265	(5th wkt) S M Nurse (137) and G St A Sobers (174), 1966
192	(1st wkt) R C Fredericks (109) and C G Greenidge (115), 1976
118*	(2nd wkt) C L Hooper (73*) and B C Lara (48*), 1995
143	(4th wkt) R B Kanhai (92) and G St A Sobers (102), 1963
108	(3rd wkt) G S Camacho (71) and B F Butcher (91), 1969
106	(1st wkt) C G Greenidge (49) and D L Haynes (43), 1984

6 BEST INNINGS ANALYSES

For England

8 for 43	R G D Willis v. Australia, 1981
8 for 59	C Blythe v. South Africa, 1907 (1st inns)
8 for 107	N A Foster v. Pakistan, 1987
7 for 40	C Blythe v. South Africa, 1907 (2nd inns)
7 for 51	G A R Lock v. New Zealand, 1958
7 for 115	A P Freeman v. South Africa, 1929

For Australia

7 for 37	J N Gilliespie, 1997
7 for 58	C G Macartney, 1909
7 for 76	G D McGrath, 2001
6 for 33	S R Watson, 2010 v. Pakistan
6 for 85	G J Gilmour, 1975
6 for 135	T M Alderman, 1981

5 WICKETS IN AN INNINGS

For India (2)

5 for 40	R M H Binny, 1986
5 for 100	Ghulam Ahmed, 1952

For New Zealand (5)

7 for 74	B L Cairns, 1983
5 for 74	R O Collinge, 1973
5 for 95	E J Chatfield, 1983
5 for 97	T B Burtt, 1949
5 for 127	J Cowie, 1949

For Pakistan (6)

7 for 40	Imran Khan, 1987
5 for 39	Sarfraz Nawaz, 1978
5 for 49	Imran Khan, 1982
5 for 117	Waqar Younis, 1992
5 for 123	Umar Gul, 2006
5 for 128	Munir Malik, 1962

For South Africa (7)

6 for 17	G A Faulkner, 1907
6 for 92	N A Quinn, 1929
6 for 54	J H Kallis, 2003
5 for 53	S M Pollock, 1998
5 for 69	T L Goddard, 1955
5 for 71	A A Donald, 1998
5 for 94	H J Tayfield, 1955
5 for 174	A M B Rowan, 1951

For West Indies (8)

7 for 53	M D Marshall, 1984
7 for 70	F M Worrell, 1957
6 for 36	C C Griffith, 1963
6 for 39	L R Gibbs, 1996
6 for 52	C E L Ambrose, 1991
5 for 32	I R Bishop, 1995
5 for 41	G.St.A Sobers, 1966
5 for 42	G.St A Sobers, 1969

10 WICKETS IN A MATCH

For England (7)

15 for 99	(8 for 59 and 7 for 40)	C Blythe v. South Africa, 1907
11 for 65	(4 for 14 and 7 for 51)	G A R Lock v. New Zeland, 1958
11 for 88	(5 for 58 and 6 for 30)	F S Trueman v. Australia, 1961
11 for 113	(5 for 58 and 6 for 55)	J C Laker v. Australia, 1956
10 for 82	(4 for 37 and 6 for 45)	D L Underwood v. Australia, 1972
10 for 115	(6 for 52 and 4 for 63)	S F Barnes v. South Africa, 1912
10 for 207	(7 for 115 and 3 for 92)	A P Freeman v. South Africa, 1929

For Australia (3)

11 for 85	(7 for 58 and 4 for 27)	C G Macartney, 1909
10 for 122	(5 for 66 and 5 for 56)	W J O'Reilly, 1938
10 for 151	(5 for 107 and 5 for 44)	T M Alderman, 1989

For New Zealand (1)

10 for 144	(7 for 74 and 3 for 70)	B L Cairns, 1983

For Pakistan (1)

10 for 77	(3 for 37 and 7 for 40)	Imran Khan, 1987

Note: Best bowling in a match for:

India:	7 for 58 (5 for 40 and 2 for 18)	R M H Binney, 1986
South Africa:	9 for 75 (6 for 17 and 3 for 58)	G A Faulkner, 1907
West Indies:	9 for 81 (6 for 36 and 3 for 45)	C C Griffith, 1963

HAT-TRICKS

J T Hearne v. Australia, 1899

P J Loader v. West Indies, 1957

TEST MATCH AT BRAMALL LANE, SHEFFIELD 1902

1902 **Australia 194** (S F Barnes 6 for 49) and **289** (C Hill 119, V T Trumper 62, W Rhodes 5 for 63) **England 145** (J V Saunders 5 for 50, M A Noble 5 for 51) and **195** (A C MacLaren 63, G L Jessop 55, M A Noble 6 for 52).
Australia won by 143 runs Toss: Australia

For England

YORKSHIRE ONE-DAY INTERNATIONAL CRICKETERS 1971-2013/14 (Correct to February 3, 2014)

Player	M	I	NO	Runs	HS	Av'ge	100s	50s	Balls	Runs	W	Av'ge	Best	4wI	Ct/St
ATHEY, C W J 1980-88	31	30	3	848	142*	31.40	2	4	—	—	—	—	—	—	16
BAIRSTOW, D L 1979-84	21	20	6	206	23*	14.71	—	—	—	—	—	—	—	—	17/4
BAIRSTOW, J M 2011-12	7	6	1	119	41*	23.80	—	—	—	—	—	—	—	—	3
BALLANCE, G S 2013-13/14	5	5	0	132	79	26.40	—	1	—	—	—	—	—	—	5
BLAKEY, R J 1992-93	3	3	1	25	25	12.50	—	—	—	—	—	—	—	—	2/1
BOYCOTT, G 1971-81	36	34	4	1,082	105	36.06	1	9	168	105	5	21.00	2-14	—	5
BRESNAN, T T 2006-13/14	81	61	18	846	80	19.67	—	1	4043	3676	101	36.39	5-48	4	20
COPE, G A 1977-78	2	1	1	1	1*	—	—	—	112	35	2	17.50	1-16	—	1
GOUGH, D 1994-2006	158	87	38	609	46*	12.42	—	—	8,422	6,154	234	26.29	5-44	10	24
HAMPSHIRE, J H 1971-72	3	3	1	48	25*	24.00	—	—	—	—	—	—	—	—	0
HOGGARD, M J 2001-06	26	8	4	17	7	4.25	—	—	1,306	1,152	32	36.00	5-49	1	5
JARVIS, P W 1988-93	16	8	2	31	16*	5.16	—	—	879	672	24	28.00	5-35	2	1
LOVE, J D 1981	3	3	0	61	43	20.33	—	—	—	—	—	—	—	—	1
McGRATH, A 2003-04	14	12	2	166	52	16.60	—	1	228	175	4	43.75	1-13	—	4
MOXON, M D 1985-88	8	8	0	174	70	21.75	—	1	—	—	—	—	—	—	5
OLD, C M 1973-81	32	25	7	338	51*	18.77	—	1	1,755	999	45	22.20	4-8	2	8
RASHID, A U 2009	5	4	1	60	31*	20.00	—	—	204	191	3	63.66	1-16	—	2
ROOT, J E ..2012/13-13/14	23	22	3	686	79*	36.10	—	5	372	385	6	64.16	2-46	—	10
SHAHZAD, A 2010-11	11	8	2	39	9	6.50	—	—	588	490	17	28.82	3-41	—	4
SIDEBOTTOM, R J 2001-10	25	18	8	133	24	13.30	—	—	1,277	1,039	29	35.82	3-19	—	6
SILVERWOOD, C E W 1996-2001	7	4	0	17	12	4.25	—	—	306	244	6	40.66	3-43	—	0
STEVENSON, G B 1980-81	4	4	3	43	28*	43.00	—	—	192	125	4	31.25	2-25	—	2
VAUGHAN, M P 2001-07	86	83	10	1,982	90*	27.15	—	16	796	649	16	40.56	4-22	1	25
WHITE, C 1994-2003	51	41	5	568	57*	15.77	—	1	2,364	1,726	65	26.55	5-21	2	12
For Scotland															
BLAIN, J A R 1999-2009	33	25	6	284	41	14.94	—	—	1,329	1,173	41	28.60	5-22	4	8
HAMILTON, G M 1999-2010	38	38	3	1,231	119	35.17	2	7	220	160	3	53.33	2-36	—	6/1
WARDLAW, I 2012/13-13/14	11	6	5	13	7*	13.00	—	—	645	553	21	26.33	4-43	1	0

YORKSHIRE PLAYERS WHO PLAYED ALL THEIR ONE-DAY INTERNATIONAL CRICKET AFTER LEAVING YORKSHIRE

For England

Player	M	I	NO	Runs	HS	Av'ge	100s	50s	Balls	Runs	W	Av'ge	Best	4wI	Ct/St
BATTY, G J 2002-09	10	8	2	30	17	5.00	—	—	440	366	5	73.20	2-40	—	4
CLOSE, D B 1972	3	3	0	49	43	16.33	—	—	18	21	0	—	—	—	1
GRAYSON, A P ...2000-01	3	2	0	6	6	3.00	—	—	90	60	3	20.00	3-40	—	1
ILLINGWORTH, R .1971-72	3	2	0	5	4	2.50	—	—	130	84	4	21.00	3-50	—	1
PLUNKETT, L E ** 2005/6-2010/11	29	25	10	315	56	21.00	—	1	1,363	1,321	39	33.87	3-24	—	7
RHODES, S J 1989-95	9	8	2	107	56	17.83	—	1	—	—	—	—	—	—	9/2
WHARF, A G 2004-05	13	5	3	19	9	9.50	—	—	584	428	18	23.77	4-24	1	1
WOOD, B 1972-82	13	12	2	314	78*	31.40	—	2	420	224	9	24.88	2-14	—	6

** before joining Yorkshire

Overseas Players
(Qualification: 24 List A matches for Yorkshire)

For Australia

Player	M	I	NO	Runs	HS	Av'ge	100s	50s	Balls	Runs	W	Av'ge	Best	4wI	Ct/St
BEVAN, M G ...1994-2004	232	196	67	6,912	108*	53.58	6	46	1,966	1,655	36	45.97	3-36	—	128
HARVEY, I J .1997/98-2004	73	51	11	715	48*	17.87	—	—	3,279	2,577	85	30.31	4-16	4	17
JAQUES, P A ...2006-2007	6	6	0	125	94	20.83	—	1	—	—	—	—	—	—	3
LEHMANN, D S .1996-2005	117	101	22	3,078	119	38.96	4	17	1,793	1,445	52	27.78	4-7	1	26

For South Africa

Player	M	I	NO	Runs	HS	Av'ge	100s	50s	Balls	Runs	W	Av'ge	Best	4wI	Ct/St
RUDOLPH, J A 2003-06	43	37	6	1,157	81	37.32	—	7	24	26	0	—	—	—	11

For West Indies

Player	M	I	NO	Runs	HS	Av'ge	100s	50s	Balls	Runs	W	Av'ge	Best	4wI	Ct/St
RICHARDSON, R B 1983-96	224	217	30	6,248	122	33.41	5	44	58	46	1	46.00	1-4	—	75

SUMMARY OF RESULTS

ENGLAND	Played	Won	Lost
v. Australia	4	2	2
v. Bangladesh	1	1	0
v. India	5	3	2
v. New Zealand	2	0	2
v. Pakistan	3	2	1
v. South Africa	2	2	0
v. Sri Lanka	4	2	2
v. West Indies	4	3	1
v. Zimbabwe	1*	0	0
Totals	26	15	10

*No result. In addition to two matches v. West Indies abandoned and one match v. Australia abandoned

AUSTRALIA	Played	Won	Lost
v. England	4	2	2
v. Pakistan	2	1	1
v. South Africa	1	1	0
v. West Indies	1	0	1
Totals	8	4	4

In addition to one match abandoned

BANGLADESH	Played	Won	Lost
v. England	1	0	1

INDIA	Played	Won	Lost
v. England	5	2	3
v. East Africa	1	1	0
v. New Zealand	1	0	1
Totals	7	3	4

NEW ZEALAND	Played	Won	Lost
v. England	2	2	0
v. India	1	1	0
v. Zimbabwe	1*	0	0
Totals	4	3	0

*No result

PAKISTAN	Played	Won	Lost
v. Australia	2	1	1
v. Canada	1	1	0
v. England	3	1	2
v. Sri Lanka	1	1	0
Totals	7	4	3

SOUTH AFRICA	Played	Won	Lost
v. Australia	1	0	1
v. England	2	0	2
Totals	3	0	3

SRI LANKA	Played	Won	Lost
v. England	4	2	2
v. Pakistan	1	0	1
Totals	5	2	3

SUMMARY OF RESULTS *(Continued)*

WEST INDIES	Played	Won	Lost
v. Australia	1	1	0
v. England	4	1	3
Totals	5	2	3

In addition to two matches abandoned

ZIMBABWE	Played	Won	Lost
v. England	1*	0	0
v. New Zealand	1*	0	0
Totals	2*	0	0

*No result

CANADA	Played	Won	Lost
v. Pakistan	1	0	1

EAST AFRICA	Played	Won	Lost
v. India	1	0	1

CENTURIES

152	S J Jayasuriya for Sri Lanka v. England, 2006
144	D P M D Jayawardene Sri Lanka v. England, 2011
128	R A Smith for England v. New Zealand, 1990
126	A J Strauss for England v. Pakistan, 2010
121	M E Trescothick for England v. Sri Lanka, 2006
120*	S R Waugh for Australia v. South Africa, 1999
112	S J Jayasuriya for Sri Lanka v. England, 2002
109	W U Tharanga for Sri Lanka v. England, 2006
108	G M Wood for Australia v. England, 1981
104*	M E Trescothick for England v. Australia, 2005
102*	Imran Khan for Pakistan v. Sri Lanka, 1983
102*	M J Greatbatch for New Zealand v. England, 1990
101	H H Gibbs for South Africa v. Australia, 1999

4 WICKETS IN AN INNINGS

7 for 36	Waqar Younis for Pakistan v. England, 2001
7 for 51	W W Davis for West Indies v. Australia, 1983
6 for 14	G J Gilmour for Australia v. England, 1975
5 for 34	D K Lillee for Australia v. Pakistan, 1975
5 for 39	A L F de Mel for Sri Lanka v. Pakistan, 1983
5 for 44	Abdul Qadir for Pakistan v. Sri Lanka, 1983
4 for 15	M Hendrick for England v. Pakistan, 1979
4 for 29	R M Hogg for Australia v England, 1981
4 for 29	A Flintoff for England v. Bangladesh, 2005
4 for 34	P D Collingwood for England v. Australia, 2005
4 for 40	Wasim Akram for Pakistan v. Australia, 1999
4 for 44	S L Malinga for Sri Lanka v. England, 2006
4 for 56	I T Botham for England v. India, 1982
4 for 81	S J C Broad for England v. Pakistan, 2010

LIMITED-OVERS INTERNATIONAL MATCHES
AT NORTH MARINE ROAD, SCARBOROUGH 1976-1978

1976 **England 202 for 8 wkts** (55 overs) (G D Barlow 80*, A M E Roberts 4 for 32).
West Indies 207 for 4 wkts (41 overs) (I V A Richards 119*).
West Indies won by 6 wickets **Award: I V A Richards**

1978 **England 206 for 8 wkts** (55 overs) (G A Gooch 94, B L Cairns 5 for 28).
New Zealand 187 for 8 wkts (55 overs) (B E Congdon 52*).
England won by 19 runs **Award: G A Gooch**

LIST OF PLAYERS AND CAREER AVERAGES IN ALL FIRST-CLASS MATCHES FOR YORKSHIRE 1863-2013

Based on research by John T Potter, Roy D Wilkinson and the late Anthony Woodhouse

The Editor and Statistics Editor welcome any information which will help in keeping this list up to date. The present compilers do not believe that we should alter the status of matches from that determined at the time they were played. Therefore, these averages include the match versus Gentlemen of Scotland in 1878, and exclude the matches versus Liverpool and District played in 1889, 1891, 1892 and 1893 in line with what appear to be the decisions of the Club at the time.

* Played as an amateur § Born outside Yorkshire

© Awarded County Cap

Player	Date of Birth	Date of Death (if known)	First Played	Last Played	M	Inns	NO	Runs	HS	Av'ge	100s	Runs	Wkts	Av'ge	Ct/St
Ackroyd, A *	Aug. 29, 1858	Oct. 3, 1927	1879	1879	1	1	0	2	2*		0	7	0		0
Allen, S *	Dec 20, 1893		1924	1924	1	2	0	8	6	4.00	0	116	2	58.00	0
Allen, W R	April4, 1893	Oct 14, 1950	1921	1925	30	32	10	475	95*	21.59	0				45/21
Ambler, J	Feb 12, 1860	Feb 10 1899	1886	1886	4	7	0	68	25	9.71	0	22	0		2
Anderson, G	Jan 20, 1826	Nov 27, 1902	1851	1869	19	31	6	520	99*	20.80	0				19
Anderson, P N	Apr. 28, 1966		1988	1988	1	1	0	0	0	0.00	0	47	1	47.00	1
Anson, C E *	Oct 14, 1889	Mar 26, 1969	1924	1924	1	2	0	27	14	13.50	0				1
Appleton, C *	May15, 1844	Feb 26, 1925	1865	1865	1	2	0	56	18	11.20	0				1
Appleyard, R	June 27, 1924		1950	1958	133	122	43	679	63	8.59	0	9,903	642	15.42	70
Armitage, C1 *	Apr 24, 1849	Apr 24, 1917	1873	1878	3	5	0	26	12	5.20	0	29	0		0
Armitage, T	Apr 25, 1848	Sept 21, 1922	1872	1878	52	85	8	1,053	95	13.67	0	1,614	107	15.08	20
Ash, D L	Feb 18, 1944		1965	1965	3	3	0	22	12	7.33	0	22	0		0
Ashman, J R	May 20, 1926		1951	1951	1	1	0	0	0*		0	116	4	29.00	0
Ashraf, Moin A ©	**Jan 5, 1992**		**2010**	**2013**	**21**	**19**	**5**	**56**	**10**	**4.00**	**0**	**1,268**	**43**	**29.48**	**2**
Aspinall, R	Oct 26, 1918	Aug 16, 1999	1946	1950	36	48	8	763	75*	19.07	0	2,670	131	20.38	18
Aspinall, W	Mar 24, 1858	Jan 27, 1910	1880	1880	2	3	0	16	14	5.33	0				1
Asquith, F T	Feb 5, 1870	Jan 11, 1916	1903	1903	1	1	0	0	0	0.00	0				2
Athey, C W J	Sept 27, 1957		1976	1983	151	246	21	6,320	134	28.08	10	1,003	21	47.76	144/2
Atkinson, G R	Sept 21, 1830	May 3, 1906	1861	1870	27	38	8	399	44	13.30	0	1,146	54	21.22	14
Atkinson, H	Feb 1, 1881	Dec 22, 1959	1907	1907	1	2	0	0	0	0.00	0	17	0		0
Azeem Rafiq	**Feb 27, 1991**		**2009**	**2013**	**21**	**24**	**2**	**497**	**100**	**22.59**	**1**	**1,607**	**46**	**34.93**	**8**
Backhouse, E N *	May 13, 1901	Nov 1, 1936	1931	1931	1	1	0	2	2	2.00	0	4	0		0
Badger, H D *	Mar 7, 1900	Aug 10, 1975	1921	1922	2	4	2	6	6*	3.00	0	145	6	24.16	1

LIST OF PLAYERS AND CAREER AVERAGES IN ALL FIRST-CLASS MATCHES FOR YORKSHIRE (Continued)

Player	Date of Birth	Date of Death (if known)	First Played	Last Played	M	Inns	NO	Runs	HS	Av'ge	100s	Runs	Wkts	Av'ge	Ct/St
Bambridge, A B	Oct 15, 1932		1961	1963	5	10	0	93	24	9.30	0	358	20	17.90	3
Baines, F E *	June 18, 1864	Nov 17, 1948	1888	1888	1	1	0	0	0	0.00	0	—	—	—	0
Bairstow, A	Aug 14, 1868	Dec 7, 1945	1896	1900	24	24	10	69	12	4.92	0	—	—	—	41/18
Bairstow, D L	Sept 1, 1951	Jan 5, 1998	1970	1990	429	601	113	12,985	145	26.60	9	192	6	32.00	907/131
Bairstow, J M	© Sept 26, 1989		2009	2013	59	98	16	3,661	205	44.64	6	—	—	—	140/5
Baker, G R	Apr 18, 1862	Feb 6, 1938	1884	1884	7	11	1	42	13	4.20	0	43	0	—	5
Baker, R *	July 13, 1849	June 21, 1896	1874	1875	3	5	1	45	22	11.25	0	45	0	—	3
Balderstone, J C	Nov 16, 1940	Mar 6, 2000	1961	1969	68	81	6	1,332	82	17.76	0	790	37	21.35	24
§ Ballance G S	© Nov 22, 1989		2008	2013	48	72	12	2,932	148	48.86	8	132	0	—	32
Barber, A T *	© June 17, 1905	Mar 10, 1985	1929	1930	42	54	3	1,050	100	20.58	1	0	0	—	40
Barber, W	Apr 18, 1901	Sept 10, 1968	1926	1947	354	495	48	15,315	255	34.26	27	404	14	28.85	169
Barraclough, E S	Mar 30, 1923	May 21, 1999	1949	1950	2	4	2	43	24*	21.50	0	136	4	34.00	0
Bates, W	Nov 19, 1855	Jan 8, 1900	1877	1887	202	331	11	6,499	136	20.37	8	10,692	637	16.78	163
Bates, W E	Mar 5, 1884	Jan 17, 1957	1907	1913	113	167	15	2,634	81	17.32	0	57	2	28.50	64
Batty G J	Oct 13, 1977		1997	1997	1	2	0	18	18	9.00	0	70	2	35.00	0
Batty, J D	May 15, 1971		1989	1994	64	67	20	703	51	14.95	0	5,286	140	37.75	25
Bayes, G W	Feb 27, 1884	Dec 6, 1960	1910	1921	18	24	11	165	36	12.69	0	1,534	48	31.95	7
Beaumont, J	Oct 14, 1916	Nov. 15, 2003	1946	1947	28	46	6	716	60	17.90	0	236	9	26.22	11
Beaumont, J	Sept 16, 1855	May 1, 1920	1877	1878	5	9	3	60	24	10.00	0	50	2	25.00	2
Bedford, H	July 17, 1907		1928	1928	5	5	1	57	24	14.25	0	179	8	22.37	2
Bedford, W	Feb 24, 1879	July 28, 1939	1903	1903	2	2	1	38	30*	38.00	0	117	2	58.50	1
Bell, J T	June 16, 1895	Aug 8, 1974	1921	1923	18	32	2	492	54	16.40	0	—	—	—	12
Berry, John	Jan 10, 1823	Feb 26, 1895	1849	1867	7	8	2	125	30	20.83	0	149	8	18.62	1
Berry, Joseph	Nov 29, 1829	Apr 20, 1894	1861	1874	3	4	2	68	31*	34.00	0	—	—	—	2
Berry, P J.	Dec 28, 1966		1986	1990	3	4	0	76	40	19.00	0	401	7	57.28	1
§ Best T L	© Aug 26, 1981		2010	2010	9	9	1	86	44*	10.75	0	793	18	44.05	2
Betts, G	Sept 19, 1843	Sept 26, 1902	1873	1874	2	4	2	56	56	28.00	0	—	—	—	4
§ Bevan, M G	© May 8, 1970		1995	1996	32	56	8	2,823	160*	58.81	9	720	10	72.00	24
Binks, J G	Oct 5, 1935		1955	1969	491	587	128	6,745	95	14.69	0	66	0	—	872/172
Binns, J	Mar 31, 1870	Dec 8, 1934	1898	1898	1	1	0	4	4	4.00	0	—	—	—	0/3
Bird, H D	Apr 19, 1933		1956	1959	14	25	2	613	181*	26.65	1	—	—	—	3

LIST OF PLAYERS AND CAREER AVERAGES IN ALL FIRST-CLASS MATCHES FOR YORKSHIRE (Continued)

Player	Date of Birth	Date of Death (if known)	First Played	Last Played	M	Inns	NO	Runs	HS	Av'ge	100s	Runs	Wkts	Av'ge	Ct/St
Birkenshaw, J.	Nov 13, 1940		1958	1960	30	42	7	588	42	16.80	0	1,819	69	26.36	21
Birtles, T J D	Oct 26, 1886	Jan 13, 1971	1913	1924	37	57	11	876	104	19.04	1	20	—	—	19
Blackburn, J D H *	Oct 27, 1924	Feb 19, 1987	1956	1956	1	2	0	18	15	9.00	0				0
Blackburn, J S	Sept 24, 1852	July 8, 1922	1876	1877	6	11	1	102	28	10.20	0				4
§ Blain J A R	Jan 4, 1979		2004	2010	10	13	6	26	6*	3.71	0	173	7	24.71	9
Blackburn, W E *	Nov 24, 1882	June 3, 1941	1919	1920	15	13	3	137	28*	13.70	0	1,113	45	24.73	4
Blake, W	Nov 29, 1854	Not known	1880	1880	2	3	0	44	21	14.66	0	1,312	38	34.52	4
Blakey, R J	© Jan 15, 1967		1985	2003	339	541	84	14,150	223*	30.96	12	17	1	17.00	768/56
Blamires, E	July 31, 1850	Mar 22, 1886	1877	1877	12	23	2	655	190	31.19	1	68	1	68.00	0
§ Blewett, G S	© Oct 29, 1971		1999	1999	2	1	0	2	2	2.00	0	82	5	16.40	5
Bloom, G R	Sept 13, 1941		1964	1964	1	2	0	14	11	7.00	0	212	5	42.40	2
Bocking, H	Dec 10, 1835	Feb 22, 1907	1865	1865	1	1	0	6	6	6.00	0				—
Boden, J G *	Dec 27, 1848	Jan 3, 1928	1878	1878	1	1	0	11	11	11.00	0				2
Bolton, B C *	Sept 23, 1862	Nov 18, 1910	1890	1891	4	6	0	25	11	4.16	0				1
Bolus, J B	© Jan 31, 1934		1956	1962	107	179	18	4,712	146*	29.26	7	252	13	19.38	45
Booth, A	Nov 3, 1902	Aug 17, 1974	1931	1947	36	36	16	114	29	5.70	0	407	13	31.30	10
Booth, M W	© Dec 10, 1886	July 1, 1916	1908	1914	144	218	31	4,244	210	22.69	2	11,017	557	19.17	114
Booth, P A	Sept 5, 1965		1982	1989	23	29	9	193	33*	9.65	0	1,517	35	43.34	7
Booth, R	Oct 1, 1926		1951	1955	65	76	28	730	55*	15.20	0				79/29
Bore, M K	June 2, 1947		1969	1977	74	78	21	481	37*	8.43	0	4,866	162	30.03	27
Borrill, P D	July 4, 1951		1971	1971	2	—	—	—	—	—	—	61	5	12.20	0
Bosomworth W E	Mar 8, 1847	June 7, 1891	1872	1880	4	7	1	20	7	3.33	0	140	9	15.55	2
Bottomley, I H *	Apr 9, 1855	Apr 23, 1922	1878	1880	9	12	0	166	32	13.83	0	75	1	75.00	1
Bottomley, T	Dec 26, 1877	Feb 19, 1977	1934	1935	6	7	0	142	51	20.28	0	188	1	188.00	5
Bower, W H	Oct 17, 1857	Jan 31, 1943	1883	1883	1	2	0	10	10	5.00	0				0
Bowes, W E	© July 25, 1908	Sept 4, 1987	1929	1947	301	257	117	1,251	43*	8.93	0	21,227	1,351	15.71	118
Boycott, G	© Oct 21, 1940		1962	1986	414	674	111	32,570	260*	57.85	103	665	28	23.75	200
Brackin, T	Jan 5, 1859		1882	1882	3	6	0	12	9	2.00	0				0
Brayshay, P B *	Jan 14, 1916	July 6, 2004	1952	1952	2	3	0	20	13	6.66	0	104	3	34.66	0
Brearley, H *	June 26, 1913	Aug 14, 2007	1937	1937	1	2	0	17	9	8.50	0				0
Brennan, D V *	© Feb 10, 1920	Jan 9, 1985	1947	1953	204	221	66	1,653	47	10.66	0				280/100

363

LIST OF PLAYERS AND CAREER AVERAGES IN ALL FIRST-CLASS MATCHES FOR YORKSHIRE *(Continued)*

Player	Date of Birth	Date of Death (if known)	First Played	Last Played	M	Inns	NO	Runs	HS	Av'ge	100s	Runs	Wkts	Av'ge	Ct/St
Bresnan, T T ...©	**Feb 28, 1985**		**2003**	**2013**	**95**	**130**	**23**	**2,760**	**116**	**25.79**	**2**	**8,072**	**261**	**30.92**	**38**
Britton, G	Feb 7, 1843	Jan 3, 1910	1867	1867	1	2	0	3	3	1.50	0				0
Broadbent, A	June 7, 1879	July 19, 1958	1909	1910	3	5	0	66	29	13.20	0	252	5	50.40	1
Broadhead, W B	May 31, 1903	Apr 2, 1986	1929	1929	2	2	0	5	3	2.50	0				0
Broadhurst, M	June 20, 1974		1991	1994	3	3	2	7	6	2.33	0	231	7	33.00	0
§ Brophy, G L ...©	Nov 26, 1975		2006	2012	73	112	12	3,012	177*	30.12	3				176/15
Brooke, J W	Feb 1, 1897		1923	1923	1	1	0					6	0		0
Brooke, B	Mar 3, 1930	Mar.3 1989	1950	1950	2	4	0	16	14	4.00	0	191	2	95.50	0
§ Brooks, J A ...©	June 4, 1984		2013	2013	12	14	7	100	33*	14.28	0	908	37	24.54	6
Broughton, P N	Oct 22, 1935		1956	1956	6	5	2	19	12	6.33	0	365	16	22.81	4
Brown, A	June 10, 1854	Nov 2, 1900	1872	1872	2	3	0	9	9	3.00	0	47	3	15.66	4
Brown, J T (Driffield) ©	Aug 20, 1869	Nov 4, 1904	1889	1904	345	567	41	15,694	311	29.83	23	5,183	177	29.28	188
Brown, J T (Darfield)	Nov 24, 1874	Apr 12, 1950	1897	1903	30	32	3	333	37*	11.48	0	2,071	97	21.35	18
Brown, W	Nov 19, 1876	July 27, 1945	1902	1908	2	2	1	2	2	2.00	0	84	4	21.00	0
Brownhill, T	Oct 10, 1838	Jan 6, 1915	1861	1871	14	20	3	185	25	10.88	0				7
Brumfitt, J *	Feb. 18, 1917	Mar 16, 1987	1938	1938	1	1	0	9	9	9.00	0				0
Buller, J S	Aug 23, 1909	Aug 7, 1970	1930	1930	1	2	0	5	5	2.50	0				2
Bulmer, J R L	Dec 28, 1867	Jan 20, 1917	1891	1891	1	2	0	0	0	0.00	0				0
Burgess, T	Oct 1, 1859	Feb 22, 1922	1895	1895	1	1	1	0	0*	0.00	0	79	1	79.00	2
Burgin, E	Jan 4, 1924		1952	1953	12	10	3	92	32	13.14	0	795	31	25.64	0
Burman, J R *	Oct 5, 1838	May 14, 1900	1867	1867	1	2	1	1	1*	1.00	0				0
Burnet, J R * ...©	Oct 11, 1918	Mar 7, 1999	1958	1959	54	75	6	889	54	12.88	0	26	1	26.00	7
§ Burrows, J *	Aug 18, 1855	May 29, 1893	1880	1880	6	10	0	82	23	8.20	0				2
Burton, D C F *	Sept 13, 1887	Sept 24, 1971	1907	1921	104	130	15	2,273	142*	19.76	2				44
Burton, R C *	Apr 11, 1891	Apr 30, 1971	1914	1914	2	2	0	47	47	23.50	0	73	6	12.16	2
Butterfield, E B *	Oct 22, 1848	May 6, 1899	1870	1870	1	2	0	18	10	9.00	0				0
Byas, D	Aug 26, 1963		1986	2001	268	449	42	14,398	213	35.37	28	727	12	60.58	351
Byrom, J L *	July, 20, 1851	Aug 24, 1931	1874	1874	2	1	0	19	11	4.75	0				0
Cammish, J W	May 21, 1921	July 16, 1974	1954	1954	2	1	0	0	0	0.00	0	155	3	51.66	0
Carrick, P ...©	July, 16 1952	Jan 11, 2000	1970	1993	425	543	102	9,994	131*	22.66	3	30,530	1,018	29.99	183

LIST OF PLAYERS AND CAREER AVERAGES IN ALL FIRST-CLASS MATCHES FOR YORKSHIRE (Continued)

Player	Date of Birth	Date of Death (if known)	First Played	Last Played	M	Inns	NO	Runs	HS	Av'ge	100s	Runs	Wkts	Av'ge	Ct/St
Carter, Rev E S *	Feb 3, 1845	May 23, 1923	1876	1881	14	21	2	210	39*	11.05	0	104	8	13.00	4
Cartman, W H	June 20, 1861	Jan 16, 1935	1891	1891	3	6	0	57	49	9.50	0	—	—	—	—
Cawthray, G	Sept 28, 1913	Jan 5, 2000	1939	1952	4	6	0	114	30	19.00	0	304	4	76.00	1
Chadwick, J P G	Nov 8, 1934		1960	1965	6	9	0	106	59	17.66	0	67	2	33.50	7
Chapman, C A	Dec 27, 1851	June 26, 1909	1876	1879	14	23	3	148	29	7.78	0	17	1	17.00	7
Chapman, C A P	June 8, 1971		1990	1998	8	13	2	238	80	21.63	0	—	—	—	13/3
Charlesworth, A P	Feb 19, 1865	May 11, 1926	1894	1895	7	12	1	241	63	21.90	0	—	—	—	2
§ Chichester-Constable, R C J *	Dec 21, 1890	May 26, 1963	1919	1919	1	1	0	0	0	0.00	0	6	0	—	0
Clarkson, A	Sept 5, 1939		1963	1963	6	8	1	80	30	11.42	0	92	5	18.40	5
Claughton, H M	Dec 24, 1891	Oct 17, 1980	1914	1919	4	6	0	39	15	6.50	0	176	3	58.66	1
§ Clayton, M E	Nov 25, 1982		2005	2006	3	4	2	38	38	19.00	0	263	3	87.66	0
§ Clayton, R O	Jan 1, 1844	Nov 26, 1901	1870	1879	70	115	23	992	62	10.78	0	2,478	153	16.19	26
§ Cleary, M F	July 19, 1980		2005	2005	2	2	0	23	12	11.50	0	250	8	31.25	0
Clegg, H	Dec 8, 1850	Dec 30, 1920	1881	1881	6	8	1	63	25*	9.00	0	—	—	—	2
Clifford, C C	July, 5, 1942		1972	1972	11	12	4	39	12*	4.87	0	666	26	25.61	5
Close, D B	Feb 24, 1931		1949	1970	536	811	102	22,650	198	31.94	33	23,489	967	24.29	564
Clough, G D	May 23, 1978		1998	1998	1	2	0	34	33	17.00	0	11	0	—	1
Collinson, R W *	Nov 6, 1875	Dec 26, 1963	1897	1897	2	3	0	58	34	19.33	0	—	—	—	—
Cooper, H P	Apr 17, 1949		1971	1980	98	107	29	1,159	56	14.85	0	6,327	227	27.87	60
Cooper, P E *	Feb 19, 1885	May 21, 1950	1910	1910	2	2	0	0	0	0.00	0	—	—	—	—
Cope, G A	Feb 23, 1947		1966	1980	230	249	89	2,241	78	14.00	0	15,627	630	24.80	64
Corbett, A M	Nov 25, 1855	Oct 7, 1934	1881	1881	1	2	0	0	0	0.00	0	—	—	—	—
Coverdale, S P	Nov 20, 1954		1973	1980	6	4	0	31	18	7.75	0	—	—	—	11/4
Coverdale, W *	July 8, 1862	Sept 23, 1934	1888	1888	2	2	0	2	1	1.00	0	—	—	—	2
Cowan, M J	June 10, 1933		1953	1962	91	84	48	170	19*	4.72	0	6,389	266	24.01	37
Cowley, J M	Feb 24, 1929	Nov 7, 1998	1952	1952	2	2	1	19	19	19.00	0	119	1	119.00	0
Coxon, A	Jan 18, 1916	Jan 22, 2006	1945	1950	142	182	33	2,747	83	18.43	0	9,528	464	20.53	124
Craven, V J	July 31, 1980		2000	2004	33	55	6	1,206	81*	24.61	0	584	15	38.93	18
Crawford, G H	Dec 15, 1890	June 28, 1975	1914	1926	9	8	0	46	21	5.75	0	541	21	25.76	3
Crawford, M G *	July 30, 1920	Dec 2, 2012	1951	1951	1	2	0	22	13	11.00	0	—	—	—	1

Player	Date of Birth	Date of Death (if known)	First Played	Last Played	M	Inns	NO	Runs	HS	Av'ge	100s	Runs	Wkts	Av'ge	Ct/St
Creighton, E	July 9, 1859	Feb 17, 1931	1888	1888	4	8	2	33	10	5.50	0	181	10	18.10	0
Crick, H	Jan 29, 1910	Feb 10, 1960	1937	1947	8	10	0	88	20	8.80	0		0		18/4
Crookes, R	Oct 9, 1846	Feb 15, 1897	1879	1879	1	2	1	2	2*	2.00	0	14	0		0
Crossland, S M	Aug 16, 1851	April 11, 1906	1883	1886	4	6	2	32	20	8.00	0				3/5
Crowther, A	Aug 1, 1878	June 4, 1946	1905	1905	1	2	0	0	0	0.00	0				1
Cuttell, W	Jan 28, 1835	June 10, 1896	1862	1871	15	27	6	271	56	12.90	0	596	36	16.55	4
Dalton, A J	Mar 14, 1947		1969	1972	21	31	2	710	128	24.48	3				6
§ Darnton, T	Feb 12, 1836	Oct 18, 1874	1864	1868	13	22	1	314	81*	14.95	0	349	12	29.08	3
© Davidson, K R	Dec 24, 1905	Dec 25, 1954	1933	1935	30	46	5	1,331	128	32.46	2				18
Dawes, J	Feb 14, 1836	Not known	1865	1865	5	9	2	93	28*	13.28	0	196	5	39.20	3
Dawood, I	July 23, 1976		2004	2005	20	31	7	636	75	26.50	0				46/3
Dawson, E	May 1, 1835	Dec 1, 1888	1863	1874	16	25	1	224	20	9.33	0				5
© Dawson, R K J	Aug 4, 1980		2001	2006	72	106	9	2,179	87	22.46	0	6,444	157	41.04	39
Dawson, W A *	Dec 3, 1850	Mar 6, 1916	1870	1870	1	2	0	0	0	0.00	0				1
Day, A G *	Sept 20, 1865	Oct 16, 1908	1885	1888	6	10	0	78	25	7.80	0				1
© Dennis, F	June 11, 1907	Nov 21, 2000	1928	1933	89	100	28	1,332	67	18.50	0	4,517	156	28.95	58
© Dennis, S J	Oct 18, 1960		1980	1988	67	62	24	338	53*	8.89	0	5,548	173	32.06	19
© Denton, D	July 4, 1874	Feb 16, 1950	1894	1920	676	1,058	61	33,282	221	33.38	61	957	34	28.14	360/1
Denton, J	Feb 3, 1865	July 19, 1946	1887	1888	15	24	1	222	59	9.65	0	15	0		6
Dewse, H	Feb 23, 1836	July 8, 1910	1873	1873	1	2	0	14	12	7.00	0				1
Deyes, G	Feb 11, 1879	Jan 11, 1963	1905	1907	17	24	4	44	12	2.20	0	944	41	23.02	6
Dick, R D *	Apr 16, 1889	Dec 14, 1983	1911	1911	1	1	0	2	2	2.00	0	37	2	18.50	1
Dobson, A	Feb 22, 1854	Sept 17, 1932	1879	1879	1	3	0	1	1	0.33	0				1
Doidge, M J	July 2, 1970		1990	1990	2						0	106	1	106.00	0
© Dolphin, A	Dec 24, 1885	Oct 23, 1942	1905	1927	427	446	157	3,325	66	11.50	0	28	1	28.00	569/260
Douglas, J S	Apr 4, 1903	Dec 27, 1971	1925	1934	23	26	8	125	19	6.94	0	1,310	49	26.73	14
© Drake, A	Apr 16, 1884	Feb 14, 1919	1909	1914	156	244	24	4,789	147*	21.76	3	8,623	479	18.00	93
Drake, J	Sept 1, 1893	May 22, 1967	1923	1924	3	4	1	21	10	7.00	0	117	1	117.00	2
Driver, J	May 16, 1861	Dec 10, 1946	1889	1889	2	4	1	24	8	8.00	0				2
Dury, T S *	June 12, 1854	Mar 20, 1932	1878	1881	13	24	1	329	46	14.30	0	21	0		3

LIST OF PLAYERS AND CAREER AVERAGES IN ALL FIRST-CLASS MATCHES FOR YORKSHIRE (Continued)

Player	Date of Birth	Date of Death (if known)	First Played	Last Played	M	Inns	NO	Runs	HS	Av'ge	100s	Runs	Wkts	Av'ge	Ct/St
Dyson, W L	Dec 11, 1857	May 1, 1936	1887	1887	2	4	0	44	23	11.00	0	—	—	—	2
Earnshaw, W	Sept 20, 1867	Nov 24, 1941	1893	1896	29	51	2	591	68	12.06	0	349	11	31.72	6/2
Eastwood, D	Mar 30, 1848	May 17, 1903	1870	1877	6	2	2	9	9*	—	0	62	0	—	16
Eckersley, R	Sept 4, 1925	May 30, 2009	1945	1945	1							—	—	—	0
Elam, F W *	Sept 13, 1871	Mar 11, 1943	1900	1902	2	3	1	48	28	24.00	0	77	1	77.00	0
§ Elliott, M T G	Sept 28, 1971		2002	2002	5	10	1	487	127	54.11	1	—	—	—	7
Ellis, J E	Nov 10, 1864	Dec 1, 1927	1888	1892	11	15	6	14	4*	1.55	0	—	—	—	11/10
Ellis, S *	Nov 23, 1851	Oct 28, 1930	1880	1880	2	3	0	12	9	4.00	0	—	—	—	2
Elms, J E	Dec 24, 1874	Nov 1, 1951	1905	1905	1	2	0	20	20	10.00	0	28	1	28.00	1
Elstub, C J	Feb 3, 1981		2000	2002	6	7	6	28	18*	28.00	0	356	9	39.55	1
Emmett, T	Sept 3, 1841	June 29, 1904	1866	1888	299	484	65	6315	104	15.07	1	15,465	1,216	12.71	179
Farrar, A	Apr 29, 1884	Dec 25, 1954	1906	1906	1	1	0	2	2	2.00	0	133	6	22.16	1
Fearnley, M C	Aug 21, 1936	July 7, 1979	1962	1964	3	4	2	19	11*	9.50	0	12	0	—	0
Featherby, W D	Aug 18, 1888	Nov 20, 1958	1920	1920	46	71	6	1,526	109	23.47	1	1,202	32	37.56	23
Fellows, G M	July 30, 1978		1998	2003	18	24	6	182	25	10.11	0	—	—	—	—
Fiddling, K	Oct 13, 1917	June 19, 1992	1938	1946	1	1	0	1	1	1.00	0	—	—	—	24/13
Firth, A *	Sept 3, 1847	Jan 16, 1927	1869	1869	8	8	5	134	67*	44.66	0	—	—	—	1
Firth, Rev E B *	Apr 11, 1863	July 25, 1905	1894	1894	52	58	14	681	76*	15.47	0	—	—	—	14/2
Firth, J	June 27, 1918	Sept 7, 1981	1949	1950	24	32	9	545	68*	23.69	0	—	—	—	22
Fisher, H	Aug 3, 1903	Apr 16, 1974	1928	1936	4	8	0	121	57	15.12	0	2,621	93	28.18	1
Fisher, I D	Mar 31, 1976		1996	2001	7	14	2	469	98	39.08	0	1,382	43	32.13	13
Flaxington, S	Oct 14, 1860	Mar 10, 1895	1882	1882	107	91	31	414	28*	6.90	0	—	—	—	25
§ Fleming, S P	©Apr 1, 1973		2003	2003	5	8	1	80	31*	11.42	0	—	—	—	4
Fletcher, S D	June 8, 1964		1983	1991	51	34	16	114	35	6.33	0	7,966	234	34.04	19
Fletcher, W	Feb 16, 1866	June 1, 1935	1892	1892	14	1	0	2	2	2.00	0	157	7	22.42	6
Foord, C W	June 11, 1924	April 16, 1956	1947	1953	1	7	1	165	63*	27.50	0	3,412	126	27.07	6
Foster, E	Nov 23, 1873		1901	1901	5	20	5	138	25	9.20	0	27	1	25.00	3
Foster, M J	Sept 17, 1972		1993	1994	14	2	0	10	7	5.00	0	—	—	—	8
§ Foster, T W	Nov 12, 1871	Jan 31, 1947	1894	1895	14	28	4	298	58	12.41	0	952	58	16.41	—
Frank, J *	Dec 17, 1857	Oct 22, 1940	1881	1881	5							—	—	—	—
©Frank R W *	May 29, 1864	Sept 9, 1950	1889	1903	18							17	1	17.00	—

Player	Date of Birth	Date of Death (if known)	First Played	Last Played	M	Inns	NO	Runs	HS	Av'ge	100s	Runs	Wkts	Av'ge	Ct/St
Freeman, G	July 27, 1843	Nov 18, 1895	1865	1880	32	54	4	752	53	14.46	0	2,079	209	9.94	16
Gale, A W	**Nov 28, 1983**		**2004**	**2013**	**104**	**164**	**13**	**5,548**	**272**	**36.74**	**14**	**238**	**1**	**238.00**	**38**
Geldart, C J *	Dec 17, 1991		2010	2011	2	2	1	51	34	25.50	0				1
Gibb, P A *©	July 11, 1913	Dec 7, 1977	1935	1946	36	54	7	1,545	157*	32.87	2	82	3	27.33	25/8
Gibson, B P **	Mar 31, 1996		2011	2011	1	1	1	—	1*	—	0	—	—	—	6/0
§ Gitkins, C J *	Feb 19, 1856	Jan 31, 1897	1880	1880	2	3	0	30	23	10.00	0	—	—	—	1
Gilbert, C R	Apr 16, 1984		2007	2007	1	2	0	64	64	64.00	0	—	0	—	1
Gill, F	Sept 3, 1883	Nov 1, 1917	1906	1906	1	2	0	18	11	4.50	0	11	0	—	—
§ Gillespie, J N *	©April 19, 1975		2006	2007	26	34	11	640	123*	27.82	1	2,013	59	34.11	4
§ Gillhouley, K	Aug 8, 1934		1961	1961	24	31	9	323	56*	13.45	0	1,702	77	22.10	16
Gough, D	© Sept 18, 1970		1989	2008	146	188	29	2,922	121	18.37	1	12,487	453	27.56	30
Goulder, A	Aug 16, 1907	June 11, 1986	1929	1929	2	1	0	3	3	3.00	0	90	3	30.00	—
§ Gray, A K D	May 19, 1974		2001	2004	18	26	3	649	104	28.21	1	1,357	30	45.23	16
Grayson, A P	Mar 31, 1971		1990	1995	25	50	10	1,958	100	48.95	2	846	13	65.07	16
Greenwood, A	Aug 20, 1847	Feb 12, 1889	1869	1880	95	166	6	2,762	91	17.93	0	36	2	18.00	33
§ Greenwood, F E *	© Sept 28, 1905	July 30, 1963	1929	1932	57	66	8	1,458	104*	25.13	1	—	—	—	37
Greenwood, L	July 13, 1834	Nov 1, 1909	1861	1874	50	84	4	885	83	12.29	0	1,615	85	19.00	24
Grimshaw, C H	May 12, 1880	Sept 25, 1947	1904	1908	50	75	4	1,219	85	17.92	0	221	7	31.57	42
Grimshaw, I	May 4, 1857	Jan 18, 1911	1880	1887	125	194	14	3,354	129*	18.63	4				76/3
Guy S M	Nov 17, 1978		2000	2011	37	52	6	742	52*	16.13	0	8	0	—	98/12
Haggas, S	Apr 18, 1856	Mar 14, 1926	1878	1882	31	47	3	478	43	10.86	0	—	—	—	10
Haigh S	Mar 19, 1871	Feb 27, 1921	1895	1913	513	687	110	10,993	159	19.05	4	29,289	1,876	15.61	276
Hall, B	Sept 16, 1929	Feb 27, 1989	1952	1952	1	2	0	10	10	7.00	0	55	1	55.00	1
Hall, C H	Apr 5, 1906	Dec 11, 1976	1928	1934	23	22	9	67	15*	5.15	0	1,226	45	27.24	11
§ Hall, H J	Nov 11, 1815	Apr 17, 1888	1844	1863	1	2	0	4	4	2.00	0	—	—	—	2
Hall, L	Nov 1, 1852	Nov 19, 1915	1873	1894	275	477	58	9,757	160	23.28	9	781	15	52.06	173
Halliday, H	© Feb 9, 1920	Aug 27, 1967	1938	1953	182	279	18	8,361	144	32.03	12	3,119	101	30.88	140
Halliley, C	Dec 5, 1852	Mar 23, 1929	1872	1872	3	5	0	27	17	5.40	0	—	—	—	2
Hamer, C	Dec 8, 1916	Nov 3, 1938	1938	1938	3	2	0	3	3	1.50	0	64	1	64.00	2

368

** At 15 years and 27 days on April 27, 2011, First Day of Yorkshire's match v. Durham MCCU, he became the youngest ever English First Class cricketer.

LIST OF PLAYERS AND CAREER AVERAGES IN ALL FIRST-CLASS MATCHES FOR YORKSHIRE *(Continued)*

Player	Date of Birth	Date of Death (if known)	First Played	Last Played	M	Inns	NO	Runs	HS	Av'ge	100s	Runs	Wkts	Av'ge	Ct/St
§ Hamilton, G M ...	©Sept 16, 1974		1994	2003	73	108	18	2,228	125	24.75	1	5,479	222	24.68	25
Hampshire, A W ...	Oct 18, 1950		1975	1975	3	2	0	18	17	9.00	0				1
Hampshire, J ...	Oct 5, 1913	May 23, 1997	1937	1937	2	2	0	5	5	2.50	0	109	5	21.80	1
Hampshire, J H ...	©Feb 10, 1941		1961	1981	456	724	89	21,979	183*	34.61	34	1,108	24	46.16	368
Hannon-Dalby, O J ...	Jun 20, 1989		2008	2012	24	25	10	45	11*	3.00	0	1,938	43	45.06	2
§ Harbord, W E * ...	Dec 15, 1908	July 28, 1992	1929	1935	16	21	1	411	109	20.55	1				7
§ Harden, R J ...	Aug 16, 1965		1999	2000	12	22	3	439	69	23.10	0				2
Hardisty, C H ...	Dec 10, 1885	Mar 2, 1968	1906	1909	38	55	5	991	84	19.82	0				18
§ Hargreaves, H S ...	Mar 22, 1911	Sept 29, 1991	1934	1938	18	20	6	51	9	3.64	0	1,145	55	20.81	3
§ Harmison, S J ...	Oct 23, 1978		2012	2012	3	3	0	25	23	8.33	0	195	8	24.37	1
Harris, W ...	Nov 21, 1861	May 23, 1923	1884	1887	4	8	2	45	25	7.50	0	18			1
§ Harrison, G P ...	©Feb 11, 1862	Sept 14, 1940	1883	1892	59	87	26	407	28*	6.67	0	3,276	226	14.49	36
Harrison, H ...	Jan 26, 1885	Feb 11, 1962	1907	1907	2	2	1	4	4*	4.00	0	39	2	19.50	0
Harrison, W H ...	May 27, 1863	July 15, 1939	1888	1888	3	6	1	12	7	2.40	0				1
Hart, H W * ...	Sept 21, 1859	Nov 2, 1895	1888	1888	1	2	0	6	6	3.00	0	32	2	16.00	0
Hart, P R ...	Jan 12, 1947		1981	1981	3	5	0	23	11	4.60	0	140	2	70.00	1
Hartington, H E ...	Sept 18, 1881	Feb 16, 1950	1910	1911	10	10	4	51	16	8.50	0	764	23	33.21	2
Hartley, P J ...	©Apr 18, 1960		1985	1997	195	237	51	3,844	127*	20.66	2	17,438	579	30.11	60
Hartley, S N ...	Mar 18, 1956		1978	1988	133	199	27	4,193	114	24.37	4	2,052	42	48.85	47
§ Harvey, S N ...	Apr 10, 1972		2004	2005	20	31	1	1,045	209*	36.03	2	831	37	22.45	12
Hatton, A G ...	Mar 25, 1937		1960	1961	3	1	1	4	4*		0	202	6	33.66	1
§ Hawke, Lord * ...	©Aug 16, 1860	Oct 10, 1938	1881	1911	510	739	91	13,133	166	20.26	10	16	0		159
Hayley, H ...	Feb 22, 1860	June 3, 1922	1884	1898	7	12	1	122	24	11.09	0	48	1	14.00	3
Haywood, W J ...	Feb 25, 1841	Jan 7, 1912	1878	1878	1	2	0	7	7	3.50	0	14	1		3
Hicks, J ...	Dec 10, 1850	June 10, 1912	1872	1876	15	25	3	313	66	14.22	0	17			12
Higgins, J ...	Mar 13, 1877	June 10, 1905	1901	1905	9	14	5	93	28*	10.33	0				10/3
Hill, A ...	Nov 14, 1843	Aug 29, 1910	1871	1882	140	223	25	1,705	49	8.61	0	7,002	542	12.91	91
Hill, H * ...	Nov 29, 1858	Aug 14, 1935	1888	1891	14	27	2	337	34	13.48	0				10
Hill, L G * ...	Nov 2, 1860	Aug 27, 1940	1882	1882	1	2	0	13	13	6.50	0				1
Hirst, E T * ...	May 6, 1857	Oct 26, 1914	1877	1888	21	33	2	328	87*	10.58	0				7
Hirst, E W * ...	Feb 27, 1855	Oct 24, 1933	1881	1881	2	3	0	33	28	11.00	0	3	0		0

Player	Date of Birth	Date of Death (if known)	First Played	Last Played	M	Inns	NO	Runs	HS	Av'ge	100s	Runs	Wkts	Av'ge	Ct/St
Hirst, G H	© Sept 7, 1871	May 10, 1954	1891	1921*	717	1,050	128	32,024	341	34.73	56	44,716	2,481	18.02	518
Hirst, T H	May 21, 1865	Apr 3, 1927	1899	1899	1	1	0	5	5*		0	27	0		0
§ Hodd, A J	Jan 12, 1984		2012	2013	13	14	2	308	68*	25.66	0				35/1
Hodgson, G	July 24, 1938		1964	1964	1	1	0	4	4	4.00	0				0/2
Hodgson, L J	Nov 15, 1828	Nov 24, 1867	1855	1866	21	35	14	164	21*	7.80	0	1,537	88	17.46	11
Hodgson, L J	Jun 29, 1986		2009	2010	3	3	0	99	34	33.00	0	158	2	79.00	1
Hodgson, P	Sept 21, 1935		1954	1956	13	6	2	33	8*	8.25	0	648	22	29.45	6
Hoggard, M J	© Dec 31, 1976		1996	2009	102	120	34	956	89*	11.11	0	8,956	331	27.05	23
Holdsworth, W E N	Sept 17, 1928		1952	1953	27	26	12	174	22*	7.92	0	1,598	53	30.15	7
Holgate, G	June 23, 1839	July 11, 1895	1865	1867	12	19	0	38	11	9.15	0				17/1
Holmes, P	© Nov 25, 1886	Sept 3, 1971	1913	1933	485	699	74	26,220	315*	41.95	60	124	1	124.00	319
Horner, N F	May 10, 1926	Dec 24, 2003	1950	1950	2	4	0	114	43	28.50	0				2
Houseman, I J	Oct 12, 1969		1989	1991	5	2	1	18	18	18.00	0	311	3	103.66	0/1
Hoyle, T H	Mar 19, 1884	June 2, 1953	1919	1919	1	1	0	7	7	7.00	0				2
Hudson, D	June 29, 1852	Nov 11, 1901	1880	1880	3	4	0	13	5	3.25	0				2
Hunter, D	© Feb 23, 1860	Jan 11, 1927	1888	1909	517	681	323	4,177	58*	11.66	0	43	0		863/323
Hunter, J	Aug 3, 1855	Jan 4, 1891	1878	1888	143	213	61	1,183	60*	7.78	0				207/102
Hutchison, P M	June 9, 1977		1996	2001	39	39	23	187	30	11.68	0	3,244	143	22.68	8
Hutton, L	© June 23, 1916	Sept, 6, 1990	1934	1955	341	527	62	24,807	280*	53.34	85	4,221	154	27.40	278
Hutton, R A	© Sept 6, 1942		1962	1974	208	292	45	4,986	189	20.18	0	10,254	468	21.91	160
Iddison, R	© Sept 15, 1834	Mar 19, 1890	1855	1876	72	108	15	1,916	112	20.60	1	1,540	102	15.09	70
Illingworth, R	June 8, 1932		1951	1983	496	668	131	14,986	162	27.90	14	26,806	1,431	18.73	286
§ Imran Tahir	Mar 27, 1979		2007	2007	1	2	0	5	5	2.50	0	141	0		0
Ingham, P G	Sept 28, 1956		1979	1981	8	14	0	290	64	20.71	0				0
Inglis, J W	Oct 19, 1979		2000	2000	1	2	0	4	2	2.00	0				0
§ Inzamam-ul-Haq	Mar 3, 1970		2007	2007	3	4	0	89	51	22.25	0				5
Jackson, Hon F S *	Nov 21, 1870	Mar 9, 1947	1890	1907	207	328	22	10,371	160	33.89	21	9,690	506	19.15	129
Jackson, S R *	July 15, 1865	July 19, 1941	1891	1891	1	2	0	9	9	4.50	0				0
Jacques, T A	Feb 19, 1905	Feb 23, 1995	1927	1936	28	20	7	162	35*	12.46	0	1,786	57	31.33	12

LIST OF PLAYERS AND CAREER AVERAGES IN ALL FIRST-CLASS MATCHES FOR YORKSHIRE (Continued)

Player	Date of Birth	Date of Death (if known)	First Played	Last Played	M	Inns	NO	Runs	HS	Av'ge	100s	Runs	Wkts	Av'ge	Ct/St
Jakeman, F	Jan 10, 1920	May 18, 1986	1946	1947	10	16	2	262	51	18.71	0	228	8	28.50	3
James, B	Apr 23, 1934		1954	1954	4	5	3	22	11*	11.00	0				
§ Jaques, P A	© May 3, 1979		2004	2013	53	82	3	4,039	243	51.12	11	112	1	112.00	46
Jarvis, P W	June 29, 1965		1981	1993	138	160	46	1,898	80	16.64	0	11,990	449	26.70	36
Johnson, J	Sept 5, 1947		1969	1979	100	152	14	2,960	107	21.44	2	265	4	66.25	50
Johnson, M	May 16, 1916		1936	1939	3	3	2	5	4*	5.00	0	27	5	5.40	1
Johnson, M	Apr 23, 1958		1981	1981	4	4	2	2	2	1.00	0	5	0	—	—
Joy, J	Sept 29, 1826	Sept 27, 1889	1849	1867	3	5	0	107	74	21.40	0	5	0	—	1
Judson, A	July 10, 1885	Apr 8, 1975	1920	1920	1	1						5	0	—	3
§ Katich, S M	Aug 21, 1975		2002	2002	1	2	0	37	21	18.50	0	25	0	—	1
Kaye, Harold S *	May 9, 1882	Nov 6, 1953	1907	1908	18	25	1	243	37	10.12	0				9
Kaye, Haven	June 11, 1846	Jan 24, 1892	1872	1873	8	14	0	117	33	8.35	0				3
Keedy, G	Nov 27, 1974		1994	1994	1	1	0	1	1	1.00	0				
§ Keighley, W G *	Jan 10, 1925	June 14, 2005	1947	1951	35	51	5	1,227	110	26.67	1	18	0	—	12
Kellett, S A	Oct 16, 1967		1989	1995	86	147	10	4,204	125*	30.68	7	7	0	—	74
Kennie, G	May 17, 1904		1927	1927	1	2	0	6	6	3.00	0				
Kettleborough, R A	Mar 15, 1973		1994	1997	13	19	2	446	108	26.23	1	153	3	51.00	9
Kilburn, S	Oct 16, 1868	Sept 25, 1940	1896	1896	1	1	0	8	8	8.00	0				
Kilner, N	July 21, 1895	Apr 28, 1979	1919	1923	69	73	7	1,253	112	18.98	2				34
Kilner, R	© Oct 17, 1890	Apr 5, 1928	1911	1927	365	478	46	13,018	206*	30.13	15	14,855	857	17.33	231
King, A M	Oct 8, 1932		1955	1955	1	1	0	12	12	12.00	0	12	0	—	0
Kippax, P J	Oct 15, 1940		1961	1962	4	7	2	37	9	7.40	0	279	8	34.87	0
§ Kirby, S P	© Oct 4, 1977		2001	2004	47	61	14	342	57	7.27	0	5,143	182	28.25	11
§ Kruis, G J	© May 9, 1974		2005	2009	54	64	31	617	50*	18.69	0	5,431	154	35.26	11
§ Lambert, G A	Jan 4, 1980		2000	2000	2	3	0	6	3*	6.00	0	133	4	33.25	
Lancaster, W W	Feb 4, 1873	Dec 30, 1938	1895	1895	7	10	0	163	51	16.30	0	29	0	—	1
§ Landon, C W *	May 30, 1850	Mar 5, 1903	1878	1882	9	13	0	51	18	3.92	0	74	0	—	7
§ Law, W *	Apr 9, 1851	Dec 20, 1892	1871	1873	4	7	0	51	22	7.28	0				3
Lawson, M A K	Oct 24, 1985		2004	2007	15	21	5	197	44	12.31	0	1,699	42	40.45	7
Leadbeater, B	© Aug 14, 1943		1966	1979	144	236	27	5,247	140*	25.10	1	5	1	5.00	80

LIST OF PLAYERS AND CAREER AVERAGES IN ALL FIRST-CLASS MATCHES FOR YORKSHIRE (Continued)

Player	Date of Birth	Date of Death (if known)	First Played	Last Played	M	Inns	NO	Runs	HS	Av'ge	100s	Runs	Wkts	Av'ge	Ct/St
Leadbeater, E	Aug. 15, 1927	Apr 17, 2011	1949	1956	81	94	29	898	91	13.81	0	5,657	201	28.14	49
Leadbeater, H *	Dec 31, 1863	Oct 9, 1928	1884	1890	6	10	2	141	65	17.62	0	11	0	—	4
§ Leaning, J A	Oct 18, 1993		2013	2013	1	1	0	0	0	0.00	0	22	0	—	0
Leatham, G A B *	Apr 30, 1851	June 19, 1932	1874	1886	12	18	5	61	14	4.69	0	—	—	—	21/7
Leather, R S *	Aug 17, 1880	Jan 31, 1913	1906	1906	1	2	0	19	14	9.50	0	—	—	—	0
Lee, C	Mar 17, 1924	Sept 4, 1999	1952	1952	2	4	0	98	74	24.50	0	—	—	—	1
Lee, F	Nov 18, 1856	Sept 13, 1896	1882	1890	105	182	10	3,622	165	21.05	3	—	—	—	53/1
Lee, G H	Aug 24, 1854	Oct 4, 1919	1879	1879	1	2	0	13	9	6.50	0	—	—	—	0
Lee, Herbert	July 2, 1856	Feb 4, 1908	1885	1885	5	6	0	20	12	3.33	0	—	—	—	2
Lee, J E *	Mar 23, 1838	Apr 2, 1880	1867	1867	2	3	0	9	6	3.00	0	—	—	—	2
Lee, J E	Dec 23, 1988		2006	2009	2	3	1	149	74	74.50	0	—	—	—	2
Lees, A Z	Apr 14, 1993		2010	2013	11	18	3	659	275*	43.93	3	—	—	—	2
Legard, A D *	June 19, 1878	Aug 15, 1939	1910	1910	4	5	0	50	15	10.00	0	26	0	—	0
§ Lehmann, D S	Feb 5, 1970		1997	2006	88	137	8	8,871	339	68.76	26	1,952	61	32.00	35
Lester, E I	Feb 18, 1923	Jan 1, 1967	1945	1956	228	339	27	10,616	186	34.02	24	160	3	53.33	106
Leyland, M	July 20, 1900		1920	1946	548	720	82	26,180	263	41.03	62	11,079	409	27.08	204
Lilley, A E	Apr 17, 1992		2011	2011	1	1	0	0	0	0.00	0	34	0	—	0
Linaker, L	Apr 8, 1885	Nov 17, 1961	1909	1909	1	2	1	36	10	3.60	0	28	1	28.00	1
Lister, B	Dec 9, 1919	Dec 3, 1919	1874	1878	7	11	0	13	7*	13.00	0	64	1	64.00	2
§ Lister-Kaye, K A *	Mar 27, 1892	Feb 28, 1955	1928	1928	2	2	0	35	16	8.75	0	—	—	—	2
Lister, J *	May 14, 1930	Jan 28, 1991	1954	1954	214	364	29	7,789	208	23.25	6	2,265	141	16.06	164/2
Lockwood, E	Apr 4, 1845	Dec 19, 1921	1868	1884	16	27	2	408	90	16.32	0	37	0	—	8
Lockwood, H	Oct 20, 1855	Feb 18, 1930	1877	1882	2	3	0	48	30	16.00	0	17	0	—	1
Lodge, J T	Apr 16, 1921	July 9, 2002	1948	1948	247	388	58	10,263	170*	31.10	13	835	12	69.58	123
Love, J D	Apr 22, 1955		1975	1989	1	1	1	5	5*	5.00	0	—	—	—	0
Love, G E	Jan 12, 1878	Aug 15, 1932	1902	1902	1	1	0	5	5	5.00	0	—	—	—	0
Lowe, J R	Oct 19, 1991		2010	2010	1	1	0	5	5	5.00	0	—	—	—	0
Lowson, F A	July 1, 1925	Sept 8, 1984	1949	1958	252	404	31	13,897	259*	37.25	30	15	0	—	180
§ Loxley-Firth, E *	Mar 7, 1886	Jan 8, 1949	1912	1912	2	4	0	43	37	10.75	0	—	—	—	0
§ Lucas, D S	Aug 19, 1978		2005	2005	1	—	—	—	—	—	—	84	8	10.50	—

372

LIST OF PLAYERS AND CAREER AVERAGES IN ALL FIRST-CLASS MATCHES FOR YORKSHIRE (Continued)

Player	Date of Birth	Date of Death (if known)	First Played	Last Played	M	Inns	NO	Runs	HS	Av'ge	100s	Runs	Wkts	Av'ge	Ct/St
Lumb, E * ...Ⓞ	Sept 12, 1852	Apr 5, 1891	1872	1886	14	23	4	311	70*	16.36	0	199	5	39.80	5
§ Lumb, M J ...Ⓞ	Feb 12, 1980		2000	2006	78	135	12	4,194	144	34.09	8	5	0	—	43
Lumb, R G ...	Feb 27, 1950		1970	1984	239	395	30	11,525	165*	31.57	22	88	0	—	129
Lupton, A W * ...	Feb 23, 1879	Apr 14, 1944	1908	1927	104	79	15	668	43*	10.43	0				25
Lynas, G G ...Ⓞ	Sept 7, 1832	Dec 8, 1896	1867	1867	2	3	1	4	4*	2.00	0				2
Lyth A ...Ⓞ	**Sept 25, 1987**		**2007**	**2013**	**77**	**126**	**6**	**4,579**	**248***	**38.15**	**7**	**452**	**7**	**64.57**	**81**
Macaulay, G G ...Ⓞ	Dec 7, 1897	Dec 13, 1940	1920	1935	445	430	112	5,717	125*	17.97	8	30,554	1,774	17.22	361
McGrath, A ...Ⓞ	Oct 6, 1975		1995	2012	242	405	29	14,091	211	37.47	34	4,652	128	36.34	168
McHugh, F P ...	Nov 15, 1925		1949	1949	3	1	0	0	0	0.00	0	147	4	36.75	1
Marshall, A ...	July 10, 1849	Aug 3, 1891	1874	1874	1	2	0	2	1	1.00	0	11	0	—	
§ Martyn, D R ...	Oct 21, 1971		2003	2003	2	3	0	342	238	171.00	1				2
Mason, A ...	May 2, 1921	Mar. 2006.	1947	1950	18	19	3	105	22	6.56	0	1,473	51	28.88	6
Maude, E * ...	Dec 31, 1839	July 2, 1876	1866	1866	2	2	0	17	16	8.50	0				
Metcalfe, A A ...Ⓞ	Dec 25, 1963		1983	1995	184	317	19	10,465	216*	35.11	25	344	3	114.66	72
Micklethwait, W H * ...	Dec 13, 1885	Oct 7, 1947	1911	1911	1	1	0	44	44	44.00	0				
Middlebrook, J D ...	May 13, 1977		1998	2001	23	31	3	485	84	17.32	0	1,458	49	29.75	14
Middlebrook, W ...	May 23, 1858	Apr 26, 1919	1888	1889	17	27	7	88	19*	4.40	0	895	50	17.90	1
Midgley, C A * ...	Nov 11, 1877	June 24, 1942	1906	1906	4	6	2	115	59*	28.75	0	149	3	49.66	3
Milburn, S M ...	Sept 29, 1972		1992	1898	6	8	2	22	7	3.66	0	431	14	30.78	
§ Milligan, F W * ...	Mar 19, 1870	Mar 31, 1900	1894	1898	81	113	10	1,879	74	18.24	0	2,736	112	24.42	40
Mitchell, A ...Ⓞ	Sept 13, 1902	Dec 25, 1976	1922	1945	401	550	69	18,189	189	37.81	39	291	5	58.20	406
Mitchell, F * ...Ⓞ	Aug 13, 1872	Oct 11, 1935	1894	1904	83	125	5	4,104	194	34.20	10	16	1	16.00	52
Monks, G D ...	Sept 3, 1929		1952	1952	1	1	0	2	2	3.00	0				
Moorhouse, R ...Ⓞ	Sept 7, 1866	Jan 7, 1921	1888	1899	206	315	45	5,217	113	19.32	3	1,232	43	28.65	92
§ Morkel, M ...Ⓞ	Oct 6, 1984		2008	2008	1	2	0	8	8	4.00	0	33	1	33.00	0
Morris, A C ...	Oct 4, 1976		1995	1997	16	23	0	362	60	17.23	0	508	9	56.44	12
Mosley, H ...	Mar 8, 1858	Nov 29, 1933	1881	1881	2	4	0	1	1	0.25	0	34	3	11.33	
Motley, A * ...Ⓞ	Feb 5, 1858	Sept 28, 1897	1879	1879	2	2	0	10	8*	10.00	0	135	7	19.28	
Mounsey, J T ...Ⓞ	Aug 30, 1871	Apr 6, 1949	1891	1897	92	145	21	1,939	64	15.63	0	444	10	44.40	45
Moxon, M D ...Ⓞ	May 4, 1960		1981	1997	277	476	42	18,973	274*	43.71	41	1,213	22	55.13	190

LIST OF PLAYERS AND CAREER AVERAGES IN ALL FIRST-CLASS MATCHES FOR YORKSHIRE (Continued)

Player	Date of Birth	Date of Death (if known)	First Played	Last Played	M	Inns	NO	Runs	HS	Av'ge	100s	Runs	Wkts	Av'ge	Ct/St
Myers, H .... ©	Jan 2, 1875	June 12, 1944	1901	1910	201	289	46	4,450	91	18.31	0	7,095	282	25.15	106
Myers, M	Apr 12, 1847	Dec 2, 1919	1876	1878	22	40	4	537	49	14.91	0	20	0	—	11
§ Naved-ul-Hasan, Rana	Feb 28, 1978		2008	2009	11	16	3	207	32	15.92	0	1,018	26	39.15	3
Naylor, J E	Dec 11, 1930	June 26, 1996	1953	1953	11							88	0	—	1
Newstead, J T ...... ©	Sept 8, 1877	Mar 25, 1952	1903	1913	96	128	17	1,791	100*	16.13	1	5,555	297	18.70	75
Nicholson, A G ...... ©	June 25, 1938	Nov 3, 1985	1962	1975	282	267	125	1,667	50	11.73	0	17,296	876	19.74	85
Nicholson, N G	Oct 17, 1963		1988	1989	5	8	3	134	56*	26.80	0	25	0	—	5
Oates, William	Jan 1, 1852	Dec 9, 1940	1874	1875	7	13	7	34	14*	5.66	0			—	5/1
Oates, W F	June 11, 1929	May 15, 2001	1956	1956	3	3	0	20	9	6.66	0			—	1
Old, C M .... ©	Dec 22, 1948		1966	1982	222	262	56	4,785	116	23.22	5	13,409	647	20.72	131
Oldham, S	July 26, 1948		1974	1985	59	39	18	212	50	10.09	0	3,849	130	29.60	18
Oldroyd, E .... ©	Oct 1, 1888	Dec 29, 1964	1910	1931	383	509	58	15,891	194	35.23	37	1,658	42	39.47	203
Oyston, C	May 12, 1869	July 15, 1942	1900	1909	15	21	8	96	22	7.38	0	872	31	28.12	3
Padgett, D E V ...... ©	July 20, 1934		1951	1971	487	774	63	20,306	161*	28.55	29	208	6	34.66	250
Padgett, G H	Oct 9, 1931		1952	1952	6	7	4	56	32*	18.66	0	336	4	84.00	5
Padgett, J	Nov 21, 1860	Aug 2, 1943	1882	1889	6	9	0	92	22	10.22	0			—	2
Parker, B	June 23, 1970		1992	1998	44	71	10	1,839	138*	30.14	2	3	0	0.00	19
§ Parkin, C H	Feb 18, 1886	June 15, 1943	1906	1906	1	1	0	0	0	0.00	0	25	2	12.50	0
Parratt, J	Mar 24, 1859	May 6, 1905	1888	1890	2	2	0	11	11	5.50	0	75	1	75.00	4
§ Parton, J W	Jan 31, 1863	Jan. 30, 1906	1889	1889	1	2	0	16	14	8.00	0	4	1	4.00	0
Patterson, S A ...... ©	Oct 3, 1983		2005	2013	73	82	28	807	53	14.94	0	5,469	192	28.48	13
Pearson, H E	Aug 7, 1851	July 8, 1880	1878	1880	4	4	1	31	10*	15.50	0	90	5	18.00	—
Pearson, J H	May 14, 1915	May 13, 2007	1934	1936	3	3	0	54	44	18.00	0			—	1
Peate, E	Mar 2, 1855	Mar 11, 1900	1879	1887	154	226	61	1,793	95	10.86	0	9,986	794	12.57	97
Peel, R .... ©	Feb 12, 1857	Aug 12, 1941	1882	1897	318	510	42	9,322	210*	19.91	6	20,638	1,311	15.74	141
Penny, J H	Sept 29, 1856	July 29, 1902	1891	1891	1	1	0	8	8*		0	31	2	15.50	—
Pickles, C S ...... ©	Jan 30, 1966		1985	1992	58	76	21	1,336	66	24.29	0	3,638	83	43.83	24
Pickles D	Nov 16, 1935		1957	1960	41	40	20	74	12	3.70	0	2,062	96	21.47	10
Pinder, G	July 15, 1841	Jan 15, 1903	1867	1880	125	199	44	1,639	57	10.57	0	325	19	17.10	145/102
Platt, R K .... ©	Dec 26, 1932		1955	1963	96	103	47	405	57*	7.23	0	6,389	282	22.65	35

LIST OF PLAYERS AND CAREER AVERAGES IN ALL FIRST-CLASS MATCHES FOR YORKSHIRE (Continued)

Player	Date of Birth	Date of Death (if known)	First Played	Last Played	M	Inns	NO	Runs	HS	Av'ge	100s	Runs	Wkts	Av'ge	Ct/St
Plunkett L E ....©	Apr 6, 1985		2013	2013	13	18	2	394	68	24.62	0	1,065	42	25.35	9
Pollard, D	Aug 7, 1835	Mar 26, 1909	1865	1865	—	2	0	3	3	1.50	0	—	—	—	—
Pollitt, C H	June 3, 1874	Not known	1899	1899	1	1	0	51	51	51.00	0	19	0	—	1
Prest, C H *	Dec 9, 1841	Mar 4, 1875	1864	1864	2	4	0	57	31	14.25	0	—	—	—	—
Preston, J M ....©	Aug 23, 1864	Nov 26, 1890	1885	1889	79	134	11	1,935	93	15.73	0	3,232	178	18.15	36
Pride, T	July 23, 1864		1887	1887	1	1	0	1	1	1.00	0	—	—	—	4/3
Priestley, I M	Sept 25, 1967		1989	1989	2	4	2	25	23	12.50	0	119	4	29.75	—
Pullan, P	Mar 29, 1857	Mar 3, 1901	1884	1884	2	2	1	14	14	14.00	0	5	—	—	—
Pyrah R M ....©	Nov 1, 1982		2004	2013	42	51	6	1,256	134*	27.91	3	2,145	49	43.77	20
§ Radcliffe, E J R H *©	Jan 27, 1884	Nov 23, 1969	1909	1911	64	89	13	826	54	10.86	0	134	2	67.00	21
Ramage, A	Nov 29, 1957		1979	1983	23	22	9	219	52	16.84	0	1,649	44	37.47	8
Ramsden, G	Mar 2, 1983		2000	2000	1	1	1	0	0*	—	0	68	1	68.00	—
Randhawa G S	Jan 25, 1992		2011	2011	1	1	0	5	5	5.00	0	62	2	31.00	—
Raper, J R S *	Aug 9, 1909	Mar 9, 1997	1936	1947	3	4	0	24	15	6.00	0	—	—	—	—
Rashid A U ....©	Feb 17, 1988		2006	2013	100	140	27	4,050	180	35.84	7	10,401	294	35.37	50
Rawlin, E R	Oct 4, 1897	Jan 11, 1943	1927	1936	8	10	2	72	35	8.00	0	498	21	23.71	2
Rawlin, J T	Nov 10, 1856	Jan 19, 1924	1880	1885	27	36	2	274	35	8.05	0	258	11	23.45	13
Rawlinson, E B	Apr 10, 1837	Feb 17, 1892	1867	1875	37	68	5	991	55	15.73	0	62	5	12.40	16
Redfearn, J	May 13, 1862	Jan 14, 1931	1890	1890	1	1	0	5	5	5.00	0	—	—	—	—
Render, G W A	Jan 5, 1887	Sept 17, 1922	1919	1919	1	1	0	5	5	5.00	0	—	—	—	—
Rhodes, A C ....©	Oct 14, 1906	May 21, 1957	1932	1934	61	70	19	917	64*	17.98	0	3,026	107	28.28	45
§ Rhodes, H E *	Jan 11, 1852	Sept 10, 1889	1878	1883	10	16	1	269	64	17.93	0	—	—	—	1
Rhodes, S J	June 17, 1964		1981	1984	3	2	1	41	35	41.00	0	—	—	—	1
Rhodes, Wilfred ......©	Oct 29, 1877	July 8, 1973	1898	1930	883	1,195	162	31,075	267*	30.08	46	57,634	3,598	16.01	586
Rhodes, William	Mar 4, 1883	Aug 5, 1941	1911	1911	1	2	1	—	1*	—	0	40	0	—	—
Richardson, J A *	Aug 4, 1908	Apr 2, 1985	1936	1947	7	12	1	308	61	30.80	0	90	2	45.00	3
§ Richardson, R B ......©	Jan 12, 1962		1993	1994	23	39	2	1,310	112	34.47	1	23	1	23.00	18
§ Richardson, S A	Sept 5, 1977		2000	2003	13	23	2	377	69	17.95	0	—	—	—	11
Riley, H	Aug 17, 1875	Nov 6, 1922	1895	1900	4	5	1	36	25*	9.00	0	54	—	54.00	—
Riley, M *	Apr 5, 1851	June 1, 1899	1878	1882	17	28	3	361	92	13.37	0	10	—	—	3
Ringrose, W	Sept 2, 1871	Sept 14, 1943	1901	1906	57	66	9	353	23	6.19	0	3,224	155	20.80	25

LIST OF PLAYERS AND CAREER AVERAGES IN ALL FIRST-CLASS MATCHES FOR YORKSHIRE (Continued)

Player	Date of Birth	Date of Death (if known)	First Played	Last Played	M	Inns	NO	Runs	HS	Av'ge	100s	Runs	Wkts	Av'ge	Ct/St
Robinson, A L	Aug 17, 1946	—	1971	1977	84	69	31	365	30*	9.60	0	4,927	196	25.13	48
Robinson, Edward * ..	Dec 27, 1862	Sept 3, 1942	1887	1887	1	2	—	23	23*	23.00	0	—	—	—	0
Robinson, Emmott ..	Nov 16, 1883	Nov 17, 1969	1919	1931	413	455	77	9,651	135*	25.53	7	19,645	893	21.99	318
Robinson, E P	Aug 10, 1911	Nov 10, 1998	1934	1949	208	253	46	2,596	75*	12.54	0	15,141	735	20.60	189
Robinson, H	May 12, 1858	Dec 14, 1909	1879	1879	1	2	0	5	5	2.50	0	20	1	20.00	0
Robinson, M A	Nov 23, 1966	—	1991	1995	90	93	36	240	23	4.21	0	6,866	218	31.49	17
Robinson, P E	Aug 3, 1963	—	1984	1991	132	217	13	6,668	189	35.84	7	238	1	238.00	96
Robinson, W	Nov 29, 1851	—	1876	1877	7	14	1	151	68	11.61	0	—	—	—	3
Roebuck C G	Aug 14, 1991	—	2010	2010	1	1	0	23	23	23.00	0	—	—	—	3
Root, J E	**Dec 30, 1990**	—	**2010**	**2013**	**34**	**57**	**7**	**2,188**	**236**	**43.76**	**5**	**490**	**8**	**61.25**	**18**
Roper, E *	Apr 8, 1851	Apr 27, 1921	1878	1880	5	7	1	85	68	14.16	0	—	—	—	2
Rothery, J W	Sept 5, 1877	June 2, 1919	1903	1910	150	236	18	4,614	161	21.16	3	44	2	22.00	45
Rowbotham, J	July 8, 1831	Dec 22, 1899	1861	1876	94	162	9	2,624	113	17.15	3	37	3	12.33	52
§ Rudolph J A	May 4, 1981	—	2007	2011	68	112	8	5,429	228*	52.20	18	311	1	311.00	79
Rudston, H	Nov 22, 1879	April 14, 1962	1902	1907	21	30	0	609	164	20.30	0	—	—	—	2
Ryan, M	June 23, 1933	—	1954	1965	150	149	58	682	26*	7.49	0	9,466	413	22.92	59
Ryder, L	Aug 28, 1899	Jan 24, 1955	1924	1924	2	2	0	1	1	1.00	0	151	4	37.75	2
Sanderson B W	Jan 3, 1989	—	2008	2010	3	2	1	6	6	6.00	0	190	6	31.66	0
Savile, G *	Apr 26, 1847	Sept 4, 1904	1867	1874	3	7	0	140	65	20.00	0	—	—	—	2
Sayers, J J *	**Nov 5, 1983**	—	**2004**	**2113**	**97**	**161**	**13**	**4,855**	**187**	**32.80**	**9**	**166**	**6**	**27.66**	**60**
Schofield, C J	Mar 21, 1976	—	1996	1996	3	1	0	25	25	25.00	0	—	—	—	0
Schofield, D	Oct 9, 1947	—	1970	1974	3	4	4	13	6*	—	0	112	5	22.40	0
Scott, E	July 6, 1834	Dec 3, 1898	1864	1864	1	1	0	8	8	8.00	0	27	1	13.50	1
Sedgwick, H A	Apr 8, 1883	Dec 28, 1957	1906	1906	3	5	3	53	34	17.66	0	327	16	20.43	0
Sellers, Arthur *	May 31, 1870	Sept 25, 1941	1890	1899	49	88	1	1,643	105	18.83	2	84	2	42.00	40
Sellers, A B *	Mar 5, 1907	Feb 20, 1981	1932	1948	334	437	51	8,949	204	23.18	4	653	8	81.62	264
Shackleton, W A	Mar 9, 1908	Nov 16, 1971	1928	1934	5	6	0	49	25	8.16	0	130	6	21.66	3
Shahzad, Ajmal	July 27, 1985	—	2006	2012	45	58	14	1,145	88	26.02	0	4,196	125	33.56	5
Sharp, K	Apr. 6, 1959	—	1976	1990	195	320	35	8,426	181	29.56	11	836	12	69.66	95
§ Sharpe, C M *	Sept 6, 1851	June 25, 1935	1875	1875	1	1	0	15	15	15.00	0	17	—	—	0

LIST OF PLAYERS AND CAREER AVERAGES IN ALL FIRST-CLASS MATCHES FOR YORKSHIRE *(Continued)*

Player	Date of Birth	Date of Death (if known)	First Played	Last Played	M	Inns	NO	Runs	HS	Av'ge	100s	Runs	Wkts	Av'ge	Ct/St
Sharpe, P J ©	Dec 27, 1936		1958	1974	411	666	71	17,685	203*	29.72	23	140	2	70.00	525
Shaw C	Feb 17, 1964		1984	1988	61	58	27	340	31	10.96	0	4,101	123	33.34	9
Shaw, J *	Mar 12, 1865		1896	1897	3	3	0	8	7	2.66	0	181	7	25.85	2
Sheepshanks, E R *	Mar 22, 1910	Dec 31, 1937	1929	1929	1	1	0	26	26	26.00	0	—	—	—	0
Shepherd, D A *	Mar 10, 1916	May 29, 1998	1938	1938	1	1	0	0	0	3.25	0	—	—	—	0
Shotton, W	Dec 1, 1840	May 26, 1909	1865	1874	2	4	0	13	7	3.25	0	—	—	—	0
Sidebottom, A ©	Apr 1, 1954		1973	1991	216	249	50	4,243	124	22.33	1	13,852	558	24.82	60
Sidebottom, R J ©	**Jan 15, 1978**		**1997**	**2013**	**96**	**124**	**31**	**1,330**	**61**	**14.30**	**0**	**7,270**	**302**	**24.07**	**29**
Sidgwick, R *	Aug 7, 1851		1882	1882	5	9	3	64	17	4.92	0	—	—	—	3
Silverwood, C E W ©	Mar 5, 1975	1934	1993	2005	131	179	33	2,369	80	16.22	0	11,413	427	27.62	30
Silvester, S	Mar 12, 1951		1976	1977	6	7	4	30	14	10.00	0	313	12	26.08	2
Simpson, E T B *	Mar 5, 1867	Mar 20, 1944	1889	1889	1	2	0	1	1	0.50	0	—	—	—	1
§ Sims, Rev H M *	Mar 15, 1853	Oct 5, 1885	1875	1877	5	10	1	109	35*	12.11	0	—	—	—	5
Slinn, W	Dec 13, 1826	June 19, 1888	1861	1864	9	14	3	22	11	2.00	0	742	48	15.45	2
Smailes, T F *	Mar 27, 1910	Dec 1, 1970	1932	1948	262	339	42	5,686	117	19.14	3	16,593	802	20.68	153
Smailes, K	Sept 15, 1927		1948	1950	13	19	3	165	45	10.31	0	766	22	34.81	4
Smith, A F	Mar 7, 1847	Jan 6, 1915	1868	1874	28	49	4	692	89	15.37	0	—	—	—	11
Smith, E (Barnsley)	July 11, 1888	Jan 2, 1972	1914	1926	16	21	4	169	49	10.56	0	1,090	46	23.69	5
Smith, Ernest (Morley) * ©	Oct 19, 1869	Feb 9, 1945	1888	1907	154	234	18	4,453	129	20.61	2	6,278	248	25.31	112
Smith, Fred (Idle)	Dec 26, 1885	Not known	1911	1911	1	1	0	11	11	11.00	0	45	2	22.50	0
Smith, Fred (Yeadon)	Dec 18, 1879	Oct 20, 1905	1903	1903	13	19	1	292	55	16.22	0	—	—	—	3
Smith, G	Jan 13, 1876	Jan 16, 1929	1901	1906	2	2	1	7	7	7.00	0	62	0	—	3
Smith, J	Mar 23, 1833	Feb 12, 1909	1865	1865	2	3	0	28	16	9.33	0	72	6	12.00	3
Smith, N	Apr 1, 1949	Mar 4, 2003	1970	1971	8	11	2	82	20	13.66	0	—	—	—	6
Smith, R	Apr 6, 1944		1969	1970	5	8	3	99	37*	19.80	0	—	—	—	14/3
Smith, Walker	Aug 14, 1847	July 7, 1900	1874	1874	9	9	1	152	59	16.88	0	—	—	—	3
§ Smith, William *	Nov 1, 1839	Apr 19, 1897	1865	1874	11	19	3	260	90	16.25	0	—	—	—	8
Smithson, G A	Nov 1, 1926	Sept 6, 1970	1946	1950	39	60	5	1,449	169	26.34	2	84	3	84.00	21
Smurthwaite, J	Oct 17, 1916	Oct 20, 1989	1938	1939	7	9	5	29	20*	7.25	0	237	12	19.75	4
Sowden, A *	Dec 1, 1853	July 5, 1921	1878	1887	8	11	0	137	37	12.45	0	22	0	—	1
Squire, J	Dec 31, 1864	Apr 28, 1922	1893	1893	1	2	0	0	0	0.00	0	25	0	—	0

LIST OF PLAYERS AND CAREER AVERAGES IN ALL FIRST-CLASS MATCHES FOR YORKSHIRE (Continued)

Player	Date of Birth	Date of Death (if known)	First Played	Last Played	M	Inns	NO	Runs	HS	Av'ge	100s	Runs	Wkts	Av'ge	Ct/St
Squires, P J	Aug 4, 1951		1972	1976	49	84	8	1,271	70	16.72	0	32	0	—	14
Stanley, H C *	Feb 16, 1888	May 18, 1934	1911	1913	8	13	0	155	42	11.92	0	—	—	—	6
§ Stanyforth, R T *	May 30, 1892	Feb 20, 1964	1928	1928	3	3	1	26	10	8.66	0	—	—	—	2
§ Starc, M A	Jan 13, 1990		2012	2012	2	1	1	28	28*	—	0	—	—	—	0
Stead, B	June 21, 1939	Apr 15, 1980	1959	1959	2	3	0	8	8	2.66	0	153	7	21.85	1
§ Stemp, R D	◎Dec 11, 1967		1993	1998	104	135	36	1,267	65	12.79	0	115	7	16.42	49
Stephenson, E	◎June 5, 1832	July 5, 1898	1861	1873	36	61	5	803	67	14.33	0	8,557	241	35.50	30/27
Stephenson, J S *	Nov 10, 1903	Oct 7, 1975	1923	1926	16	19	2	182	60	10.70	0	65	0	—	6
Stevenson, G B	◎Dec 16, 1955		1973	1986	177	217	32	3,856	115*	20.84	2	13,254	464	28.56	73
Stott, W B	◎July 18, 1934		1952	1963	187	309	19	9,168	186	31.61	17	112	0	—	91
Stringer, P M	Feb 23, 1943		1967	1969	19	17	8	101	15*	11.22	0	696	32	21.75	7
Stuchbury, S	June 22, 1954		1978	1981	3	3	2	7	4*	7.00	0	236	8	29.50	7
§ Sugg, F H	Jan 11, 1862	May 29, 1933	1883	1883	3	12	1	80	13*	10.00	0	—	—	—	4/1
§ Sugg, W	May 21, 1860	May 21, 1933	1881	1881	1	1	0	9	9	9.00	0	—	—	—	—
Sullivan, J H B *	Sept 21, 1890	Feb 8, 1932	1912	1912	1	2	0	41	26	20.50	0	43	0	—	—
Sutcliffe, H	Nov 24, 1894	Jan 22, 1978	1919	1945	602	864	96	38,558	313	50.20	112	381	8	47.62	402
Sutcliffe, W H H *	Oct 10, 1926	Sept 16, 1998	1948	1957	177	273	34	6,247	181	26.13	6	152	6	25.33	80
Swallow, I G	Dec 18, 1962		1983	1989	61	82	18	1,296	114	20.25	1	3,270	64	51.09	28
§ Swanepoel, P J	Mar 30, 1977		2003	2003	2	3	0	20	17	6.66	0	129	3	43.00	1
§ Tait, T	Oct 7, 1872	Sept 6, 1954	1898	1899	2	3	1	7	3	3.50	0	—	—	—	1
§ Tasker, J *	Feb 4, 1887	Aug 24, 1975	1912	1913	31	43	4	586	67	15.02	0	—	—	—	14
Tattersall, G *	Apr 21, 1882	June 29, 1947	1905	1905	1	2	0	26	26	13.00	0	—	—	—	0
Taylor, C R	Feb 21, 1981		2001	2005	16	27	3	416	52*	17.33	0	—	—	—	8
Taylor, H	Dec 18, 1900	Oct 28, 1988	1924	1925	9	13	0	153	36	11.76	0	—	—	—	1
Taylor, H S	Dec 11, 1856	Nov 16, 1896	1879	1879	3	5	0	36	22	7.20	0	—	—	—	—
Taylor, J	Apr 2, 1850	May 27, 1924	1880	1881	9	13	1	107	44	8.91	0	—	—	—	4
Taylor, K	◎Aug 21, 1935		1953	1968	303	505	35	12,864	203*	27.37	16	3,680	129	28.52	146
Taylor, N S	◎June 2, 1963		1982	1983	8	6	1	10	4	2.00	0	720	22	32.72	2
Taylor, T L *	◎May 25, 1878	Mar. 16, 1960	1899	1906	82	122	10	3,933	156	35.11	8	195	4	48.75	47/2
§ Tendulkar, S R	◎Apr 24, 1973		1992	1992	16	25	2	1,070	100	46.52	1	—	—	—	10

Player	Date of Birth	Date of Death (if known)	First Played	Last Played	M	Inns	NO	Runs	HS	Av'ge	100s	Runs	Wkts	Av'ge	Ct/St
Thewlis, H	Aug 31, 1865	Nov 30, 1920	1888	1888	2	4	1	4	2*	1.33	0	—	—	—	2
Thewlis, John Jun.	Sept 21, 1850	Aug 9, 1901	1879	1879	3	4	0	21	10	5.25	0	—	—	—	0
Thewlis, John Sen.	Mar 11, 1828	Dec 29, 1899	1861	1875	44	80	3	1,280	108	16.62	1	—	—	—	21/1
Thornicroft, N D	Jan 23, 1985		2002	2007	7	10	4	50	30	8.33	0	545	16	34.06	2
Thornton, A	July 20, 1854	Apr 18, 1915	1881	1881	3	4	0	21	7	5.25	0	—	—	—	2
Thornton, G *	Dec 24, 1867	Jan 31, 1939	1891	1891	3	4	0	21	16	5.25	0	74	2	37.00	0
Thorpe, G	Feb 20, 1834	Mar 2, 1899	1864	1864	1	2	1	14	9*	14.00	0	—	—	—	2/1
Threapleton, J W	July 20, 1857	July 30, 1918	1881	1881	1	1	0	8	8*	—	0	—	—	—	1
Tinsley, H J	Feb 20, 1865	Dec 10, 1938	1890	1891	9	13	0	56	15	4.30	0	57	4	14.25	1
Townsley, R A J	June 24, 1952		1974	1975	2	4	0	22	12	5.50	0	0	0	—	1
Towse, A D	Apr 22, 1968		1988	1988	1	1	0	1	1	1.00	0	50	3	16.66	—
Trueman, F S	© Feb 6, 1931	July 1, 2006	1949	1968	459	533	81	6,852	104	15.15	2	29,890	1,745	17.12	325
Tunnicliffe, J	© Aug 26, 1866	July 11, 1948	1891	1907	472	768	57	19,435	243	27.33	22	388	7	55.42	665
Turner, A	Sept 2, 1885	Aug 29, 1951	1910	1911	9	16	1	163	37	10.86	0	—	—	—	7
Turner, B	July 25, 1938		1960	1961	2	4	2	7	3*	3.50	0	47	4	11.75	2
Turner, C	Jan 11, 1902	Nov 19, 1968	1925	1946	200	266	32	6,132	130	26.20	2	5,320	173	30.75	181
Turner, F	Sept 3, 1894	Oct 18, 1954	1924	1924	5	7	0	33	12	4.71	0	—	—	—	2
Tyson, C T	Jan 24, 1889	Apr 3, 1940	1921	1921	3	5	2	232	100*	77.33	1	—	—	—	1
Ullathorne, C E	Apr 11, 1845	May 2, 1904	1868	1875	27	46	8	283	28	7.44	0	—	—	—	19
Ulyett, G	Oct 21, 1851	June 18, 1898	1873	1893	355	618	31	14,157	199*	24.11	15	8,181	457	17.90	235
§ Usher, J	Feb 26, 1859	Aug 9, 1905	1888	1888	1	2	1	7	5	3.50	0	31	2	15.50	1
van Geloven, J	Jan 4, 1934	Aug 21, 2003	1955	1955	2	2	1	16	16	17.00	0	224	6	37.33	2
§ Vaughan, M P *	© Oct 29, 1974		1993	2009	151	267	14	9,160	183	36.20	20	4,268	92	46.39	55
§ Verelst, H W *	July 2, 1846	Apr 5, 1918	1868	1869	3	4	1	66	33*	22.00	0	—	—	—	1
Verity, H	© May 18, 1905	July 31, 1943	1930	1939	278	294	77	3,898	101	17.96	1	21,353	1,558	13.70	191
Waddington, A	© Feb 4, 1893	Oct 28, 1959	1919	1927	255	250	65	2,396	114	12.95	1	16,203	835	19.40	222
Wade, S	© Feb 8, 1858	Nov 5, 1931	1886	1890	65	111	20	1,438	74*	15.80	0	2,498	133	18.78	31
Wainwright, D J	© Mar 21, 1985		2004	2011	29	36	11	914	104*	36.56	0	2,480	69	35.94	6
Wainwright, E	© Apr 8, 1865	Oct 28, 1919	1888	1902	352	545	30	11,092	228	21.53	18	17,744	998	17.77	327

Player	Date of Birth	Date of Death (if known)	First Played	Last Played	M	Inns	NO	Runs	HS	Av'ge	100s	Runs	Wkts	Av'ge	Ct/St
Wainwright, W	Jan 21, 1882	Dec 31, 1961	1903	1905	24	36	3	648	62	19.63	0	582	19	30.63	21
Wake, W R *	May 21, 1852	Mar 14, 1896	1881	1881	3	3	0	13	11	4.33	0	—	1	—	2
Walker, A *	June 22, 1844	May 26, 1927	1863	1870	9	16	1	138	26	9.20	0	74	2	74.00	2
Walker, C	June 26, 1919	Dec 3, 1992	1947	1948	5	9	2	268	91	38.28	0	71	2	35.50	1
Walker, T	Apr 3, 1854	Aug 28, 1925	1879	1880	14	22	2	179	30	8.95	0	7	0	—	3
Waller, G	Dec 3, 1864	Dec 11, 1937	1893	1894	3	4	0	17	13	4.25	0	70	4	17.50	1
Wallgate, L *	Nov 12, 1849	May 9, 1887	1875	1878	3	3	1	17	9	3.00	0	17	1	17.00	—
Ward, A	Nov 21, 1865	Jan 6, 1939	1886	1886	4	7	1	41	22	6.83	0	1	0	—	1
Ward, F	Aug 31, 1881	Feb 28, 1948	1903	1903	1	1	1	0	0*	—	0	—	—	—	—
Ward, H P *	Jan 20, 1899	Dec 16, 1946	1920	1920	1	1	0	10	10*	10.00	0	16	0	—	1
Wardall, T A ©	Apr 19, 1862	Dec 20, 1932	1884	1894	43	73	2	1,003	106	14.12	2	489	23	21.26	25
Wardlaw, I	June 29, 1985		2011	2012	4	3	2	31	17*	31.00	0	368	4	92.00	2
Wardle, J H ©	Jan 8, 1923	July 23, 1985	1946	1958	330	418	57	5,765	79	15.96	0	27,917	1,539	18.13	210
Waring, J S	Oct 1, 1942		1963	1966	28	27	15	137	26	11.41	0	1,122	53	21.16	17
Waring, S	Nov 4, 1838		1870	1870	2	1	0	9	9	9.00	0	—	—	—	—
Washington, W A1	Dec 11, 1879	Apr 17, 1919	1900	1902	44	62	6	1,290	100*	23.03	1	—	—	—	18
Watson, H	Sept 26, 1880	Nov 24, 1951	1908	1914	29	35	11	141	41	5.87	0	—	—	—	46/10
Watson, W ©	Mar 7, 1920	Apr 24, 2004	1939	1957	283	430	65	13,953	214*	38.22	26	75	0	—	170
Waud, B W *	June 4, 1837	May 31, 1889	1862	1864	6	10	1	165	42	18.33	0	—	—	—	2
Webster, C	June 9, 1838	Jan 6, 1881	1861	1868	3	5	1	30	10	7.50	0	—	—	—	1
Webster, H H	May 9, 1844	Mar 5, 1915	1868	1868	2	3	0	10	10	3.33	0	—	—	—	—
§ Weekes, L C	July 19, 1971		1994	2000	2	2	0	20	10	10.00	0	191	10	19.10	1
West, J	Oct 16, 1844	Jan 27, 1890	1868	1876	38	64	13	461	41	9.03	0	853	53	16.09	14
Wharf, A G	June 4, 1975		1994	1997	7	9	1	186	62	23.25	0	454	11	41.27	2
Whatmough, F J	Dec 4, 1856	June 3, 1904	1878	1882	7	11	1	51	20	5.10	0	111	5	22.20	4
Wheater, C H *	Mar 4, 1860	May 11, 1885	1880	1880	2	4	1	45	27	15.00	0	—	—	—	3
White, Sir A W * ©	Oct 14, 1877	Dec 16, 1945	1908	1920	97	128	28	1,457	55	14.57	0	7	0	—	50
White, C ©	Dec 16, 1969		1990	2007	221	350	45	10,376	186	34.01	19	7,649	276	27.71	140
Whitehead, J P ©	Sept 3, 1925	Aug 15, 2000	1946	1951	37	38	17	387	58*	18.42	0	2,610	96	27.47	11
Whitehead, Lees ©	Mar 14, 1864	Nov 22, 1913	1889	1904	119	172	38	2,073	67*	15.47	0	2,408	99	24.32	68

LIST OF PLAYERS AND CAREER AVERAGES IN ALL FIRST-CLASS MATCHES FOR YORKSHIRE (Continued)

Player	Date of Birth	Date of Death (if known)	First Played	Last Played	M	Inns	NO	Runs	HS	Av'ge	100s	Runs	Wkts	Av'ge	Ct/St
Whitehead, Luther	June 25, 1869	Jan 16, 1931	1893	1893	2	4	0	21	13	5.25	0	—	—	—	—
Whiteley, J P	Feb 28, 1955		1978	1982	45	38	17	231	20	11.00	0	2,410	70	34.42	21
Whiting, C P	Apr 18, 1888	Jan 14, 1959	1914	1920	6	10	2	92	26	11.50	0	416	15	27.73	2
Whitwell, J F *	Feb 22, 1869	Nov 6, 1932	1890	1890	1	2	0	8	4	4.00	0	11	1	11.00	2
§ Whitwell, W F *	Dec 12, 1867	Apr 12, 1942	1890	1890	10	14	4	67	26	5.58	0	518	25	20.72	5
Widdup, S	Nov 10, 1977		2000	2001	11	18	1	245	44	14.41	0	22	1	22.00	5
Wigley, D H	Oct 26, 1981		2002	2002	1	2	1	19	15	19.00	0	116	1	116.00	0
§ Wilkinson, A J A *	May 28, 1835	Dec 11, 1905	1865	1868	5	6	0	129	53	21.50	0	57	0	—	1
Wilkinson, F	May 23, 1914	Mar 26, 1984	1937	1939	14	14	1	73	18*	5.61	0	590	26	22.69	12
Wilkinson, H *	Dec 11, 1877	Apr 15, 1967	1903	1905	48	75	3	1,382	113	19.19	1	121	3	40.33	19
Wilkinson, R	Nov 11, 1977		1998	1998	1	1	0	9	9	9.00	0	35	1	35.00	0
Wilkinson, W H ©	Mar 12, 1881	June 4, 1961	1903	1910	126	192	14	3,812	103	21.41	1	971	31	31.32	93
Williams, A C	Mar 1, 1887	June 1, 1966	1911	1919	12	14	0	95	48*	23.75	0	678	30	22.60	6
§ Williamson K S ...	**Sept 8, 1990**		**2013**	**2013**	**5**	**9**	**1**	**403**	**97**	**50.37**	**0**	**247**	**4**	**61.75**	**4**
Wilson, B B	Dec 11, 1879	Sept 14, 1957	1906	1914	185	308	12	8,053	208	27.50	15	278	2	139.00	53
Wilson, C E M *	May 15, 1875	Feb 8, 1944	1896	1899	8	13	3	256	91*	25.60	0	257	12	21.41	7
Wilson, D	Aug 7, 1937	July 21, 2012	1957	1974	392	502	85	5,788	83	13.88	0	22,626	1,104	20.49	235
Wilson, E R *	Mar 25, 1879	July 21, 1957	1899	1923	66	72	18	902	104*	16.70	1	3,106	197	15.76	30
Wilson, Geoffrey *	Aug 21, 1916	Nov 29, 1960	1919	1924	92	94	14	983	70	12.28	0	11	0	—	33
Wilson, G A *	Feb 2, 1916	Sept 24, 2002	1936	1939	15	25	5	352	55*	17.60	0	138	1	138.00	7
Wilson, John *	June 30, 1857	Nov 11, 1931	1887	1888	4	5	1	17	13*	4.25	0	165	12	13.75	3
Wilson, J P *	Apr 3, 1889	Oct 3, 1959	1911	1912	9	14	1	81	36	6.23	0	24	1	24.00	2
Wilson, J V ©	Jan 17, 1921	June 5, 2008	1946	1962	477	724	75	20,548	230	31.66	29	313	3	104.33	520
Wood, A ©	Aug 25, 1898	Apr 1, 1973	1927	1946	408	481	80	8,579	123*	21.39	1	33	1	33.00	612/243
Wood, B	Dec 26, 1942		1964	1964	5	7	2	63	35	12.60	0	—	—	—	—
Wood, C H	July 26, 1934	June 28, 2006	1959	1959	4	4	1	22	10	7.33	0	319	11	29.00	1
Wood, G W	Nov 18, 1862	Dec 4, 1948	1895	1895	2	2	0	2	2	1.00	0	—	—	—	0/1
Wood, H *	Mar 22, 1855	July 31, 1941	1879	1880	10	16	1	156	36	10.40	0	212	10	21.20	8

LIST OF PLAYERS AND CAREER AVERAGES IN ALL FIRST-CLASS MATCHES FOR YORKSHIRE (Continued)

Player	Date of Birth	Date of Death (if known)	First Played	Last Played	M	Inns	NO	Runs	HS	Av'ge	100s	Runs	Wkts	Av'ge	Ct/St
Wood, J H *			1881	1881	2	1	0	14	14	14.00	0	—	—	—	0
Wood, M J	Apr 6, 1977 ©		1997	2007	128	222	20	6,742	207	33.37	16	27	2	13.50	113
Wood, R	June 3, 1929	May 22, 1990	1952	1956	22	18	4	60	17	4.28	0	1,346	51	26.39	5
Woodford, J D	Sept 9, 1943		1968	1972	38	61	2	1,204	101	20.40	1	185	4	46.25	12
Woodhead, F E *	May 29, 1868	Aug 25, 1943	1893	1894	4	8	0	57	18	7.12	0	—	—	—	3
Woodhouse, W H *	Apr 16, 1856	Mar 4, 1938	1884	1885	9	13	0	218	63	16.76	0	—	—	—	6
Wormald, A	May 10, 1855	Feb 6, 1940	1885	1891	7	11	3	161	80	20.12	0	—	—	—	10/2
Worsley, W A * ©	Apr 5, 1890	Dec 4, 1973	1928	1929	60	50	4	722	60	15.69	0	—	—	—	32
Wrathmell, L F	Jan 22, 1855	Sept 16, 1928	1886	1886	1	2	0	18	17	9.00	0	—	—	—	0
Wright, R	July 19, 1852	May 25, 1891	1877	1877	2	4	1	28	22	9.33	0	—	—	—	0
Wright, T J *	Mar 5, 1900	Nov 7, 1962	1919	1919	1	1	0	12	12	12.00	0	—	—	—	0
Yardley, N W D * ©	Mar 19, 1915	Oct 4, 1989	1936	1955	302	420	56	11,632	183*	31.95	17	5,818	195	29.83	220
Yeadon, J	Dec 10, 1861	May 30, 1914	1888	1888	3	6	2	41	22	10.25	0	—	—	—	5/3
§ Younus Khan	Nov 29, 1977 ©		2007	2007	13	19	2	824	217*	48.47	3	342	8	42.75	11
§ Yuvraj Singh	Dec 12, 1981		2003	2003	7	12	2	145	56	14.50	0	130	3	43.33	12

In the career averages it should be noted that the bowling analysis for the second Cambridgeshire innings at Ashton-under-Lyne in 1865 has not been found. G R Atkinson took 3 wickets, W Cuttell 2, G Freeman 4 and R Iddison 1. The respective bowling averages have been calculated excluding these wickets.

MOST FIRST-CLASS APPEARANCES FOR YORKSHIRE

Matches	Player	Matches	Player
883	W Rhodes (1898-1930)	477	J V Wilson (1946-1962)
717	G H Hirst (1891-1929)	472	J Tunnicliffe (1891-1907)
676	D Denton (1894-1920)	459	F S Trueman (1949-1968)
602	H Sutcliffe (1919-1945)	456	J H Hampshire (1961-1981)
548	M Leyland (1920-1947)	445	G G Macaulay (1920-1935)
536	D B Close (1949-1970)	429	D L Bairstow (1970-1990)
517	D Hunter (1888-1909)	427	A Dolphin (1905-1927)
513	S Haigh (1895-1913)	425	P Carrick (1970-1993)
510	Lord Hawke (1881-1911)	414	G Boycott (1962-1986)
496	R Illingworth (1951-1983)	413	E. Robinson (1919-1931)
491	† J G Binks (1955-1969)	411	P J Sharpe (1958-1974)
487	D E V Padgett (1951-1971)	408	A Wood (1927-1946)
485	P Holmes (1913-1933)	401	A Mitchell (1922-1945)

† Kept wicket in 412 consecutive Championship matches 1955-1969

MOST TOTAL APPEARANCES FOR YORKSHIRE
(First-Class, Domestic List A and t20)

Matches	Player	Matches	Player
883	W Rhodes (1898-1930)	512	M D Moxon (1980-1997)
827	D L Bairstow (1970-1990)	510	Lord Hawke (1881-1911)
727	P Carrick (1970-1993)	500	P J Sharpe (1958-1974)
717	R J Blakey (1985-2004)	485	P Holmes (1913-1933)
717	G H Hirst (1891-1929)	477	J V Wilson (1946-1962)
687	J H Hampshire (1961-1981)	472	J Tunnicliffe (1891-1907)
676	D Denton (1894-1920)	470	F S Trueman (1949-1968)
674	G Boycott (1962-1986)	467	J D Love (1975-1989)
602	H Sutcliffe (1919-1945)	451	D Wilson (1957-1974)
580	A McGrath (1995-2012)	449	A Sidebottom (1973-1991)
577	D Byas (1986-2001)	445	G G Macaulay (1920-1935)
568	D B Close (1949-1970)	440	C M Old (1966-1982)
548	M Leyland (1920-1947)	427	A Dolphin (1905-1927)
545	C White (1990-2007)	413	E Robinson (1919-1931)
544	D E V Padgett (1951-1971)	411	P J Hartley (1985-1997)
536	R Illingworth (1951-1983)	408	A Wood (1927-1946)
521	J G Binks (1955-1969)	401	A Mitchell (1922-1945)
517	D Hunter (1888-1909)	401	A G Nicholson (1962-1975)
513	S Haigh (1895-1913)		

FRIENDS PROVIDENT TROPHY, CHELTENHAM & GLOUCESTER TROPHY, GILLETTE CUP AND NATWEST TROPHY 1963-2009

WINNERS 1965, 1969 AND 2002
SEMI-FINALISTS 1980, 1982, 1995, 1996, 1999, 2004, 2005 AND 2008

Played 137, Won 77 (in Yorkshire 36, Away 41). Lost 54 (in Yorkshire 21, Away 33).
No Result 4 (in Yorkshire 3, Away 1). Abandoned 2 (in Yorkshire 1, Away 1)

Highest Score:	By Yorkshire:	411:6 v. Devon at Exmouth, 2004
	Against Yorkshire:	339:7 by Northamptonshire at Northampton, 2006
†Lowest Score:	By Yorkshire:	76 v. Surrey at Harrogate, 1970
	Against Yorkshire:	53 by Ireland at Leeds, 1997
Highest Individual Score:	For Yorkshire:	160 M J Wood v. Devon at Exmouth, 2004
	Against Yorkshire:	177 S A Newman for Surrey at The Oval, 2009

Highest Partnerships: For Yorkshire:

1st wkt	242*	M D Moxon (107*) and A A Metcalfe (127*) v. Warwickshire at Leeds, 1990
2nd wkt	202	G Boycott (87) and C W J Athey (115) v. Kent at Leeds, 1980
3rd wkt	164	A McGrath (105*) and J A Rudolph (82) v. Scotland at Leeds, 2008
4th wkt	207	S A Kellett (107) and C White (113) v. Ireland at Leeds, 1995
5th wkt	160*	G M Fellows (80*) and C White (73*) v Surrey at Leeds, 2001
6th wkt	128*	A McGrath (72*) and G M Fellows (68*) v. Essex at Chelmsford, 2002
7th wkt	102	D L Bairstow (92) and C M Old (55*) v. Worcestershire at Leeds, 1982
8th wkt	79	P J Hartley (83) and D Gough (46) v. Ireland at Leeds, 1997
9th wkt	66	T T Bresnan (55) and A Shahzad (33) v. Durham at Chester-le-Street, 2008
10th wkt	29*	R Illingworth (32*) and A G Nicholson (15*) v. Warwickshire at Birmingham, 1968

Best Bowling:	For Yorkshire:	7 for 27 D Gough v. Ireland at Leeds, 1997
	Against Yorkshire:	7 for 33 R D Jackman for Surrey at Harrogate, 1970
Most Economical Bowling:	For Yorkshire:	12-9-4-1 D Wilson v. Norfolk at Lakenham, 1969
	Against Yorkshire:	12-6-10-0 D L Underwood for Kent at Canterbury, 1981
Most Expensive Bowling:	For Yorkshire:	10-0-82-3 T T Bresnan v. Northamptonshire at Northampton, 2006
	Against Yorkshire:	12-1-96-0 M E Waugh for Essex at Chelmsford, 1995

†Lowest score is either the lowest all-out score or the lowest score at completion of 60 overs (65 overs in 1963. 50 overs from 1999)

Centuries (23)

C W J Athey	115	v. Kent at Leeds, 1980
G Boycott	146	v. Surrey at Lord's, 1965
M T G Elliott	128*	v. Somerset at Lord's, 2002
J H Hampshire	110	v. Durham at Middlesbrough, 1978
S A Kellett	107	v. Ireland at Leeds, 1995
D S Lehmann (2)	105	v. Glamorgan at Cardiff, 1997
	118*	v. Northamptonshire at Northampton, 2006
A McGrath (3)	135*	v. Lancashire at Manchester, 2007
	100	v. Durham at Leeds, 2007
	105*	v. Scotland at Leeds, 2008
A A Metcalfe	127*	v. Warwickshire at Leeds, 1990
M D Moxon (2)	107*	v. Warwickshire at Leeds, 1990
	137	v. Nottinghamshire at Leeds, 1996
J A Rudolph (2)	100	v. Leicestershire at Leeds, 2007
	118	v Gloucestershire at Leeds, 2009
M P Vaughan	116*	v Lancashire at Manchester, 2004
C White (4)	113	v. Ireland at Leeds, 1995
	100*	v. Surrey at Leeds, 2002
	112	v. Northamptonshire at Northampton, 2006
	101*	v. Durham at Chester-le-Street, 2006
M J Wood (2)	118*	v. Cambridgeshire at March, 2003
	160	v. Devon at Exmouth, 2004
Younus Khan	100	v. Nottinghamshire at Nottingham, 2007

5 Wickets in an Innings (8)

D Gough (2)	7 for 27	v. Ireland at Leeds, 1997
	5 for 30	v. Yorkshire CB at Harrogate, 2000
P J Hartley	5 for 46	v. Hampshire at Southampton, 1990
M J Hoggard	5 for 65	v. Somerset at Lord's, 2002
R Illingworth	5 for 29	v. Surrey at Lord's, 1965
A Sidebottom	5 for 27	v. Glamorgan at Leeds, 1987
G B Stevenson	5 for 27	v. Berkshire at Reading, 1983
F S Trueman	6 for 15	v. Somerset at Taunton, 1965

Man of the Match Awards

M D Moxon	5
J H Hampshire	4
C White	4
M P Vaughan	2
C W J Athey	2
M G Bevan	2
G Boycott	2
G L Brophy	2
D Gough	2
A McGrath	2
A A Metcalfe	2
P J Sharpe	2
C E W Silverwood	2
M J Wood	2

D L Bairstow, T T Bresnan, P Carrick, D B Close, M T G Elliott, G M Fellows, S D Fletcher, P J Hartley, P M Hutchison, R Illingworth, S A Kellett, B Leadbeater, D S Lehmann, M J Lumb, R M Pyrah, A Sidebottom, G B Stevenson, F S Trueman (1 each). (54 Awards: 32 Players).

versus Derbyshire: Played 5, Won 3 (in Yorkshire 1, Away 2), Lost 1 (in Yorkshire), No Result 1 (Away)

Highest Score:	By Yorkshire	253:4	at Derby, 2007
	By Derbyshire	251:6	at Leeds, 2006
Lowest Score:	By Yorkshire	219:8	at Lord's, 1969
	By Derbyshire	94	at Leeds, 2008
Highest Individual			
Score:	For Yorkshire	81	J A Rudolph at Derby, 2007
	For Derbyshire	100	C R Taylor at Leeds, 2006
Best Bowling:	For Yorkshire	3-16	A McGrath at Leeds, 2008
	For Derbyshire	3-31	A Ward at Lord's, 1969

versus Durham: Played 9, Won 5 (in Yorkshire 3, Away 2), Lost 4 (in Yorkshire 2, Away 2)

Highest Score:	By Yorkshire	268:7	at Chester-le-Street, 2009
	By Durham	266:8	at Leeds, 2007
Lowest Score:	By Yorkshire	135	at Harrogate, 1973
	By Durham	166	at Leeds, 2009
Highest Individual			
Score:	For Yorkshire	110	J H Hampshire at Middlesbrough, 1978
	For Durham	124*	J P Maher at Chester-le-Street, 2006
Best Bowling:	For Yorkshire	4-9	C M Old at Middlesbrough, 1978
	For Durham	5-15	B R Lander at Harrogate, 1973

versus Essex: Played 4, Won 2 (in Yorkshire 1, Away 2), Lost 1 (Away)

Highest Score:	By Yorkshire	307:3	at Chelmsford, 1995
	By Essex	285:8	at Chelmsford, 2008
Lowest Score:	By Yorkshire	198	at Chelmsford, 2008
	By Essex	132	at Leeds, 1982
Highest Individual			
Score:	For Yorkshire	92	S A Kellett at Chelmsford, 1995
	For Essex	95	A N Cook at Chelmsford, 2008
Best Bowling:	For Yorkshire	3-21	A Sidebottom at Leeds, 1982
	For Essex:	3-30	R N ten Doeschate at Chelmsford, 2008

versus Glamorgan: Played 2, Won 1 (in Yorkshire), Lost 1 (Away)

Highest Score:	By Yorkshire	236:8	at Cardiff, 1997
	By Glamorgan	237:9	at Cardiff, 1997
Lowest Score:	By Yorkshire	—	
	By Glamorgan	83	at Leeds, 1987

Highest Individual

Score:	For Yorkshire	105	D S Lehmann at Cardiff, 1997
	For Glamorgan	62	M P Maynard at Cardiff, 1997
Best Bowling:	For Yorkshire	5-27	A Sidebottom at Leeds, 1987
	For Glamorgan	3-26	D A Cosker at Cardiff, 1997

versus Gloucestershire: Played 7, Won 2 (Away 2), Lost 5 (in Yorkshire 2, Away 3)

Highest Score:	By Yorkshire	243:6	at Bristol, 2004
		243:8	at Bristol, 1993
	By Gloucestershire	269	at Leeds, 2009
Lowest Score:	By Yorkshire	217:9	at Bristol, 2009
	By Gloucestershire	201	at Bristol, 2008

Highest Individual

Score:	For Yorkshire	118	J A Rudolph at Leeds, 2009
	For Gloucestershire	143*	C M Spearman at Bristol, 2004
Best Bowling:	For Yorkshire	4-31	T T Bresnan at Bristol, 2008
	For Gloucestershire	4-21	M J Procter at Leeds, 1976

versus Hampshire: Played 5, Won 2 (in Yorkshire 1, Away 1), Lost 3 (in Yorkshire 0, Away 3)

Highest Score:	By Yorkshire	233:6	at Bradford, 1974
	By Hampshire	261	at Bournemouth, 1977
Lowest Score:	By Yorkshire	118	at Southampton, 1990
	By Hampshire	192	at Bradford, 1974

Highest Individual

Score:	For Yorkshire	93*	C W J Athey at Southampton, 1980
	For Hampshire	100	S M Ervine at Southampton, 2005
Best Bowling:	For Yorkshire	5-46	P J Hartley at Southampton, 1990
	For Hampshire	5-35	J M Rice at Bournemouth, 1977

versus Kent: Played 3, Won 1 (in Yorkshire 1, Away 0), Lost 2 (in Yorkshire 0, Away 2)

Highest Score:	By Yorkshire	279:6	at Leeds, 1980
	By Kent	233	at Leeds, 1980
Lowest Score:	By Yorkshire	148	at Canterbury, 1971
	By Kent	233	at Leeds, 1980

Highest Individual

Score:	For Yorkshire	115	C W J Athey at Leeds, 1980
	For Kent	118*	C J Tavaré at Canterbury, 1981
Best Bowling:	For Yorkshire	4-35	A Sidebottom at Leeds, 1980
	For Kent	5-25	B D Julien at Canterbury, 1971

versus Lancashire: Played 12, Won 5 (in Yorkshire 2, Away 3), Lost 6 (in Yorkshire 1, Away 5), No result 1 (in Yorkshire)

Highest Score:	By Yorkshire	292:4	at Leeds, 2006
	By Lancashire	293:9	at Manchester, 1996
Lowest Score:	By Yorkshire	173	at Leeds, 1974
	By Lancashire	169	at Leeds, 1995

Highest Individual

Score:	For Yorkshire	135*	A McGrath at Manchester, 2007
	For Lancashire	141*	B J Hodge at Manchester, 2007
Best Bowling:	For Yorkshire	4-18	G S Blewett at Manchester, 1999
	For Lancashire	4-17	P Lever at Leeds, 1974

versus Leicestershire: Played 7, Won 3 (in Yorkshire 1, Away 2), Lost 4 (in Yorkshire 3, Away 1)

Highest Score:	By Yorkshire	310:5	at Leicester, 1997
	By Leicestershire	284:4	at Leeds, 2007
Lowest Score:	By Yorkshire	109	at Leeds, 1975
	By Leicestershire	168	at Leicester, 1965

Highest Individual

Score:	For Yorkshire	100	J A Rudolph at Leeds, 2007
	For Leicestershire	90	I J Sutcliffe at Leicester, 1997
Best Bowling:	For Yorkshire	4-18	H P Cooper at Leeds, 1975
	For Leicestershire	5-34	P A J DeFreitas at Leeds, 1987

versus Middlesex: Played 5, Won 2 (in Yorkshire 2, Away 0), Lost 3 (in Yorkshire 1, Away 2)

Highest Score:	By Yorkshire	205:9	at Leeds, 1986
	By Middlesex	225:7	at Leeds, 1988
Lowest Score:	By Yorkshire	90	at Lord's, 1964
	By Middlesex	151	at Lord's, 1964

Highest Individual

Score:	For Yorkshire	73*	D Byas at Leeds, 1996
	For Middlesex	104	P N Weekes at Leeds, 1996
Best Bowling:	For Yorkshire	4-29	H P Cooper at Lord's, 1979 and C Shaw at Leeds, 1988
	For Middlesex	4-24	N G Cowans at Leeds, 1986

versus Northamptonshire: Played 8, Won 4 (in Yorkshire 2, Away 2), Lost 4 (in Yorkshire 2, Away 2)

Highest Score:	By Yorkshire	341:3	at Northampton, 2006
	By Northamptonshire	339:7	at Northampton, 2006
Lowest Score:	By Yorkshire	165	at Leeds, 1983
	By Northamptonshire	211:7	at Leeds, 1983

Highest Individual

Score:	For Yorkshire	118*	D S Lehmann at Northampton, 2006
	For Northamptonshire	161	D J G Sales at Northampton, 2006
Best Bowling:	For Yorkshire	4-36	D Gough at Northampton, 2000
	For Northamptonshire	5-33	B J Griffiths at Leeds, 1983

versus Nottinghamshire: Played 6, Won 5 (in Yorkshire 4, Away 1), Lost 0, Abandoned 1 (in Yorkshire)

Highest Score:	By Yorkshire	345:5	at Leeds, 1996
	By Nottinghamshire	243	at Nottingham, 2007
Lowest Score:	By Yorkshire	191	at Scarborough, 1969
	By Nottinghamshire	123	at Scarborough, 1969

Highest Individual

Score:	For Yorkshire	137	M D Moxon at Leeds, 1996
	For Nottinghamshire	100*	J B Bolus at Middlesbrough, 1963
Best Bowling:	For Yorkshire	4-30	F S Trueman at Middlesbrough, 1963
	For Nottinghamshire	4-33	K Gilhouley at Middlesbrough, 1963

versus Somerset: Played 5, Won 2 (in Yorkshire 0, Away 2), Lost 3 (in Yorkshire 2, Away 1)

Highest Score:	By Yorkshire	260:4	at Lord's, 2002
	By Somerset	256:8	at Lord's, 2002
Lowest Score:	By Yorkshire	150	at Taunton, 1966
	By Somerset	63	at Taunton, 1965

Highest Individual

Score:	For Yorkshire	128*	M T G Elliott at Lord's, 2002
	For Somerset	87*	I V A Richards at Leeds, 1985
Best Bowling:	For Yorkshire	6-15	F S Trueman at Taunton, 1965
	For Somerset	4-33	R Palmer at Taunton, 1966

versus Surrey: Played 9, Won 5 (in Yorkshire 2, Away 3), Lost 4 (in Yorkshire 2, Away 2)

Highest Score:	By Yorkshire	330:6	at The Oval, 2009
	By Surrey	329:8	at The Oval, 2009
Lowest Score:	By Yorkshire	76	at Harrogate, 1970
	By Surrey	134	at The Oval, 1969 and 134:8 at Harrogate, 1970
Highest Individual Score:	For Yorkshire	146	G Boycott at Lord's, 1965
	For Surrey	177	S A Newman at The Oval, 2009
Best Bowling:	For Yorkshire	5-29	R Illingworth at Lord's, 1965
	For Surrey	7-33	R D Jackman at Harrogate, 1970

versus Sussex: Played 6, Won 2 (in Yorkshire 1, Away 1), Lost 4 (in Yorkshire 2, Away 2)

Highest Score:	By Yorkshire	270	at Hove, 1963
	By Sussex	292	at Hove, 1963
Lowest Score:	By Yorkshire	125	at Leeds, 1986
	By Sussex	212:9	at Hove, 1996
Highest Individual Score:	For Yorkshire	82	M P Vaughan at Leeds, 2009
	For Sussex	90	J M Parks at Hove, 1963
Best Bowling:	For Yorkshire	4-35	T T Bresnan at Leeds, 2009
	For Sussex	4-17	G S Le Roux at Leeds, 1986

versus Warwickshire: Played 10, Won 2 (in Yorkshire 1, Away 1), Lost 6 (in Yorkshire 3, Away 3), No Result 1 (in Yorkshire), Abandoned 1 (Away)

Highest Score:	By Yorkshire	242:0	at Leeds, 1990
	By Warwickshire	245	at Leeds, 1993
Lowest Score:	By Yorkshire	123	at Birmingham, 1991
	By Warwickshire	157	at Birmingham, 1965
Highest Individual Score:	For Yorkshire	127*	A A Metcalfe at Leeds, 1990
	For Warwickshire	113	K D Smith at Birmingham, 1982
Best Bowling:	For Yorkshire	3-26	P Carrick at Leeds, 1990
	For Warwickshire	4-16	A A Donald at Birmingham, 1991

versus Worcestershire: Played 5, Won 2 (in Yorkshire), Lost 2 (Away), No Result 1 (in Yorkshire)

Highest Score:	By Yorkshire	290:7	at Leeds, 1982
	By Worcestershire	286:5	at Leeds, 1982
Lowest Score:	By Yorkshire	177	at Worcester, 2003
	By Worcestershire	215:7	at Leeds, 2007
Highest Individual Score:	For Yorkshire	92	D L Bairstow at Leeds, 1982
	For Worcestershire	105	G M Turner at Leeds, 1982
Best Bowling:	For Yorkshire	3-41	I J Harvey at Leeds, 2005
	For Worcestershire	5-49	M Hayward at Worcester, 2003

versus Ireland: Played 4, Won 4 (in Yorkshire 3, Away 1), Lost 0

Highest Score:	By Yorkshire	299:6	at Leeds, 1995
	By Ireland	228:7	at Leeds, 1995
Lowest Score:	By Yorkshire	249	at Leeds, 1997
	By Ireland	53	at Leeds, 1997
Highest Individual Score:	For Yorkshire	113	C White at Leeds, 1995
	For Ireland	82	S J S Warke at Leeds, 1995
Best Bowling:	For Yorkshire	7-27	D Gough at Leeds, 1997
	For Ireland	3-26	P McCrum at Leeds, 1997

versus Scotland: Played 5, Won 5 (in Yorkshire 3, Away 2)

Highest Score:	By Yorkshire	259:8	at Edinburgh, 2007
	By Scotland	244	at Leeds, 2008
Lowest Score:	By Yorkshire	—	
	By Scotland	193:8	at Edinburgh, 2008
Highest Individual			
Score:	For Yorkshire	105*	A McGrath at Leeds, 2008
	For Scotland	73	I L Philip at Leeds, 1989
Best Bowling:	For Yorkshire	3-22	T T Bresnan at Edinburgh, 2007
	For Scotland	3-62	J A R Blain at Edinburgh, 2007

versus Bedfordshire: Played 1, Won 1 (Away)

Highest Score:	By Yorkshire	212:6	at Luton, 2001
	By Bedfordshire	211:9	at Luton, 2001
Highest Individual			
Score:	For Yorkshire	88	D S Lehmann at Luton, 2001
	For Bedfordshire	34	O J Clayton at Luton, 2001
Best Bowling:	For Yorkshire	4-39	R J Sidebottom at Luton, 2001
	For Bedfordshire	4-54	S Rashid at Luton, 2001

versus Berkshire: Played 2, Won 2 (Away 2)

Highest Score:	By Yorkshire	131:3	at Reading, 1983
	By Berkshire	128:9	at Reading, 1983
Lowest Score:	By Yorkshire	Have not been dismissed, nor batted through entire overs	
	By Berkshire	105	at Finchampstead, 1988
Highest Individual			
Score:	For Yorkshire	74*	A A Metcalfe at Finchampstead, 1988
	For Berkshire	29	G R J Roope at Reading, 1983
Best Bowling:	For Yorkshire	5-27	G B Stevenson at Reading, 1983
	For Berkshire	1-15	M Lickley at Reading, 1983

versus Cambridgeshire: Played 3, Won 3 (in Yorkshire 2, Away 1)

Highest Score:	By Yorkshire	299:5	at March, 2003
	By Cambridgeshire	214:8	at March, 2003
Lowest Score:	By Cambridgeshire	176:8	at Leeds, 1986
Highest Individual			
Score:	For Yorkshire	118*	M J Wood March, 2003
	For Cambridgeshire	85	J D R Benson at Leeds, 1986
Best Bowling:	For Yorkshire	3-11	A G Nicholson at Castleford, 1967
	For Cambridgeshire	3-53	Ajaz Akhtar at March, 2003

versus Cheshire: Played 1, Won 1 (Away)

Highest Score:	By Yorkshire	160:0	at Oxton, 1985
	By Cheshire	159:7	at Oxton, 1985
Highest Individual			
Score:	For Yorkshire	82*	M D Moxon at Oxton, 1985
	For Cheshire	46	K Teesdale at Oxton, 1985
Best Bowling:	For Yorkshire	2-17	G B Stevenson at Oxton, 1985
	For Cheshire	No wicket taken	

versus Devon: Played 4, Won 4, (Away 4)

Highest Score:	By Yorkshire	411:6	at Exmouth, 2004
	By Devon	279:8	at Exmouth, 2004
Lowest Score:	By Devon	80	at Exmouth, 1998
Highest Individual			
Score:	For Yorkshire	160	M J Wood at Exmouth, 2004
	For Devon	83	P M Roebuck at Exmouth, 1994
Best Bowling:	For Yorkshire	4-26	D S Lehmann at Exmouth, 2002
	For Devon	2-42	A O F Le Fleming at Exmouth, 1994

versus Dorset: Played 1, Won 1, (Away)

Scores:	By Yorkshire	101:2	at Bournemouth, 2004
	By Dorset	97	at Bournemouth, 2004
Highest Individual			
Score:	For Yorkshire	71*	M J Wood at Bournemouth, 2004
	For Dorset	23	C L Park at Bournemouth, 2004
Best Bowling:	For Yorkshire	4-18	C E W Silverwood at Bournemouth, 2004
	For Devon	2-31	D J L Worrad at Bournemouth, 2004

versus Herefordshire: Played 1, Won 1 (Away)

Highest Score:	By Yorkshire	275:8	at Kington, 1999
	By Herefordshire	124:5	at Kington, 1999
Highest Individual			
Score:	For Yorkshire	77	G S Blewett at Kington, 1999
	For Herefordshire	39	R D Hughes at Kington, 1999
Best Bowling:	For Yorkshire	2-22	G M Hamilton at Kington, 1999
	For Herefordshire	2-41	C W Boroughs at Kington, 1999

versus Norfolk: Played 2, Won 2 (in Yorkshire 1, Away 1)

Highest Score:	By Yorkshire	167	at Lakenham, 1969
	By Norfolk	104	at Leeds, 1990
Lowest Score:	By Yorkshire	167	at Lakenham, 1969
	By Norfolk	78	at Lakenham, 1969
Highest Individual			
Score:	For Yorkshire	56*	M D Moxon at Leeds, 1990
	For Norfolk	25	R J Finney at Leeds, 1990
Best Bowling:	For Yorkshire	3-8	P Carrick at Leeds, 1990
	For Norfolk	6-48	T I Moore at Lakenham, 1969

versus Northumberland: Played 1, Won 1 (Away)

Highest Score:	By Yorkshire	138:2	(51.3 overs) at Leeds, 1992
	By Northumberland	137	at Leeds, 1992
Highest Individual			
Score:	For Yorkshire	38	S A Kellett at Leeds, 1992
	For Northumberland	47	G R Morris at Leeds, 1992
Best Bowling:	For Yorkshire	3-18	M A Robinson at Leeds, 1992
	For Northumberland	2-22	S Greensword at Leeds, 1992

versus Shropshire: Played 2, Won 1 (Away 1), Lost 1 (Away 1)

Highest Score:	By Yorkshire	192	at Telford, 1984
	By Shropshire	229:5	at Telford, 1984
Lowest Score:	By Yorkshire	192	at Telford, 1984
	By Shropshire	185	at Wellington, 1976
Highest Individual			
Score:	For Yorkshire	59	J H Hampshire at Wellington, 1976
	For Shropshire	80	Mushtaq Mohammed at Telford, 1984
Best Bowling:	For Yorkshire	3-17	A L Robinson at Wellington, 1976
	For Shropshire	3-26	Mushtaq Mohammed at Telford, 1984

versus Wiltshire: Played 1, Won 1 (Away)

Highest Score:	By Yorkshire	304:7	at Trowbridge, 1987
	By Wiltshire	175	at Trowbridge, 1987
Highest Individual			
Score:	For Yorkshire	85	A A Metcalfe at Trowbridge, 1987
	For Wiltshire	62	J J Newman at Trowbridge, 1987
Best Bowling:	For Yorkshire	4-40	K Sharp at Trowbridge, 1987
	For Wiltshire	2-38	R C Cooper at Trowbridge, 1987

versus Yorkshire Cricket Board: Played 1, Won 1 (Away)

Scores:	By Yorkshire	240:5	at Harrogate, 2000
	By Yorkshire CB	130	at Harrogate, 2000
Highest Individual			
Score:	For Yorkshire	70	M P Vaughan at Harrogate, 2000
	For Yorkshire CB	31	R A Kettleborough at Harrogate, 2000
Best Bowling:	For Yorkshire	5-30	D Gough at Harrogate, 2000
	For Yorkshire CB	1-25	A E McKenna at Harrogate, 2000

CAREER AVERAGES FOR YORKSHIRE

FRIENDS PROVIDENT TROPHY, CHELTENHAM & GLOUCESTER TROPHY, GILLETTE CUP AND NATWEST TROPHY 1963-2009

Player	M	Inns	NO	Runs	HS	Av'ge	100s	50s	Runs	Wkts	Av'ge	Ct/St
Athey, C W J ..	15	15	2	485	115	37.30	1	2	41	1	41.00	2
Bairstow, D L ..	34	27	5	492	92	22.36	—	2	—	—	—	38/3
Balderstone, J C	5	3	0	65	34	21.66	—	—	10	1	10.00	1
Batty, J D	3	2	0	7	4	3.50	—	—	97	1	97.00	1
Bevan, M G	8	8	2	388	91*	64.66	—	4	89	3	29.66	—
Binks, J G	16	10	1	107	22	11.88	—	—	—	—	—	15/6
Blain, J A R	3	2	0	13	7	6.50	—	—	63	3	21.00	—
Blakey, R J	48	35	13	516	75	23.45	—	2	—	—	—	54/5
Blewett, G S ...	3	3	0	83	77	27.66	—	1	57	7	8.14	1
Booth, P A	1	1	1	6	6*	—	—	—	33	0	—	—
Bore, M K	3	2	1	0	0*	0.00	—	—	98	5	19.60	—
Boycott, G	40	39	4	1378	146	39.37	1	9	238	8	29.75	9
Bresnan, T T ..	**36**	**20**	**4**	**309**	**55**	**19.31**	**—**	**1**	**1360**	**47**	**28.93**	**8**
Brophy, G L	23	19	7	437	68	36.41	—	4	—	—	—	29/3
Byas, D	34	32	3	912	73*	31.45	—	8	23	1	23.00	23
Carrick, P	32	23	3	320	54	16.00	—	1	741	24	30.87	6
Chapman, C ...	1	—	—	—	—	—	—	—	—	—	—	1
Claydon, M E ..	7	2	0	15	9	7.50	—	—	293	8	36.62	—
Close, D B	15	15	4	407	96	31.30	—	2	357	22	16.22	6
Cooper, H P	11	9	4	49	17	9.80	—	—	347	15	23.13	2
Cope, G A	4	2	2	1	1*	—	—	—	130	5	26.00	3
Craven, V J	4	3	1	38	26	19.00	—	—	41	2	20.50	2
Dawson, R K J .	22	7	0	77	24	11.00	—	—	762	15	50.80	9
Dawood, I	4	3	0	26	23	8.66	—	—	—	—	—	1/1
Dennis, S J	5	2	0	14	14	7.00	—	—	202	6	33.66	—
Elliott, M T G ..	1	1	1	128	128*	—	1	—	—	—	—	—
Fellows, G M ..	12	8	3	230	80*	46.00	—	2	55	0	—	3
Fisher, I D	3	1	0	5	5	5.00	—	—	87	3	29.00	2
Fletcher, S D ...	15	7	4	36	16*	12.00	—	—	576	15	38.40	2
Gale, A W	**26**	**22**	**4**	**567**	**69***	**35.43**	**—**	**4**	**—**	**—**	**—**	**2**
Gilbert, C R	3	2	0	9	6	4.50	—	—	134	6	22.33	—
Gillespie, J N ..	11	2	1	15	15*	15.00	—	—	363	9	40.33	3
Gough, D	44	20	3	251	46	14.76	—	—	1596	86	18.55	9
Gray, A K D ...	3	1	0	0	0	0.00	—	—	152	5	30.40	3
Grayson, A P ..	7	6	0	91	29	15.16	—	—	241	4	60.25	3
Guy, S M	12	7	1	45	22	7.50	—	—	—	—	—	17/3
Hamilton, G M .	9	8	3	146	39	29.20	—	—	254	15	16.93	2
Hampshire, A W	1	1	0	0	0	0.00	—	—	—	—	—	1
Hampshire, J H .	32	31	5	877	110	33.73	1	6	4	0	—	10
Harden R J	4	4	0	54	37	13.50	—	—	—	—	—	—
Hartley, P J	28	17	8	250	83	27.77	—	2	1108	45	24.62	2
Hartley, S N ...	15	12	0	263	69	21.91	—	2	114	1	114.00	5
Harvey, I J	4	4	0	151	74	37.75	—	2	184	6	30.66	2
Hoggard, M J ..	16	4	4	8	7*	—	—	—	555	23	24.13	1
Hutchison, P M .	3	1	1	4	4*	—	—	—	62	5	12.40	—
Hutton, R A	13	10	2	136	61	17.00	—	1	341	13	26.23	3
Illingworth, R ..	15	10	7	150	45	50.00	—	—	260	8	32.50	7
Jaques, P A	6	6	1	211	55*	42.20	—	2	—	—	—	2
Jarvis, P W	16	9	2	86	16	12.28	—	—	655	19	34.47	3
Johnson, C	4	4	0	62	44	15.50	—	—	—	—	—	—
Katich, S M	1	1	1	40	40*	—	—	—	—	—	—	—
Kellett, S A	9	7	0	246	107	35.14	1	1	—	—	—	6
Kirby, S P	2	1	0	0	0	0.00	—	—	74	2	37.00	—
Kruis, G J	25	9	5	42	11	10.50	—	—	774	26	29.76	3
Leadbeater, B ..	9	9	0	155	76	17.22	—	1	47	3	15.66	2

391

Player	M	Inns	NO	Runs	HS	Av'ge	100s	50s	Runs	Wkts	Av'ge	Ct/St
Lehmann, D S ..	23	19	5	853	118*	60.92	2	6	462	20	23.10	4
Lester, E I	1	1	0	0	0	0.00	—	—	—	—	—	—
Love, J D	21	18	3	266	67	17.73	—	3	39	2	19.50	5
Lumb, M J	20	18	3	628	89	41.86	—	4	—	—	—	6
Lumb, R G	12	12	0	222	56	18.50	—	1	—	—	—	—
Lyth, A	**11**	**9**	**1**	**218**	**83**	**27.25**	**—**	**1**	**—**	**—**	**—**	**4**
McGrath, A	60	54	8	1879	135*	40.84	3	15	732	22	33.27	19
Metcalfe, A A ..	20	20	3	714	127*	42.00	1	5	44	2	22.00	4
Middlebrook, J D	2	1	1	6	6*	—	—	—	38	0	—	3
Morris, A C ...	1	1	1	1	1*	—	—	—	43	1	43.00	—
Moxon, M D ...	34	34	6	1316	137	47.00	2	10	68	4	17.00	12
Nicholson, A G .	17	12	4	42	15*	5.25	—	—	467	21	22.23	6
Old, C M	28	23	3	268	55*	13.40	—	1	799	43	18.58	7
Oldham, S	8	5	3	35	19	17.50	—	—	309	15	20.60	—
Padgett, D E V .	17	15	1	309	46	22.07	—	—	—	—	—	4
Parker, B	6	4	0	87	69	21.75	—	1	—	—	—	—
Patterson, S A .	**9**	**3**	**3**	**17**	**14***	**—**	**—**	**—**	**320**	**7**	**45.71**	**—**
Pickles, C S ...	3	2	0	15	12	7.50	—	—	111	4	27.75	1
Pyrah, R M ...	**28**	**18**	**5**	**273**	**67**	**21.00**	**—**	**1**	**1015**	**40**	**25.37**	**12**
Ramage, A	4	1	0	14	14	14.00	—	—	167	4	41.75	1
Rana Naved -ul-Hasan	7	7	1	134	53*	22.33	—	1	324	10	32.40	4
Rashid, A U ...	**18**	**11**	**2**	**105**	**41***	**11.66**	**—**	**—**	**466**	**13**	**35.84**	**5**
Richardson, R B .	5	5	0	194	90	38.80	—	2	—	—	—	—
Robinson, A L ..	5	2	1	18	18*	18.00	—	—	179	9	19.88	1
Robinson, M A .	11	4	3	1	1*	1.00	—	—	390	12	32.50	—
Robinson, P E ..	8	5	0	113	66	22.60	—	1	—	—	—	3
Rudolph, J A ...	26	25	3	873	118	39.68	2	5	8	0	—	16
Ryan, M	3	2	1	7	6*	7.00	—	—	149	5	29.80	3
Sayers, J J	6	6	0	111	51	18.50	—	1	—	—	—	1
Shahzad, A	8	6	2	110	43*	27.25	—	—	292	7	41.71	2
Sharp, K	17	13	2	228	50	20.72	—	1	47	4	11.75	6
Sharpe, P J	22	20	1	331	68	17.42	—	2	—	—	—	18
Shaw, C	6	5	2	10	6*	3.33	—	—	194	11	17.63	—
Sidebottom, A ..	25	16	5	192	45	17.45	—	—	700	37	18.91	9
Sidebottom, R J .	14	2	1	13	7*	13.00	—	—	432	20	21.60	4
Silverwood,CEW	26	12	3	161	61	17.88	—	1	841	27	31.15	7
Smith, N	1	1	0	5	5	5.00	—	—	—	—	—	—
Squires, P J ...	2	2	0	46	42	23.00	—	—	—	—	—	1
Stemp, R D	11	3	2	1	1*	1.00	—	—	406	14	29.00	1
Stevenson, G B .	19	13	1	190	34	15.83	—	—	612	30	20.40	5
Stott, W B	2	2	0	30	30	15.00	—	—	—	—	—	—
Stringer, P M ...	2	2	2	7	5*	—	—	—	21	4	5.25	—
Swallow, I G ...	2	1	1	17	17*	—	—	—	16	0	—	—
Taylor, C R ...	1	—	—	—	—	—	—	—	—	—	—	—
Taylor, K	10	10	0	135	30	13.50	—	—	168	11	15.27	3
Tendulkar, S R .	2	2	1	53	32*	53.00	—	—	—	—	—	1
Thornicroft, N D	2	1	1	10	10*	—	—	—	97	1	97.00	1
Trueman, F S ..	11	9	1	127	28	15.87	—	—	348	21	16.57	5
Vaughan, M P ..	41	40	3	1356	116*	36.64	1	10	333	6	55.50	10
Wainwright, D J	7	4	3	50	15*	50.00	—	—	237	7	33.85	4
Waring, J	1	1	1	1	1*	—	—	—	11	0	—	—
White, C	60	55	14	1809	113	44.12	4	10	1130	40	28.25	19
Whiteley, J P ..	1	—	—	—	—	—	—	—	48	0	—	—
Wilson, D	15	13	1	72	16	6.00	—	—	391	21	18.62	10
Wood, M J	28	28	6	908	160	41.27	2	3	45	3	15.00	11
Woodford, J D ..	1	1	0	15	15	15.00	—	—	—	—	—	—
Younus Khan ...	7	6	0	234	100	39.00	1	0	124	2	62.00	3
Yuvraj Singh ...	1	1	0	27	27	27.00	—	—	27	0	—	—

WINNERS OF THE GILLETTE CUP, NATWEST TROPHY, CHELTENHAM & GLOUCESTER TROPHY AND FRIENDS PROVIDENT TROPHY 1963-2009

GILLETTE CUP

1963 **Sussex**, who beat Worcestershire by 14 runs
1964 **Sussex**, who beat Warwickshire by 8 wickets
1965 **Yorkshire**, who beat Surrey by 175 runs
1966 **Warwickshire**, who beat Worcestershire by 5 wickets
1967 **Kent**, who beat Somerset by 32 runs
1968 **Warwickshire**, who beat Sussex by 4 wickets
1969 **Yorkshire**, who beat Derbyshire by 69 runs
1970 **Lancashire**, who beat Sussex by 6 wickets
1971 **Lancashire**, who beat Kent by 24 runs
1972 **Lancashire**, who beat Warwickshire by 4 wickets
1973 **Gloucestershire**, who beat Sussex by 40 runs
1974 **Kent**, who beat Lancashire by 4 wickets
1975 **Lancashire**, who beat Middlesex by 7 wickets
1976 **Northamptonshire**, who beat Lancashire by 4 wickets
1977 **Middlesex**, who beat Glamorgan by 5 wickets
1978 **Sussex**, who beat Somerset by 5 wickets
1979 **Somerset**, who beat Northamptonshire by 45 runs
1980 **Middlesex**, who beat Surrey by 7 wickets

NATWEST TROPHY

1981 **Derbyshire**, who beat Northamptonshire by losing fewer wickets with the scores level.
1982 **Surrey**, who beat Warwickshire by 9 wickets
1983 **Somerset**, who beat Kent by 24 runs
1984 **Middlesex**, who beat Kent by 4 wickets
1985 **Essex**, who beat Nottinghamshire by 1 run
1986 **Sussex**, who beat Lancashire by 7 wickets
1987 **Nottinghamshire**, who beat Northamptonshire by 3 wickets
1988 **Middlesex**, who beat Worcestershire by 3 wickets
1989 **Warwickshire**, who beat Middlesex by 4 wickets
1990 **Lancashire**, who beat Northamptonshire by 7 wickets
1991 **Hampshire**, who beat Surrey by 4 wickets
1992 **Northamptonshire**, who beat Leicestershire by 8 wickets
1993 **Warwickshire**, who beat Sussex by 5 wickets
1994 **Worcestershire**, who beat Warwickshire by 8 wickets
1995 **Warwickshire**, who beat Northamptonshire by 4 wickets
1996 **Lancashire**, who beat Essex by 129 runs
1997 **Essex**, who beat Warwickshire by 9 wickets
1998 **Lancashire**, who beat Derbyshire by 9 wickets
1999 **Gloucestershire**, who beat Somerset by 50 runs
2000 **Gloucestershire**, who beat Warwickshire by 22 runs

CHELTENHAM & GLOUCESTER TROPHY

2001 **Somerset**, who beat Leicestershire by 41 runs
2002 **Yorkshire**, who beat Somerset by 6 wickets
2003 **Gloucestershire**, who beat Worcestershire by 7 wickets
2004 **Gloucestershire**, who beat Worcestershire by 8 wickets
2005 **Hampshire**, who beat Warwickshire by 18 runs
2006 **Sussex**, who beat Lancashire by 15 runs

FRIENDS PROVIDENT TROPHY

2007 **Durham**, who beat Hampshire by 125 runs
2008 **Essex**, who beat Kent by 5 wickets
2009 **Hampshire**, who beat Sussex by 6 wickets

YORKSHIRE BANK 40, CLYDESDALE BANK 40, PRO40, NATIONAL AND SUNDAY LEAGUES 1969-2013

JOHN PLAYER SPECIAL LEAGUE WINNERS 1983

Played 684, Won 304 (in Yorkshire 168, Away 136), Lost 319 (in Yorkshire 143, Away 176)
Ties 4   No Result 24   Abandoned 33

Highest Score:	By Yorkshire	352:6 v. Nottinghamshire at Scarborough, 2001
	Against Yorkshire	375:4 by Surrey at Scarborough, 1994
†Lowest Score:	By Yorkshire	54 v. Essex at Leeds, 2003
	Against Yorkshire	23 by Middlesex at Leeds, 1974
Highest Individual		
Score:	For Yorkshire	191 D S Lehmann v. Nottinghamshire at Scarborough, 2001
	Against Yorkshire	155* B A Richards for Hampshire at Hull, 1970
Most Runs in a Season:		851 J A Rudolph in 2010

†Lowest score is the lowest all-out score or the lowest score at completion of allotted overs

Highest Partnerships: For Yorkshire

1st wkt	233*	A W Gale (125*) and J A Rudolph (101*) v. Essex at Chelmsford, 2010
2nd wkt	172	D Byas (86) and D S Lehmann (99) v. Kent at Maidstone, 1998
3rd wkt	176	R J Blakey (86) and S R Tendulkar (107) v. Lancashire at Leeds, 1992
4th wkt	198*	M T G Elliott (115*) and A McGrath (85*) v. Kent at Leeds, 2002
5th wkt	190	R J Blakey (96) and M J Foster (118) v. Leicestershire at Leicester, 1993
6th wkt	110	B Leadbeater (69) and C Johnson (51*) v. Nottinghamshire at Hull, 1972
7th wkt	129*	D Byas (74*) and D Gough (72*) v. Leicestershire at Leicester, 1991
8th wkt	89	R J Blakey (60) and R K J Dawson (41) v. Leicestershire at Scarborough, 2002
9th wkt	88	S N Hartley (67) and A Ramage (32*) v. Middlesex at Lord's, 1982
10th wkt	64	R J Blakey (47) and R J Sidebottom (30*) v. Glamorgan at Leeds, 2002

Best Bowling:	For Yorkshire	7 for 15 R A Hutton v. Worcestershire at Leeds, 1969
	Against Yorkshire	6 for 15 A A Donald for Warwickshire at Birmingham, 1995
Most Economical Bowling:		
	For Yorkshire	8-5-3-3 A L Robinson v. Derbyshire at Scarborough, 1973
	Against Yorkshire	8-4-6-2 P J Sainsbury for Hampshire at Hull, 1970
		8-5-6-3 M J Procter for Gloucestershire at Cheltenham, 1979
Most Expensive Bowling:		
	For Yorkshire	9-0-87-1 T T Bresnan v. Somerset at Taunton, 2005
	Against Yorkshire	9-0-78-1 Mohammed Akram for Surrey at The Oval, 2005
Most Wickets In A Season:		37 M J Hoggard in 2000

Centuries (58)

	C W J Athey	118	v. Leicestershire at Leicester, 1978
	J M Bairstow	114	v. Middlesex at Lord's, 2011
	G S Ballance (2)	103*	v. Unicorns at Scarborough, 2012
		139	v. Unicorns at Leeds, 2013
	M G Bevan (2)	103*	v. Gloucestershire at Middlesbrough, 1995
		101	v. Worcestershire at Scarborough, 1995
	G Boycott (2)	104*	v. Glamorgan at Colwyn Bay, 1973
		108*	v. Northamptonshire at Huddersfield, 1974

Centuries *(Continued)*

R J Blakey (3)	100*	v. Gloucestershire at Cheltenham, 1990
	130*	v. Kent at Scarborough, 1991
	105*	v. Warwickshire at Scarborough, 1992
D Byas (3)	106*	v. Derbyshire at Chesterfield, 1993
	101*	v. Nottinghamshire at Leeds, 1994
	111*	v. Lancashire at Leeds, 1996
M T G Elliott (2)	109	v. Leicestershire at Leicester, 2002
	115*	v. Kent at Leeds, 2002
S P Fleming	139*	v. Warwickshire at Leeds, 2003
M J Foster	118	v. Leicestershire at Leicester, 1993
A W Gale (2)	125*	v Essex at Chelmsford, 2010
	112	v. Kent at Canterbury, 2011
J H Hampshire (6)	108	v. Nottinghamshire at Sheffield, 1970
	119	v. Leicestershire at Hull, 1971
	106*	v. Lancashire at Manchester, 1972
	111*	v. Sussex at Hastings, 1973
	100*	v. Warwickshire at Birmingham, 1975
	114*	v. Northamptonshire at Scarborough, 1978
P A Jaques	105	v Sussex at Leeds, 2004
S A Kellett	118*	v. Derbyshire at Leeds, 1992
D S Lehmann (3)	103	v. Leicestershire at Scarborough, 2001
	191	v. Nottinghamshire at Scarborough, 2001
	104	v. Somerset at Taunton, 2002
J D Love (3)	100*	v. Gloucestershire at Gloucester, 1985
	104*	v. Nottinghamshire at Hull, 1986
	118*	v. Surrey at Leeds, 1987
R G Lumb	101	v. Nottinghamshire at Scarborough, 1976
A Lyth	109*	v Sussex at Scarborough, 2009
A McGrath (2)	102	v. Kent at Canterbury, 2001
	148	v. Somerset at Taunton, 2006
A A Metcalfe (2)	115*	v. Gloucestershire at Scarborough, 1984
	116	v. Middlesex at Lord's, 1991
M D Moxon (3)	105	v. Somerset at Scarborough, 1990
	129*	v. Surrey at The Oval, 1991
	112	v. Sussex at Middlesbrough, 1991
R B Richardson	103	v. Nottinghamshire at Nottingham, 1993
J A Rudolph (7)	127	v. Somerset at Scarborough, 2007
	120	v. Leicestershire at Leeds, 2008
	101*	v Essex at Chelmsford, 2010
	105	v. Derbyshire at Chesterfield, 2010
	124*	v. Middlesex at Scarborough, 2010
	106	v. Warwickshire at Scarborough, 2010
	132*	v. Sussex at Scarborough 2011
K Sharp (2)	112*	v. Worcestershire at Worcester, 1985
	114	v. Essex at Chelmsford, 1985
S R Tendulkar	107	v. Lancashire at Leeds, 1992
M P Vaughan	116*	v. Kent at Leeds, 2005
C White	148	v. Leicestershire at Leicester, 1997
M J Wood (2)	105*	v. Somerset at Taunton, 2002
	111	v. Surrey at The Oval, 2005

5 Wickets in an Innings (32)

C W J Athey	5 for 35 v. Derbyshire at Chesterfield, 1981	
M G Bevan	5 for 29 v. Sussex at Eastbourne, 1996	
P Carrick (2)	5 for 22 v. Glamorgan at Leeds, 1991	
	5 for 40 v. Sussex at Middlesbrough, 1991	
H P Cooper (2)	6 for 14 v. Worcestershire at Worcester, 1975	
	5 for 30 v. Worcestershire at Middlesbrough, 1978	
D Gough (2)	5 for 13 v. Sussex at Hove, 1994	
	5 for 25 v. Surrey at Leeds, 1998	
G M Hamilton (2)	5 for 16 v. Hampshire at Leeds, 1998	
	5 for 34 v. Sussex at Scarborough, 2000	
P J. Hartley (2)	5 for 38 v. Worcestershire at Worcester, 1990	
	5 for 36 v. Sussex at Scarborough, 1993	
M J Hoggard (2)	5 for 28 v. Leicestershire at Leicester, 2000	
	5 for 30 v. Northamptonshire at Northampton, 2000 (consecutive matches)	
R A Hutton	7 for 15 v. Worcestershire at Leeds, 1969	
P W Jarvis (3)	6 for 27 v. Somerset at Taunton, 1989	
	5 for 18 v. Derbyshire at Leeds, 1990	
	5 for 29 v. Northamptonshire at Northampton, 1992	
J A Leaning	5 for 22 v. Unicorns at Leeds, 2013	
A G Nicholson (2)	6 for 36 v. Somerset at Sheffield, 1972	
	5 for 17 v. Nottinghamshire at Hull, 1972 (Consecutive matches).	
C M Old (2)	5 for 33 v. Sussex at Hove, 1971	
	5 for 38 v. Northamptonshire at Sheffield, 1972	
S A Patterson	6 for 32 v. Derbyshire at Leeds, 2010	
C Shaw	5 for 41 v. Hampshire at Bournemouth, 1984	
R J Sidebottom (2)	6 for 40 v. Glamorgan at Cardiff, 1998	
	5 for 42 v. Leicestershire at Leicester, 2003	
G B Stevenson	5 for 41 v. Leicestershire at Leicester, 1976	
S Stuchbury	5 for 16 v. Leicestershire at Leicester, 1982	
N D Thornicroft	5 for 42 v. Gloucestershire at Leeds, 2003	
C White	5 for 19 v. Somerset at Scarborough, 2002	
D Wilson	6 for 18 v. Kent at Canterbury, 1969	

versus Derbyshire: Played 43, Won 23 (in Yorkshire 13, Away 10), Lost 16 (in Yorkshire 8, Away 8), Tied 1 (Away), No Result 1, Abandoned 2

Highest Score:	By Yorkshire	276:6 at Chesterfield, 2010	
	By Derbyshire	268:6 at Chesterfield, 2010	
Lowest Score:	By Yorkshire	117	at Huddersfield, 1978
	By Derbyshire	87	at Scarborough, 1973
Highest Individual Score:	For Yorkshire	118* S A Kellett at Leeds, 1992	
	For Derbyshire	109* C J Adams at Derby, 1997	
Best Bowling:	For Yorkshire	6-32 S A Patterson at Leeds, 2010	
	For Derbyshire	4-14 A E Warner at Chesterfield, 1995	

versus Durham: Played 15, Won 7 (in Yorkshire 4, Away 3) Lost 6 (in Yorkshire 3, Away 3), No Result 1, Abandoned 1

Highest Score:	By Yorkshire	269:5 at Chester-le-Street, 2002	
	By Durham	256:4 at Chester-le-Street, 2005	
Lowest Score:	By Yorkshire	122	at Chester-le-Street, 2007
	By Durham	121	at Scarborough, 1997
Highest Individual Score:	For Yorkshire	83 A W Gale at Scarborough, 2009	
	For Durham	114 W Larkins at Leeds, 1993	
Best Bowling:	For Yorkshire	4-18 C White at Scarborough, 1997	
	For Durham	4-20 S J E Brown at Leeds, 1995	

versus Essex: Played 38, Won 16 (in Yorkshire 9, Away 7)
                          Lost 19 (in Yorkshire 10, Away 9), Abandoned 3

Highest Score:	By Yorkshire	264:6 at Ilford, 1997
	By Essex	262:9 at Ilford, 1997
Lowest Score:	By Yorkshire	54 at Leeds, 2003
	By Essex	108 at Leeds, 1996
Highest Individual Score:	For Yorkshire	125* A W Gale at Chelmsford, 2010
	For Essex	114 N Hussain at Leeds, 1999
Best Bowling:	For Yorkshire	4-21 C White at Leeds, 1996
	For Essex	6-18 R E East at Hull, 1969

versus Glamorgan: Played 38, Won 16 (in Yorkshire 8, Away 8),
                          Lost 20 (in Yorkshire 8, Away 12), Abandoned 2

Highest Score:	By Yorkshire	257 at Colwyn Bay, 2013
	By Glamorgan	285:7 at Colwyn Bay, 2013
Lowest Score:	By Yorkshire	139 at Hull, 1981
	By Glamorgan	90 at Neath, 1969
Highest Individual Score:	For Yorkshire	104* G Boycott at Colwyn Bay, 1973
	For Glamorgan	97* G P Ellis at Leeds, 1976
Best Bowling:	For Yorkshire	6-40 R J Sidebottom at Cardiff, 1998
	For Glamorgan	5-16 G C Holmes at Swansea, 1985

versus Gloucestershire: Played 44, Won 17 (in Yorkshire 11, Away 6),
                          Lost 22 (in Yorkshire 7, Away 15), No Result 3, Abandoned 2

Highest Score:	By Yorkshire	262:7 at Bristol, 1996
	By Gloucestershire	294:6 at Cheltenham, 2010
Lowest Score:	By Yorkshire	115 at Leeds, 1973
	By Gloucestershire	90 at Tewkesbury, 1972
Highest Individual Score:	For Yorkshire	115* A A Metcalfe at Scarborough, 1984
	For Gloucestershire	146* S Young at Leeds, 1997
Best Bowling:	For Yorkshire	5-42 N D Thornicroft at Leeds, 2003
	For Gloucestershire	5-33 M C J Ball at Leeds, 2003

versus Hampshire: Played 34, Won 13 (in Yorkshire 7, Away 6),
                          Lost 19 (in Yorkshire 9, Away 10), No Result 1, Abandoned 1

Highest Score:	By Yorkshire	264:2 at Southampton, 1995
	By Hampshire	257:6 at Middlesbrough, 1985
Lowest Score:	By Yorkshire	74:9 at Hull, 1970
	By Hampshire	122 at Leeds, 1994
Highest Individual Score:	For Yorkshire	98* M G Bevan at Leeds, 1996
	For Hampshire	155* B A Richards at Hull, 1970
Best Bowling:	For Yorkshire	5-16 G M Hamilton at Leeds, 1998
	For Hampshire	5-31 D W White at Southampton, 1969

versus Kent: Played 49, Won 19 (in Yorkshire 11, Away 8),
                          Lost 27 (in Yorkshire 10, Away 17) No Result 1, Abandoned 2

Highest Score:	By Yorkshire	299:3 at Leeds, 2002
	By Kent	266:5 at Maidstone, 1998
Lowest Score:	By Yorkshire	75 at Leeds, 1995
	By Kent	105 at Canterbury, 1969
Highest Individual Score:	For Yorkshire	130* R J Blakey at Scarborough, 1991
	For Kent	118* M H Denness at Scarborough, 1976
Best Bowling:	For Yorkshire	6-18 D Wilson at Canterbury, 1969
	For Kent	6-32 M T Coles at Leeds, 2012

versus Lancashire: Played 34, Won 10 (in Yorkshire 4, Away 6),
Lost 19 (in Yorkshire 11, Away 8), No Result 3, Abandoned 2

Highest Score:	By Yorkshire	260:6 at Leeds, 1992	
	By Lancashire	264:3 at Leeds, 1992	
Lowest Score:	By Yorkshire	81	at Leeds, 1998
	By Lancashire	68	at Leeds, 2000
Highest Individual Score:	For Yorkshire	111* D Byas at Leeds, 1996	
	For Lancashire	102* N J Speak at Leeds, 1992	
Best Bowling:	For Yorkshire	4-14 C White at Leeds, 2000	
	For Lancashire	6-25 G Chapple at Leeds, 1998	

versus Leicestershire: Played 49, Won 21 (in Yorkshire 14, Away 7),
Lost 24 (in Yorkshire 12, Away 12), Tie 1, No Result 2, Abandoned 1

Highest Score:	By Yorkshire	318:7 at Leicester, 1993	
	By Leicestershire	302:7 at Leeds, 2008	
Lowest Score:	By Yorkshire	89:9 at Leicester, 1989	
	By Leicestershire	53	at Leicester, 2000
Highest Individual Score:	For Yorkshire	148 C White at Leicester, 1997	
	For Leicestershire	108 N E Briers at Bradford, 1984	
Best Bowling:	For Yorkshire	5-16 S Stuchbury at Leicester, 1982	
	For Leicestershire	5-24 C W Henderson at Leeds, 2004	

versus Middlesex: Played 39, Won 20 (in Yorkshire 12, Away 8),
Lost 15 (in Yorkshire 3, Away 12), No Result 4

Highest Score:	By Yorkshire	275-4 at Lord's 2011	
	By Middlesex	273:6 at Southgate, 2004	
Lowest Score:	By Yorkshire	94	at Lord's, 1969
	By Middlesex	23	at Leeds, 1974
Highest Individual Score:	For Yorkshire	124* J A Rudolph at Scarborough, 2010	
	For Middlesex	125* O A Shah at Southgate, 2004	
Best Bowling:	For Yorkshire	4-6 R Illingworth at Hull, 1983	
	For Middlesex	4-22 K P Dutch at Lord's, 1998	

versus Northamptonshire: Played 39, Won 26 (in Yorkshire 12, Away 14),
Lost 9 (in Yorkshire 5, Away 4), No Result 2, Abandoned 2

Highest Score:	By Yorkshire	262-8 at Northampton, 2012	
	By Northamptonshire	282:4 at Middlesbrough, 1982	
Lowest Score:	By Yorkshire	112	at Northampton, 1975
	By Northamptonshire	109	at Northampton, 2000
Highest Individual Score:	For Yorkshire	114* J H Hampshire, Scarborough, 1978	
	For Northamptonshire	104* P Willey at Bradford, 1976	
Best Bowling:	For Yorkshire	5-29 P W Jarvis at Northampton, 1992	
	For Northamptonshire	5-15 Sarfraz Nawaz, Northampton, 1975	

YORKSHIRE BANK 40, CLYDESDALE BANK 40, PRO40, NATIONAL AND SUNDAY LEAGUES 1969-2013 *(Continued)*

versus Nottinghamshire: Played 37, Won 16 (in Yorkshire 11, Away 5),
Lost 16 (in Yorkshire 6, Away 10), Tie 1, No Result 3,
Abandoned 1

Highest Score: By Yorkshire   352:6 at Scarborough, 2001
By Nottinghamshire   291:6 at Nottingham, 2004
Lowest Score: By Yorkshire   147   at Nottingham, 1975
By Nottinghamshire   66   at Bradford, 1969

Highest Individual
Score: For Yorkshire   191   D S Lehmann at Scarborough, 2001
For Nottinghamshire   123   D W Randall at Nottingham, 1987
Best Bowling: For Yorkshire   5-17 A G Nicholson at Hull, 1972
For Nottinghamshire   5-41 C L Cairns at Scarborough, 1996

versus Somerset: Played 45, Won 21 (in Yorkshire 13, Away 8),
Lost 22 (in Yorkshire 9, Away 13), No Result 1, Abandoned 1

Highest Score: By Yorkshire   343:9 at Taunton, 2005
By Somerset   345:4 at Taunton, 2005
Lowest Score: By Yorkshire   110   at Scarborough, 1977
By Somerset   139   at Taunton, 2004

Highest Individual
Score: For Yorkshire   148   A McGrath at Taunton, 2006
For Somerset   140* P D Trego at Taunton, 2013
Best Bowling: For Yorkshire   6-27 P W Jarvis at Taunton, 1989
For Somerset   5-27 J Garner at Bath, 1985

versus Surrey: Played 39, Won 15 (in Yorkshire 9, Away 6),
Lost 22 (in Yorkshire 8, Away 14), Abandoned 2

Highest Score: By Yorkshire   334:5 at The Oval, 2005
By Surrey   375:4 at Scarborough, 1994
Lowest Score: By Yorkshire   91   at Scarborough, 1970
By Surrey   90   at Leeds, 1996

Highest Individual
Score: For Yorkshire   129* M D Moxon at The Oval, 1991
For Surrey   136   M A Lynch at Bradford, 1985
Best Bowling: For Yorkshire   5-25 D Gough at Leeds, 1998
For Surrey   5-22 R D Jackman at The Oval, 1978

versus Sussex: Played 41, Won 17 (in Yorkshire 9, Away 8),
Lost 19 (in Yorkshire 9, Away 10), Abandoned 5

Highest Score: By Yorkshire   302:4 at Scarborough, 2011
By Sussex   272:6 at Arundel, 2000
Lowest Score: By Yorkshire   89   at Hove, 1998
By Sussex   108   at Hove, 1971

Highest Individual   For Yorkshire   132* J A Rudolph at Scarborough, 2011
For Sussex   129   A W Greig at Scarborough, 1976
Best Bowling: For Yorkshire   5-13 D Gough at Hove, 1994
For Sussex   4-10 M H Yardy at Hove, 2011

versus Warwickshire: Played 44, Won 15 (in Yorkshire 8, Away 7),
Lost 22 (in Yorkshire 11, Away 11), Tied 1, No Result 1,
Abandoned 5

Highest Score:	By Yorkshire	274:3 at Leeds, 2003
	By Warwickshire	309:3 at Birmingham, 2005
Lowest Score:	By Yorkshire	56 at Birmingham, 1995
	By Warwickshire	59 at Leeds, 2001
Highest Individual Score:	For Yorkshire	139* S P Fleming at Leeds, 2003
	For Warwickshire	137 I R Bell at Birmingham, 2005
Best Bowling:	For Yorkshire	4-21 C E W Silverwood at Leeds, 2001
	For Warwickshire	6-15 A A Donald at Birmingham, 1995

versus Worcestershire: Played 44, Won 22 (in Yorkshire 7, Away 15),
Lost 20 (in Yorkshire 13, Away 7), No Result 1, Abandoned 1

Highest Score:	By Yorkshire	231:4 at Leeds, 2011
	By Worcestershire	251:4 at Scarborough, 1995
Lowest Score:	By Yorkshire	90 at Worcester, 1987
	By Worcestershire	86 at Leeds, 1969
Highest Individual Score:	For Yorkshire	112* K Sharp at Worcester, 1985
	For Worcestershire	113* G A Hick at Scarborough, 1995
Best Bowling:	For Yorkshire	7-15 R A Hutton at Leeds, 1969
	For Worcestershire	5-30 R J Chapman at Worcester, 1998

versus Netherlands: Played 4, Won 2 (in Yorkshire 1, Away 1),
Lost 2 (in Yorkshire 1, Away 1)

Highest Score:	By Yorkshire	204:6 at Leeds, 2010
	By Netherlands	200:8 at Leeds, 2010
Lowest Score:	By Yorkshire	123 at Amsterdam, 2011
	By Netherlands	154:9 at Rotterdam, 2010
Highest Individual Score:	For Yorkshire	83* J A Rudolph at Leeds, 2010
	For Netherlands	62 M G Dighton at Leeds, 2010
Best Bowling:	For Yorkshire	4-24 R M Pyrah at Rotterdam, 2010
	For Netherlands	3-26 Mudassar Bukhari at Leeds, 2011

versus Scotland: Played 4, Won 4 (in Yorkshire 2, Away 2)

Highest Score:	By Yorkshire	240:5 at Leeds, 2004
	By Scotland	203:9 at Edinburgh, 2005
Lowest Score:	By Yorkshire	199:8 at Edinburgh, 2004
	By Scotland	140 at Edinburgh, 2004
Highest Individual Score:	For Yorkshire	88* D S Lehmann at Leeds, 2004
	For Scotland	78 J A Beukes at Edinburgh, 2005
Best Bowling:	For Yorkshire	4-20 R K J Dawson at Edinburgh, 2004
	For Scotland	3-47 Asim Butt at Edinburgh, 2004

versus Unicorns: Played 4, Won 4 (in Yorkshire 3, Away 1)

Highest Score:	By Yorkshire	268:6 at Leeds, 2013
	By Unicorns	234 at Leeds, 2013
Lowest Score:	By Unicorns	150-6 at Leeds 2012
Highest Individual Score:	For Yorkshire	139 G S Ballance at Leeds, 2013
	For Unicorns	107 M S Lineker at Leeds, 2013
Best Bowling:	For Yorkshire	5-22 J A Leaning at Leeds, 2013
	For Unicorns	2-25 R J Woolley at Leeds, 2012

YORKSHIRE BANK 40, CLYDESDALE BANK 40, PRO40, NATIONAL AND SUNDAY LEAGUE RECORDS 1969-2013

Player	M	Inns	NO	Runs	HS	Av'ge	100s	50s	Runs	Wkts	Av'ge	Ct/St
Ashraf, M A ...	21	5	4	3	3*	3.00	—	—	857	23	37.26	3
Athey, C W J ...	94	86	8	2560	118	32.82	1	18	315	14	22.50	30
Azeem Rafiq ..	14	10	4	111	34*	18.50	—	—	453	12	37.75	4
Bairstow, D L ..	279	227	51	3677	83*	20.89	—	16	—	—	—	234/23
Bairstow, J M .	30	26	3	645	114	28.04	1	3	—	—	—	18/1
Baker, T M	1	0	0	0	0	—	—	—	22	1	22.00	1
Balderstone, J C	8	8	2	108	46	18.00	—	—	28	1	28.00	2
Ballance, G S ..	29	28	6	1259	139	57.22	2	8	—	—	—	12
Batty, J D	31	13	6	41	13*	5.86	—	—	1091	40	27.27	16
Best, T L	5	1	1	8	8*	—	—	—	166	10	16.60	1
Bevan, M G	29	27	5	1108	103*	50.36	2	7	399	23	17.34	9
Binks, J G	14	11	2	140	34	15.55	—	—	—	—	—	11/2
Blain, J A R	11	6	3	21	11*	7.00	—	—	364	11	33.08	3
Blakey, R J	249	218	52	5531	130*	33.31	3	27	—	—	—	244/48
Blewett, G S ...	11	11	0	178	48	16.18	—	—	116	4	29.00	6
Booth, P A	2	—	—	—	—	—	—	—	67	1	67.00	1
Bore, M K	44	18	7	67	15	6.09	—	—	1300	37	35.13	14
Boycott, G ...	163	157	24	5051	108*	37.97	2	37	611	14	43.64	69
Bresnan, T T .	90	67	18	827	61	16.87	—	2	3110	91	34.17	26
Broadhurst, M ..	1	—	—	—	—	—	—	—	27	0	—	—
Brophy, G L ...	45	38	5	803	93*	24.33	—	5	—	—	—	38/11
Byas, D	217	211	27	5352	111*	29.08	3	28	463	19	24.36	88
Carrick, P	210	143	42	1481	48*	14.66	—	—	5030	170	29.58	53
Chapman, C A ..	7	6	3	89	36*	29.66	—	—	—	—	—	2
Cleary, M F	4	3	1	50	23*	25.00	—	—	159	2	79.50	—
Close, D B	17	16	0	224	50	14.00	—	1	118	1	118.00	8
Coad, B O	6	2	2	1	1*	—	—	—	244	3	81.33	3
Cooper, H P ...	103	50	24	358	29*	13.76	—	—	3038	120	25.31	20
Cope, G A	28	14	7	61	16*	8.71	—	—	750	18	41.66	6
Coverdale, S P .	3	3	2	18	17*	18.00	—	—	—	—	—	3
Craven, V J	36	34	4	540	59	18.00	—	2	297	18	16.50	11
Dalton, A J	17	16	1	280	57	18.66	—	1	—	—	—	7
Dawood, I	20	16	4	212	57	17.66	—	1	—	—	—	17/7
Dawson, R K J .	65	46	9	303	41	8.18	—	—	1914	70	27.34	20
Dennis, S J	41	19	11	87	16*	10.87	—	—	1188	27	44.00	6
Elliott, M T G ..	5	5	1	266	115*	88.66	2	—	—	—	—	—
Elstub, C J	9	3	3	4	4*	—	—	—	259	11	23.55	—
Fellows, G M ..	62	52	8	893	67	20.29	—	4	589	13	45.30	21
Fisher, I D	24	11	3	63	20	7.87	—	—	595	25	23.80	3
Fisher, M D ...	2	1	0	10	10	10.00	—	—	85	1	85.00	—
Fleming, S P ...	7	7	1	285	139*	47.50	1	1	—	—	—	3
Fletcher, D G .	86	19	11	53	11*	6.62	—	—	3136	114	27.50	26
Foster, M J	20	14	1	199	118	15.30	—	1	370	6	61.66	6
Gale, A W	84	80	6	2404	125*	32.48	2	12	—	—	—	20
Gibson, R J	3	2	1	10	6	10.00	—	—	98	3	32.66	—
Gilbert, C R	1	1	0	9	9	9.00	—	—	40	2	20.00	—
Gillespie, J N ..	7	2	0	14	11	7.00	—	—	238	9	26.44	3
Gough, D	129	80	24	845	72*	15.08	—	1	3929	159	24.71	23
Gray, A K D ...	24	14	6	111	30*	13.87	—	—	612	17	36.00	5
Grayson, A P ...	49	35	6	367	55	12.65	—	1	1051	31	33.90	14
Guy S M	18	14	3	188	40	17.09	—	—	—	—	—	18/8
Hamilton, G M .	74	52	12	743	57*	18.57	—	2	2033	81	25.09	12

YORKSHIRE BANK 40, CLYDESDALE BANK 40, PRO40, NATIONAL AND SUNDAY LEAGUE RECORDS 1969-2013 *(Continued)*

Player	M	Inns	NO	Runs	HS	Av'ge	100s	50s	Runs	Wkts	Av'ge	Ct/St
Hampshire, A W	3	2	0	3	3	1.50	—	—	—	—	—	—
Hampshire, J H .	155	152	15	4505	119	32.88	6	26	22	1	22.00	47
Hannon-Dalby, O J												
	5	1	1	21	21*	—	—	—	202	5	40.40	3
Harden, R J	12	10	2	133	42	16.62	—	—	—	—	—	1
Hartley, P J ...	145	102	31	1164	52	16.39	—	2	4778	174	27.45	26
Hartley, S N ..	130	119	25	2087	83*	22.20	—	9	1587	48	33.06	40
Harvey, I J	24	23	2	486	69	23.14	—	1	766	24	31.91	7
Hodd, A J	7	6	1	56	21	11.20	—	—	—	—	—	8/1
Hodgson, D M .	10	8	1	216	90*	30.85	—	2	—	—	—	8/1
Hodgson L J ..	6	2	0	9	9	4.50	—	—	161	4	40.25	1
Hoggard, M J ..	56	21	12	23	5*	2.55	—	—	1777	82	21.67	5
Hutchison, P M .	23	8	5	8	2*	2.66	—	—	670	28	23.92	3
Hutton, R A ...	77	60	19	761	65	18.56	—	3	2215	94	23.56	19
Illingworth, R ..	23	4	3	12	8*	12.00	—	—	453	26	17.42	7
Ingham, P G ...	12	10	4	312	87*	52.00	—	2	—	—	—	2
Inzamam-ul-Haq	3	3	0	69	53	23.00	—	1	—	—	—	—
Jaques, P A ...	36	35	1	1298	105	38.17	1	10	—	—	—	17
Jarvis, P W	94	49	21	316	38*	11.28	—	—	2914	138	21.11	25
Johnson, C	100	81	17	1186	67*	18.53	—	3	5	2	2.50	24
Johnson, M	10	4	1	30	15*	10.00	—	—	317	5	63.40	2
Katich, S M	2	2	1	39	39*	39.00	—	—	—	—	—	2
Kellett, S A	30	30	2	697	118*	24.89	1	3	16	0	—	6
Kettleborough, R A	10	6	3	71	28	23.66	—	—	72	3	24.00	4
Kirby, S P	25	10	3	38	15	5.42	—	—	919	22	41.77	6
Kruis, G J	30	13	6	96	31*	13.71	—	—	1019	36	28.30	6
Lawson, M A K.	4	4	0	30	20	7.50	—	—	141	3	47.00	1
Leadbeater, B ..	73	68	14	1423	86*	26.35	—	6	38	2	19.00	18
Leaning, J A ...	4	4	1	96	60	32.00	—	1	60	6	10.00	3
Lee, J E	4	0	0	0	0	—	—	—	116	7	16.57	—
Lees, A Z	6	6	1	190	63	38.00	—	2	—	—	—	1
Lehmann, D S ..	77	77	11	3091	191	46.83	3	24	1222	47	26.00	24
Love, J D	157	146	18	2919	118*	22.80	3	10	83	3	27.66	32
Lucas, D S	5	2	0	40	32	20.00	—	—	187	3	62.33	1
Lumb, M J	71	69	4	1838	92	28.27	—	14	28	0	—	22
Lumb, R G	87	75	10	1588	101	24.43	1	9	—	—	—	15
Lyth, A	61	57	5	1626	109*	31.26	1	8	100	1	100.00	20
McGrath, A	179	165	29	4448	148	32.70	2	24	1772	55	32.21	60
Metcalfe, A A ..	140	135	7	3529	116	27.57	2	23	—	—	—	32
Middlebrook, J D	14	9	2	52	15*	7.42	—	—	417	13	32.07	1
Milburn, S M ..	4	2	1	14	13*	14.00	—	—	118	2	59.00	1
Miller, D A	3	3	0	45	44	15.00	—	—	—	—	—	—
Morris, A C. ...	23	15	3	208	48*	17.33	—	—	362	15	24.13	4
Moxon, M D ...	151	143	8	4128	129*	30.57	3	24	868	21	41.33	46
Nicholson, A G .	83	28	14	97	13*	6.92	—	—	1998	117	17.07	8
Nicholson, N G .	2	2	1	1	1*	1.00	—	—	—	—	—	2
Old, C M	143	112	27	1711	82*	20.12	—	6	3847	192	20.03	38
Oldham, S	71	26	15	144	38*	13.09	—	—	2064	83	24.86	10
Padgett, D E V .	40	39	2	760	68	20.54	—	2	25	1	25.00	9
Parker, B	56	49	6	723	42	16.81	—	—	18	0	—	8
Patterson, S A .	40	17	11	110	25*	18.33	—	—	1484	54	27.48	8
Pickles, C	56	38	17	259	30*	12.33	—	—	1896	53	35.77	20
Plunkett, L E ..	5	4	1	89	53	29.66	—	1	221	7	31.57	3
Pyrah, R M ...	71	48	12	629	69	17.47	—	1	2073	77	26.92	20

Player	M	Inns	NO	Runs	HS	Av'ge	100s	50s	Runs	Wkts	Av'ge	Ct/St
Ramage, A	20	12	5	90	32*	12.85	—	—	658	14	47.00	—
Ramsden, G	1	—	—	—	—	—	—	—	26	2	13.00	—
Rana Neved -ul-Hasan .	10	9	0	241	74	26.77	—	2	357	16	22.31	1
Rashid, A U . . .	54	38	13	541	46*	21.64	—	—	1890	63	30.00	17
Rhodes, S J	2	1	0	6	6	6.00	—	—	—	—	—	3
Rhodes, W M H	7	6	1	53	19*	10.60	—	—	133	4	33.25	2
Richardson, R B	21	21	6	740	103	49.33	1	5	—	—	—	5
Robinson, A L . .	69	28	14	94	14	6.71	—	—	1904	81	23.50	11
Robinson, M A .	65	21	11	35	7	3.50	—	—	2030	63	32.22	7
Robinson, O E .	3	2	1	16	12*	—	—	—	66	0	—	4
Robinson, P E . .	104	100	12	2194	78*	24.93	—	11	—	—	—	37
Root, J E	16	15	2	443	63	34.07	—	2	222	7	31.71	9
Rudolph J A . . .	39	37	7	2217	132*	73.90	7	14	29	0	—	16
Sanderson B W .	10	2	1	14	12*	—	—	—	247	8	30.87	5
Sayers, J J . . .	24	23	2	466	62	22.19	—	4	79	1	79.00	1
Scofield, D	3	1	0	0	0	0.00	—	—	111	2	55.50	1
Shahzad, A . . .	21	15	4	125	59*	11.36	—	1	839	22	38.13	5
Sharp, K	141	135	13	3392	114	27.80	2	20	1	0	—	45
Sharpe, P J	52	50	0	871	81	17.42	—	4	11	0	—	22
Shaw, C	38	14	7	113	26	16.14	—	—	1142	45	25.37	8
Sidebottom, A .	156	86	33	835	52*	15.75	—	—	4561	149	30.61	29
Sidebottom, R J	79	42	19	270	30*	11.73	—	—	2577	92	28.01	12
Silverwood, CEW	106	64	27	555	58	15.00	—	2	3168	146	21.69	11
Smith, N	6	1	1	0	0*	—	—	—	—	—	—	2
Smith, R	3	2	0	17	17	8.50	—	—	—	—	—	1
Squires, P J	47	39	4	602	79*	17.20	—	3	4	0	—	8
Starc, M A	4	2	2	5	4*	—	—	—	181	8	22.62	1
Stemp, R D	60	21	7	114	23*	8.14	—	—	1978	67	29.52	13
Stevenson, G B .	153	116	16	1275	81*	12.75	—	2	4641	186	24.95	25
Stringer, P M . . .	9	6	4	22	13*	11.00	—	—	235	11	21.36	—
Stuchbury, S . . .	20	7	3	15	9*	3.75	—	—	588	26	22.61	2
Swallow, I G . . .	2	1	0	2	2	2.00	—	—	31	0	—	—
Swanepoel, P J .	3	2	2	9	8*	—	—	—	100	3	33.33	—
Tattersall, J A .	1	1	0	0	0	0.00	—	—	—	—	—	—
Taylor, C R	5	5	0	102	28	20.40	—	—	—	—	—	—
Tendulkar, S R .	13	13	1	464	107	38.66	1	1	102	3	34.00	1
Thornicroft, N D	11	6	3	42	20	14.00	—	—	447	15	29.80	1
Townsley, R A J	5	4	1	81	34	27.00	—	—	62	0	—	1
Vaughan, M P . .	101	99	7	2344	116*	25.47	1	11	988	34	29.05	34
Wainwright D J .	40	16	10	100	26	16.66	—	—	1145	29	39.48	12
Wardlaw, I	16	9	4	38	17*	7.60	—	—	659	22	29.95	3
Warren, A C . . .	1	1	0	3	3	3.00	—	—	35	1	35.00	—
Wharf, A G	4	1	1	2	2*	—	—	—	87	3	29.00	1
White, C	185	168	18	3643	148	24.28	1	13	3479	159	21.88	50
Whiteley, J P . . .	5	4	0	19	14	4.75	—	—	147	2	73.50	1
Widdup, S	4	4	0	49	38	12.25	—	—	—	—	—	—
Williamson, K S	1	1	0	45	45	45.00	—	—	42	1	42.00	—
Wilson, D	39	32	7	352	46	14.08	—	—	958	42	22.80	11
Wood, M J	103	94	6	2053	111	23.32	2	10	26	0	—	41
Woodford, J D . .	60	50	12	834	69*	21.94	—	2	1401	60	23.35	20
Younus Khan . .	4	2	0	14	14	7.00	—	—	20	0	—	2
Yuvraj Singh . . .	8	8	0	169	50	21.12	—	1	170	3	56.66	1

CAREER AVERAGES FOR YORKSHIRE

ALL LIMITED-OVERS COMPETITIONS (LIST A) OF 40 TO 65 OVERS 1963-2013

Player	M	Inns	NO	Runs	HS	Av'ge	100s	50s	Runs	Wkts	Av'ge	Ct/St
Ashraf, M A	21	5	4	3	3*	—	—	—	857	23	37.26	3
Athey, C W J	138	127	14	3653	118	32.32	2	25	431	19	22.68	45
Azeem Rafiq	14	10	4	111	34*	18.50	—	—	453	12	37.75	4
Bairstow, D L	398	313	70	5114	103*	21.04	1	19	17	0	—	389/31
Bairstow, J M	30	26	3	645	114	28.04	1	3	—	—	—	18/1
Baker, T M	4	1	0	3	3	3.00	—	—	89	4	22.25	3
Balderstone, J C ..	13	11	2	173	46	19.22	—	—	38	2	19.00	3
Ballance, G S ...	29	28	6	1259	139	57.22	2	8	—	—	—	12
Batty, J D	38	16	7	50	13*	5.55	—	—	1297	42	30.88	18
Berry, P J	1	0	0	0		—	—	—	28	0	—	—
Best, T L	5	1	1	8	8*	—	—	—	166	10	16.60	1
Bevan, M G	47	44	11	2040	103*	61.82	2	18	513	27	19.00	10
Binks, J G	30	21	3	247	34	13.72	—	—	—	—	—	26/8
Blain, J A R	14	8	3	34	11*	6.80	—	—	427	14	30.50	3
Blakey, R J	371	317	83	7355	130*	31.43	3	35	—	—	—	369/59
Blewett, G S	17	17	0	345	77	20.29	—	2	196	11	17.81	7
Booth, P A	5	2	1	7	6*	7.00	—	—	147	3	49.00	1
Bore, M K	53	23	10	80	15	6.15	—	—	1591	50	31.82	15
Boycott, G	260	251	37	8481	146	39.63	6	62	1076	24	44.83	92
Bresnan, T T ...	132	91	25	1159	61	17.56	—	3	4589	141	32.54	35
Broadhurst, M ...	1								27	0	—	—
Brophy, G L	68	57	12	1240	93*	27.55	—	9	—	—	—	67/14
Byas, D	309	298	35	7691	116*	29.24	5	43	641	25	25.64	128
Carrick, P	302	204	52	2141	54	14.08	—	2	7361	236	31.19	68
Chapman, C A ...	8	6	3	89	36*	29.66	—	—	—	—	—	3
Claydon, M E ...	7	2	0	15	9	7.50	—	—	293	8	36.62	—
Cleary, M F	4	3	1	50	23*	25.00	—	—	159	2	79.50	—
Close, D B	32	31	2	631	96	21.75	—	3	475	23	20.65	14
Coad, B O	6	2	2	1	1*	—	—	—	244	3	81.33	3
Cooper, H P	142	74	34	483	29*	12.07	—	—	4184	177	23.63	26
Cope, G A	36	20	13	96	18*	13.71	—	—	1011	24	42.12	9
Coverdale, S P ...	3	3	2	18	17*	18.00	—	—	—	—	—	3
Craven, V J	41	38	5	579	59	17.54	—	2	338	20	16.90	14
Dalton, A J	17	16	1	280	55	18.66	—	1	—	—	—	7
Dawood, I	24	19	4	238	57	15.86	—	1	—	—	—	18/8
Dawson, R K J ...	90	56	11	396	41	8.80	—	—	2711	90	30.12	30
Dennis, S J	55	23	11	111	16*	9.25	—	—	1717	40	42.92	7
Elliott, M T G ...	6	6	3	394	128*	131.33	3	—	—	—	—	4
Elstub, C J	9	9	3	4	4*	—	—	—	259	11	23.54	—
Fellows, G M	94	78	15	1342	80*	21.30	—	6	836	22	38.00	27
Fisher, I D	28	12	3	68	20	7.55	—	—	708	29	24.41	6
Fisher, M D	2	1	0	10	10	10.00	—	—	85	1	85.00	0
Fleming, S P	7	7	1	285	139*	47.50	1	1	—	—	—	3
Fletcher, S D	128	32	18	109	16*	7.78	—	—	4686	164	28.57	34
Foster, M J	20	14	1	199	118	15.30	1	—	370	6	61.66	6
Gale, A W	110	102	10	2971	125*	32.29	2	16	—	—	—	22
Gibson, R	3	2	1	10	6	10.00	—	—	98	3	32.66	0
Gilbert, C R	4	3	0	18	9	6.00	—	—	174	8	21.75	—
Gillespie, J N	18	4	1	29	15*	9.66	—	—	601	18	33.38	6
Gough, D	212	119	33	1273	72*	14.80	—	1	6770	290	23.34	43
Gray, A K D	30	18	7	128	30*	11.63	—	—	814	23	35.39	8
Grayson, A P	65	48	7	575	55	14.02	—	1	1410	38	37.10	19
Guy, S M	30	21	4	233	40	13.70	—	—	—	—	—	35/11

404

Player	M	Inns	NO	Runs	HS	Av'ge	100s	50s	Runs	Wkts	Av'ge	Ct/St
Hamilton, G M	100	70	18	1059	57*	20.36	—	2	2761	118	23.39	15
Hampshire, A W	4	3	0	3	3	1.00	—	—	—	—	—	1
Hampshire, J H ..	231	220	24	6248	119	31.87	7	36	26	1	26.00	69
Hannon-Dalby, O J ..	5	1	1	21	21*	—	—	—	202	5	40.40	3
Harden, R J	19	16	2	230	42	16.42	—	—	—	—	—	1
Hartley, P J ..	216	145	49	1609	83	16.76	—	4	7425	280	26.51	40
Hartley, S N ..	170	153	31	2810	83*	23.03	—	13	2122	67	31.67	52
Harvey, I J	28	27	2	637	74	25.48	—	3	950	30	31.66	8
Hodd, A J	7	6	1	56	21	11.20	—	—	—	—	—	8/1
Hodgson, D M ...	10	8	1	216	90	30.85	—	2	—	—	—	8/1
Hodgson, L J	6	2	0	9	9	4.50	—	—	161	4	40.25	1
Hoggard, M J ...	83	28	19	41	7*	4.55	—	—	2682	118	22.72	7
Hutchison, P M ..	32	11	8	18	4*	6.00	—	—	844	43	19.62	3
Hutton, R A ..	105	78	24	1015	65	18.79	—	4	2990	128	23.35	27
Illingworth, R ...	40	15	11	171	45	42.75	—	—	764	39	19.58	14
Ingham, P G	12	10	4	312	87*	52.00	—	2	—	—	—	—
Inzamam-ul-Haq ..	3	3	0	69	53	23.00	—	1	—	—	—	—
Jaques, P A	42	41	2	1509	105	38.69	1	12	—	—	—	16
Jarvis, P W ..	142	72	27	512	42	11.37	—	—	4575	209	21.88	32
Johnson, C ..	127	101	22	1614	73*	20.43	—	4	28	2	14.00	33
Johnson, M	14	6	3	34	15*	11.33	—	—	455	12	37.91	2
Katich, S M	3	3	2	79	40*	79.00	—	—	—	—	—	2
Kellett, S A	53	49	3	1182	118*	25.69	2	4	16	0	—	12
Kettleborough, R A .	10	6	3	71	28	23.66	—	—	72	3	24.00	4
Kirby, S P	28	12	3	38	15	4.22	—	—	1036	24	43.16	6
Kruis, G J	55	22	11	138	31*	12.54	—	—	1793	62	28.91	9
Lawson, M A K ..	4	4	0	30	20	7.50	—	—	141	3	47.00	1
Leadbeater, B ..	103	98	19	2179	90	27.58	—	11	95	5	19.00	25
Leaning, J A	4	4	1	96	60	32.00	—	1	60	6	10.00	3
Lee, J E	4	0	0	0	0	—	—	—	116	7	16.57	—
Lees, A Z	6	6	1	190	60	38.00	—	2	—	—	—	2
Lehmann, D S ..	130	126	20	5229	191	49.33	8	38	1990	79	25.18	41
Lester, E I	1	1	0	0	0	0.00	—	—	—	—	—	—
Love, J D ..	220	203	33	4298	118*	25.28	4	18	129	5	25.80	44
Lucas, D S	5	2	0	40	32	20.00	—	—	187	3	62.33	1
Lumb, M J ..	102	96	8	2592	92	29.45	—	18	28	0	—	31
Lumb, R G ..	135	121	13	2747	101	25.43	1	16	—	—	—	21
Lyth, A	72	66	6	1844	109*	30.73	1	9	100	1	100.00	24
McGrath, A ..	272	250	39	7067	148	33.49	6	44	2514	79	31.82	90
Metcalfe, A A ..	191	186	14	5520	127*	32.09	4	36	44	2	22.00	44
Middlebrook, J D ..	18	11	3	61	15*	7.62	—	—	530	13	40.76	5
Milburn, S M	4	2	1	14	13*	14.00	—	—	118	2	59.00	1
Miller, D A	3	3	0	45	44	15.00	—	—	—	—	—	3
Morris, A C	25	16	4	209	48*	17.41	—	—	409	16	25.56	5
Moxon, M D ..	235	227	21	7307	141*	35.47	7	48	1178	34	34.64	77
Nicholson, A G ..	119	45	22	154	15*	6.69	—	—	2943	173	17.01	16
Nicholson, N G ..	2	2	1	1	1*	1.00	—	—	—	—	—	2
Old, C M ..	218	166	37	2550	82*	19.76	—	10	5817	306	19.00	56
Oldham, S ..	105	40	21	192	38*	10.10	—	—	3136	142	22.08	17
Padgett, D E V ..	57	54	3	1069	68	20.96	—	2	25	1	25.00	13
Parker, B	72	60	8	964	69	18.53	—	1	18	0	—	11
Patterson, S A ..	49	20	14	127	25*	21.16	—	—	1804	61	29.57	8
Pickles, C S	69	47	19	370	37*	13.21	—	—	2355	62	37.98	22
Plunkett, L E	5	4	1	89	53	29.66	—	1	221	7	31.57	3
Pyrah, R M	99	66	17	902	69	18.41	—	2	3088	117	26.39	32
Ramage, A	34	17	8	134	32*	14.88	—	—	1178	30	39.26	3

Player	M	Inns	NO	Runs	HS	Av'ge	100s	50s	Runs	Wkts	Av'ge	Ct/St
Ramsden, G	1								26	2	13.00	—
Rana Naved												
-ul-Hasan	17	16	1	375	74	25.00	—	3	681	26	26.19	5
Rashid, A U	**72**	**49**	**15**	**646**	**46***	**19.00**	—	—	**2356**	**76**	**31.00**	**22**
Rhodes, S J	2	1	0	6	6	6.00	—	—	—	—	—	3
Rhodes, W M H . . .	**7**	**6**	**1**	**53**	**19***	**10.60**	—	—	**133**	**4**	**33.25**	**2**
Richardson, R B . . .	28	28	6	993	103	45.13	1	8	—	—	—	5
Robinson, A L	92	36	19	127	18*	7.47	—	—	2588	105	24.64	14
Robinson, M A	86	30	16	41	7	2.92	—	—	2725	89	30.61	7
Robinson, O E	**3**	**2**	**2**	**16**	**12***	—	—	—	**66**	**0**	—	**4**
Robinson, P E	134	123	15	2738	78*	25.35	—	14	—	—	—	47
Root, J E	**16**	**15**	**2**	**443**	**63**	**34.07**	—	**2**	**222**	**7**	**31.71**	**9**
Rudolph, J A	65	62	10	3090	132*	59.42	9	19	37	0	—	32
Ryan, M	3	2	1	7	6*	7.00	—	—	149	5	29.80	3
Sanderson, B W	10	2	1	14	12*	14.00	—	—	247	8	30.87	5
Sayers, J J	30	29	2	577	62	21.37	—	5	79	1	79.00	2
Scofield, D	3	1	0	0	0	0.00	—	—	111	2	55.50	1
Shahzad, A	29	21	6	235	59*	15.66	—	1	1131	29	39.00	7
Sharp, K	203	188	18	4693	114	27.60	3	27	48	4	12.00	66
Sharpe, P J	89	84	4	1499	89*	18.73	—	8	11	0	16.50	52
Shaw, C	48	20	10	127	26	12.70	—	—	1396	58	24.06	8
Sidebottom, A	233	129	47	1273	52*	15.52	—	—	6841	258	26.51	51
Sidebottom, R J . . .	**113**	**51**	**22**	**303**	**30***	**10.44**	—	—	**3631**	**124**	**29.28**	**24**
Silverwood,C E W . .	164	93	32	866	61	14.19	—	4	5145	223	23.07	25
Smith, N	7	2	1	5	5	5.00	—	—	—	—	—	2
Smith, R	3	2	0	17	17	8.50	—	—	—	—	—	1
Squires, P J	56	48	5	708	79*	16.46	—	3	4	0	—	10
Starc, M A	4	2	2	5	4*	—	—	—	181	8	22.62	1
Stemp, R D	88	28	10	118	23*	6.55	—	—	2996	100	29.96	14
Stevenson, G B	216	157	23	1699	81*	12.67	—	2	6820	290	23.51	38
Stott, W B	2	2	0	30	30	15.00	—	—	—	—	—	—
Stringer, P M	11	8	6	29	13*	14.50	—	—	256	15	17.06	—
Stuchbury, S	22	8	4	21	9*	5.25	—	—	677	29	23.34	2
Swallow, I G	8	5	3	37	17*	18.50	—	—	198	2	99.00	5
Swanepoel, P G	3	2	2	9	8*	—	—	—	100	3	33.33	—
Tattersall, J A	**1**	**1**	**0**	**0**	**0**	**0.00**	—	—	—	—	—	**0**
Taylor, C R	6	5	0	102	28	20.40	—	—	—	—	—	—
Taylor, K	10	10	0	135	30	13.50	—	—	168	11	15.27	3
Tendulkar, S R	17	17	2	540	107	36.00	1	1	167	6	27.83	3
Thornicroft, N D . . .	13	7	4	52	20	17.33	—	—	544	16	34.00	2
Townsley, R A J	5	4	1	81	34	27.00	—	—	62	0	—	1
Trueman, F S	11	9	1	127	28	15.87	—	—	348	21	16.57	5
Vaughan, M P	182	177	13	4890	125*	29.81	3	28	1836	59	31.11	56
Wainwright, D J	47	20	13	150	26	21.42	—	—	1382	36	38.38	16
Wardlaw, I	**16**	**9**	**4**	**38**	**17***	**7.60**	—	—	**659**	**22**	**29.95**	**3**
Waring, J	1	1	1	1	1*	—	—	—	11	0	—	—
Warren, A C	1	1	0	3	3	3.00	—	—	35	1	35.00	—
Wharf, A G	6	1	1	2	2*	—	—	—	176	8	22.00	1
White, C	291	265	39	6376	148	28.21	5	28	6088	246	24.74	84
Whiteley, J P	6	4	0	19	14	4.75	—	—	195	2	97.50	1
Widdup, S	4	4	0	49	38	12.25	—	—	—	—	—	2
Williamson, K A . . .	**1**	**1**	**0**	**45**	**45**	**45.00**	—	—	**42**	**1**	**42.00**	**0**
Wilson, D	59	45	8	424	46	11.45	—	—	1502	74	20.29	22
Wood, M J	143	132	14	3209	160	27.19	5	14	71	3	23.66	56
Woodford, J D	72	57	14	890	69*	20.69	—	2	1627	77	21.12	25
Younus Khan	11	8	0	248	100	31.00	1	—	144	2	72.00	5
Yuvraj Singh	9	9	0	196	50	21.77	—	1	197	3	65.66	1

YORKSHIRE T20i CRICKETERS 2003-2013 (Correct to February 3, 2014)

For England

Player	M	I	NO	Runs	HS	Av'ge	100s	50s	Balls	Runs	W	Av'ge	Best	4wI	Ct/St
BAIRSTOW, J M .2011-12/13	18	14	4	194	60*	19.40	—	1	—	—	—	—	—	—	21
BRESNAN, T T ..2006-13/14	28	17	6	123	23*	11.18	—	—	556	703	21	33.47	3-10	—	8
RASHID, A U ...2009	5	2	1	10	9*	10.00	—	—	84	120	3	40.00	1-11	—	—
ROOT, J E ...2012/13-13/14	7	5	2	152	90*	50.66	—	1	42	80	3	26.66	1-13	—	4
SHAHZAD, A 2010-11	3	1	1	0	0*	—	—	—	66	97	3	32.33	2-38	—	1
VAUGHAN, M P ...2005-7	2	2	0	27	27	13.50	—	—	—	—	—	—	—	—	—

For Scotland

Player	M	I	NO	Runs	HS	Av'ge	100s	50s	Balls	Runs	W	Av'ge	Best	4wI	Ct/St
BLAIN, J A R 2007-8	6	3	1	4	3*	2.00	—	—	120	108	6	18.00	2-23	—	1
HAMILTON, G M ..2007-10	12	8	0	90	32	11.25	—	—	—	—	—	—	—	—	3
WARDLAW, I .2012/13-13/14	4	1	0	1	1	1.00	—	—	96	145	9	16.11	4-40	—	—

YORKSHIRE PLAYERS WHO PLAYED ALL THEIR T20i CRICKET AFTER LEAVING YORKSHIRE

For England

Player	M	I	NO	Runs	HS	Av'ge	100s	50s	Balls	Runs	W	Av'ge	Best	4wI	Ct/St
BATTY, G J 2009	1	1	0	4	4	4.00	—	—	18	17	0	—	—	—	—
GOUGH, D 2005-06	2	0	0	0	—	—	—	—	41	49	3	16.33	3-16	—	—
LUMB, M J ...2010-13/14	20	20	0	410	53*	21.57	—	2	—	—	—	—	—	—	7
PLUNKETT, L E **...2006	1	0	0	0	—	—	—	—	24	37	1	37.00	1-37	—	—
SIDEBOTTOM, R J .2007-10	18	1	0	5	5*	—	—	—	367	437	23	19.00	3-16	—	5

** before joining Yorkshire

Overseas Players

(Qualification: 24 t20 matches for Yorkshire)

For South Africa

Player	M	I	NO	Runs	HS	Av'ge	100s	50s	Balls	Runs	W	Av'ge	Best	4wI	Ct/St
RUDOLPH, J A 2006	1	1	1	6	6*	—	—	—	—	—	—	—	—	—	—

TWENTY20 CUP 2003-2013

BEST SEASON — LOSING FINALIST 2012

Played 111, Won 48 (in Yorkshire 27, Away 20, Neutral 1)
Lost 52 (in Yorkshire 21, Away 30, Neutral 1)
Tied 3 (in Yorkshire 2 Away 1), No Result 4 (in Yorkshire 1, Away 3)
Abandoned 4 (in Yorkshire 3, Away 1)

Highest Score:	By Yorkshire	213:7 v. Worcestershire at Leeds, 2010
	Against Yorkshire	222:5 by Derbyshire at Leeds, 2010
†Lowest Score:	By Yorkshire	90:9 v. Durham at Chester-le-Street, 2009
	Against Yorkshire	98 by Durham at Chester-le-Street, 2006
Highest Individual		
Score:	For Yorkshire	109 I J Harvey v. Derbyshire at Leeds, 2005
	Against Yorkshire	111 D L Maddy for Leicestershire at Leeds, 2004

†Lowest score is the lowest all-out score or the lowest score at completion of 20 overs

Highest
Partnerships: For Yorkshire

1st wkt	131	A Lyth (78) and P A Jaques (64) v. Derbyshire at Leeds, 2012
2nd wkt	137*	A W Gale (60*) and H H Gibbs (76*) v. Durham at Leeds, 2010
3rd wkt	121	J A Rudolph (56) and A McGrath (59) v. Leicestershire at Leicester, 2008
4th wkt	93	P A Jaques (92) and T T Bresnan (42) v. Leicestershire at Leeds, 2004
5th wkt	91	D A Miller (54) and G S Ballance (42) v. Lancashire at Leeds, 2012
6th wkt	65	A McGrath (39) and A U Rashid (34) v. Worcestershire at Worcester, 2010
7th wkt	56	V J Craven (44) and R J Blakey (18) v. Durham at Chester-le-Street, 2004
8th wkt	43*	R M Pyrah (22*) and C J McKay (21*) v. Worcestershire at Worcester, 2010
9th wkt	33*	A U Rashid (5*) and D Gough (20*) v. Lancashire at Leeds, 2008
10th wkt	28*	A U Rashid (28*) and G J Kruis (12*) v. Durham at Chester-le-Street, 2009

Best Bowling:	For Yorkshire:	5 for 16 R M Pyrah v. Durham at Scarborough, 2011
	Against Yorkshire	4 for 9 C K Langerveldt for Derbyshire at Leeds, 2008

Most Economical Bowling (4 overs):

	For Yorkshire	4-0-12-2 T T Bresnan v. Lancashire at Manchester, 2008
	Against Yorkshire	4-0-9-4 C K Langeveldt for Derbyshire at Leeds, 2008

Most Expensive Bowling:

	For Yorkshire	4-0-65-2 M J Hoggard v. Lancashire at Leeds, 2005
	Against Yorkshire	4-0-58-0 G Welch for Derbyshire at Leeds, 2003

versus Derbyshire: Played 17, Won 11 (in Yorkshire 4, Away 7), Lost 5 (in Yorkshire 5)
No Result 1 (Away)

Highest Score:	By Yorkshire	210:3 at Derby, 2006
	By Derbyshire	222:5 at Leeds, 2010
Lowest Score:	By Yorkshire	109 at Derby, 2012
	By Derbyshire	119:7 at Leeds, 2007
Highest Individual Score:		
	For Yorkshire	109 I J Harvey at Leeds, 2005
	For Derbyshire	100* G M Smith at Leeds, 2008
Best Bowling:	For Yorkshire	4 for 21 B W Sanderson at Derby, 2011
	For Derbyshire	4 for 9 C K Langeveldt at Leeds, 2008

versus Durham: Played 20, Won 10 (in Yorkshire 6, Away 4), Lost 8 (in Yorkshire 3, Away 5), Tied 1 (in Yorkshire), No Result 1 (Away)

Highest Score:	By Yorkshire	198:4 at Leeds, 2003
	By Durham	215:6 at Chester-le-Street, 2013
Lowest Score:	By Yorkshire	90:9 at Chester-le-Street, 2009
	By Durham	98 at Chester-le-Street, 2006
Highest Individual Score:		
	For Yorkshire	76* H H Gibbs at Leeds, 2010
	For Durham	91 P Mustard at Chester-le-Street, 2013
Best Bowling:	For Yorkshire	5 for 16 R M Pyrah at Scarborough, 2011
	For Durham	4 for 38 S J Harmison at Leeds, 2008

versus Essex: Played 1, Lost 1 (Away)

Scores:	By Yorkshire	143:7 at Chelmsford, 2006
	By Essex	149:5 at Chelmsford, 2006
Highest Individual Score:		
	For Yorkshire	43 G L Brophy at Chelmsford, 2006
	For Essex	48* J S Foster at Chelmsford, 2006
Best Bowling:	For Yorkshire	2 for 22 A Shahzad at Chelmsford, 2006
	For Essex	2 for 11 T J Phillips at Chelmsford, 2006

versus Hampshire: Played 1, Lost 1 (Neutral)

Scores:	By Yorkshire	140-6 at Cardiff, 2012
	By Hampshire	150-6 at Cardiff, 2012
Highest Individual Score:		
	For Yorkshire	72* D A Miller at Cardiff, 2012
	For Hampshire	43 J H K Adams at Cardiff, 2012
Best Bowling:	For Yorkshire	2 for 20 R J Sidebottom at Cardiff, 2012
	For Hampshire	3 for 26 C P Wood at Cardiff, 2012

versus Lancashire: Played 20, Won 9 (in Yorkshire 6, Away 3), Lost 8 (in Yorkshire 2, Away 6), Tied 1 (in Yorkshire) Abandoned 2 (in Yorkshire 1, Away 1)

Highest Score:	By Yorkshire	180:6 at Leeds, 2012
	By Lancashire	207 at Manchester, 2005
Lowest Score:	By Yorkshire	97 at Manchester, 2005
	By Lancashire	104:3 at Manchester, 2003
Highest Individual Score:		
	For Yorkshire	108* I J Harvey at Leeds, 2004
	For Lancashire	101 S G Law at Manchester, 2005
Best Bowling	For Yorkshire	4 for 26 A U Rashid at Leeds, 2011
	For Lancashire	3 for 10 D G Cork at Manchester, 2005

versus Leicestershire: Played 17, Won 6 (in Yorkshire 3, Away 3), Lost 10 (in Yorkshire 4, Away 6), Abandoned 1 (in Yorkshire)

Highest Score:	By Yorkshire	211:6 at Leeds, 2004
	By Leicestershire	221:3 at Leeds, 2004
Lowest Score:	By Yorkshire	105 at Leicester, 2013
	By Leicestershire	113:9 at Leeds, 2013
Highest Individual Score:		
	For Yorkshire	92 P A Jaques at Leeds, 2004
	For Leicestershire	111 D L Maddy at Leeds, 2004
Best Bowling:	For Yorkshire	5 for 21 J A Brooks at Leeds, 2013
	For Leicestershire	3 for 3 J K H Naik at Leeds, 2011

versus Northamptonshire: Played 4, Won 1 (Away), Lost 1 (in Yorkshire), Tied 1 (Away), Abandoned 1 (in Yorkshire)

Highest Score:	By Yorkshire	180:3 at Northampton, 2010
	By Northamptonshire	180:5 at Northampton, 2010
Lowest Score:	By Yorkshire	144 at Northampton, 2011
	By Northamptonshire	132-7 at Northampton, 2011
Highest Individual Score:	For Yorkshire	101* H H Gibbs at Northampton, 2010
	For Northamptonshire	53 W P U J C Vaas at Northampton, 2010
Best Bowling:	For Yorkshire	3 for 23 A U Rashid at Leeds, 2010
	For Northamptonshire	4 for 23 A J Hall at Northampton 2011

versus Nottinghamshire: Played 20, Won 7 (in Yorkshire 4, Away 3), Lost 12 (in Yorkshire 5, Away 7), No Result 1 (In Yorkshire)

Highest Score:	By Yorkshire	207:7 at Nottingham, 2004
	By Nottinghamshire	215:6 at Nottingham, 2011
Lowest Score:	By Yorkshire	112:7 at Nottingham, 2010
	By Nottinghamshire	136:8 at Nottingham, 2008
Highest Individual Score:	For Yorkshire	96* M J Wood at Nottingham, 2004
	For Nottinghamshire	91 M A Ealham at Nottingham, 2004
Best Bowling:	For Yorkshire	4 for 23 Rana Naved-ul-Hasan at Leeds, 2009
	For Nottinghamshire	3 for 17 S R Patel at Nottingham, 2013

versus Sussex: Played 2, Won 1 (Neutral), Lost 1 (Away)

Highest Score:	By Yorkshire	172:6 at Cardiff, 2012
	By Sussex	193:5 at Hove, 2007
Lowest Score:	By Yorkshire	155 at Hove, 2007
	By Sussex	136:8 at Cardiff, 2012
Highest Individual Score:	For Yorkshire	68* J M Bairstow at Cardiff, 2012
	For Sussex	80* C D Nash at Cardiff, 2012
Best Bowling:	For Yorkshire	2 for 22 T T Bresnan at Cardiff, 2012
	For Sussex	3 for 22 S B Styris at Cardiff, 2012

versus Warwickshire: Played 4, Lost 3 (in Yorkshire 2, Away 1), No Result 1 (Away)

Highest Score:	By Yorkshire	161:8 at Leeds, 2011
	By Warwickshire	164:5 at Leeds, 2011
Lowest Score:	By Yorkshire	121:9 at Leeds, 2010
	By Warwickshire	145:8 at Birmingham, 2010
Highest Individual Score:	For Yorkshire	54 A W Gale at Leeds, 2011
	For Warwickshire	64 W T S Porterfield at Leeds, 2011
Best Bowling:	For Yorkshire	3 for 22 R M Pyrah at Leeds, 2010
	For Warwickshire	4 for 19 K H D Barker at Birmingham, 2010

versus Worcestershire: Played 5, Won 3 (in Yorkshire), Lost 2 (Away)

Highest Score:	By Yorkshire	213:7 at Leeds, 2010
	By Worcestershire	208:7 at Worcester, 2010
Lowest Score:	By Yorkshire	142 at Worcester 2011
	By Worcestershire	109 at Leeds, 2010
Highest Individual Score:	For Yorkshire	65 J E Root at Leeds, 2012
	For Worcestershire	80* P J Hughes at Leeds, 2012
Best Bowling:	For Yorkshire	4 for 21 R M Pyrah at Leeds, 2011
	For Worcestershire	4 for 31 Shakib al Hasan at Worcester, 2011

Player	M	Inns	NO	Runs	HS	Av'ge	100s	50s	Runs	Wkts	Av'ge	Ct/St
Ashraf, M A ...	13	1	0	4	4	4.00	—	—	387	15	25.80	1
Azeem Rafiq ..	45	22	14	114	21*	14.25	—	—	1172	43	27.25	16
Bairstow, J M ..	38	33	5	532	68*	19.00	—	1	—	—	—	10/2
Ballance, G S ..	38	34	6	753	68	26.89	—	1	—	—	—	21
Best, T L	8	3	2	10	10*	10.00	—	—	243	7	34.71	4
Blakey, R J	7	5	1	119	32	29.75	—	—	—	—	—	5/1
Bresnan, T T ..	50	35	12	412	42	17.91	—	—	1228	51	24.07	15
Brooks, J A ...	8	0	0	0	0	—	—	—	189	13	14.53	3
Brophy, G L ...	54	46	9	717	57*	19.37	—	2	—	—	—	25/7
Claydon, M E ..	7	2	2	14	12*	—	—	—	188	5	37.60	2
Craven, V J ...	6	6	4	76	44*	38.00	—	—	67	0	—	3
Dawood, I	11	8	3	44	15	8.80	—	—	—	—	—	5/2
Dawson, R K J ..	22	8	3	71	22	14.20	—	—	558	24	23.25	7
Fleming, S P ...	4	4	0	62	58	15.50	—	1	—	—	—	1
Gale, A W	76	70	7	1770	91	28.09	—	14	—	—	—	25
Gibbs, H H	15	15	3	443	101*	36.91	1	2	—	—	—	8
Gilbert, C R ...	13	9	2	107	36*	15.28	—	—	—	—	—	7
Gillespie, J N ..	17	4	2	14	8*	7.00	—	—	422	17	24.82	5
Gough, D	17	7	3	42	20*	10.50	—	—	416	16	26.00	2
Gray, A K D ...	8	3	0	17	13	5.66	—	—	211	9	23.44	4
Guy, S M	10	6	1	44	13	8.80	—	—	—	—	—	2
Hamilton, G M .	3	3	1	41	41*	20.50	—	—	—	—	—	1
Harvey, I J	10	10	1	438	109	48.66	2	2	258	10	25.80	4
Hodd, A J	6	5	2	29	11	9.66	—	—	—	—	—	2/1
Hodgson, D M ..	10	10	1	177	52*	19.66	—	1	—	—	—	5/1
Hodgson, L J ..	2	1	1	39	39*	—	—	—	59	2	29.50	1
Hoggard, M J ..	15	2	1	19	18	19.00	—	—	472	13	36.30	4
Jaques, P A	29	28	3	817	92	32.68	—	6	15	0	—	5
Kirby, S P	3	—	—	—	—	—	—	—	119	4	29.75	1
Kruis, G J	20	5	3	41	22	20.50	—	—	486	19	25.57	6
Lawson, M A K .	2	1	1	4	4*	—	—	—	87	3	29.00	1
Leaning, J A ...	3	3	0	14	8	4.66	—	—	18	0	—	—
Lees, A Z	2	2	0	33	32	16.50	—	—	—	—	—	—
Lehmann, D S ..	9	9	3	252	48	42.00	—	2	180	8	22.50	4
Lumb, M J	26	26	3	442	84*	19.21	—	4	65	3	21.66	8
Lyth, A	46	41	1	805	78	20.12	—	2	16	1	16.00	16
McGrath, A	66	61	12	1403	73*	28.63	—	8	698	23	30.34	26
McKay, C J	8	6	3	54	21*	18.00	—	—	258	10	25.80	1
Miller, D A	12	11	3	390	74*	48.75	—	4	—	—	—	4
Patterson, S A .	20	4	3	3	3*	3.00	—	—	653	17	38.41	3
Plunkett, L E ..	9	9	1	101	30	12.62	—	—	277	8	34.62	3
Pyrah, R M ...	84	59	17	510	42	12.14	—	—	1812	88	20.59	31
Rana Naved-ul-Hasan	8	8	2	63	20*	10.50	—	—	159	11	14.45	2
Rashid, A U ...	53	37	7	318	34	10.60	—	—	1345	53	25.37	17
Rhodes, W M H .	2	2	0	13	13	6.50	—	—	14	0	—	—
Root, J E	21	18	4	347	65	24.78	—	1	148	2	74.00	8
Rudolph, J A ...	39	35	5	710	61	23.66	—	3	145	6	24.16	7
Sanderson, B W .	4	—	—	—	—	—	—	—	74	6	12.33	—
Sayers, J J	17	14	0	253	44	18.07	—	—	—	—	—	5

Player	M	Inns	NO	Runs	HS	Av'ge	100s	50s	Runs	Wkts	Av'ge	Ct/St
Shahzad, A	22	16	4	129	20	10.75	—	—	576	17	33.88	5
Sidebottom, R J	**28**	**13**	**8**	**82**	**16***	**16.40**	**—**	**—**	**731**	**26**	**28.11**	**8**
Silverwood, C E W	9	5	2	32	13*	10.66	—	—	264	7	37.71	4
Swanepoel, P ...	2	1	1	2	2*	—	—	—	60	3	20.00	1
Starc, M A	10	2	1	0	0*	0.00	—	—	218	21	10.38	1
Taylor, C R	2	2	1	10	10*	10.00	—	—	—	—	—	—
Vaughan, M P ..	16	16	1	292	41*	19.46	—	—	81	1	81.00	2
Wainwright, D J	26	9	6	23	6*	7.66	—	—	551	21	26.23	9
Wardlaw, I	8	1	1	1	1	—	—	—	133	2	66.50	—
Warren, A C ...	2	—	—	—	—	—	—	—	70	4	17.50	—
White, C	33	31	0	570	55	18.38	—	2	132	2	66.00	8
Wood, M J	15	15	3	328	96*	27.33	—	2	32	2	16.00	11
Younus Khan ...	2	2	0	55	40	27.50	—	—	32	2	16.00	0
Yuvraj Singh ...	5	5	0	154	71	30.80	—	1	51	5	10.20	0

SECOND ELEVEN RECORDS
in the
SECOND ELEVEN CHAMPIONSHIP 1959-1961 AND 1975-2013

SUMMARY OF RESULTS BY SEASON

Season	Played	Won	Lost	Drawn	Tied	Abandoned	Position in Championship
1959	10	4	1	5	0	0	7
1960	10	1	3	6	0	0	14
1961	9	2	2	5	0	1	11
1975	14	4	0	10	0	0	4
1976	14	5	5	4	0	0	5
1977	**16**	**9**	**0**	**7**	**0**	**1**	**1**
1978	15	5	2	8	0	0	4
1979	16	5	0	11	0	0	3
1980	14	5	2	7	0	1	5
1981	16	2	3	11	0	0	11
1982	16	2	3	11	0	0	14 =
1983	11	5	1	5	0	3	2
1984	**15**	**9**	**3**	**3**	**0**	**0**	**1**
1985	14	3	3	8	0	1	12
1986	16	5	1	10	0	0	5
1987	**15**	**5**	**2**	**8**	**0**	**1**	**1 =**
1988	16	4	1	11	0	0	9
1989	17	2	3	12	0	0	9 =
1990	16	1	6	9	0	0	17
1991	**16**	**8**	**1**	**7**	**0**	**0**	**1**
1992	17	5	2	10	0	0	5
1993	17	6	1	10	0	0	3
1994	17	6	2	9	0	0	2
1995	17	7	1	9	0	0	5
1996	17	6	3	8	0	0	4
1997	16	8	5	3	0	1	2
1998	15	4	2	9	0	0	9
1999	16	3	8	5	0	1	14
2000	14	5	2	7	0	1	5
2001	12	8	2	2	0	1	2
2002	12	5	1	6	0	0	3
2003	**10**	**7**	**1**	**2**	**0**	**0**	**1**
2004	7	2	0	5	0	1	8
2005	12	2	4	6	0	0	10
2006	14	6	4	4	0	0	3
2007	12	4	5	3	0	0	10
2008	12	4	4	4	0	2	5
2009	9	5	0	4	0	0	(Group A) 2
2010	9	2	4	3	0	0	(Group A) 8
2011	9	0	4	4	1	0	(Group A) 10
2012	7	1	2	4	0	2	(North) 9
2013	9	3	4	2	0	0	(North) 4
Totals	566	185	103	277	1	17	

Matches abandoned without a ball being bowled are not counted as a match played.
The Championship was divided into two groups from 2009, each team playng each other
once. The two group winners played for the Championship

ANALYSIS OF RESULTS AGAINST EACH OPPONENT

County	Played	Won	Lost	Drawn	Tied	Abandoned	First Played
Derbyshire	53	12	8	33	0	3	1959
Durham	29	10	6	13	0	2	1992
Essex	13	9	2	2	0	0	1990
Glamorgan	39	11	3	25	0	2	1975
Gloucestershire	10	3	3	4	0	0	1990
Hampshire	12	4	1	7	0	0	1990
Kent	26	5	4	17	0	1	1981
Lancashire	65	14	18	33	0	3	1959
Leicestershire	27	11	5	10	1	1	1975
MCC Young Cricketers	4	3	1	0	0	0	2005
MCC Universities	2	1	0	1	0	0	2011
Middlesex	18	7	2	9	0	0	1977
Northamptonshire	46	13	6	27	0	1	1959
Nottinghamshire	56	17	11	28	0	2	1959
Scotland	2	1	0	1	0	0	2007
Somerset	18	9	3	6	0	0	1988
Surrey	36	9	9	18	0	2	1976
Sussex	16	6	5	5	0	0	1990
Warwickshire	58	21	12	25	0	0	1959
Worcestershire	37	19	5	13	0	0	1961
Totals	567	185	104	277	1	17	

Note: Matches abandoned are not included in the total played.

Highest Total

By Yorkshire: 538 for 9 wkts dec v. Worcestershire at Stamford Bridge, 2007
Against Yorkshire: 567 for 7 wkts dec by Middlesex at RAF Vine Lane, Uxbridge, 2000

Lowest Total

By Yorkshire: 67 v. Worcestershire at Barnt Green, 2013
Against Yorkshire: 36 by Lancashire at Elland, 1979

Highest Individual Score

For Yorkshire: 273* by R J Blakey v. Northamptonshire at Northampton, 1986
Against Yorkshire: 235 by O A Shah for Middlesex at Leeds, 1999

Century in Each Innings

For Yorkshire:	C White	209* and 115*	v. Worcestershire at Worcester, 1990
	K Sharp	150* and 127	v. Essex at Elland, 1991
	A A Metcalfe	109 and 136*	v. Somerset at North Perrott, 1994
	R A Kettleborough	123 and 192*	v. Nottinghamshire at Todmorden, 1996
	C R Taylor	201* and 129	v. Sussex at Hove, 2005
	A W Gale	131 and 123	v. Somerset at Taunton, 2006
	J J Sayers	157 and 105	v. Lancashire at Leeds, 2007
Against Yorkshire:	N Nannan	100 and 102*	for Nottinghamshire at Harrogate, 1979
	G D Lloyd	134 and 103	for Lancashire at Scarborough, 1989
	A J Swann	131 and 100	for Northamptonshire at York, 1998
	G J Kennis	114 and 114	for Somerset at Taunton, 1999

Best Bowling in an Innings

For Yorkshire: 9 for 27 by G A Cope v. Northamptonshire at Northampton, 1979
Against Yorkshire: 8 for 15 by I Folley for Lancashire at Heywood, 1983

Best Bowling in a Match

For Yorkshire: 13 for 92 (6 for 48 and 7 for 44) by M K Bore v. Lancashire at Harrogate, 1976
Against Yorkshire: 13 for 100 (7 for 45 and 6 for 55) by N J Perry for Glamorgan at Cardiff, 1978

Totals of 450 and over

By Yorkshire (26)

Score	Versus	Ground	Season
538 for 9 wkts dec	Worcestershire	Stamford Bridge	2007
534 for 5 wkts dec	Lancashire	Stamford Bridge	2003
530 for 8 wkts dec	Nottinghamshire	Middlesbrough	2000
514 for 3 wkts dec	Somerset	Taunton	1988
509 for 4 wkts dec	Northamptonshire	Northampton	1986
502	Derbyshire	Chesterfield	2003
501 for 5 wkts dec	MCC Young Cricketers	Stamford Bridge	2009
497	Derbyshire	Chesterfield	2005
495 for 5 wkts dec	Somerset	Taunton	2006
488 for 8 wkts dec	Warwickshire	Harrogate	1984
486 for 6 wkts dec	Glamorgan	Leeds	1986
480	Leicestershire	Market Harborough	2013
476 for 3 wkts dec	Glamorgan	Gorseinon	1984
475 for 9 wkts dec	Nottinghamshire	Nottingham	1995
474 for 3 wkts dec	Glamorgan	Todmorden	2003
474	Durham	Stamford Bridge	2003
470	Lancashire	Leeds	2006
469	Warwickshire	Castleford	1999
462	Scotland	Stamford Bridge	2007
461 for 8 wkts dec	Essex	Stamford Bridge	2006
459 for 3 wkts dec	Leicestershire	Oakham	1997
459 for 6 wkts dec	Glamorgan	Bradford	1992
457 for 5 wkts dec	Kent	Canterbury	1983
456 for 5 wkts dec	Gloucestershire	Todmorden	1990
456 for 6 wkts dec	Nottinghamshire	York	1986
454 for 9 wkts dec	Derbyshire	Chesterfield	1959
452 for 9 wkts dec	Glamorgan	Cardiff	2005

Against Yorkshire (12)

Score	For	Ground	Season
567 for 7 wkts dec	Middlesex	RAF Vine Lane, Uxbridge	2000
555 for 7 wkts dec	Derbyshire	Stamford Bridge	2002
525 for 7 wkts dec	Sussex	Hove	2005
493 for 8 wkts dec	Nottinghamshire	Lady Bay, Nottingham	2002
488 for 8 wkts dec	Warwickshire	Castleford	1999
486	Essex	Chelmsford	2000
485	Gloucestershire	North Park, Cheltenham	2001
477	Lancashire	Headingley	2006
471	Warwickshire	Clifton Park, York	2010
458	Lancashire	Bradford	1997
454 for 7 wkts dec	Lancashire	Todmorden	1993
450 for 7 wkts (inns closed)	Derbyshire	Bradford	1980

Completed Innings under 75

By Yorkshire (3)

Score	Versus	Ground	Season
67	Worcestershire	Barnt Green (1st inns)	2013
68	Worcestershire	Barnt Green (2nd inns)	2013
69	Lancashire	Heywood	1983
74	Derbyshire	Chesterfield	1960
74	Nottinghamshire	Bradford	1998

Against Yorkshire (10)

Score	By	Ground	Season
36	Lancashire	Elland	1979
49	Leicestershire	Leicester	2008
50	Lancashire	Liverpool	1984
60	Derbyshire	Bradford	1977
60	Surrey	Sunbury-on-Thames	1977
62	MCC YC	High Wycombe	2005
64	Nottinghamshire	Brodsworth	1959
66	Leicestershire	Lutterworth	1977
72	Sussex	Horsham	2003
74	Worcestershire	Barnsley	1978

Individual Scores of 150 and over (60)

Score	Player	Versus	Ground	Season
273*	R J Blakey	Northamptonshire	Northampton	1986
238*	K Sharp	Somerset	Taunton	1988
233	P E Robinson	Kent	Canterbury	1983
221*	K Sharp	Gloucestershire	Todmorden	1990
219	G M Hamilton	Derbyshire	Chesterfield	2003
218*	A McGrath	Surrey	Elland	1994
212	G S Ballance	MCC Young Cricketers	Stamford Bridge	2009
209*	C White	Worcestershire	Worcester	1990
205	C R Taylor	Glamorgan	Todmorden	2003
204	B Parker	Gloucestershire	Bristol	1993
203	A McGrath	Durham	Headingley	2005
202*	J M Bairstow	Leicestershire	Oakham	2009
202	M J Wood	Essex	Stamford Bridge	2006
201*	C R Taylor	Sussex	Hove	2005
200*	D Byas	Worcestershire	Worcester	1992
200*	A McGrath	Northamptonshire	Northampton	2012
192*	R A Kettleborough	Nottinghamshire	Todmorden	1996
191	P E Robinson	Warwickshire	Harrogate	1984
191	M J Wood	Derbyshire	Rotherham	2000
191	M J Lumb	Nottinghamshire	Middlesbrough	2000
189*	C S Pickles	Gloucestershire	Bristol	1991
186	A McGrath	MCC Universities	York	2011
184	J D Love	Worcestershire	Headingley	1976
183	A W Gale	Durham	Stamford Bridge	2006
174	G L Brophy	Worcestershire	Stamford Bridge	2007
173	S N Hartley	Warwickshire	Edgbaston	1980
173	A A Metcalfe	Glamorgan	Gorseinon	1984
173	B Parker	Sussex	Hove	1996
173	R A Kettleborough	Leicestershire	Oakham School	1997

Individual Scores of 150 and over *(Continued)*

Score	Player	Versus	Ground	Season
172	A C Morris	Lancashire	York	1995
170*	R A J Townsley	Glamorgan	Harrogate	1975
169	J E Root	Warwickshire	York	2010
168	M J Wood	Leicestershire	Oakham School	1997
166	A A Metcalfe	Lancashire	York	1984
166	C A Chapman	Northamptonshire	York	1998
165*	A Lyth	Durham	Stamford Bridge	2006
165	J J Sayers	Sussex	Hove	2006
164*	A W Gale	Leicestershire	Harrogate	2002
164	J C Balderstone	Nottinghamshire	Harrogate	1960
163*	J E Root	Leicestershire	Oakham	2009
163	A A Metcalfe	Derbyshire	Chesterfield	1992
162*	D Byas	Surrey	Scarborough	1987
160	A A Metcalfe	Somerset	Bradford	1993
157	J J Sayers	Lancashire	Headingley	2007
155	S M Guy	Derbyshire	Chesterfield	2005
154*	C R Taylor	Surrey	Whitgift School	2005
153*	A A Metcalfe	Warwickshire	Bingley	1995
153	C White	Worcestershire	Marske-by-the-Sea	1991
153	R A Stead	Surrey	Todmorden	2002
152	A A Metcalfe	Gloucestershire	Bristol	1993
151*	P E Robinson	Nottinghamshire	York	1986
151*	S J Foster	Kent	Elland	1992
151*	J J Sayers	Durham	Stamford Bridge	2004
151	P J Hartley	Somerset	Clevedon	1989
151	A McGrath	Somerset	Elland	1995
151	V J Craven	Glamorgan	Todmorden	2003
150*	K Sharp	Essex	Elland	1991
150*	G M Fellows	Hampshire	Todmorden	1998
150*	S M Guy	Nottinghamshire	Headingley	2005
150*	J A Leaning	Worcestershire	Worcester	2011
150	K Sharp	Glamorgan	Ebbw Vale	1983
150	S N Hartley	Nottinghamshire	Worksop	1988
150	C R Taylor	Derbyshire	Chesterfield	2003

7 Wickets in an Innings (30)

Analysis	Player	Versus	Ground	Season
9 for 27	G A Cope	Northamptonshire	Northampton	1977
9 for 62	M K Bore	Warwichshire	Scarborough	1976
8 for 53	S J Dennis	Nottinghamshire	Nottingham	1983
8 for 57	M K Bore	Lancashire	Manchester	1977
8 for 79	P J Berry	Derbyshire	Harrogate	1991
7 for 13	P Carrick	Northamptonshire	Marske-by-the-Sea	1977
7 for 21	S Silvester	Surrey	Sunbury-on-Thames	1977
7 for 22	J A R Blain	Surrey	Purley	2004
7 for 32	P W Jarvis	Surrey	The Oval	1984
7 for 34	P Carrick	Glamorgan	Leeds	1986
7 for 37	P M Hutchison	Warwickshire	Coventry	2001

7 Wickets in an Innings *(Continued)*

Analysis	Player	Versus	Ground	Season
7 for 39	G M Hamilton	Sussex	Leeds	1995
7 for 40	M K Bore	Worcestershire	Old Hill	1976
7 for 44	M K Bore	Lancashire	Harrogate	1976
7 for 44	J P Whiteley	Worcestershire	Leeds	1979
7 for 51	J D Middlebrook	Derbyshire	Rotherham	2000
7 for 53	J P Whiteley	Warwickshire	Birmingham	1980
7 for 55	C White	Leicestershire	Bradford	1990
7 for 58	K Gillhouley	Derbyshire	Chesterfield	1960
7 for 58	P J Hartley	Lancashire	Leeds	1985
7 for 63	M J Hoggard	Worcestershire	Harrogate	1998
7 for 65	M K Bore	Nottinghamshire	Steetley	1976
7 for 70	J D Batty	Leicestershire	Bradford	1992
7 for 71	J D Batty	Hampshire	Harrogate	1994
7 for 81	K Gillhouley	Lancashire	Scarborough	1960
7 for 84	I J Houseman	Kent	Canterbury	1989
7 for 88	I G Swallow	Nottinghamshire	Nottingham	1983
7 for 90	A P Grayson	Kent	Folkestone	1991
7 for 93	D Pickles	Nottinghamshire	Nottingham	1960
7 for 94	K Gillhouley	Northamptonshire	Redcar	1960

12 Wickets in a Match (6)

Analysis		Player	Versus	Ground	Season
13 for 92	(6-48 and 7-44)	M K Bore	Lancashire	Harrogate	1976
13 for 110	(7-70 and 6-40)	J D Batty	Leicestershire	Bradford	1992
13 for 111	(4-49 and 9-62)	M K Bore	Warwickshire	Scarborough	1976
12 for 69	(5-32 and 7-37)	P M Hutchison	Warwickshire	Coventry	2001
12 for 120	(5-39 and 7-81)	K Gillhouley	Lancashire	Scarborough	1960
12 for 163	(5-78 and 7-84)	I J Houseman	Kent	Canterbury	1989

Hat-tricks (4)

Player	Versus	Ground	Season
I G Swallow	Warwickshire	Harrogate	1984
S D Fletcher	Nottinghamshire	Marske-by-the-Sea	1987
I G Swallow	Derbyshire	Chesterfield	1988
M Broadhurst	Essex	Southend-on-Sea	1992

ANNUAL REPORT
and
Statement of Account
for the year ended
December 31, 2013

CHAIRMAN'S REPORT

COLIN GRAVES

The Club held several commemorative events throughout 2013, beginning with the Sesquicentennial Soiree on January 8, 150 years to the date that Yorkshire County Cricket Club was formed at The Adelphi Hotel in Sheffield.

Following that, the 150th Anniversary Lunch took place in early April, when we welcomed over 600 of the Club's members, players and guests to Headingley's Long Room for an afternoon of great food, excellent company and entertainment from Yorkshire greats past and present.

In June we had our special Service of Thanksgiving at York Minster, led by the Dean and Chapter of York Minster. Suffragan Bishop of Hull The Right Reverend Richard Frith and the President of Marylebone Cricket Club, Mike Griffith, gave an address. It was very satisfying to see the Minster full of Yorkshire supporters and dignitaries.

In September a commemorative match was held at Abbeydale Cricket Ground, where a Yorkshire XI faced a Sheffield Collegiate Invitational XI. It was another entertaining day, and all players thoroughly enjoyed the experience of being present at such a memorable occasion.

The year came to a grand finale with the 150th Gala Dinner in October — when almost 800 supporters, colleagues, players past and present, partners and commercial friends celebrated Yorkshire County Cricket Club at Elland Road. The Gala Dinner was the pinnacle of Yorkshire's incredible 150th year and helped to celebrate the greatness of Yorkshire County Cricket Club.

It was without doubt a year to remember, and I must place on record my thanks and gratitude to the 150th Anniversary Committee for providing an outstanding array of events. History and tradition is what Yorkshire cricket is all about. We have achieved so many great things over the years. Success is part of our fabric, and it was truly rewarding to capture these moments throughout 2013.

On the field it was another progressive year in the LV=County Championship. After gaining promotion the previous season we had set ourselves the tough objective of trying to clinch the title in our anniversary year. We made a good fist of it, and missed out in the final month of the season, finishing runners-up to Durham after leading the Championship for most of the season.

Our County Championship performance was consistently brilliant. We scored big runs when it mattered, Gary Ballance excelling with the bat. He amassed over 1,300 Championship runs at an average of 64.90, which inevitably earned him a call-up to the England squad for the *Ashes* tour of Australia. He was equally supported by captain Andrew Gale, who showed glimpses of his real quality, including a superb career-best 272 against Nottinghamshire at Scarborough in June.

Admittedly, as with every team, we found ourselves with more drawn results than we would have liked, but the team performances could rarely be knocked. Our attack was among the strongest in the country, and the very reliable pairing of Ryan Sidebottom and Steve Patterson showed their qualities with 53 and 51 wickets respectively. They were enhanced by the inseparable pairing of Jack Brooks and Liam Plunkett in their first season with the Club, alongside Adil Rashid who had one of his best seasons for a while with both bat and ball.

In the shorter form of the game our form was disappointing, and there will be a lot of effort among players and coaches during the winter months to get this right in 2014. I can assure members that we will improve, and will not see a repeat of 2013 where we fell well short of our high standards in *T20* and limited-overs cricket. I do not want to dwell on this, and Martyn Moxon will outline his thoughts in his report.

Under Martyn and Jason Gillespie we are building a squad that is capable of competing against the best clubs in the country, and I have every confidence both in them and the players. I am certain that 2014 will be a positive year across all cricketing disciplines. Consistency is the key for Yorkshire. We will be aiming to try and win the LV=County Championship crown this year following our impressive performance last year. We will also be looking to compete in one-day cricket, and have aspirations of winning a trophy in the shorter form. Whatever happens it should be very exciting following the fortunes of the Club.

On the international scene we continue to be the envy of the county game in respect of the number of players we are producing at elite level. Four featured for England in 2013. Jonny Bairstow, Gary Ballance, Tim Bresnan and Joe Root all played their part in a mixed year of success for the national team. The less said about the winter series in Australia the better, but you have to admire England's resolve in the summer, where they defeated New Zealand in the Test series in May — winning the final match at Headingley before going on to to win the *Ashes* for a third successive series later in the summer. The highlight for me was seeing Joe Root record his maiden Test century in May in front of a partisan crowd at Headingley. He has a big future in the game.

In the other national set-ups we continue to flourish. Alex Lees is now firmly established in the England Lions squad. He had a brilliant first season in county cricket, averaging 47.76 with the bat, including an imperious 275 not out against Derbyshire at Chesterfield — the second highest score by a Yorkshire batsman since the Second World War.

We had five players representing England Under-19s. Exciting all-rounder Will Rhodes captained the side, and 15-year-old seamer Matthew Fisher, who made his senior debut with the Club in the Yorkshire Bank 40 competition in the summer, proved himself to be a

---

We continue to be the envy of the county game in respect of the number of players we are producing at elite level.

---

star in the making. The England Under-17s currently have two Yorkshire representatives, with many more players ready to come through. I have to say that the conveyor belt of emerging elite players is relentless and will provide the backbone of Yorkshire cricket for many years to come.

Away from the domestic side we have hosted two internationals in the past 12 months. Unfortunately, the weather played its part in both. The opening day of the Test match against New Zealand was a washout, and we had a repeat dose of the inclement weather later in the year when our one-day international between England and Australia was abandoned without a ball bowled. It is frustrating, and unfortunate for everyone connected with the venue when we are faced with difficulties beyond our control. A full year of preparation and planning can fall by the way-side due to the adverse conditions. As I have said on numerous occasions international cricket is the lifeblood of the organisation.

A detailed review of the Club's finances can be found in Charles Hartwell's report, but for the Club to prosper and grow it is vital that we all continue to support international cricket at Headingley. Internationals are guaranteed every year until 2019, but we cannot afford to be com-placent. For Headingley to flourish and retain its international status in what is becoming a very competitive market we have to demonstrate to the ECB that we are capable of staging matches of this magnitude. We need the support of the whole of the Yorkshire cricket community for international cricket to prosper in the county, and ultimately the public to support us by buying tickets. Headingley is a special venue that has an atmosphere not matched by most venues around the world. We are continually upgrading facilities and, just as important, looking to enhance the matchday experience. This is being led and delivered by Chief Executive Mark Arthur. He joined us in May from Nottingham Forest, but with vast amounts of experience in cricket, having worked with Nottinghamshire and the ECB in the past. He has a vision that can lead us forward and deliver success across all our business disciplines.

At this point I must also thank our retiring President, Geoffrey Boycott, who has made an outstanding contribution during his two years in office. It has been a privilege and a pleasure to have worked with a true legend of both Yorkshire and world cricket. Geoffrey has been immense in his role, and has been a faultless ambassador — promoting, with enthusiasm and pride, our great Club to all and sundry across the world through his role as a broadcaster and column writer.

To my fellow Board members, I would like to thank you for your efforts and unwavering support throughout the year. Your encouragement and advice is most invaluable and makes me more determined than ever to see the Club prosper. My long-term ambition is for us to be financially secure and to eradicate the debt. It will be a painful journey, but over time, and with the help and support of everyone involved in Yorkshire cricket, we will achieve sustained success for many years to come.

Undoubtedly, the next few years are going to be challenging. I am confident that we can deliver some long overdue silverware on the playing front and continue to develop the infrastructure off the pitch.

May I wish you all a very enjoyable 2014 season, and I look forward to seeing you at Headingley and Scarborough throughout the campaign.

COLIN GRAVES
Executive Chairman
The Yorkshire
County Cricket Club

FINANCE DIRECTOR'S REPORT

CHARLES HARTWELL

In broad terms, the financial success or failure of Yorkshire County Cricket Club revolves around three factors: the opposition for our England internationals, the weather and the attractiveness of our Club to commercial sponsors.

Over the past four years international match and commercial sponsorship income, including advertising revenues, accounted for nearly 70 per cent of the Club's controllable income (total income less the fixed and performance-related fee payments received from the ECB). Although the cost base of the Club can be budgeted with a high degree of certainty these three factors are, to a large degree, outside of the Club's control.

The Club is reporting total income of £6.8m for 2013, a deficit before taxation and exceptional items (trading deficit) of £1.2m and a bottom-line deficit of £0.6m. Unfortunately, this is not an improvement over 2012, when the Club reported income of £7.8m, a trading deficit of £43k and a bottom-line deficit of £0.1m.

International match revenue in 2013 was £2.2m (33 per cent of total income) which was £900k down on 2012 and accounts for the lion's share of the fall in total year-on-year income. The fall can be attributed to the fact that we were allocated a May Test Match against New Zealand in an *Ashes* year, with Australia playing all around us later in the summer. The weather in Yorkshire in May is not always kind, and this did not help to drive advance ticket sales, despite the Club offering various incentives for early purchase.

The Club, therefore, had to rely on good weather to attract significant walk-up ticket sales if budget was to be achieved. Unfortunately, day one was completely rained off, and therefore generated no walk-up income. The match was then forced into a fifth day through Alastair Cook's controversial decision not to enforce the follow-on and, with the contest effectively over, the fifth day offered no incentive for people to attend. Only 500 people watched the assured England victory, with the Club consequently losing in the region of £50,000 for the day.

Although the One Day International was totally washed out all tickets were sold well in advance as the opposition and timing were highly attractive. This meant that the Club retained all ticket revenue, and the ECB's insurance scheme refunded ticket-holders. The Club also took the decision to offer, instead of a refund, an exchange of tickets for the 2014 ODI – an initiative that was very well received by both ticket-holders and the ECB, with nearly 4,000 tickets being exchanged.

The Club is reporting commercial income of £1.6m, a reduction of £150k over 2012. The Club's 150th-anniversary celebrations were a great success on all counts, and the Gala Dinner auction made a welcome contribution to the Club's finances. In addition, the Club agreed new partnership deals with Wensleydale Creamery and Puma. That being said, the economy is still in a fragile state and the market for major commercial investment remains challenging. The Club did not secure a new ground naming-rights partner in 2013, and this is the primary reason why overall commercial income fell compared to 2012. The Club is working hard to secure a naming rights partner in 2014.

As predicted, income from the ECB remained consistent with 2012, and income of £1.8m has been reported. Due to the strength and age profile of the Club's playing squad ECB income can be budgeted with relative certainty.

The Club is run on an extremely lean basis, and costs are very tightly controlled. That being said, a ground of Headingley's size needs a considerable sum spent on it to maintain and continually improve its facilities. The cost of Infrastructure and Ground Operations rose by 18 per cent over 2012 to £846k. This increase is attributable to the increases in business rates and various repairs around the ground, including the installation of additional pigeon netting underneath the North Stand, repairs to the East Stand roof and also the player's gym. In addition, the costs of the commercial and administrative departments have increased by £174k to £1.3m, due to the costs of bringing the Club's PR and Communications resource in-house and the recruitment of a Chief Executive in May 2013.

During the year the Club took on a further £3m of interest-bearing loans, but also repaid £1m of loans and reduced the overdraft by a further £1m. The Club's net interest-bearing borrowings therefore increased by £1m. The resulting incremental interest burden has been partially mitigated by negotiating a one per cent reduction in the rate of interest charged by the Graves Trusts. The additional net borrowings were used to fund the budget shortfalls from the Test match and ground naming rights.

In addition to the interest-bearing loans the ECB made available a £1m Business Plan loan, which is effectively interest free and of which £0.9m was drawn down in 2013. This loan has been made available to all FCCs once they have submitted a robust business plan to the ECB. The loans can only be used for investment in ground improvements or to accelerate the repayment of debt, and will be repaid in 2015 through the payment by the ECB of an expected one-off fee payment, making the loan cash neutral to the Club. Yorkshire's loan has been used to make a £0.5m advance capital-loan repayment to Leeds City Council (part of the £1m loan repayment previously mentioned) to install a new score-board and to finance the planning application for permanent floodlights. The balance of the loan will be drawn down in 2014, and will be used to segregate the West Stand ready for the 2014 season.

Elsewhere on the Balance Sheet, the main movements of note from 2012 to 2013 relate to Creditors: amounts falling due within one year which have fallen by £1.8m to £3.5m. This reflects the loans, paying down £1m of the Club's overdraft and the finalisation of the loan repayment schedule with Leeds City Council, which have reduced the capital-loan repayments due within the next 12 months by £0.6m.

As a result of the negotiations with the bank regarding our interest-rate hedge 2013 debtors include an expected one-off £0.6m interest credit from HSBC. This is also treated as an exceptional item on the Income and Expenditure Account.

Looking forward to 2014, I feel that the Club will report a better financial performance. However, I do not expect a bottom-line surplus to be reported, and I expect the pressure on working capital to continue. I feel that the timing of the Test match, coupled with the strength of the opposition and the fact that 2014 is not an *Ashes* year, will help to increase attendances and revenue for the June Test. This is supported by the fact that ticket purchases as at December 31, 2013, for both the Test and ODI are higher than at the same time last year, and we have an additional month to sell the Test compared to last year. The expansion of the *T20* from five to seven home matches and the fact that Headingley will be staging no fewer than five on Friday nights is also very welcome from a financial perspective. This scheduling will create an appointment to view, and I expect this to significantly increase domestic attendances and revenues for 2014.

Yorkshire are fortunate to have our Chairman personally guaranteeing the Club's debts. But, looking at the financial state of cricket as a whole, we have had nine Test match grounds for a number of years now and, in my opinion, this has not delivered a healthy and vibrant environment. Many grounds have taken on massive levels of debt and financial risk in order to try and secure the biggest matches, and this model cannot be sustained. Sooner or later some extremely difficult decisions will have to be made, and action needs to be taken now.

2014 will be extremely tough, but we have a number of initiatives that will help to attract cricket fans and commercial sponsors to our Club. As always, we need our members to continue to help by bringing people to watch our team and our internationals, and by spreading the word about our Club.

To conclude, I would like to thank our members, supporters and commercial partners who continue to back our Club. In particular I would like to thank HSBC, Leeds City Council, The Yorkshire Cricket Foundation, the Supporters' Association, the Players' Association and the Yorkshire Cricket Taverners' Club for their continued support. We are very fortunate at Yorkshire to have such hard-working, dedicated and talented staff both on and off the field, and I would personally like to thank them all for their efforts during 2013.

I wish you all an enjoyable and prosperous 2014 season.

CHARLES HARTWELL ACA
Director of Finance
Yorkshire County Cricket Club

DIRECTOR OF PROFESSIONAL CRICKET'S REPORT

As 2013 saw the Club celebrate its 150th Anniversary it was always our intention to prioritise the County Championship. The fact that we ended the season in second place, while undoubtedly slightly disappointing, should still be regarded as a fantastic achievement, given that it was also our first season back in Division 1.

MARTYN MOXON

Considering the excellent cricket that followed, losing the first game against Sussex perhaps provided the team with an extra shot of motivation. They bounced back in terrific style at the Riverside, and chased-down a challenging fourth-innings total. Many of the batsmen made valuable contributions to the cause. However, Joe Root's 182 was a truly magnificent innings which only served to further highlight his potential.

This was followed by a remarkable game against Derbyshire at Headingley, in which both Root and Jonny Bairstow shone with the bat. Their partnership of 233 took the game away from our opponents, and some outstanding bowling, particularly from Jack Brooks, in the second innings saw us win by an innings and 39 runs. It was an incredible result when you consider that Derbyshire scored 475 in their first innings.

Those two victories gave the team a huge amount of confidence and belief. Excellent wins at Edgbaston, Lord's, Chesterfield and Trent Bridge followed, where we dominated the opposition, and we gave ourselves an excellent opportunity to win the competition.

Unfortunately, our title chance slipped away against Durham at Scarborough. In all honesty we were outplayed. Credit must go to Durham for the way they dominated the game and stuck to their task, when it looked as though we might get away with a draw. Following that crucial victory, they blew the opposition away in their remaining games and went on to become deserved Champions. We were hampered by the weather at Hove and beat Middlesex at Headingley, but it was not quite enough. I think it is fair to say that it was a case of Durham winning the title, rather than us losing it.

As I've already said, the team played some fantastic cricket during the season with eight different players scoring centuries — equalling the

Club record. The bowlers also played their part, with the regular quartet of Sidebottom, Brooks, Patterson and Plunkett being particularly impressive. It was especially pleasing to see both Jack Brooks and Liam Plunkett fitting into the squad so seamlessly and producing a number of match-winning performances. They are both fantastic lads, and have a great desire to succeed at Yorkshire. The pride they felt when awarded their First Eleven caps was plain to see. It meant an awful lot to them.

We also recruited Kane Williamson towards the end of the season. He, too, fitted into the squad very well and played some fine innings. We're delighted that he'll be returning to the Club for the majority of the forthcoming season. He will be a great asset to us as we try and build on the success of 2013.

Although our performances in four-day cricket were very pleasing, our one-day form was disappointing in the same measure. We make no excuses for having used the *YB40* competition to blood some of our younger players and rest Sidebottom and Patterson in particular. Nonetheless, we expected better performances and results from those who did play. The young players actually produced some really encouraging moments. However, the senior players did not always perform, and we often found ourselves either 15-20 runs short of a winning total or unable to see the game out with the ball.

Similarly, in the *T20* competition we did not bat well throughout, and again were not able to close games out from potentially winning positions with the ball. We lost the first three games when we were in positions to possibly win, a costly over at the death swinging the game in the opposition's favour. Our skills were not as sharp as they had been in 2012, and we clearly missed a number of our key performers from the previous season. As a result of this we will be working hard on our one-day skills this winter, and one-day cricket will form a greater proportion of our pre-season tour this year than has been the case in the past.

I've always said that I want to build a team that's competitive in all forms of the game. Although the Championship will always be our main objective we are all eager to experience *T20* Finals Day once again and remain determined to end our long wait for a Lord's final berth.

I am certain that the potential to achieve all of our aims exists within the current squad. However, we face the challenge of bringing through the next generation of Yorkshire cricketers over the next 12-18 months as we find ourselves in a situation where we may potentially lose a number of players to the national sides. As I'm sure you know, we had four players involved in the winter *Ashes* squad, and we also have Alex Lees now playing for the England Lions. We are lucky to have a phenomenally exciting crop of young players coming through, five of whom have been involved with the England Under-19s squad for the past 12 months and two playing for England Under-17s.

I believe the years that lie ahead for the Club will be exceptionally exciting, and I would like to thank all our support staff for the work they have done and continue to do in trying to fully realise this potential. Over the last two years Jason Gillespie, Paul Farbrace, Ian Dews, Richard Damms, Tony Pickersgill, Tom Summers, Scot McAllister and Chris Liversidge have helped to create an environment in which the players can flourish.

Since the end of last season we have had to replace Paul, Tom and Scot. Paul was appointed Sri Lanka's Head Coach, an opportunity he could not ultimately turn down; Tom has moved to Hong Kong along with his wife who was offered a fantastic career opportunity, and Scot has taken up a position with the Scottish Rugby Union 7s team. All three men played a big part in developing a strong and effective team of support staff, and I thank them sincerely for their contributions and wish them all well for the future.

At the time of writing have just recruited former Yorkshire off-spinner Richard Dawson to replace Paul, and I am delighted that we have been able to appoint Ian Fisher as our Senior Strength and Conditioning Coach with Blaine Clancy working alongside him. We are the first county to have two full time S&C coaches, and this means that players from the Academy and age group teams will have greater exposure to supervised training sessions. We truly believe this will pay dividends in the future. We have also recruited Kunwar Bansil from Hull Rugby League to replace Scot. All three have fitted in really well and are already producing some excellent work.

Everything is set for an exciting season ahead. There will obviously be challenges, but I feel that the Club is in good shape. It is being well run by the Chairman, Board and Chief Executive off the field and they give the Cricket Department tremendous support. It is our job to maintain the progress on the field.

Finally, thank you for your continued support. All the players and staff appreciate it and I hope we can entertain you in all forms of the game during 2014.

MARTYN MOXON
Director of Professional Cricket
Yorkshire County Cricket Club

MEMBERS' COMMITTEE
CHAIRMAN'S REPORT

The following served on the Members' Committee during the year.

Chairman:	**Mr S J Mann**
Elected Members:	**Mrs C Evers**
	Mr R Levin
	Mr S J Mann
	Mr E Stephens
Appointed Members:	**Mr G Clark**
	Mr A Kilburn
	Mr R W Stott
In Attendance:	**Mr M Arthur,** Chief Executive
	Mr A Dawson, Commercial Director
In Attendance:	**Mr R Smith,** Board Director

There were seven full committee meetings during the year. The minutes of these meetings are passed to the Board and a summary of the key issues continues to be posted on the Club website for the information of Members. Three Member Forums were held in the Long Room through the season. There were no changes to the elected or appointed members of the committee during the year. The Chief Executive joined the committee on his appointment in the spring.

As in previous years the concept of Member Forums continues to be a key component of the communication process between the Club and the membership, and long may it continue to be so. However, it has to be reported that the committee have become increasingly concerned that the style, tone and content is a good deal less than productive or constructive. The objective has always been to provide a platform for members to raise topics and questions of a substantive nature, but increasingly the issues raised do not fit this definition. The forums have never had the objective of providing a conduit merely for complaints, yet some members seem to think this is the only reason for attending.

In addition to the forums a member-help desk manned by committee colleagues was provided during the luncheon interval on several occasions. It is disappointing to report that this initiative was a good deal less than successful. The opportunity for a personal discussion became an opportunity to reiterate matters already raised at forums. Such helpdesks will not be provided in the future.

At the November meeting of the committee all of these concerns were debated and a number of decisions taken. Firstly, forums will still be held in 2014, but a different venue to the Long Room will be utilised. The meetings will not be used for complaint-making but for discussion on topics of a "substantive" nature. More details and the actual schedule will be announced on the website prior to the start of the 2014 season.

Through the middle of the year the main topic of debate at committee meetings was the membership scheme and Test/ODI pricing, with particular emphasis on spectator choice and value. Having provided members with a

STEPHEN MANN

reduced pricing structure for 2013 to help to celebrate the 150th anniversary, it was considered necessary and appropriate to return to more commercial prices for 2014. Thus a minimal increase on 2012 was agreed.

The committee were consulted throughout the process of preparing a member package for 2014, and while there has been this small increase on 2012 it is felt that membership of Yorkshire CCC still provides amazing value, both in terms of watching Division 1 cricket and in the excellent facilities provided for spectators at Headingley and Scarborough.

The 150th-anniversary celebrations have been a tremendous success, befitting the most famous cricket club in the world. The varied programme of events was developed to enable the involvement of members, and particularly well supported were the opening evening at the Crucible in Sheffield, the service at York Minster and the lunch in April at Headingley.

Finally, I would like to record my sincere appreciation to all the Members' Committee for their support throughout the year. All the committee give a considerable amount of personal time on a voluntary basis to work for the Club and the membership.

STEPHEN MANN,
Chairman,
Members' Committee
Yorkshire County Cricket Club

YORKSHIRE CRICKET FOUNDATION CHAIRMAN'S REPORT

Cricket in Yorkshire is represented by three main bodies:

The Yorkshire County Cricket Club (YCCC) focuses on elite cricket, the Yorkshire Cricket Board (YCB) focuses on league and amateur cricket development, and the Yorkshire Cricket Foundation (YCF) delivers cricket-based initiatives focusing on education, community engagement, and heritage.

These three organisations are referred to as the *Yorkshire Cricket Partners* or *Yorkshire Cricket.*

DAVID GENT

2013 was a great year for the YCF, and we have continued to grow and expand our reach at pace. To that end we have been able to employ a full-time project manager in Nick Robinson, who together with Will Saville takes care of the day-to-day operations of the Foundation. The YCF is looking to take permanent offices at Headingley early in 2014.

I am very excited about the close working relationship that the YCF has built with the YCCC and YCB. The Partners have agreed an out-comes-focused strategy of engagement, inclusion, and excellence within all aspects of cricket in Yorkshire, and this will bear fruit very soon, with a number of exciting projects and initiatives on the horizon.

Turning to YCF's work on Yorkshire's rich cricketing heritage, we secured funding from the Heritage Lottery Fund which has enabled a mobile cricket museum to be built. This took to the road in May, and has proven to be a great success visiting schools, cricket clubs and events throughout the county. The Archives Committee came under the YCF in January, which cements the Foundation's intention to protect and grow the archive for future generations and provide a platform for tax-efficient giving of monies and memorabilia so that the archive can grow, become easily accessible, and be safeguarded for future generations.

To summarise some of the other achievements throughout the year:

• 4,000 primary school children took part in our flagship scheme, *Cricket in the Classroom*, our highest number to date.

• 6,000 people attended Children's Day, a free, family-activity day at Headingley Cricket Ground.

• We developed the *Yorkshire Elite Leaders Academy* in partnership with the YCB, which mentors and rewards young people involved in cricket-based volunteering within their community

• We launched our new website *www.yorkshirecricketfoundation.com* which has provided us with an excellent platform to promote our work and communicate with the Yorkshire community

We plan to continue our growth and development in 2014, developing further community initiatives and reaching new audiences, but all of our income still comes from donations, legacies, and specific grants that we apply for. If you would like to make a donation the easiest way is to donate online at *www.justgiving.com/yorkshirecricketfoundation.*

If you would like to consider making a legacy or donating any memorabilia, please contact Will Saville on 0113-2033620. I would like to end by thanking everyone who made a donation to the YCF during the year, and specifically the generosity of the Emerald Foundation.

DAVID GENT
Chairman of the Board of Trustees
Yorkshire Cricket Foundation

YORKSHIRE CRICKET MUSEUM DIRECTOR's REPORT

The 150th Anniversary Year provided the opportunity for us to feature in the Museum and the Long Room displays which highlighted the illustrious history of the Club, with particular emphasis on the decades of exceptional achievement.

A new film featuring an abridged *History of Yorkshire County Cricket Club* was introduced in the Museum cinema.

We were delighted to welcome some distinguished guests to the Museum during the season, including the Leader of the Opposition, Ed Miliband and the Home

DAVID HALL

Secretary, Theresa May. Interest in the Museum has spread beyond the county, and we were pleased to show round some other clubs who are exploring the possibility of setting up a museum on their own grounds.

Unfortunately, in September an incident involving a car seriously damaging the *Great Games* and *War of the Roses* zones of the Museum. These sections are having to be completely rebuilt, and we hope to have them ready in time for the new season.

In 2014 new displays will recall highlights from the Anniversary Year, *1914 – start of the Great War*, *Bat Making Tools* recently gifted to the Club and an updated *Tie Presentation*.

During the year the manufacture of our Mobile Museum, funded by a Heritage Lottery Grant, was completed. Displays featuring the heritage of the Club are shown in it, and it has visited the Great Yorkshire Show and Scarborough Cricket Festival among its outings. We plan to broaden its visits to clubs, schools and special events around the county to encourage interest in the history of cricket, which is so interconnected with our social history, and widen interest in the game.

DAVID HALL CBE TD
Museum Director

INDEPENDENT AUDITORS' REPORT

TO THE MEMBERS OF THE YORKSHIRE COUNTY CRICKET CLUB

We have audited the financial statements of The Yorkshire County Cricket Club for the year ended December 31, 2013, set out on Pages 439 to 448. The financial reporting framework that has been applied in their preparation is applicable in law and UK Accounting Standards (UK Generally Accepted Accounting Practice).

This report is made solely to the Club's members, as a body, in accordance with Section 9 of the Friendly and Industrial and Provident Societies Act 1968. Our audit work has been undertaken so that we might state to the Club's members those matters we are required to state to them in an auditor's report and for no other purpose. To the fullest extent permitted by law we do not accept or assume responsibility to anyone other than the Club and the Club's members, as a body, for our audit work, for this report, or for the opinions we have formed.

Respective responsibilities of directors and auditor

As more fully explained in the Statement of Directors' Responsibilities set out on Page 438 the Club's directors are responsible for the preparation of financial statements which give a true and fair view. Our responsibility is to audit, and express an opinion on, the financial statements in accordance with applicable law and International Standards on Auditing (UK and Ireland). Those standards require us to comply with the Auditing Practices Board's Ethical Standards for Auditors.

Scope of the audit of the financial statements

A description of the scope of an audit of financial statements is provided on the Financial Reporting Council's website at www.frc.org.uk/auditscopeukprivate

Opinion on financial statements

In our opinion the financial statements:

- give a true and fair view, in accordance with UK Generally Accepted Accounting Practice, of the state of the Club's affairs as at 31 December, 2013, and of its deficit for the year then ended; and
- have been properly prepared in accordance with the Industrial and Provident Societies Acts 1965 to 2003.

Matters on which we are required to report by exception

We have nothing to report in respect of the following.

Under the Industrial and Provident Societies Acts 1965 to 2003 we are required to report to you if, in our opinion:

- a satisfactory system of control over transactions has not been maintained; or
- the association has not kept proper accounting records; or
- the financial statements are not in agreement with the books of account; or
- we have not received all the information and explanations we need for our audit.

ANDREW SILLS (Senior Statutory Auditor) for and on behalf of KPMG LLP, Statutory Auditor
Chartered Accountants,
Leeds   FEBRUARY 10, 2014

CORPORATE GOVERNANCE

The Board is accountable to the Club's members for good corporate governance, and this statement describes how the principles of governance are applied.

THE BOARD

The Board is responsible for approving Club policy and strategy. It meets monthly, or more frequently if business needs require, and has a schedule of matters specifically reserved to it for decision, including all significant commercial issues and all capital expenditure.

The Executive Management Team supply the Board with appropriate and timely information, and the Board Members are free to seek any further information they consider necessary.

NOMINATIONS COMMITTEE

The Nominations Committee is formally constituted with written terms of reference, which are defined in the Club Rules and reviewed regularly. It consists of the President, Secretary and two other Board members, currently C J Graves and R A Smith.

RELATIONS WITH MEMBERS

The Club encourages effective communication with its members, and a specific Committee, as defined in the Club Rules, is appointed for that purpose.

INTERNAL CONTROL

The Board acknowledges its responsibility to maintain a sound system of internal control relating to operational, financial and compliance controls and risk management to safeguard the members' interests and the Club's assets, and will regularly review its effectiveness. Such a system, however, is designed to manage and meet the Club's particular needs and mitigate the risks to which it is exposed, rather than eliminate the risk of failure to achieve business objectives, and can provide only reasonable and not absolute assurance against material mis-statement or loss.

The Club considers its key components to provide effective internal control and improve business efficiency are:

- Regular meetings with senior management to review and assess progress made against objectives and deal with any problems which arise from such reviews.
- A financial reporting system of annual budgets, periodic forecasts and detailed monthly reporting which includes cash-flow forecasts. Budgets and forecasts are reviewed and approved by the Board.
- A defined management and organisation structure with defined responsibilities and appropriate authorisation limits and short lines of communication to the Executive Chairman.

ACCOUNTABILITY AND AUDIT

The Board's responsibilities

The following statement, which should be read in conjunction with the Report of the Independent Auditors, is made with a view to distinguishing for members the respective responsibilities of the Board and of the auditors in relation to the accounts:

The Board is required by UK law to prepare accounts which give a true and fair view of the state of affairs of the Club at the end of the financial year and of the surplus or deficit of the Club for the financial year then ended.

The Board is also responsible for maintaining adequate accounting records and for taking reasonable steps to safeguard the assets of the Club and detect irregularities and fraud.

The Board confirms that in preparing the Club's accounts appropriate policies have been consistently applied and applicable accounting standards complied with. Further, in all material respects the accounts are supported by prudent judgments and estimates made by reference to information available at the time of their preparation.

All Board members bring independent judgment to bear on their deliberations concerning strategy and performance. The Board is satisfied that it has had access to sufficient information to enable it to make proper decisions in a timely manner, and the Chairman has ensured that Board Members were kept properly briefed.

INCOME AND EXPENDITURE ACCOUNT
for the year ended 31st December, 2013

	Note	2013 £	2012 £
Income			
International ticket and hospitality revenue		2,239,656	3,135,963
Domestic ticket and hospitality revenue		442,126	451,669
Subscriptions		520,234	491,558
England and Wales Cricket Board		1,832,574	1,874,697
Commercial income		1,633,442	1,783,957
Other income		105,975	37,816
		6,774,007	7,775,660
Cost of sales			
International match and hospitality expenditure		1,096,811	1,461,424
Domestic match and hospitality costs (home fixtures)		153,975	214,907
Retail		107,131	113,924
Catering		41,053	39,557
		(1,398,970)	(1,829,812)
Cricket expenses			
Staff remuneration and employment expenses		2,242,983	2,144,045
Match expenses (away fixtures)		301,606	258,845
Development expenses		357,089	279,845
Other cricket expenses		36,085	61,297
		(2,937,763)	(2,744,032)
Overhead			
Infrastructure and ground operations		846,013	717,462
Commercial		691,477	608,648
Administration *1		592,537	500,956
Ticket and membership office		156,972	136,116
		(2,286,999)	(1,963,182)
Earnings before interest, tax, depreciation and amortisation		150,275	1,238,634
Below the line expenditure:			
Loan Interest *1		(478,106)	(1,010,811)
Depreciation		(457,794)	(540,057)
Release of Capital Grants		146,195	159,496
		(789,705)	(1,391,372)
(Deficit) before taxation and exceptional items		(1,165,984)	(43,201)
Exceptional items *1		526,554	(109,537)
(Deficit) before taxation		(639,430)	(152,738)
Taxation	4	81,720	35,091
(Deficit) for the year after taxation		(557,710)	(117,647)

*1 As a result of negotiations with the bank regarding an interest-rate hedge, it is expected that the Club will receive a one-off interest rebate of £563,741, and this has been accounted for as an exceptional item (income). In 2012 exceptional costs amounting to £109,537 were incurred in relation to staff-restructuring. There were no other gains and losses in the current or preceding year other than stated above. The accompanying notes form an integral part of these accounts.

BALANCE SHEET

as at 31st December, 2013

	Note	2013 £	2013 £	2012 £	2012 £
Assets employed:					
Fixed Assets	5		28,493,028		28,650,114
Current assets:					
Stocks		68,628		64,198	
Debtors	6	1,865,416		1,176,541	
Cash at bank and in hand		—		—	
		1,934,044		1,240,739	
Creditors: amounts falling due within one year	7	(3,521,551)		(5,333,632)	
Net current liabilities			(1,587,507)		(4,092,893)
Total assets less current liabilities			26,905,521		24,557,221
Funded by:					
Creditors: amounts falling due after more than one year	8		(25,095,448)		(22,043,243)
Deferred income — capital grants	9		(4,697,933)		(4,844,128)
			(29,793,381)		(26,887,371)
Capital and Reserves					
Called up share capital	11		(219)		(264)
Capital redemption reserve	12		(671)		(626)
Income and expenditure account	12		2,888,750		2,331,040
			2,887,860		2,330,150
			26,905,521		24,557,221

These accounts were approved by the Board on 10th February 2014

C J GRAVES, Chairman

R A SMITH, Director

The accompanying notes form an integral part to these accounts. There were no other gains and losses in the current or preceding year other than those stated above.

440

CASH FLOW STATEMENT

for the year ended 31st December, 2013

	Note	2013 £	2012 £
Cash (outflow)/inflow from operating activities	13	**(519,886)**	285,671
Returns on investments and servicing of finance	14	**(1,004,660)**	(1,010,811)
Capital expenditure and financial investment	14	**(300,708)**	(209,710)
Cash (outflow) before financing		**(1,825,254)**	(934,849)
Financing	14	**2,804,311**	964,899
Increase in cash in the period		**979,057**	30,050

Reconciliation of net cash flow to movement in net debt

	2013	2012
Increase in cash in period	**979,057**	30,050
HSBC loan repayment	**200,000**	700,000
Leeds City Council loan repayment	**700,000**	200,000
Additional C J Graves loan	**(1,000,000)**	(2,100,000)
Additional Graves Trust loans	**(2,000,000)**	—
Additional debentures	**(40,783)**	(2,000)
Other loans - ECB net repayment	**(899,296)**	40,000
New finance leases	**—**	(23,011)
Capital element of finance lease repayments	**235,723**	197,050
	(1,825,299)	(957,911)

ANALYSIS OF NET DEBT

	At 1 Jan 2013 £	Cash flow 2013 £	Other changes 2013 £	At 31 Dec 2013 £
Cash at bank and in hand	—	—	—	—
Overdraft - current	(1,280,306)	979,057	—	(301,249)
	(1,280,306)	**979,057**	**—**	**(301,249)**
Debt due within one year:				
HSBC loan	(200,000)	200,000	(200,000)	(200,000)
Leeds City Council loan	(797,000)	200,000	397,000	(200,000)
Other loans ECB	(110,000)	40,000	—	(70,000)
Finance leases less than one year	(217,203)	235,723	(216,212)	(197,692)
Debt due after one year:				
HSBC loan	(3,269,014)	—	200,000	(3,069,014)
Leeds City Council loan	(7,510,000)	500,000	(397,000)	(7,407,000)
Other Loans ECB	—	(939,296)	—	(939,296)
Pride Appeal Loan	(5,000)	—	—	(5,000)
Graves Family Trusts loans	(3,600,000)	(2,000,000)	—	(5,600,000)
C J Graves loan	(3,500,000)	(1,000,000)	—	(4,500,000)
Debentures	(325,896)	(40,783)	—	(366,679)
Finance leases more than one year	(1,428,867)	—	216,212	(1,212,655)
	(20,962,980)	**(2,804,356)**	**—**	**(23,767,336)**
Total	**(22,243,286)**	**(1,825,299)**	**—**	**(24,068,585)**

NOTES TO THE ACCOUNTS

for the year ended 31st December, 2013

1. Accounting policies

The accounts have been prepared in accordance with applicable accounting standards and under the historical cost convention. The principal accounting policies of the Club have remained unchanged from the previous year.

The format of the Income and Expenditure Account has been changed in the year to provide more meaningful analysis of the Club's financial performance. Comparatives have been adjusted accordingly.

(a) Income

All income is accounted for on an accruals basis, except for donations which are accounted for in the year of receipt.

Income represents amounts receivable from the Club's principal activities. Income is analysed between international-ticket and hospitality revenue, domestic-ticket and hospitality revenue, subscriptions, England and Wales Cricket Board, commercial and other income.

Subscriptions

Subscription income comprises amounts receivable from members in respect of the current season. Subscriptions received in respect of future seasons are treated as deferred income.

Domestic-ticket and hospitality revenue

Relate to amounts received from gate charges, ticket sales, hospitality and guarantees directly attributable to staging domestic-cricket matches in Yorkshire.

International-ticket and hospitality revenue

Relate to amounts received from gate charges, ticket sales, hospitality and guarantees directly attributable to staging international cricket matches in Yorkshire.

England and Wales Cricket Board (ECB)

ECB income relates to fees receivable, including performance-related elements, in the current season distributed from central funds in accordance with the First Class Memorandum of Understanding. ECB fees received in respect of future seasons are treated as deferred income. ECB distributions receivable to fund capital projects are treated as deferred income and are released to the Income and Expenditure Account by equal instalments over the expected useful lives of the relevant assets in accordance with accounting policy (b) Fixed assets and depreciation, as set out below.

Commercial and other income

Commercial income relates to amounts received, net of related expenditure, from ground advertising, catering guarantees, box lettings, facility hire, dinners and other events.

Advertising income received in respect of future seasons is treated as deferred income.

Other income relates to amounts received, net of related expenditure, from retail, Cricket Centre bar, Taverners' Club, fund-raising activities and other sundry items.

(b) Fixed assets and depreciation

All expenditure in connection with the development of Headingley Carnegie Cricket Ground and the related facilities has been capitalised. Finance costs relating to and incurred during the period of construction were also capitalised. Depreciation is only charged once a discrete phase of the development is completed.

Depreciation is calculated to write down the cost of fixed assets by equal annual instalments over their expected useful lives.

The periods generally applicable are:

Headingley Carnegie Cricket Ground and Cricket Centre

Buildings	Carnegie Pavilion	125 years
	Other buildings	50 years
Fixtures		4 years
Plant & Equipment	Between 4 and 10 years	
Office equipment		
— telephone system		4 years
Computer equipment		2 years

442

Freehold land is not depreciated.

All other expenditure on repairs to Headingley Carnegie Cricket Ground and other grounds is written off as and when incurred.

(c) Carnegie Pavilion

The Club's contribution towards the design and build cost of the Carnegie Pavilion is £3m, of which £1.5m is payable over 20 years under a 125-year lease agreement. The £3m, together with the associated legal, professional and capital fit-out costs of the areas within the Pavilion that the Club occupies, have been capitalised and depreciated over the 125-year lease term. The £1.5m payable under the lease agreement has been treated as a finance lease within the financial statements with the capital element reported within Creditors (Finance leases), and the interest element charged to the Income and Expenditure Account on a straight-line basis over the 20-year term.

(d) Stocks

Stocks represent goods for resale, and are stated at the lower of cost and net realisable value.

(e) Grants

Capital grants relating to the development of Headingley Carnegie Cricket Ground (including the Yorkshire Cricket Museum) and Cricket Centre are included within the Balance Sheet as deferred income, and are released to the Income and Expenditure Account by equal instalments over the expected useful lives of the relevant assets in accordance with accounting policy (b) Fixed assets and depreciation, as set out above.

Grants of a revenue nature are credited to the Income and Expenditure Account in the same period as their related expenditure.

(f) Disclosure of information to Auditor

The members of the Board who held office at the date of approval of the Annual Report and Accounts confirm that, so far as they are aware, there is no relevant information of which the Club's auditor is unaware; or each member has taken all the steps that he ought to have taken as a member to make himself aware of any relevant audit information or to establish that the Club's auditor is aware of that information.

2. Financial Position

The Club is in a net current liability position of £1.6m (2012: £4.1m). This includes deferred income of £1.6m (2012: £1.6m). Details of the loan and overdraft maturity analysis which impact on the financial position can be found in Note 8.

The Club is not expecting to generate a cash surplus in 2014, and therefore Mr C J Graves has agreed to provide such cash-flow support as the Club requires during 2014.

The Board therefore considers it appropriate to prepare the financial statements on a going-concern basis.

3. Directors' remuneration

	2013	2012
	£	£
Wages and salaries	—	40,000
Social security costs	—	5,089
Pension costs	—	—
	—	45,089

	2013 £	2012 £
4. Taxation		
UK corporation tax	—	—
Current tax on income for the period	—	—
Adjustments in respect of prior periods	—	—
Total current tax	—	—
Deferred tax (see Note 10)	(81,720)	(35,091)
Tax on (deficit) on ordinary activities	(81,720)	(35,091)
(Deficit) on ordinary activities before taxation	(639,430)	(152,738)
Current tax at 23.25% (2012: 24.5%)	(148,667)	(37,421)
Effects of:		
Expenses not deductible for taxation purposes	27,992	34,797
Non taxable income	(78,168)	(77,332)
Depreciation for the period		
in excess of capital allowances	(27,456)	56,882
Losses not utilised	226,299	23,074
Total current tax (see above)	£ —	£ —

5. Fixed assets (See next page)

6. Debtors		
Trade debtors	194,341	185,838
Deferred tax asset (see Note 10)	840,306	758,586
Other debtors	830,769	232,117
	1,865,416	1,176,541

7. Creditors: amounts falling due within one year		
Leeds City Council loan	200,000	797,000
Bank loan	200,000	200,000
Bank overdraft (secured)	301,249	1,280,306
ECB loans	70,000	110,000
Trade creditors	252,503	557,266
Finance leases	197,692	217,203
Social security and other taxes	272,162	262,067
Other creditors	203,808	318,166
Accruals	245,825	18,627
Deferred income	1,578,312	1,572,997
	3,521,551	5,333,632

| | Cricket Centre | | Headingley Carnegie Cricket Ground | | | | |
	Freehold Land and Buildings £	Plant & Equipment £	Freehold Land and Buildings £	Plant and Equipment £	Improvements to Leasehold Property £	Office Equipment £	Total £
Cost							
At January 1, 2013	601,124	773,176	25,293,079	4,638,912	4,584,662	371,737	36,262,690
Additions	—	—	—	277,266	—	23,442	300,708
At December 31, 2013	601,124	773,176	25,293,079	4,916,178	4,584,662	395,179	36,563,398
Depreciation							
At January 1, 2013	106,412	759,329	2,130,653	4,149,177	114,324	352,681	7,612,576
Provided in the year	16,414	1,853	245,481	137,972	43,569	12,504	457,794
At December 31, 2013	122,826	761,182	2,376,134	4,287,149	157,893	365,185	8,070,370
Net book value							
At December 31, 2013	478,298	11,994	22,916,945	629,029	4,426,769	29,993	28,493,028
At December 31, 2012	**494,712**	**13,847**	**23,162,426**	**489,735**	**4,470,338**	**19,056**	**28,650,114**

445

Improvements to Leasehold Property consist of the Club's share of the costs associated with the design and build of the Carnegie Pavilion. This cost includes a £3m base-capital contribution (£1.5m of which has been treated as a finance lease, with the outstanding capital balance shown within creditors). The remaining £1.3m represents costs associated with fit-out, structural amendments, legal and consultancy fees. The total cost is depreciated over 125 years, which represents the term of the lease.

	2013 £	2012 £
8. Creditors: amounts falling due after more than one year		
Leeds City Council loan	**7,407,000**	7,510,000
Bank loan	**3,069,014**	3,269,014
ECB Loan	**939,296**	—
Pride Appeal loans	**5,000**	5,000
Debentures	**366,679**	325,691
Finance Leases	**1,212,656**	1,428,868
Deferred income	**1,995,803**	2,404,670
	14,995,448	14,943,243
CJ and J Graves Accumulation and Maintenance Trusts loans	**5,600,000**	3,600,000
C J Graves loan	**4,500,000**	3,500,000
	25,095,448	22,043,243
Loan and overdraft maturity analysis:		
In one year or less or on demand	**968,941**	2,604,510
In more than one year but not more than two years	**1,465,986**	4,925,721
In more than two years but not more than five years	**7,625,000**	4,353,690
In more than five years	**14,008,659**	10,359,161
	24,068,586	22,243,082

The Leeds City Council loan is repayable by December 15, 2025, at an interest rate of 4.5 per cent per annum. The Club has given a First Legal Charge over the freehold property known as Headingley Cricket Ground, St Michael's Lane, Leeds, to Leeds City Council in respect of this loan. Mr C J Graves has provided a shortfall guarantee in respect of this loan. The Club has also given a First Legal Charge to HSBC Bank plc over the Cricket Centre known as 41/43 St Michael's Lane, Headingley, Leeds, and a Second Legal Charge over the property known as Headingley Cricket Ground, St Michael's Lane, Leeds, in respect of the bank loan and overdrafts. HSBC Bank plc also has a fixed and floating charge over all the assets of the Club, subject to the Legal Charges referred to above. This loan is repayable by April 30, 2020, and bears an interest rate of four per cent over the Bank's base rate. Mr C J Graves has also provided a personal guarantee in respect of the indebtedness to HSBC Bank plc. The loan from Mr C J Graves bears interest at the rate of four per cent plus the Bank of England Base Rate. The loan is repayable on demand with 12 months notice. The Club has given Mr C J Graves a Fourth Legal Charge over the property known as Headingley Cricket Ground. The C J Graves Accumulation and Maintenance Trust and J Graves Accumulation and Maintenance Trust each bear interest at the rate at the higher of four per cent above the Bank of England Base Rate and 4.5 per cent per annum. However, interest is capped at seven per cent. These loans are repayable in October 2016, and the Club has given a Third Legal Charge over the property known as Headingley Cricket Ground.

The Loan from the ECB represents a loan which was made available to all 18 First Class counties. The purpose of these loans is to support capital improvements and accelerate capital-debt repayments that are identified as strategic priorities under each FCCs Business Plan. The total available loan is £1m, and the Club had drawn down £939,296 during the year. The loan will be repaid in 2015 using the proceeds of an expected one-off fee payment from the ECB. The loan bears a notional level of interest which equates to less than one per cent. The main applications of the Club's loan have been to make a £500k additional loan repayment to Leeds City Council, install a new state-of-the-art scoreboard and finance the planning application in respect of the plan to install permanent floodlights at the ground.

9. Deferred income -capital grants		
At January 1, 2013	**4,844,128**	5,003,624
Received in year	**—**	—
Received in year	**—**	—
Released to Income and Expenditure Account	**(146,195)**	(159,496)
At December 31, 2013	**4,697,933**	4,844,128

	2013	2012
	£	£

10. Provision for Liabilities
   — **Deferred Taxation (Asset) / (Liability)**

	2013	2012
At January 1, 2013	**(758,586)**	(723,495)
(Credit) to Income and Expenditure Account for the year	**(81,720)**	(35,091)
At December 31, 2013	**(840,306)**	(758,586)

The elements of deferred taxation are as follows:

	2013	2012
Difference between accumulated depreciation and capital allowances	**219,690**	162,925
Tax losses	**(1,059,996)**	(921,511)
	(840,306)	(758,586)

11. Share capital

	2013	2012
Allotted, called up and fully paid Ordinary shares of 5p each	**219**	264

During the year there was a net reduction in qualifying members of 904. The total number of qualifying members as at December 31, 2013, was 4,374 (2012: 5,278). Each member of the Club owns one Ordinary share, and the rights attached thereto are contained within the Club's rules which can be found on the Club's website or from the Secretary on request.

12. Reserves.

	Income and Expenditure Account	Capital Redemption Reserve
At January 1, 2013	**(2,331,040)**	626
Deficit for the year	**(557,710)**	—
Shares in respect of retiring members	**—**	45
At 31 December 2013	**(2,888,750)**	671

13. Reconciliation of operating Surplus (Deficit) to cash flow

(Deficit) for the year before taxation	**(639,430)**	(152,738)
Loan interest and similar amounts payable	**1,004,660**	1,010,811
Operating Surplus	**365,230**	858,073
Depreciation of tangible assets	**457,794**	540,057
Release of capital grants	**(146,195)**	(159,496)
(Increase) / decrease in stock	**(4,430)**	(24,155)
(Increase) / decrease in debtors	**(607,155)**	(158,825)
Increase / (decrease) in creditors	**183,652**	122,889
(Decrease) / increase in deferred income	**(403,552)**	(892,872)
Cash (outflow)/inflow from operating activities	**(519,886)**	285,671

14. Analysis of cash flows

Returns on investment and servicing of finance

Loan interest and facility fees	**(1,004,660)**	(1,010,811)
	(1,004,660)	(1,010,811)

Capital expenditure and financial investment

Purchase of tangible fixed assets	**(300,708)**	(209,709)
	(300,708)	(209,709)

| | | 2013 | 2012 |
| | | £ | £ |

14. (Continued)

Financing

Other loans received in year:

	2013 £	2012 £
ECB	1,009,296	192,500
Debentures	40,783	2,000
C J Graves	1,000,000	2,100,000
Graves Trust	2,000,000	—
ECB loan repayment	(110,000)	(232,500)
HSBC loan repayment	(200,000)	(700,000)
LCC loan repayment	(700,000)	(200,000)
Capital element of finance lease rental payments	(235,723)	(197,050)
Issue of ordinary share capital	—	1 1
Repurchase of ordinary share capital	(45)	(62)
	2,804,311	964,899

15. Leasing commitments

Operating lease payments amounting to £40,163 (2012: £43,273) are due within one year. The leases to which these amounts relate expire as follows:

	2013 Land and buildings £	2013 Other £	2012 Land and buildings £	2012 Other £
In one year or less	—	221	—	3,360
Between two and five years	—	9,142	—	9,913
In five years or more	30,000	—	30,000	—
	£30,000	£10,163	£30,000	£13,273

16. Related party transactions

Mr C J Graves was the Chairman of Costcutter Supermarkets Group Limited during part of the year ended December 31, 2012. The Club has purchased printing and software maintenance and a new till system from Costcutter Supermarkets Group Limited. The turnover for the year is £3,000 (2012: £8,860) of which £1,000 remains outstanding at December 31, 2013 (2012: £nil). Costcutter are also sponsors of the Club and boxholders at Headingley Cricket Ground under the Club's normal commercial terms.

During the year Mr R A Smith was a Board Member and Trustee of the Yorkshire Cricket Foundation (YCF). During 2013 the YCF awarded non-capital grants of £13,294 (2012: £14,283).

17. Pensions

The Club operates defined contribution-pension schemes for the benefit of certain employees. The amounts paid during the year were £195,075 (2012: £174,763). The assets of these schemes are administered in funds independent from those of the Club.

18. Audit Fee

The Club paid its auditor £16,500 (2012: £16,500) in respect of the audit of its Financial Statements.